Calibano
8

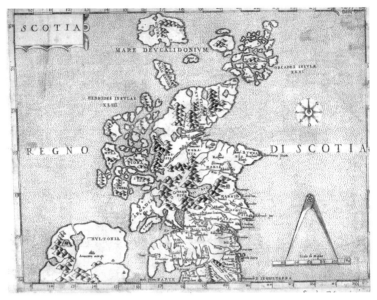

The map above (Paolo Forlani?, Regno di Scozia, *ca. 1560) is reproduced by permission of the Trustees of the National Library of Scotland.*

The publisher acknowledges a subsidy from the 'Dipartimento di Studi Linguistici e Letterari Europei e Postcoloniali' of the University of Ca' Foscari (Venice) towards the publication of this volume.

The publisher and the author also acknowledge financial assistance from the Royal Society of Edinburgh towards the project and the research carried out in Edinburgh in 2001.

ALBA LITERARIA

A History of Scottish Literature

Edited and introduced by
Marco Fazzini

[handwritten signature: Marco Fazzini]

[handwritten note: Grazie for reading this block of paper !]

[handwritten signature: Marco]

AMOS EDIZIONI

First published 2005
by Amos Edizioni
s.a.s. of Michele Toniolo and C.

Printed in Italy
by cooperativa Litografica COM

Available directly from:
AMOS EDIZIONI
VIA SAN DAMIANO, 11 - 30174 VENEZIA MESTRE
PHONE AND FAX: 041.989980 - CELL PHONE: 333.6457682
www.amosedizioni.it
e-mail: info@amosedizioni.it

ISBN 88-87670-12-9

Table of Contents

MARCO FAZZINI

Alba Literaria and the New Canon:
An Introduction

If the Scottish nation has widely been associated with its football or
rugby representatives playing abroad, with tartanry or with that
Edinburgh folk military show known as the Tattoo, it has been
questionable until some years ago how a nation without a
Parliament can be a credible nation, and how Scottish literature
can get rid of the 'British', or better still, 'English' labels attached to
it by the United Kingdom literary politics. For centuries, at least
since 1707 when the Scottish Parliament was absorbed into the
London institutions, the ambiguities generated by such terms as
'English' or 'British' have obfuscated the particularity of more than
one marginalized culture. Scottish literature, like Welsh, Irish, and
any other non-canonical literary productions outside England, has
been neglected because of its supposed provincial or barbarous
condition.[1] This is the reason why all the attempts to define the situation of 'minor' cultures, or the oppositional acts made against the
Canon supported by the Centre, have tended towards the destruction of a 'major' literature, and a 'major' language from within.[2]

According to Robert Crawford, Scottish literature 'offers the
longest continuing example of a substantial body of literature produced by a culture pressurized by the threat of English cultural domination'.[3] The critic also points out that Scottish universities, as mainstream channels of higher education, helped to promote English
studies, attempting 'suppression of native tradition in a process of
cultural conversion that was thought of as a move from the barbarous Scottish to the polite British'.[4] So, while on the one hand the
internal colony of Scotland has helped to provide the basis of
English studies around the world, on the other it has constructed a
new strategy of opposition involving not only Welsh and Irish but

also Caribbean, Canadian, African, American and Australian literatures.[5] Noting that the discussion of Scottish nationality and culture
is not included in one of the most popular books about post-colonial theory, Colin Nicholson underlines how this fact should not prevent us from either acknowledging the historical truism of English
domination upon Scottish languages, or ignoring the possible links
existing among the literary productions of Scotland, Ireland, Wales,
South Africa, Nigeria, Kenya, Australia and the Caribbean islands.[6]

Alba Literaria is the first history of Scottish literature planned
and produced outside Scotland. It is made up of 48 essays written
on single authors or single aspects of the Scottish literary production, dating from medieval times to some of the latest writers working nowadays in the country (or, partly, outside it); yet, the volume
and its chapters do not want to be exhaustive in any way. Each
contribution to the volume insists on some of the key works or key
authors of Scottish literary history, and it focuses on particular
aspects of those works or writers, so as to analyse the fracture
zones where the Canon and its linearity is questioned or subverted.
This means that the reader will not be able to read the usual presentation of biographical details, succession of works and their
contextualization. Only a partial view of that writer, or of his or her
production, or of the period or problem under focus is offered
here; at the same time, each chapter wants to be representative of
some of the core problems attached to a 'minor' and 'colonised'
country such as Scotland: the loss of national identity, the schizophrenic contradictions linked to its multi-linguistic reality, the psychic and cultural anxiety determined by its 'marginalization', the
tragedies of the Scottish Clearances and Diaspora, the contamina-
tions and the divergences between the English and the Scottish
canons, the role played, through various centuries, by translation.
No general bibliography is offered in the volume; yet each essay
lists a partial bibliographical note (made of primary and secondary
sources on the topic or period) meant to be the starting point for
further researches and readings. This kind of decentred discussion
of the Scottish canon welcomes, at times, a counter-discursive or
post-colonial approach, and it seems to be particularly useful to
read and study writers such as Douglas Dunn, Edwin Morgan,
Hugh MacDiarmid, Thomas Pringle, and even some of the tradi-

tional authors of the recent and distant past, such as Michael Scot, Robert Henryson, Blind Harry, or Gavin Douglas.

All the collaborators are, obviously, experts on their topics, and their inclusion in *Alba Literaria* is an acknowledgement of both their dedication to their fields of research and of the innovative contribution of several of their ideas about the non-English, and non-British peculiarities of the Scottish canon. It is still a controversial matter if writers such as Thomas Pringle, or George Gordon Byron or Thomas Carlyle have any right to appear under such a literary and national label; or if Lady Anne Barnard's notebooks, or the women's Gaelic songs can face the high results of Walter Scott's prose books, or of Burns' compositions written with musical and poetic aims. Yet, this perfectly suits the literary agenda pursued by intellectuals, writers and academics working during the last 50 years in the various Scottish fields: literature, folk tradition, politics and music. And it is no surprise, for example, that any reader of folk traditions or any fan of Scottish music has now access to a huge collection of folk material at the University of Edinburgh, where Hamish Henderson, and others after him have worked since the end of the last war, leaving poetical and musical documents which are still to be investigated in their larger meanings. From a strictly literary point of view, The National Library of Scotland represents a brilliant mine where one can delve for years, studying and researching not only on the mapping (both cartographic and literary) of that national heritage through the centuries, but also and mostly on an alternative canon which is partly contained in letters, manuscripts, rare editions of art-books.

This is the reason why the re-definition of the Scottish canon which *Alba Literaria* proposes in each of its contributions can relocate and subvert the old centre, so that the energy of the new literatures written in English can make 'new centres out of old peripheries'.[7] After the experience, under MacDiarmid's guidance, of that phase that is generally defined as the Scottish Renaissance, or denial of the privilege of 'English', with the consequent re-introduction of the use of the Scots language, English has been later appropriated and renovated from within through a slow process of contamination operated by the writers belonging to the First and Second Wave of the Scottish Renaissance. MacDiarmid himself, in

the late 1920s and early 1930s, after his theorization for the renovated role of the Scots language, proposed some general directions
for the manipulation of the colonizer's language and the emergence of a new phase in which the local, barbarian and peripheral
Scottish accent and language could build a bridge towards the
other post-colonial literatures in English.

Concentrating on a literary production which covers nearly seven
centuries, and discussing, in various ways and through diverse
approaches, the different strategies through which a sense of cultural
identity is created by counter-exercising power and self-constitution,
Alba Literaria is not only concerned with the many 'englishes' born
after the collapse of the British Empire but with the more general
collision of the many facets of Otherness those languages have
brought into play in a near and distant past. When linguistic dislocation and literary hybridity are involved, the counter-discourse of the
marginalized Other proposes the rejection of the organic wholeness
of the imperial discourse for the re-constitution of a national identity.
To look at Scotland in terms of a counter-discursive theory means
not only to place the country within the general discussion about the
marginalization of the peripheral literatures written in the English
language, but to observe how the Empire has been condemned to
collapse because of the introduction of a large number of new and
subversive voices inside its system. The literatures in English that
Riach speaks about, and which have been introduced, not without a
certain ideological debate in some universities,[8] have imposed new
aesthetic values and a new literary project for a future of oppositional criticism, in order to learn not just 'the overt thematic declarations
of anti-colonial resistance in "ex-centric" post-colonial writing, but
also the counter-discursive investments of post-colonial figuration on
the level of genre and mode'.[9]

It seems undeniable that in contemporary Scotland we face an era
in which we must pay attention to the question of multiculturalism
because Scottish literature(s) contains one of the most heterogeneous productions coming out of the ex-Empire, and one which can
properly be defined as multilingual and syncretic, being written in
Scots, Gaelic, and English respectively. Looking for a model for
Scotland, Angus Calder observes that since Scottish culture is
remarkably diverse within a relatively small area, 'any suggestion

that it has ever been or should be "racially" homogeneous can only
be dismissed with contempt. Like Russian culture, it is marked by a
fierce sense of difference, but this is not difference from sharply distinct tartars and Catholics but more elusive divergence from English
people close in many ways, delimited by a border which has always
been more like a revolving door than a portcullis'.[10]

The flexibility of the border has been both a weakness and a
strength for Scotland. The transformation and the adaptation of
Scottish literature to its multi-linguistic realities have contributed to
the shaping of an ambiguous character which Hugh MacDiarmid
defined by using G. Gregory Smith's phrase 'Caledonian Antisyzygy'.
Noting that in his or her literature the Scot presents a contradictory
character which reflects the 'stress of foreign influence and native
division, almost a zigzag of contradictions', Smith admits that two
sides of the matter must be considered when studying the oxymoronic restlessness of the local culture.[11] Both seem to refer to the
idea of a Scottish mixture of contraries, a diversity-in-unity which
opens itself to the multifarious influences deriving from a variety of
heritages. However, beyond every kind of polarization of opposites,
it seems that MacDiarmid's model for twentieth century Scottish culture more clearly responds to the post-colonial idea of a hybridized
dynamic creativity. From this point of view, MacDiarmid's words go
beyond a mere reconciliation or clash of contraries when he underlines that 'the abiding myth of our people' is represented by the synthesis of East and West, multi-linguistic interests, internationalism,
world-consciousness.[12] What MacDiarmid longs for is the recupera-
tion not only of Scots culture but of the hidden Celtic heritage of the
Highlands in order to underline the hybrid character of his national
identity and confront it with other international realities. Bhabha's
proposal of the existence of a 'third space', an interstice opening up
new possibilities for literary and sociological aims, seems to have
most to offer to those interested not just in the Caledonian
Antisyzygy combination of opposites but in MacDiarmid's programme of a polyphonic comprehensiveness which could include
Scots, Gaelic, English, Russian, Italian, and other influences.

The foundation of any individual identity for many of the writers
examined in this volume rests less on a closure than on an openness to the contradictory textures of the world and of language in

particular, leaving both writers and readers in a world where paradox might be a relevant basis of one's being. Here the ambiguities
of the World become the ambiguities of the Word so that this half-
way position within language and identity subverts not only any
authoritarian and institutionalised discourse but also the hegemony
of the Subject. Crossing the borders of a national and cultural
exclusivity, as we can clearly see in Lenta's essay on Lady Anne
Barnard, in Tony Voss's contribution on Thomas Pringle or in all
the diaspora poets discussed by G. Ross Roy or, again, in the inter-
nationality of the medieval poet Michael Scot or in an innovator
such as MacDiarmid, means to do without any kind of linguistic
and perceptive appropriation of reality, so that translation can
become an all-important tool of literary and intellectual struggle.
Supported by both MacDiarmid and Muir in the twentieth century,
translation has represented an essential part of the contemporary
Scottish writer's work, especially in the last 50 years. For Bhabha,
the notion of hybridity comes out of the genealogy of difference
and the idea of translation. Both help the attainment of the awareness of multiculturalism as a denial of essentialism and
originary/original culture. The hybrid for Bhabha also avoids the
simplistic dichotomies ruler/ruled, coloniser/colonised so that from
two original moments a third entity emerges. This 'third space'
helps to displace 'the histories that constitute it, and sets up new
structures of authority, new political initiatives, which are inade-
quately understood through received wisdom'.[13]

Bhabha's 'third space' is reflected in McCarey's description of the
'third tiger',[14] that half-way condition reserved for both poetry and
translation when writing has much to do with the trans-national and
supra-national character of the writer's median state. It is this balanced position which can subvert the two original moments from
which, as Bhabha says, the third emerges. Translation is one of the
possible means to approach the Other, responding to the call of a
kind of elective affinity and refusing the authority of the standard-
ized language and the canonized prescriptions imposed by the
Centre. In Scotland, a similar process of abrogation has given way to
the First Wave of the Scottish Renaissance, and the appropriation of
the coloniser's language and culture has given impulse to the so-
called Second Wave, performing that disruptive role which has

achieved the imposition of an ex-centric vision of contemporary literature. As a direct consequence of the process of abrogation that MacDiarmid inaugurated in the 1920s with his 'Synthetic Scots', Bhabha's 'third space' emerges from the interstice created by the friction of two contrasting cultures. As the authors of *The Empire Writes Back* point out, there is no hope 'that cultural practices can return to some "pure" and unsullied cultural condition, and that such practices themselves, such as the use of vernacular terms or grammatical forms in English literature, can embody such an authenticity'.[15]

Where, as Wilson Harris – a writer of Scottish origins – notes in the last page of his novel *The Palace of the Peacock*, an alchemic mixture of opposites engenders a 'starred peacock who was instantly transported to know and to hug to himself his true invisible otherness and opposition, his true alien spiritual love without cruelty and confusion in the blindness and frustration of desire',[16] there is still the possibility of enjoying the enriching reality of syncretic discourses: here the subject can confront its alterity and speak a language which re-establishes not only a national identity but a sense of completeness in local languages, history and place.

SELECTED BIBLIOGRAPHY: 2000-2005

Anderson, Carol, and Christianson, Aileen, *Scottish Women's Fiction 1920 to 1960s: Journeys into Being*, East Linton: Tuckwell Press, 2000.
Angeletti, Gioia, *Eccentric Scotland: Three Victorian Poets*, Bologna: Clueb, 2004.
Bell, Eleanor, *Questioning Scotland: Literature, Nationalism, Postmodernism*, London: Palgrave Macmillan, 2004.
Bell, Eleanor, and Miller, Gavin, *Scotland in Theory: Reflection on Culture and Literature*, Amsterdam and New York: Rodopi, 2004.
Carruthers, Gerard, Goldie, David, and Renfrew, Alastair eds., *Beyond Scotland: New Contexts for Twentieth-century Scottish Literature*, Amsterdam and New York: Rodopi, 2004.
Cavecchi, Mariacristina, Rose, Margaret, and Soncini, Sara eds., *Caledonia Dreaming: la nuova drammaturgia scozzese*, Salerno: Oedipus, 2001.
Christianson, Aileen, and Lumsden, Alison eds., *Contemporary Scottish Women Writers*, Edinburgh: Edinburgh University Press, 2000.

Devine, T.M. ed., *Scotland's Shame: Bigotry and Sectarianism in Modern Scotland*, Edinburgh and London: Mainstream, 2000.

Fazzini Marco, *Crossings: Essays on Contemporary Scottish Poetry and Hybridity*, Venezia: Supernova, 2000.

Findlay, Bill ed., *Scots Plays of the Seventies: An Anthology*, Dalkeith: Scottish Cultural Press, 2001.

Gifford, Douglas, Dunnigan, Sarah, and MacGillivray, Alan, *Scottish Literature in English and Scots*, Edinburgh: Edinburgh University Press, 2002.

Görlach, Manfred, *A Textual History of Scots*, Heidelberg: Winter, 2002.

Gray, Alasdair, *A Short Survey of Classic Scottish Writing*, Edinburgh: Canongate, 2001.

Hassan, Gerry, and Warhurst, Chris eds., *Anatomy of the New Scotland: Power, Influence and Change*, Edinburgh and London: Mainstream, 2002.

Kirk, John, and Baoill, Dónall P Ó eds., *Language Links: The Languages of Scotland and Ireland*, Belfast: Cló Ollscoil na Banríona/Queen's University Belfast, 2001.

Leigh March, Cristie, *Rewriting Scotland*, Manchester: Manchester University Press, 2002.

Macaulay, Ronald K.S., *Extremely Common Eloquence: Constructing Scottish Identity Through Narrative*, Amsterdam and New York: Rodopi, 2005.

Marinelli, Sara, *Corpografie femminili: gli sconfinamenti della scrittura in tre autrici scozzesi*, Napoli: Liguori, 2004.

Poggi Ghigi, Valentina, and Rose, Margaret, *A Theatre That Matters: Twentieth-Century Scottish Drama and Theatre*, Milano: Unicopli, 2000.

Prillinger, Horst, *Family and the Scottish Working-Class Novel 1984-1994*, Frankfurt am Main and Oxford: Peter Lang, 2000.

Sassi, Carla, *'Imagined Scotlands': saggi sulla letteratura scozzese*, Trieste: Edizioni Parnaso, 2002.

Sassi, Carla, *Why Scottish Literature Matters,* Edinburgh: Saltire Society, 2005.

Van Heijnsbergen, Theo, and Royan, Nicola eds., *Literature, Letters and the Canonical in Early Modern Scotland*, East Linton: Tuckwell, 2002.

Whyte, Christopher, *Modern Scottish Poetry*, Edinburgh: Edinburgh University Press, 2004.

NOTES

[1] See Craig Beveridge and Ronald Turnbull, 'Inferiorism', *Cencrastus*, vol. 8, Spring 1982, pp. 4-5.

[2] See Gilles Deleuze and Félix Guattari, 'What is Minor Literature?', in Russell Ferguson, Martha Gever, Trinh T. Minh-ha, Cornel West eds., *Out There: Marginalization and Contemporary Cultures*, New York: The New Museum of Contemporary Art, 1990, p. 59 and p. 67.

[3] Robert Crawford, *Devolving English Literature*, Oxford: Oxford University Press, 1992, p. 8. See also John E. Schwarz, 'The Scottish National Party: Non-violent Separatism and Theories of Violence', in I.K. Feierabend et al. eds., *Anger, Violence and Politics*, London: Prentice-Hall, 1972, pp. 325-341.

[4] Robert Crawford, *op. cit.*, p. 22.

[5] See the following articles: Alan Riach, 'Tradition and the New Alliance: Scotland and the Caribbean', in Raoul Granqvist ed., *Major Minorities: English Literatures in Transit*, Amsterdam and Atlanta: Rodopi, 1993, pp. 9-17; Manfred Görlach, *Englishes: Studies in Varieties of English 1984-1988*, Amsterdam and Philadelphia: John Benjamin's Publishing Company, 1991, pp. 69-89; Susan Bassnett, 'Comparative Identities in Post-colonial World', in *Comparative Literature: A Critical Introduction*, Oxford (UK) and Cambridge (Mass.): Blackwell, 1983, pp. 70-91.

[6] Colin Nicholson, *Poem, Purpose and Place*, Edinburgh: Polygon, 1992, p. xix.

[7] See Marshall Walker, 'The Age of Periphery: An Ex-paranoiac's Thoughts on the Literary Canon', *Scotlands*, vol. 2, no. 1, 1995, p. 20.

[8] See Helen Tiffin, '"Lie Back and Think of England": Post-Colonial Literatures and the Academy', in Hena Maes-Jelinek, Kirsten Holst Petersen and Anna Rutherford eds., *A Shaping of Connections: Commonwealth Literary Studies – Then and Now*, Sydney: Dangaroo Press, 1989, pp. 116-126. With regard to the study of Scottish literature abroad, see the following articles: Isabel Carrera Suàrez, 'Scottish Studies in Spanish Universities', *Scottish Literary Journal*, vol. 16, no.1, May 1989, pp. 59-64; Valentina Poggi, 'Scottish Studies in Italy', *Scottish Literary Journal*, vol. 17, no. 1, May 1990, pp. 85-90; Alan Riach, 'Scottish Studies in New Zealand', *Scottish Literary Journal*, vol. 18, no. 2, November 1991, pp. 63-70; Alan Riach, 'Scottish Studies in Australia: An Interim Report', *Scottish Literary Journal*, vol. 20, no. 1, May 1993, pp. 49-61.

[9] Stephen Slemon, 'Monuments of Empire: Allegory/Counter-discourse/Post-colonial Writing', *Kunapipi*, vol. 9, no. 3, 1987, p. 14.

[10] Angus Calder, 'A Descriptive Model of Scottish Culture', *Scotlands*, vol. 2, no. 1, 1995, p. 6.

[11] G. Gregory Smith, *Scottish Literature: Character and Influence*, London: Macmillan, 1919, pp. 1-9. For a critical appreciation of G. Gregory Smith's proposal of a 'Caledonian Antisyzygy' for Scottish Literature see W.N. Herbert, 'The Significance of Gregory Smith', in W.N. Herbert and Richard Price eds., *Gairfish: Discovery*, Bridge of Weir: Gairfish, 1991, pp. 16-27.

[12] Hugh MacDiarmid, *Lucky Poet*, London: Jonathan Cape, 1972, p. 187.

[13] Homi Bhabha, 'The Third Space', in Jonathan Rutherford ed., *Identity, Community, Culture, Difference*, London: Lawrence and Wishart, 1990, p. 211.

[14] Peter McCarey, 'Edwin Morgan the Translator', in Robert Crawford and Hamish Whyte eds., *About Edwin Morgan*, Edinburgh: Edinburgh University Press, 1990, pp. 97-98. See also Edwin Morgan's use of the phrase 'third tiger' in his paper, delivered at Glasgow University on 3rd June 1988, called 'The Third Tiger: The Translator as Communicative Creator'.

[15] Bill Ashcroft, Gareth Griffiths, and Helen Tiffin eds., *The Empire Writes Back: Theory and Practice in Post-colonial Literatures*, London: Routledge, 1989, pp. 41-42.

[16] Wilson Harris, *The Palace of the Peacock*, London: Faber & Faber, 1960, p. 116.

Acknowledgments

Above all I should like to thank all the collaborators for having provided the kind of competence and support that is not easily found.

My greatest debt is to some of my friends, such as Valerie Gillies, Christopher Whyte, Ronnie Jack, Edwin Morgan, Douglas Dunn and G. Ross Roy, because their response to my idea of dealing with Scottish works and writers and analysing the fracture zones where the Canon and its linearity is questioned or subverted was particularly encouraging.

For help of various kinds I am also grateful to William Gillies, Roberta Cimarosti, Michele Toniolo, Anna Lukianowicz, Armando Pajalich, and to the following institutions: The Edinburgh Institute for Advanced Studies in the Humanities, The School of English at the University of Edinburgh, The National Library of Scotland, The Edinburgh University Library, The Royal Society of Edinburgh, the *Studies in Scottish Literature* journal, The University of Columbia (South Carolina) and the Rare Book Collection of the Thomas Cooper Library, the Department of Modern Languages at the University of Macerata, and the Department of European and Postcolonial Studies at the University of Ca' Foscari (Venice).

ALBA LITERARIA

Tom Hubbard

Michael the Wandering Scot: *'Preziosissimo fra i miei Maestri'*

Licet autem scientia animae sit gravis et periculosa
[omni inquisitori tamen aliqua
hic dicemus de ipsa ut de nostro et alieno, sicut deus
[auctor omnium et
singulorum gratiam concedet nobis, nec ad nostri laudem,
[sed ad honorem dei et
ad utilitatem scolarium modernorum in hac arte astronomiae.

Although the theory of the soul is difficult and dangerous
[for every researcher,
nevertheless we shall say something here about the soul,
[as about something
familiar to us and to everyone else, as far as God,
[the creator of every single
thing, will grant us his grace, not to our own praise,
[but to the honour of God and
for the use of modern scholars in this art of astrology.[1]

In this volume the reader will encounter many examples of Scottish writers who lived and worked overseas, enriching and enriched by the cultures in which they found themselves. Mediterranean and central Europe; north America; the South Pacific islands; these are among the most prominent destinations of the Scottish literary 'diaspora', to cite the term favoured by G.Ross Roy in the following pages. Alternatively, there is the phrase 'wandering Scot', which has established itself as something of a popular idiom: conveniently, the earliest celebrated literary example bears his nationality in his surname.

Michael Scot (c. 1175-1235),[2] a native of the Scottish border country, went on to become one of the greatest polymaths of mediaeval Europe. He was a physician, mathematician, musicologist, astrologer/astronomer, alchemist, early psychologist, translator and much else; his scientific studies made him the target of legend-makers, who conferred on him the dubious alter ego of a wizard in league with the devil. He is believed to have studied at the Universities of Oxford, Paris and Bologna, and to have subsequently worked as a churchman in Italy. At some stage he entered the service of Frederick II, King of Sicily and Holy Roman Emperor, to whom he became 'preziosissimo fra i miei Maestri'. Officially, he was the imperial tutor and astrologer; he could be described even more expansively, it seems, as the young monarch's sage and mentor.

During and around the year 1217 he was based at Toledo, where he was a key figure in the importation of Arabic learning to Europe, as well as the reimportation of Greek texts which had been preserved and annotated by Arab scholars. He translated into Latin treatises by the astrologer/astronomer Alpetragius (Al-Bitruji),[3] Aristotle (via Arabic intermediary versions), and the philosophers Averroës and Avicenna; this work influenced his own original writing on physiognomy, that early form of what we now call psychology.

The legendary Michael Scot, while a fascinating persona, has for non-specialists (even the serious ones) obscured his real-life counterpart. It was inevitable, in his time, that science would be confused with magic; Scot himself denounced the latter, but in his writing he criss-crossed the undemarcated frontier between the two. Both his native and adopted countries – Scotland and Italy – have created a veritable industry of Michael Scot folklore.[4] This Faustian wizard, we are told, set the devil the impossible task of making rope from the sand of Kirkcaldy beach; Walter Scott, in *The Lay of the Last Minstrel* (1805), makes much of the story that his near-namesake (again with infernal assistance) 'cleft in three' the Eildon Hills in southern Scotland. The sixteenth century Italian poet Folengo informs us that Scot could call up devils from the four quarters of heaven, ride an enchanted horse, sail in an enchanted ship, and wrap himself in a cloak of invisibility. A Neapolitan tradition has it that he invented a metallic contrivance within which he would place an egg; the movement – or, worse, the breakage – of the egg could predict earthquakes of varying magnitude. It may come as no surprise, then, that Dante consigns this flawed paragon to the eighth circle of the 'Inferno':

> Quell'altro che ne' fianchi è così poco,
> Michele Scotto fu, che veramente
> de le magiche frode seppe il gioco.

> [The other, so slight about the flanks,
> Was Michael Scot, who in truth
> of magic frauds knew well the game.] [5]

At which point it is well to return to the historical Michael Scot, or at least to the little that we know about him for certain. His magnum opus, which exists in numerous manuscript versions, is the unfinished trilogy *Liber Introductorius, Liber Particularis,* and the *Liber Physionomiae* (also known as the *Physionomia* or *De Secretis Naturae*). These were presented to Frederick in 1228; the *Physionomia* – to use its shortest title – was published in 1477. These dates remain conjectural. The first text, as its name suggests, is for beginners, and discusses astrology and other sciences; the second offers a more advanced approach; the third concerns anatomy, physiology, reproduction, zoology, and, as mentioned above, psychology. The progression is logical for a belief-system which maintains that the stars influence the composition and development of the human soul. Michael – he is normally cited by his forename – defines 'physiognomy' as 'the science of nature by whose insinuation one sufficiently skilled in it recognises the differences of animals, and the vices and virtues of persons of all sorts'.[6]

The *Physionomia* is concerned with human development, both pre- and post-natal, with much to advise on the best conditions and timing for conception. The stars are of course given their due credit for their influence on the whole process, but the author offers counsel on the kind of food which a man must eat to achieve good quality semen. There are people of both sexes who require frequent intercourse in order to maintain health; Michael advises them to carry with them a jasper or topaz, as a kind of talisman.[7] (Here we have more than a hint of his geological-alchemical interests). Anticipating Freud by some seven hundred years, Michael devotes much space to dreams and their interpretation. In his 1965 monograph on our author, Lynn Thorndike summarises his thinking as follows:

> Some [dreams] are true; some false. Some signify as to the past; some as to the present; some as to the future. Some signify nothing but fancy. The age and food of the dreamer and the stage of the moon should be taken into account. A boy sees dreams in one way; a young man otherwise; an old man, still differently; and a woman, yet otherwise. A dream before food is digested signifies nothing or concerns the past. A dream while digestion is going on, but is not yet completed, signifies as to present affairs. A dream after complete digestion signifies wholly concerning the future. One is advised to arise immediately and make a note of a dream which seems of great significance, or not sleep longer on the side on which one dreamt, 'and then he will recall it, when day comes, unless he saw many dreams [Michael]'. If he has forgotten part of the dream he should rub the back of his head, where the virtue of memory is located. Subsequent chapters are concerned with dreams signifying the dominance of each of the four humours, each of the four qualities – hot, cold, dry, and moist – repletion of humours, and bad humours.[8]

Curiously, as if it is all part of the magic which he professes to abhor, he denounces elsewhere those who claim to read the meaning of dreams.

However, Michael has been praised for his open-mindedness, his intellectual amplitude. It goes with a tendency to be modest rather than magisterial, as when he refers to one of his manuscripts as a mere pamphlet or opuscule.[9] The *Liber Introductorius* aims to entertain as well as enlighten: he appeals to non-specialists, as if he recognised the potential of (pre-)democratic intellect. This very antithetical Scot, in considering matters cosmic, can be touchingly homely in his choice of imagery. The axis of the heavens is likened to the axle of the wheel of a mill or a wagon. Anticipating one of the most memorable tropes in the poetry of Rainer Maria Rilke, he tells us that the universe is a round, whole apple which contains the hidden seeds of future development. Stars do not so much determine the future as indicate it: a tavern sign which represents wine is not the wine itself. God created the universe as a unity, but also in separate parts, as a baker makes many loaves of bread from a single mass of dough.[10] Michael incorporates a mini-

narrative, a species of folktale both comic and tragic in its grotes-
querie; when preparing a piece on Michael for theatre performance, I made a verse paraphrase of the story:

> [...] This monkey had three bairns.
> Hunters chased her through every wood in Africa.
> Well, Madam Ape takes her favourite brat by the hand,
> And tucks the second one under her arm.
> What of the third? She likes it least of all,
> Lets it drop to await the hunter's spear.
> Aha! The fly wee bugger jumps on her back.
> It's the one to escape when she loses hold of the others.[11]

He has a mind that is both poetic and tidy, given to neat categori-
sations as befits a pioneer of scientific classification. The trinity of
God is reflected in that of the human soul: will; reason; memory.
(An unholier trinity is that of the magus, who is trickster [illusor],
sorceror [maleficus], and sage [sapiens]). His notions of
national/regional difference, as evident in cultural, linguistic, and
even physical varieties of European peoples, may anticipate the
equally engaging (and questionable) ethnicities expounded by a
later wandering Scot of pan-European reputation – John Barclay
(1582-1621), in his *Icon Animorum* of 1614.

The prolific translator was himself much translated. The earliest
recorded vernacular version of the *Physionomia* (Saragossa, 1494)
is in Spanish (appropriately, in view of his Toledan labours almost
three centuries earlier). The same work appeared in Italian in
Venice in 1514 and was much reprinted in that language. It is at
least a reasonable speculation that the Moscow translation of 1781
owed its existence to the Russian Enlightenment and an accelerated interest in western culture.[12]

NOTES

[1] [Michael Scot], MS Escorial, f. 34ra, as quoted and translated in Dag
Nikolaus Hasse, *Avicenna's De Anima in the Latin West: the Formation
of a Peripatetic Philosophy of the Soul 1160-1300*, London and Torino:
The Warburg Institute and Nino Aragno Editore, 2001, p. 25. Dr

Hasse's section on Michael (pp. 23-30) can be warmly recommended.

[2] During consultation of library catalogues and the internet, it is advisable to bear in mind the various forms of Michael's surname – Scot, Scott, Scotus. In books he is usually indexed under Michael.

The Michael Scot Research Project, established in May 2000, aims 'to research and publish his works in English for the first time, in both print and electronic versions'. For further information, see: HYPERLINK http://www.historytoday.com/index.cfm?articleid=403 http://www.historytoday.com/index.cfm?articleid=403

In addition to the secondary material cited in the following footnotes, the reader might consult the chapter on Michael Scot in Lynn Thorndike's *A History of Magic and Experimental Science during the first Thirteen Centuries of our Era*, vol. 2, London: Macmillan, 1923, pp. 307-337. His monograph (1965), cited below, is indispensable. I would also recommend J. Read, 'Michael Scot: A Scottish Pioneer of Science', *Scientia*, octobre-novembre, 1938, pp. 190-197.

[3] Michael dates the completion of his version of Al-Bitruji's *De Motibus Celorum* very precisely at '18° die ueneris augusti hora tertia [...] anno incarnationis Ihesu Christi 1217'. A critical edition, prepared by Francis J. Carmody, was published by the University of California Press, Berkeley, 1952.

[4] I must confess my own part in nurturing these stories. In 1992 the Scottish Arts Council awarded me a grant to write verse dramas on the legendary Michael; these were subsequently performed by theatre groups in France and the USA. My shorter poems on Michael are collected in Tom Hubbard, *Scottish Faust*, Newtyle, Angus: Kettillmin, 2004.

[5] Dante Alighieri, *Divina Commedia,* 'Inferno', XX, 115-117.

[6] As quoted and translated in Lynn Thorndike, *Michael Scot*, Edinburgh: Nelson,1965, p. 87.

[7] *Ibidem*, p. 87.

[8] *Ibidem*, pp. 89-90.

[9] Nikolaus Hasse, *op. cit.*, p. 25.

[10] The foregoing summarises and annotates Lynn Thorndike (1965), pp. 17ff.

[11] Tom Hubbard, 'From the Verse Drama *The Devil and Michael Scot*, *Skinklin' Star: The Scottish Poetry and Graphics Broadsheet*, 1, Glasgow: Postgraduate School of Scottish Studies, University of Glasgow, May 1996.

[12] For records of translations of Michael Scot, see the Bibliography of Scottish Literature in Translation (BOSLIT) at HYPERLINK http://boslit.nls.uk

Barbour's Brus: *Epic Poetry and the National Resistance of the Admirable Warrior King*

In 1375, John Barbour, Archdeacon of Aberdeen, completed his epic poem *Brus*: a momentous event not only in the life's work of its author but in the history of Scottish literature, and even in that of the national identity of Bruce's kingdom.

Barbour's life story cannot be reconstructed in detail; but more is known, or can be reasonably deduced, about him than about many mediaeval figures. The post of Archdeacon (a church official second in rank to a bishop, with responsibility for distributing charities, presiding over meetings of the church court and supervising appointments to lower orders, including priesthood) was in his hands from 1357 till his death in 1395. The earlier period of his life is obscure: we know that he was precentor of the cathedral at Dunkeld in 1355, and very little else: neither the date nor the place of his birth is recorded. We cannot even say with certainty that he was an Aberdonian, except by adoption: there are, indeed, powerful arguments for the view that he came originally from the South-West, in that his name is to this day much commoner in that part of Scotland than in Aberdeenshire; that several people mentioned in his poem were certainly from the South-West; and that the episodes in the poem which take place south of the Forth-Clyde line are described in more detail, and with more apparent knowledge of the terrain, than those set further north.

As Archdeacon of Aberdeen, Barbour earned high renown. He travelled widely throughout the extensive diocese, and must have become a well-known figure among its parishioners. Shortly after his appointment he went to Edinburgh as the bishop's representative at a meeting of the National Council, held to discuss the ransoming of King David II from English captivity. Later, he visited Oxford to study, travelling on a safe-conduct from Edward III: this courtesy of the English king was utilised on several subsequent occasions, when he returned to Oxford or travelled through England to Paris or St Denis. These trips may have been for study, to buy books for St Machar's Cathedral library, for church business or for pilgrimage: we cannot be certain, but they clearly suggest the activity of an energetic and conscientious churchman. When David II died in 1371 and was succeeded by his nephew Robert II (the first of the Stewarts), Barbour was appointed auditor of the Royal Exchequer, with a substantial salary. Many charters bear his name among the list of witnesses; many documents relating to church administration or national government testify to his presence; the Pope accorded him the singular privilege of appointing a deputy if he was prevented by illness from travelling on church business. By the time of his death, Barbour as Archdeacon of Aberdeen had earned a reputation that spread far beyond the bounds of his diocese. His principal legacy to posterity, however, is his epic poem.

For many reasons, the *Brus* is one of the greatest landmarks in Scottish literary history. First, it is the earliest surviving work of importance in the Scots tongue. Intriguingly, this is an issue which could never have occurred to Barbour himself: neither he nor any of his contemporaries used the term 'Scots' of their language; and they would have had difficulty in understanding the patriotic attachment to it felt by later generations. For the importance of this aspect of Barbour's achievement to become clear, two facts should be borne in mind: that in the Scotland of the early Stewarts Gaelic was still spoken by at least half the population and over more than half the land area of the kingdom; and that the dialects descended from the tongue of the ancient Anglo-Saxons formed a continuously varying series from the Moray Firth to the English Channel. There was as yet no question of a standard literary 'English' carrying an aura of cultural imperialism to which Scottish writers could proclaim their opposition by writing in 'Scots', in the vein of Allan Ramsay and Robert Burns in the eighteenth century or Hugh MacDiarmid and his great successors in the twentieth. Chaucer and Gower, Barbour's contemporaries, by the splendour of their writings laid the foundations for the literary pre-eminence of the London dialect; but the same period saw poets of almost equal

gifts demonstrating the expressiveness of other forms of English:
William Langland wrote his moral allegory *Piers Plowman* in the
dialect of the Cotswolds and the Malvern Hills, and an anonymous
genius known as the Gawain-Poet[1] utilised the rugged rhythms of
Lancashire or Cheshire. To Barbour, his medium was *Inglis*; and
the differences between it and the language of Chaucer, though
unmistakable, were not nearly significant enough to obscure what
he would have seen as their essential identity. Indeed, if Barbour
and Chaucer ever met – and though there is no evidence that they
did, nothing makes it unlikely – they could have conversed together with greater ease than a Londoner and an Aberdonian of today.

Nonetheless, events which Barbour could not have predicted
resulted in his work coming to be seen, with justice, as the foun-
tainhead of the great tradition of literature in Scots. As the fifteenth
century progressed and the English monarchy became, finally, an
English-*speaking* monarchy,[2] the London dialect gradually eclipsed
all others from literary use: the dialects of Langland, the Gawain-
Poet, the Yorkshire mystic Richard Rolle and other great English
poets from beyond the metropolis declined in range and status,
and eventually disappeared. In Scotland, however, the language of
Barbour's poem set out on a course of brilliant and dynamic development. His poetic example was immediately and enthusiastically
taken up: his younger contemporary Andrew of Wyntoun used the
same style and metre, as well as the same language, to write a
verse history of Scotland from the Creation to his own time. James
I recorded his Acts of Parliament in the vernacular instead of Latin,
and had the Acts of his predecessors translated into it: Gaelic
ceased to be the language of the monarchy as the Stewarts, with
Edinburgh as their capital, identified themselves increasingly with
the Lowlands. Successive Stewart kings gave their patronage to a
series of gifted poets, of whom one of the greatest, Gavin Douglas,
proclaimed (more than a century after Barbour's death) that his
language was not *Inglis* but *Scottis*. And a cumulative series of
developments in the language itself, both from within (gradual
changes in pronunciation and grammar) and because of external
influences (borrowings from French, Dutch, Gaelic and other languages) caused Scots to become increasingly unlike the language
of England's court and culture. Scots – a fact which is far too sel-

dom appreciated, even in Scotland – is the vehicle of one of Europe's great vernacular literatures, and the only one of the many speech-forms descended from Old English, other than standard literary English itself, to claim the status of a language in its own right. Barbour could not even have imagined such a development; but his contribution to it is fundamental.

Next, Barbour's interpretation of the events he describes has shaped our picture of a key episode in Scottish history, and consequently our entire national self-image, from his own time to the present. Here the poet *did* know what he was doing: namely, presenting Robert Bruce as the admirable warrior king who, assisted by loyal followers and by the devotion of the Scottish peasantry, led a heroic and (ultimately) gloriously successful national resistance to English aggression. This is the historical view of Bruce which has prevailed; and even in our deracinated times, every Scot takes a well-founded patriotic pride in the achievements of the hero-king. Yet it must be recalled that Barbour was a *writer*: his presentation of Robert Bruce is a literary construction. This does not mean that it is invalid. No possible re-interpretation of the historical evidence can call in question Bruce's amazing personal courage, his Scottish patriotism, his military genius, his political skill or his charismatic personality. But it does entitle, indeed oblige, Barbour's contemporary readers to examine his assumptions and motives, and the influence he has exerted on later perceptions of events.

Barbour wrote in the service of the reigning house: he received a pension from Robert II, later confirmed by Robert III, for writing the *Brus*; and he is known to have composed a poem, now lost, on the origins of the Stewart dynasty. The history of Bruce's royal descendants, however, had not been a distinguished one: Barbour lived during one of the least glorious periods of Scottish history. Bruce's achievement in securing Scotland's independence had been almost undone during his son's minority; and David II's reign was a gloomy period of disorder at home and chronic warfare with England. Robert II, elderly and almost blind when he came to the throne, was an even weaker ruler; and with his son Robert III, who succeeded him in 1390, royal authority reached a nadir: not the least remarkable aspect of James I's reign was his success in restoring order and stability to a Scotland crippled by almost a century of wars and feeble kings. Barbour's poem had a complex and forceful political relevance to his own time. Firstly, it underpinned the House of Stewart by emphasising the glorious achievement of the king from whom they derived their claim to the throne – to do which, Barbour was obliged to be highly selective in his telling of Bruce's story. In actual fact, the life of Robert Bruce is one of the most spectacular examples in all history of a career justified by its success. His assumption of the throne was a usurpation almost as blatant as that of England's Richard III in a later age. John Balliol, inadequate as he had proved, was legally Scotland's reigning king: all the efforts of William Wallace had been directed towards his restoration. And if Balliol's deposition by Edward Langshanks was regarded as having *de jure* status, this meant that the rightful King of Scots was his son Edward Balliol (who indeed, after Bruce's death, made a vigorous attempt to enforce his claim to the throne). Bruce's kingship was by no means universally recognised in Scotland: his ultimate success becomes even more astonishing when it is remembered that for several years he was fighting a full-scale civil war, brought on by his murder of Balliol's nephew John Comyn, at the same time as the war with England. Barbour presents Bruce's seizure of the throne in a far more favourable light than the circumstances of the time actually warranted. He gives a cursory dismissal to Balliol, and diminishes his moral standing by relating a story, of very doubtful authenticity, that Edward first offered the kingdom to Bruce[3] on condition that he held it as Edward's vassal and, angered by his proud refusal to hold the Scottish throne except as an independent sovereign, then bestowed it on the weaker Balliol who had no such reservation. He also exonerates Bruce, as far as possible, for the killing of Comyn by a decidedly 'official' version of the story wherein Comyn proposes to support him in claiming the throne in exchange for his family lands, and then – Barbour here interpolating a lofty discourse, with numerous examples, on heroes who have been shamefully betrayed – reveals the plan to Edward.[4] Having thus underplayed, re-interpreted or ignored the very dubious background to Bruce's assumption of the kingship, he devotes his powerful literary talent to relating how Bruce *thereafter* earned the unchallengeable status of a great national leader.

Barbour's account of Robert I was clearly intended to cast some reflected glory on the much inferior Robert II, who had gained very little by his own endeavours. Yet it would be an over-simplification to consider his purpose as merely to flatter his royal patron. In Bruce's time, a brave, generous and dynamic warrior-king had earned the loyalty of his subjects and fought successfully, with their assistance, to secure Scotland's freedom. David II had fallen far short in all aspects of this; Robert II even further. It is not pushing conjecture beyond its permissible limits to imagine that Barbour wrote to inspire the inept kings of his own time to rule in a manner more worthy of their great predecessor, and their lawless subjects to display the loyalty which Bruce's lords had shown to him. Robert II appears to have been chronically handicapped by the fact that his claim to the throne was through his mother.[5] Barbour's poem must have pointedly reminded him of the fact that his grandfather had technically no claim at all, but had brilliantly justified his kingship by his success as a national leader.

Barbour, therefore, wrote with the deliberate aim of enhancing Scotland's pride in its history and its heroic achievements, in order to keep the national spirit high during a sad period and to present an inspiring standard for the men of his time to emulate. These are noble aims; and his artistic success can be measured by the place held in the national consciousness to this day by the people and events he describes.

Thirdly, Barbour's poem set Scottish literature on a new course of development by adopting and naturalising a poetic form already widely popular in continental Europe. The type of poem known as 'romance', in which the deeds of a hero such as Hector of Troy, King Arthur or Charlemagne were recounted on an epic scale, was a well-developed genre; and the tales embodied in the romances fell into three sets: the Matter of Rome (stories of Troy and the legendary founding of Rome by Aeneas), the Matter of France (stories of Charlemagne and his Twelve Peers), and the Matter of Britain (stories of Brut, the mythical founder of Britain, and the Arthurian cycle). The *Brus* is the first Scottish exemplar of the tradition.[6] However, Barbour's choice and treatment of his subject is highly innovative. Firstly, he wrote in Scots, until then a relatively undeveloped vernacular tongue, instead of Latin (the universal language of historical chronicles) or a language with a well-established literary tradition like French. Next, his hero is not a semi-legendary figure or one from a remote historical period, but a man whose exploits had occurred within living memory. That is, Barbour was writing for a popular audience, not only the learned and courtly hearers of traditional romances; and about events which many of them would have known at first or second hand: he states specifically on several occasions that he had got his information from men who had been present at the action. (Not the least important aspect of his poem is as a source of historical evidence: Barbour was a more conscientious researcher than many historians of his period, even on occasions giving two accounts of the same event with the explanation that he has been unable to ascertain which of them was true.) His transplanting of a poetic genre associated with the heroes of antiquity to his own place and time had far-reaching results. It enabled him to place his Scotland in a universal context, and to aggrandise his protagonists by citing classical precedents for their deeds and their heroic virtues. Barbour is fond of comparing his characters to mighty predecessors: Bruce, his brother Edward, his lieutenants Douglas and Randolph, measure favourably against Hector, Tydeus, King David or Judas Maccabeus; and by contrast Comyn is likened to Mordred and Caesar's assassins. Barbour's achievement, indeed, is nothing less than the foundation of a literary Matter of Scotland: a foundation at once built upon by other writers, of whom the greatest after Barbour is Blind Harry with his epic of Wallace; and on which our Scottish patriotic feelings today are very firmly founded.

A further innovation in Barbour's treatment of the romance genre is that his presentation of warfare is ruthlessly realistic. Bruce in the poem is as heroic as Hector or Sir Lancelot, but his heroism consists not simply in an ability to fight bravely: he is a military commander up against almost impossible odds, forced to seize the advantage as and when he can. We read in Barbour more about the bloodshed, disorder and terror of battle than about its pageantry and imposing spectacle; and the cold, discomfort and physical strain of guerrilla warfare form a background to much of the poem. It is in this context that some of its characteristic

episodes occur, such as that of Bruce, waiting with his men while
they are being rowed, a few at a time, across Loch Lomond, keeping their spirits high by telling them stories from the heroic
romances; or that of a French knight expressing surprise that
Bruce, at the siege of Perth, should join his men in wading through
the city's filthy moat. (Barbour would have appreciated the disillusionment of the imposing French troop which arrived in Scotland
during the minority of David II to help their allies in the renewed
war against Edward III's England: expecting to win glory in big
pitched battles, they were sadly disappointed to find that the Scots
preferred their own less impressive but more reliable guerrilla tac-
tics!)

Barbour's moral outlook on events, too, is less simple than in
the traditional romance world. His characters, great as they are, are
fallible human beings: Edward Bruce is sometimes rash and hasty,
Randolph can make military errors, even Bruce can act unwisely,
listen to bad advice or give way to temporary loss of heart; and by
contrast, English knights can show chivalry and valour, and receive
the poet's praise for it. And though Barbour is among the most
ardently patriotic of poets, he does not naively equate Bruce's or
Scotland's cause with the right side. He is at pains to argue that the
English have put themselves morally in the wrong by making an
unprovoked attack on a smaller and weaker country which had
shown no hostility to them. Patriotism is a virtue in Barbour's
poem and inspires men to great deeds; but patriotism operates in
the service of a higher moral imperative: the duty to fight against
those who would break God's law by acts of oppression and rob-
bery. On many occasions in the poem Barbour sees God's hand in
the events described: Bruce's early misfortunes in the war are
implicitly attributed to the fact that he killed Comyn in a church,
thus breaching sanctuary; but later he can confidently say to his
men before Bannockburn 'We haf the rycht, And for the rycht ay
God will fycht'.

For all those reasons, the significance of Barbour's poem is
enormous. Yet it would not have survived in popular memory, or
exerted its far-reaching influence, had it not been plainly and simply a great poem. And the last point to be made about the *Brus* is
the most essential one of all: the poem which initiates the splendid

pageant of literature in the Lowland tongue is of a quality worthy of its subject. Rapid and lively in its action, abounding in realistic dialogue passages, full of exciting and vividly-described scenes of combat ranging in scale from Bruce's single-handed defeat of three traitors to the Battle of Bannockburn, it is the work of a master story-teller. The tales familiar to generations of Scottish schoolchildren – Bruce's escape from the bloodhound at the ford, the taking of Edinburgh Castle, the Douglas Larder, the felling of Henry de Bohun – are all here, in memorable detail. His dramatic characterisation of Bruce, an admiring but realistic portrait of a great warrior king, is worthy of – a writer with whom he has much in common, and who would have appreciated the comparison – Walter Scott: besides the episodes which show the king's indomitable courage, his ferocity in battle and his tactician's ability to turn the most daunting of military situations to his advantage, we see the humanity of a leader who delays the departure of his troop while a camp laundress gives birth. And though on a first reading the poem is likely to suggest a sequence of thrilling episodes, it has in fact a carefully-planned large-scale structure. Barbour's brief summary of the background to Bruce's assumption of the throne leads to his famous apostrophe to freedom, a keynote passage for the entire poem; the ensuing story of Bruce's initial defeat and the resulting misfortunes befalling him and his followers gives place to his, and Scotland's, gradual recovery, and the climactic Battle of Bannockburn. The scene then shifts to Ireland as Edward Bruce attempts, unsuccessfully, to establish a kingdom there;[7] and returns to the King's story with his successful prosecution of the war, now largely on English soil, the triumphant peace negotiations, and Bruce's death. As a sort of coda, Barbour rounds off the story with Douglas's departure on crusade bearing Bruce's heart in a casket, and his death in battle against the Moors in Spain.[8]

Barbour's theme is a worthly focus for Scottish patriotic pride; so is his poem. The extensive, brilliant and strongly national corpus of literature in the Lowland Scots tongue could have no more fitting overture than the epic of *Brus*.

NOTES

[1] From the greatest of his four extant poems, *Sir Gawain and the Green Knight.*

[2] A fact which sometimes causes surprise is that the first fully English-speaking monarch after the Norman Conquest was Henry IV, who succeeded in 1399. His predecessor Richard II was an ardent Francophile who disdained the English language. Edward Langshanks, Bruce's great antagonist, certainly knew no English.

[3] *This* Bruce – Robert Bruce the Competitor, whose claim to the throne was considered by Edward – was, of course, the grandfather of the future hero-king. Critics have almost universally assumed that Barbour either confused or deliberately amalgamated the two; but the fact that he does not say specifically that the Competitor was *not* the same man as the hero of the poem, which would be perfectly well known to his original readers, is hardly evidence that he actually believed or wished to suggest that he *was.*

[4] The true facts regarding Bruce's pact with Comyn, if indeed there was one, have never been ascertained: in the nature of things it is unlikely that their conversations would have been recorded in durable form.

[5] David II was childless. Robert II was the son, born posthumously, of Bruce's daughter Marjorie, who had married Walter the Great Steward of Scotland.

[6] Thomas of Ercildoune (the historical 'Thomas the Rhymer') is recorded as having written a poem of Sir Tristram, which may have been an example of the same genre; but it has not survived.

[7] This is one of the most controversial and variously-interpreted episodes in the whole history of the period: in Ireland it is regarded to this day as an unmitigated disaster.

[8] Spanish chronicles of the period testify to Douglas's valour and the high regard in which he was held by the Spanish King and nobles.

R.D.S. JACK

The Wallace

Among native writers, Robert Burns and Walter Scott have had the greatest influence in formulating visions of Scotland abroad. While both read the works of their medieval and renaissance predecessors with admirable thoroughness, each unequivocally places John Barbour's *Bruce* (c.1375) and the *Wallace* of Henry the Minstrel (c.1476) at the epicentre of their own and their nation's concern. Scott notes in his Preface to *The Lord of the Isles*, 'I could hardly have chosen a subject more popular in Scotland, than anything connected with Bruce's history, unless I had attempted that of the Wallace'.[1] For Burns, the later of these long, historical Romances was the more influential. Writing to Dr. John Moore, he lists it along with Plutarch's *Life of Hannibal*, as the earliest written influence on his boyish imagination. 'The story of Wallace poured a Scottish prejudice in my veins, which will boil along there till the flood-gates of life shut in eternal rest'.[2]

In the context of post-colonial theory, Burns's evaluation of the *Wallace*, has three important implications:

Historical Relativity: Burns knew the textual pedigree of the poem he was reading. Hamilton of Gilbertfield's eighteenth century translation of Henry's poem, which was his immediate source, normally kept very close to the original but did make some changes to it.[3] As a minstrel, the author of the original had, in his turn, poetically adapted the 'truth' of history from earlier chronicle evidence, principally that provided by Wyntoun and Bower.[4] Burns, therefore, accepted that literary versions of history would alter known facts in relation to changing audience tastes.

Pity and Patriotism: Burns was also trained as a 'makar' or rhetorical word-builder. He does not, therefore, expect to read a factual

account. From a base in chronicled history, the bard may imaginatively arrange, adapt and delete events in order to arouse the pity
necessary for Aristotelian catharsis on behalf of his chosen hero.
Both Plutarch and the *Wallace*, are welcomed in these terms, as
sentimental evocations of warfare, designed to make their audience
wish themselves soldiers. 'Prejudice' and a call to arms against the
English are the emotional and active aims which the latter hopes to
evoke. This presents an early variation on Fanon's theme, that the
coloniser 'turns to the past of the oppressed people, and distorts,
disfigures and destroys it'.[5] Those who believe that the principles
of post-colonial theory are only applicable to Scottish literature
once the national parliament was sacrificed in 1707, forget that
even in its days of independence, this was a people under constant
threat from the feudal claims of their larger neighbour. For three
centuries before that event Scottish poets had used the techniques
outlined by Fanon in a counter-colonising defence of this fragile
freedom.

Origins and Anagogy. Derek Walcott's comments on the 'Old World'
and 'its longing for innocence' have to be carefully refined, when
considering the medieval interest in national origins.[6] The makars,
in common with poets in other ages, may wish for innocence now
and imagine it in the past. But, as Christian writers, they had no
belief in it. For them, fallen actions and fallen words were the lot of
humankind since the days of Adam. When they literally 'make up'
the different courses[7] of their allegorical texts, they are only too
aware that God normally concealed himself beyond time, offering
only oblique signs by way of guidance. Revealed visions alone
might fictively suggest participation within the knowledge of the
first Maker of all. More usually, their artifice confined itself to the
realm of pragmatic moral guidance. Barbour, indeed, denied any
direct concern with final (anagogical) concerns, leaving such matters to academics and 'thaim that ar of mar renown' (I, 260).

Three major questions follow on this evidence. Most basically,
does knowledge of the *Wallace* and its author broadly confirm this
theory that the 'makars' might re-organize or alter the facts of history? And, if this is so, why and how are the changes made – literally
and allegorically? Finally, are the mysterious intentions for
Scotland's patriot avoided or revealed?

Background knowledge of hero, text and minstrel provide a clear answer to the first query. Sir William Wallace (1270-1305) is still regarded by many as the founder of Scottish nationalism. Brought up in a period of English occupation, he entered historical records at the age of 27 as a leader in the frequent uprisings against the occupiers. In the same year, 1297, he killed the English Sheriff of Lanark. This event drew him into the nationalist army then led by Andrew Murray. He was prominent in the Scottish victory over English forces at Stirling Bridge and rose to the rank of Guardian of Scotland. But his end was tragic. Betrayed in 1305, he faced a charge of treason before an English court at Westminster Hall. Found guilty, he was hanged, disembowelled and beheaded on 23 August of that year. His limbs were then variously dispatched to Newcastle, Berwick, Perth and Stirling to warn other would-be patriots of their likely fate.

The *Wallace* was composed in the late 1470s. At this time, James III's unpopular policy of appeasing England was causing widespread anger in the country. The poem, therefore, speaks out in favour of the past and of stern patriotism at a particularly apposite time. If he opposed James III, James IV seems to have valued his services, as records show him in attendance on that monarch in Linlithgow.[8] While his identity remains shadowy, his twelve book poem proves that he was well educated and widely read, not only in his own language but in Latin and French. As he was well versed in what Dr. Johnson termed 'the faith of chronicles', when he departs from their evidence, it may be assumed that he does so knowingly.

Normally, of course, this is not the case. Most of the historical events he records did happen, although those highlighted may be carefully selected. This principle of selective truthfulness applies to the factual event used to introduce the vulnerability of Scotland's royal succession to claims from the south:

Quhen Alexander our worthi king had lorn°   lost
Be aventur° his liff besid Kyngorn...   By chance (I, 41-42)[9]

The accidental death of Alexander III initiated doubts over hereditary rights to the Scottish throne. As English kings could now advance their own genealogical claims to the crown, attempts to

annex the northern kingdom increased from that day on. But
Alexander's tragic fall from his horse is also an ideal opening for
any 'counter-colonising' attempt to warn Scots of the dangers
implied by this situation. It is significant, therefore, that Henry
echoes his bardic predecessor, John Barbour, not only in the event
he chooses, but in the phraseology he employs to describe it.[10] If
Henry follows Barbour in using the norm of historical verisimili-
tude as a foundation for the presentation of other kinds of persuasive 'truth' entirely, he also proves the more inventive of the two.
As James Goldstein rightly notes, the many overt references to the
historical accuracy of the text seem

> [...] all the more significant once we recognize the extent to which he is,
> in fact, lying through his teeth. The battles of Loudon Hill, Biggar, and
> Linlithgow, the invasion of England as far as St. Albans in York, the Barns
> of Ayr incident, Wallace's threefold rescue of Scotland: these are just
> some outstanding examples of what modern historians would instantly
> recognize as departures from 'real' history.[11]

The principle of historical relativism does, therefore, characterise
the Wallace.

The second task – to explain why a fifteenth century Scottish
poet believed he could manipulate history and how this principle
betrays itself in the text's narrative, characterisation and structure –
is much more challenging. To begin the process, some understanding of the ways in which a fifteenth century bard's art and education differed from to-day's is needed. First of all, Henry worked in
a predominantly oral culture, as the narrator's language confirms.

Off Inglismen sum-part speke I will   (III, 444)
Of Wallace end to her°...   to hear   (XII, 302)

When references to reading do occur, they either mean 'reading
aloud', or 'interpreting' the written text. The poet's art, therefore,
remains within the broader, classical remit of oratorical persuasion.
In the fifteenth century university curriculum, Aristotle (especially)
and Cicero dominated thinking in this area.

The limitations of human memory become a crucial consideration for authors composing under these auspices. To that end, both
classical and medieval commentators advised poets to make their
topic clear from the outset. Henry's 'sententia' is as clear as it is

bloodthirsty. His poem will warn Scots not to follow James III in trusting the English 'in their mychty pryde' (I, 12) because

| Our auld ennemyis cummyn of° Saxonys blud | are descended from |
| That° nevyr yeit to Scotland wald° do guid. | Who; wished to (I, 7-8) |

The need to defend Scotland martially against attack from the south will be the steadfast persuasive aim of his poem. In the final book the narrator even explicitly confirms that his boasts of truthfulness refer to that proposed topic: 'In this sentence, I had na will to le' means 'In relation to this theme [rather than to the facts of history] I have no wish to lie' (XII, 1438).

Literary 'truthfulness' for late medieval authors, as evaluated against the normative curricular teachings of Aristotle, Horace and the medieval grammarians, was not equated with representing facts alone. Horace in particular urged the moral remit of history as a vehicle for teaching, while Aristotle granted to the poetic imagination, freedom to explore issues across the entire disciplinary range. At this stage, it is the literal story line which is our major concern, however, and even there the causal line of rhetorical craftsmanship equated the end of mimetic 'making' with achieving a specified audience response. Henry is doing no more than follow the most revered authorities of his day, when he opens by defining a theme and suggesting an appropriate response to it.

Even the means by which his Epic-cum-Romance will achieve this end is conventional. It is pity for which the narrator and characters overtly appeal. After describing this uneven, national contest over the centuries, the bard proclaims that it 'pitte was to se' such slaughter (I,107). The character of Wallace is then shown to agree, for he 'Gret pitte thocht that Scotland tuk sic harmys' (I,182). Fear is also invoked in this early account of Wallace's cruel treatment at English hands, in a land ruled by foreign forces obeying Edward I. Throughout the poem these two emotions are counterpointed in tacit agreement with the cathartic theories, deemed appropriate for tragedy by Aristotle, 'The tragic pleasure is that of pity and fear, and the poet has to produce it by a work of imitation'.[12] In the end, as in the beginning, the pitiful appeal of the work is reiterated, 'Off Wallace end to her it is pete'. (XII, 302).

The apparent simplicity of this claim belies an obvious problem.

In Epic and martial Romance, the modes whose conventions
Henry's poem most regularly draws upon, the balance between
pity and fear is particularly problematic. In both modes, honour
and martial courage are the emotions to be encouraged by the
cathartic movement. While it is proper to evoke pity for the hero,
however, the question naturally arises as to whether an audience
will still be keen to embark on a war, however righteous, after
being vividly reminded of the hero's gruesome death! Intelligently,
the author of the *Wallace* meets this dilemma by avoiding it. He
may talk of the pity his hero's barbaric death should evoke but the
facts of execution, disembowelling and limb-dispersal are rhetorically circumvented:

Bot Wallas end in warld was displesans°,	distress	
Tharfor I ces° and puttis nocht in rym.	cease	(XII, 1230-1231)

There are some instances when pity may intensify fear rather than
purify it. The good makar has to know when a cathartic imbalance
of this sort is likely.

Wallace's early days as an innocent under English rule offer no
restraints of this sort. The melodramatic conventions of the legends
of the saints, are used to evoke pity for him as one of the many
vulnerable Scots, forced to endure contempt and cruelty at the
hands of the occupying army. It is unsurprising, therefore, that
Burns who admits that 'his favourite authors are of the sentimental
kind', finds this section of the poem particularly affecting. Writing
to one of Wallace's ancestors, he recalls the account, in Book II, of
young Wallace retreating into Leglen woods. He even went to the
spot 'with as much devout enthusiasm as ever Pilgrim did to
Loretto'.[13] Burns's patriotic desire to see for himself the place
where Scotland's future Guardian overpowered an evil English
'churll' may be touching. But he is only worshipping the poetic
powers of another patriot-bard, as the entire incident is almost certainly imaginary.

If the strengthening of sentiment justifies inventions with no
secure base in history, it also allows historical possibilities to
become fictive certainties. For example, the possibility that Wallace
killed the Sheriff of Lanark to avenge the death of his wife
becomes, in Book VI, an established fact whose pitiful ramifica-

tions are exhaustively explored with Mrs. Wallace inevitably becoming as pure and innocent as the Sheriff is vile.

As this incident implies, simplified persuasive patterns carry over from the events described into the realm of characterisation. Here, exaggerated contrasts between heroes and villains is the name of the game. First, Henry elevates the moral and spiritual qualities of his Scottish heroes so far above the evidence of chronicles that they threaten to become stereotypes of virtue. Wallace, in particular, must be the perfect patriot-warrior. To this end, the victories of Robert Bruce at Loudon Hill and of Douglas at Stanhope are fictively transferred to him. In this iconic guise, his deeds are appropriately judged against the highest examples available in classical Epic or medieval Romance. In generosity he becomes 'lik Alexander the king', in courage 'the rycht Ector was he' (X, 1242-1244).

This makes him at once an individual to be admired and an icon whose behaviour may become a model for others. To aid this effect, the major heroes and villains become type characters, assessed (positively or negatively) against the defining characteristics of Epic heroism. The criteria of courage (fortitudo) and strategic wisdom (sapientia) demanded within the classical Epic become an alliterative formula in Middle Scots – Wallace is always both 'wicht' and 'wys'.[14] This is only one side of the 'colonising' mindset as described by Fanon. To empty England's history of its claims to honour, the author of the *Wallace* makes most of the English usurpers just as cowardly and foolish as their Scottish foes are brave and wise. The additional Virgilian characteristic of *pietas* is also introduced and it is this sense of moral duty, which memorably distinguishes Wallace from his most powerful foe – Edward I, Hammer of the Scots. Edward does not fail the tests of courage or cleverness, but morally and spiritually, he is set on the side of Satan. The first martial confrontation between the two clearly confirms the methodology. A Christlike Wallace commands a pious army, who kneel before God prior to the conflict while Edward's host imitate their leader's devilish characteristics of 'prydefull Ire'.

These moral and spiritual associations remind us that, so far, this study has confined itself almost entirely to the literal level of interpretation. But the poet in particular has the imaginative power to refract questions across all levels of allegorical exploration political, moral and divine. In fact, Horace uses the kind of epic characterisation discussed above as a means of discussing the way in which Homer uses history to teach such lessons. Ulysses in his 'power of worth and wisdom... sets before us an instructive pattern'.[15]

The author of the *Wallace*, whose narrator offers 'parablys' (I,16) as well as history, provides an ambitious example of this type of craftsmanship. His hero's temporal tragedy will be considered morally and divinely as well as personally and historically. A change of focus from characterisation to structuring will demonstrate how the various levels of this poetic building may retain their formal unity, yet teach at different levels in different ways. To use the historical facts of the past to sign the intentions of God was, of course, an accepted medieval approach in chronicle as well as history, while Aristotle's extension of the poet's mimetic domain to include potentiality and Platonic Ideas gave the bard freedom to pose questions across the entire allegorical range.[16]

How, then, does Henry construct the allegorical message of his text? At the foundation level of the word-building, Wallace's life is divided into two parallel sections. Books I-VI trace the hero's youth while Books VII-XII deal with his mature career. Within these divisions, events are often grouped in threes. Wallace, for example is made Guardian three times. While there is no historical authority for this, the number of joy and the Trinity provides a mysterious reminder that higher authorities exist and may offer Scotland's patriots a kinder final judgement.

If Wallace's biography is *per se* tragic, its political and natural configurations provide a more explicit form of comfort than the numerological symbolism noted above. From these perspectives, regenerative schemes dominate. Politically, Wallace's life is framed within a mythological account of Scotland's origins, which at once confirms that country's just cause and its divine origins as God's chosen nation. Thus, he inherits 'The haly linage and trew line of Scotland' (I, 21) from Fergus, the country's first mythical king. That nátion's odyssey 'Fra Spane Quhen Iber Scot fyrst in-till Irland come' (I, 121) is also seen as a time served in the wilderness, prior to arrival in a promised land.

Natural signs reaffirm the hopeful message of this larger tale.

Each transient life, like Wallace's, must end in the winter of death.
But a series of formal seasonal introductions (Books III-VI) establish the unchanging, re-creative pattern which lies behind this.
These open with one joyous season (summer) and end with another (spring). Even autumn becomes a hopeful sign within this
divinely comic pattern. As a colder season than summer, it fittingly
provides the backdrop for the young hero's exile in the 'wildernes
so wyde' of Book IV. But it also furnishes man with the mature
fruits of the earlier season:

In September, the humyll° moneth swete,	modest
Quhen passyt by the hycht° was off the hette°,	extremity; heat
Victaill° and froyte° ar rypyt in aboundance	food; fruit
As god ordans to mannys governance°.	government (IV, 1-4)

Within this divine 'governance' bad fortune makes the strong,
stronger – a lesson which Wallace learns in Book IV.

   Spiritually, prophecies are the main device employed to move
beyond past into future. Prospective in nature, artistically they have
a retrospective force allowing Wallace's mature achievements to be
assessed triumphantly at the outset. In Books I and II, Scotland's
final victory over the English is anticipated and Wallace's crucial
role within that process evaluated. Ironically, English soothsayers
are the first to prophesy that one of the Wallace family will, later,
overthrow Edward II. With commendable ingenuity, they identify
Isabel Valois as a 'Wallis'. Isobel and her son will defeat Edward
and, in driving the English out of Scotland for ever, fulfil the
prophecy that: 'A Wallace suld putt thame of Scotland' (I, 352):
In Book II, the Scottish seer, Thomas the Rhymer confirms these
beliefs with more enthusiasm:

Then Thomas said, 'Forsuth, or he deces°,	before he dies
Mony° thousand in field sall mak thar end.	Many
Off° this regioune he sall the Southron° send,	Out of; English
And Scotland thris° he sall bryng to the pes°¹	thrice; peace (II, 346-349)

Thus, divine comedy for Wallace and Scotland's cause encloses and
counterpoints the hero's tragic death prophetically, as well as historically, naturally and politically.

   In Biblical and doctrinal terms, Wallace's early life as leader in a
wilderness has already been noted. If comparisons with Moses and

John the Baptist are aptly drawn in at this stage, it is with Christ
that the Scottish hero is most regularly compared in the poem as a
whole. Like the young Christ, he sets off about his father's business
and leaves his mother weeping. When he is put in prison and
thought to be dead in Book III, echoes of the Harrowing of Hell
and of the empty tomb lead into a series of appearances to those
who thought him dead. His cousin, Robert Boyd, with his refusal
to believe a female account of their hero's victory over death, even
provides a Scottish type of doubting Thomas.

In a work designed to evoke hatred of the English, contrasts are
deemed necessary at the associative level as well as the dramatic.
When Wallace is seen as a latter-day Moses, Edward I and his
occupying forces become their Biblical counter-types in villainy –
'King Herodis part thai playit in-to Scotland' (I, 165). When the
Scottish hero is associated with Christ, the English king's character
is defined by Satanic subtlety and the devil's dedicated sins of
pride, wrath and envy.

Doctrinally, the calendar of the Christian church is used to
impose order on the necessarily chaotic time scheme of the war.
Historical facts again have to accommodate themselves to this
divinely significant time-scheme. Most obviously major battles are
re-assigned to holy days. The Battle of Stirling Bridge (1297) is re-
dated on Assumption Day, August 15, 1298. The Battle of Falkirk is
even further backdated – from 1298 until St Magdalen's Day, 1303.

All this, the audience is told, should teach them similar faith.
That statement in its turn introduces the ontological issue raised in
the last of the three questions set at the start of the chapter. How
far does the *Wallace* venture fictively beyond time into the mysterious intentions of God? Indeed, given its theme, this question might
be re-phrased. 'Can Henry afford to do otherwise in a religious
age?' After all, his hero in his vengeful bloodthirstiness is scarcely a
model candidate for entry into a patient, merciful Christian heaven.

And Henry does provide answers. Two mysterious visions dominate the first and last books (VII and XII) of the poem's second
section. In Book VII, the sleeping hero is taken by St. Andrew to a
mountain, which signifies knowledge of right and wrong. From
there he sees the entire, glorious history of Scotland laid out before
him. He dies, therefore, knowing that his cause will eventually tri-

umph. If this provides temporal comfort, divine approval is not lacking either. The Virgin, in person, assures him that he will be her chosen love in heaven (VII, 96-104).

Book XII confirms these conclusions. The narrator reinterprets Wallace's vengeful mission in terms of the Day of Judgement – harsh justice may be necessary as a means to mercy. A theological debate then addresses the same problem in terms of the hero's own salvation. Can a man who loved killing Englishmen – 'I lik better to see the Sothren de/Than gold or land' (V, 397) – be granted extreme unction without repenting for this? An English priest argues that it is a sin and must be expiated; a Scottish priest argues the counter-case and absolves him without penance on that score. The second revealed vision enacts these conclusions. A holy monk, on accelerated passage through heaven, is told that even he must give precedence to 'a gret slaar of men' (XII, 1278). This beatified soul proves to be no other than the unapologetically vengeful Wallace. In this way, personal tragedy becomes part of a higher comedy and the fifteenth century audience are encouraged to believe that they too may enjoy killing Saxons on their way to bliss!

Later versions of the *Wallace* tend to play down or omit these anagogical movements. Hamilton, in an age dominated by protestantism and rationalism certainly does so and it is his version on which the twentieth-century film *Braveheart*, is based.[17] Within the allegorical structure of their source, however, they are crucial, providing as they do the last and highest course of all. This serves to warn the critic against concepts derived from later post-colonial theory simplistically. At the same time, the intense national self-consciousness of the *Wallace* (and the *Bruce*) as well as their call for all classes to rally to the standard, make them exceptions to the general rules drawn up by Anderson in *Imagined Communities*, when arguing that concepts of nationhood usually post-date feudalism.[18] Henry follows Barbour in demanding that the class loyalties of noble to noble, merchant to merchant encouraged across geographical boundaries encouraged by that hierarchical system be waived in certain cases. As the justification proves to be 'The haly linage and trew line of Scotland' (I, 21), it follows that the community of Scotland in the 1370s and in the 1470s exists and may be appealed to in those terms. Any 'imagining' of that community by way of glorifying its past to influence its present, remains in the hands of the bards. And their re-'making' of history, given this shared ground, will bear careful comparison with the practice and the theory of later days.

NOTES

[1] In the Introduction to the 1833 edition. The medieval wars of liberty remain a major rallying call for the Scottish nationalist consciousness to-day.

[2] *The Letters of Robert Burns*, edited by G. Ross Roy, Oxford: Clarendon Press, 1985, I, 136. no. 125. He read it in translation; see no. 3.

[3] William Hamilton (c.1665-1751) was a poet and soldier. His translation of the *Wallace* was hugely popular. A convenient edition is William Hamilton of Gilbertfield, *Blind Harry's Wallace*, Edinburgh: Luath Press, 1998.

[4] See *The Original Chronicle of Andrew of Wyntoun*, edited by F.J. Amours, Scottish Text Society, 6 vols., Edinburgh and London: Blackwood, 1902-1906; *Scotichronicon*, general editor: D.E.R. Watt, 9 vols., Edinburgh: Mercat Press, 1990-1999.

[5] Franz Fanon, 'On National Culture', in Bill Ashcroft, Gareth Griffin and Helen Tiffin eds., *The Post-Colonial Studies Reader*, London: Routledge, 1997, (pp. 153-156) p. 154.

[6] Derek Walcott, *What the Twilight Says*, London: Faber & Faber, 1998, p. 40.

[7] The image of the text as a house, built upwards on various distinct but interrelated levels is a commonplace in the medieval commentary tradition. See, for example, *The Didascalicon of Hugh of St Victor*, translated by Jerome Taylor, New York: Columbia University Press, 1991, VI. 4, pp. 139-45.

[8] The fullest background account is given by Matthew MacDiarmid (editor) in his introduction to *Harry's Wallace*, Scottish Text Society, 2 vols. Edinburgh and London: Blackwood, 1968; 1969, I, pp. ix-cxxxii.

[9] Quotations are based on MacDiarmid's edition with some normalisation to aid understanding.

[10] 'Quhen Alexander the king wes deid/That Scotland had to steir and leid' (*Bruce*, I, 37-38).

[11] R. James Goldstein, *The Matter of Scotland*, Lincoln, Neb.: University of Nebraska Press, 1993, p. 252.

[12] *The Complete Works of Aristotle*, 2 vols. edited by Jonathan Barnes, Princeton NJ: Princeton University Press, II, 2326: Poetics, 1453b.

[13] Robert Burns, *Letters*, I, 62. no. 54.

[14] See for example I, 184; II, 436. His loyal supporters and friends are similarly evaluated. See III, 390 for the case of his cousin, Robert Boyd.

[15] Horace, *Satires, Epistles, Ars Poetica*, edited by H.R. Fairclough, Loeb Library edition, London and New York: Heinemann, 1926, p. 18. Epistle I.ii, lines 17-18.

[16] '...the poet's function is to describe, not the thing that has happened but a kind of thing that might happen'. *Poetics* 1451a1.

[17] *Braveheart* was produced in 1997 by Twentieth Century Fox.

[18] Benedict Anderson, *Imagined Communities*, London: Verso, 1936.

R.D.S. Jack

Robert Henryson

Robert Henryson (c.1450-1505) is now recognized as one of
Scotland's major poets. This chapter's purpose is the critical sub-
stantiation of that claim through analysis of his major narrative
poems – *Orpheus and Eurydice*, *The Testament of Cresseid* and *The
Morall Fabillis of Esope the Phrygian*. But his position as Scot and
European, from artistic, sociological, biographical and linguistic
perspectives, will initially be established.

In Scottish literary history, he is viewed as, chronologically, the
first in a trinity of late fifteenth and early sixteenth century poets.
His moral narratives, when grouped along with the lyrics of
William Dunbar (c.1480-1520) and the *Eneados* of Gavin Douglas
(1476-1522), form a body of work, which compares favourably
with contemporary writing in England. As 'makars' or word-
builders, they work within the traditions of Classical Rhetoric as
conditioned by Christian Scholastic thought.[1] But viewing
Henryson's work from a Southern European perspective also highlights crucial differences. In Italy, Renaissance humanism challenged the ideas of the Middle Ages. In Northern Europe, that transition was significantly delayed and much more gradual. The terms
Medieval or Renaissance as applied to Henryson are, therefore, seldom helpful.[2]

Sociologically, it might seem surprising that a small, poor, war-
torn nation could provide literature of quality. Henryson, after all,
lived most of his life during the reign of James III when visitors
from Southern Europe usually confirmed the opinion of Matthew
Paris, that Scotland was a country, fit only for cattle and shepherds.[3]
The king, who succeeded to the throne after the violent death of
his father, was murdered by a group of rebels, including his own

son, in 1488. But barbarism and internecine strife were not the whole picture. The Universities of Glasgow (1451) and Aberdeen (1495) were founded in that period, as were many of the country's major grammar schools.[4]

While James IV strove to make the Edinburgh court a cultural centre, Henryson's scant biographical records place him within another developing social area – that of the burgh and the educated middle class associated with it. He was certainly a schoolmaster (probably headmaster) of the Abbey school in Dunfermline in the early 1470s and may have retained that position in later life. If he can be identified with the Robert Henryson, who taught law at Glasgow University prior to this, then he held the degrees of Master of Arts and Bachelor of Canon Law – probably from a European University. His neoplatonism, rhetorical skills and detailed knowledge of legal and burgh life are certainly consistent with that life pattern.

For a long time, Henryson's reputation was overshadowed by that of Dunbar due to the greater linguistic virtuosity of his fellow makar. As professional court poet, Dunbar was paid to demonstrate the full stylistic range of Middle Scots at a time when it could match the Chaucerean dialect of Middle English in subtlety. Henryson, by contrast, is firmly based within the Middle Style. This is not because extremes are beyond him; the complex internal rhyme and Latinate diction of 'Ane Prayer for the Pest' reveal his ability to match high topic with High Style:

> Superne lucerne, guberne this pestilens,
> Preserve and serve that we nocht sterf thairin,
> Declyne that pyne be thy devyne prudens,
> For trewth, haif rewth, lat nocht oure slewth us twyn.[5]

For successful use of the Low Style, one need only turn to 'Sum Practysis of Medecyne':

> Put all thir in ane pan with pepper and pik.
> Syne sett in to this,
> The count of ane cow kis;
> Is nocht better, I wis,
> For the collik.   ('Practysis', 35-39)

His preference derives from his rhetorical training; the Horatian laws of decorum advise the Middle Style for poets, who wish to teach clearly.

He has also been called a Scottish Chaucerean. True, he admires Chaucer as poet and as originator of the vernacular movement in British verse. Henryson's 'The Cock and the Fox' is a reworking of 'The Nun's Priest's Tale' and *The Testament of Cresseid* derives from *Troilus and Criseyde*. But the debt confessed at the beginning of the latter poem, written more than a century later, sets limits on his discipleship. He is enthusiastic about Chaucer's depiction of Troilus:

> For worthie Chauceir in the samin buik,
> In gudelie termis and in joly veirs,
> Complyit hes his cairis...   (*Testament*, 58-60)

but questions whether the Englishman's word should simply be acccpted – 'Quha wait gif all that Chauceir wrait was trew?' (64). His own poem will derive from 'inventioun' (67) and concentrate on the fate of the heroine, whose later disappearance from the centre of Chaucer's concern disturbs his critical sensibilities.

His shorter lyrics, most of which deal with religious or philo-sophical themes, also match rhetorical skill to didactic intent. 'The Prologue' to his thirteen *Morall Fabillis of Aesope the Phrygian*, which are based on various sources including Gualterus Anglicus, Lydgate's *Fabules* and *Le Roman de Renart*, also offers 'ane morall sweit sentence' (12). Following Boethius, he identifies these 'polite termes of sweit rhetore' (3) as the means of making learning plea-surable. Then, using Aquinas's argument that a bowstring should not be kept taut all the time, he reassures his readers that 'sad materis' will mix with 'merines' (26).

Those who hope to derive this pleasure easily are quickly dis-abused. Each fable will present its own unique hermeneutic chal-lenge. Indeed he has chosen the form because animals, sharing a bestial soul with us but lacking its rational counterpart, are espe-cially suited to the analogic mode of poetry (43-56). Concentration first on the common ground and then on human distinctiveness will set up such obvious dislocations between narrative and moral logics that the reader, faced with the Scottish equivalent of Dante's *versi strani*,[6] must till at the rough earth of the story if the flower of knowledge is to flourish in his mind (8-14). He must crack a 'schell... hard and teuch' before the 'kirnell sweit' of 'doctryne wyse' will emerge (15 -17).

The medieval writer was taught to establish theme and method clearly at the outset. In his opening tale of the starving cock who discovers a jewel, Henryson does both. The focus on starvation unites animal and human reactions. We are encouraged to share the cock's sad rejection of the jewel as inappropriate to his imme-diate needs. But the moral overtly moves the hermeneutic goal-posts. A series of possible applications for the jewel image are fol-lowed by an injunction to think specifically of the rational soul and re-translate our conclusions on the premise that the jewel represent knowledge. This allows Henryson to foreshadow the *versi strani* method in extreme form at the outset but also to reconfirm his own authorial position. The question, 'Quha can governe ane realme, cietie, or hous/Without science?' (136-137) challenges the learned to involve themselves in worldly problems. 'The Prologue' had defined the entire pedagogic purpose of the *Fabillis* in these terms.

In seeing the end of poetry as effective audience persuasion and by claiming imagination as the proper (quidditative) focus for fic-tion, Henryson places himself firmly within the Scholastic commen-tating tradition from Aristotle through Augustine to Dante.[7] This inheritance had indeed been confirmed in the first stanza of the *Fabillis*. Henryson's justification of the allegorical method ('be fig-ure of ane uther thing') as a necessary means of guiding fallen man towards helpful truths and a better life ('to repreif the of thi misleving-ing') is identical in theory and spirit to 'The Epistle to Can Grande'.

The tales, which most evidently comment on Scottish society are 'The Two Mice', 'The Sheep and the Dog' and 'The Lion and the Mouse'. The story of town and country mouse, each experiencing the other's life, mirrors the growth of the Scottish burgh. The inno-cent sheep's appeal for justice before a court of powerful enemies is closely modelled on Scottish legal practice. James III's problems in controlling his nobles and the common people are clearly fore-shadowed in Henryson's version of King Lion's strange alliance with one of his most insignificant subjects. Vocabulary and situa-tion point beyond the animal example in each case. The town mouse is a Scottish 'gild brother' and 'fre burges', who lives 'toll-fre' (172-173) and owns her own home unlike her outlawed, country cousin. The procedures and language followed in the sheep's farcical trial imitate those procedures followed in a Scottish consistorial court. The problems faced by the slothful lion so closely shadow the political difficulties of James III, that a Scottish audience would easily relate the two.

Nonetheless, the rough soil of each story has to be tilled differently. The human details ascribed to animals in 'The Two Mice' are the only signs of a specialised political meaning. There is no other obvious mismatch between story and generalised moral. In 'The Lion and the Mouse', by contrast, the national application is reserved for the moral and *versi strani* abound. The lion is punished only after he has ceased to be slothful; the hunters of the tale would seem to prefigure the nobility but are not so defined in the *Moralitas*. 'The Sheep and the Dog' offers no clear break between fable and moral but latterly reinforces the legal satire by moving from terminology based on consistorial practice to the diction of civil law.

The principle of variety also allows Henryson to focus his lessons differently across the entire allegorical range of reference. Fittingly, the final fable, 'The Paddock and the Mouse', embraces all of the perspectives covered by that method. The mouse's efforts to avoid the kite and cross a stream on the paddock's back is variously proposed as a sign of the proper relationship between body and soul, a moral lesson in avoiding hypocrites, a doctrinal image of the Fall and an anagogical metaphor of our exile from the true home of heaven. 'The Preiching of the Swallow' covers the same allegorical range but its sermon mode allows the different allegorical applications to build up gradually from the outset. The Swallow itself overtly reads the signs of Nature as a code designed to teach practical, moral and fideistic lessons, leaving the narrator free to concentrate on the higher levels of the allegorical ladder and offer a neat quadruple summation, ending with 'perfite cheritie' and 'blis with angelis' (1944-1950).

Most of the remaining tales have morals couched primarily at one allegorical level of application. Moral philosophy (general tropology) is taught by 'The Cock and the Fox' and 'The Wolf and the Wether' where the dangers of pride, flattery and presumption are wittily enacted. Christian doctrine (allegory) is explained in the Marian conclusion of 'The Trial of the Fox' and the patient, merciful lesson of 'The Wolf and the Lamb'. The final mysteries (anagogy) form the 'doctrine wyse' in the three fox and wolf tales.

Modern readers, puzzled by the ingenuity with which Henryson appends apparently farfetched morals to his narratives, should remember that the Christian God created a world where everything was potentially both good and useful. This gave the well-intentioned writer, to whom the full range of imaginative application was quidditatively open, freedom to interpret stories in any way likely to ease that audience's passage from this life to the next. The opening lines of Henryson's moral sections, therefore, never say that the chosen lesson 'is' or 'must be' the tale's meaning, only that it 'may' offer a helpful interpretation to those willing to listen:

Friendis, heir may ye ye find, will ye tak heid,
In this fabill ane gude moralitie.   ('The Two Mice')

Richt so under ane fabill figurall
Sad sentence men may seik and, efter, fyne.   ('The Trial of the Fox')

Henryson's minor lyrics confirm many of these characteristics. In particular, almost all relate form to meaning in the manner advocated by the grammarians.[8] The same situation, character or story line is often recapitulated, using a change in narrative voice to highlight both parallels and variations. That technique, exemplified in the narrative-moral disjunction of the *Fabillis*, is lyrically re-translated in the debate form of 'The Ressoning betwix Deth and Man' and 'The Ressoning betwix Aige and Yowth'. More subtly, in the pastourelle 'Robene and Makyne', Henryson counterpoints male and female arguments to give dramatic poignancy to the proverb 'The man that will not quhen he may, Sall haif nocht quhen he wald' (89-92).

The longer mythical narratives *Orpheus and Eurydice* and *The Testament of Cresseid* also employ conscious structural patterning to emphasize the principle of similarity and variation. Orpheus is probably the earlier of the two, and it is closer methodologically to the *Fabillis*. The narrator, in admitting that his first source for the story is Boethius (414), evokes a context of metaphysical questioning. Under the governing image of the harmony of the spheres, this version of Orpheus' story may, therefore, also be read as the story of Everyman within a mode of interpretation which legitimizes apparently discordant interpretations by nicely distinguishing the allegorical angle of approach. This is explicitly admitted in the *Moralitas*, where Henryson's reliance on the Dominican commentator Nicholas Trevet is also admitted (421). Had his readers used apparent oddities in the story line to look under the 'cloke' (420) of literalism? Had they anticipated the revelations of the *Moralitas*, by seeing early on that the story was being manipulated in a manner suggesting Trevet's neoplatonic reading of the myth as a psychomachia between reason and sensuality (425-434)?

The clues can first be demonstrated structurally. Broadly, the story has been divided into two parallel sequences, marked off by changes in narrative mode:

Descriptive: Stanzas 1-10: Orpheus's Genealogy.
Dramatic: Stanzas 11-19: Orpheus marries Eurydice, Arestaeus' assault and her death.
Lyrical: Stanzas 20-24: Orpheus's first lament in innocence.
Descriptive: Stanzas 25-48: Orpheus seeks Eurydice in heaven and hell.
Dramatic: Stanzas 49-54: Orpheus meets Pluto and loses Eurydice.
Lyrical: Stanzas 55-57: Orpheus's second lament in experience.

The descriptive sections establish the Boethean universalising intention by tracing, respectively, the hereditary and experiential influences on Orpheus' character. His grandparents' marriage (god with mortal) first suggests a conflict between reason and passion, while his mother Calliope, as goddess of music, teaches him how to harmonise them. The second descriptive section turns Orpheus' search for Eurydice into an otherworldly journey. Using the Scholastic via negativa/via positiva method, Henryson follows his hero down the hierarchy of the pagan gods in heaven. While this reacquaints Orpheus positively with divine intentionality and the music of the spheres, it does not reveal Eurydice's place in the metaphysical scheme. Blinded by love, he is looking for her in the wrong place. An added journey into Hell is needed to provide the dual counterbalance of negative metaphysical and positive personal knowledge. Tuning his harp to heavenly melodies, he finds her with Pluto in the realm of chaos. For Orpheus as god, the two sides of divine justice thus enacted would be enough. Significantly, the chronological and moral details necessary to relate his story to total *human* knowledge are reserved for the *Moralitas*. There, the young hero passes the three-headed Cerberus of youth, maturity and age and meets the three Fates of thought, word and deed. The last moral escape-hatches permitting the excuse of inadequate evidence close on reader as well as god.

The dramatic passages highlight key moments in Orpheus/Mankind's journey through innocence and experience, while the lyrical setpieces use Orpheus' music as a leitmotiv-check on the prevalent balance between reason and passion in his soul. The classical topos of *varius sis sed tamen idem* remains the governing principle. Such a structure invites comparisons between the drama of Orpheus' first, temporal loss of Eurydice in youthful innocence and his second, eternal, desertion in knowledge and experience. The song and complaint which, respectively, follow these sections are formally counterpointed. As passionate disharmony is less excusable once the entire divine scheme has been revealed to you, so his first song, marked off by a distinctive nine line stanza, misses the heavenly register alone – 'ces of all thi subtell sangis sweit' (136). Orpheus can still charm the sub-lunar world. For the second lament, the harp has been set aside and all eloquence lost. Orpheus expresses his despair in stilted commonplaces. Anyone who does not learn to place reason above passion in the knowledgeable soul will be damned eternally.

The strangest configurations of the literal story are reserved for the dramatic sections. It seems odd, for example, that Orpheus, a male god, should be 'requyr(ed)' to marry by Eurydice, who is only a mortal. Equally strange is her death. After the shepherd Aresteus has failed to rape her, she stands on a serpent and so perishes. But the whole purpose of 'strange lines' is to use literal dissatisfaction to encourage a search for allegorical sense. When the *Moralitas* explains that a pure mind would have seen Eurydice's command and Orpheus' obedience as passion overthrowing the rational harmony of the soul, we cannot plead the lack of clues. Equally, Aresteus literally kept his beasts in order, and so should have suggested the properly harmonized Platonic soul. In the moral, there-fore, he represents 'gude vertewe' (436) whose failure to 'rape' passion, leads to sin (serpent/devil) and death (the wages of sin). This witty yoking together, at one referential point, of logics which otherwise are extremely disparate is the dialectical equiva-lent of the conceits practised by Donne and the English Metaphysical poets.

His other major narrative poem, the *Testament*, returns to the theme of lost harmony in a tragic pagan soul during early life and later experience. As noted earlier, it derives from Henryson's criti-cal reaction to Chaucer's *Troilus and Criseyde*. Foreseeably, he wishes to judge the English poet's heroine as well as provide a sat-isfactory ending to her story. Allegorical categories close in on her at once. Diomede is associated with 'appetyte' (71); Cresseid with 'fleschelie lust' (80). A 'voiced' pattern, similar to but less tight than that used in Orpheus,[9] also replaces the freer, dramatic form of the English poem:

Descriptive: Lines 1-91: The Narrator explains his reasons for writ-ing about Cresseid.
Dramatic: Lines 92-125: Cresseid tells Calchas of her life until Diomede's desertion.
Lyrical: Lines 126-140: Cresseid's first lament.
Descriptive: Lines 141-173: She dreams of being called before a parliament of gods.
Dramatic Lines 174-406: Tried and found guilty, she awakens. Calchas agrees to her joining a leper colony.
Lyrical: Lines 407-469: Cresseid's second lament.
Dramatic: Lines 470-537: A leper lady counsels self-reliance; she meets Troilus again.
Lyrical: Lines 538-609: Cresseid's testament.

Instead of a long *Moralitas*, the final seven lines teach Christian women how to profit from Cresseid's example.

Crucially, however, the critical challenge has changed. Instead of inviting us to identify Cresseid and Troilus with moral qualities and then re-read their tragedy in these terms, Henryson asks us to con-sider whether the spiritual viewpoint need confirm the tragic read-ing of temporality at all. The image of the harmony of the spheres, translated hermeneutically, not only allows a worldly tragedy to be a divine comedy; in a sense it determines that it must be.

Certainly the first descriptive-dramatic-lyrical movement stresses that tragic disorder exists at all levels. In a wintry Scottish spring, the aged narrator thinks back to his own springtime in order to write about Cresseid blighting her youthful beauty. The ensuing dramatic discussion between Cresseid and Calchas economically recapitulates that early biography in terms of continued exile and desertion – by Troilus, by Troy, by Diomede and by society. As Calchas was the first in this line, her reconciliation with him is at once joyous, pathetic and ironic. This highly emotive context introduces the heroine's first lament. In this, she appropriates the narrator's winter-spring leitmotiv in order to lament her loss of physical beauty – 'the seid' of her beauty 'with froist is slane' already (137, 139).

Major variations are reserved for the second descriptive-dramatic-lyrical movement. The pagan gods of 'Orpheus' return at the equivalent stage in this poem, but in dream form. Crucially, the vision reflects Cresseid's current understanding of her own past. Her current concern with lost physical beauty logically translates itself into images of those gods who govern physical process – 'all thing generabill' (148). The dramatic prosecution by Cupid on behalf of Venus results in her dream-judges – Saturn and Cynthia – decreeing that she suffer the supposedly venereal form of leprosy, whose early symptoms she had just lamented before falling asleep. In modern terms, this is the dreamwork by which she strives to understand her situation. Translated via the attributes of the named gods, her premature ugliness has come via misuse of beauty and love (Venus; Cupid) and so has outraged the normal processes of time and change (Saturn; Cynthia). Winter possesses both the body and the soul of Spring.

The acceptance that she has wasted both the Gifts of Fortune and of Nature makes her more worldly-wise. It does not alter her moral outlook and so her second soliloquy remains, formally and materially, a complaint. She still blames the gods rather than herself and, although she does warn others against following her example, her concerns remain the worldly ones of appearance and reputation (452-469). Cresseid's dramatic meetings with the leper lady and Troilus begin her penitential quest. As in 'Orpheus', single moments represent crucial stages in life's journey. After the lady's blunt advice to accept her fate stoically, Cresseid journeys 'Fra place to place, quhill cauld and hounger sair Compellit hir to be ane rank beggair' (482-530). Therefore, when Troilus half-recognizes her and donates gold, her newfound moral maturity is to be understood as having been forged through a long, dark night of the soul. The woman, who would earlier have bemoaned the unfairness of others, now praises her erstwhile lover's spiritual generosity and unequivocally blames herself, 'O fals Cresseid and trew knight Troylus' (546).

Of Cresseid's three parallel soliloquys, then, only the last is not a self-centred complaint. It is a 'testament' in two senses, both of which introduce the stages of Christian penance and, therefore, lead towards divine comedy. In the sense of a covenant, her testament enacts contrition and a full confession of sin. As a will, that testament allows a Christian audience to see a pagan, in the Age of Justice, anticipating the third stage of the sacrament by offering full satisfaction through benevolent bequests. This dual conclusion also allows Henryson to offer to his chosen audience – the 'worthie women' of his own day – a two-way moral mirror. While Cresseid's 'sore conclusioun' warns them against following her tragic worldly example – 'Ming not youre lufe with fals deceptioun' (613) – her penitential regaining of the ways of 'cheritie' (612) provides a positive emblem of the way to spiritual joy, more unequivocally available in the Age of Mercy.

Despite Henryson's apparent linguistic conservatism and his controlled formal structures, he offers a stunningly wide range of helpfully persuasive images and ideas. Those who are willing to enter his value system and share the open discourse of persuasive effectiveness may not only learn how a cock may at once treat a jewel sensibly and foolishly or a poem be a comedy and a tragedy simultaneously; they may also enjoy the challenge.

NOTES

1 See Robert L. Kindrick, *Henryson and the Medieval Arts of Rhetoric*,

Kalamazoo, Mich.: University of Western Michigan Press, 1993.

[2] See John MacQueen, *Robert Henryson, The Major Narrative Poems,* Oxford: Oxford University Press, 1967, p. 22.

[3] Cited by Douglas Gray, *Robert Henryson,* Leiden: Brill, 1979, p. 4.

[4] John MacQueen, *Henryson,* cit., pp. 1-23.

[5] *The Poems of Robert Henryson,* edited by Denton Fox, Oxford: Oxford University Press, 1981, p. 169. Further references to this edition are given after quotations in the text.

[6] Dante Alighieri, *Divina Commedia,* 'Inferno', IX, 61-63: 'O voi ch'avete li 'ntelletti sani,/mirate la dottrina che s'asconde/sotto il velame de li versi strani'.

[7] Helpfully explained and illustrated in *Medieval Literary Theory and Criticism,* edited by A.J. Minnis et al., Oxford: Oxford University Press, 1988.

[8] *Poetria Nuova of Geoffrey of Vinsauf,* edited by M.F. Nims, Toronto: Pontifical Institute of Medieval Studies, 1967, p. 14f.

[9] See John MacQueen, 'Neoplatonism and Orphism in Fifteenth-Century Scotland', *Scottish Studies,* vol. 20, 1976, pp. 69-89.

STEFANIA D'AGATA D'OTTAVI

Dunbar's The Goldyn Targe *and* *The Question of the 'Auctoritates'*

Intertextuality seems to be one of the main features of medieval texts, although the term should be understood in its correct meaning, which is not exactly the one modern theory has developed. The wealth of sources a medieval text normally offers finds a theoretical justification in such concepts as *imitatio*, *continuatio*, *amplificatio*, etc, which become important *topoi* in the course of the history of medieval literature. It has, however, long been recognized[1] that the use of such devices does not actually prevent innovation, but is often the screen which hides new ideas and techniques, exactly in the same way as the literal meaning of a text is believed to be the *integumentum* which covers the higher levels of interpretation, e.g. the allegorical, the tropological, the anagogical. From this point of view, the constant mention of the *auctoritates* in medieval writings appears to be the price an author has to pay to the main *topoi* of the culture of his time and his homage to the ancient writers, of whom he claims to be the imitator and whose works he pretends to continue, becomes a formal device which only shows the distance the writer is anxious to take from the official modes of expression in order to allow his own voice to emerge.

The works of William Dunbar, though coming at the end of the Middle Ages, are no exception. Moreover, in his case, in addition to the traditional practice of his time, this author's frequent mention of other writers and the variety of the sources he uses are easily interpreted as the homage to the dominating *intelligentsia* from a provincial author writing at the outskirts of the real centre of culture. I would like to suggest, however, that what the poet really does, in spite of the formal recognition of his *auctoritates*, is the search for the creation and the establishment of a Scottish tradition.

Within this framework, *The Goldyn Targe*, probably composed about 1506, seems, in the great wealth of Dunbar's production, to be especially significant, for a number of reasons. First, it is a dream poem, that is, a kind of composition belonging to a genre that had received a great impulse during the later Middle Ages, both in France and in England, and could well be considered representative of the leading paradigms of the official culture. Second, it combines the lyrical with the narrative mode, allowing a great wealth of registers to create a really polyphonous work. Third, it allows a versatile use of rhetoric, so that the ability of the *makar* may shine forth, at the same time encouraging originality and the rising of a native voice. In short, it is a genre which easily consents innovation to be concealed within an apparently traditional approach.

Metapoetical interpretations of this poem have already been suggested and the manipulation of the language it shows has been persuasively ascribed to the habit of reflecting about poetry and the art of writing in general.[2] I would like to take a step further and argue that the actual outcome of the highly formalized lines the poem presents and of the frequent quotations from, or allusions to, literary texts, while following apparently traditional patterns, achieve in the end completely original results. The mention of poets or recognized authorities, implicit in the first stanzas, more direct toward the end of the poem, and culminating in the formal homage to Chaucer and the other authors of dream narratives at the very end, emphasises the distance that separates the older composition from the more modern one, the creation of a Scottish literary tradition which is perfectly aware of the English achievements, but is at the same time eager to find its own voice.

Before analysing *The Goldyn Targe* in detail, I shall try to show that the result the Scottish poet is after is perfectly consistent with the main issues of the medieval mentality and with a consciousness on the part of the writers of the fictitious character of their work much greater than the insistence, on the part of both authors and critics, on the seriousness of their claims has generally been able to acknowledge.

Comparison, confrontation and analogy are among the leading cultural parameters throughout the Middle Ages. A culture of the double if ever there was one, the medieval civilisation unceasingly experiences and re-elaborates the dichotomy between heathen and Christian, Old and New Testament, oral and written production, Latin and vernacular, authority and experience, etc. To create the conditions for these 'contraries' to exist is the constant effort of medieval intellectuals who strive to arrive at a *concordia discors*, that is unity out of diversity, and being it often impossible to achieve a complete unity, there comes the function of analogy, which does not eliminate differences, but bridges the gap between concepts normally considered as irreconcilable by devising a series of intermediate ideas which bring the two 'contraries' as near as possible. Confrontation and comparison are therefore felt as ways of establishing some sort of continuity with tradition, thus over-coming any uncanny feelings of alterity innovation may cause. The entire Medieval literary tradition can be interpreted from this point of view and thrives in the paradox of the new which is discarded as such, but presented as part of tradition, and therefore automatically endowed with truthfulness. A great number of well-known consequences derive from this attitude. First of all, the idea that 'continuity' can be interpreted as 'continuation', and the claim of many writers that their work simply 'continues' an older and more authoritative one. This, in turn, has the important implication of establishing tradition as the real referent of medieval literary production.[3] And exactly in the same way as the new tends to be con-cealed in the old, the modern author tends to hide his name in order to make room, as it were, for the writer he has chosen to 'continue', and confer authority upon his own work by making it appear as closely related as possible to the more famous one. The most interesting consequence of this situation is the fact that the idea of 'continuation' being so common and widespread, tends to become a *topos* in itself, and part of the world the medieval author is faced with and toward which he exerts all the technical devices of imaginative re-elaboration he is capable of. Hence, the invented source, the non-existent authority, the manipulated quotation. A closer analysis of the concept of *auctoritas* will provide interesting results.[4] This word normally indicates both the authoritative person whose wisdom makes his word worthy of imitation and the work he has produced. From this point of view, the *auctoritates* are not

only models of writing, but produce literature in various forms, as
well: glosses, commentaries, essays and, of course, new poetry or
prose claiming a relationship with them. The important consequence deriving from this is the fact that even the traditional
homage to the authorities becomes part of the literary convention
and is often a way of getting rid of a cumbersome tradition, which
done, the author is free to follow his own inclinations.

The distorted use of *auctoritates* the meanings of which everybody can twist as he likes is lamented by Alain de Lille: 'Auctoritas
cereum habet nasum, id est in diversum potest flecti sensum',[5] and
Walter Map, at the end of the XII century, complains that he cannot be considered an *auctoritas* as he is still alive, immediately
adding, however, that he has no intention of dying in order to
become one.[6] Adelard of Bath admits of having attributed his own
ideas to important Arabic authors in order to make them more
authoritative and more acceptable to his readers.[7] This shows that
auctoritas and *auctoritates* become in the end literary *topoi* and as
such can be manipulated to become part of the conventions of literature. To quote an author in order to change, even radically, his
meaning, to present novelty as the continuation of somebody's
work, to invent an author's name to conceal one's true source, as
Chaucer does when he replaces Boccaccio with the non-existent
'Lollius' in *Troilus and Criseyde*, is the way by which medieval
intellectuals show their conscious use of literary conventions, and
the close relationship they establish between texts fulfils the aim of
analysing the mechanisms of their construction and the way literature actually works.

The Goldyn Targe can be considered a masque,[8] that is a courtly
entertainment, composed on some important occasion for James
IV. Various assumptions have been made, but what is certain is that
both the complex aureate language and the subject of the poem
make the Scottish court the ideal addressee of the composition.
This interpretation is enforced by the observation that two important objects, uncommon in dream poetry, which however play an
important part in the poem, i.e. the ship and the gun, may allude
to James the IV's efforts in order to establish a powerful Scottish
navy, and to his passion for arms, respectively.[9] It would therefore
be strange if a courtly poet had produced as a homage to his king

a mere imitation of the works of other poets, however illustrious, belonging to a country which had been the enemy of his own for such a long time. In fact, *The Goldyn Targe* shows an actively conscious re-elaboration of current themes and forms. The very number of works that have been recognized as possible sources of the poem makes close imitation impossible.[10] The conventional form of the dream vision, besides providing the author with a certain freedom in the choice of subject and composition, is an excellent example of courtly poetry as a genre long practised both in England and in Scotland. It has been argued that *The Goldyn Targe* is a poem about poetry. To this one may add that it is a poem about the creation of a Scottish poetic tradition. In order to do this, the poet must be confronted with the other specimens of the genre, which he quotes and even praises, only to diverge from them in subject and method. Indeed, at times he seems positively eager to upset the conventions of the genre: the *topos* of the *locus amoenus* – just to quote one example – which is developed in the first four stanzas of the poem brings together different traditions. The poetic persona wakes up early and in broad daylight goes to the 'rosere' where he falls asleep. In this way, the traditional 'obeysance' to the month of May, which can be found in Chaucer (*The Legend of Good Women* and *The Knight's Tale*) and originally derives from the *Roman de la Rose*, is the source of the dream. In the *Prologue* to *The Legend of Good Women* the narrator falls asleep, or rather asks that his bed should be prepared, in a beautiful garden. Other Chaucerian narrators (in *The Book of the Duchess*, *The House of Fame* or *The Parliament of Fowls*) fall asleep in their beds and the *locus amoenus* is part of the dream. In *The Goldyn Targe* the two traditions are brought together and the scene is described in a much more vivid manner than the usual dream setting normally allows. Colours dominate: 'goldyn', 'purpur', 'qwite', 'rede', while the quick movements ('wyth skyppis and with hoppis') and the singing of the birds make the scene a particularly lively one.

The emphasis on colours gives the description a miniature-like quality which seems to allude to the fact that it is a not a mere imitation, but a representation of nature through the re-elaboration of sense perception in the work of art, exactly as miniatures and illuminations are art, not 'nature', but nature transfigured by art. But the vivid colours and the liveliness of the scene have also the function of justifying, as it were, through the intoxication of the senses, the fact that the narrator should fall asleep when everything around him seems to conspire to keep him awake. This description of the *locus amoenus* is comparatively longer than the usual ones. Critics do not mention *Pearl* (with the exception of line 77), but a writer from the West Midlands such as the Gawain-Poet might very well have been known to Dunbar, and there are important analogies between the descriptions of the two gardens, which in *Pearl* also occupies part of the dream. The vivid colours, the constant comparison with precious stones (which in *Pearl* is obviously thematic) are features common to both poems to an extent that can hardly be ascribed to mere chance, as I will try to show later.

The most constant comparison is, however, with Chaucer, not only the Chaucer of the dream poems, but also the poet of the *Canterbury Tales.* In what follows I shall argue that Dunbar makes a very personal use of Chaucer's poetry and that similarities and even at times quotations from the elder poet's works, while formally acknowledging his authority, fulfil other aims and achieve results that are altogether different.

The metre, to start with. It is generally understood that it imitates the one Chaucer uses in the central part of *Anelida and Arcite*, i.e. in the actual complaint (*Proem, Strophe*, with its seven stanzas, and six stanzas of the *Antistrophe*), and this is interesting because *The Goldyn Targe* may be considered some kind of complaint in itself, namely the narrator's against the unhappiness of love. But once this formal analogy has been recognized and the use of the same metre has acquired the importance of an acknowledgement of thematic similarity ('I am a writer of complaints'), it is immediately evident that the overall result points toward different directions. The line is much more regular and formally 'closed', in length and beat and above all there is a much greater use of the alliteration (119 lines out of 279 alliterate more less strongly), thus combining the new metrical form with the more traditional one, common to Northern poetry and to the so-called alliterative revival, possibly with an eye at the Gawain-Poet. Chaucer is the creator of well-known *topoi*, especially as far as dream poetry is concerned, and it is only natural that a poet writing more than a century later should look to him as a model. Sometimes Dunbar gives the impression of using Chaucer's expressions as formulae, as markers of a literary genre that has such a noble ancestor, to which he gives new meanings in the different contexts he has created. References to Chaucer's works have punctually been pointed out by critics, but never fully analysed in order to understand the actual use the Scottish poet has made of his chief *auctoritas*. Just to give one example, at the very beginning of *The Goldyn Targe*, the sun is called the 'goldyn candill matutyne', an epithet which can be found in *The Complaint of Mars* where it is the 'sunne, the candel of jelosye'.[11] It is interesting to remark that the sun, which is mentioned three times ('the stern of day', l. 1; 'the goldyn candill matutyne', l. 4; 'Phoebus', l. 7) is only alluded to metaphorically, as if it were unnecessary to explain what the epithets chosen referred to. In Chaucer, however, the expression receives a negative connotation, since sunlight is feared by the lovers who are more likely to be found out ('lest wikked tonges yow espye', l. 6.). The expression, decontextualized, in Dunbar's poem emphasises the brilliant colours the poet is about to describe. Colour and movement characterize Dunbar's *locus amoenus*, while the direct counterparts in Chaucer are somewhat more static. Compare, for example, the second stanza of *The Goldyn Targe* with Chaucer, *Canterbury Tales*, I, 1491-1499:[12]

> Full angellike thir birdis sang thair houris
> Within thair courtnys grene in to thair bouris,
> Apparilit quhite and rede wyth blomes swete;
> Anamalit was the felde wyth all colouris.
> The perly droppis schuke in silvir schouris,
> Quhill all in balme did branch and leuis flete.
> Depart fra Phebus did Aurora grete-
> Hir cristall teris I saw hyng on the flouris,
> Quhilk he for lufe all drank up wyth all his hete.
>
> The bisy larke, messager of day,
> Salueth in hir song the morwe gray,
> And firy Phebus riseth up so bright
> That all the orient laugheth of the light,
> And with his stremes dryeth in the greves

The silver dropes hangynge on the leves.
And Arcita, that in the court roial
With Theseus is squier principal,
Is risen and looketh on the myrie day.

Chaucer is interested in providing a frame for Arcite's actions, while in Dunbar the description is part of a magic atmosphere which reminds us of *Sir Orfeo*'s fairyland, a glossy and unreal world where supernatural events are likely to occur which only poetry can narrate.

Chaucerian 'quotations' are also frequent in *The Goldyn Targe*, and seem to be used only as witnesses that Chaucer's poetry is well known to Dunbar and that some of the expressions the English poet uses have by now become commomplaces. This is the case with 'Ther saugh I, Mars armypotent, O chaste goddes of the wodes grene', the invocation to Clio, which comes directly from *Troilus and Criseyde* (II, 8-11), but in Chaucer is much more elaborated, while in Dunbar's poem it is simply part of a list.

In some cases, the meaning of the original seems to be thouroughly reversed and a suspicion of irony arises. For example, the simile relating stars and the frosty night (36) is almost identical with ll. 266-268 in Chaucer's *Prologue* to the *Canterbury Tales*, but while in Dunbar it is a poetical way of describing the sky at night, Chaucer uses it to mention the sparkling and shrewd eyes of the friar. The word 'attempre', the usual term to indicate the sweetness of the air, which can be found in Chaucer (*The Parliament of Fowls*, 249, *The Book of the Duchess*, 340) and in *The Romaunt of the Rose*, 130-131, emphasises in Dunbar the background against which the lovely colours of his description are exalted.

The function of background some quotations from Chaucer, Gower, and *The Romaunt of the Rose* acquire throughout Dunbar's poem is, I believe, essential, for it shows what other poetry is really for him, i.e. the starting point for new developments and in some cases for the new directions his art is going to take. Once more, a comparison can prove interesting to understand the poet's method. At the benninnig of *The Goldyn Targe*, the following (already quoted) lines can be compared to similar expressions in *The Canterbury Tales*, *The Legend of Good Women* and *Troilus and Criseyde*:

Depart fra Phebus did Aurora grete–
Hir cristall teris I saw hyng on the flouris,
Quhilk he for lufe all drank up wyth all his hete

The Canterbury Tales, I, 1493-1496:

And firy Phebus riseth up so bright
That all the orient laugheth of the light,
And with his stremes dryeth in the greves
The silver dropes hangynge on the leves.

Troilus and Criseyde, III, 1464-1470:

And ek the sonne, Titan, gan he chide,
And seyde, "O fool, wel may men the dispise,
That hast the dawyng all nyght by thi syde,
And suffrest hire so soone up fro the rise
For to disese loveris in this wyse.
What, holde youre bed ther, thow, and ek thi Morwe!
I bidde god, so yeve yow bothe sorwe!"

The Legend of Good Women, 773-775:

Tyl on a day, whan Phebus gan to clere–
Aurora with the stremes of hire hete
Hadde dreyed up the dew of herbes wete.

In the lines from *The Canterbury Tales* it is Phebus who dries with his rays the 'silver dropes', while in *The Legend of Good Women* the action is ascribed to Aurora. In much more complex lines, Pandarus in *Troilus and Criseyde* reproaches Titan (Tithonus) because he lets Aurora go away from him. Dunbar combines the different elements present in his sources and the result is a deeply re-elaborated form, where Phebus is said to dry Aurora's tears with his heat. Moreover, Chaucer's lines belong to different textual aspects: description in *The Canterbury Tales*, invective in *Troilus and Criseyde*, part of a story in *The Legend of Good Women*. The separation betweeen Aurora and Phebus reminds the poet of other separations alluded to in Chaucer's works, those between Piramus and Thisbe, and Troilus and Criseyde, respectively, and more indirectly the final separation between Arcite and Emelye, which is going to occur shortly in *The Knight's Tale*. Thus, stories of unhap-

py love have given rise to a rhetorical form where nature anticipates the events to be narrated. The participation of nature in the
story is one of the main features of Dunbar's poem and an important difference with respect to his source. In Chaucer the *locus
amoenus* generally provides the frame of the story and one element is usually singled out to be described in greater detail.
Dunbar's descriptions normally extend to the whole of nature and
all the elements seem to cooperate in creating the atmosphere for
the actions the poetic persona is going to narrate. In *The
Parliament of Fowls* Chaucer describes the garden where Nature
will appear with great care and many details, even making a list of
the various kinds of trees the dreamer sees there, and then mentioning the flowers with their colours, the river with its fish, etc.
Dunbar uses all the wealth of Chaucer's description, but the result
he obtains is completely different, for the imagery of his poem
tends to give an idea of the actions of the elements on each other:

> The cristall air, the sapher firmament,
> The ruby skyes of the orient
> Kest beriall bemes of emerant bewis grene.
> The rosy garth, depaynt and redolent,
> With purpur, azure, gold and goulis gent
> Arayed was by dame Flora, the quene,
> So nobil that joy was for to sene
> The roch again the riwir resplendent,
> As low enlumynit all the leues schene.
>
> But, Lord so I was glad and well begoon!
> For overal where that I myne eyen caste
> Were trees clad with leves that ay shal laste,
> Ech in his kynde, of colour fresh and grene
> As emeraude, that joie was to sene.
>
> The byldere ok, and ek the hardy asshe,
> The piler elm, the cofre unto carayne,
> The boxtree pipere, holm to whippes lashe,
> The saylynge fyr, the cipresse deth to playne;
> The shetere ew; the asp for shaftes pleyne;
> The olyve of pes and ek the dronke vyne;
> The victor palm, the laurel to devyne.

> A garden saw I ful of blosmy bowes
> Upon a ryver, in a grene mede,
> There as swetness evermore inow is,
> With foures white, blewe, yelwe and rede,
> And colde welle-stremes, nothyng dede,
> That swymmen ful of smale fishes lighte,
> With fynnes rede and skales sylver brighte.

These lines show, I think, better than others, the way Dunbar creates his text on the basis of previous authorities. Chaucer's lines describe the garden, so to speak, step by step, taking its various aspects into consideration one after the other, while Dunbar is interested in showing the effects of one object on the others: it is the red light of the eastern sky that radiates on the trees and makes them glitter, and this establishes a relationship between sky and earth, while water and rock are related by the complex imagery of the light reflected from the sky on the river and from the rocks on the leaves of the trees. In this way all the elements are simultaneously involved.

This aspect of Dunbar's poetry is once more strongly reminiscent of *Pearl*, the influence of which on *The Goldyn Targe* has, I think, been greatly underestimated. Mention of this poem can only be found in the critical literature as an analogue for the meaning of 'lef' (27) as 'foliage'. But in analysing possible sources one should do what John Livingston Lowes did with S.T. Coleridge's *Notebooks* when he tried to trace the imagery of *The Rime of the Ancient Mariner* and *Kubla Khan*, that is, one should read some lines before and after the quotation considered. If we do this and compare *The Goldyn Targe* with *Pearl* we find that the concept expressed by Dunbar at ll. 26-27 is similar in idea and images to *Pearl*, ll. 77-80 and that such a debt may provide an explanation of the difficult l. 25 of 'The Goldyn Targe':[13]

> The rosis yong, now spreding of thair knopis,
> War powderit brycht with hevinly beriall droppis,
> Throu bemes rede birnyng as ruby sperkis.
> The skies rang for schoutyng of the larkis,
> The purpur hevyn, ourscailit in silvir sloppis,
> Ourgilt the treis branchis, lef and barkis.
>
> As bornyst syluer the lef on slydez,

That thike con trylle on uch a tynde;
Quen glem of glodez agaynz hem glydez,
Wyth schymeryng schene ful schrylle thay schynde.

The liveliness of the description, the glossy colours, the mention of precious stones seem to make *Pearl* an important referent of Dunbar in this poem, not only for the lines I have just quoted, but for the whole natural setting.

When the dream begins (46), the relationship with the sources becomes more complex and less straightforward, and the poet seems to use suggestions from other texts only as fairly distant reminders of a literary genre, but within contexts generally very different. The simile describing the sails of the ship that carries the ladies who appear to the narrator in his dream ('als quhite as blossum upon spray') has been compared to *Canterbury Tales* ('As whit as is the blosme upon the rys', I, 3323), which, however, describes Absolon's gown in *The Miller's Tale*. The aspect of the ladies is usually compared to a similar passage in *The Romaunt of the Rose*, where the tresses of the women are also mentioned. But if we look at Chaucer's tale a bit more closely, we find that, just before describing Absolon's surplice, the narrator has mentioned his hair ('Crul was his heer, and as the gold it shoon/And strouted as a fanne large and brode', 3314-3315); Dunbar's ship has 'merse of gold brycht as the stern of day' (52), while, as far as the ladies are concerned, 'Thair brycht hairis hand gleting on the strandis,/In tressis clere wyppit wyth goldyn thredis' (61-62). The brightness of the colours has evidently caught the Scottish poet's attention, and two sources, *The Miller's Tale* and *The Romaunt of the Rose* have been brought together and freely transferred from people to objects, and back.

A slight difference in an otherwise similar quotation shows another aspect of Dunbar's use of sources. In *Troilus and Criseyde*, II, 50, May is called 'that moder of monthes glade', an expression which in Dunbar (82) becomes 'Thare saw I May, of myrthfull monetis quene'. The epithets are commonplace enough, but the difference between the two lines is subtle: in Dunbar the month is personified, being one of the people who are in the ship, so that the shift from 'mother' to 'quene' is justified, but the creation of a royal character also indicates that Dunbar is interested in emphasising the courtly nature of his poem, and the idea of family link ('mother') is transformed into some kind of hierarchical relationship between a queen and her subjects, the idea of family being, however, recovered in the definition of April and June as May's 'sisters'.

The predominance of brilliant colours is also evident in Dunbar's brief description of Nature. The model is, of course, Alain de Lille's *De Planctu Naturae*, but in *The Goldyn Targe* Nature is only mentioned as the one who gives May a rich gown (87-88). The mind immediately goes to *The Parliament of Fowls*, where Nature is equally just mentioned and said to appear as Alain de Lille describes her (316-317). The analogy might not be of great importance, as Nature is often mentioned in dream poetry, but if we read a bit further on in both poems we immediately see that Dunbar re-arranges Chaucer's lines according to his own engagement:

> The mery foulis blisfullest of chere
> Salust Nature, me thoucht, on thair manere;
> And ewiry blome on branch and eke on bonk
> Opnyt and spred thair balmy leuis donk,
> Full low enclynyng to thair quene so clere,
> Quham of thair noble norising thay thonk.
> Thair hony throtis opnyt fro the splene
> With werblis swetedid perse the hevinly skyes,
> Quhill loud resownyt the firmament serene.   (DUNBAR)

> And right as Aleyn, in the Pleynt of Kynde,
> Devyseth Nature of aray and face,
> In swich aray men myghte hire there fynde.
> This noble emperesse, full of grace,
> Bad every foul to take his owne place.   (CHAUCER)

The long list of birds Chaucer makes after the lines I have quoted is obviously avoided by Dunbar, whose story is different, but the *brevitas* which characterizes his description with respect to Chaucer's is counterbalanced by a greater generality when the homage to Nature is mentioned. It is not without purpose, in fact, that Dunbar dismisses the subject by saying that birds greet Nature 'on thair manere'. Immediately afterwards he shows the 'manere' of the flowers in paying homage to their queen. Once more, Dunbar's consideration of Nature seems to involve it in its entirety. The poet is not interested in singling out one element, but in showing the way they interact with one another and with man, as it appears very clearly when the forces of Nature are personified in the various characters, who provide a list so 'complete' to risk confusion. The switch from the literal to the metaphorical, ending in the definition of 'Mercurius' as the one who 'Of rhetorick fand the flouris faire' finally relates the natural to the human, and the language of nature (flowers, birds) to that of man (rhetoric).

The principle of *brevitas* is often used by Dunbar when quoting from the *auctoritates*. It shows that the poet is aware of their existence, and can afford to dismiss them to follow other paths. The long list of the effects Saturn can have on nature (I, 2469-2477), which in *The Knight's Tale* has the function of emphasising the god's power, is reduced to a line and a half ('crabbit Saturn, ald and haire/His luke was lyke for to perturb the aire', 114-115) in *The Goldyn Targe*, in agreement with the fact that here Saturn is only one of the gods of Dunbar's heathen Paradise. The same can be said of Priapus, mentioned also in *The Merchant's Tale* and in *The Parliament of Fowls*, as well as of Fanus (*Faunus*), present in *Troilus and Criseyde*, and of Janus ('god of entree') who can be found in the same poem, IV, 1544, while the 'unstable' aspect of Eolus is of course reminiscent of *The House of Fame*. To a different and perhaps less known tradition, but very important and consistent with the atmosphere of *The Goldyn Targe*, belongs the way Pluto is presented ('the erlich incubus/In cloke of grene- his court usit no sable', 125-126), that is, as a demon. In this definition part of the tradition is retained: Chaucer gives him and Proserpina a fairy train in *The Merchant's Tale* (2038) and later in the same tale calls him 'kyng of Fayrye' (2226) in telling part of the story of this god and of Proserpina. The contexts are in both cases nature and gardens, where the king and the queen dance. The underworld part of the story can be found in *The House of Fame*, where the poet Claudian is said to bear up 'all the fame of helle/Of Pluto and of Proserpyne/That quene ys of the derke pyne' (1510-1512). Dunbar seems to combine the two traditions: he makes Pluto a demon, but denies him the use of dark colours, which would reduce the liveliness of the nature he has been describing so far.

As soon as the climax approaches, the use of the sources becomes more original and idiosyncratic, as the transformation of the well-known *topos* concerning the effects of love clearly shows. Lines 133-135 of *The Goldyn Targe* have been compared to lines 253-255 of Chaucer's Anelida and Arcite:

Than crap I throu the leus and drew nere,
Quhare that I was rycht sudaynly affaryt,
All throu a luke, quhilk I haue boucht full dere.   (DUNBAR)

Alas! Is ther now notherword ne chere
Ye vouchen sauf upon myn hevynesse?
Ales! Youre love, I bye al to dere.   (CHAUCER)

In Chaucer, it is Anelida who complains of having bought Arcita's love too dear, while in Dunbar it is the narrator's indiscretion which is paid too dear: he is punished by falling in love. In Chaucer, love is a cause, in Dunbar, it is a consequence, and the expression anticipates what will come. But love is traditionally related to sight (Andreas Capellanus), and the narrator, punished because he has spied upon the ladies, uses Chaucer's sentence in a context so different that it might even sound ironical, since Anelida is complaining of paying too dear not her falling in love, but the desertion of her lover. In a similar way, the shower of arrows coming from the Queen of Love and her court may be considered an ironical *amplificatio* of the Black Knight's confession in *The Book of the Duchess* when he tells the narrator that Love saw him and hit him with the desire for White (838-840).

The canonical contrast between Love and Reason, which in *The Romaunt of the Rose* is expressed by the long dialogue between Raison and Amant is deeply re-elaborated by Dunbar, who prefers 'more matter with less art' and avoids Raison's long explanations, merely showing how the narrator is hit by the arrows of all the ladies in the train of the Queen of Love and how Reason, whose 'goldyn targe' seems to avail him nothing, is beaten and, in the end, blinded. So Love, which is first conveyed through sight, needs the blinding of Reason to prevail. The long list of allegorical figures has a distant relation to *The Romaunt of the Rose*, where the personifications of virtues and vices are described at length and their modes of action fully explained. Dunbar is only intersted in showing how powerful the Queen of Love's attack is, and does not stop to describe her train in detail. Once more, totally reversing his source, however, in *The Goldyn Targe* he makes Reason become mad because of the powder which is thrown into his eyes, while in *The Romaunt of the Rose* it is Amant who, abandoned by Raison, becomes 'wood'.

Moreover, Dunbar's intentions seem to be more general: the slavery of love does not concern one person in particular, but involves 'Beauty', perhaps implying that whenever Reason is blinded, irrational passions prevail. The whole process is presented in terms of warfare, and therefore the usual oxymoronic epithet for love 'swete helle/sorrowful paradys' is discarded: love without reason is simply hell, even if at times it may appear as paradise. The death of Blanche, i.e. the loss of love, had for the Black Knight turned joy into its opposite to the point of making him feel one and the same with sorrow ('I am sorwe and sorwe ys me', 345); in Dunbar there is no loss, but it is love itself to cause 'hevinesse' and no woman is mentioned, but 'Beautee', an abstract feature (his own? his woman's?) that is said to depart from the narrator because of 'Dangere'.

The wind storm recalls *The House of Fame* (1636-1654), but Aeolus here is no longer the messenger of Fame, but a *deus ex machina* that indirectly helps the unhappy lover, at the cost of creating a desert. The tempest that follows is now one of guns, and the deafening noise once more involves all nature. The awakening brings again the vivid colours described at the beginning, but the repetition now achieves the purpose of comparing the perfection and the purity of colours in nature to the language and the poetry of Chaucer. The imagery the poet uses in stanza 28, where nature is described, has a direct counterpart in stanza 29, where Chaucer's poetry is praised:

28
And as I did awake of my sueving,
The ioyfull birdis merily did syng
For myrth of Phebus tender bemes schene.
Suete war the vapouris, soft the morowing,
Halesum the vale depaynt wyth flouris ying,
The air attemperit, sobir and amene.
In quhite and rede was all the felde besene,

Throu Naturis nobil fresch anamalyng
In myrthfull May of ewiry moneth quene.

29
O reuerend Chaucere, rose of rhetoris all
(As in oure tong ane flour imperiall)
That raise in Britane ewir, quho redis rycht,
Thou beris of makaris the tryumph riall,
Thy fresch anamalit termes celicall
This mater could illumynit haue full brycht.
Was thou noucht of oure Inglisch all the lycht,
Surmounting ewiry tong terrestriall,
Alls fer as Mayes morow dois mydnycht?

Flowers, birds and precious stones bring joy into the natural world, exactly as poetry does into the world of man. The usual homage to Chaucer is immediately followed by the envoy, containing the customary modesty *topos*. But it is evident that in spite of the derogatory expressions he uses for his own work, Dunbar is implicitly comparing himself to Chaucer. He has used themes and language of the older poet in a very personal way, deeply modifying the sources he claims to admire so much. The central part of his poem, especially, has much more to do with the life of the Scottish court of his time and with the tastes of King James IV than with Chaucer or Lydgate. The king's love for arms, his interest in a powerful navy have been mentioned as elements the courtier Dunbar must have known very well.

All these elements justify, I think, the assumption I made at the beginning of this paper. Dunbar is anxious to show that he is familiar with the most important sources of the literary genre he has adopted in his poem, pays them a formal homage, and then develops his own themes in his own ways. Consciously or unconsciously recollecting the metaphor the medieval intellectuals had created to solve the contrast between tradition and innovation, namely that of the 'moderni' as dwarfs sitting on giants' shoulders, Dunbar shows his referent and removes it from his poetry by giving it a completely different context, quoting it only to show that his purposes lie elsewhere. But there is probably more in this than the mere ostentation of a new poetic voice. In showing that he is aware of the tradition of the literary genre he is practising and in distorting his sources to create innovation out of tradition, the poet also emphasises his aspiration to become 'the Chaucer of Scottish poetry', i.e. the courtly poet who gives Middle Scots the same literary dignity Chaucer had given 'oure Inglish'.

NOTES

[1] Roger Dragonetti, *Le mirage des sources*, Paris: Seuil, 1987. Umberto Eco, 'Sviluppo dell'estetica medievale', in *Momenti e problemi di storia dell'estetica*, Milano: Marzorati, 1983. Jacques Le Goff, *La civilisation de l'Occident médiéval*, Paris: A. Artaud, 1964.

[2] Denton Fox, 'Dunbar's "The Golden Targe"', *English Literary History*, vol. 26, 1959, pp. 311-334. Frank Shuffleton, 'An Imperial Flower: Dunbar's "The Goldyn Targe" and the Court Life of James IV of Scotland', *Studies in Philology*, vol. 72, 1975, pp.193-207.

[3] Paul Zumthor, *Essai de poétique médiévale*, Paris: Seuil, 1972.

[4] A.J. Minnis, *Medieval Theory of Authorship*, London: Scolar Press, 1984.

[5] Alain de Lille, 'De fide catholica', *Patrologia Latina*, ccxx.

[6] Walter Map, *De nugiis curialium*, edited by M.R. James, Oxford: Clarendon Press, 1983, *Distinctio* iv, cap. 5, p. 312.

[7] Adelard of Bath, *De eodem et diverso*, Oxford: Clarendon Press, 1985.

[8] P.M. King, 'Dunbar's "The Golden Targe": A Chaucerian Masque', *Studies in Scottish Literature*, vol. 19, 1984, pp. 115-131.

[9] See the already quoted papers by Denton Fox and Frank Shuffleton.

[10] The editions of Dunbar's works by W. Mackay Mackenzie (1932), James Kinsley (1979), and the most recent one by Priscilla Bawcutt (1998) carefully mention all the possible sources of Dunbar's poetry, although the way the poet uses them is never extensively taken into account.

[11] If not otherwise stated, all quotations from 'The Goldyn Targe' refer to *The Poems of William Dunbar*, edited by Priscilla Bawcutt, Glasgow: ASLS, 1998.

[12] All quotations from Chaucer's works refer to *The Riverside Chaucer*, edited by L.D. Benson, Oxford: Oxford University Press, 1988. *The Roman de la Rose* is also quoted in Chaucer's translation, and therefore mentioned as *The Romaunt of the Rose*.

[13] The lines from *Pearl* are quoted from the edition by Malcom Andrew and Ronald Waldron: *The Poems of the Pearl Manuscript*, Exeter: University of Exeter Press, 1996. Line 25 of *The Goldyn Targe* has always been considered a *crux* by editors. I think comparison with lines 77-70 of *Pearl* (see also the editors' explanation, p. 58 of the edition quoted) may help to understand the rather obscure *brevitas* which Dunbar has chosen to express a similar concept.

ANNA TORTI

The Poetry of Gavin Douglas: Memory, Past Tradition and Its Renewal

In the Preface to his book, *The Identity of the Scottish Nation, A Historic Quest*,[1] William Ferguson begins by asking the essential question 'Who are the Scots?' and has to admit, sadly, that 'At different times answers have changed as circumstances have altered'. The time I am here concerned with is that of the 'Scottish Renaissance' as represented by the excellent poet and translator Gavin Douglas. Even the term 'Renaissance' raises its own problems, as R.D.S. Jack has extensively demonstrated,[2] since the simple utterance of the expression with or without the qualifier 'Scottish' opens the way to a twofold understanding. Moreover, the definition '(Scottish) Renaissance' could well be applied to both the Later Middle Ages – or rather the Early Modern Age – and the Twentieth Century, and it is undeniable that the two 'Renaissances' are characterized by a strong interest in the European literary models. But if the group of authors who form the modern 'Renaissance' movement are 'doubly praised for literary skill *and* patriotic confirmation of the current devolutionist war-cry "Scotland in Europe"',[3] could the same be said of Gavin Douglas?

Douglas's *Eneados*, which was completed in 1513, is the first full-length translation of a classical work in Britain and earned him widespread fame. His cultural background seems to suggest a profound personal involvement in the identity of Scotland as a nation and as a centre of literary production. As Priscilla Bawcutt[4] and Ruth Morse[5] point out, his biography throws light on his literary career which, though short – it occupied the years between 1501 (the date of *The Palice of Honour*) and 1513 (when the translation of the *Aeneid* was completed) – is marked by a strong awareness of the important role Scottish poetry had acquired. Gavin Douglas

belonged to a powerful and ambitious family. He was the third son
of the fifth Earl of Angus, Archibald 'Bell the Cat', an aristocrat with
remote claims to the Scottish throne, and of Elizabeth, daughter of
Lord Boyd, who had been Chamberlain of Scotland until 1469,
when he lost his position of power. We know very little about the
early years of his life, except that he entered the University of St
Andrews in 1490 and graduated in 1494, but we have plenty of
records of his involvement in promoting the interests of the
Douglas family.

He possibly spent some time studying in Paris and visiting the
continent before settling down in Scotland. He completed his most
famous work, the *Eneados*, in 1513, shortly before the Battle of
Flodden. After Flodden Douglas's political activity increased in the
hope of obtaining an ecclesiastical appointment in line with the
status of his family. The marriage of his nephew, heir to the Angus
title, with Margaret Tudor, widow of James IV, added to the political influence of the Douglases. Within a context of never ending
competition among the ruling families, Gavin Douglas was granted
a bishopric at Dunkeld, but he had first to experience trial, imprisonment, battles and various other obstacles. This brief survey of
Douglas's complicated life in a troubled historical period clearly
illustrates the poet's central role in the political affairs of his country. Unfortunately, his family's and personal intrigues turned out to
be difficult to control and in the end, after being accused of alignment with the English, Douglas had to flee to London, where he
died of plague in 1522 while trying to win Wolsey's support in
order to regain his social position in Scotland.

The uncertainty of his life, marked by an obsession for promotion, did not prevent Douglas from writing two works among the
most representative in Scottish literary history. His first known
poem, *The Palice of Honour*, dedicated to James IV, belongs to the
dream allegorical tradition which was commonly exploited in the
Later Middle Ages. The poem has structural affinities with many
works, in particular with Chaucer's *House of Fame*, and might have
inspired Skelton's *Garlande of Laurell*, poems which are both concerned with the true significance of poetry. But Chaucer's long
investigation of the various aspects of Fame, and Skelton's self-
praise for being crowned poet laureate, are in many ways more

related to each other than to Douglas's poem, since the quest of
the Scottish poet leads not to earthly Fame but to Honour, which is
supernatural, just, and eternal. If the *Palice of Honour* was written
well before the translation of the *Eneados*, Douglas, in following
the path of the dream-vision convention laid open by Chaucer, was
even then in search of a language which could express the concept of Honour renewed by his poetry, and which could possibly
represent its classical embodiment in Aeneas, the perfect exemplary figure for the king. His words at the beginning of the poem
are clear: from the poetic aridity he finds himself in ('in that desert
terribill', 136)[6] he is saved by the intervention of Calliope in the
'...Court Rethoricall/of Poet termis, singand Poeticall,/And constant
ground of famous storeis sweit' (835-837). It is the comfort of that
Court which redirects the poet's inspiration from the theme of
mutable love, linked to Venus and to the love poets of the past, to
a concept of poetry understood as a combination of high style and
noble deeds offered as a mirror to a worthy audience. The language Douglas uses to describe Calliope,

> [...] of Nobill fatis hes the steir
> To write thair worschip, victorie and prowes
> In Kinglie stile, quhilk dois thair fame Incres,
> Cleipit in Latine Heroicus, but weir,
> Cheif of all write like as scho is Maistres.   (875-879)

shows, within the context of a dream-vision poem in the
Chaucerian tradition, a search for a kind of poetry which could
lead man to virtue and honour as is the case in the *Eneados* – at
least in the way Douglas interprets Virgil.

A fascinating aspect of dream-vision poetry is the dual interest
that lies in the dream experience unfolding before the poet's and
the reader's eyes: on the one hand that experience is an event
(whether real or imagined) to which the dreamer is a party; on the
other it is an account of that event, a transposition of it into words
by the narrator-poet. Within the narrator-dreamer-poet interchange
typical of medieval dream poetry, Douglas inserts the later
medieval humanistic views of poetry and of the poet, thus construing a narrative which, through the restoration of his poetic powers,
guides the poet to the goal of poetry, Honour. Douglas's quest,
then, relies on the authority of past authors, but at the same time

adds to it the ennobling function of poetry both for the poet and for the reader. This is made clear when the poet sees the rock on which the Palace of Honour stands: after a long journey, Douglas the dreamer, together with the great poets of the ancient past, is there and: '... at last in lifting vp our Ene/We se the finall end of our trauaill' (1247-1248). The words used to describe the vision taken literally point to the grievous events which had accompanied the dreamer, but metaphorically the strong 'sense of an ending'[7] implies that Honour is the ultimate aim of all poets and poetry.[8]

Douglas's work is different from the *House of Fame* not only for the supernatural meaning of Honour in contrast with the earthly character of Fame, but also for the profound faith in the ethical function of poetry. The nymph sent by Calliope to help the dreamer defines both Honour and Virtue in highly spiritual terms:

'Honour,' quod scho, 'to this heuinlie King
Differris richt far fra warldlie gouerning,
Quhilk is bot Pompe of eirdlie dignitie,
Geuin for estait of blude, micht or sic thing.
... ...
For eirdlie gloir is nocht bot vanitie
That as we se sa suddanelie will wend,
Bot verteous Honour neuer mair sall end.
... ...
For vertew is a thing sa precious,
Quhairof the end is sa delicious,
The warld can not considder quhat it is.
It makis folk perfite and glorious,
It makis Sanctis of pepill vitious,
It causis folk ay liue in lestand blis,
It is the way to hie Honour, I-wis.   (1972-2005)

And here we understand that the literary works of the past consti-tute the substance and the model for writing poetry – and in fact the dreamer will perform this act when he wakes up and begins his poem –, but we also become aware of the strong moral respon-sibility the poet has towards the reader. After the long quest through knowledge and after the partial view of God, the supreme embodiment of Honour, and the imperfect understanding of the nymph's sermon, the poet's *earthly* education is complete. In order to be called a poet, Douglas has to write a book out of his visionary experience: *The Palice of Honour*. This long poem with its 'tour de force' and often loose structure is there to demonstrate how Douglas has learnt the lessons given by the various guides of the old tradition, and how he has redirected that tradition towards a new purpose. In order to set about his most original 'trauaill', the translation of the *Aeneid*, Douglas has to master the poet's craft in the same ways as the older poets of the 'Court Rethoricall' did ('...thair purpois to expres/In ornate wise, prouokand with glaidnes/All gentill hartis to thair lair Incline.', 847-849), but having in mind the moral aim, that is the achievement of honour through virtue. Poetry is therefore both the memory of past tradition and the renewal of that tradition through the mediation of the poet Douglas, who has arrived at the point where 'All eirdlie thing me thocht barrane and vile' (2100). Here the twofold function, episte-mological and narrative, of the dream is elicited by the dream poem. If an epistemological enquiry is at the root of the dream poem and it takes the form of metalinguistic reflection on the relating of the dream, then the narrator-dreamer-poet, more or less consciously (in the case of Douglas, quite consciously), acquires a certain authority with regard to the cognitive problems posed and to the narrative form in which they are embodied. The content of the dream gives 'authority' to the poem and to the poet, but the narrator's painful movement from a hell-like desert, which repre-sents his former poetic failure, to the realization of the true style and subject-matter when he sees the Palace of Honour, suggests the difficult passage from a traditional poetry linked with love and pleasure to an innovative one celebrating honour and virtue. It is only after *this* book, which is Douglas's *Bildungsroman* and which in Venus's words alludes to *the* very book he is bound to write, that the *Eneados* can be translated.

Douglas's poetry is authenticated by his admission to the Court of Rhetoric and to the fellowship of classical and modern writers with the consequent renewal of his poetic powers, but his sudden vision of God/Honour after the long 'literary' journey is there to indicate a new way of poetizing. If Chaucer, who appears in the usual trio with Gower and Lydgate, is singled out among the poets Douglas sees in the Court as 'A per se sans peir/In his vulgare' (919-920), then from what follows: 'Of this Natioun I knew also anone/Greit Kennedie and Dunbar ʒit vndeid,/And Quintine with ane Huttok on his heid.' (922-924), the significant deictic *this* blatantly inserts Scotland and Scots poetry in the modern tradition. Furthermore, Venus's order that he should 'put in Ryme that proces than quite tint' (1752), coming after the dreamer has completed his earthly education, but *before* the thorough explanations of the nymph on the true function of poetry, suggests a future projection into the consciousness of an authority that the poet Douglas, himself 'of this Natioun', is entitled to. The long 'proces' of rendering the highest example of poetry in English, which started with Chaucer in the opening lines of the *House of Fame* and the summary of events contained there and continued with Caxton's 'unworthy' translation, will be accomplished by Douglas.

Douglas's *Eneados* is, therefore, seen as the fulfilment of the full assimilation of English medieval poetry to the classical tradition and also as the starting-point for a new philological understanding of the tradition represented by Virgil. After the various medieval reworkings of material from the *Aeneid* for moral and didactic discourses[9] connected with the widespread interest in the 'matter of Troy'[10] and Caxton's version, though 'Hys febil proys beyn mank and mutulate' (Prol. V, 51),[11] Douglas's is the first true translation of Virgil's epic. Although Caxton, in his Prologue, makes it clear that his is not a direct translation but is derived from a French source,[12] Douglas nevertheless strongly criticizes Caxton for the rudeness of his language and style and in general for his infidelity to the Latin text. And here, I think, lies the answer to the vexed question of Douglas's assertion of the existence of 'Scottis' as distinct from 'Inglis'.[13] For a moment let us go back to where this analysis started, in the sixteenth-century Renaissance. As has often been claimed, the sixteenth century witnessed a flourishing literary tradition which was marked by an increasing concern with translation, as Douglas first and later King James VI and his Castalian Band testify.[14] Behind the search for continental models and the inclination to translate classical, French, and Italian works lies a nationalistic project which undoubtedly unites Douglas and James, whose ideal is to create a Scottish tradition comparable to the best European literature, including the English tradition yet seen as separate. In his *Testament of the Papyngo*, written shortly after Douglas's death, Sir

David Lyndsay praises the contemporary poet precisely for the same
qualities Chaucer had been admired for in the fifteenth and sixteenth centuries and lays emphasis on his achievements in rhetoric:

> Allace for one, quhilk lampe wes of this land,
> Off Eloquence the flowand balmy strand,
> And, in our Inglis rethorick, the rose,
> As of Rubeis the Charbunckle bene chose:
> And, as Phebus dois Synthia presell,
> So Gawane Dowglas, Byschope of Dunkell,
>
> Had, quhen he wes in to this land on lyue,
> Abufe vulgare Poetis prerogatyue,
> Boith in pratick and speculatioun.
> I saye no more: gude redaris may discryue
> His worthy workis, in nowmer mo than fyue,
> And, speciallye, the trew Translatioun
> Off Uirgill, quhilk bene consolatioun
> To cunnyng men, to knaw his gret Ingyne,
> Als weill in Naturall Science as Deuyne.[15]   (22-36)

We could easily dismiss the eulogy as conventional, but we cannot
fail to notice how the translation, 'true' to Virgil and of comfort to
wise men, stands out among Douglas's works. The motives behind
his 'wark', the word Douglas repeatedly uses to refer to his translation, are many and are openly declared in the Prologue to the first
Book: his response to the request of his patron, Lord Sinclair, his
desire to achieve fame since, unlike Caxton and Chaucer, he is 'to
Virgillis text ybund' (Prol. I, 299), the pedagogic aim of making the
'sentence' of the Latin text available to people with no knowledge
of the classical language.[16] The first Prologue contains therefore an
analysis of what the art of translation means. As in the *Palice of
Honour*, the poet is aware of the difficulties he has to face in performing his task, since his linguistic medium is inadequate to render Virgil's 'sle poetry' (Prol. I, 108) and to disclose 'the rycht sentens' (Prol. I, 133), but to avoid the failures of Caxton's and even
Chaucer's attempts he constructs his own original way in order to
reveal the meaning of the *Aeneid*.

First Douglas creates the audience appropriate to his endeavour,
an aristocratic group of readers, 'beaw schirris' (Prol. I, 105), who
will share with him the language of the Scottish nation, which he

learnt when he was a page. In so doing he also makes clear that
his use of Scots, although interspersed with 'sum bastard Latyn,
French or Inglys' (Prol. I, 117) to add to its resources, is dictated by
the desire to reach a wider audience and to offer them not a word
for word translation but the sentence of the text which could only
be conveyed by the native tongue. The attack against Caxton and
the distance from Chaucer are best understood then as a critique of
medieval adaptations of classical texts and the continuous reference to Scots should be interpreted in the same way. The other
vernaculars – French and English – had till then been the language
of reworkings with insertions and omissions or plain imitation of
the *Aeneid*: through Scots Douglas cannot and must not imitate the
Latin of Virgil, his 'eloquens', but be able to express the 'sentens',[17]
the essence of the text in terms of a content which is morally ele-
vating. Douglas is aware of the limitations of Scots compared with
the excellence of Latin, this being more concise, yet richer in
vocabulary and full of *gravitas*, but his native language will be the
only means to capture Virgil's *sens*:

> For thar be Latyn wordis mony ane
> That in our leyd ganand translatioun has nane
> Less than we mynys thar sentens and grauyte
> And ȝit scant weill exponyt.   (Prol. I, 363-366)

And yet without the examples offered by his English predecessors,
Caxton, Lydgate, and Chaucer, he would not have been able to
master the language he uses to recreate the life of Virgil's poetry.
After the long exposition of the problems raised by such a translation, torn as he is between a desire to adhere to the true meaning
of the text, 'to follow a fixt sentens or mater' (Prol. I, 289), and a
pedagogic aspiration for a 'sentens diuers to heir' (Prol. I, 352),
Douglas finally finds an explanation and a justification for his work
in his prayer to God, 'prynce of poetis' (Prol. I, 452), to Christ,
through the intercession of the Virgin Mother, that is within a 'correct' Christian use of the translation to be delivered to a Christian
audience. In this final Christian address it is impossible not to hear
the echo of the prayer at the end of Chaucer's *Troilus* and yet, as
Douglas will show in the various Prologues, his reading of the
Aeneid is similar to the views shared by Italian humanists such as

Cristoforo Landino, who sees Aeneas as the perfect model for virtuous life.[18] In aiming at the 'sentens', Douglas tries to overcome
the problem of Virgil's paganism: once the inner meaning has been
disclosed, the story of Aeneas could become a paradigm for the
quest of man, of the prince, and of the poet himself. But, instead
of inserting moral comments and allegorical interpretation in the
text, the Scottish poet uses prologues, epilogues and postscript to
convey his explanations of the problems connected with form and
content. Douglas does not renounce the didactic role, which he
combines with fine observations on the art of translation, and all is
assigned to the various forms of paratext. The Prologues II-VI are
concerned with the relation between the narrator and the text he is
translating with a particular emphasis on the distance of the Scots
translation from the original. Douglas's divided attitude is nevertheless evident in the way he revives medieval modes of writing like
the dream-vision tradition with a strange man appearing in
Prologue VIII and complaining that the world is turned upside
down, and like the Christian allegorization of Aeneas's quest in
Prologue VI. And yet this Prologue which, following Servius,
Ascensius, and Landino refers to Virgil as a philosopher and to his
works as describing the 'stait of man' (Prol. VI, 34), represents the
turning-point in the step-by-step commentary offered by the paratext, since it demonstrates how the *Aeneid*, if the 'sentens' is
grasped, could be interpreted as an allegory of human life in a way
that anticipates Christianity. And it is significant that the shift from
a view of the transitory world to the experience of the afterlife corresponding to Aeneas's descent into the underworld is given
strength by originally transforming the 'Sibilla Cumane' (146) in
'our Sibill, Crystis moder deir' (145), implying that the ancient
prophecy has become true in Christ through the Incarnation.

In Prologues VII-XII Douglas focuses his attention on his poetical art, Prologue VII being one of the three nature prologues but
also a new starting-point for writing.[19] Unlike Aeneas who in his
descent to Hell discovers the sense of his wanderings, the poet
fails to grasp, within a dream-vision frame marked by the presence
of a strange man and by resorting to the alliterative style, the function of poetry in a world gone mad. Whereas the majority of people
described in the Prologue are preoccupied with worldly affairs, the

poet wishes he could 'haue our buke done' (Prol. VIII, 142), but
the man dismisses his request by pointing out the uselessness of
the enterprise. On his awakening the narrator finds himself striving
to complete the book seen as a possible 'bute' (solace) to his
conflicts. Prologues IX-XII are all concerned with the poetical
work in its content and style. Prologue IX, with its emphasis on
the moral significance of poetry, clearly states the exemplary
function of the Virgilian text while the sudden reference to the
'ryall style' (21) fully represents the poet's awareness, as expressed
in the following lines, of the need for a language consonant with it:

> The sayar eik suld weil considir thys,
> Hys mater, and quhamto it entitilit is:
> Eftir myne authouris wordis, we aucht tak tent
> That baith accord, and bene conuenient,
> The man, the sentens, and the knychtlyke stile.   (Prol. IX, 27-31)

The necessary correspondence between theme, language, and
audience is a classical commonplace, but here Douglas is also
showing his faith in the ennobling force of the epic within Scottish
society. The didactic function of his translation, after the strong
affirmation of God as the only source of inspiration in Prologue X,
is reinforced in Prologue XI where the construction of the audience is completed through recourse to St Paul's popular image of
the Christian knight (Ephesians vi, 13-17) and to the Flesh/Spirit
debate, the core of man's struggle between vice and virtue. And
the poet's dilemma – the condemnation of pagan poetry and its
exemplary figures as in Prologue X[20] and the admiration for
Aeneas as a mirror for the perfect knight – is reconciled in the
moral reading of Aeneas whose adventures are likened to man's
struggle to flee vice and pursue virtue. If in Prologue I the poet
refers to Aeneas as the *summa* of earthly chivalry, at least in
Virgil's *descriptio*,[21] in Prologue XI, after the redirection of
Douglas's poetical art, Aeneas's 'feill dangeris' (179) and 'stryfe in
stour' (180) *sub specie temporum* are seen as pressing us 'to wyn
the kynryk ay lestyng' (183).

Prologue XII to Virgil's last Book is a hymn to renewal and
regeneration both in nature and in human craft: the wonder of the
sun's rising highlights the architectural frames of 'Towris, turettis,
kyrnellis, pynnaclys hie/Of kyrkis, castellis and ilke fair cite' (Prol.

XII, 69-70), which stand as painted in a conscious metalinguistic interchange, and affects Nature and all her creatures, from the blossoming flowers and the singing birds to human beings in love within a spring setting.[22] To rejoicing Nature inundated by the sunlight and aroused by the generative forces of the spring season corresponds the narrator's poetical activity renewed after the darkness of sleep.[23] The minutely detailed *tableau vivant* describing a conventionally diffuse *locus amoenus* emphasizes the beauty of *natura naturans* by means of an aureate language which mirrors an idealized setting. Here Douglas is not interested in a realistic picture of a typically Scottish landscape as his nature Prologues are often praised for, but in stating a close partnership between Nature's work and man's work, in this special case the poet's work, his translation. The view that Prologue XII represents a crucial assertion of Douglas's concern with poetics is confirmed by the recurring images of weaving: the ground, in a profusion of colours, is 'naturis tapestreis' (102), while 'Full bissely Aragne wevand was,/To knyt hir nettis and hir wobbys sle' (170-171) and the narrator's reference to Procne's and Philomela's lamentations recall yet other examples of tapestry. Within such a context is placed the poet's precious artifact, a 'lusty crafty preambill, "perle of May"' (307), which is both the Prologue to the last Book and the translation itself, his 'langsum wark' (270), which, as he declares, was completed in May. The likeness of Douglas's text to a tapestry is appropriate if, together with the Virgilian epic, the paratext formed of Prologues, a 'Conclusio', a letter to Sinclair, an 'Exclamatioun', and of 'tyme, space and dait' is taken into account. Douglas is, by virtue of his various insertions, a medieval poet who feels he has to comment on the text, but, in his profound respect for the integrity of the *Aeneid* whose 'sentence' he tried to grasp in the translation, he is a man of the Renaissance.

We have already seen how Douglas incorporates in his translation, at least in his Prologues, the commentary tradition handed down as a companion to the *Aeneid*: he goes further and adds to his *Eneados* Maphaeus Vegius's Christian allegorical conclusion as Book XIII, which is also preceded by the usual Prologue.[24] Prologue XIII contains Douglas's justification for translating Maphaeus's *Supplementum* by the dream encounter with the Italian

poet, who literally forces him to acknowledge what the Scot
already knows – Virgil's relevance to a Christian audience –, and to
consider his own booklet as the right allegorical guidance. And yet
this Prologue is more than the medieval recourse to the *locus
amoenus* and to the prophetic dream vision with the appearance
of an authoritative figure:[25] it is a way both of paying a debt to the
humanistic practice of inserting Maphaeus's thirteenth Book in editions of Virgil for a very long time and of mirroring the poet's own
doubts about the meaning and value of his translation. Priscilla
Bawcutt has shown how the motive of the poet's being asked by
another to write is of long standing, and significantly Henryson is
indicated as a model.[26] Maphaeus is in fact described 'Lyke to sum
poet of the ald fasson' (Prol. XIII, 88), almost in the same terms as
Aesop and Mercury in, respectively, Henryson's *Fables* and
Testament of Cresseid, clearly pointing to Douglas's aim to confront
his poetic skill with tradition while assessing his own poetic identity. It is significant that in the final stage of his work Douglas's
thought goes to a great Scots poet of the near past and to the one
who had extensively dealt with the authority of classical authors
and with the theme of pagan antiquity and of Britain's Trojan
inheritance. In his *Testament of Cresseid* Henryson had questioned
Chaucer's authority as *the* model for any future retelling of the
Troilus and Criseyde story, thus clearly establishing his own role of
auctor of a poem that would remain with the readers not only as a
moral warning, but also as a monument to his fame.[27] Like
Henryson Douglas has drawn on the classical past to make classical texts available to Scottish as well as to English readers, but
unlike Henryson's reworkings Douglas's *Eneados* is a translation
which as 'wlgar Virgill' ('Exclamatioun' 37) will 'with euery gentill
Scot be kend,/And to onletterit folk be red on hight,/That erst was
bot with clerkis comprehend.' ('Exclam.' 43-45). Through the examples of the learned Maphaeus and the distinguished Scots poet
Henryson Douglas seems to have solved the dilemma which has
been constantly present in his writing, whether a pagan text in a
vernacular as near as possible to his native language could be useful to Christian readers. Although in his 'Directioun' he recalls his
kinsman and patron, Lord Sinclair, the audience he has in mind is
not restricted to Scotland, but as he had boldly stated in the

'Conclusio', 'Throw owt the ile yclepit Albyon/Red sall I be, and
sung with mony one' (11-12). In order to reach such a wide audience and to make the 'sentens' of Virgil's Latin available in Middle
English, in order to be 'British', Douglas the poet must, as he often
points out in the Prologues and Epilogues, be 'Scottish'.[28] His work
therefore goes beyond the limitations of a nationalistic *querelle* in
that it aims at offering a 'faithful' text of a poem closely connected
with the foundation of Britain to those who were not at ease with
Latin.

NOTES

[1] William Ferguson, *The Identity of the Scottish Nation, A Historic
Quest*, Edinburgh: Edinburgh University Press, 1998. Interestingly he
quotes Douglas's expression, 'Lang desparit work', in order to thank
his family for their support. On the myth of a separate Scottish identity
in the Middle Ages, see E.J. Cowan, 'Myth and Identity in Early
Medieval Scotland', *Scottish Historical Review*, vol. 63, 1984, pp. 111-
135 and Adrian Hastings, *The Construction of Nationhood: Ethnicity,
Religion and Nationalism*, Cambridge: Cambridge University Press,
1997, pp. 70-73.
[2] R.D.S. Jack, '"Translating" the Lost Scottish Renaissance', *Translation
and Literature,* vol. 6, 1997, (pp. 66-80) p. 66. He purposely asks himself why if invited to a Renaissance conference in English Literature
one expects it to deal with sixteenth- and seventeenth-century authors,
while a Scottish Literature 'Renaissance' conference must be associated
with twentieth-century authors. Among the many articles devoted to
the question of a Scottish literary identity, see, by the same author,
'Which Vernacular Revival? Burns and the Makars', *Studies in Scottish
Literature,* vol. 30, 1998, pp. 9-17.
[3] R.D.S. Jack, '"Translating" the Lost Scottish Renaissance', cit., p. 66.
[4] Priscilla Bawcutt, *Gavin Douglas*, Edinburgh: Edinburgh University
Press, 1976, pp. 1-22. See also her 'New Light on Gavin Douglas', in
A.A. MacDonald, Michael Lynch and I.B. Cowan eds., *The Renaissance
in Scotland: Studies in Literature, Religion, History and Culture
Offered to John Durkan*, Leiden: E.J. Brill, 1994, pp. 95-106 and 'The
Correspondence of Gavin Douglas', in Janet Hadley Williams ed.,
Stewart Style 1513-1542: Essays on the Court of James V, East Linton:

Tuckwell Press, 1996, pp. 52-61.

[5] Ruth Morse, 'Gavin Douglas: "Off Eloquence the flowand balmy strand"', in Ruth Morse and Barry Windeatt eds., *Chaucer Traditions: Studies in Honour of Derek Brewer*, Cambridge: Cambridge University Press, 1990, (pp. 107-121) pp. 107-109.

[6] All quotations are from the Edinburgh text of the *Palice of Honour* in Priscilla Bawcutt ed., *The Shorter Poems of Gavin Douglas*, STS, Edinburgh and London: Blackwood, 1967. A new edition (STS, 2003) with an updated bibliography is now available, but, since the Introduction, Texts and Apparatus have remained unaltered, quotations are still taken from the 1967 edition.

[7] The expression is to be understood according to Frank Kermode, *The Sense of an Ending*, Oxford: Oxford University Press, 1967 (especially chapter 5).

[8] This idea is further exploited by G.B. Kinneavy in 'The Poet in *The Palice of Honour*', *Chaucer Review*, vol. 3, 1969, pp. 280-303, where the poem is seen as an illustration of the poetic act: 'First the poet must have the vision of the subject matter; his imagination must first of all operate to acquire the materials of the poem. And secondly, it must operate to order and express that vision', p. 295.

[9] For the study of translation from antiquity to the Middle Ages within the theoretical systems of rhetoric and hermeneutics, see Rita Copeland, *Rhetoric, Hermeneutics, and Translation in the Middle Ages: Academic Traditions and Vernacular Texts*, Cambridge: Cambridge University Press, 1991 (especially chapter 7 on Chaucer and Gower). On the various reworkings of the *Aeneid*, see J.E. Singerman, *Under Clouds of Poesy: Poetry and Truth in French and English Reworkings of the Aeneid, 1160-1513*, New York and London: Garland, 1986, and Arturo Cattaneo, *Tecniche traduttive nell'Umanesimo inglese: L'Eneide in Gran Bretagna da Lydgate a Surrey*, Brescia: La Scuola, 1990. See also Colin Burrow, 'Virgil in English Translation', in Charles Martindale ed., *The Cambridge Companion to Virgil*, Cambridge: Cambridge University Press, 1997, pp. 21-37.

[10] See the now classical studies of C.D. Benson, *The History of Troy in Middle English Literature*, Woodbridge: D.S. Brewer, 1980, and Piero Boitani ed., *The European Tragedy of Troilus*, Oxford: Clarendon Press, 1989.

[11] All quotations are from D.F.C. Coldwell ed., *Virgil's Aeneid Translated into Scottish Verse by Gavin Douglas*, 4 vols., STS, Edinburgh and London: Blackwood, 1957-1964.

[12] *Eneydos*, Prologue: 'whiche booke as me semed sholde be moche requysyte to noble men to see as wel for the eloquence as the historyes'; the quotation is from W.J.B. Crotch ed., *The Prologues and Epilogues of William Caxton*, EETS OS 176, London: Oxford University Press, 1928, Klaus Reprint, 1978, p. 108.

[13] On the question of either an essential identity or an essential distinctiveness of Scots and English, compare J.D. McClure, 'Scottis, Inglis, Suddroun: Language Labels and Language Attitudes', in R.J. Lyall and Felicity Riddy eds., *Proceedings of the Third International Conference on Scottish Language and Literature (Medieval and Renaissance)*, Stirling and Glasgow: University of Glasgow, 1981, pp. 52-69 and John Corbett, 'Writtin in the Language of the Scottis Natioun: Literary Translation into Scots', in Susan Bassnett ed., *Translating Literature, Essays and Studies*, Cambridge: D.S. Brewer, 1997, pp. 95-118.

[14] See John Corbett, 'Writtin in the Language of the Scottis Natioun', cit., pp. 99-103 and R.D.S. Jack's Introduction (pp. xi-xxxix) to R.D.S. Jack and P.A.T. Rozendaal eds., *The Mercat Anthology of Early Scottish Literature 1375-1707*, Edinburgh: Mercat Press, 1997. A critique of the common view concerning the Castalian Band is in Priscilla Bawcutt, 'James VI's Castalian Band: A Modern Myth', *Scottish Historical Review*, vol. 80, 2001, pp. 251-259.

[15] *The Works of Sir David Lindsay of the Mount 1490-1555*, edited by Douglas Hamer, 4 vols., STS, Edinburgh and London: Blackwood, 1931-1936, I, pp. 56-57. The poem is dated 1530.

[16] According to Priscilla Bawcutt (*Gavin Douglas*, cit., pp. 98-100) the text used by Douglas is the edition of the printer Badius Ascensius, from which he derived the commentary and most likely the text itself.

[17] The distinction between 'eloquens' and 'sentens' is thoroughly discussed in C.R. Blyth, *'The Knychtlyke Stile': A Study of Gavin Douglas' Aeneid*, New York and London: Garland, 1987, pp. 122-130; Blyth, however, reads the *Eneados* within the context of medieval narrative style.

[18] See Priscilla Bawcutt, *Gavin Douglas*, cit., pp. 74-77. For a discussion of Landino's representation of Aeneas as the embodiment of virtue, see the Introduction in Timothy Hampton, *Writing from History: The Rhetoric of Exemplarity in Renaissance Literature*, Ithaca and London: Cornell University Press, 1990 (especially pp. 19-30).

[19] On Douglas's view of nature in the Prologues, see Priscilla Bawcutt, *Gavin Douglas*, cit., pp. 175-190.

[20] 'Lat Virgill hald hys mawmentis to him self;/I wirschip nowder ydoll,

stok nor elf,/Thocht furth I write so as myne autour dois'., Prol. X, 153-155.

[21] 'For euery vertu belangand a nobill man/This ornate poet bettir than ony can/Payntand discryvis in person of Eneas –/Not forto say sikane Eneas was/ʒit than by hym perfytely blasons he/All wirschip, manhed and nobilite,/With euery bonte belangand a gentill wycht,/Ane prynce, ane conquerour or a valʒeand knycht.', Prol. I, 325-332, echoing Ascensius's words, *speculum atque exemplum perfecti viri.* See Priscilla Bawcutt, *Gavin Douglas,* cit., p. 84.

[22] See Priscilla Bawcutt, *Gavin Douglas,* cit., p. 177. Her analysis of Prologue XII convincingly focuses on the blend of convention and love for naturalistic detail.

[23] The narrator can also allude to the aridity of his poetical art as represented in the *Palice of Honour* and in the first Prologue.

[24] The inclusion of Maphaeus's addition has been variously interpreted. On the one hand, Robert Cummings, in '"To the cart the fift quheill": Gavin Douglas's Humanist Supplement to the *Eneados*', *Translation and Literature,* vol. 4, 1995, pp. 133-156, sees Douglas's work as a mirror for King James and Maphaeus would provide a summary of political issues present in Virgil's *Aeneid;* on the other, Kantik Ghosh in '"The Fift Quheill": Gavin Douglas's Maffeo Vegio', *Scottish Literary Journal,* vol. 22, 1995, pp. 5-21 understands the poet's acceptance of the *Supplement* as a way of emphasizing the ambivalent attitude Douglas has towards the *Aeneid,* representative of a pagan flawed world and hinting at a pre-Christian vision of hidden truths. The fortune of Maphaeus's book is outlined in the introduction to the edition by Anna Cox Brinton, pp. 29-32 (*Maphaeus Vegius and his Thirteenth Book of the Aeneid. A Chapter on Virgil in the Renaissance,* Stanford: Stanford University Press, 1930).

[25] Priscilla Bawcutt (*Gavin Douglas,* cit., pp. 188-189) notes that the association of Douglas's dream with Jerome's also alludes to the fact that the saint himself was a translator, the translator of the Vulgate.

[26] *Ibidem,* p. 189.

[27] See Anna Torti, 'Henryson's *Testament of Cresseid:* Deconstructing the *Auctoritas*', *Textus,* vol. 5, 1992, pp. 3-11.

[28] On the literary relations between England and Scotland, see Gregory Kratzmann, *Anglo-Scottish Literary Relations 1430-1550,* Cambridge: Cambridge University Press, 1980, and, more recently, Priscilla Bawcutt, 'Crossing the Border: Scottish Poetry and English Readers in the Sixteenth Century', in Solly Mapstone and Juliette Wood eds., *The*

Rose and the Thistle: Essays on the Culture of Late Medieval and Renaissance Scotland, East Linton: Tuckwell Press, 1998, pp. 59-76. On the term 'Great Britain', see Denys Hay, *Europe: The Emergence of an Idea*, Edinburgh: Edinburgh University Press, 1968, pp. 128-144. See also John Smyth, *The Making of the United Kingdom 1660-1880*, London: Longman, 2001, for a useful introduction to 'British' history between the Restoration and the creation of the United Kingdom of Great Britain and Ireland in 1800.

KEVIN MCGINLEY

The Poetry of Sir David Lyndsay: Reforming the Nation

Sir David Lyndsay of the Mount (c.1485-1555) is chiefly famed for his pro-reformation play, *Ane Satyre of the Thrie Estaitis*. Yet between 1528 and 1553 Lyndsay also produced a substantial body of poetry which has perhaps been overshadowed by the success of his dramatic work. Lyndsay's poems, while lacking the technical virtuosity of Dunbar or Gavin Douglas, show his fine rhetorical command of verse form across a considerable range of genres. Moreover, the poems deal with many of the key concerns to which Lyndsay returns in *The Thrie Estaitis*. They promote a view of national well-being as depending on monarch, court, clergy and general populace (merchants, artisans, peasants) all recognising their interdependence and mutual responsibilities. Lyndsay's poetry and drama express the idea that Scottish society, if rightly governed, can be an orderly and unified hierarchy, beneficial to all its members.

Lyndsay was born around 1485. Little is known of his early life, but he entered the service of King James IV sometime towards the end of the first decade of the sixteenth century. In 1512 he was appointed usher to the infant prince James (later James V) a post which entailed the roles of tutor, entertainer, and almost surrogate father.[1] Lyndsay retained this role after the death of James IV at Flodden and through the period of regency until 1524. At this point he was stripped of his position as usher when the King's mother, Margaret Tudor, gained control of the crown and began to rule in her son's name. In 1528, after further turmoil, which involved James being held by the Douglases, the King began to rule in his own name and Lyndsay's position at court was restored. Between 1528 and 1530 he wrote three long poems: 'The Dreme', 'The Complaynt', and 'The Testament of the Papyngo'. Around 1530 he was appointed Snowdon Herald and in 1543 was appointed Lyon King of Arms. This was the most important heraldic position and one in which Lyndsay had apparently served unofficially several times in the 1530s. In his capacity as herald Lyndsay arranged a number of court entertainments (a pageant for the celebrations of the King's second marriage being a notable instance). He also served on diplomatic missions, including a journey to France with the royal envoys to negotiate James' first marriage to the Princess Magdalen (who died not long after the marriage) and other embassies to Denmark, the Netherlands, France, and England. After the death of James V in 1542 Lyndsay spent considerably less time at court though he was still involved in some diplomatic duties. He may also have served as a member of the parliament in the fifteen-forties. In the period from 1448 to 1555 Lyndsay produced four substantial literary works: 'The Tragedie of the Cardinall', 'Squyer Meldrum', *The Thrie Estaitis* and 'The Monarche'. He died in 1555.

Lyndsay's earliest extant poem, 'The Dreme' (1528) is, as its title indicates, a dream-vision, and it establishes a set of concerns that continues, with modifications, throughout Lyndsay's work. The narrator is led by Dame Remembrance on a Dantesque journey through Hell, Purgatory, Heaven and Earth (in that order), concluding with an account of the current state of Scotland. The progress from cosmic visions of Hell and Heaven, through a global account of the Earth's regions, to a localised focus on Scotland, makes clear that Lyndsay, like Dante, insists on referring his visionary subject matter back to the actual political circumstances of this world.[2]

The vision of Hell opens with a depiction of damned clergymen (176-238), placed there because of neglect of their spiritual duties in pursuit of secular interests and their spending of the Church's income, exacted from their congregations, on worldly pleasures such as 'cartis, and dyce, on harllotrie and huris' (207). This highlighting of the clergy's failure to carry out their pastoral duties and condemnation of the abuse of the wealth they obtain from their benefices is a persistent theme in Lyndsay's attacks on the Church. Lyndsay is writing at a time when popular dissatisfaction with the established Church was growing in Scotland and reforming ideas were beginning to spread. In 'The Dreme', as throughout his work, Lyndsay is strongly in sympathy with these urgings for change.

Lyndsay's attacks on the clergy, however, show little interest in doctrinal issues. While in later years he becomes more clearly Lutheran, his focus is predominantly on the clergy's immorality and social abuses.[3]

The depiction of Hell in 'The Dreme' also condemns the injustice and licentiousness of the nobility (239-301). The attention that Lyndsay devotes to the nobility is hardly surprising given the political situation in Scotland when he was writing 'The Dreme'. In 1528, King James V of Scotland had reached his majority after fifteen years in which the government of Scotland had been remarkably unstable, largely due to conflicts over the regency, strife between different family factions and antagonism between pro-French and pro-English groupings.[4] Lyndsay's 'The Complaynt' (1529) notes the events of the period disapprovingly:

> That tyme, in court, rais gret debait,
> And euerilk lord did stryue for stait,
> That all the realme mycht mak no reddyng,
> Quhyll on ilk syde thare was blude scheddyng [...] ('The Complaynt', 351-354)

The social disorder that results from the misdeeds of the nobility is thus as pressing an issue as the corruption of the clergy. Indeed, the misconduct of the clergy and nobility are given much greater weight than the failings of the rest of society. 'The Dreme' contains only two stanzas devoted to the vices of common people, briefly noting the dishonesty of merchants, lawyers and craftsmen. Lyndsay thus identifies the clergy and the nobility as the key figures responsible for the condition of society.

The concluding section of 'The Dreme' returns the narrator to the disorder of contemporary Scotland. Here Lyndsay introduces the figure of John the Commonweal, who appears again in *Ane Satyre of the Thrie Estaitis*. John the Commonweal, or 'common good' narrates how he has wandered throughout Scotland seeking shelter only to find that each region, the Borders, the Highlands and Islands, and the Lowlands, rejects him: 'singulare proffeit gart me soune disluge' (969). A key opposition between commonweal and singular profit is introduced here. The concept of the commonweal designates the joining of the various parts of society in a bond of common interests and mutual obligations. The poem's diffraction of Scotland into regions, all of which reject the common-weal, indicates that the concept denotes a sense of community, and indeed of political and national identity, that has been lost through the pursuit of factional interests, or 'singulare proffect'. It is this sense of commonalty that the clergy's corruption and the dissension among the nobility undermine. What is needed to reinstate it, as the Commonweal's concluding remarks indicate, is a strong and just monarch:

> Quod he: thare sall na Scot haue confortyng
> off me, tyll that I see the countre gydit
> Be wysedome of ane gude auld prudent kyng [!] ('Dreme', 1103-1108)

The need for an effective ruler to set the kingdom in order is, again, a theme to which Lyndsay returns.

Lyndsay's finest early poem, 'The Testament and Complaynt of our Soverane Lordis Papyngo' (1530), elaborates the themes of 'The Dreme'. The poem combines a range of generic forms: beast-fable, chanson d'aventure, the parliament of birds tradition, the *De Casibus* tradition, and the *De Regimine Principum*. Lyndsay turns these materials to didactic and satirical ends. The main narrative section of the poem has the parrot of the title climbing on a tree against advice from the narrator. She subsequently falls, mortally wounding herself. Two 'epistles' follow, in which the parrot addresses words of advice to James V and his courtiers. The final section contains a debate between the parrot and the magpie, the raven, and the kite. These birds represent the Augustinian canons, the monks, and friars, respectively. In a passage that recalls the darker moments of Robert Henryson's *Fabillis*, the poem concludes with these spiritual counsellors squabbling over the parrot's corpse as they tear it to shreds.

The narrative of the Papyngo's fall presents a general lesson about the dangers of ambition and pride, but the epistles invite different understandings of and responses to that lesson according to the social role of the audience. The epistle to the king recommends various leisure pastimes and studies that will enable the king to properly fulfil his duties. Lyndsay urges this educational program to remind James that he is merely an officer of God and must learn to perform his role in accordance with His will (248-

254). In warning the king against governing by personal desire rather than by consideration of his divinely ordained responsibilities, the poem identifies the specific form of pride most appropriate to its royal addressee. The epistle to the courtiers states a single theme at the outset, which it elaborates and illustrates with historical examples:

> To preis ouer heych I pray yow not pretend yow,
> The vaine ascens of court quho wyll considder,
> Quho sittith moist hie sal fynd the sait most slidder. ('Papyngo', 350-352)

Lyndsay outlines the specific modes of behaviour which make the court so 'vntraist and transitorie' (367), all of which show the courtiers' pride in using their positions for personal advancement rather than common good. The greatest outrage is reserved for those who, to promote their own interests, lead the king into sensuality: 'bernes of Baliall,/Full of dissimilit payntit flatterie,/Prouocande, be Intoxicat counsall,/Prencis tyll huredom and tyll hasardrie' (395-398). These reprobates combine the vices of all the other bad courtiers: dissimulation, flattery and bad counsel. They thus appear as the summit of courtly vice. Lyndsay affirms that such self-interested courtiers 'Sulde puneist be abufe all strang tratouris' (401) and counsels an ethos of humble service:

> Conforme your trust in God alluterlie;
> Ayne serue your Prince, with enteir hart, trewlie;
> And, quhen ye se the court bene at the best,
> I counsall yow, than draw you to your rest. ('Papyngo', 601-604)

In this, the epistle to the courtiers restates the theme of the commonweal, showing how instability results when common profit is ousted by singular profit.

The structure of 'The Papyngo', in having a simple narrative open onto different levels of meaning which apply to different audiences, expresses a central concern of Lyndsay's didactic method. Indeed, Lyndsay echoes the structure of 'The Papyngo' seventeen years later in *The Tragedie of the Cardinall* (1547), which again features a main narrative followed by expository addresses to the princes and to the prelates. This device allows his work, which is consistently directed towards the regulation of human actions, to address itself to the backgrounds and concerns

of different levels of society, showing the specific implications
which exemplary values have in different contexts. In this,
Lyndsay's literary technique is adapted to relate his moral themes
to the experiences and concerns of different levels of audience.
This is a vital feature for a writer whose work is so consistently
aimed at engaging his audience in order to effect moral and social
reform. The discussion of the clergy in the final section of 'The
Papyngo' extends the poem's moral focus to emphasise the suffering that the clergy inflicts on the wider community:

> I did persaue, quhen preuelye ye did pyke
> Ane chekin frome ane hen, vnder ane dyke.
> I grant, said he; that hen was my gude freind,
> And I that chekin tuke, bot for my teind. ('Papyngo', 678-681)

Lyndsay is referring to the teind system whereby the clergy claimed
tithes for their upkeep from the community. By associating this
practice with the predatory kite Lyndsay presents it as a source of
exploitation. A few stanzas later the parrot tells the kite that 'The
wyffis of the village cryis, with cair,/Quhen thai persaue your
muow ouirthort thar medis' (712-714). These references to the
teind system and to the life of the village balance Lyndsay's earlier
focus on the divinely decreed requirements of the monarch's role
with a broader consideration of the practical effects of misgovern-
ment in the world beyond the court.

'The Testament of the Papyngo' features a powerful attack on the
Church's abuse of its wealth. Love of property, the parrot argues,
leads the Church to become subject to riches and sensuality:

> This royall Ryches and Lady Sensuall
> Frome that tyme furth tuke hole the gouernance
> Off the moste part of the stait spiritual. ('Papyngo', 850-852)

Soon, we are told, 'thay foryet to study, praye and preche' (857). In
'The Papyngo', the correct use of the wealth of churchmen is
defined as being to aid them in the spiritual duties of study, prayer,
and preaching. The poem envisions an ideal world where clerical
positions are given to men of learning and wisdom:

> Gret plesour war to heir ane Byschope preche,
> One Dane, or Doctour in Diuinitie,

One Abbote quhilk could weill his conuent teche,
One persoun flowyng in Phylosophie. ('Papyngo', 1032-1035)

Lyndsay here indicates that the spiritual duties of the clergymen are
primarily to give the people spiritual guidance by preaching to the
community directly, as a part of it. Indeed, he attacks the upper
clergy specifically for relying on the friars to provide such pastoral
care ('Papyngo', 1036-1038).

Lyndsay's views here may reflect a Protestant stress on preaching and pastoral care. But the proposed reforms also have clear
political connotations. Lyndsay's attack on the clergy's excessive
concern with temporal matters, and his definition of their duties as
primarily pastoral and requiring them to work among the general
populace, tend to marginalise them with regard to the business of
political administration, which becomes reserved for the nobility.
The upper clergy had traditionally played an important part in
affairs of state, but Lyndsay stresses their more mundane duties in
the world at large. This exclusion of the clergy from affairs of state
is also evident in the poem's insistence that reform can be effected
by the secular rulers taking greater care over whom they place in
ecclesiastical office. The raven comments thus:

Prencis, I pray yow, be no more abusit,
To verteous men hauyng so small regarde.
Quhy sulde vertew, throuch flattrye, be refusit,
That men, for cunnyng, can get no rewarde? ('Papyngo', 1011-1014)

In making this appeal Lyndsay invites the crown and the secular
authorities under it to exercise control over the spiritual estates.
This emphasis is implicit in the very structure of 'The Papyngo'.
While the monarch and the court are addressed as part of the
poem's audience, the clergy are presented only as part of its narrative. Ecclesiastical opinion is not solicited.

Lyndsay's program of reform, then, is similar to the actual
reform effected in England by Henry VIII in 1534. The Henrician
reforms brought the English Church thoroughly under the control
of the state, with the crown in fact being enriched considerably by
the appropriation of Church goods and revenues. Lyndsay's proposed reforms also tend in this direction and are clearly in tune
with the Henrician laicisation of government and subjection of the

Church to secular authority.

Lyndsay's literary output diminished in the 1530s and 1540s and his first major poem after 'The Papyngo' is 'The Tragedie of the Cardinall' (1547).[5] This poem opens with the narrator perusing Boccaccio's *De Casibus Virorum Illustrium*, which recounts the tragic fates of a series of great figures from history, highlighting the instability of worldly glory. The prologue thus places the poem in a tradition of literary historiography in which history is combined with moral edification. As the narrator reads, the spirit of Cardinal David Beaton, who was stabbed to death by reformers in 1546, appears before him wounded and bleeding. Beaton condemns himself out of his own mouth as he proceeds to narrate his own history of misdeeds and consequent fall.[6]

In 'The Tragedie', Lyndsay accentuates the social effects of the clergy's vices and demands that, in the light of those abuses, the secular authorities reform the ways in which they dispense ecclesiastical benefices. The poem depicts Beaton not merely as an example of pride and ambition, but of specifically clerical forms of pride and ambition. Much is made of his interference in politics, as he subordinates Scottish interests to the interests of the French and to the Catholic Church, and of his neglect of spiritual duties in favour of temporal interests. Beaton, consequently, appears not merely as a vain and ambitious man, but as a vain and ambitious member of the Scottish clergy in the mid-sixteenth century. In condemning Beaton's role in recent political events the poem presents Lyndsay's moral points as immediately pertinent to contemporary life. Clerical vice is thus not merely condemned as immoral: Lyndsay foregrounds the malign social effects of such vice as a major motive for reform.

While the focus of 'The Tragedie' is almost wholly on the clergy, 'Squyer Meldrum' (1550) takes the nobility as its subject matter. The poem is a chivalric romance which eulogises William Meldrum, who was a friend of Lyndsay. Lyndsay focuses on two main periods of Meldrum's life. The first period covers Meldrum's military exploits in France, and on his journeys there and back; the second period relates Meldrum's greatest love affair and its tragic denouement, as Meldrum is almost killed by an envious foe and recovers to find that his beloved has been married to another. The narrative concludes with a short account of Meldrum's peaceful final years.

The chivalric ideals of Romance are consistently presented positively in the poem. For instance, when Meldrum takes up the proud challenge of the English knight, Talbert, the latter's discourteous and boastful demeanour causes even his own comrades to look askance at him (297-336). Meldrum's genteel treatment of Talbert, on the other hand, wins him acclaim even from the English side:

> The Capitane of the Inglis band
> Tuke the young squyer be the hand,
> And led him to the Pailyeoun
> And gart him mak collatioun. ('Squyer Meldrum', 567-570)

Chivalry is thus shown to have an ameliorating influence on conflict as Meldrum's courtesy inspires reciprocal courtesy from even his opponents in warfare.[7]

As is common with romance protagonists, Meldrum is presented as a type, an embodiment of virtue, rather than as an individual. Indeed, he is introduced as 'ane Nobill Squyer' (29), discussed and praised in general terms, and only named forty-one lines later. Lyndsay's priorities are neatly demonstrated by his defining Meldrum within a class before individuating him: what is of key importance in Meldrum's character is what is general and shared in it, not what is unique. This concern with general, shared values is connected with a desire in the poem to see those values promulgated. Echoing the opening of Robert Henryson's *Orpheus and Eurydice*, the poem invites the members of its audience to apply depicted virtues in their own lives:

> Quho that Antique Stories reidis
> Consider may the famous deidis
> Of our Nobill Progenitours,
> Quhilk suld to vs be richt mirrouris,
> Thair verteous deides to ensew,
> And vicious leuing to eschew.   ('Squyer Meldrum', 1-6)

In this it suggests that one should actually aim to live the values depicted in Romance. In evoking a set of ideal chivalric values and indicating that these should be put into practice, 'Squyer Meldrum' invites its noble readers to regulate their behaviour according to a common system of values. The poem thus encourages a form of class-consciousness, reminding the nobility of collective values and interests beneficial to them all. Given the conflicts among the nobility that characterised the first half of the sixteenth century, the poem might be viewed as Lyndsay's attempt to reinstate a sense of social cohesion. If the clergy, then, are seen in 'The Tragedie' as the chief source of social disorder, 'Squyer Meldrum' indicates that the conduct of the nobility is a hope for the repair of that disorder.

Ane Satyre of the Thrie Estaitis (1553),[8] undoubtedly Lyndsay's most important work, is the only surviving Scottish morality play. The play falls into two parts with an intervening interlude. The first part presents a typical morality play narrative in which the inexperienced protagonist, Rex Humanitas, is led into sin by Dame Sensualitie and an array of Vices, until Divine Correction enters and sets right the situation by ousting the Vices and restoring the Virtues. The second part depicts a parliamentary setting in which the three estates of society (the nobility, the clergy and the common people) meet to decide on a program of social reform which will oust vice from the kingdom as a whole.

In keeping with the morality tradition, Lyndsay employs allegorical representation so that the action of the play has two distinct levels of meaning. Rex Humanitas, for instance, is an everyman figure, while Wantoness, Placebo, Solace and Sensualitie, represent general immoral temptations, as do Falset, Flatterie and Dissait. Equally though, Rex Humanitas is not just any human being, but quite specifically a king. Nor are the Vices simply general moral forces. Wantoness, Placebo, Solace and Sensualitie are the king's courtiers, while Falset, Flatterie and Dissait are his false counsellors. Lyndsay thus not only provides a generally applicable morality, but also outlines the specific temptations that threaten a king and the specific consequences of the monarch's subjection to sin.

The play also draws on the conventions of farce and of fabliaux.[9] These genres deal not with allegorically represented moral forces, but with familiar social types (e.g. the lecherous monk, the domineering wife). Again, this permits Lyndsay to combine general morality with precise social reference. For instance, when Chastitie goes seeking shelter throughout the kingdom all the estates reject her. But the play complements this highlighting of widespread immorality in the kingdom by showing that the lack of chastity among the spiritual estates has particular consequences ensuing from their social status. The Vices, in persuading Rex Humanitas to lechery, cite the example of the Catholic church, supposedly the guardians of morality, as proof that sensuality is no sin:

> Believe ye, Sir, that lecherie be sin?
> Na trow nocht that! This is my ressoun quhy:
> First at the Romane court will ye begin,
> Quhilk is the lemand lamp of lechery [...] (235-238)

The clergy's rejection of Chastitie is thus presented not merely as an offence against the moral law, but as having specific evil results due to the clergy's social role, and is shown as fundamental to the disorder which sees the king given over to Sensualitie and incapable of proper governance. Indeed, by stating that they saw no harm in lechery, the first trio of Vices escape punishment and are allowed to maintain a role in court, leading the king in harmless recreations (1829-1858). Given that, in 'The Papyngo', Lyndsay states that courtiers who lead the monarch into vice should receive harsher punishment even than traitors, this suggests a hardened attitude towards the clergy, whose immorality is now seen as the chief cause of social disorder.

The interaction, then, between allegorical representations of universal moral forces, such as Chastitie and Sensualitie, and social types such as the Abbot and the Persone, enables Lyndsay to spell out the socio-political implications of his general moral points. This social and political emphasis perhaps also underlies the choice of Correctioun, rather than 'Wisdom' or 'Grace', as the figure of divine intervention. Correctioun suggests action with regard to the behaviour of others, indeed even punishment. Correctioun in fact leads the parliament in Part Two of the play, where reform is extended from a merely personal basis to be enforced through state legislation. This concern with the practical, social application of general morality is also evident in Lyndsay's overt association of moral reform with Protestantism. The character of Veritie, in particular, has strong Protestant associations: the Persone refers to her as a Lutheran (1126), and her concern with making the word of God clearly known to all reflects the priority placed by Protestants on making vernacular Bibles generally available. The Virtues are thus not just general moral dispositions, but are associated with a precise politico-religious grouping.

In the second part of the play Lyndsay is even more pointedly social in his emphasis, urging moral regeneration through parliamentary legislation. This is signalled in the interlude, which opens with the entry of the Pauper, who enters the audience begging. The Pauper's exchange with Diligence is a fierce attack on the entitlements of the clergy to enrich themselves at the expense of the community through death duties and the teind system (1978-2014). The pardoner, who sells indulgences which reduce one's time in purgatory after death, is another example of the Church at its most exploitative, taking advantage of the people's concern for their own salvation in order to enrich himself (2044-2296). The corruption of the clergy is shown to exacerbate the poverty and famine that plagued the land in the early 1550s.

In keeping with this marked concern with the deleterious social effects of moral corruption on the nation, Part Two of the play has John the Commonweal enter to represent the complaints of the realm of Scotland. Over one thousand lines of the play are devoted to outlining the program of reform with which the parliament proposes to remedy those complaints. These proposals are nominally directed at all of society. Lyndsay condemns the deceitfulness of merchants and the nobility's ruthlessness (2678-2687). The acts of parliament target the nobility as well as the clergy, demanding that their lands be rented directly to labourers, and that they take responsibility in their own lands for the proper carrying-out of justice (3839-3854). The reforms, however, concentrate chiefly on clerical misconduct and greatly restrict the privileges and powers of the churchmen. They include disbanding convents, with the rents of their lands being appropriated as funding new secular Courts of Justice; depriving ecclesiastical courts of any temporal jurisdiction; forcing bishops to reside within their diocese in order to properly administer their pastoral duties; stipulating that only one ecclesiastical benefice may be held at a time and that Rome should receive no payment for these.

These reforms are clearly geared towards reducing the Church's power and affirming the political dominance of the secular estates.

The secular authorities of Scotland are in fact invited to override the Pope's authority in deciding how the Church should be run. To the Scottish clergy's objections, Temporalitie replies 'We cure nocht quhidder ye consent or nocht' (3107). Lyndsay's reforms thus have the temporal estates serving the interests of the commonweal by acting through parliament, so as to bring the spiritual estates firmly under their authority.

In *The Thrie Estaitis*, then, the commonweal becomes a much more active concept than in Lyndsay's earlier writings. Rather than relying on the direct intervention of the king and his administration at court, the general community, whose mutual interests the commonweal embodies, are themselves urged to take action, identifying abuses and remedying them through legislation by a parliament in which they themselves participate. Rex Humanitas is a spectator rather than a participant in Part Two of the play and his presence seems almost a ceremonial formality. *The Thrie Estaitis* thus sees a significant development in Lyndsay's political thought. The commonweal, rather than merely designating a bond of interdependence and mutual responsibility which should bind the populace and govern each member's conduct, becomes a principle which urges the community to take united political action in order to protect itself, with parliament being the institutional expression of this common will. While the concept of the commonweal is present throughout Lyndsay's work, in *The Thrie Estaitis* it finds its fullest expression as a political concept.

After the hanging and expulsion of the Vices towards the end of Part Two, with reform having been effected within the play, Lyndsay startlingly reintroduces a Vice figure, Foly, who dominates until the conclusion. Foly indulges in irreverent horseplay and mocks the parliament before announcing to kings, clergy, nobility, and commons alike, 'Ye ar all fuillis' (4867), and distributing folly hats. The intrusion of the character at this late stage call into question the success of the reforms instituted previously in the play. The introduction of Foly may express a pessimism about the possibility of achieving any lasting solution to social problems or injustices.[10] But it may also remind the audience that reform, once achieved, cannot be taken for granted: its maintenance requires constant vigilance. If Lyndsay suggests the precariousness of reform in the Foly episode, this may be aimed at alerting his audience to the constant need to guard against the forces of disorder.

Lyndsay's final poem, 'The Monarche' (1555), provides a fitting conclusion to his career. The work outlines the whole of human history and identifies the Papacy as the rule of the Anti-Christ, presaging the day of Judgement and the establishment of Christ's kingdom on Earth. The poem's attacks on the corruption of the Papal rule restate Lyndsay's familiar complaints against the clergy for their dedication to sensuality and their exploitation of the common people. 'The Monarche' thus introduces to Lyndsay's analysis of the social ills of sixteenth-century Scotland an apocalyptic dimension in which the nation's suffering is imaged as a stage in the historical unfolding of the providential design. The poem's eschatological vision aims to affirm a perception of national destiny in despite of social fragmentation. In this respect, 'The Monarche' continues Lyndsay's perennial concern: to promote the ideal of the commonweal of Scotland in defiance of socially divisive forces; to reforge, after the disintegrative disaster of Flodden, a unifying sense of Scottish national identity.

NOTES

[1] See Lyndsay's own brief account of his role in 'The Dreme' (lines 8-14). All references to Lyndsay's poems are taken from *The Works of Sir David Lindsay of the Mount, 1490-1555*, edited by Douglas Hamer, 4 vols., Edinburgh: Blackwood, 1931-1936.

[2] On this aspect of Dante's poetics, see Eric Auerbach, *Dante: Poet of the Secular World*, translated by Ralph Mannheim, Chicago: University of Chicago Press, 1961.

[3] On the background to Lyndsay's reforming ideals, and the humanistic rather than religious bias of his early works, see Carol Edington, *Court and Culture in Renaissance Scotland: Sir David Lyndsay of the Mount*, East Linton: Tuckwell, 1994, pp. 145-162.

[4] See Rosalind Mitchison, *A History of Scotland,* 2nd edn, London: Methuen, 1982, pp. 88-92.

[5] Minor poems from the 1530s and 1540s are 'The Deploratioun of the Deith of the Quene Magdalene' (1537); 'The Justing between James

Watson and Jhone Barbour' (1538); 'Ane Supplicatioun in Contemptioun of Syde Taillis'; 'The Complaint and Publict Confessioun of the Kingis Auld Hound callit Bagsche'; 'The Answer to the Kingis Flyting'. The last three cannot be dated with any certainty.

6 On Beaton's life and career, see M.H.B. Sanderson, *Cardinal of Scotland: David Beaton c.1494-1546* , Edinburgh: J. Donald, 1986.

7 For an opposing view of how Lyndsay depicts Meldrum, see Carol Edington, *Court and Culture*, cit., pp. 122-125.

8 *Ane Satyre of the Thrie Estaitis*, edited by R.J. Lyall, Edinburgh: Canongate, 1989. For discussion of the dating of the play see J.S. Kantarowitz, *Dramatic Allegory: Lindsay's Ane Satyre of the Thrie Estaitis,* Lincoln NA: University of Nebraska Press, 1975, pp. 12-23; R.J. Lyall, 'The Linlithgow Interlude of 1540', in Jean-Jacques Blanchot and Claude Graf eds., *Actes du 2e Colloque de Langue et de Littérature* (Moyen Age et Renaissance), Strasbourg: Institut d'études anglaises Strasbourg, 1978, pp. 409-421.

9 On the play's generic affiliations and literary antecedents and analogues, see Lyall's introduction to his edition, pp. xxii-xxvi.

10 See Sandra Billington, 'The Fool and the Moral in English and Scottish Morality Plays', in F.G. Andersen et al. eds., *Popular Drama in Northern Europe in the Later Middle Ages*, Odense: Odense University Press, 1988.

SARAH M. DUNNIGAN

A New Critical Cartography:
pre and post-Union Scottish Renaissance

Uncertainty and reluctance has characterised any quest to identify the precise location of a 'Renaissance' in Scotland; after all, early twentieth-century Scottish literature has, perhaps hubristically, asserted its right to that title. Although the idea of a single, all-encompassing 'Renaissance', such as that espoused in the nineteenth-century by Jacob Burkhardt and others, has long fallen from favour, that of a 'Northern Renaissance', which embraces Scotland and not simply England and the Low Countries, still requires justification in certain intellectual contexts, despite recent theoretical explorations in Renaissance literary studies.[1] One can quibble exactly when the first Scottish Renaissance begins and ends; 1495, the year that Erasmus, as John Durkan puts it, 'is first found in touch with a Scot' [Hector Boece],[2] might justly be claimed as the defining Scottish 'early modern' or 'Renaissance' moment. In the context of this account, however, it encompasses the period from 1561 until 1625: from the return of Mary, Queen of Scots until the death of James VI. This is not, and should not be taken as, an irrefutably fixed demarcation. Yet the decades spanning the Marian and Jacobean reigns are barely visible on the artistic and cultural cartography of the 'British', not least the European, Renaissance, and conventionally receive only perfunctory attention in canonical histories, or the *grand histoire*, of Scottish literature. Their aesthetic, linguistic, and political forms do not fit seamlessly into any unitary, essentialist narrative.[3] Renaissance Scottish literature, however temporally imagined, has endured many forms of displacement. Yet it is precisely its liminal and exiled status which renders it ripe for rediscovery at the present theoretical moment. This account does not attempt to be exhaustive or comprehensive but identifies particular writers and texts which are markedly influential in the shaping of a Scottish Renaissance poetics.[4] It offers three consecutive historical and cultural 'moments' in the creation of the first Scottish Renaissance, each differently founded upon acts of reconstitution, redefinition, and re-imagining.

THE MARIAN RENAISSANCE: BEAUTY AND VIOLENCE

In 1548, political and diplomatic reasons dictated that Marie Stewart (1542-1587), the daughter of Marie de Guise and James V, be taken from Scotland to France; on 19 August 1561, she returned aged nineteen to resume her sovereign power as Queen of Scotland. It was an auspicious moment, eagerly commemorated in verse such as Alexander Scott's 'Ane New Yeir Gift to the Quene Mary, quhen scho come first hame, 1562'.[5] Mary's incarnation in French poetry and painting had promised beauty, sensitivity, and well-attested artistic gifts. If a Renaissance, a *rinascimento* of the arts, had suffered during the uncertainty of the years since James V's death, then Mary's return augured well for its desired fruition. It is one of the poignant ironies of Mary's reign, and of the intermittent struggles of monarchy in sixteenth-century Scotland, that this was never enduringly attained. Ample evidence suggests that French royal culture nurtured her intellectually, aesthetically, and spiritually. Yet in Mary's reign, the conflict between religion, politics, and art takes bitter root. Of course, all European Renaissance culture is affected, enlarged, or circumscribed by such vicissitudes; but in Scotland, and in Mary's brief, seven-year reign, secular artistic culture could not wholly survive the religious and political turmoil engendered by a young female sovereign who was Catholic in a country which had entered into a religious reformation endorsed by most of the political establishment, or elite ruling nobility. The zealous intensities of the reformers, such as the (in)famous John Knox (?1512-1572), and their hostility to the visual and verbal arts is well-known, and contentious: had this Reformation not occurred, might Scottish artistic culture have properly flourished? While such alternative historical narratives can only be imagined, Knox's rhetorically skilful prose work, *The Historie of the Reformatioun in Scotland* (1559-1567), offers vivid tableaux of conflicts between himself and Mary which Romantic and Victorian artists would dramatise, as if an allegory of Marian Catholicism versus Knoxian Calvinism; artistic sensibility in opposition to artistic dereliction; and, underpinning these and other symbolic oppositions, feminine power in conflict with masculine. Antifeminism became a powerful political and cultural force in the Marian decade.[6] In such apparent simplifications lie grains of truth. What remains provocative is firstly the extent to which secular culture *did* endure the cultural privations of religious and political conflict; and secondly the ways in which such conflict fostered new and interesting forms of literary discourse.

Marian court culture, as Renaissance court cultures in general, perceived harmony between visual, verbal, and musical cultures. Court entertainment sought to cultivate beauty aurally, visually, and sensually; accordingly, court masque was a popular form of entertainment. At Mary's court, several masques were devised to commemorate both her marriage to Lord Darnley, Henry Stewart (a marriage which would end in tragic and politically injurious circumstances two years later), and the birth of her son, James. These masques were chiefly composed by George Buchanan (1506-1582), humanist, scholar, and neoLatin poet.[7] Ironically, he would shortly become one of the chief architects of the antiMarian party, the political faction who sought to discredit and injure Mary. The transformation in Buchanan's art, from the composition of pieces of theatre essentially designed to praise Mary through the devices of elaborate visual ritual and language, to that of the *Detectioun* (1571), the fiercely denunciatory prose polemic, is testament to the queen's changeful fortunes aesthetically, no less than politically. It is a far cry from the masques staged at Holyrood in 1564, 'In Castitatem' and 'Mutuus Amor', to the *Detectioun* which dramatically inverts such allegorical iconography.[8]

The evident popularity of masques at the Marian court, with their emphasis upon spectacle and performance, surprisingly may explain the popularity of lyric too, which the contemporary French writer, Pierre de Ronsard (1524-1585) concisely defined as the genre of 'les [...] petitz pôësmes'.[9] In Mary's reign, perhaps inevitably given that its early years saw anxiety regarding a suitable marriage partner for her, it was the small poem of love which flourished:

O lusty may w^t flora queen   *with*
The balmy dropis frome phebus schene
Prelucia[n]d bemes befoir the day
Be that diana growis grene
Throwch glaidnes of this lusty may[10]   *through*

Frequently, such poetry was set to music, drawing out in allusive, punning form the erotic implications of such realisation.[11] These texts may also have been 'declaimed' or recited before a courtly or other intimate audience. In this sense, they can be considered 'performative'; a performance or invocation of desire which can be endlessly recreated. Ample evidence of this lyric form is found in manuscript collections of the period, particularly in that known as the Bannatyne manuscript associated with the Edinburgh merchant, George Bannatyne (1545-1606).[12] Bannatyne's erotic section bears resemblances to the French florilegium, *Le Jardin de Plaisance et la Fleur de Rhetorique*, published in 1501; the *balades amoureuses* of both exemplify a late medieval courtly lyric style. Such lyrics are characteristically short and beautiful, almost incantatory in the language and conceits which the corpus endlessly reworks. These qualities may deceptively conceal their rhetorical and 'psychic' subtlety: their explorations of erotic interiority and of the imperfect, self-betraying powers of a lover's language:

ffayne wald I speik and speiking my^t awaill   *might*
And scho for speiking wald speik to me agane
I spair to speik for spilling of my taill
Than I my speiking spendit hes in vane
To speik and speid not it is ane lestand pane...[13]

Such lyrics, in accordance with the increasing emphasis in Renaissance rhetorical treatises on the role of the passions, demand that love-words compel *perturbationes*.

Justifiably, the most well-known of lyricists at the Marian court is Alexander Scott (c1515–c1582). While Scott sustained 'close professional connections with the [principally Marian] court and the nobility',[14] he is identified in the extant records as a musician, the canon and organist of the priory of Inchmahome, and with that particular royal centre of culture, the Chapel Royal at Stirling. In Scott's poetry, the language of eros is sharply attenuated:

> I wilbe plane/and lufe affane/ffor as I mene/so tak me...
> It is bot waist/mo wird[is] to taist/ye haif my laist/so tak me words
> I mak it plane/for luve agane ...[15]

Such avowed rhetorical plainness (itself ironic, given the literary culture of feigning or dissimulation from which such lyrics arise) may be viewed through the lens of Castiglionian *sprezzatura*: 'che nascona l'arte e dimostri ciò che si fa e dice venir fatto senza fatici e quasi senza pensarvi. Da questo creda io che derivi assai la grazia... Però si po dir quella esser vera arte che non pare esser arte...'.[16] Yet such *sprezzatura* is held in tension with the emotional fragility which markedly defines Scott's love poems; the ideal of courtly *grazia* is precariously sustained. Many explore the difficult articulation of love which has only inward existence (the reluctance to violate the secrecy of desire, the lover's 'inwart tho[t] [thought] and mynd').[17] Only in 'Vp helsum hairt',[18] indebted to the medieval *alba* or dawn-song, is communion achieved between lovers. In other lyrics, the darker moral and theological conflict between 'reson' and 'lathly lust' is broached:

> ffra raige of yow[t] the rynk hes rune   *yowth*
> And ressone tane the man to tune
> The brukle body than Is Wune
>   And maid ane veschell new.
> ffor than thruch grace he is begune
> The well of wisdome for to kune
> Than is his weid of vertew spune
>   Trest weill this taill Is trew[19]

Scott's profane poetry arguably fulfils Bannatyne's requirement of 'richt reformation'.[20] His lyric 'selves' seek anxiously to preserve in the face of destructive sensuality the precarious unity of 'body honor and substance../and saule in perrell':[21] to perform the transformation of the 'hairt oppressit' into one spiritually cleansed and 'Immaculat'.[22] Scott's erotic corpus reveals a new juxtaposition of the secular and the sacral in Scottish poetry;[23] it is therefore significant that versions of the first and fiftieth Psalms ('Wesche me and mak my sawle serene...') are preserved.[24] Scott's poetry, imbued with the inflexions of protestant devotion, exemplifies the spirit of devotional lyric popular in Scotland in the mid 1560s: lyrics, such as those printed in the *Gude and Godlie Ballatis* which proclaim the new reformed devotion, constitute religious 'reworkings' of secular songs, or propound a doctrinal and theological point, however crudely expressed. In these respects, art and the new protestantism bore fruit; indeed, a new book industry grew out of Scotland's religious schisms.

But when religion is directly bound up with eros and politics in the figure of Mary the image of a sustainable Renaissance court culture is shattered. When the queen herself is believed to have composed erotic poetry, love-words lose their courtly playfulness and become a 'performance' of adulterous desire, murderous intent, and grave political fallibility:

O Dieux ayez de moy compassion,
Et m'enseignez quelle preuue certain
Ie puis donner qui ne luy semble vain
De mon amour & ferme affection.
Las n'est il pas ia en possession
Du corps, du coeur qui ne refuse paine
Ny deshonneur, en la vie incertaine,
Offense de parentz, ne pire affliction?
Pour luy tous mes amis i'estime moins que rien,
Et de mes ennemis je veux esperer bien.
I'ay hazardé pour luy & nom & conscience;
Ie veux pour luy au monde renoncer:
Ie veux mourir pour luy auancer.
Que reste il plus pour prouuer ma constance?

O Goddis haue of me compassioun,
And schew quhat certaine profe
I may geif, which shall nat seme to him vaine,
Of my loue and feruent affectioun.
Helas, is he nat alredy in possessioun
Of my bodie, of hart, that refusis no payne,
Nor dishonour in the life uncertaine,
Offence of frendes, nor worse afflictioun,
For him I esteme all my frends les then nathing,
And I will haue gude hope of my enemeis.
I haue put in hasard for him baith fame & conscience,
I will for his sake renounce ye world,
I will die to set him forwart.
Quhat remayneth to geif proof of my constancie?[25]

The love poems ascribed to Mary may be read as a dark, intricate, and unorthodox meditation on feminine, and queenly, desire; their instrumentality in the political process which worked to depose Mary from the throne ironically corroborates this. While their structural form and conceitful discourse embed these sonnets in Renaissance female erotic modes of Petrarchism and neo-Platonism (comparable in that sense to the love poetry of Gaspara Stampa or Veronica Gambara), they were recontextualised and reinterpreted by the queen's enemies: as evidence of her love for Lord Bothwell, James Hepburn; of her desire to destroy her sovereign husband, Darnley; and of her incapacity to govern her kingdom. Though the so-called 'casket sonnets' are both a powerful and poignant epilogue to the decade's love poetry, Mary herself continued to write in the subsequent years of her imprisonment. Poetry survives which enshrines her Catholic faith; there are inscriptions in her prayer book, and elaborate emblems and allegories stitched in tapestry.[26] But the publication of the sonnets in 1571 is an apposite moment at which to consider the 'end' or dissolution of the 'Marian Renaissance'. Much is absent which should be mourned. Had Mary's reign endured beyond 1567 and reforming protestantism not taken root, another literary narrative might have emerged. But both historical contingencies laid the foundation for another renaissance, centred round the figure of James VI, the son who was forcibly estranged from his mother, Mary.

THE JACOBEAN RENAISSANCE: DIFFERENCE AND (RE)INVENTION

If the Marian Renaissance proved incomplete and imperfect, then the Jacobean period (c1579-1603) offers a vision of relative unity. James was characteristic of the Scottish Stewart monarchy in his intellectual and aesthetic proclivities. Yet the artistic reinvigoration which James orchestrated was by this time a political prerequisite. The strength of the monarchy needed assertion after the 'Ruthven Raid' of 1582 when James was temporarily under the control of the pro-English, extreme Protestant faction. The first, most important expression of an appropriately invulnerable sovereign word was the *Essayes of a Prentise in the Divine Arte of Poesie* (1584). In the most well-known of its pieces, the prose treatise called *The Reulis and Cautelis to be observit and eschewit in Scottis poesie*, James proscribes or legislates how a Scottish *rinascimento* should be achieved. Though it is perhaps unjust to ascribe the diversity of literary production in this period (sonnet sequences, elegies, epithalamia, panegyric, allegories, translations) solely to the *Reulis'* influence, the text presents a fruitful source by which to trace the development of a 'national poetics':[27]

> Thairfore, quhat I speik of Poesie now, I speik of it, as being come to mannis age and perfectioun, quhair as then, it was bot in the infancie and chyldheid.[28]

This is one of the eighteen-year old James's most paradoxical performances of rhetorical command, characteristic of a king who would perpetuate his own personae in court art and culture (the mythological Apollo, the biblical David), and of the novice-writer who would frequently confess his own ingenuousness.[29] It is also a work of considerable technical precision, expounding the virtues of 'Ryming in Termis' and 'vocabula artis'. Above all, literary identity is enshrined within language which in turn confers on 'Scottis poesie' its unique linguistic and ideological value. This is the clearest expression of a contemporary Scottish national poetics which limpidly articulates the idea of aesthetic and linguistic sovereignty:

> ...That as for thame that hes writtin in it of late, there hes neuer ane of thame that hes writtin in our language. For albeit sindrie hes writtin of it in English, quhilk is lykest to our language, yit we differ frome thame in sindrie reulis of poesie...[30]

Of course, as James himself acknowledged, he was indebted to theoretical ideas about vernacular language which the French Pléiade in particular had espoused. Scotland's alterity or 'otherness' at this moment was shaped by other literary movements intent on cultivating forms of difference. James's treatise is irrefutably important but the king's aesthetic ideals are also illuminated by the sonnets published in the *Essayes*:

> Or when I lyke my pen for to imploy
> Of fertile Harvest in description trew:
> Let Readers think, they instantly conuoy
> The busie shearers for to reap their dew...

Let Readers think, thy eloquence deuyne
O Mercure, in my Poems doth appeare:
And that Parnassis flowing fountaine fyne
Into my works doth shyne lyke cristall cleare...[31]

Still, the *Reulis* helps to disclose two important aspects of Jacobean Renaissance culture: its most precious achievements are produced by an elite coterie at the heart of James's court; and these were produced in a period of relative political stability in contrast to the turbulence of Mary's reign. The art of the Jacobean coterie – produced by courtier writers of whom the most well-known are Alexander Montgomerie, William Fowler, John Stewart of Baldynneis, William Alexander, and a number of other associated but less prolific writers and musicians – is characterised by poetic performances of extraordinary intimacy between sovereign and courtier. In practice, the creative relationship between James and these writers depended upon mutual inspiration. Absolute poetic obedience may be overtly proclaimed but poetry of this period reveals a delicate interplay between conformity and innovation (or even dissent). Two important principles which James employs in the *Reulis* help crystallise this shift, and also the rhetorical and philosophical nature of the Jacobean Renaissance as a whole:

> Bot sen Inuention, is ane of the chief vertewis in a Poete, it is best that ye inuent your awin subiect, your self, and not to compose of sene subiectis...
> Ye man also be warre with composing ony thing in the same maner, as hes bene ower oft vsit of before. As in speciall, gif ye speik of loue...[32]

In the context of Renaissance literary theory, imitation can be defined as a faithful replication of the original text, which strives for parity with the original; and invention as the effort to produce a new text, self-reflexively aware and often grounded in an acute historical awareness of the literary past. James's poets readily imitate the pre-eminent examples of European literary art: for example, Petrarch, as attested by the popularity of the Petrarchan-style love sequence; Ariosto's *Orlando Furioso*; the French Pléiade. The king's own poetry of this period is a sustained homage to the French poet Guillaume de Salluste Du Bartas (1544-1590) whose moral and religious epics he assiduously translated. Though

James's largely unpublished, poetry is eclectic, ranging from sonnets on the Danish astronomer Tycho Brahe to antifeminist satire,
erotic wit to translations of the psalms, it was Du Bartas's protestant vision, however, which spiritually and ideologically inspired
James. This, indeed, was James's own literary path to invention;
but the practice of translation enabled other Jacobean poets to cultivate their own forms of difference. Though collections of neo-
Petrarchan love poetry so proliferated in Renaissance Europe by
this period that in portraiture the clandestine insertion of a miniature book of Petrarch's love verse was a sign of the subject's fash-
ionableness, the canonicity of such poetry offered the opportunity
for distinctive 'national' inflections, or rewritings. In short, the *Rime
sparse* or *Canzoniere* served as a locus of both origin and departure. William Fowler's erotic sonnet sequence, *The Tarantula of
Love* (circa early 1580s), attests this in its renegotiation of the
Rime's final apotheosis of profane into sacred love. Though
Fowler's lover may 'write' as Petrarch does, 'diffused in ryme and
sad disordred verse',[33] he wrestles with the Catholic transfiguration
of the Petrarchan original. In so doing, he creates a new version
imbued with the current preoccupations and anxieties of the
Scottish Jacobean sensibility. Fowler's theological or spiritual
engagement with Petrarch is sustained in his translation of the first
three of the poet's *Trionfi*.[34]

The transformative nature of translation can also be seen in John
Stewart's partial version of Ariosto's *Orlando Furioso* (1532). As if
overwhelmed by the imaginative spaciousness of the Italian epic
(this 'lairge prolixit histoir'[35]), Stewart concentrates upon a small
range of exemplary narratives, chief of which is the story of
Angelica:

O Angelique, quhais fame begins to feed,
The quhilk sa lang hes flurist far and fair,
I do lament thir lothsum lyns to leed
Of thy betrappit persone in thus snair,
Thy luifers all And Chastetie preclair
Quhy sould thow for ane sempill sulart lois?[36]

Stewart's intense, almost empathic, fascination for Angelica is perhaps best understood within the translation's wider context which
is the meticulously embellished manuscript, presented as a gift to

James: a triptych composed of the *Roland Furious*, a lyric collection known as the *Rapsodies*, and a religious allegory, *Ane Schersing out of Trew Felicitie*. Stewart's loving annotation of Angelica's trials mirrors the ebullience and préciosité of his new-fashioned Ariosto as a whole, 'not strictly a translation but a free adaptation', as R.D.S. Jack comments;[37] but the endangered chastity motif, and the extended rhetorical exaltations of beauty and love anticipate the deepening spiritual and philosophical preoccupations of the manuscript's later poems.

The final quality of invention in Scottish Jacobean verse suggested here can be perceived in its frequent resort to verbal extravagance; a kind of cult of rhetorical magnificence which is often held in formal tension with the constraining exactitude of the sonnet scheme:

OF THE QUALITIES OF LOVE

Luif is ane aigre douce delyt and greif:
Greif is in luif ane lustie langing lyf:
Lyf may not last Quhair luif pretends mischeif:
Mischeif of luif is euirlasting stryf:
Stryf reuling luif, than rancor raidgeis ryf:
Ryf raidge is not, gif luifers luif abound:
Aboundng luif is scharp as scharpest knyf:
Knyf may not kill moir scharplie vith ane vound:
Vound deip vith vo, And schortlie haill and sound,
Sound syn to suell in syching sour and sueit,
Sueit luif heirvith dois suffer monie stound:
Stound both vith cair And confort lairge repleit:
Repleit vith luif hes bein both gods and men:
Men luif obeyis Gods vill not luif misken.[38]

The deliberate importation of French rhyme schemes, often those popularised by the late medieval grands rhétoriqueuers (thus exemplifying the coterie's love of literary *bricolage*) means that the verbal mannerism or *manierismo* of Petrarchan-style verse, for example, is further enhanced or intensified: these bizarrely beautiful word-sculptures, intent on unveiling the 'lustre of a poem',[39] render Scottish literary practice entirely distinct from English.

Perhaps the most inventive Jacobean writer of all is Alexander Montgomerie (?1555-1597), whom James called his 'prince of poets', but one defined by paradox.[40] One of the earliest to offer poetic adoration of James (in an allegorical masque-like poem called *The Navigatioun*), and an exemplar of many Jamesian literary ideals in the *Reulis*, he most fiercely registers dissent from kingly approbation in poems which attest a breach between sovereign and courtier that cannot be healed. Writing for a protestant king and patron, he is himself a Catholic convert. Montgomerie's poetry is generically and modally diverse, reinvoking the Scottish medieval flyting technique in the popular *Flyting or Invective*, and visionary narrative in *The Cherrie and the Slae* (1597),[41] a work which echoes allegories such as Colonna's *Hypnerotomachia* (1499). It may also veil a contemporary allegorical labyrinth about the 'choice' between Catholicism and the Reformed faith beneath the surface allegoresis of profane versus spiritual love. Intellectual and rhetorical puns proliferate in Montgomerie's poetry, disquisitory and playful; his love poetry is dominated by an extraordinary quality of dark tenderness such as the lyric, 'Evin dead behold I breathe', and an insouciant will to parody can turn Petrarchan conventions upside down; other lyrics are criss-crossed by the myriad voices of coterie verse so that there are sonnets which are dedications, petitions, and requests to putative friends and lovers, patrons and, in one instance, his lawyer. Montgomerie's rich lyric corpus as a whole constitutes an absorbing emotional theatre. Though the emotional *veritas* or authenticity of Montgomerie's lyric voices may only be the consequence of skilful rhetorical 'illusioning', their drama is frequently arresting such as in the song-lyric, 'Come my children dere draw near me', a hymn of love sung by a Bride of Christ (Montgomerie's religious voice is less ideologically codified than other Jacobean writers), and the sonnet sequences *en miniature*, 'To his Majestie for his Pensioun', and 'To Robert Hudsone', which suggest that the subject-position of a monarch's courtier, much as a lover, leaves one open and vulnerable to receiving 'love' but also pain.

Scottish Jacobean literature, then, successfully invented or performed its own Renaissance, the richness of which can only be contoured here. It owed much to James, who in one sense was compelled to atone for the supposed sins of his mother, but more to the coterie of writers who managed to transcend the Jamesian literary vision. In 1603, the crowns of Scotland and England were united; by then, Montgomerie was dead, Stewart had ceased writing. When Elizabeth I died and James left Scotland to govern a newly twinned isle, the reign of Scottish Jacobean literature seemingly ended.

POST-UNION LITERATURE: MELANCHOLY AND MOURNING?

Like the Reformation, the Union of 1603 has proven a thorn in the side of Scottish literary history; another reason why Scotland's Renaissance was made impossible. The removal of king and court to London is taken to mean that the cultural heart of Renaissance Scotland was torn out and that the force of anglicisation, which was actually manifest as early as the 1560s and the period of Reformation, took ineradicable hold. The king who had once instigated the renaissance of 'Scottis poesie' now assured Scotland of a long period of cultural and aesthetic dereliction. So engrained is this perception of post-Union Scottish literature that reinterpretation, or redemption, of the period is urgently needed. It is impossible to do justice here to a period which saw the prodigious flourishing of neoLatin poetry (the origin of many Scottish literary classicists lay in the Catholic and Episcopalian North East[42]), the first entrance into print of women writers in Scotland, and the Rabelaisian translations of Sir Thomas Urquhart (1611-1660). Rather, the remainder of this chapter argues for the complexity of the response to the Union as embodied in a poetics of melancholy and mourning that depends on the power of literary equivocation. The 'lost' nation is reinvented or reimagined through the emergence of a new poetic-political mode. It is the genre of pastoral which forges a new relationship with the absent monarch by those writers who chose to accompany their monarch south (such as Alexander Craig [?1568-1627]) and William Drummond (1585-1649) who remained in Scotland.

Craig's love of intellectually abstruse conceits provides a suitable language by which to encode mixed political sentiment. Adept at royal panegyric, intended for Queen Anna as well as James, Craig seemingly offers up orthodox poems to the Union's altar such as the 'Epistle Congratulatorie & Peroenetic' or the 'Sonet' which proclaims 'Keepe Britaine whole'.[43] Yet found within the same collection, the *Poeticall Essayes* of 1604 (printed in London), are the poems 'Scotlands Teares' and 'Calidons Complaint', where the portrait of a betrayed nation in mourning questions whether a royal readership or audience could ever have been intended as its recipient:

> Shall *Scotland* hensforth haue againe no cround K. of their owne?
> Shall wee from King, Queene, Prince, & all their brood disseuer?
> And shall not *Scotland* be againe inhabited for euer?[44]

> *Eliza* faire is gone, into the land of rest,
> To that *Elisium* predecried and promis'd to the blest;
> And *England* for her sake now weaires the sabill weede,
> But *Scotland* of thou rightly looke thou has more cause indeede.
> The for a *Dian* dead, *Apolloes* beames enioy...
> And we are but *Cymmerian* slaues with gloomy clouds ou'rcled.[45]

Such texts challenge the entrenched perception that post-Union Scottish writing subscribed to an ideological consensus but instead wrestled with the implication of its possible status as an inferior or subordinate, rather than equal, kingdom. Most commonly, Scotland is depicted as bereaved or widowed; melancholic loss is the defining mood of these veiled political elegies. The impulses of mourning and dissent are often found in fragmentary form, located between the interstices of metaphor and conceit; even an isolated sonnet such as Robert Ayton's 'Upon the River Tweed', whose final couplet celebrating 'that religious place, whose stately walls/Does keepe the heart which all our hearts inthralls', may suggest that the holy place which holds a loyal sovereign heart is not Westminster Abbey, with the newly anointed James, but Melrose Abbey, with the heart of Robert the Bruce.[46] A sonnet which opens in ostensible royal praise ends as a reliquary.

The visit of James to Scotland in 1618, the only return journey he made, offered Scottish writers another opportunity for monarchical eulogy but of a kind which accommodated reflection and irony; the preoccupation with the figural or symbolic nation in exile or mourning returns. In Drummond's poem, *Forth Feasting*, as in his earlier lament on the death of the young Prince Henry (in which the River Forth and its landscape sustains a collective, personified mourning), the conventions of classical pastoral are harnessed to the creation of a new, entirely Scottish, elegiac topography. This may conform to a definition of 'national allegory', the eternal aesthetic or mythological abstraction of the nation, but it possesses a contemporary political specificity.[47] In Seamus Deane's phrase, 'the naming of the land' is paramount:[48]

Ah, why should Isis only see thee shine?
Is not thy Forth, as well as Isis, thine?
Though Isis vaunt she hath more wealth in store,
Let it suffice thy Forth doth love Thee more.[49]

The intricately worked series of imaginative correspondences unfold to transform the river Isis into England, the river Forth into Scotland; the superficial, meretricious beauty of the former, in terms of the conceit's feminine personifications, is outdone by the pure, loving integrity of the latter.[50] In Drummond's poem, then, the intrinsic political potential of pastoral is renewed in the wake of Scotland's condition. Invoking the classical myth of the Golden Age (Scotland has lost hers because her 'lover', her king, abandoned her), Drummond composes another elegy, this time not for a dead prince, but for Scotland, a nation itself, or for its power as symbolically incarnate in its absent monarch. Political critique is therefore displaced and veiled by the non-mimetic mode of Renaissance allegory. Three decades earlier, James had articulated a series of literary desires in the name of 'Scottis poesie'; none of the post-Union writers can summon up such an aesthetic identity but collectively they now mourn new-found forms of fragmentation.

The critical reflectiveness of Scottish post-Union pastoral is seldom perceived by the vein of Scottish 'essentialist' criticism which cannot see beyond its anglified discourse and apparently unquestioning royalism. Post-Union literature, of course, is not composed of such overtly political verse; the seams of religious and erotic literature continued to be mined by writers such as Drummond, Craig, Ayton, William Mure of Rowallan and many others whose work is still relatively unknown. Its complexity cannot be justly accounted for here; but it is not easily accommodated or neatly embraced by the conventional, predominantly Anglocentric literary categories and canons which are usually invoked (such as 'meta-

physical', or 'Cavalier'). The aesthetics and emotionality of
Drummond's religious poetry, for example, has striking affinities
with poets of the European Counter-Reformation baroque. The
apparent critical exile into which most seventeenth-century Scottish
literature has been cast ironically works to shaken up or loosen the
dominant critical narratives or paradigms. If post-Union Scotland
was politically decentred, it still granted 'freedom' for the creation
of aesthetically, and linguistically, diverse 'communities' such as the
NeoLatin writers, as well as the motivation to write in the 'new'
idiom of English.

* * *

The return of this Renaissance literature to the fold of Scottish literary history demonstrates that any unitary definition of 'Scottish' is
impossible. The sign of 'cultural authenticity', spurious anyway,
should not rest upon linguistic identity. Renaissance Scottish writing succumbs to anglicisation in the early seventeenth-century
because of a number of different 'pressures', not purely political,
and these decades are arguably the most linguistically and rhetorically diverse within Scottish literature. In the period also, one can
perceive the kinds of national 'reimaginings' more usually ascribed
to eighteenth-century, Romantic and twentieth-century Scotland;
namely, that in some way, nations are created through writing, and
that literature can invent the idea of a nation. Neither is really possible and Scottish Renaissance literature demonstrates why. The
desire to incarnate a symbolic 'Scottish identity' in literature haunts
Scottish Jacobean poets but, particularly in the case of James himself, depends upon the refutation, or simply the wilful elision, of
what went before: Mary, and the troubling, politically provocative
literature she engendered. Post-Union Scottish poetry exemplifies
in its manifestations of fragmented nationhood that any idea of
unity usually carries the seeds of its own potential frailty.

Renaissance, and in particular post-Union, Scottish literature
offers an interesting case for postcolonial interpretation. Unlike
Ireland in the same period, it was not violently colonized by
English imperialist and religious expansion (indeed, James VI
orchestrated the Plantation of Ulster); a union implies a bond

entered into equally. An interesting position of hybridity therefore emerges for post-Union Scottish literature. Scottish sovereignty, however, was annulled; the royal centre of artistic and cultural power and patronage which had flourished since the fourteenth century disappeared; and the linguistic hegemony of literary English over Scots was estlabished. Post-Union Scottish literature can be richly opened up to a series of post-colonial theoretical concerns. In itself it may not fulfill the position of the abject colonised but it can justly be defined as a culture affected by the imperial process. The idea of nationhood, political and aesthetic, has securely entered literary discourse; there is recognition, implicit and explicit of the politics of language choice; and pre and post-Union, there is a deep and abiding concern with place and displacement in the work of these writers.[51] The different journeys undertaken by Scotland's Renaissance monarchs, Mary and James – from France to Scotland, Scotland to England – and the different imaginative, intellectual, and spiritual journeys of the literature they nurtured, should persuade of the need to redraw the current critical cartography.

NOTES

[1] Cf. Jacob Burckhardt, *Die Cultur der Renaissance in Italien* (1869). In the past decade, Renaissance studies have been influenced by post-colonial theory which has resulted in explorations of imperialism, nation, and race in early modern culture. While Ireland has been embraced by such investigations, Scotland has not. Cf. R.D.S. Jack, '"Translating' the Lost Scottish Renaissance', *Translation and Literature*, vol. 6, 1997, pp. 66-80.

[2] John Durkan, 'The Beginnings of Humanism in Scotland', *Innes Review*, vol. 4, 1953, pp. 5-24.

[3] Cf. Gerard Carruthers, 'The Construction of the Scottish Critical Tradition', in Neil MacMillan and Kirsten Stirling eds., *Odd Alliances*, Glasgow: Cruithne Press, 1999.

[4] This essay examines predominantly court-based literature but it should be observed that cultural production is not confined to the court, increasingly so in the later period. For comprehensive surveys,

see the essays by R.D.S. Jack and Michael Spiller in the first volume of Cairns Craig's *History of Scottish Literature* (4 vols., Aberdeen: Aberdeen University Press, 1988), and the recommended bibliographies. For the most recent essay collection on the period, see Nicola Royan and Theo van Heijnsbergen eds., *Literature, Letters and the Canonical in Early Modern Scotland*, East Linton: Tuckwell Press, 2002.

For reasons of accessibility, readers are also referred to the most recent anthology of the period, R.D.S. Jack and P.A.T. Rozendaal eds., *The Mercat Anthology of Early Scottish Literature*, Edinburgh: The Mercat Press, 1997; 2000; much writing is still only available in early editions of the Scottish Text Society.

[5] See R.D.S. Jack and P.A.T. Rozendaal eds., *op. cit.*, pp. 198-199, for extract; the full text can be found in James Cranstoun ed., *The Poems of Alexander Scott*, STS, Edinburgh: Blackwood, 1886, pp. 1-8.

[6] See Helen Smailes, *The Queen's Image*, Edinburgh: Scottish National Portrait Gallery, 1987; S.M. Dunnigan, 'The creation and self-creation of Mary Queen of Scots: rhetoric, sovereignty and femininity in sixteenth-century Scottish poetry', *Scotlands*, vol. 5, no. 2, 1998, pp. 65-88.

[7] Cf. I.D. MacFarlane, *Buchanan*, London: Duckworth, 1981.

[8] Joseph Robertson ed., *Inuentaires de la Royne Descosse Douairiere de France: Catalogues of the Jewels, Dresses, Furniture, Books and Paintings of Mary Queen of Scots, 1556-69*, Edinburgh: 1863, p. lxxxiii.

[9] Bernard Weinberg ed., 'Abbregè de l'Art Poétique François' (1565), in *Critical Prefaces of the French Renaissance*, Evanston: Northwestern University Press, p. 202.

[10] W.T. Ritchie ed., *The Bannatyne Manuscript*, 4 vols., Edinburgh: Blackwood, 1928-1934, III, p. 300 (anonymous). Some orthographical modernisation has been introduced in the transcription here. See note 12 below for further details.

[11] Cf. the lyric, 'My mistres is in Musik passing skilfull', in W.T. Ritchie ed., *op. cit.*, III, p. 239. For context and sources on Scottish Renaissance music and literature, see Helena Shire and Kenneth Elliott eds., *Music of Scotland 1500-1700: Musica Brittanica*, vol. XV, London: Stainer and Bell, 1975; and Elliott's most recent edition, *Musica Scotica*, 2 vols., Glasgow: University of Glasgow Music Department Publications, 1996, vol. 1; W.H. Rubsamen, 'Scottish and English Music of the Renaissance in a Newly Discovered Manuscript', *Festschrift Heinrich Besseler*, Veb Deutscher Verlag fur Musik Leipzig, 1961; D.J. Ross, *Musick Fyne: Robert Carver and the Art of Music in*

Sixteenth Century Scotland, Edinburgh: Mercat Press, 1993; Theo van Heijnsbergen, 'The Scottish Chapel Royal as Cultural Intermediary between Court and Capital', in J.W. Drijvers and A.A. MacDonald eds., *Centres of Learning: Learning and Location in Pre-Modern Europe and the Near East,* Leiden and New York: E.J. Brill, 1995, pp. 299-313.

[12] This voluminous manuscript, probably compiled between 1565 and 1568, preserved in the National Library of Scotland, is divided into five sections: devotional, moral, comic, and erotic verse, and finally fables. See A.A. MacDonald, 'The printed book that never was: George Bannatyne's poetic anthology (1568)', in J.M.M. Hermans and K. van der Hoek eds., *Boeken in de late Middeleeuwen,* Groningen: Egbert Forsten, 1993, pp. 101-110.

[13] W.T. Ritchie ed., *op. cit.,* vol 3, p. 259, anon.

[14] John MacQueen, 'Alexander Scott and Scottish Court Poetry of the Middle Sixteenth Century', *Proceedings of the British Academy,* vol. 54, 1968, (pp. 93-116) p. 106.

[15] James Cranstoun ed., *op. cit.,* pp. 38-40. The principle source for Scott's poetry is the Bannatyne manuscript where they are made to encompass the entire generic range of Bannatyne's classification of the *luve-ballattis;* as a body of work, they are associated with the 1550s and 1560s.

[16] Castiglione, *Il Libro del Cortegiano,* Venice, 1541, f. 19v.

[17] The most recent work on Scott's poetry is by Theo van Heijnsbergen; see, for example, his 'Love in the lyrics of Alexander Scott', *Studies in Scottish Literature,* vol. 26, 1991, pp. 366-379.

[18] James Cranstoun ed., *op. cit.,* pp. 44-45.

[19] *Ibidem,* pp. 76-77.

[20] 'The Wryttar to the reidaris', in W.T. Ritchie ed., *op. cit.,* vol 2, p. 1.

[21] 'Quhome suld I wyt of my mischance', in W.T. Ritchie ed., *op. cit.,* vol 3, pp. 83-84.

[22] From the lyrics 'Oppressit hairt endure', James Cranstoun ed., *op. cit.,* pp. 55-57, and 'Lord God deliver me allace', p. 94.

[23] Theoretically at least, the Reformation theology of personal penitence can be perceived in those recantatory poems that confess the remoteness of divine grace for the penitent encumbered with the knowledge of human love's irredeemably fallen state.

[24] James Cranstoun ed., *op. cit.,* pp. 91-96.

[25] From *Ane detectioun of the duinges of Marie Quene of Scottes, touchand the murder of hir husband, and hir conspiracie, adulterie, and*

pretensed mariage with the Erle Bothwell (London, 1571).

[26] Cf. S.M. Dunnigan, 'Scottish Women Writers c.1560-c.1650', in Douglas Gifford and Dorothy McMillan eds., *The History of Scottish Women's Writing*, Edinburgh: Edinburgh University Press, 1997, pp. 15-43.

[27] For the most thorough and wide-ranging analysis of James's work, see the essay collection edited by Daniel Fischlin and Mark Fortier, *Royal Subjects: The Writings of James V and I*, Detroit, Michigan: University of Wayne State Press, 2001.

[28] James Craigie ed., *The Poems of James VI of Scotland*, 2 vols., Edinburgh: Blackwood, 1955, vol 1, p. 67.

[29] Such contrived self-abasement is best seen in the prefaces to his printed literary work.

[30] James Craigie ed., *op. cit.*, vol 1, p. 67. See R.D.S. Jack, 'Poetry under King James VI', in Cairns Craig ed., *History of Scottish Literature*, cit., I, pp. 127-128, for exposition of the formal sonnet-scheme used by Jacobean writers which pre-dates English usage.

[31] From sonnets 5 and 11, James Craigie ed., *op. cit.*, vol 1, pp. 11, 14; for further comment on James's aesthetic *trompe l'oeil*, see R.J. Lyall, 'James VI and the sixteenth-century cultural crisis', in Julian Goodare and Michael Lynch eds., *The Reign of James VI*, East Linton: Tuckwell Press, 2000, pp. 55-70.

[32] James Craigie ed., *op. cit.*, vol 1, p. 79.

[33] The manuscript copies are reproduced in H.W. Meikle, James Craigie, and John Purves eds., *The Works of William Fowler*, 3 vols., Edinburgh: Blackwood, 1912-1939, vol 1.

[34] See R.D.S. Jack, 'William Fowler and Italian Literature', *Modern Language Review*, vol. 65, 1970, pp. 481-492.

[35] Thomas Crockett ed., *Poems of John Stewart of Baldynneis*, Edinburgh: Blackwood, 1913, p. 30.

[36] *Ibidem*, p. 71.

[37] R.D.S. Jack, *The Italian Influence on Scottish Literature*, Edinburgh: Edinburgh University Press, 1972, p. 58. See also Donna Rodger, 'John Stewart of Baldynneis: ane maist perfyt prentes', in Neil MacMillan and Kirsten Stirling eds., *op. cit.*, pp. 2-10.

[38] Thomas Crockett ed., *op. cit.*, p. 157.

[39] James Craigie ed., *James VI, Basilicon Doron*, Edinburgh: Blackwood, 1944-1950, p. 186.

[40] For the best account of Montgomerie's writing, see R.D.S. Jack,

Alexander Montgomerie, Edinburgh: Scottish Academic Press, 1985; *Scottish Literary Journal,* vol. 26, no. 2, 1999, is a special issue of recent critical essays on Montgomerie.

[41] See David Parkinson ed., *Alexander Montgomerie: Poems,* 2 vols., Edinburgh: The Scottish Text Society, 2000, pp. 141-274.

[42] Cf. the collection compiled by Arthur Johnston (1587-1641), *Delitiae poetarum Scotorum aevi illustrium* (Amsterdam, 1637), and the series, *Musa latina Aberdonensis,* 3 vols., edited by Sir William Duguid Geddes (Aberdeen, 1892-1910).

[43] *Poeticall Essayes of Alexander Craige, Scotobritane,* reprinted from the first edition (Hunterian Club, 1873), p. 25.

[44] *Ibidem,* p. 21.

[45] *Ibidem,* pp. 18-19.

[46] R.D.S. Jack and P.A.T. Rozendaal eds., *op. cit.,* p. 364. See Morna Fleming, 'Renaissance Poetry', in Douglas Gifford, Sarah Dunnigan, and Alan McGillivray eds., *Scottish Literature,* Edinburgh: Edinburgh University Press, 2002, for detailed analysis of Ayton's sonnet.

[47] Cf. Neil Larsen, 'Imperialism, Colonialism, Postcolonialism', in Henry Schwarz and Sangeeta Ray eds., *A Companion to Postcolonial Studies,* Oxford: Blackwell, 2000, p. 37ff.

[48] Seamus Deane, *Celtic Revivals: Essays in Modern Irish Literature 1880-1980,* London: Faber & Faber, 1985, p. 13.

[49] R.D.S. Jack and P.A.T. Rozendaal eds., *op. cit.,* p. 387.

[50] See further Gerard Carruthers and Sarah Dunnigan, '"A reconfused chaos now": Scottish Poetry and Nation from the Medieval Period to the Eighteenth Century', *Edinburgh Review,* vol. 100, 1999, pp. 81-94.

[51] Cf. the provisional definition of postcolonial concerns in Bill Ashcroft, Gareth Griffiths, and Helen Tiffin, *The Empire Writes Back: Theory and Practice in Post-colonial Literatures,* London: Routledge, 1989, pp. 4-8.

DERICK THOMSON

Alexander Macdonald, William Ross and Duncan Macintyre: Gaelic Poetry in the Eighteenth Century

ALEXANDER MACDONALD[1]

Alexander MacDonald (in Gaelic Alasdair Mac Mhaighstir Alasdair, c. 1695 c. 1770).

The eighteenth century was a period of considerable turbulence in Scotland and especially in the Highlands. The Scottish Parliament was dismantled in 1707 and attempts by the direct descendants of the Stuart monarchs to regain the throne resulted in two main risings in 1715 and 1745, which had disastrous consequences for the Highlands. Alasdair Mac Mhaighstir Alasdair was deeply involved in the 1745 Rising and possibly was involved in 1715, and he produced a diverse body of Gaelic poetry that throws much light on the political and social mores of the time and in various ways transforms the tradition of Gaelic verse. This is the result both of political and social change in his time and of his own tempestuous and strongly individual character.

Alexander MacDonald was probably born about 1695, or possibly a little earlier, the son of Alexander MacDonald, Episcopal clergyman at Islandfinnan in Moidart (West Invernessshire). His father had graduated M.A. at the University of Glasgow in 1674, thus acquiring the title Maighstir Alasdair (i.e. Alexander Master of Arts). The title Maighstir was commonly used of clergymen at this time and for long afterwards. The family home was at Dalilea, by Loch Shiel. The clergyman was born and reared in South Uist, and his family was closely related to the MacDonald chiefs of Clanranald, and the famous Flora MacDonald was a niece of his. Two of the poet's brothers farmed in the islands closely associated with the Clanranald chiefs (South Uist and Benbecula), and the Clanralds also held extensive lands in West Invernessshire, and in the islands of Canna and Eigg. The poet's mother was a MacLachlan from

Morven, and his wife was Jane MacDonald of Dalness. Her family had also produced Gaelic poets.

This background helps to explain the poet's deep commitment to Gaelic poetry and politics. It is conjectured that the poet spent some time at the University of Glasgow, possibly before the 1715 Rising, and he may have acquired some legal skills in Edinburgh in the decade following 1715. Some references in his poetry, and influences that show up in it, suggest continuing contacts with Edinburgh, and a document in the Clanranald papers was written and witnessed by him in 1727 in Benbecula, suggesting that he was employed for a time in a semilegal capacity.

Documentary evidence for the poet's activities is largely concentrated on the period 1729 to 1745. During this period he was employed as a preacher and catechist, under the auspices of the General Assembly of the Church of Scotland. He worked in Ardnamurchan, at Islandfinnan and Kilmory, and Kilchoan and Corryvullin, ending his teaching career in 1745 when he became involved in preparations for the Rising. Evidence from Presbyterial records of these years was assembled by William Mackay in a detailed paper which was published in the *Transactions of the Gaelic Society of Inverness* (vol. XI), in 1885. He converted to Roman Catholicism about 1745, though this may have been more a political than a religious decision. Evidence for his detailed involvement in the 1745 Rising and subsequent events appears in the *Lockhart Papers* (vol. 11), in 1817, and in *The Lyon in Mourning*, edited by Henry Paton in 1895.

His Edinburgh contacts surface clearly in these documents, especially in reports of his visits to the Rev. Robert Forbes, an Episcopalian clergyman in Leith, later to become a Bishop. Such Edinburgh contacts are further underlined in his poetry, as in his use of Lowland song airs for some of his poems, and the controlled influence of James Thomson's poems on the Seasons on Nature poems which Mac Mhaighstir Alasdair wrote, probably around the early 1740s. He seems also to have been influenced, at least marginally, by the Scots poetry of Gavin Douglas, and by the work of Allan Ramsay whom he may have known in Edinburgh.

In subjects and styles Mac Mhaighstir Alasdair's poetry has a wide range, and it is clear that he moved consciously away from some of the established topics and techniques of the Gaelic poetry of his times, exploring new territory, though it is equally clear that he was familiar with the earlier traditions, even to some extent with the classical Gaelic verse of the earlier professional poets. An early poem entitled 'The Author's Prayer to the Muses' shows some familiarity with Classical (Latin and Greek) models and very probably with Gavin Douglas's *The Palice of Honour*, which dates from the earliest years of the sixteenth century. Mac Mhaighstir Alasdair addresses the Muses in turn, and after this asks them to discourage him from producing verse that relies overmuch on its sound patterns, neglecting sense and understanding. This can probably be interpreted as a criticism of some existing Gaelic verse traditions at the time. He goes on to apologise for his lack of that training which the professional Gaelic bards used to have, but we can perhaps take this with a grain of salt. Another early poem, his 'Elegy for a Pet Dove', was probably influenced by Catullus's poem on a Sparrow, and Classical references occur in his Nature poems. But his poetry is never dominated by earlier models: he continually brings his own individuality to bear.

   Current political influences played an important part throughout his writing, with reflections on the events of the 1715 Rising and the turmoil of the following forty years. There are two poems which probably date from c. 1725, one in praise of the Lion (i.e. the MacDonalds) and another in dispraise of the Deer's Antler (referring to the Mackenzies who avoided supporting the Jacobites in 1715 and after). The main body of political verse dates from c. 1744 to c. 1749, with detailed references to the 1745 Rising and its aftermath. His 'Song of the Highland Clans' is a pre-1745 appeal to a wide range of clans, even the Campbells, to support the Jacobite campaign. In another poem, dating from 1746, before and after the Culloden disaster, he analyses in detail the themes of Stuart legitimacy and Hanoverian illegitimacy, showing his strong disapproval of the Act of Settlement of 1701, and satirising the Hanoverian dynasty in a series of fierce comparisons to pigs, boars and ravens. In spite of these references, this is on the whole a controlled and skilful political assessment, constantly enlivened by vivid imagery. Two colourful stanzas from this poem are quoted here in translation:

Slender the string, O George,
you played on to three kingdoms;
guileful the act and cloak
with which they made you king;
there are fifty men and more
closer in blood and claim,
in Europe, than you are;
remote and weak and devious
is the female line you came from
at the outside of the tree.

The boar who's called King George,
son of the German sow,
his friendship and his love
is the raven's for the bone;
he pulled us from our pelt;
the traitor caught and plundered us
and then killed us outright.
We're not his people anyway
and so he doesn't care
if we beat each other up.

Other poems from the 1745 campaign are designed to enthuse
Jacobite supporters, with hope of victory and spoils, or are simply
drinking songs which celebrate the troops' cameraderie. A poem
which probably dates from the later 1740s ('The Ark') describes a
ficticious dream that a gentleman had of a flood in Argyll, and
urges Alexander Campbell of Ardslignis, who is described in the
poem as the Campbell Noah, to build an Ark, excluding many who
took the Hanoverian side in the 1745 Rising, but allowing some
Campbells on board. This poem has a strange mixture of fun and
bitterness and it has a controlled overall structure, as though the
poet is reasserting himself over the politician.

He returns periodically to the theme of Nature description. This
is a recurrent theme in Gaelic poetry and song, but Mac Mhaighstir
Alasdair gave it a new focus, especially in his poems on the
Seasons. Two of these survive, one on Summer and one on Winter,
and probably date from the early 1740s. He was influenced, but in
no sense dominated, by James Thomson's *Seasons*, which were
appearing in the 1720s, and in extended form in the late 1730s. He
may well have written poems on the other two seasons but they

do not survive. His work inspired a succession of such poems in the second half of the century. The poem about Summer is richly descriptive of plant and bird and animal life, darting impressionistically from one description to another, with this variety and movement symbolising the reactions Nature produced in the poet. The poem on Winter follows a fairly similar pattern, but at some points has a more jocular tone, as in this stanza quoted in translation:

The bare month of colds and of coughs
when heroes' black brose is much sought;
month that's mutched, coated, tawny and brown,
breeched, stockinged, breast
hooded fast,
booted, white
vested and gloved,
bready, crowdie
less, buttery, cheesy,
fond of brose, of beef and of kail,
and of anything else if it's warm.

Another long Nature poem, 'Allt an t-Siùcair' (Sugar Burn) was set in the southern part of Ardnamurchan, and probably dates from the early 1740s also, and he returned to the Nature theme in much later poems, when he lived in Eigneig and Morar in his final years.

It was probably about 1727 that the poet married Jane MacDonald, and he composed a rather formal love song for her at that time. Some years later he wrote a long poem entitled 'Moladh Mòraig' (Praise of Morag), which describes, whether factually or ficticiously, a passionate affair with a 'country lass'. This was followed by 'Mìmholadh Mòraig' (Dispraise of Morag), a satirical and bawdy work. It is not clear whether these poems record an actual affair or a literary fiction or indeed both. Another set of very bawdy pieces is centred on an outbreak of sexual disease in Ardnamurchan. And, a little later, there are virulently satirical pieces directed largely against the Campbells, including satire of an Oban woman poet. A vivid mixture of satire and Nature description occurs in a poem describing his movement from Eigneig to Inbhir-Aoidh. This includes fierce satire of a priest and a factor, and is one of many examples in his work where strong emotion produces a wealth of descriptive language which has probably never been equalled in the history of Scottish Gaelic verse.

He produced another tour-de-force of a different kind in the long poem 'Birlinn Chlann Raghnaill' (The Clanranald Galley) which describes in lavish detail a stormy journey (probably imaginary) between Islay and Northern Ireland, with vivid detail of the storm and the activities of the crew, and the activities of wild life in the sea and on the seabed. This poem also draws on early Gaelic legend and verse. It is sometimes interpreted as an elaborate praise poem for the Clanranald and their chiefs. It may be that in one sense, or can be interpreted in that way, but it is primarily a work of poetic imagination. Mac Mhaighstir Alasdair seems in general to have avoided the genre of chief-praise that was a prominent choice of many earlier Gaelic poets. The 'Birlinn' poem was probably written close to the year 1750, after he had recovered to some extent from the deep disappointment of the failed 1745 campaign. The earliest published version is in the Eigg Collection, compiled by the poet's son and published in 1776. It did not appear in the collection of his poetry published in 1751, but it had probably been largely completed by then. He uses a variety of traditional Gaelic metres in the poem, which is carefully and logically constructed, and shows an extraordinary wealth of Gaelic vocabulary. In the Mòrag poems he had used metres based in part on the movements of classical pipe music (ceòl mòr), and this innovation was used by some later poets also.

The 1751 book was in fact the earliest published collection of secular verse in Gaelic. Mac Mhaighstir Alasdair had produced another 'first' in 1741, with the publication of his Gaelic vocabulary, *Leabhar a theagasc: Ainiminnin no Nuadhfhocloir Gaoidheilg & Béurla*.

His poems were frequently reprinted and re-edited, for example in 1764, 1802, 1806, 1809, 1813, 1839, 1874. A comprehensive edition was published in 1924 by the Revs. A. and A. MacDonald. This includes translations, but it is deficient as to editorial apparatus. A detailed edition of the 'Birlinn' was produced by Angus MacLeod in 1933, and the political poems were edited by J.L. Campbell in 1933, and revised in 1984. A selection of the poems, with more detailed editorial apparatus, appeared in my edition *Alasdair Mac*

MACDONALD/ROSS/MACINTYRE 127

Mhaighstir Alasdair: Selected Poems, in 1996.

WILLIAM ROSS[2]
William Ross (in Gaelic Uilleam Ros, 1762-1791?) was born at
Sìthean, in the Isle of Skye.

His father was a travelling merchant or pedlar, and his mother
was the daughter of John Mackay, who is known as Am Pìobaire
Dall (the Blind Piper) and was well known both as a poet and a
piper. William Ross lived with his family for some years in Forres
(Morayshire) and was educated there. He then moved to Gairloch
(in Wester Ross), his mother's home region, and worked as a
teacher and catechist there. His knowledge of Classical literature,
and of the work of Lowland Scottish writers, especially Burns,
shows clearly in his poems, and he was marginally influenced by
James Macpherson's Ossianic writings. He seems also to have been
familiar with various strands of Gaelic poetry, but he brings his
own individuality and sensitivity into his work, producing a varied
and innovative body of verse in his short life. It is said that he
destroyed most of his poetry before his death, but fortunately some
of it survived in the memories of friends and contemporaries.

To some extent memory of his work is dominated by the story
that he fell deeply in love with a girl from Stornoway, called Mòr
Ros, whom he met on a visit to Lewis with his father about 1780.
She married a Captain Clough from Liverpool in 1782. The legend
was that Ross died of a broken heart, but that was some nine years
later. Three of his poems refer to this attachment. 'Feasgar Luain'
(Monday Evening) describes their first meeting, and gives a
detailed description of Mòr's beauty, and of her distinguished forebears: this is considerably influenced by traditional Gaelic praise
poetry, and has a number of references to Classical icons (Diana,
Venus, Cupid), while emphasising his own enchantment with Mòr.
This poem was composed some time after the meeting in
Stornoway, and may even be post-1782. The other two poems
were clearly composed after Mòr married Captain Glough. 'Oran
Cumhaidh' (A Lament) describes his anguish, again using Classical
references and also an extended passage about a legendary love
affair between Cormac and Finne. The third song, 'Oran Eile'

(Another Song) is the most effective of the three, with the poet's personal anguish showing through poignantly, and not deflected by the poetic conventions of the other two poems. The opening lines and the final stanza ara quoted in translation:

Overburdened with sorrow now
I can drink no dram with joy,
a maggot broods in my mind
telling my secrets to all

. . . .

No ode to beauty comes forth,
I can't put a poem in place,
I cannot pick out a tune,
I hear no young laughing cry,
no longer climb in the hills
with zest as at one time I did,
I must journey to final sleep
in the hall of the poets who are dead.

Fortunately Ross's talent did not die at this point. His surviving work includes poems on a good range of topics and in a variety of styles. His song about Summer is influenced by Mac Mhaighstir Alasdair but is in no way dominated by it. Another song is in praise of whisky, and there are several light hearted and sometimes ribald songs about chasing girls. He reworked an earlier song 'Cuachag nan Craobh' (The Cuckoo/Ringletted Girl of the Wood) which exists in a MS dated 1765, but he adds lively stanzas to it. He records the death of Prince Charlie in 1788, in another song. A rhymed debate between the Poet and the Hag makes fun of some of the conventional love imagery:

...to cotton
grass you compare her,
but what is its use?
If love brings death to you
have a good final year.

. . . .

My love is a peacock
who over hundreds excels,
fair-faced, slender
eyebrowed,

with warm, soft blue eyes...

And the Hag responds:

> Were it not for the feathers
> a peacock wouldn't attract,
> it does no good and no mischief,
> simply pleasing the eye,
> its claws and its legs
> detract from its image,
> though its clothing is foppish
> it's a bird of no worth.

Some of Ross's poems appeared in A. and D. Stewart's Collection of 1804. They were extensively published by John Mackenzie in the early 1830s, and edited with translations by George Calder in 1937.

Duncan Macintyre[3]

Duncan Macintyre (in Gaelic Donnchadh Bàn i.e. Fairhaired Duncan, 1724-1812).

He was born in Glen Orchy, Argyllshire, Scotland, and lived in that area until 1766, working as a forester or gamekeeper between Glen Etive and Glen Lochay. He moved to Edinburgh in 1766, and served in the City Guard there until 1793. After that he served for about six years in the Breadalbane Fencibles, a military regiment, but Edinburgh remained his home.

His principal clan allegiance was to the Campbells, who were very prominent in his home area, and he composed a number of praise songs and laments for Campbell chiefs and other prominent Campbells, from about 1746 to 1793. He seems to have been able to produce songs at the drop of a hat, and sometimes over indulges, as in his series of six songs in praise of Gaelic and the bagpipes, composed for the London Highland Society's competitions between 1781 and 1789. He fought briefly on the Hanoverian side in 1746, but shows Jacobite sympathies elsewhere.

These Campbell connections no doubt helped him in various ways to make a living, and may have encouraged him to visit Killin in Perthshire, where he made the acquaintance of the Stewart minister there, and his son. The Rev. James Stewart had translated the New Testament from Greek to Gaelic, and this was published in 1767, while his son the Rev. John Stuart, together with another minister, the Rev. Donald MacNicol, helped Macintyre to publish a collection of his poetry in 1768. Macintyre himself was not literate, though he had an extensive knowledge of oral Gaelic tradition. The Rev. MacNicol is said to have written down the poet's songs from his recitation, and the Rev. Stuart helped to edit and publish them. It is probable too that these Stewart contacts made him more closely aware of the work of Alasdair Mac Mhaighstir Alasdair, published in 1751, and this influence is clearly seen in his poetry.

Macintyre's poetry can be assigned to two broad categories: a predominantly public one, and a more private one closely connected with his years working in the glens and mountains of Argyllshire and Perthshire. The public poems are associated with Campbells of influence, with his work as a City Guard and soldier, and his entries for song competitions, and there are a number of drinking songs that fit into this category. Many of these show considerable linguistic and metrical fluency, and some humour and satire, and this explains his wide popularity in his lifetime and afterwards. His attitude to the increase of sheep farming in the countryside he knew, and the increasing dominance of new fangled factors in that society, show some radicalism which would also have increased his popularity. There is, however, little evidence of intellectual depth in this work.

The poems associated with his work and experiences in Argyll and Perthshire, and especially his reactions to Nature and landscape, have a much richer texture. His poem on Summer is probably over influenced by Mac Mhaighstir Alasdair's poem on this subject, and his long poem 'Moladh Beinn Dòbhrain' (Praise of Ben Doran) was influenced by the overall shape and the metrics of Mac Mhaighstir Alasdair's Mòrag poems, but this does not inhibit his own originality and his vivid observation and emotional reactions to the landscapes and natural life he encountered there.

Two poems describe Coire a' Cheathaich, a corrie some six miles north of Crianlaraich and five miles east of Ben Doran. These are elaborate and sensitive descriptions of the landscape, its vegetation and flowers, nuts and fruit, birds and fish and animals. Two stanzas are quoted in translation from one of these poems:

> On calm clear mornings, at time of waking,
> beneath the peak, what a joy it was
> to hear the moor
> hen, with husky cackle,
> and the courtly cock, making murmuring beck,
> the lively wren with his tuneful chanter
> letting it rip, agile and sweet,
> starling and robin, with busy bustle
> cheerfully warbling swift
> moving staves.
>
> ....
>
> The yellow doe roves in the thicket,
> peeling the base of the saplings bare,
> the morose buck with his curving hoof
> busily scraping a courtly bed,
> while the brindled fawn, so smoothly sided,
> with twitching nostrils and wildest head,
> lies cosy, sleeping in lonely hollow,
> a rounded bunch under rushes' tips.

Macintyre's major work is undoubtedly the long poem in praise of Ben Doran. This runs to just over 550 lines, with different sections using a variety of metres which are linked to the movements of classical pipe music. There are detailed descriptions of the landscape and its plant and flower life, but it is clear that the poet's major fascination was with the deer that inhabited this landscape. He continually returns to references and long detailed descriptions of does, hinds, stags, their movements, their reactions to their surroundings and their own species, and to the functions of the gamekeeper. His admiration for the animals does not deter him from giving close descriptions of the guns that are used at times to kill them. This combination of emotion and practicality may seem strange to modern readers, but it was probably normal in Macintyre's times and circumstances.

The poem has a rich texture, in terms of language and vocal music, exploiting the wide and diverse range of sound that is one of the striking characteristics of Scottish Gaelic. In these respects it is probably one of the outstanding achievements in Gaelic poetry. This richness is difficult to reproduce in translation, but an accessible translation, with an interesting introduction, was made by I.C. Smith, and published in 1969 by Akros Publications. D.J. MacLeod had much earlier published French translations of the poetry, with a detailed French introduction.

NOTES

[1] A select bibliography on Alexander MacDonald includes the following books: Priscilla Bawcutt, *Gavin Douglas: A Critical Study*, Edinburgh: Edinburgh University Press, 1976; Ronald Black, *Mac Mhaighstir Alasdair: The Ardnamurchan Years*, Isle of Coll, Argyll: Society of West Highland and Island Historical Research, 1988; J.L. Campbell, *Highland Songs of the Forty Five*, Edinburgh: Scottish Gaelic Texts Society, 1933-1984; Edinburgh: Eigg Collection, 1776; Alexander MacDonald, *Aiseiridh na sean chanain Albanaich*, Glascho: Clò-Bhuailte le Miur, Gobhan, 1834; Rev. A and Rev A. MacDonald, *The Poems of Alexander MacDonald*, Inverness: [s.n.], 1924; Derick Thomson, *Gaelic Poetry in the Eighteenth Century*, Aberdeen: Association for Scottish Literary Studies, 1993; Derick Thomson, *Alasdair Mac Mhaighstir Alasdair: Selected Poems*, Edinburgh: Scottish Gaelic Texts Society, 1996.

[2] A select bibliography on William Ross includes George Calder, *Gaelic Songs of William Ross*, Edinburgh: Oliver & Boyd, 1937 and Derick Thomson, *An Introduction to Gaelic Poetry*, London: Gollancz, 1974; Edinburgh: Edinburgh University Press, 1990.

[3] A select bibliography on Duncan Macintyre includes the following books: George Calder, *The Gaelic Songs of Duncan Macintyre*, Edinburgh: John Grant, 1912; Angus MacLeod, *The Songs of Duncan Bàn Macintyre*, Edinburgh: Scottish Gaelic Texts Society, 1952; D.J. MacLeod, *Donnchadh Bàn Mac an t-Saoir*, Inverness: Northern Countries Newspaper and Printing and Publishing Company, 1929?; I.C. Smith, *Ben Dorain*, Preston: Akros, 1969.

FRANCO BUFFONI

Allan Ramsay [1]

Within the Scottish literary context, Allan Ramsay is a figure whose importance transcends the mere artistic value of his work. *The Evergreen* and *The Tea-Table Miscellany*, the two collections which included re-elaborations and actual re-creations carried out within the popular poetic tradition, were a key factor in the evolution of Scottish poetry. We can comprehend the extent to which Scottish culture and civilization are indebted to Ramsay if we consider the impulse he gave to theatrical activity in Edinburgh. He supported, also financially, The Edinburgh Company of Players, whose activity extended from 1733 to 1735. In 1736 he instituted, in Carrubber's Close, the New Theatre, the first regular theatre in Edinburgh; an initiative which was destined to be short-lived, however. He also established the first circulating library and was one of the founders of the Easy Club, the most famous cultural club in the city. All this was done in open challenge to the authorities.

Ramsay was born in Leadhills, Lanarkshire, on 15 October 1685. Shortly after the death of his father, his mother, Alice Bower, remarried and Allan grew up a country lad in a barely well-to-do family. The poet was little over fourteen when his mother died, also; it is not difficult to understand, therefore, why his studies were necessarily limited. However, the period of life and work on the farm revealed itself fruitful in the long run: for the setting of *The Gentle Shepherd* he looked back to the experiences of those years.

In the capital, Ramsay became apprentice wigmaker and in 1710 he opened his own shop as master wigmaker. Also in 1710 he married Christian Ross, who belonged to an illustrious family in decline and who gave him seven children. Ramsay obtained his first affirmation as poet in 1721 with the publication of *Poems*, a

collection of lyrics dedicated 'to the most Beautiful, the Scots
Ladies'. But even prior to this, in 1718 and 1719, he had published
some *Scots Songs* and, still earlier, 'A Poem to the Memory of
Famous Archibald Pitcairn, M.M.', which appears to be his first
composition.

Just as Fergusson and Burns afterwards, at the beginning of his
poetic career Ramsay dedicated himself to versification in the
English language without obtaining better results than his successors. His most significant work in the line of the Genteel English
Tradition is the mock heroic poem, 'The Morning Interview', clearly
inspired by Pope's *The Rape of the Lock*. In 1724 the first of the
four volumes which compose the collection *The Tea-Table
Miscellany* appeared, and the following year the pastoral work *The
Gentle Shepherd* was sent to the printer. Also in 1724 the two vol-
umes of the other collection, *The Evergreen*, were published. *The
Evergreen*, as the title suggests, was entirely dedicated to the great
Makars (Henryson, Dunbar, Lyndsay). Finally, in 1725, *Orpheus
Caledonius* appeared, a collection of fifty Scottish songs complete
with text and music.

As Fergusson and Burns, Ramsay, too, was a Jacobite, although
political passion never *got* the better of his inborn common sense.
His patriotism emerges clearly in the preface to *The Evergreen*,
where he observes: 'The poetry of these good old Bards is the
product of their own Country. [...] We are not carried to Greece or
Italy for a Shade, a Stream or a Breeze. The Groves rise in our own
Valleys; the Rivers flow from our own Fountains, and the Winds
blow upon our own Hills'. More traces of patriotism, or chauvinism, are found in 'A Tale of Three Bonnets' and in 'Tartana: Or,
The Plaid'. In this last work Ramsay portrays a fierce aversion for
foreign influences which pollute Scottish traditions and custom.

Ramsay had opponents not only among political men but also
in the midst of religious authority (the dividing line between the
two was certainly not well defined). Calvinism numbered poetry,
as well, among the immoral amusements; but if, on the one hand,
the Church sought to prohibit dance, in 1723 Ramsay composed
'Fair Assembly', a lively poem in defense of dance.

It was in such an atmosphere dense with decrepit moral values
that Allan Ramsay worked, and today he appears as the first per-

sonality of lower middle-class extraction that succeeded in the artistic field in spite of the sectarian mentality in the Scotland of his day. Nevertheless, the times were ripe for a change: the Act of Union had achieved the effect of rekindling ancient Scottish pride, thus augmenting an interest for tradition which had never been actually suppressed. Ramsay was aware of this and he was able to move in the most careful and productive manner. A.M. Kinghorn writes: 'As a poet, clubman, urban reformer, patriot, promoter of civic amenities, shop-keeper and encourager of the fine arts, Ramsay sums up in his own personality the first phase of a national movement towards cultural recovery'.[2] He found worthy successors in Fergusson and, above all, Burns: untiring critics of religious hypocrisy and Calvinist orthodoxy.

In reality, Ramsay portrayed little rebellion (unlike his successors he was always self-controlled and well-balanced), but he opposed fanaticism and excesses. Above all, he could not tolerate limits on his artistic activity. Declaring himself a believer he should have been a member of the Whig party; but the baseness and the hypocrisy of many members of that party discouraged him. So the poet preferred to take a neutral stance: neither Whig nor Tory. But Ramsay's contradictions are summed up by David Daiches: 'A Gentleman of the Augustan Age and an ardent Scottish patriot; an admirer of Pope and Gay and Matthew Prior and devoted champion of the older Scottish makars and of the use of vernacular Scots by contemporary Scottish poets [...] A sentimental Jacobite and a prudent citizen who cannily absented himself from Edinburgh when Prince Charlie held court in Holyrood in 1745'.[3]

Notwithstanding opposition and contrasts, Ramsay's shop became one of the fulcrums of the political and literary activity of the city. Soon his fame extended beyond local boundaries, to the point that he attracted illustrious visitors. Even John Gay paid a lengthy visit to his shop while visiting Scotland in the company of the Duchess of Queensbury.

In those years the intelligentsia of Edinburgh was divided into two 'factions', both nationalist but separated by the 'question of language'. Ramsay became the most prominent figure among those who affirmed, in more or less fiery terms, the need to keep alive a Scottish language. The other current centered around David Hume.

Both groups sought to sustain Scottish thought and culture, but while Hume and his followers thought to fight the English by using the language of the adversary, Ramsay and his friends held that, in order to keep national unity alive, they had to work from within tradition, maintaining the ancient Scottish language in use.

In reality it was a utopian aspiration since it seemed that the Scottish language did not possess the lexical qualities necessary to aspire once again to the position of national idiom. It was, indeed, employed on the domestic level, but no one would have seriously thought to write a novel in the vernacular. Besides being a vernacular which does not consist of a single idiom, for there are nine dialectal regions in Scotland, as William Grant demonstrates.[4] In each of these it is possible to observe various sub-divisions. The written dialect was, therefore, adapt only for poetical expression, but with necessary limits. It is within those limits that Ramsay produced poetically. If Ramsay had not undertaken his careful and meticulous work of collection and re-elaboration, besides that of original poetic production, his two successors, Fergusson and Burns, would not have been able to express themselves as they did. Burns himself recognized his indebtedness with great modesty; he harbored a veritable veneration for Ramsay. 'The Merry Beggars' and 'The Happy Beggars', in particular, witness the deep dependence of Burns on his predecessor's collection.

A literary genre that had much influence on the developments of poetry in Scotland, and of which Ramsay may be considered initiator, is the genre of verse epistles. We are not dealing with great poetry; nonetheless, it represents, as Daiches observes, 'a craftsmanlike handling of the familiar style, an exercising of the vernacular which was to stand Burns in good stead, and it further helped to provide both a social and a metrical convention for Scots verse'.[5] Even the genre of flyting poems, which had much fortune in the second half of the eighteenth century with the compositions of Fergusson and Burns, has a worthy representative in Allan Ramsay. In this composition two animals, two objects or two abstractions are given conspicuous human traits and they are made to converse in order to underline the vices, defects, incongruencies – and sometimes even the virtues – of man. Ramsay wrote various works which have as protagonists animals with anthropomorphous characteristics; this is the case with 'The Chamaleon', 'The Ape and the Leopard', 'The Two Cats and the Cheese'. Ramsay's work fits well within the typically Scottish tradition that sees in the stories of animals a biting and persuasive manner to represent the tragicomedy of interpersonal relationships.

The influence of Ramsay on Fergusson and Burns is not limited to theme alone. The two successors often looked to Ramsay for the metrical and rhythmic structure, also. An example is the use of the Habbie Stanza (or Standard Habbie), a stanza of six verses (of which four – the first, second, third, and fifth – composed of eight syllables, and two – the fourth and sixth – composed of four; and often the last verse is repeated in every stanza, forming a sort of refrain). The name derives from Habbie Simpson, a seventeenth century player, to whom Robert Sempill dedicated a half-serious epitaph. Traditionally, this stanza was used exclusively in the comic-elegiac genre and in verse epistles. Ramsay collected and re-elaborated the sixteenth and seventeenth century poems written according to this model and he himself composed several works with it; 'The Elegy on Maggie Johnston' is the best example of the use of the Habbie Stanza by Ramsay. Ramsay served as model for Burns even for the eight verse stanza which was practically ignored by Fergusson.

In relation to Ramsay's attempts in the pastoral genre prior to *The Gentle Shepherd*, David Daiches points out that 'the combination of conversational idiom with classical allusion comes off better than one might expect'.[6] We think that the two conflicting aspects must be underlined immediately since the conventionality of the occasion and of the situation and the originality of the language are essential traits of Ramsay's pastoral production. In the pastoral 'Richy and Sandy', composed by Ramsay in 1720 on the death of Addison, the author adheres completely to a scheme which had already belonged to Milton in *Lycidas*: to mourn the death of a poet one must represent him as shepherd in an ideal Arcadia.

Similarly to Theocritus's use of Doric, even Ramsay uses the vernacular to confer liveliness and originality to his plots. Again, it is the language that supports Ramsay's other two early pastorals: 'Pastoral Dialogue Between Patie and Roger' and 'Jenny and Peggy'. Encouraged by the success he obtained, Ramsay would later com-

pose the more ambitious *The Gentle Shepherd* following the structures of the two earlier works.

The Gentle Shepherd appeared in 1725 and Boswell defined it as
'the best pastoral that has ever been written'. In observance with
the rules of the three unities, the action takes place in a village of
shepherds within the classical twenty-four hour time span: the first
act describes the happenings of the morning, the second act
describes those of the afternoon, the third ends at dusk, in the
fourth the night is described, in the fifth dawn appears. The protagonist, Patie (the noble shepherd), is in love with Peggy, grand-
daughter of Glaud; Glaud is an old shepherd who, together with
Symon, is in charge of the lands of Sir William Worthy.

The early audience of *The Gentle Shepherd* belonged to a country totally lacking in literary theatrical experience and tradition.
Before Ramsay, Scotland did not possess original antecedents in
this field. Ramsay's work appears, therefore, quite distant from that
pastoral convention that reached its peak of hypocrisy during the
period of the Restoration; but, it seems to us, equally distant in
spirit from the nostalgic return of the eighteenth century towards
rural innocence (the poet townsman who rediscovers lost incanta-
tions). This is because Ramsay himself was practically a farmer, no
doubt urbane and cultivated, but with a solid villatic background.
For this reason, his love for the country does not appear ambiguous. Beneath his apparent ingenuity we are led to notice Ramsay's
capability to depict with craftsmanship the typical mentality of the
aristocracy. We certainly do not wish to ascribe to him critical
capacities which he did not possess. In any case, we do not consider it just to disregard the intuitions of which, perhaps, he was
unaware.

Ramsay is only indirectly associated with the classical tradition,
but if we wanted to propose a link of a pathological nature, we
would think of returning to Theocritus. Theocritus, whose shepherds are not abstract creations of the imagination, but real shepherds, real people. If, as is true in general during the eighteenth
century, Dafni and Cloe, Tirsi and Menalca became 'manifold and
interchangeable names for a unique type, the shepherd in love
who, beyond these qualities, of being a shepherd, of being in love,
does not possess any individual character, any personality',[7]

Ramsay seems to represent an exception, undoubtedly peripheral and modest, but a sapid and accomplished exception.

Ramsay has a certain manner of establishing situations and characters that reminds us of Theocritus. Theocritus who was the first 'to write rustic poetry based on the life of the shepherds of Sicily, a life that he knew well and partook of, with the songs heard from their mouths, with the adored landscapes, with his dreamed-of ideal of farmer-poet'.[8] But another association, of an economic and political nature, seems to ideally link the two poets. The simple men, whose loves Theocritus described and idealized to cheer up the refined citizens of Alexandria, were subjected in that period to a condition of total bondage on the immense estates of the island; the poet was aware of this, and perhaps the acute sense of regret for a lost happy past which delicately rises from the verses may be ascribed to this. Similarly, in Scotland in 1725, with the ratification of the Act of Union still painfully near, institutions and traditions were fatally subjugated and scoffed at by the new landlords; a glorious nation was slipping to the rank of a poor province of a future empire. Of course, Ramsay could not imagine that his farmers were becoming poorer since they had always lived with great difficulty; but he was deeply aware that, together with the entire nation, they were losing their freedom. For this reason, even when we detect, in his verses, melancholy and regret, it is not fatuous allusion to a ghostly golden age, but the regret for a much more concrete and immediate loss of national identity.

The overall impression we are given, however, is that, for Ramsay, this suffering remains on a substantially sentimental level, removed from any sort of awareness of a political nature, strictly speaking. With Ramsay we are quite distant from the revolutionary radicalism that other authors would later manifest. Rebels are against the 'law of nature'; one must fight them with all the violence possible. The law of the king, of the nation, of the landlord is the law of conscience. The right of property is a law of nature. His thought, therefore, finds its place in a perspective of dynastic law and of privileges by birth, of social status solidly defined for each person from birth. The only possibility of emancipation is to be found in the rêverie of fairy tales, in the fortuitous action of a *deus ex machina* who can rest his gaze on a humble person and, thus, admit him among the powerful.

Therefore, Ramsay sets himself apart from the townsman intellectual who hypocritically sublimates his own alienation by narrating the life of the humble, because he is himself a former countryman; but he makes manifest his cultural and ethical limits succumbing to the fashion of the bucolic regret. Rather than nostalgia for the rural condition, we have here the regret of the mature man for the age of simplicity and carefreeness. It has nothing to do with the wishful attempt by Pope to recover the golden age; it is only something ambiguous and mediated, *sui generis*.[9] Looking at the past, we find nothing of the refinements of Guarini or Garcilaso, Fletcher or Lodge, of the Tirsi or of the Aminta; and equally nothing, or very little, of the comic and popular realism of the rustic farce: no Ruzzante, in other words.

Ramsay composed *The Gentle Shepherd* as *Gulliver's Travels* was about to go into print and six years after the appearance of the modern novel (*Robinson Crusoe*, 1719). How can we classify Ramsay's work? Certainly not among those works that succeeded in capturing the ferment of the new century, but neither among those characterized by a suffocating mannerism. The reason is that in Ramsay, beneath the form, it is not difficult to apprehend a plebean substance that confers a certain rigor to the work, a style of its own, with due reservations.

The work of Ambrose Philips is closer to Ramsay's in that it is simply more human: and it is exactly for that naiveté and that substantial mediocrity that Gay criticized him bitterly. Of course, with Gay we are at the threshold of genius; he cannot tolerate the intellectual limits of a Philips because he feels the imperious impulse to give a faithful image of reality. With Gay, with Swift, we feel that the century will lead to Rousseau and his contract, to Beccaria, to Wordsworth's poetic theory. However, even with Gay and Swift we perceive limits because, in spite of the new artistic perspective with which they stand before the humble, theirs is still the attitude of the aristocrat who observes the rural world from atop his pedestal; he sees it as another world, different, to which he feels he has to grant his genius but certainly not an emotional participation to foster a possibility of liberation. Therefore, despite the artistic limits of his work, let us re-evaluate Philips. And let us re-evaluate Ramsay. We think we can discern in their line of mediocrity and honest simplicity the germ that, towards the end of the century, characterized Crabble's answer in relation to what these farmers, these shepherds, actually were.

'After Cartesio', says Basil Willey, 'poets inevitably wrote with the sensation that their constructions were not true and this deprived their work of the necessary seriousness'.[10] Besides, in 1699 Jean le Clerc wrote that the reader 'opening a book of poetry must remember that he is about to read the work of a liar, that he intends to entertain him with falseness'.[11] If this observation concerns, generally speaking, all authors, it is especially true for 'the pastoral writer', 'whose first duty', as Lytton Strachey observes,[12] 'was to be unoriginal'.

What we should underline is how, with *The Gentle Shepherd*, Ramsay – according to Rayner Unwin's definition – was able to bring 'freshness and life to the time-worn pastoral theme'.[13] He succeeded in doing this, first of all, by avoiding to insert in his plot the usual artifice of the love-sick poet. Even Pope, in *The Rape of the Lock*, avoids this theme, artfully poking fun at it. With Pope we are dealing with the perfection of the minuet, with the mannerism of mannerism; we witness the destruction of a 'genre' out of the voluntary abuse of substance (that is, of metaphor); with Ramsay, on the other hand, the genre recovers itself, recycling its own substance. The reason is that even in *The Gentle Shepherd*, Roger and Bauldy suffer the pains of love. However, it is they who suffer, and they suffer rustically. The poet simply waits for the events to change and make them happy as their status and the 'genre' call for.

Thanks to *The Evergreen*, Ramsay had acquired a profound expertise of Scottish lore; the poet followed a rather efficacious method in the choice of the musical motifs for his pastoral: he would take an ancient song whose contents suggested a certain change in the plot, he would compose verses which were fitting to the melody, finally, he would leave some trace of the original text (a verse or a significant expression) so that the audience could recognize it more easily and recollect it.

It is interesting to note that in the original version of *The Gentle Shepherd* only four songs appeared;[14] the other eighteen were

added later (in 1728), when the author, in tune with the times –
and particularly with the success of Gay –, decided to transform
the dramatic pastoral in a ballad opera. This interpolation attracted
to the theatre – censorship permitting – an audience that otherwise
would not have attended. We must remember the success that the
work encountered during the eighteenth and, still, during the nineteenth century, especially with provincial audiences.

The palinodes of traditional songs appeared to Ramsay as the
most practical means to enliven his pastoral in a period when the
melodic element was undoubtedly penetrating ever deeper into the
poetic, but in England melodrama in the true sense of the word
was having difficulty taking root. We can mention, in this regard,
the chauvinistic aversion towards Italian musical innovations. We
can, thus, say that in peripheral Scotland, theatrically in ruins,
Ramsay's operation may be assimilated to the late Renaissance Italian
attempts (Poliziano, for example, had composed *Orfeo* to be recited,
but later some passages were put into music). For in Ramsay, also,
just as in the beginnings of the Italian melodrama, music intervenes
occasionally. Once we have understood the Scottish delay with
regards to the evolution of melodrama (and, naturally, once we have
determined that the principle causes of this are to be found in the
Calvinist mentality and in the local philosophic disposition), we can
recall that in Italy, also, the appearance of true melodrama was preceded by musical and harmonic comedies. As often happens,
although the delay in relation to the times is, 'technically' speaking,
evident, we cannot say the same for the contents: if, roughly
speaking, we think we can distinguish two veins in Ramsay's work,
then these are represented by the roman feuilleton and the operetta.

The decadent language of Scotland that flows for the length of
five acts confers originality to the work, even more so than the
mise-en-scéne. Ramsay did not need to make use, as Spenser in
Arcadia, of apparently rough archaisms to bestow credibility to the
rusticity of his milieu. He already had at his disposal a characteristic idiom which he used in the most careful and productive manner. (It is a fact that the dialectal expression, besides giving the dialogues greater vivacity, is able to render acceptable certain considerations and concepts that, otherwise, in the official language
would appear shamefully commonplace).

It is because the vernacular presents a limited lexical extension that Ramsay could work with a wider range of syntactic and rhythmic solutions than other British poets. In fact, he used the English term, not only to make up for the natural deficiencies of the vernacular, but also and often, for mere reasons of rhyme or to reach more effectual semantic eversions; to the point of neologism, we may add, without, however, making an excessive use of it. Ramsay was certainly not guided by whim, but by a serious intention to make manifest, through the 'truth' of language, witty aspects of a pastorally mediated Scottish reality. A seriousness that is evinced even in his search (at least in the vernacular, if not in the 'language') of the most appropriate term to refer to the natural element, to the humble botanic datum. An attention that we may encounter, not by chance, even in Dyer and in the Thomsonian *Seasons*, and that does not appear in many of the eighteenth century pastoral works (not only English, but also Italian and French).

The seventeenth century had witnessed the irremediable decline of the Scottish language and its relegation to the rank of dialect. The nationalistic upsurge provoked by the ratification of the Act of Union could not turn the tide: the nation's linguistic identity had been corrupted at the roots. Authors like Boswell and Thomson contributed to this definitive decline by disdaining the common language, preferring the more refined English idiom. If there was a revival, it was thanks to the patient work of James Watson and, above all, Allan Ramsay, who collected and transcribed all they could of the ancient poetic tradition, re-elaborating it in a sufficiently organic manner. Ramsay's collections (*The Evergreen* and *The Tea-Table Miscellany*) allowed Fergusson and Burns to draw from the folkloric heritage.

NOTES

[1] Summarized and translated from: Franco Buffoni, *Ramsay e Fergusson: Precursori di Burns*, Milano: Guerini, 1992. Summarized and translated by Nello Quattrociocchi.

[2] *The Works of Allan Ramsay*, edited by A.M. Kinghorn and Alexander Law, Edinburgh: Scottish Text Society, 1945-1974, p. 163.

[3] David Daiches, 'Eighteenth Century Vernacular Poetry', in James Kinsley ed., *Scottish Poetry: A Critical Survey*, London: Cassell, 1955, p. 155.

[4] William Grant, *Dialect Map of Scotland*, Edinburgh: Edinburgh University Press, 1971, p. 11.

[5] David Daiches, *Robert Burns*, New York: Reinehart, 1950, p. 159.

[6] See David Daiches 'Eighteenth Century Vernacular Poetry', cit., p. 157.

[7] See André Bonnard, *La civiltà greca*, Milano: Garzanti, 1961, p. 674.

[8] *Ibidem*, p. 671.

[9] According to Rayner Unwin (*The Rural Muse: Studies in the Peasant Poetry of England*, London: Allen and Unwin, 1954, p. 150): 'The Scottish writers, under Allan Ramsay, then as always were pursuing an independent course'.

[10] Basil Willey, *La Cultura inglese del Seicento e del Settecento*, Bologna: Il Mulino, 1975, p. 92; italian edition of *The Seventeenth Century Background: Studies in the Thought of the Age in Relation to Poetry and Religion*, London: Chatto and Windus, 1934 and *The Eighteenth Century Background: Studies on the Idea of Nature in the Thought of the Period*, London: Chatto and Windus, 1940.

[11] Quoted by Basil Willey, *op. cit.*, p. 328.

[12] Lytton Strachey, *Spectatorial Essays*, London: Chatto and Windus, 1964, p. 78 (The quotation is taken from the essay 'The Pastoral', 1906).

[13] See Rayner Unwin, *op. cit.*, p. 29.

[14] 'Peggy, now the King's come', 'By the Delicious Warmness of the Month', 'Jocky said to Jenny' and 'My Patie is a Lover Gay'.

FRANCO BUFFONI

Robert Fergusson [1]

Robert Fergusson was born on 5 September 1750 in Cap-and-Feather Close in the district of Edinburgh; he was the second son of William Fergusson, a modest clerk, and of Elizabeth Forbes, both born in the county of Aberdeen. Between 1758 and 1762 Robert studied at Edinburgh Secondary School but even then his bad health forbade him from attending regularly. He went on to the Grammar School in Dundee thanks to a scholarship which was renewed in 1764 for four more years at St. Andrews University. At St. Andrews the young Robert completed his first poetic experiments: for the most part satirical verses – many of which in the Scottish language – aimed at teachers and classmates. Of these we have still 'The Elegy on the Death of Mr David Gregory', a mathematics teacher. Belonging to this period are also compositions of a scholastic nature, as the Scottish version of 'Ode XI' of Horatio.

The standard of life at St. Andrews was rather poor but culturally stimulating. Robert was considered a 'light-hearted prankster' for the vivacity of his spirit and, above all, for the 'witty verse-satires' already mentioned. His favourite readings were Latin, English and Scottish poetry. All the biographers underline 'his electrifying a college congregation by his conduct'.[2] We are reminded of 'his masquerading, Sganarelle-like, as a doctor, and prescribing for patients'[3] and 'that Robert Fergusson and some others, who had appeared the most active' during a 'scuffle', 'were expelled'.[4] These characteristics would not be so worthy of mention if they did not appear so much in contrast with the career to which, in his early adolescence, the poet had been destined. It had, in fact, been decided 'to train him for the Ministry'.[5]

The Secondary School he attended in Edinburgh was actually a *seminary*. With the passing of time, however, 'his inborn Bohemianism'[6] surfaced forcefully, together with an actual rebellion towards any form of imposition: 'So it seems that the notion of a clerical career', concludes Sir George Douglas, 'came tacitly to be dropped'.[7] Fergusson, as many Scotsmen of the eighteenth century – and in reference to the poets, we can mention Robert Burns and Campbell –, was Jacobite and nationalist at the same time. Thus, while on the one hand he tended to 'celebrate' and idealize the Scottish heroes (like Wallace), with the intention of stimulating his fellow countrymen to rebellion against the Act of Union, on the other hand he did not hesitate to lament the fall of the Stuarts.[8]

At the expiration of the scholarship, Fergusson left St. Andrews (May 1768) and returned to Edinburgh, where he had to seek employment to support his mother and sister. His qualification was 'Copyst of legal documents' for the Commissary Office (a government legal office). This poorly paid and unsatisfying activity was the only employment he held on a regular basis. However, he did not lose the habit acquired at St. Andrews and continued writing poems, especially pastorals, elegies and *burlesques.*

In 1771 eight compositions in 'neo-classical English' appeared in the *Weekly Magazine.* Among these can also be found the pastorals 'Morning, Noon and Night' that make up the best of his production at the time. In January, 1772, Fergusson published the first poem in Scottish, 'The Daft-Days', which was followed in the same year by eight more compositions in vernacular. The poet, however, did not abandon immediately his production in English; in fact, seventeen poems, which were imitative in nature and composed in English, appeared in the same year in the *Weekly Magazine.* The fame which he encountered did not assure him financial security, thus he was forced to continue working in order to live. He often found himself suddenly interrupting his work, in the throes of inspiration, and jotting down a few verses, at times a whole poem.

The immediacy of the inspiration manifested itself particularly in a genre which is typical enough of Scottish poetry: the epigram. The story goes that once, rushing back towards his office, he observed the young helper of the bookseller Sommers earnestly reading a poem on creation. Robert recited these verses on the spur of the moment:

Tom Sommers is a gloomy man,
His soul is dark with sin;
O holy J... s glaze his soul
That light may enter in.[9]

To justify Fergusson's poetic ardor we must consider the extreme importance that poetry had at that time in Scotland on all levels: from the popular ballad to verse satire, from euologistic poetry to poetry of elite.

Although retaining his position within the same administration, for a few months Fergusson worked in a different office: the Sheriff-clerk's office. This bit of information that biographers often neglect is, in reality, very important for the influence that this experience had on his formation and, consequently, on his artistic activity. As a matter of fact, particularly in the poems in Scottish there are frequent polemic attacks against the police, the prefecture, the city administration. More than anything else, Fergusson rebels against the often violent methods of the police officers and the criteria used for maintaining public order. His 'anger' was partly a result of what he saw happen every day in his office. All types of individuals passed through: alcoholics, disturbers of the peace, petty thieves, prostitutes.

In 'The Daft-Days' the poet defines the City Guard, which acted as a military police force, as 'that black banditti'. Besides Fergusson's opinion, which may be partial, other sources testify that in the second half of the eighteenth century arbitrary and excessive use of force by law enforcers was more or less frequent in Edinburgh. The police were, therefore, disliked by the people; they were both feared and ridiculed. Fergusson harbored a veritable aversion towards them. In another poem written in vernacular, 'The King's Birth-Day in Edinburgh', the poet indulges in the description of the mockeries, the jests, and even the stone and rubbish throwing that the men of the City Guard became the objects of as they marched in their bright uniforms. The clash between the two Fergussonian worlds, that of reality, of social injustices, of work, and that of fantasy, of friends, of poetry, the one frustrating, the other exalting, was always very violent. 'His song', says Sir George Douglas, 'remained the captive lark's'.[10]

Within a few months of that same year, 1772, Fergusson was

acclaimed new Scottish national poet. Considering the period and the conditions, his success was truly extraordinary. In October he was admitted to the Cape Club.[11] 'Is Allan risen frae the deid?', was what the men of letters of Edinburgh wondered, remembering the success of Allan Ramsay. In January of the following year, Fergusson published a small volume of poems of which nine were written in Scottish. The publication marked the summit of his career. In any event, 'to live of poetry was for him, of course, out of the question'.[12] Later, in the same year, 'Auld Reikie' appeared together with sixteen poems in Scottish and twelve in English, all in the *Weekly Magazine*. It was also a period of intense social and mundane activity, especially with the Cape Club.

In the meantime, Robert Fergusson's health kept declining, in spite of his young age. In October the seriousness of the mental and physical exhaustion manifested itself completely and the poet was forced to leave his employ at the Commissary Office before the end of the year, thus throwing the family into a state of misery.

There is an anecdote that helps to clarify the man's character and the drama that befell him. As we know, Robert often exceeded in drinking and it often happened that he would end the evening drunk in some tavern. One night someone reproached him for his vice, trying to make him understand that he would ruin himself if he continued along that path. The poet, with dazzled eye, glass in hand, exploded with a shout: 'Anything to forget my mother!' That 'anything' Robert found in madness. But his was not total madness; he had intense moments of lucidness, then folly would return to assist him. In 1774, in a Scottish mental institution prison, a twenty-four-year-old malnourished and delirious poet died. It is not an overstatement to say that Fergusson had 'the saddest fate recorded in Scottish letters'.[13]

Yet, in 1772 he had become one of the most important figures in Edinburgh thanks not only to his penmanship, but also to his versatility. He possessed very affable manners; he was lively, loquacious and of pleasing aspect; his conversation was that of the gentleman and scholar. He was the animator of any convivial reunion, so much so that he was nicknamed *Sir Precentor.* Fergusson was blinded by his success in society and he was not able to comprehend to what extent this could damage him. As

Burns afterwards, Fergusson did not understand that the society of
Edinburgh was ruthlessly exploiting him. Consequently, we see the
gay and mocking image of Fergusson take shape, the *Sir Precentor*
of social occasions. A *mask* that we also encounter in the poems. If
we were to define him in a few words as a poet, we could say he
was an extremely acute, almost detailed, observer of objective reality, but also capable of capturing subjective and, at times, very
emotional images. Where else could he exercise this great quality
of his of observer of men and objects if not in the streets of the
city? The street is the prime element and motor of Fergussonian
poetics, the street with its distractions, its miseries, its pain, perhaps even its pleasures. The street and public places, the taverns,
the clubs, the brothels: and all these events were chaotic, impetu-
ous. Reflection, recollection and, therefore, poetry, so alive, immediate, spontaneous; this was the direct consequence.[14] Still today,
in Princess Street, the reader of Fergusson cannot help but rediscover the spirit. Douglas rightly says: 'The impression produced by
reading his best-known poems is very much that of walking in a
crowded thoroughfare with a sprightly, malicious companion on
one's arm, whispering remarks'.[15] Fergusson assumes, therefore, a
critical stance, at times veiled, often ruthless, but always permeated
with sympathy for the object of his attention and, thus, of his poetic narration. Besides, his irony rarely degenerates into base satire.
This is why Fergusson remains 'the gayest'[16] of the Scottish poets,
even if his tragic end sheds a sombre light over his figure.

The poet was buried in the Canongate Churchyard in
Edinburgh. The grave of a poor man, without inscription. Thirteen
years passed before someone 'worthy' enough, disturbed by the
carelessness with which his remains were treated, decided to inter-
vene. That 'worthy' person was Robert Burns. He visited the grave
and forwarded a petition[17] to the municipality of Edinburgh that he
be permitted to privately erect a 'stone' over Fergusson's grave. On
the grave Burns had the following words engraved:

> No sculptur'd marble here, nor pompous lay,
> No storied urn nor animated bust,
> This simple stone directs pale Scotia's way,
> To pour her sorrows o'er her Poet's dust.

If it is not difficult to discern in the figure of Robert Fergusson the traits of the preromantic hero that so much literature has provided us with; in him we may also recognize the pride of Scotland. Not in the sense that Scotland has been or is particularly proud of him (the Establishment always seeks out those it favors from among less disturbing, more flexible figures: in Scotland, for example, Ramsay has always been the more 'celebrated' of the two), but in the sense that we may see the pride of the people of Scotland in him.

The years of poetic activity were two: 1772-1773. His abilities revealed themselves almost by surprise. Still in 1771, in fact, Fergusson's production (poems of his appeared regularly in the *Weekly Magazine*) was of modest level. More than anything else, it consisted of imitations of Shenstone.[18] Then, with 'The Daft-Days',[19] began the grand season: thirty-one very brisk poems in the Scottish language that were to have so much impact on Robert Burns.

In Robert Fergusson's work it is possible to trace clearly-defined themes that emerge more or less explicitly in many compositions. All together they form a complete picture of the interests of the poet. Two biographical elements that had a determining influence on his formation – poverty and poor health – appear in a fragmentary and rather elusive manner in his work for the reason that Fergusson shied away from any form of self-pity. It is possible, however, to discover the essence of them. A joking epigram may at times be more revealing than an entire poem. This is the feeling evoked when considering 'On the Author's Intention of Going to Sea':

Fortune and Bob, e'er since his birth,
Could never yet agree;
She fairly kicked him from the earth,
To try his fate at sea.[20]

'Fortune and Bob'... 'Fortune' is the expression behind which Fergusson normally hides his personal dilemma, the autobiographical revelations. Actually, there are two more explicit compositions in this respect and, for this reason, at least in appearance, less desperate, more sarcastic: 'My last Will' and 'Codicil to Robert Fergusson's Last Will'. In them the author mentions with tact and sense of humour the beneficiaries of his 'inexistent' fortune. In the same manner, the terror of death appears explicitly in only one work: 'Auld Reikie', and even there it is well concealed by a desperate sarcasm.

Fergusson dedicated neither a short sonnet nor a composition of manners or in the vernacular to a woman. Like the sea or ancient traditions or whisky, the poet considers girls as part of the array of 'things' that make life pleasant. Nothing more. However, the references to women seen as a symbol of beauty are full of energy and enthusiasm. On the other hand, Fergusson often adopts an objective position, registering the pleasures of others: the girls and boys that seek one another and spend the holiday afternoon together ('the joes and lasses loe to frisk it') are a recurrent image in many poems. And he is a very acute observer of the movements of the girls ('Some [girls] tak a great delight to place the modest bon-grace owre the face'). Generally, it is the woman-as-object that has the upper hand, the woman that can be compared with or exchanged for other 'pleasures' (food, company, drink...); not to mention the woman who makes 'whoredom her trade' and 'vice her end'. When the poet has to give an account of how evenings are spent in Edinburgh, he exclaims: 'Now, some [men] to porter, some to punch – Some to their wife, and some their wench, retire'. The wife, the girl-friend, the lover, the tavern or the club.

Only one female figure differs significantly from the others. In 'Auld Reikie', speaking of the flowers in the market scene, Fergusson designates their most worthy function: to adorn the breasts of girls. In that occasion he mentions a girl: Mary. But the reader understands that it is a symbolic name. Mary has the exclusive function of representing all young and beautiful women. Immediately after, the poet returns to his generalizations.

The young poet manifests deeper constancy in his expressions of civic love and respect for tradition. These expressions are almost always set in opposition to the indifference and corruption of the municipal administration and of rulers in general, and they stand as solemn admonition, conferring to the author an aura almost of poet-prophet. The most complete attack against the administrators and the most forceful exhaltation of the greatness of Scotland appear in the XXII stanza of 'Auld Reikie' ('Let me to Arthur's Seat pursue/Lamenting what auld Scotland knew'). But Fergusson's accusations are more effective when they refer to particular arguments such as, for example, the discontinuation of the restructuring of a bridge (the famous 'North Bridge'), the exploitation of the funds for orphanages (in 'The Ghaists'). In such occasions his criticism is steadfast and socially advanced in concept, and these verses place him in the foreground of eighteenth century criticism of exploitation.

Where Fergusson appears weaker in the eyes of the modern reader is in his chauvinism, in his extreme nationalism, that brings him to harshly condemn foreign forms and modes of expression as, for example, Italian music ('Banish vile Italian Tricks!' in 'The Daft-Days'; 'Sounds fresh sprung frae Italy, a bastard breed' in 'The Elegy on the Death of Scots Music'),[21] foreign drinks, such as Cognac or Champagne ('Braw days for you, whan fools, newfangle fain, like ither countries better than their ain', in 'A Drink Eclogue'), and even voyages abroad ('Lord kens how awa! At Italy, or Well o'Spa, or to Montpelier's safter air', 'the Arno and the Tiber lang', in 'Hame Content'). These attacks are, in reality, less base than they may appear since they not only show scorn for everything foreign, but they also entail the praise of Scottish values and customs. The poet opposes the ancient dances of the Highlands to Italian music, Whisky to Cognac, sojourns in the Scottish countryside to voyages abroad. Besides, Fergusson was preceded by Ramsay and succeeded by Burns along the same line of defense of traditional values.

Fergusson, however, is also a satirical poet and, thereby, his attacks often result in mockery; in 'Auld Reikie', for example, the object of his discontent is the stench that fills the morning air in Edinburgh due to the lack of an adequate sewage system. But the purest and most significant verses remain those that exhalt the idea of freedom and national independence against English domination. The image given us is, therefore, on the whole that of a young man endowed with great patriotic love and extreme civic dignity.

Dignity, modesty, consciousness of his limitations, all these emerge as essential elements in Fergusson, also in relationship to his manner of 'being a poet'. Several verse epistles are undeniable proof of this. It was customary among devotees of verse to address poems of praise, of encomium, of encouragement to the established poet through newspapers or magazines. Fergusson, too, indulged in this custom on several occasions. In 1772 a certain Mr. J.S. exalted him as the heir and custodian of poetic tradition; Fergusson replied kindly, but also with sincere firmness: 'Awa', ye wylie fleetchin fallow' ('Away, you wily flattering fellow') and, also trying not to offend the writer, he defined his praises as 'butter'd words'. With a modesty that likens him to Burns (Ramsay, on the other hand, was immune enough to this), Fergusson defines himself a simple artisan of verse and, above all, an ordinary man of letters who subjects himself daily to a 'weary practice' in order to be worthy of the name of poet. Considering the enormous success he obtained in a very short time span and his young age, we can justify the insistence on the term dignity in defining the character of the artist.

The close tie between Fergusson and the world of taverns and clubs requires special attention because the image we obtain in observing his work is that of a Rabelaisian Fergusson, an epicurean; and this is the image that critics and biographers put greater emphasis on.[22] There is reason for this because we can say that Fergusson did all he could to be remembered in this manner:

Hear, O ye host of Epicurus! Hear!
To you I consecrate the sond adventurous![23]

Undoubtedly, there exists a fundamental truth behind this *mask*. If we consider Fergusson's character and vicissitudes more carefully, we begin to suspect that verses like the ones just quoted show us only the falser, albeit the more noticeable, aspect of the poet. Equally frequent are 'confessions' such as this:

Then, come and gie's the tither blaw
O' reaming ale,
Mair precious than the Well o' Spa,
Our hearts to heal   (from 'The Daft-Days')

Come hostesses and pour us so much more beer, more precious than spring water to silence the hearts. To drown the drama and anguish of all kind. A desperate existential drama that manifests itself in a relentless search for oblivion through alcohol and sex. In spite of this, Fergusson remains the poet 'attracted by the magic of the bowl',[24] the exalter *par excellence* of whisky and of hearty eating.

Fergusson also remains the poet of solitude and meditation; the young man who had instinctively understood the illusory nature of ambitions and how human evils derive from conceit and pride. This is a less known aspect of his personality, but certainly not less worthy of consideration. The 'dissipated' poet also wrote that on a sunny day a young swan with coaxing voice told him:

Ye, who to wisdom would devote your hours,
And far from riot, far from discord stray!
Look back disdainful on the city's towers,
Where Pride, where Folly, point the slippery way.[25]

The 'dissipated' poet wrote grandiose praises to nature, to contemplative life, to meditation ('Meditation! Sweeter than shady groves in Summer's pride!'); he sought with all his might – although constitutionally incapable of attaining it – peace of mind ('Let me to Arthur's seat pursue, Whare bonny pastures meet the view'); he was able to find powerful moral imperatives from the careful observation of nature. Fergusson is certainly contradictory, but he is aware of this and honest enough to admit it. It is out of the question that he dedicated himself to certain themes simply because the pastoral genre was popular. He is against materialism, he is scourger of men's habits, and he is two centuries ahead of his time for certain ideas related to consumerism:

Ye sages, tell! Was man e'er made
To dree this hatefu' sluggard trade,
Steekit frae Nature's brauties a'
That daily on his presence ca',
At hame to grin, and whinge, and pine
For favourite dishes, favourite wine?[26]

Recognized as 'citizen' poet *par excellence*, Fergusson knew and loved nature in all its manifestations, and he shouted his ferocious protest against all those who, even at the time, betrayed it. Pagan, in the most classical and intimate sense, he bows down to adore its essence, 'the winsome flowers frae Nature's lap'.[27]

The dissipated poet who dedicates himself to the pleasures of

the night also knows how to seek out its most delicate and spiritual aspects, as well as its tenebrous, ghostly fascination and Biblical
reminiscences of punishment. He loves tradition for its purity, irra-
tionality, naturalness, and spontaneousness; he hates meaningless
rites, defining them as hypocritical, superstitious, or 'religious'. His
attitude towards religious hypocrisy is courageous and in advance
of the times. For this reason he praises the life of the farmers (in
'The Farmer's Ingle') and violently condemns ancient rites transported to the city and clothed with middle-class falseness ('Auld Reikie',
stanza XV).

   To change this world, and then to change the world transformed, and rediscover the primeval, uncorrupted essence. The
essence that Fergusson virtually shows that he possesses, thanks to
nature and philosophic intelligence. So, his attitude towards the
city and its citizens is one of love and hate; it continually portrays
the cyclical alternation: hope-frustration, dream-disillusionment.
Even when it seems that he participates in the 'new rites' of the
city, he is, in reality, far away in search of the hypothetical
absolute.

   Nonetheless, Fergusson is a careful, scrupulous observer of city
life. There is no social allegory or characteristic personality that
escapes his analysis. An analysis that proceeds with simplicity from
compositions that we may define as 'partial' (because mirrors of
particular moments of the life of the city: 'The Daft-Days', 'Hallow
Fair', 'The King's Birthday', 'Leith Races') to the 'summa' poem
'Auld Reikie', which includes every aspect of the activity of the
capital. All these poems together make up a picture of the time
and place whose vivacity and wit was equalled but not surpassed by
Burns. Fergusson transmits the essence of every type of manifestation
with very elastic language, from solemn civil and military ceremonies
to the most corrupt sides of night life.[28] What strikes us most is his
ability to adhere emotionally to the subject of his narration. At
times this adherence is elegantly implied, and the reader can
understand intuitively the poet's feelings of pity, indignation,
understanding or sympathy only thanks to the grace with which
the various sketches are presented, whatever their content.
Fergusson's attitude is naturalistic. Everything men do, say, think or
hide is dictated by an interior motive that is always worthy of

being analyzed. Why hide the most revolting, basest behavior? Just as heroic or generous actions, these, too, are 'human'. Therefore, they have a cause and, possibly, an end. The end is absurd, the cause remote? Deep within him, man is always without guilt.

Naturally, his sympathy goes to the humble, simple people, the exploited (the fisher wives, the burden-bearers, the barefoot housemaids). His attention lingers on simple, daily 'rituals'. He condemns the arrogance of the rich. He mentions high-class public places, but reserves his enthusiasm for the taverns inhabited by violent characters reminiscent of Hugo. He enlivens the features of the landladies, but winks at the young maids. Pompous barristers do not escape his analysis, nor do merchants, whose frauds he does not hesitate to reveal, or the police, with whom he does not harbor good relations; but he dedicates verse upon verse to 'errand-boys', to drivers, to sedan-chair bearers. The reader is, thus, introduced into the fast-paced, unveiled life of a northern capital in the second half of the eighteenth century: the Edinburgh of alleys and slums, smelling and swarming; the Edinburgh of marketplaces, of fairs, of commerce and cultural activities; the elegant city of Princess Street, of the walks to the castle, of horse races... it all seems to want to erupt from the verses of 'its' poet. Perhaps it is sad to think that the monument in Princess Street was erected only to the memory of Ramsay, or that only Burns is considered the 'poet' of Scotland.

Of the thirty-one brisk poems written in the Scottish language, and that would have so much influence on Robert Burns, 'Auld Reikie' is unanimously recognized as the masterpiece. 'Auld Reikie' is the name with which the Scottish affectionately refer to Edinburgh. 'Auld' means old, 'reikie' means smoky (from 'reik', smoke). Therefore, the old smoky lady. Fergusson completed the work in the autumn of 1773, a few months before his collapse. It is the last of his poems, and also the longest and most ambitious. An original poem, not only within the Scottish literary context, but also in British literature. 'Auld Reikie' is not actually a poem, particularly for its ample and heterogenous contents. It represents a complete picture, not only as representation of a city, but also as interesting mirror of the Fergussonian 'truths' in all their splendor.

Fergusson is always alone in his relationship with the city; he avoids mentioning himself as much as possible. And when he does, he resorts to stratagems such as *the writer* or *the poet*, as if a sort of modesty restrains him. The continuous changes of mood, of tone, and even of theme – in certain strident passages – denote the intention, perhaps not entirely conscious, of not going completely all the way, of not wanting to erase the quality of the sketch, almost as if the author feared losing his poetic power if he pushed certain analyses or certain attacks too far (like he does in the final attack against the municipality).

The initial theme is very simple: when winter comes, Auld Reikie is the only refuge; when nature betrays man, Edinburgh offers him welcoming places where he can drink and converse and enjoy the pleasures of life. However, there is a greater rhythmic elasticity with respect to many previous works, a greater mastering of the verse and of the images. How much looser, in relation to the corresponding passage in 'The Daft-Days', appears the description of nature in decline, which finds its emblem in the disappearance of the sweet song of the bird:

And now frae nouther bush nor brier
The spreckled mavis greets your ear;
Nor bonny blackbird skims and roves
To seek his live in yonder groves.

The limitation, so to speak, of the work is perhaps a certain fragmentary quality in its layout. The various parts have great value if taken separately, but taken as a whole they lack an organic nature. Naturally, there is always the common denominator of the city or the inhabitants, but at times this does not seem sufficient. The poet, perhaps, saw himself submerged by various sketches of Edinburgh life and he decided to enclose them in a single work. In any case, the fact that we can read and appreciate any single part disregarding the rest may also be seen as a quality.

Once we have considered the first fifty verses we become aware of an interesting characteristic: compared to other works like 'Hallow Fair'[29] and 'The Daft-Days', Fergusson's language in 'Auld Reikie' contains a very limited number of vernacular expressions, as if in this last work the poet had undergone an involution; as if, in other words, although remaining faithful to the theme (or themes)

of dialectal poetry (Edinburgh, the people of Edinburgh), he tended to return to English versification. We observe, however, that in
the work Fergusson does make abundant use of dialectal expressions when he deals with certain themes (for example, in stanza
XVII, the market). We could desume, from this, that his familiarity
with the two 'languages' and with versification in general allowed
him to disregard any division between English language poetry
and dialectal poetry. At this point he was only interested in saying
certain things, in communicating certain impressions in the most
efficacious manner, making use of the instrument – the type of language – that at the moment appeared to him most proper for his
purpose. We may add that he was aided in this by the 'tetrameter
couplet' that, among the various forms of meter Fergusson
employed, remains the one that reveals him most powerfully.

In reality, Robert Fergusson's 'mother tongue' was not Scottish
vernacular. First of all, as is also true for Ramsay, there is not just
one Scottish vernacular, but dozens, and they all have more or less
marked differences one from the other. Whereas Burns formed his
dialectal rhythmic movements solely on the basis of the Ayrshire
phonemes, Fergusson absorbed different popular ways of speaking. 'He had North-East family ties, holidayed in Aberdeenshire,
studied in Fife, lived in contact with the Lothians and Borders, and
mingled with Highland police and chairmen, Edinburgh cadies and
the wits and roughs of the city'.[30] Furthermore, since childhood the
poet received a strict classical education in the English language.
Thus, all of his cultural, scientific and moral 'discoveries' (from the
reading of the Bible to mathematical and philosophic speculation)
took place outside the vernacular. The composition of poems in
dialect acquires, therefore, the characteristics of a courageous cultural operation. Henderson observes: 'Fergusson had a subtler
knowledge of vernacular Scots than Burns – or rather his Scots was
the Scots not of the rustic but of the educated classes'.[31] If we
briefly reflect on the classical distinction between popular poetry
and dialectal poetry, we can state that Fergusson set off from the
former (the reading of the Ballatyne, Maitland, Watson and Ramsay
collections) to arrive at the latter. We can notice a passage, a
change in Fergusson: from the popular song to the dialectal song,
from immediacy to elaboration, from his first becoming a poet by

instinct to the creation of a philosophy of life (that could be expressed efficaciously also by making use of expressions from the vernacular vocabulary).

'It is not in a poet's nature to confine himself to pure dialect, for metrical writing demands an extensive and elastic vocabulary which dialect is unlikely to yield'. This affirmation by A.D. Mackie[32] has been proven true precisely by the Scottish poet who has been pointed out by many critics as the heir (otherwise we would have to mention Stevenson) of Fergusson: Robert Garioch. When asked why, in his opinion, Fergusson fused together within the same composition – but also within the same stanza and within the same verse – vernacular and English expressions and words, Garioch answered: 'I myself have attempted many times – I say myself because Fergusson certainly underwent the same suffering – not to "contaminate" certain compositions of mine with words not belonging to the vernacular. I must say that I have given up: I remember, the last time I needed the dialectal word corresponding with the adjective "private"; well, it does not exist in our vernacular'. Fergusson's so-called poems in vernacular are, therefore, actually written in a hybrid Anglo-Scottish. Let's consider three ordinary verses from an ordinary composition: 'Mourn ilka nymph and ilka sawin,/Ilk sunny hill and dowie glen;/Let weeping streams and Naiads drain their fountain head';[33] we can see how the poet makes use of English not only where there is no dialectal term (nymph, Naiads), but also to obtain a more effective syntactical result ('Let weeping streams...') or for rhythmic purposes ('Their fountain head'). From this we can deduce that, owing to the fact that the vernacular is limited, Fergusson – just as Ramsay before him and Burns after – had at his disposal a greater number of words, of syntactic and rhythmic solutions than any other English poet. The worthy use he made of so much 'abundance' totally justifies, in any case, the artifice inherent in the process.

Fergusson mixed 'his' dialects freely to give greater elasticity to the verses. Folk, for example, is expressed with 'fouk' (in use in northern Scotland), but also with 'fock', typical of the Lowlands. 'Nae', in place of 'not' after the verb (negation form of the Highlands) is frequent enough; so also 'no', contraction of the ancient 'nocht' in use among the Lothians. Furthermore, there have been numerous changes even within the same dialects in the course of two centuries. 'Skelf for shelf and skair for share are two words Fergusson uses which would nowadays be considered Northern'. These forms, however, Mackie suggests, 'may have been lingering on in the South in his time'.[34] At times the poet chooses a term from the vocabulary of a particular dialect in order to better define a given character. Consequently, it is clear that precise rules of pronunciation cannot be indicated.

A basic rule which we can adhere to is suggested by Fergusson's adoption of English spelling even for Scottish words (a method also employed by Ramsay). When the spelling of a word is the same in the two languages, we must remember that Fergusson, although adhering to the English spelling, suggests the Scottish pronunciation. In this manner, 'creature' rhymes with 'nature', but we must read 'craitur' and 'naitur'; 'shoulder' rhymes with 'powder' (pr. 'Shoother' and 'poother'), 'ground' with 'wind' ('grund' and 'wund') and so on. 'Spelt as English, with apostrophes where necessary, the words are recognised with more facility by those more accustomed to reading English. It is in this spirit of meeting the reader half-way', Mackie acutely observes, 'that owre becomes o'er'.[35]

For obvious reasons of rhyme, at times, however, the poet resorts to the English spelling and pronunciation of words. So we find the English 'clay' instead of the Scottish 'cley' (pr. Clai) in order to rhyme with 'they'; 'too' that rhymes with 'mou' (in Scottish, on the other hand, we would have 'tae' and 'moo'). As we have already seen, thanks to such 'licences', Fergusson's rhythmic possibilities (but also those of Ramsay and Burns, we must add) were nearly unlimited. Only more recent criticism (David Daiches, Alan MacLaine) seems to recognize in Fergusson those artistic and human qualities that traditional criticism had underestimated for decades. From Angellier to Ritter, from Chambers to Meyerfield, nineteenth-century criticism tended, almost unanimously, to consider Fergusson in a rather negative light. We must remember that, differently from Ramsay, Fergusson was too disturbing a figure, morally speaking, for certain Victorian, and not only Victorian, pruderies. Too disturbing a figure to be recognized for what he was: an innovator with ingenious intuitions that he was able to put into practice completely. Fergusson used every type of meter existing in previous Scottish poetry, but never passively: he always added a personal touch; arriving, at times, at actual 'inventions', thus paving the way for Burns.

NOTES

[1] Summarized and translated from: Franco Buffoni, *Ramsay e Fergusson: Precursori di Burns*, Milano: Guerini, 1992. Summarized and translated by Nello Quattrociocchi.

[2] Sir George Douglas, *Scottish Poetry: Drummond of Hawthornden to Fergusson*, Glasgow: J. Maclehose and Sons, 1911, p. 165.

[3] *Ibidem*, p. 166.

[4] Alexander Peterkin, *The Works of Robert Fergusson*, London: Printed for S.A. & H. Oddy, 1807, pp. 19-20.

[5] See Sir George Douglas, *op. cit.*, p. 167.

[6] *Ibidem*, p. 168.

[7] *Ibidem*, p. 167.

[8] 'Fergusson's was a disappointed nationalism, and (as often in Scotland since the Stuart cause ceased to be an actual political danger) it took the form of romantic jacobitism. Though scarcely a defeatist, Fergusson was culturally and politically on the defensive, and (if only because the dividing line between national and foreign could no longer be taken completely for granted) highly suspicious of foreign influences'. See Kurt Wittig, *The Scottish Tradition in Literature*, Edinburgh: Oliver & Boyd, 1958, p. 177.

[9] See *The Works of Robert Fergusson*, edited by A. & H. Oddy, London: s.i.c., 1807. Hereafter cited for all quotations from Fergusson's works. See p. 257 for this quotation.

[10] See Sir George Douglas, *op. cit.*, p. 169.

[11] The members of the club had defined themselves as The Knights Companions of the Cape. Members of the new group were, among others, the painters Alexander Runciman and Alexander Nasmyth, the authors Thomas Lancashire (to whom Fergusson dedicated an epitaph) and William Woods, the critic James Sibbald and the musician Stephen Clarke.

[12] See Sir George Douglas, *op. cit.*, p. 170.

[13] *Ibidem*, p. 173.

[14] The rhythm of Fergusson's poetry is the rhythm of ancient dances, an unique expression of an *ars dramatica* of remote, pre-christian origins that in Fergusson's time survived in the folk festival, in the fairs, in the rustic holidays of which even today there are traces especially in the north-western part of the Highlands. 'Even those poems of Fergusson which do not specifically describe and celebrate feasts, fairs and holidays', observes John Speirs, 'still carry in their rhythm the original impulse of the dance'.

[15] See Sir George Douglas, *op. cit.*, p. 176.

[16] *Ibidem*, p. 162.

[17] Robert Burns addressed 'Hon.ble The Bailies of the Canongate, Edinburgh' in the following manner: 'Gentlemen, I am sorry to be told that [...] I petition you then, Gentlemen, for your permission to lay a simple stone over his revered ashes, to remain an unalienable property to his deathless fame'. Edinburgh – 6th Feb. 1787. *The Letters of Robert Burns*, edited by J. de L. Ferguson, Oxford: Oxford University Press, 1931, I, p. 72.

[18] William Shenstone (1714-1763), author of pastorals, ballads, songs, elegies. Notable are 'The Landskip, Written at an Inn at Hanley' and a pastoral ballad in fourteen stanzas subdivided in two sections, 'Absence and Hope'.

[19] Published in January 1772, it is the first poem in vernacular by Fergusson: The Daft Days are the days between Christmas and New Year.

[20] See *The Works of Robert Fergusson*, cit., p. 214.

[21] 'The Elegy on the Death of Scots Music' belongs to the genre of the burlesque elegy that had much fortune with Burns (Poor Mailie's Elegy...). Introduced into Scottish literature by Robert Semple (or Sempill) (1595 ca.–1660 ca.) with the poem 'The Piper of Kilbarchan', the genre was continued by Ramsay with 'The Elegy on Lucky Wood' and 'The Elegy on John Cowper'. Other Fergussonian burlesque elegies are 'The Elegy on the Death of Mr David Gregory' and 'Elegy on John Hogg'.

[22] 'For social life, he possessed an amazing variety of qualifications. With the best good-nature, and a great degree of modesty, he was always sprightly, always entertaining. His powers of song were great in a double capacity. When seated, with some select companions, over a friendly bowl, his wit flashed like lightening, struck the hearers irresistibly, and set the table in a roar. But alas! These engaging, nay, bewitching qualities proved fatal to their owner, and shortened the period of his rational experience'. From *The Edinburgh Weekly*

Register, October 1774.

23 From 'Good Eating'. See *The Works of Robert Fergusson*, cit., p. 171.

24 From 'A Tavern Elegy'.

25 From 'Retirement', in *The Works of Robert Fergusson*, cit., p. 115.

26 From 'Hame Content', in *The Works of Robert Fergusson*, cit., p. 356.

27 From 'Ode to the Bee', in *The Works of Robert Fergusson*, cit., p. 20.

28 'Fergusson's main gift to Scots poetry was – or at least might have been – the contemporary and metropolitan character of his work. He was a man of the city, acutely aware of what went on around him and spontaneously writing down his experience with a new freedom from limitations. All his predecessors had been content, since Scots had become a vernacular, only to express in it the "hamely", humorous, mocking side of their nature. In his verse, Fergusson sought to express the wholeness of experience, and used Scots to emphasise its actuality'. See Kurt Wittig, *op. cit.*, p. 177.

29 Together with 'Auld Reikie' and 'The Daft-Days', 'Hallow Fair' is part of the trilogy of works dedicated expressly to the city and its inhabitants.

30 A.D. Mackie, *Fergusson's Language: Brid Scots Then and Now*, Edinburgh: Edinburgh University Press, 1952, p. 124.

31 T.F. Henderson, *Scottish Vernacular Literature*, London: David Nutt, 1900, p. 424.

32 See A.D. Mackie, *Fergusson's Language*, cit., p. 123.

33 See 'Elegy on the Death of Scots Music', in *The Works of Robert Fergusson*, cit., p. 250.

34 See A.D. Mackie, *Fergusson's Language*, cit., p. 137.

35 *Ibidem*, p. 134.

WILLIAM GILLIES

Traditional Gaelic Women's Songs

Present-day Gaelic singers and their audiences can mean different things when they refer to 'traditional' Gaelic songs. They may mean to suggest that a song is unpublished and owes its life entirely to oral transmission. Or they may mean that the song was composed and sung without reference to the musical intervals and pitch of the modern pianoforte, or to the regular rhythm of the 'educated' Western European musical tradition (as is the case with most contemporary compositions). Or again, 'traditional' can simply mean 'old', an imprecise term that could include compositions as recent as the late 19th-century songs of Mary MacPherson or the First World War songs of Domhnall Ruadh Chorùna (i.e. in contradistinction to songs by living bards and commemorating remembered individuals and occurrences); plus, of course, anything earlier than that.

These connotations of medium, style and age are all relevant to the body of songs to be discussed in the present essay. But to specify them completely we have to add a further ingredient: their metrical-musical form. For the metrical-musical units (or verses) of these songs, consisting of one or two lines of text combined with an often complex refrain, stand distinct from the four-line or longer stanzas of most Gaelic poetry. They constitute what has been termed a 'sub-literary' tradition of Gaelic song, in opposition to a 'literary' tradition which is more public and official in its connotations, and whose productions tend to be composed by named bards with identifiable patrons.[1] Whereas in the other branches of the literature women are very much in the minority, the sub-literary tradition of songs is quite the opposite. Although they are mostly anonymous, we are left in no doubt that they were composed by women, a perception which is borne out whenever the tradition does associate a composer's name with a song.[2]

A further distinctive feature of these songs raises the question of their function. As they have come down to us, they have an obvious affinity with labour songs, i.e. songs which were sung in conjunction with certain set activities. For a great number of them have survived as waulking songs, through the persistence in the Outer Hebrides, down to the twentieth century, of the hand-waulking of the home-made tweed cloth. This was a communal activity accompanied by songs.[3] Yet it is reasonably clear that the association between the songs and the waulking is in most cases not original, but something that happened subsequent to their composition. We shall have to return to this point.

For present purposes, then, we can talk about a recognisable body of old, mostly anonymous women's songs in Gaelic. The factors that unite them are partly formal, but partly based on their content, i.e. their tone and outlook and the political and social world and material culture that they consistently portray. It is sometimes said that their hey-day was in the seventeenth century: certainly it can hardly have been later than that.[4] They started to be gathered from oral recitation in the late nineteenth and twentieth century, having previously suffered neglect at the hands of the early collectors and anthologists, who saw them as being less valuable than the courtly ('bardic') poetry or the heroic lays.[5] They are perhaps most familiar nowadays amongst the recordings of such Hebridean singers as Kitty MacLeod, Joan Mackenzie and Flora MacNeill, and feature in some of the Scottish Tradition series issued by the School of Scottish Studies. In fact, they are perhaps more widely known nowadays than ever before, in an age which has more respect for richness and variety in musical performance – one of their principal glories – and is less inclined to grant automatic primacy to the text, where their relative lack of verbal complexity presumably caused them to suffer by comparison with the more polished genres and styles.

They may also claim to be of special interest to us today on the grounds that they offer a glimpse into the all too often suppressed world of women's literature, and to the frank, unbuttoned underworld of the 'Dionysian tendency', at an opposite extreme from the polite masculine virtues of the 'court' tradition of poetry, with its liability to succumb to over-elaboration and insincerity.

I propose in what follows to broach three important questions raised by the 'old songs':[6] 1. authorship, including relationships between the 'old songs' and the other genres of Gaelic poetry with which they co-existed; 2. literary quality, including claims that they are the most powerful and authentic voice of Gaelic poetry; and 3. their relationship with the 'women's world', including reference to the question whether they contain evidence for a distinct Gaelic women's aesthetic and mind-set. These brief discussions will lead to certain conclusions regarding the place of the 'old songs' in Gaelic literature and their value as literature. To anticipate, I shall show that they provide thought-provoking insights into the survival of oral Gaelic literature and into the effects of oral transmission on textual integrity; and they give breadth, depth, and life to the literature, including some convincing snatches of the elusive *vox feminea*.

We face a serious difficulty when investigating the authorship of the traditional song-poetry. Since these poems mostly remained orally preserved until relatively late, but seem genuinely to have been composed relatively early, they were vulnerable to the natural attrition of oral transmission, in this case exacerbated by political struggle, social disruption and linguistic change. There was ample opportunity for the authorship of a song to be lost if, for example, it survived only at a distance from the place where it was composed. Equally, authorship could be gained or altered, if an anonymous song or a song composed by an obscure poet came to be seen as typical of the work of a known poetic figure.[7]

When we turn to the 'old songs', some challenging questions are raised, as we would expect. The vast majority of them are simply *anonymous*, and the class as a whole has sometimes been differentiated by calling them the anonymous tradition of Gaelic poetry. Nevertheless, some songs are traditionally ascribed to named, or at least specified women, such 'the sister of Iain Garbh MacGille-Chaluim (of Raasay)', or 'Fraser of Reelig's daughter', or 'the wife of MacGregor of Glenstrae'. Things get more complicated, however, when we turn to the poetry ascribed to Mary MacLeod (Màiri nighean Alasdair Ruaidh), the long-lived poetess of the seventeenth-century MacLeod chiefs of Dunvegan. The songs ascribed to Mary include some which fall squarely within the literary (as opposed to the sub-literary) tradition. But her editor also included in the canon an item which, although ascribed to Mary in one source, belongs at least as securely with the sub-literary songs. Moreover, there is another composition traditionally ascribed to Mary which the editor excluded from the canon; and there are songs that are anonymous in the tradition, but in which the speaker refers to being exiled in a way that is strongly reminiscent of the exile in Scarba which the historical Mary MacLeod experienced at one point in her life.[8] And whereas there is every reason to believe that Mary Macleod existed, despite the lack of documentary references attesting to her existence, the same cannot be said about the mysterious 'Nic Iain Fhinn' and 'Nic a' Mhanaich', who are traditionally credited with the authorship of waulking songs which embodied a flyting between women from different clans or islands. They may well have been real persons, but are now no more than names in the tradition, or perhaps merely a cipher for a particular genre of poetry.[9] Our problem is brought to a fine point by the well-known waulking song 'Ailein Duinn, ó hì, shiùbhlainn leat' ('Brown-haired Allan, I would go with you'), which is ascribed in Hebridean oral tradition to an Annie Morrison of Scalpay, whose fiancé was drowned in 1786. This cannot be the whole story, since related texts contain material that clearly ante-dates that time.[10]

At all events, there is at least a thoroughly consistent assumption of women's authorship. Not only is this ubiquitous in the oral tradition that accompanies the songs, but it is overwhelmingly present in the internal evidence of the songs themselves: women speak to us. In this case the exceptions prove the rule. 'A' bhean iadach' ('The jealous woman'), in which the speaker is a dead woman, may worry us a little. And 'Cailin òg an stiùir thu mi' ('Young girl, will you steer me?') is clearly spoken by a man. But these are genuinely exceptional.[11]

These problems of authorship have led some Gaelic scholars to invoke the idea of 'folk' or 'communal' authorship, an explanation sometimes linked with suggestions of extempore composition. This was an understandable response to the carnivalesque atmosphere of the waulkings and the disjointed texts of the waulking songs. However, as our understanding of the dynamics of orality has progressed, scholars have tended to discard folk composition in general as an explanation for the genesis of popular songs and poetry. As to extempore composition, that clearly can occur in a wide range of contexts in oral literature – a Gaelic example would be verse-capping duels between rival poets – but it would be rash to assume it without question, in view of the widespread aspiration of poets to compose poetry that *appears* to be extempore.

Therefore, while acknowledging that the songs in question often have a 'weathered' feel to them, in the form of textual gaps and repetitions, and overlapping and variant versions, we need mostly, if not entirely, to associate this incoherence with the circumstances of their transmission rather than their composition. People do not usually compose incoherent and fragmentary poems in the first place. Also, we have to be clear that although waulking songs bulk large in the collections, this does not necessarily mean that they all originated as waulking songs. The proportion of waulking songs that actually refer to the waulking process is pretty small, considering the number of texts that have been collected. Mostly, they speak of anything but the waulking of the cloth.[12] And when we consider the pathos and sensibility glimpsed in so many of the waulking-songs, it is hard to see the actual waulking as a likely place for these qualities to have been brought to light.[13]

The explanation for this difficulty is not hard to find. Some songs are found both inside and outside the waulking tradition, i.e. in 'fast' versions sung with a thumping 'beat' corresponding to the practical need to get the cloth thoroughly waulked, and in slower versions in which speech rhythm and musical rhythm are more in harmony and less at war.[14] Very many of the waulking songs must have originated as lyrics independent of the waulking tradition, and been pressed into service subsequently as waulking songs. In circumstances that are now obscure, the waulking process has preserved old songs, but at the expense of adapting them to its practical needs. Therefore, when addressing questions of composition and authorship we must be prepared to regard the waulking songs as a special case, and not use them lightly as a basis for generalisation about women's traditional songs.

There are, in fact, many questions still to be addressed in relation to extemporisation. Thus, for instance, there is evidence in relation to the traditional keening of the dead to suggest that simple, strongly formulaic exclamations of grief were indeed 'extemporised' by keening women; and at the same time we seem to have evidence for women's laments which were contemporaneous with the loss of the deceased, but composed, rather than uttered.[15] Again, the question of extemporisation in the waulking songs has been recast in a more sophisticated and perhaps sustainable guise. For it has been suggested that, in the classic case where sequences of identical lines crop up as sections of two or more different songs, these groups of thematically related lines are themselves the units or building blocks which were slotted in *ad libitum* by extemporising singers. This explanation can help us to understand the reason for the 'kaleidoscope' effect which the waulking songs sometimes seem to present. But it cannot be the whole answer to the problem, since the songs have been fixed in their form, *non sequiturs* and all, for a considerable period of time. Yet it has a certain attraction, not least in its recognition that transmission is not simply a process of degeneration and decline.[16]

Occasionally, where the tradition is strongest and most settled and other factors are favourable, we may feel that we are in close contact with the circumstances of composition. Thus, the South Uist song 'A mhic Iain 'ic Sheumais' ('O son of John son of James') can be related very closely to an occurrence which took place in 1601. It is attributed to the foster-mother (*muime*) of Donald (son of John, son of James) MacDonald, who had been wounded while leading a counter-attack on a band of marauding MacLeods encamped at Carinish in North Uist. In this case documentary sources help us understand the politics, traditional North Uist accounts detail the course of the battle, and the song contains details which give an even more intimate glimpse of its subject's part in the action and in its aftermath.[17] For the majority of the traditional songs, however, we cannot be anything like so sure how close we are to real historical events and characters, and how literally we may take the traditional ascription and explanatory statement (*seanchas*) that – if we are lucky – accompanies such songs. For the waulking song texts, we may also have to allow for a wholly anonymous phase of aesthetic re-treading in the course of their importation into the waulking song tradition, and our gratefulness at receiving glimpses of the riches of an older, more diversified spectrum of women's lyrics should not obscure the fact that this relatively profound process of adaptation has taken place.

To resume, then, traditional Gaelic song-poetry includes a powerful nucleus of songs attributed to, and presumably performed by and for women. Their form or content may cause us to classify some of them as labour songs or lullabies or laments, but scholars have seen them as possessing certain literary or aesthetic qualities which may also be regarded as distinguishing features.[18] As such, they have attracted critical attention and acclaim, especially amongst critics whose intellectual framework included dissatisfaction with the canonical literary genres. Thus C.I. MacLean, writing as a professional folklorist trained in Scandinavia and Ireland, praised them as part of an unjustly neglected popular heritage.[19] Their most redoubtable champion, adding a refined literary-critical sensibility to historical learning and a committed socialist political outlook, was Sorley MacLean, who returned repeatedly to these songs in his essays.[20]

According to this school of thought, Scottish Gaelic literary criticism had concentrated excessively on its Apollonian strengths and virtues, i.e. the 'establishment' figures who clustered around the Gaelic aristocracy of old. Traditional critics had, understandably but unforgivably, praised the affected, inflated, mercenary poetry of the bardic world at the expense of its unaffected, starkly realist, spontaneously poetic heritage in the Old Songs. Similarly, the eighteenth- and nineteenth-century bards were tainted with a whiff of toadying and quietism in the face of the destruction of the society they claimed to speak for, where the Old Songs were ablaze with direct, hot-blooded emotional responses to powerful real-life events in a violent world. Naturally, critics like Sorley MacLean fully acknowledged the strengths of seventeenth- and eighteenth-century poets like Iain Lom and Alexander MacDonald and William Ross. But the sense that Gaelic possessed a neglected trove of popular literature to be rediscovered and reinstated was understandable in Scotland in an age of revolt against traditional politics and religion and the literature of the Kailyard.

For in the same way that Scots ballads and popular songs offered a twentieth-century alternative to saccharine and trivialising tendencies in Scots poetry, so the Gaelic traditional songs provided

an abundance of poetic qualities that were otherwise in short supply in Gaelic. Amongst these, three deserve particular mention.
First, every commentator has been struck by their emotional intensity: these poets can communicate emptiness or distraction or
vengeful fury – and sometimes more complex and intriguing psychological states – resulting from tragic accidents, slayings and
other violent happenings. In fact, as Sorley MacLean pointed out, if
these lyrics are the authentic statements of those who have newly
experienced such violence, the real marvel is not the emotion but
the artistic control that enabled the poetry to be distilled from it.[21]
Second, the Old Songs clearly possessed a degree of rhythmic variety and subtlety which is rare in post-Classical Gaelic verse. Few
Gaelic poets had the linguistic gifts of a Duncan Bàn Macintyre to
disguise the tyranny of the rhythmically regular, four-square
amhran metre. But the Old Songs achieved a happy accommoda-
tion between words and music, by reason of the fundamental
respect they gave to natural speech rhythms. Interestingly, William
Matheson's music-based research led him to draw similar conclusions: the Old Songs were musically richer and more varied –
rhythmically and melodically – than the songs of the *amhran*
type.[22] In the third place, scholars have responded positively to the
verbal qualities of the Old Songs: simplicity, directness, purity of
idiom, poignancy, under-statement. This can obviously be connected with their effectiveness as a stark, explicit means of communicating reality, provided we remember that simplicity can itself be
deceptive. For instance, ostensibly 'simple' terms such as 'ceò'
(mist), 'oidhche' (night), 'madainn' (morning), 'gleann' (glen) can be
used in a complex way in this poetry, to convey generic coding,
emotional colouring and so forth.[23]

To sum up so far, the traditional songs possess an arresting and
appealing directness and openness, however grim the speaker's situation and however stark the choices. They touch on flesh-and-
blood, sometimes earthy issues, and they call a spade a spade. On
these grounds, and because they often seem to represent the voice
of the 'outsider' (i.e. the non- or anti-establishment voice), they
appeal as much to modern taste as they caused difficulty to the
Victorian critics, who as a consequence tended to avoid them.

Scottish Gaelic literature has also received attention as a literature in which the voice of women is not suppressed, and critics have asked whether there were features of Gaelic (or Celtic) society that were especially favourable for this to happen. Although Gaelic poetesses are very much a minority, it is true that they are relatively well represented by comparison with most other European countries.[24] We also have many more than Gaelic Ireland, which hints that the question is not a simple one. Here I will only remark that a satisfactory answer must take into account the circumstances in which literature is preserved, and not just questions of literary practice. Certainly, the waulking as such was an important women's event in sociological terms. Even if a lot of the material preserved by it did not originate with the waulking, it has given us a great deal of unique material; and the ambience is located unequivocally in women's territory, right down to the present day revivals.[25] A couple of features may be mentioned in demonstration of this last point.

Socially speaking, some of those who speak to us through the songs are, as they make clear to us, the women of the castle, including both those of noble lineage themselves and those who surround the aristocracy, i.e. relatives and companions, nurses and servants. We are reminded that this is not simply a folk-literature, at least in origin. These women are strongly aware of their rightful station; often the songs are triggered by the demotion or exile that can arise from death or rejection. They are sociable, and resent isolation from their proper society. They are keenly interested in the eligible 'young bloods' – the desirable males of the Gaelic nobility. The world they inhabit is a wide one, in which a network of aristocracy embraces the Northern and Southern Hebrides and the Western seaboard. Ireland sometimes figures as part of it. Reference is frequent to the MacDonalds, MacLeods and MacNeills as powers in the land. People sail the sea in birlinns, are entertained by the music of the clarsach, drink wine and brandy, and wear silk from Galway. This is, in short, the same world as that presented in the predominantly men's poetic tradition of courtly eulogy and elegy. Indeed, the women's songs contain just a few 'literary' references to the characters of Gaelic romances and mythology. This is also the world glimpsed from the outside in contemporary references in the Acts of the Scots Parliament and

Privy Council, which not infrequently allude to feuds, forays and abductions, and to chieftains' wives being put away as new political alliances are made. Yet these lyrics undoubtedly represent a different viewpoint from the one we pick up in all other sources.

Another way in which these songs bear comparison with the main body of the Gaelic literary tradition is in their expression of personal feeling, which is a prime concern of their authors. They often externalise love and hatred by objectifying it in expressions of praise or dispraise, which they convey by means of sets of poetic symbols for the qualities being admired or derided. When one analyses these, it is clear that this poetry idealised its objects of praise just as much as the literary genres do. One can classify the conventional attributes and construct a consistent picture of the women's *beau idéal* from the recurrent references to his physical figure and prowess, his beauty, his mental qualities of leadership and education, his liberality, and his sporting and martial prowess. They clearly bear comparison with the equally conventional virtues and vices praised or satirised in the men's poetry of panegyric, though there are some differences.

One highly significant point of contact with the men's world is a sense of frustration that sometimes comes through in our songs. If the speaker were a man she would be able to arrange or expedite or avenge (or whatever). In real life we occasionally find powerful Highland women taking over the reins of power at a time of emergency, or catch a glimpse of them orchestrating the political games of their men-folk; but in general their freedom of action was constrained in a men's world, and it is not surprising that it shows through here and there in their literature. This whole area is one that could be explored much further than has been done so far, either from the perspective of Women's Studies or from within Gaelic Studies.

The traditional women's songs give food for thought when we ponder how high a proportion of women's songs must have been lost, both in the Highlands and more generally. In the case of Gaelic, it is depressing to consider the extent to which they were passed over in favour of more prestigious forms of literature by the early collectors, at periods when a much wider range of material and much fuller and more coherent versions would presumably have been available. It is cautionary to recall our dependence on the waulking tradition for the preservation (not without leaving its mark on them) of such a high proportion of the songs.

More positively, they supply us with generous measures of poetry distinguished by directness of communication and palpable emotional empathy, qualities which appeal to modern taste and can often seem to be missing in the more sophisticated courtly and political poetry. They thus help us towards a more rounded vision and appreciation of the life, thought and feeling of Gaels in earlier times. They take us back to a time when Gaelic society itself was more complete and self-sufficient, when song-making of an appropriate sort was a natural accomplishment for aristocratic ladies like Sìleas na Ceapaich, and for women of lower station but with a place and a stake in aristocratic society like Màiri nighean Alasdair Ruaidh or Maighread nì Lachainn, and for the female members of the *cliar* ('poetic band'), not to mention the milkers of cows and spinners of thread, the wet-nurses of the nobility, and the bands of waulking and keening women.

Those best qualified to judge have opined that the truly creative phase of the Old Songs came to an end in the seventeenth century, with the crumbling of traditional, 'heroic' Gaelic society, whose lynch-pin was the patronage of Gaelic arts by the Gaelic aristocracy. There are a few items in the waulking song corpus which have an explicit connection with Bonnie Prince Charlie and the 1745 Jacobite Rising. It may be that we glimpse here the death-throes of the old song tradition, a last-gasp revival of heroic values to coincide with the last throw of the Jacobite dice.[26] It may be more than coincidental that the same 1745 Rising saw the appropriation of the waulking-song form by Alexander MacDonald, who used it for literary-political purposes.[27]

For all that, the waulking of the cloth continued, and indeed flourished as a focus for women's group bonding right down to the twentieth century in some parts of the Outer Hebrides and occasionally elsewhere. Even if waulking the cloth is no longer a functioning institution, enough of its social aura has survived to commend waulking songs to such contemporary women performers as Talitha Mackenzie, Sìleas and Karen Matheson. They are attractive both musically and as a window onto the 'wild side' of older

Gaelic culture. Despite their venerable age, they still appear relevant today: tokens of an alternative culture handed down to us
against the odds.

NOTES

[1] The term 'sub-literary' was coined by James Ross. See 'The sub-literary tradition in Scottish Gaelic Song-poetry', *Éigse*, vol. 7, 1954-55, pp.
217-39 and vol. 8, 1955-1956, pp. 1-17. For remarks on the different
traditions in general, using a combination of social-functional and metrical-musical criteria, see the preliminary remarks of William Matheson
in his *An Clàrsair Dall: The Songs of Roderick Morison and His Music*,
Edinburgh: Scottish Gaelic Texts Society, 1970, pp. 149-153.

[2] John MacInnes has argued that a choral dimension is also integral to
the women's song tradition: see 'The Choral Tradition in Scottish
Gaelic Songs', *Transactions of the Gaelic Society of Inverness* [hereafter
TGSI], vol. 46, 1969-1970, pp. 44-65.

[3] Gaelic *luadhadh a' chlò* 'waulking of the tweed cloth'. For descriptions of the waulking process and its special aura as a communal
women's activity, see J.L. Campbell and Francis Collinson eds.,
Hebridean Folksongs, 3 vols., Oxford: Oxford University Press, 1969-
1981, I, pp. 3-16 and III, pp. 2-5.

[4] See J.L. Campbell and Francis Collinson eds., *op. cit.*, I, pp. 17-23 and
III, pp. 5-10.

[5] The greatest monument in print to these songs is J.L. Campbell and
Francis Collinson eds., *op. cit.*, see I, pp. 24-26 for earlier collections.

[6] Sorley MacLean used 'Old Songs' as a quasi-technical term in his critical writings, for which see William Gillies ed., *Ris a' Bhruthaich: The
Criticism and Prose Writings of Sorley MacLean*, Stornoway: Acair,
1985.

[7] This can be a problem even in regard to well-known poets. See, for
example, William Matheson ed., *The Songs of John MacCodrum*,
Edinburgh: Oliver & Boyd, 1938, pp. 176-181 for Banais Mhic Asgaill
('MacAskill's Wedding'); and George Calder ed., *Gaelic Songs by
William Ross*, Edinburgh: Oliver & Boyd, 1937, pp. 120-125 and 184-
185 for 'Cuachag nan Craobh' (understood as 'The Cuckoo of the
Trees').

[8] *Gaelic Songs of Mary MacLeod*, edited by J.C. Watson, Edinburgh:

Blackie, 1934. See further William Matheson, 'Notes on Mary MacLeod', *TGSI*, vol. 41, 1951-1952, pp. 11-25; John MacInnes, 'Gaelic Songs of Mary MacLeod', *Scottish Gaelic Studies*, vol. 11, no. 1, 1966, pp. 3-25; J.L. Campbell, 'Notes on the Poems ascribed to Mary MacLeod in D.C. MacPherson's Duanaire', *Scottish Gaelic Studies*, vol. 11, no. 2, 1968, pp. 171-91 (pp. 171-174); J.L. Campbell and Francis Collinson eds., *op. cit.*, I, pp. 94-97 and 174-176.

[9] See J.L. Campbell and Francis Collinson eds., *op. cit.*, II, pp. 112-121, 124-131 and 226-237.

[10] See M.F. Shaw ed., *Folksongs and Folklore of South Uist*, London: Routledge and Kegan Paul, 1955, pp. 258-261; J.L. Campbell and Francis Collinson eds., *op. cit*, I, pp. 44-49 and 161-162; cf. III, p. 300.

[11] See M.F. Shaw, *Folksongs and Folklore*, cit., pp. 254-257; J.L. Campbell and Francis Collinson eds., *op. cit.*, II, pp. 44-53 and 200-209.

[12] See M.F. Shaw, *Folksongs and Folklore*, cit., pp. 206-207; J.L. Campbell and Francis Collinson eds., *op. cit.*, I, pp. 94-97 and 174-176.

[13] As it happens, we do have a genuine extempore tradition within the waulking songs corpus, and its textual 'feel' is quite different. See the *òran basaidh* ('clapping song') beginning 'Cò bheir mi leam air an Long Èireannach' ('Whom shall I take with me on the Irish Ship?'), in which successive singers would take turns to choose a lover for a fellow waulker at the end of the waulking: see M.F. Shaw, *Folksongs and Folklore*, cit., p. 268.

[14] E.g. J.L.Campbell and Francis Collinson eds., *op. cit.*, I, pp. 54-57 and 164 ('Cairistìona').

[15] See John MacInnes, 'Choral Tradition', cit., (no. 2). An Irish parallel is provided by 'Caoineadh Airt Uí Laoghaire' ('The Lament for Art O' Leary') and the scholarship thereon: see J.E.C. Caerwyn Williams and P.K. Ford, *The Irish Literary Tradition*, Cardiff: University of Wales Press/Belmont MA: Ford and Bailie, 1992, pp. 238-240.

[16] See J.L. Campbell and Francis Collinson eds., *op. cit.*, III, pp. 6-9. John MacInnes, 'Choral Tradition', cit., makes a bold attempt to explain the abrupt switches of subject as part of the aesthetic appeal of the songs. Such switches are, of course, integral to the appeal of present-day pop videos.

[17] J.L. Campbell and Francis Collinson eds., *op. cit.*, III, pp. 94-99 and 250-256.

[18] The case for a multi-dimensional approach to Gaelic folk literature is made and put into effect in James Ross, 'A Classification of Gaelic Folk Songs', *Scottish Studies*, vol. 1, 1957, pp. 95-151.

[19] 'Traditional Songs from Raasay and their Value as Folk-literature', *TGSI*, vol. 39/40, 1942-1950, pp. 176-192. See also, from the standpoint of a Gaelic linguistic scholar and poet, George Campbell Hay's 'Gaelic and Literary Form', *The Voice of Scotland*, vol. 2, no. 1, Summer 1939, pp. 14-18. Cf. Michel Byrne ed., *Collected Poems and Songs of George Campbell Hay*, 2 vols., Edinburgh: Edinburgh University Press, 2000, II, pp. 65-67.

[20] See Sorley MacLean, *Ris a' Bhruthaich*, cit.; cf. William Gillies, 'The Poet as Critic', in R.J. Ross and Joy Hendry eds., *Sorley MacLean: Critical Essays*, Edinburgh: Scottish Academic Press, 1986, pp. 185-200.

[21] Sorley MacLean, *Ris a' Bhruthaich*, cit., p. 112; cf. William Gillies, 'Poet as Critic', cit., p. 192.

[22] Personal communication. Matheson was not spared to complete the full treatment of these matters which he had promised in *An Clàrsair Dall* (see note no. 1).

[23] See John MacInnes, 'The Panegyric Code in Scottish Gaelic Poetry and its Historical Background', *TGSI*, vol. 50, 1976-1978, pp. 435-498. Many aspects of Gaelic poetic diction have simply not been explored in print.

[24] For Mary MacLeod (Màiri nighean Alasdair Ruaidh) see the sources cited at note no. 8 above. Essays by Sorley MacLean on the poetry of Juliet MacDonald (Sìleas na Ceapaich), Margaret MacDonald (Maighread nì Lachainn) and Mary MacPherson (Màiri Mhòr nan Òran) are included in Sorley MacLean, *Ris a' Bhruthaich*, cit.

[25] In Gaelic-speaking parts of Nova Scotia waulking songs became central to social gatherings known as 'millings' which were not confined to women as the waulkings were in Scotland: see J.L. Campbell ed., *Songs Remembered in Exile*, Aberdeen: Aberdeen University Press, 1990, pp. 42-43. Here, perhaps, cultural dislocation made it more important for there to be a traditional communal occasion than for the gender-differentiated version to survive.

[26] See J.L. Campbell and Francis Collinson eds., *op. cit.*, I, pp. 136-139 and 186-187 and III, pp. 220-227 and 294-298; J.L. Campbell, *Highland Songs of the 'Forty-five*, revised edition, Edinburgh: Scottish Academic Press, 1984, p. 336; William Gillies, 'Gaelic Songs of the 'Forty-five', *Scottish Studies*, vol. 30, 1991, pp. 19-58 (pp. 44-45).

[27] See J.L. Campbell, *op. cit.*, pp. 144-153; J.L. Campbell and Francis Collinson eds., *op. cit.*, III, pp. 132-139 and 267-721. See also *ibidem*, I, pp. 24-25, for another eighteenth-century male poet (Duncan Bàn Macintyre) exploiting the waulking song genre and characteristics for his own purposes.

DAVID W. PURDIE

James Boswell

James Boswell was a child of landed privilege, one of the brethren of the Scottish Enlightenment and the father of modern biography. If, as Charles Wetherall mused, biography has added a new terror to death, this was directly due to Boswell's bringing a literary species to renewed life.

BIOGRAPHY AS GENRE

There was, of course, nothing intrinsically new about the genre. It had rudimentary beginnings in the character sketches and purported speeches of Themistocles, Pausanias and Pericles in Thucydides' *History of the Peloponnesian War*.[1]

It developed with Xenophon's accounts of the activities of Socrates and Cyrus and found its highest expression in classical antiquity with the successors of Aristotle at the Lyceum in Athens. Their traditions were followed in Hellenistic times by the scholars of the great library of Alexandria, founded by Ptolemy I – one of the generals of Alexander. Here, such as Demetrius of Phalerum and Aristophanes of Byzantium clearly directed that biographical data on classical authors facilitated the process of criticism. Although only fragments survive physically, the concept flourished and two hundred years later, in the second century AD, it was to illuminate the *Lives* of Plutarch.[2] These biographies, descriptive and morally didactic as they are, mark the conclusion of ancient Greek contributions to the genre – save for the compendium of lives of the Greek philosophers produced in the third century AD by Diogenes Laertius.[3]

Rome was to continue the development of biography which evolved from the Graeco-Roman tradition of epideictic oratory at state funerals. This emerged full-blown as autobiographies by such Republican leaders as Sulla and such holders of the Imperial purple as Augustus and Tiberius. These works are lost to us but we do possess the classic biographical compendium, *De viris illustribus* of Cornelius Nepos who treats of such as Miltiades the victor of Marathon, Hannibal and Cato.[4]

Particularly fine biographical writing in the Roman imperial period is found in the account of the general Cn. Julius Agricola by his son-in-law, the historian Tacitus. Here, incidentally, occurs the first reported speech by a native of Scotland, the Caledonian leader Calgacus who, with that terse objectivity ever characteristic of the Scots, is made to flay the Roman imperial policy towards his homeland with the words *solitudinem faciunt, pacem apellant* – they make a desert and call it peace. Incidentally, one of Agricola's camps was at Loudon Hill in present-day Ayrshire, visible from the northern boundary of James Boswell's Auchinleck estate. Roman biography culminated in the salacious – and probably accurate – *De vita Caesarum* – the Lives of the Caesars, covering Julius Caesar and eleven subsequent emperors ending with Domitian.[5] Suetonius is our link with the Middle Ages. The invariable sequence in which he dealt first with his subjects' family and early years, then public career, physical appearance and finally private life was the model which was, effectively, to end – and begin anew – with Boswell.

As it is neither possible, nor indeed appropriate to attempt a comprehensive review of the evolution of biography in English Literature, the following summary will be necessarily conceptual rather than descriptive since it was the very mould of the genre which Boswell, influenced by Johnson himself, was to shatter.

Medieval biography having been a virtual literary desert, the art experiences something of a renaissance in 16th century England with Sir Thomas More's *History of Richard III*[6] and the biography of More himself by his son-in-law William Roper.[7] Fully one third of Richard III is composed of dialogue which is reported – rather than verbatim from life – a problem for authenticity which goes back to Thucydides. It was to be tackled by Boswell whose recording apparatus consisted of his own brain with its quasi-photographic memory for dialogue – sometimes at a distance of weeks.

In the 17th century, as in the 16th, the continuing evolution of biography carried with it the inherent possibility of political or actual physical retaliation from a grandee – or monarch – whose opinion of his own character or actions, might be at serious variance with that of the biographer. As Sir Walter Raleigh put it in the introduction[8] to his *Historie of the World* (1614), 'Whosoever shall follow the truth too near... it may haply strikke out his teeth' or, as in Raleigh's case, strike off his head. Professional biography may be said to have arrived in mid-century with the anecdotal but very informative *Brief Lives* of John Aubrey, Shakespeare's first biographer, and the work of Izaak Walton, best known today for his *Compleat Angler,* whose principal subjects were the poets John Donne (1640) and George Herbert (1670). These presage Johnson and Boswell himself with their attempts to reconcile the perennial tension of biography itself – the need to illuminate, by literary art, the facts of a career and the personality of a life actually lived. The intrinsic difficulty imposed by the marriage of truth to an imaginative vivifying of the subject was, and will ever remain, a central challenge of the genre.

The principal biographers of the 18th century prior to Boswell were Roger North – who also wrote the first major critical essay on biography – and Johnson himself. Not only did he produce in his *Lives of the English Poets*, a valuable contribution to the genre but his essays and conversations also illuminate his views on the nature of biography and the duties of biographers. These opinions are of great value, both in themselves and in their clear influence on the approach which Boswell was to take in what he himself described as his 'presumptious task' – *The Life.*[9] First and above all, Johnson required that the biographer tell the factual truth. A biography should be decidedly a work of non-fiction. In order to maintain the necessary precision in recording the events of a life and career Johnson, commenting on the *Life of Parnell* by Oliver Goldsmith, observed that 'no one could furnish the life of a man but those who had eat and drank and lived in social intercourse with him'.[10]

Boswell had then known Johnson for nearly ten years and here we find for the first time the concept of a biography of his friend described as a 'constant' i.e. firm, plan. As Frank Brady has pointed out, this firmness came by degrees. On his earlier European Tour,

Boswell, his acquaintance with Johnson barely a year old, had written to say that, if permitted, he intended to 'do honour to his memory'.[11] He wrote this melodramatically lying on the tomb of the great German protestant reformer Philip Melancthon – the Greek surname a literal translation of the original German Schwarzerd – who was revered by the Scots Kirk and its Calvinist adherents for his association with Luther and his authorship of the Augsburg Confession. It is thus clear that from an early date, Boswell's reverence for Johnson was to be given substance by some form of memoir. Four years later, Boswell was cautioned by Johnson for publishing, without permission, an extract from one of his letters in Boswell's first notable work *A Journal of a Tour in Corsica* (1768). 'Who', enquired Johnson in a latter of March 23 that year 'would write to men who published the letters of their friends....?' Boswell took the bull by the horns and asked, explicitly, if it would be improper to publish his letters – presumably not just their personal correspondence – after his death. Johnson replied that he might do with them as he wished. Thus, by 1771 the plan for a Life was constant and perhaps had been so for some time. As Brady succinctly puts it – Johnson, having been Boswell's mentor, was now also his subject.

Johnson also gave a useful insight into the function of biography during the celebrated interview between himself and Lord Monboddo, one of Lord Auchinleck's peers on the bench of the Court of Session. This took place at Monboddo House in Angus with Boswell, as usual, acting as starter and umpire in the conversation. Johnson opined that he esteemed biography as an essential practical adjunct to the history of social behaviour – which he referred to as manners – because it is of ethical utility. 'Biography' said Johnson, 'comes near to ourselves – what we can turn to use'. Thus, the purpose of biography is ultimately ethical. It seeks to interpolate a life of behaviour into the social ambience of its time so that the reader may utilise the observed consequences for the direction of his own conduct. Plutarch would have approved.

Thus with Boswell, the time was ripe for a synthesis of the moral Plutarchian system of biography and the anecdotal system of vignettes going back to Suetonius and beyond. It was indeed a time of syntheses – by Kant in philosophy, seeking to unite the traditions of the rational and empirical schools, by Gibbon uniting the concrete and the abstract in history for his *Decline & Fall,* and by the whole ramshackle, splendid Age of Enlightenment as it struggled to harness revealed religion to the revelations of science. In similar mode, Boswell was also to unite the moralistic and the descriptive traditions of biography into a new whole, and one incomparably greater than the sum of its parts.

THE MAN AND HIS TIME

James Boswell was a child of Edinburgh and the son and heir to the 8,000 hectare estate of Auchinleck in the County of Ayrshire. Born in Scotland's capital in 1740 to one of her senior Judges, he was educated privately and at the Universities of Edinburgh and Glasgow. By the age of 20 he was an educated young man with a thorough grounding in the classics, literature and philosophy, and with a major interest in the proclivities of actresses. He was hauled back by his sternly moralist father, Lord Auchinleck, from his first escapade to London in 1760, but that visit bred in him a passion for the manners and activities of the metropolis with which not even Enlightenment Edinburgh could compete. He was sensible enough to see eventually that a military career – his first choice – was beyond him and having proceeded to qualify in Civil Law, he was allowed back to London in 1762. Here occurred what was to be the most momentous occasion of his life, his celebrated meeting with Samuel Johnson in Davies' bookshop in May 1763. Thus began a friendship which was to last twenty years till Johnson's death and was to produce, in 1791, the greatest biography in literature.

A year after the meeting, Boswell set off on a Grand Tour of the Continent which was to take him to Holland, Germany, Italy and finally to Corsica.[12]

Here he met the great Corsican patriot Pasquale Paoli whose cause – the independence of the island – he was to advocate in his first successful publication *An Account of Corsica,* in 1768. On the Tour Boswell's character developed into that which permeates the *Life.* He was by nature extrovert, gregarious and witty. People instinctively liked him. He was also socially ambitious, solicitous of the acquaintance of the good and the great and was as proud as a peacock of his ancestry and the social standing of his family. He was also a hedonist whose stern intentions to reform were as fragile as they were frequent, his fondness for conviviality, claret and coupling – often with streetwalkers – being meticulously recorded in his Journals. Physically he was 5 feet 6 inches tall and weighed 11 st 12 lb (66 kg) when weighed at Wilton in April 1775 by Lord Herbert.[13] He had a robust constitution, which was just as well, since it had to endure not just malaria, contracted in Corsica, but also scurvy – probably a skin condition – and no less than nineteen bouts of what he described in euphemistic terms as the malady inflicted by Venus upon her votaries. In other words, gonorrhoea or 'the clap' as Boswell often refers to it. His old schoolfriend, William Temple,[14] now a vicar in a country parish in Cornwall, spoke for most of his circle in a letter to Boswell in January 1767 'Your libation to Bacchus is excusable, but you might have omitted the sacrifice to Venus'.[15]

Nor was his mental state entirely stable. Although generally of an outgoing and pleasant disposition, he was subject to recurrent bouts of what are known today as cyclothymia. This is an alteration of normal moods with bouts of severe depression – called by Boswell melancholia – and thought in his time to be due to an excess of black bile. This disorder, when of serious degree, shades into the much more serious psychotic condition of manic depression. There is no specific test for manic-depression but modern psychiatry uses the practical test of whether the cyclic depressions render the patient incapable of working. On this test Boswell occasionally fails. In his *Journal* during November 1780 we hear, for example, that he is so 'sunk' as to be virtually unable to read or think – a severe disability in a professional advocate required to master legal depositions.[16] However, he was never certifiably insane. Indeed, as has been often remarked, Boswell spent his entire life teetering on the edge of absolute sanity.

From the time he was admitted to the Faculty of Advocates in 1766 until he departed, *en famille,* to London twenty years later, Boswell practised with reasonable success at the Edinburgh Bar. The generous intervals between the Sessions or sittings of the Court allowed him potential freedom from mid-March to mid-June and from September to November, to travel to London and rejoin

Johnson and his coterie. And of course on one famous occasion in the summer of 1773, the mountain came to Mahomet. Johnson arrived in Edinburgh, inspected – and was inspected by – the *illuminati* of that city and set out with Boswell on their remarkable journey through the highlands and the Hebridean islands, described by Johnson in *A Journey to the Western Isles of Scotland*. This was itself followed over a decade later, and after Johnson's death, by Boswell's much more racy and entertaining *Journal of a Tour to the Hebrides with Samuel Johnson*. Johnson never returned to Edinburgh and as the 1780s advanced Boswell grew increasingly dissatisfied with his life in Scotland, a situation unaffected by Johnson's death in 1784. His wife Margaret whom he had married in 1769 was a stoical long-suffering cousin of his own, who had to put up with his long absences, his frosty relations with his father and, most embarrassingly, his frequent drunken confession to dalliances with prostitutes in London and Edinburgh. Progressively weakened by the tuberculosis which was to kill her in 1789, she seems to have habitually scolded and then forgiven him even his grossest excesses. These frequently left him suffering the physical and social agonies of gonorrhoea, a condition for which – in that pre-antibiotic era – there was no effective treatment.

Seeking work at the English Bar, Boswell removed the family to London in the winter of 1786, but despite his best efforts neither legal nor political patronage came his way. He was spurned by the English lawyers and effectively ignored politically by such as Henry Dundas – who had been his school fellow – and who was now, as President of the Board of Control, the dispenser of considerable patronage on behalf of the Pitt administration.

However, by allying himself to the demagogic James Lowther, Earl of Lonsdale, Boswell did receive the position of Recorder of Carlisle, a rather pathetic and short-lived legal achievement for one who had aspired to appear before the ancient Court of King's Bench in London – and did not despair of being a Judge upon it.

Boswell's London friends from the literary and the artistic circles were, however, of a more supportive and understanding nature. In April 1773 Johnson had had Boswell accepted for membership of The Club – also known as the Literary Club and unquestionably the foremost assemblage of its day of men from politics and the literary, performing and visual arts. Apart from Johnson, the member-ship included Sir Joshua Reynolds, Edmund Burke, Oliver Goldsmith, C.J. Fox, Edward Gibbon, Adam Smith and Edmond Malone.[17] The latter is perhaps the key associate of Boswell's latter years, particularly in respect to his *magnum opus, The Life.* For it was Malone who kept him – and the project going. Malone who cajoled and encouraged him through his backsliding, his depres-sions and fear of failure. And in the end, it was with Malone's edi-torial help that, on the twenty eighth anniversary of his meeting with Johnson, *The Life* was finally published in May 1791.[18]

Boswell's later years were a curious amalgam of rising literary fame and declining physical health. The success of *The Life* did nothing to prevent his recurrent melancholia and neither did the Government's final refusal to give him an appointment – he had solicited to be Commissioner in Corsica – again in revolt against France. He continued to attend to the estate at Auchinleck, appointing a minister to the parish, settling disputes between his tenants and his estate factor and trying to reduce some of the debt with which the estate was saddled. In April 1795 he was taken seri-ously ill at the club. A urinary obstruction provoked an acute pychronephritis – infection of the kidneys – which proceeded, as his son said, to 'mortification' – gangrene. A few days later he was dead. 'How I miss' said Malone 'his noise, his hilarity and his per-petual good humour – which had no bounds'.[19] Thankfully, since *The Life of Samuel Johnson* is also in a real sense the Life of Boswell, he is with us yet.

THE MAN AS BIOGRAPHER

For a man dead only two centuries Boswell's reputation has under-gone more serious revisions than many an author of antiquity. One great paradox about Boswell which lasted well into the 20th centu-ry was simply this: the man was widely believed to be a libertine, a dilettante, a whoremonger and a drunk. Perceived wisdom had it that his association with the Olympians of The Club was simply due to his superior birth and his friendship with Johnson, a friend-ship contingent on his being Johnson's foil and fool. His master-piece *The Life* was successful simply because it was a new literary experiment produced by a player with a good memory for dialogue and a mania for seeking out complementary information from all possible sources. Boswell, it was said, had been lucky in the fame of his subject, the memorability of his sayings and the breadth of his learning. Any fool could have made a silk purse from such material – and Boswell was that fool.

It took time for this attitude to fade. It began when the folk memory of Boswell's foibles dimmed and *The Life* stood out alone, no longer coloured by the eccentricities of its author. The next and major revision was to come with the discovery of the Boswell papers – and in particular his *Journals*. Well recounted by David Buchanan in *The Treasure at Auchinleck*,[20] the story of the Boswell papers constitutes one of the great literary detective stories of last century. In summary, Boswell's Journals, his manuscripts of *The Life* and a mass of correspondence came to light at Malahide Castle in Ireland and at Fettercairn House in Scotland. Eventually, the entire archive was secured by Yale University, which published 12 'Trade' editions of the *Journals* between 1950 and 1989 – all but the last edited or co-edited by F.A. Pottle. In addition, there have been seven Yale 'Research' Editions of the correspondence, and two definitive biographies of Boswell's early and later years by Pottle and Brady respectively.

The illumination delivered by the edited *Journals* was penetrating. Boswell reappeared in the light not only of his own writing but in that of the objective literary criticism which the Journals spawned. He had need of that objectivity. Within his own family, his memory was an embarrassment. His daughter-in-law the dowager Lady Boswell, widow of his son and heir Sir Alexander ('Sandy'), stated publicly that he had degraded himself and the family by acting as Johnson's toady. The literary world seemed to agree. J.W. Croker brought out, in 1831 a five-volume edition of *Boswell's Life* containing much new material but containing also numerous notes, many highly critical of the author.[21] This edition was savagely attacked by Macaulay in the Whig *Edinburgh Review*, the historian vilifying Croker, a Tory, for his mutilation of Boswell's original text and his arrangement of the material. Although Macaulay lauded Boswell as the author of the supreme biography, he actually abetted Croker in the blackening of Boswell as a man. According to Macaulay, he was a shallow, hedonistic, bigoted alcoholic who claimed to be a gentleman but was in effect little more than a common eavesdropper. If the latter jibe was vicious, it was also not new. One of Boswell's central assets in preparing *The Life,* his recall of – and use of – verbatim conversation was the subject of trenchant criticism in his own day.

Used as we are now to the public report and publication of all but the most libellous conversations, it is difficult for us to appreciate what a mould Boswell was breaking with his passion for reporting personal conversation and correspondence. In the 18th century all communications, oral and written, were deemed to be intensely private unless that privacy was expressly waived and Boswell's airy use of what others believed to be confidential often got him into trouble. 'You must know, Mr James Boswell... that I am very much out of humour with you for publish(ing) in a book... what you pretend, or claim, I told you in private conversation'.[22] Thus did the great empirical philosopher David Hume discharge his mind to Boswell on the subject. Given that Hume was a friend, a fellow member of the gentry, and a companion whose social geniality matched Boswell's own, the degree of the perceived offence may be conjectured.

In the wider context, it should also be remembered that in the year of Boswell's death, criticism of governmental policy could invoke a charge of seditious libel, the punishment for which included both transportation to Botany Bay and the gallows.

Johnson himself, while doubtless aware that his sayings and doings were being recorded, was averse to any outwardly visible sign of the process. Once, at dinner at the Thrales' at Streatham,[23] he was reported by Fanny Burney to have discovered Boswell seated behind him, inclining forwards, writing materials at the ready. 'What do you do *there*, Sir?' thundered the sage. 'Go to the *table*, Sir!'.

Thomas Carlyle concurred that Boswell had somehow written a masterpiece by accident. He was, however, rather more merciful to Boswell, ascribing his success not to sycophancy and shameless reproduction of conversation but to sincere admiration and a desire for preservation of character and example. Both critics however agreed that Boswell's achievement was not underpinned by any literary artistry, he was decidedly not a true author but, as

Shakespeare had put it – a rude mechanical. They were both wrong – and in the highest degree. What they reckoned to be little more than stenography – was in fact the new biographical art, with that art cloaked by layers of innovation – *ars est celare artem* brought to such a degree as to completely fool Macaulay and Carlyle, two of the greatest historians and essayists of their age.

The final rehabilitation of Boswell as artist came with the scholarly analysis of his *Journals* and his letters. Beginning with Percy Fitzgerald in 1874 and continuing with George Birbeck Hill a decade later, Boswell began to be presented as a writer who had deliberately conceived, gestated and brought to birth *The Life*, a work of true literary artistry. Hill's work was to be revised in the 20th century by L.F. Powell, whose six-volume edition of *The Life* is now the standard. As Adam Sisman has it in his perceptive work *Boswell's Presumptious Task* – the making of *The Life of Dr Johnson* – Boswell's text is now protected within a fortress of scholarly apparatus and safe from further ravage.[24]

And so is Boswell's reputation; he stands as one of the great *illuminati* of the Enlightenment alongside those remarkable Scots who evolved those arts and sciences which were to underpin our modern world – David Hume in empirical philosophy; Adam Smith in economics; Burns in lyric poetry; and Boswell in biography – a man imperfect but a man touched with a genius which led even the critical Macaulay[25] to assert that 'Shakespeare is not more decidedly the first of dramatists, Demosthenes not more the first of orators than Boswell is the first of biographers'.

On the pediment of the southern façade of Auchinleck House in Ayrshire is a quotation from Horace[26] engraved in the stone, just as Lord Auchinleck hoped that it would become engraved in the soul of his errant eldest son. It is from the *Epistles: quod petis hic est./est Ulubris, animus si te non deficit aequus* – 'What you seek is here, it is at Ulubrae, if you lose not the balance of your mind'. Macaulay had, for succeeding generations, announced Boswell's arrival at Ulubrae.[27] What he had sought, he had found.

NOTES

[1] A.S Way, *Speeches in Thucydides*, London: MacMillan, 1934.

[2] Plutarch of Chaeronea, *The Lives of Noble Greeks and Romans Compared,* translated by Thomas North, Boston and New York: Houghton & Mifflin, 1928.

[3] Diogenes Laertius, *The Lives of Eminent Philosophers,* translated by R.D. Hicks, Harvard: Harvard University Press, 1925.

[4] Cornelius Nepos, *De viris illustribus*, translated by C.R. Rolfe, Harvard: Harvard University Press, 1929.

[5] C. Suetonius Tranquillus, *De vita Caesarum,* translated by Michael Grant, New York: Penguin, 1979.

[6] Sir Thomas More, *The History of King Richard III*, edited by Richard Bear, Eugene: University of Oregon Press, 1997.

[7] William Roper, *The Life of Sir Thomas More*, edited by C.W. Eliot, New York: P.F. Collier and Son, 1909.

[8] Sir Walter Raleigh, *The Historie of the World*, in five books, London: printed for Robert White, John Place and George Dawes; and to be sold by Thomas Rookes at the Lamb and Ink-bottle at the East-end of St. Pauls, MDCLXVI, 1628.

[9] James Boswell, *The Life of Samuel Johnson LLD*, edited by G.B. Hill, revised by L.F. Powell, Oxford: Oxford University Press, 1934-1950, p. 1

[10] Oliver Goldsmith, 'The Life of Thomas Parnell', in *The Works of Oliver Goldsmith*, edited by P. Cunningham, London: John Murray, 1854, p. 216.

[11] Frank Brady, *Boswell, The Later Years 1769-95*, New York: Heinemann, 1984, pp. 35-36.

[12] James Boswell, 'Boswell on the Grand Tour: Germany & Switzerland, 1764', in the Yale 'trade' editions of the *Journal of James Boswell*, edited by F.A. Pottle et al., New York: Heinemann 1950-1989, pp. 1-191

[13] James Boswell, *op. cit.,* V, p. 79.

[14] James Boswell, 'Boswell: The Ominous Years', in *Journal of James Boswell*, cit., p.154.

[15] Frank Brady, *op. cit.,* p. 469.

[16] *The correspondence of James Boswell & Wm Johnson Temple 1756-95*, I, 1756-1777, edited by Thomas Crawford, Edinburgh: Edinburgh University Press, 1997, p 67.

[17] James Boswell, 'Boswell, Laird of Auchinleck', in *Journal of James Boswell*, cit., p. 271.

[18] See note no. 9.

[19] *The Windham Papers*, I, edited by Lewis Melville, London: Herbert Jenkins, 1913, pp. 297-298.

[20] David Buchanan, *The Treasures of Auchinleck*, New York: McGraw-Hill, 1974.

[21] James Boswell, *The Life of Samuel Johnson LLD*, a new edition by J. W. Croker, 8 vols., London: John Murray, 1831.

[22] *New Letters of David Hume,* edited by Raymond Klibansky and Ernest Mossmer, (Letter 34), Oxford: Oxford University Press, 1954, p. 68.

[23] Charlotte Barrett and Austin Dobson eds., *Diary and Letters of Madame D'Arblay*, I, London: MacMillian & Co., 1904, p. 511.

[24] Adam Sisman, *Boswell's Presumptious Task*, New York: Hamish Hamilton, 2000, pp. 286-314.

[25] T.B. Macaulay, *Edinburgh Review*, vol. 54, September 1831, p 16.

[26] Q. Horatius Flaccus (Horace) I, *Epistles*, XI, 29.

[27] T.B. Macaulay, *Edinburgh Review*, vol. 76, March 1843, p. 313.

VALENTINA BOLD

Ossian and James Macpherson

By the side of a rock on the hill, beneath the aged trees, old Oscian sat on the moss; the last of the race of Fingal. Sightless are his aged eyes; his beard is waving in the wind. Dull through the leafless trees he heard the voice of the north. Sorrow revived in his soul: he began and lamented the dead.[1]

Ossian, also known as Oisín or Oiséan, is a legendary warrior Bard of Scotland. His father was Finn (Fionn ma Cumhaill, or Fingal), his grandfather was the giant Comhal, king of Morven in modern Argyll and his son, Oscar, was also an heroic warrior. Ossian, like the classical blind bards Thamyris and Tiresias, had prophetic powers. These heroes were celebrated in the Gaelic literature of Scotland and Ireland: the Fenian, or *Ossianic, heroic cycle*, set in the third century, focusses on Finn and his warriors, the *fianna*; the *Ulster*, or *Cù Chulainn, cycle*, is based around the first century Cù Chulainn. From an early period, motifs associated with the Cù Chulainn cycle were often incorporated into the Fenian, along with additional elements from legends about the Viking period. By the eighteenth century, the two cycles were very often mixed.

In the Scottish tradition, early examples of Gaelic Ossianic ballads include those in the 'Book of the Dean of Lismore' manuscript (c.1512), the Ardchonaill MSS (1690) and the Turner MS. Important collections of Ossianic texts also include those made by Jerome Stone (1727-1756), Eobhan MacDiarmaid (1762 and 1769), Archibald Fletcher of Achalder (born c.1735), the Rev Donald MacNicol (1736-1802) and the Rev James Maclagan. Many of their ballads are reprinted in J.F. Campbell's *Leabhar na Fèinne* (1872) and in Alexander Cameron's *Reliquiae Celticae* (1892-94).

James Macpherson (1736-96) was Ossian's literary translator. Born at Invertromie on Spey, in Badenoch, he was related to the Jacobite Ewan Macpherson of Cluny. His castle burnt after Culloden, Cluny spent nine years in hiding – his adventures feature in *Kidnapped* (1866) – before finally escaping for France. As Fiona Stafford suggests in her critical biography, *The Sublime Savage*, the repression Macpherson experienced in his childhood no doubt influenced his mythopoetic imagining of a lost golden age.[2] His upbringing in the Highlands, equally, made Macpherson familiar with the Gaelic language and tales of the *fiana*, transmitted by local *seanchaidhean*, or tradition bearers.

Macpherson also drew on the polite culture of Enlightenment Scotland. As a student at the University of Aberdeen (1752-55) he was influenced by Thomas Reid and James Beattie and the Common sense input on his work should not be underestimated. An interest in the vitality of early societies, as expressed in William Duncan's translation of Caesar's *Commentaries* (1753) and Blackwell's *Enquiry into the Life and Writings of Homer* (1735), perhaps led Macpherson towards seeking a social and poetic prototype. Primitive cultures, such as the ancient Highlanders', were thought to express themselves in specific ways: Edmund Burke stated in *A Philosophical Enquiry into the Origin of our Ideas of the Sublime and the Beautiful* (1757) that: 'uncultivated people are but ordinary observers of things... but, for that reason, they admire more, and are more affected with what they see, and therefore express themselves in a warmer and more passionate manner'.[3] Macpherson's 'noble savage' Ossian draws directly on such eighteenth century notions.

Macpherson was a pioneering fieldworker who, as Thomas McKean says, 'not only helped preserve valuable Gaelic manuscripts but also contributed to the emergence of the proper study of Celtic literature, drawing attention in particular to its ballad heritage.'[4] His active collecting may have begun when, after a period in Edinburgh in 1756, he was a schoolmaster at the Charity School at Ruthven, near his home. He returned to Edinburgh and, by 1758, was a tutor to the Grahams of Balgowan. At this time, he was definitely collecting in earnest.

In 1758 Macpherson combined his interests in Gaelic and Enlightenment cultures, publishing *The Highlander*, an heroic poem. Its story bears similarities to the legend of Fingal and there are allusions to the *Iliad*, the *Aeneid* and *Paradise Lost*. As Colin Kidd has shown, this poem exhibits dual affiliations to 'both the libertarian freedoms of the ancient Caledonians and the glories of the Anglo-Saxon constitution'.[5] Adam Ferguson, whom Macpherson met in 1758, provided Macpherson with an introduction to John Home, the author of the *Douglas* (1757) and, when the writers met in 1759, Macpherson showed Home 'The Death of Oscur', partly modelled on Jerome Stone's Gaelic translations in the *Scots Magazine*.[6] Home showed this, and additional pieces, to his *literati* friends in Edinburgh. Encouraged, in particular by Hugh Blair, Macpherson published his *Fragments of Ancient Poetry* in 1760.

Fragments reflect Enlightenment aesthetics, making unfamiliar, and hence exotic, Gaelic idioms accessible to its polite audience. As was the convention, Macpherson created composite texts. At times, he followed his sources closely; using Gaelic forms such as dialogue and parallelism, and even enhancing their dramatic style. Elsewhere, he sometimes misinterpreted Gaelic orthography and, at times, tampered with texts to their detriment. In a profound sense, in translating for an English-reading audience unfamiliar with Gaelic idioms or tales, Macpherson attempted to mediate between two cultures.

He establishes an affiliation with classical writers with a quote from Lucan and the work is presented as evidence of a national epic cycle, composed by a group of Bards. The Preface sets out an agenda shared by Macpherson and the *literati*: 'though the poems now published appear as detached pieces in this collection... most of them were originally episodes of a greater work which related to the wars of Fingal'. The imitative and non-interventionist nature of Macpherson's translation is emphasised, presumably to establish credibility: 'the translation is extremely literal. Even the arrangement of the words in the original has been imitated; to which must be imputed some inversions in the style'.[7]

Macpherson, then, was charged with restoring Scotland's national epic to its original purity, ancitipating nineteenth-century nationalist reconstructions, such as Finland's *Kalevala* (1835) edited by Elias Lönnrot. The lost, long 'heroic poem' had a straightforward plot. Swarthan King of Lochlyn (Denmark) had invaded Ireland. Cuchulaid, the Irish general, was forced to submit. Fingal 'The Desert of the Hills' and King of Scotland arrived, triumphed over the Danes, and returned home. It was the work of a poet who had accompanied Fingal, and 'of greater antiquity' than the other *Fragments*. The final three *Fragments*, 'tho' very imperfect' were supposedly parts of this Epic: 'if the whole were recovered, it might serve to throw considerable light upon the Scottish and Irish antiquities'. Blair stresses that these pieces were 'not set to music, nor sung', presumably to stress the epic over their ballad associations.[8]

Oscian, in the *Fragments*, is the most prominent of a group of bards including Carryl (*Fragments*, III), Alpin 'the son of song' (*Fragments*, XII) and Armyn, 'last of his race' (*Fragments*, XIII). Their collective memory is negatively selective; the young die and the old live on, in small numbers, to grieve. Oscian is presented as tearful, elderly and melancholic: 'Memory, son of Alpin, memory wounds the aged. Of former times are my thoughts... The race of the king return into my mind, and wound me with remembrance'. The poet bewails the loss of Oscur, while recalling his heroism in killing the murderer Ullin, who had bound Fingal's three younger sons, 'Carryl expert in the bow; Fillan beloved of the fair; and Fergus first in the race' (*Fragments*, VI). This combination of eulogy and despair is highly characteristic of the Ossianic style.

The *Fragments* are loosely-grouped. They are self-sufficient episodes except in two cases: XIV is a fragment of a call to war; XVI, ends the book in cliff-hanger fashion, with a battle in the making. Some are interlinked: *Fragment* VII, explains the death of Oscur, bewailed by Oscian in VI; Dargo, in V, is the enemy of Connal; Dargo's death at the hands of Oscur and Dermid features in VII. In a non-linear way which is typical of oral histories, there is no chronological order: Oscur's killing of Ullin is recalled in VI but Ullin is a current menace in XVI.

This is a narrative of loss: 'the cry of the hunter is over. The voice of war is ceased' (*Fragments*, VIII). The bards' mission is to remember those who have been lost to the living and, in this respect, Macpherson acts along with his readers. Death is not straightforward. Warriors in combat expire simultaneously. One death leads to another, sometimes through error. In *Fragment* IX, Ronnan kills Connan, the lover of his sister Rivine, by mistake, and dies, with his rival Durstan. Rivine dies too. Oscur tricks his lover, the daughter of Dargo, into killing him when he has killed his friend; she is 'well pleased' to die and kills herself (*Fragments,* VII). Women die for their lost lovers: Vinvela for Shilric; the wife of Malcolm; Crimora for Connal (*Fragments,* II, III, IV). The natural and supernatural worlds exist alongside: 'my ghost shall stand in the wind, and mourn the death of my friends. The hunter shall hear from his booth. He shall fear, but love my voice. For sweet shall my voice be for my friends; for pleasant were they both to me' (*Fragments,* X). Even those who have no mourners left are commemorated: Alpin celebrates Morar who has no mother or child left: 'the song shall preserve thy name. Future times shall hear of thee' (*Fragments,* XII).

Despite their lugubrious nature, most of the *Fragments* are brisk and economical, paced out by genealogies, formulae and epithets. Formulae include phrases such as: 'the hope of the isles, Malcolm'; 'Ullin famous in war... His stature like the oak of Morven' (*Fragments,* III, VI). Lovers, like Carmor, are 'like a sun-beam on the hill, in the day of the gloomy storm' or 'white as the driven snow' like Daur (*Fragments,* XV, XI). There are epic-style similes which, although not as lengthy as the *Iliad*'s, are still substantial: 'I saw them return from the chase, like a stream of light... like a ridge of fire' (*Fragments,* IV); Morar was 'swift... as a roe on the hill; terrible as a meteor of fire' ('meteor' is an image also used in *Paradise Lost*). As Stafford has noted, Macpherson also, 'appears to have been using the Bible as a model.[9] The description of the daughter of Dargo – 'fair as the morn; mild as the beam of night. Her eyes, like two stars in a shower: her breath, the gale of spring: her breasts, as the new-fallen snow' – for example recalls the 'Song of Songs' (*Fragments,* VII).

In a form of pathetic fallacy, perhaps reflecting Macpherson's experiences of the post-Culloden atmosphere, storms and winds surround the *fianna*: 'Autumn is dark on the mountains' and misty 'grey mist rests on the hills' (*Fragments,* V). King Lear's rants are recalled when Armyn bewails the loss, through the trickery of Earch, of his daughter Daur, her lover Armor, and his son Arindel: 'rise, winds of autumn, rise; blow upon the deark heath!... howl, ye tempests, in the top of the oak... bring to my mind that sad night, when all my children fell' (*Fragments*, XI). In passages like this, Macpherson achieves a high level of poignancy.

Fragments was hugely successful; it ran into a second edition within a year. Supported by Blair and Henry Mackenzie, Macpherson then made two collecting tours of the Highlands: in August 1760, accompanied by Lachlan Macpherson of Strathmashie (c.1723-c.1797), throughout the North West Highlands, Glenelg and Skye; in June 1761, with John Home, to the West Central Highlands, including Argyll and probably Mull. These tours led to the publication of *Fingal: An Ancient Epic Poem* (1761-62) and *Temora: an Ancient Epic Poem* (1763). *The Works of Ossian* was published, as a collection, in 1765. Derick Thomson, reviewing the sources for *Fingal*, suggests that Macpherson used relatively late material, as can be seen by the way the texts mix the Norse and Fenian heroes and, in particular, fourteen or fifteen Gaelic source ballads.[10]

Fingal (1761) develops the semi-classical bard of the *Fragments* into the major author of a national epic. Its melancholia and sentimental retrospection are even more highly developed than in the *Fragments*, anticipating Mackenzie's *The Man of Feeling* (1771). Here, for instance, Cuchullin bemoans his losses:

> O ye ghosts of the lonely Cromla! ye souls of chiefs that are no more! be ye the companions of Cuchullin, and talk to him in the cave of his sorrow. For never more shall I be renowned among the mighty in the land. I am like a beam that has shone; like a mist that fled away, when the blast of the morning came, and brightened the shaggy side of the hill... departed is my fame. (*Fingal*, Book IV)

The plot of *Fingal* complies with the expectations of the *Fragments* 'Preface'. It opens at the same point as *Fragments* XIV, where Cuchulaid was warned, by the scout Moran, that the ships of Garve and sons of Lochlyn are landing. In essence, the *Fingal* passage is the same, although there are additional details: Cuchullin, for instance, now sits by Tura's wall, rather than 'by the wall', as Swaran's ship lands. Cuchullin – commanding the Irish tribes while Cormac is in his minority – then assembles his forces to oppose the invaders. The consequent war, including councils and engagements, lasts six days and nights, for the six books of the poem. Cuchullin is defeated but Fingal, king of Scotland, arrives, wins the day, and routs the invaders. Unlike the disparate *Fragments*, this poem not only has a unified plot, but also a happy ending, as Fingal comforts Cuchullin: 'we feasted, and we sung. The soul of Cuchullin rose. The strength of his arm returned; and gladness brightened on his face' (*Fingal*, Book VI).

Fingal's plot is largely drawn from two ballads: 'Garbh mac Stairn' and 'Magnus' or Manus'; the main episodes are derived from 'Fingal's Visit to Norway', 'Duan na h-Inginn' (The Maid of Craca) and 'Ossian's Courtship', with elements from, 'Sliabh nam Ban Fionn', the 'Praise of Gol', and other oral and literary sources dealing with the Ulster and Fenian heroes. As Thomson says, 'Macpherson took considerable pains in constructing "Fingal"'.[11] Episodes are cleverly interwoven into the plot, such as the story of Grudar and Brassolis (Book I); the appearance of the ghost of Crugal (Book II); Carril's songs relating Fingal's actions in Lochlin, and the death of Swaran's sister, Agandecca (Book III); Ossian's description of his actions at the lake of Lego, and courtship of Evirallin, the mother of Oscar (Book IV). The style is slightly more elaborate than that of the *Fragments* – Ossian now has the honorific 'king of songs' – the speeches are lengthier and the sentiments, on the whole, more fullsomely expressed. The title poem is accompanied by sixteen 'Other Poems'. These sustain the gloomy atmosphere, and storyline, of the main poem.

The plot of *Temora* (1763) is more complex than that of *Fingal*. Its action takes place over four days and nights. In the First Book Cairbar, the son of Borbar-duthul, lord of Atha in Connaught, has murdered Cormac the son of Artho, the young king of Ireland, at Temora, the royal palace. Fingal, who is related to Cormac, enters Ireland and Cairbar assembles his troops to fight them. He calls a feast, resolving to kill Oscar the son of Ossian; Oscar and Cairbar kill each other. Fingal arrives, and the Irish fall back to the army of Cathmor, the brother of Cairbar. In Book II, Ossian mourns Oscar and, meeting Cathmor, promises to sing an elegy over the grave of Cairbar, thereby ensuring his soul will be content; the bard Carill the son of Kinfena is sent to sing the elegy over Cairbar's tomb. In Book III, Fingal passes the command to Gaul, the son of Morni, and the king and Ossian watch the conflict from the rock of Cormul. Gaul, kills Tur-lathon, chief of Moruth; Foldath, the Irish commander, kills Connal, chief of Dun-lora (by now we are up to the second day from the poem's opening). In Book IV, at the feast, Fingal tells the tale of his first expedition to Ireland, and his marriage with Ros-cr·na, the daughter of the Irish king Cormac. The ghost of Caurbar appears to Cathmor and foretells the outcome of the war. In Book V, Ossian describes the arrangement of the forces by the river Lubar; Foldath commands the army of the Fir-bolg, Fingal gives his command to Fillan and orders Gaul to aid him. Fillan kills Foldath and puts the army of the Fir-bolg to flight. In Book VI the king sends Ossian to aid Fillan, then retires behind the rock of Cormul, so as not to see Ossian fight Cathmor. Fillan dies and Ossian lays him to rest. The Caledonian army return to Fingal, who hears that his son has died. The book ends with the song of Sul-malla. In Book VII, a mist rises by night from the lake of Lego, where the souls of the dead stay between their decease and funeral song. The Ghost of Fillan speaks to Fingal, and the king strikes the shield of Trenmor, which means he will take arms. Sul-malla wakes Cathmor and asks him to sue for peace but he resolves to fight. She retires to the valley of Lona, where an old Druid stays, till the next day's battle is over. In Book VIII, on the fourth morning, Fingal orders Gaul, Dermid and the bard Carril to the valley of Cluna, and to conduct Ferad-artho, the son of Cairbre, to the Caledonian army. The king prepares for battle, and marches to the cave of Lubar, where Fillan's body lay, with his dog Bran guarding the entrance to the cave. In the conflict, the Fir-bolg are routed and the kings engage. Cathmor is killed and Fingal gives the spear of Trenmor to Ossian. Cathmor's spirit appears to Sul-malla. A feast is prepared and the poem ends with a speech by Fingal.

The main poem of 'Temora', like 'Fingal', was accompanied by additional material; here there are five shorter pieces ('Cath-loda', one of these, is in three duans), as well as 'A Specimen of the Original of Temora. Book Seventh' and 'A Critical Dissertation on the Poems of Ossian, the Son of Fingal' by Hugh Blair, reprinted from *A Critical Dissertation on the Poems of Ossian, The Son of*

Fingal (1763), and an expanded 'Appendix' which appeared in 1765, just before *The Works of Ossian* (it was included in the second volume). Blair emphasised Ossian's position as a leading representative of the Celtic college of bards, equivalent to the Homeric *rhapsoḍes*, who exhibited a particularly developed emotional sensibility.

This material should be set beside *The Report of the Committee of the Highland Society of Scotland, appointed to inquire into the nature and authenticity of the poems of Ossian* (1805), convened by Mackenzie. It included testimonies from witnesses to Macpherson's collecting, as well as evaluative comments. It distinguishes traditional materials from Macpherson's interpolations and, as Thomson comments, 'seems to have been realised that Macpherson used his materials freely. Dr Blair admits this, nor, he says, did Macpherson himself seem to disavow it'. Mackenzie argued that, 'such poetry did exist... in great abundance... of a most impressive and striking sort, in a high degree eloquent, tender, and sublime', even if Macpherson had added, 'what he conceived to be dignity and delicacy'. It seemed, then, that Scotland had its own Ossianic epic; collected and corroborated, if not authenticated. As Thomson says, Macpherson's 'most important tenet was that Fingal and his followers were of Scottish rather than of Irish origin, and he was concerned to refute the arguments of Irish historians... In place of this Irish system he strives to establish a Scottish one based on true, as opposed to corrupt, tradition'.[12]

Some scholars of course, including David Hume, suspected Macpherson of forgery. There were negative responses from Ireland, from Charles O' Connor and Sylvester O' Hallohan, based on Macpherson's use of traditional materials. Famously, Johnson attacked Macpherson's Ossian as a fraud, in *Journey to the Western Islands of Scotland* (1775). Ossian was cruelly parodied in the anonymous 1762 *Gisbal, An Hyperbolean Tale*. In contrast, James Boswell, Lord Kames, and Thomas Gray, were all great admirers of the Ossianic works.[13]

The Ossianic verses were equally popular, if not more so, outside Britain and translated into German, Italian, French, Spanish, Dutch, Danish, Russian, Swedish and Polish. Herder, Schiller and Goethe were all admirers of Ossian, as was Napoleon. As Susan

Manning has observed: '*The Poems of Ossian...* became a source text for European Romanticism'. In America, too, Macpherson's work was hugely popular. His famous admirers including Thomas Jefferson. He was a literary influence on poets as diverse as Joel Barlow, H.H. Brackenbridge and Whitman, as well as being parodied in John Trumbull's *McFingal.* Andrew Hook has suggested convincing reasons for the enthusiastic, international response to Ossian, commenting that readers appreciated: 'the vision of a strange, remote, exotic ancient world' and, especially, 'the note of Ossianic gloom and melancholy'.[14]

Macpherson profited from the success of his work. He moved to London and, through the patronage of the Earl of Bute – and perhaps because of a perceived affinity with primitive peoples – in 1763 Macpherson was granted a sinecured post in the newly created province of West Florida, as Surveyor General and provincial Secretary to Governor George Johnstone. He was part of a literary coterie around Johnstone's resented administration. Stationed in Pensacola, then a violent and disease-ridden frontier town, Macpherson soon fell out of favour with the irascible Johnstone. He spent less than a year in the province, although he retained his salary for seventeen years, and spent some time travelling, including to the West Indies, before returning to Britain in 1766.[15]

Macpherson's later work includes *Original Papers,* containing the *Secret History of Great Britain from the Restoration to the Accession of the House of Hanover, with Memoirs of James II* (1775) and *The Rights of Great Britain asserted against the claims of America: being an answer to the declaration of the General Congress* (1776). He published a revised edition of *Ossian,* and translated *The Iliad* (1773) in an Ossianic style. He became London agent for the Nabob of Arcot and, in 1780, Member of Parliament for Camelford, Cornwall. By the late 1780s he had a house in Westminster, a villa on Putney common and a Robert Adam-designed house, Belleville, on his Badenoch estates. He died at Belleville in 1796 and was buried, at his own expense, in Westminster Abbey.

Macpherson left a rich legacy in the Ossianic works, particularly for Scottish writers. Burns visited Ossianic sites during his 'Tour of the Highlands' and counted Macpherson's *Ossian* among his formative influences. Scott pastiched the bardic Ossian in his *The Lay of the Last Minstrel* (1805). James Hogg drew on *Ossian* for his Highland Bard Gardyn in *The Queen's Wake* (1813) and used Ossianic material in his long narrative poem, *Queen Hynde* (1825). As Hugh Cheape has shown, the visual imagery of Ossian left a lasting mark on images of the Highlander at home, and for visitors. Visiting Ossianic sites became an important act for tourists, as Paul Baines has discussed. Intriguingly, Ossianic verse survived in oral tradition and, as Joseph Nagy argues: 'Macpherson's is but one chapter in a long-lived, and perhaps still not concluded, saga of the Gaelic use of Fenian story as a way to introduce cultural and political change, and to mediate between "native" and "foreign", and "old" and "new"'.[16] Macpherson's stance, as Nagy suggests, is deeply ambivalent. His genius lay in drawing together Gaelic culture and the culture of the *literati*, to present the matter of Ossian in a comprehensible, and accessible, form.

NOTES

[1] James Macpherson, *Fragments of Ancient Poetry collected in the Highlands of Scotland, and translated from the Galic or Erse Language*, Edinburgh: G. Hamilton and J. Balfour, 1760, p. viii.

[2] F.J. Stafford, *The Sublime Savage: James Macpherson and the Poems of Ossian*, Edinburgh: Edinburgh University Press, 1988. See too Bailey Saunders, *The Life and Letters of James Macpherson*, London and New York: Swann Sonnenschein, 1894.

[3] Edmund Burke, *A Philosophical Enquiry into the Origin of our Ideas of the Sublime and the Beautiful*, (1757), rpt, edited by Adam Phillips, Oxford: Oxford University Press, 1990, pp. 113-114, 160.

[4] T.A. McKean, 'The Fieldwork Legacy of James Macpherson', *Journal of American Folklore* (Special Issue: James Macpherson and the Ossian Epic Debate), vol. 114, no. 454, Fall 2001, pp. 447-463.

[5] Colin Kidd, 'Macpherson, Burns and the Politics of Sentiment', *Scotlands* (Special Issue: Macpherson's Ossian), vol. 4, no.1, 1997, p. 29. See *The Scots Magazine*, XVIII, 1756, pp.15-17.

[6] Qtd. from James Macpherson, *The Poems of Ossian and related works*, edited by Howard Gaskill with an introduction by F.J. Stafford,

Edinburgh: Edinburgh University Press, 1996, pp. 5-6.

[7] *Ibidem*, p. 6.

[8] See Jan Vansina, *Oral Tradition as History*, Madison Wisconsin: University of Wisconsin Press, 1985.

[9] F.J. Stafford, *op. cit.*, p. 90.

[10] D.S. Thomson, *The Gaelic Sources of Macpherson's Ossian*, Edinburgh: Oliver & Boyd, 1952, pp. 10ff.

[11] *Ibidem*, p. 14.

[12] *Ibidem*, p. 74. *Report of the Committee of the Highland Society of Scotland, Appointed to inquire into the nature and authenticity of the poems of Ossian*, edited by Henry Mackenzie, Edinburgh: Constable, 1805, pp. 151-152. D.S. Thomson, *op. cit.*, p. 69.

[13] F.J. Stafford, 'Introduction', *The Poems of Ossian and Related Works*, cit., p. vii. F.J. Stafford, *The Sublime Savage*, cit., pp. 163-176; qtd. Chauncey Brewster Tinker, *Nature's Simple Plan*, Princeton: Princeton University Press, 1922, p. 66.

[14] Susan Manning, *Fragments of Union*, Basingstoke, Hampshire: Palgrave, 2002, p. 149. See Valentina Bold, '"Rude Bard of the North": James Macpherson and the Folklore of Democracy', *Journal of American Folklore* (Special Issue: James Macpherson and the Ossian Epic Debate), vol. 114, no. 454, Fall 2001, pp. 464-477. Andrew Hook, 'Scotland and Romanticism: The International Scene', in Andrew Hook ed., *The History of Scottish Literature: Volume 2. 1660-1800*, Aberdeen: Aberdeen University Press, 1987, p. 316.

[15] See Paul Gategno, 'The Sublime Savage in America: James "Ossian" Macpherson's Tour of Duty in West Florida', *Scotia*, vol. 16, 1992, pp. 1-20.

[16] See Valentina Bold, '"Poor as a Poet": Macpherson, Burns and the Peasant Poet', *Scotlands* (Special Issue: Macpherson's Ossian), vol. 4, no. 1, 1997, pp. 109-118. Hugh Cheape, 'The Culture and Material Culture of Ossian, 1760-1900', *Scotlands*, vol. 4, no. 1, 1997, pp. 1-24. Paul Baines, 'Ossianic Geographies: Fingalian Figures on the Scottish Tour, 1760-1830', *Scotlands*, vol. 4, no. 1, 1997, p. 44. Joseph Nagy, 'Observations on the Ossianesque in Medieval Irish Literature and Modern Irish Folklore', *Journal of American Folklore* (Special Issue: James Macpherson and the Ossian Epic Debate), vol. 114, no. 454, Fall 2001, pp. 436-446. See too Howard Gaskill ed., *Ossian Revisited*, Edinburgh: Edinburgh University Press, 1991.

G. ROSS ROY

Robert Burns: Poet of the People

There are very few examples in the sweep of English/Scottish literature of an author whose beginnings were so humble, rising to
preeminence in his or her lifetime. Although William Wordsworth
employed what he called 'the real language of men' and celebrated
working-class occupations, he had benefited from a university education. Robert Burns, on the other hand, was a true autodidact,
having had very little formal schooling. In a famous letter to Dr.
John Moore of August 1787, the poet listed his early reading,
which shows that by age seventeen he had studied a large number
of the standard works of the time. We can follow his voracious
reading in his letters, when he orders books from a dealer, or discusses authors with correspondents.

Burns's father was a tenant farmer, and when he died in 1784
Robert became the head of the family. According to his testimony
he began rhyming in 1774 and this, together with a busy social life
as a member of the Bachelor's Club and his own amorous life,
kept him occupied. The unanticipated outcome of his love for Jean
Armour, whose father refused permission for the couple to marry,
decided Burns to emigrate to Jamaica. Before this, he developed a
passionate love for Mary Campbell ('Highland Mary') and the two
were planning to sail to the West Indies together. Mary went to bid
her family adieu but she died at Greenock, and Burns gave up his
plan, going instead to Edinburgh. Mary was the inspiration for one
of the most beautiful songs the poet ever wrote, which begins:

> Will ye go to the Indies, my Mary,
>   And leave auld Scotia's shore;
> Will ye go to the Indies, my Mary,
>   Across th' Atlantic roar.[1]

Burns decided to publish a selection of his poems before he emi-
grated, and to this end subscription bills were circulated. On July
31, 1786, there was published by John Wilson at Kilmarnock
Poems, Chiefly in the Scottish Dialect, a work that was to make
Robert Burns famous throughout the English-speaking world.
Fortunately for him, copies found their way to Edinburgh, and
Henry Mackenzie reviewed the book in his publication *The
Lounger*, where he called Burns a 'Heaven-taught ploughman'. This
idea takes its base from Jean-Jacques Rousseau's claim that man
was pure in his natural state, but had been corrupted by society.
And so in Mackenzie's phrase this 'rustic bard' was perceived to
have much to teach the literati of Edinburgh. Encouraged by the
favorable reception of his volume, Burns gave up his plans to emigrate and went instead to Edinburgh to see a second, enlarged edition of his poems through the press with the well-known publisher
William Creech. He arrived there in late November 1786, and on
December 9 Mackenzie's review appeared. Suddenly he was the
toast of the town, an esteemed guest in the salons of Edinburgh
and to the rowdy social society of the city's taverns. In both of
these milieus Burns was notable for his brilliant repartee; almost
everyone who knew him commented on the conviviality of his
conversation.

   The poet was not, however, taken in by this adulation; he knew
that he was a kind of plaything for the literati and society of
Edinburgh, and that they would eventually tire of this fascinating
young peasant, and so he made plans for a career. The occupation
which he knew best was farming, and before the appearance of
the second edition of his poems, in April 1787, he had entered into
negotiations with Patrick Miller for the lease of a farm near
Dumfries. In Edinburgh Burns met James Johnson, editor of *The
Scots Musical Museum*, and from then until he died the poet contributed to the work.

   Burns was indefatigable in gathering words and airs for inclusion in the *Museum*. Where there were no words for a tune, he
wrote them; where there were words which were inappropriate,
he wrote new ones. In the last letter which he wrote to Johnson,
Burns said: 'Your Work is a great one; & though, now that it is near
finished, I see if we were to begin again, two or three things that

might be mended, yet I will venture to prophesy, that to future ages your Publication will be the text book & standard of Scottish Song & Music'.[2] Two centuries after he wrote these words, *The Scots Musical Museum* remains the largest and most important collection of Scottish songs with their music.

On December 4, 1787, Burns met Agnes M'Lehose (called Nancy), who was separated from her dissolute husband, and it was love at first sight for both of them. So began a correspondence to which Burns contributed fifty-two known letters (it would appear that a few may be missing), with the participants taking Arcadian names – Robert became Sylvander, Nancy became Clarinda. Most of the letters were written while Burns was in Edinburgh; after he signed the lease for Ellisland in March 1788, and settled there in June, they tapered off significantly.

In March Jean Armour again gave birth to twins, but both of the girls died that month. Uncertain that he would be able to make a living by farming, Burns had also arranged to be appointed to the Excise. He began work on September 1, 1789. His Excise work was very demanding, necessitating that he ride over 300km per week in addition to running his farm.

Not far from his farm lived the Riddells at Friars Carse, and Burns became very friendly with Robert Riddell and his sister-in-law Maria Riddell. Together Robert Riddell and Burns founded a communal library called the Monkland Friendly Society, and Burns ordered a number of books for it from Edinburgh. At the request of his friend, Burns transcribed fifty-three unpublished poems of his in one volume and in the other a selection of twenty-seven letters he had written to various people. Included was the poet's famous long autobiographical letter to Dr. Moore mentioned earlier. This letter gives a detailed account of the poet's life up to the time of writing, and is the basis of much of what we know about his early life.

With Maria Riddell Burns formed a very close friendship, bordering almost on love. Her husband Walter was a wastrel, who dissipated his fortune, and left for the West Indies to try (unsuccessfully) to repair it. Maria was a woman of substantial attainments and author of *Voyages to the Madeira and Leeward Caribbean Isles* (1792). She and the poet shared a love of reading and of the theatre. The result of a drunken frolic involving Burns and several other people at Friars Carse estranged the two friends, but before long they made up. When Burns died, Maria wrote a *Memoir Concerning Burns* which appeared in the *Dumfries Journal* for August 1796; it is recognized as the best account of Burns by a contemporary. She was prescient in her statement that:

> Scotland shall long cherish his memory with delight and gratitude. Proudly she will remember that beneath her cold sky, a genius was ripened without care or culture, that would have done honour to climes more favourable to the development of those luxuriances of fancy and colouring in which he so eminently excelled.[3]

In September 1792 George Thomson wrote to Burns asking if he would participate in a plan he had to collect and publish the national songs of Scotland, with accompaniments. Initially, as Thomson described it, Burns was to remove 'nonsense and doggerel... [and] rhymes so loose and indelicate as cannot be sung in decent company' (Douglas, VI, p. 216).[4] Thomson, who lived in Edinburgh, obviously knew of Johnson's *Scots Musical Museum*, so that his further statement to the poet that his edition would be 'infinitely more interesting than any that has yet appeared'[5] (Douglas, VI, p. 216) was surely not lost on Burns. Thus began the poet's collaboration on *A Select Collection of Original Scotish Airs*. Initially the arrangements were to be done by I.J. Pleyel, but as the work progressed J.A. Kozeluch and finally Haydn and Beethoven were added. Although there were others supplying lyrics to Thomson, Burns remained his principal source, but he also sent in work by other poets, some named, others unknown.

For nearly four years Burns supplied words to both Johnson and Thomson, sometimes even the same songs. Johnson was a very modest person and he let the poet have his own way with the material he supplied for the *Museum*, but Thomson was active in the editing of his *Select Collection of Original Scotish Airs*, and he and Burns occasionally disagreed on a text. In one well-known case Thomson tried to alter the wording of one of Burns's most famous songs – 'Robert Bruce's March to Bannockburn' – which would have weakened the quality of the song. Although the *Select Collection* is an important work, Thomson appears to have been something of a dilettante, because Beethoven also complained when Thomson altered one of his arrangements. It must be said, however, that the editor forced Burns to think through his approach to the writing of songs; sometimes we can see how Thomson caused him to improve a song.

Trying to run a farm and fulfill his Excise duties proved too arduous for Burns and he arranged a transfer to the nearby port city of Dumfries, moving his family there in November 1791. The next February Burns was promoted to the Port Division which meant that he no longer had to travel in exercising his functions.

In 1792 a republican society called the Friends of the People became active in Scotland and there was considerable support for the French Revolution. In one famous case Burns was accused of having sung 'Ça ira' (a French revolutionary song, later replaced by the 'Marseillaise') at the Dumfries theatre, and he was obliged to write a humiliating letter to the Excise Commissioner, Robert Graham of Fintry, denying the charge.

In 1793 Creech decided to reissue Burns's poems and asked the poet for enough new material to make a two-volume set. The most notable work to appear in this edition was 'Tam o' Shanter', and the venture was a success, reissued four times by 1800.

There is a touching story about how Burns composed his first song. As a youth the poet was put to work at the harvest paired with Nellie Kilpatrick, whom Burns described as a 'bewitching creature' who among 'other love-inspiring qualifications... sung sweetly'.[6] The result of this infatuation was Burns's 'O Once I lov'd a bonnie lass'. He sums it up, 'Thus with me began Love and Poesy',[7] which were to remain his passions for the next two decades of his life.

Much of the chronology of the poems and the three songs which went into his 1786 edition is uncertain, because Burns had published nothing before the volume appeared. Subsequently he occasionally sent works of his to newspapers, and he was generous with manuscript copies of poems and songs which pleased him, and these too sometimes found their way into print, allowing us to date them more precisely.

In the Kilmarnock edition Burns displayed his mastery of 'standard Habbie', a Scottish stanza form which takes its name from a seventeenth-century poem by Robert Sempill (c.1595-c.1665) enti-

tled 'The Life and Death of Habbie Simpson, the Piper of
Kilbarchan', a verse form much used by Allan Ramsay and perfected by Burns. It rhymes aaabab, with the a lines in tetrameter, and
the b usually in dimeter. Two of the best-known poems establish
Burns as a consummate master of the poem of nature. In 'To a
Mouse, On turning her up in her Nest, with the Plough, November,
1785' the poet addresses the wee creature who has seen all its
efforts to lay in store laid waste by his plough. In touching phrases
he tells the mouse that it is welcome to the few grains it has stolen
from Burns's harvest, continuing the poem with the oft-quoted passage, 'The best laid schemes o' *Mice* an' *Men*,/Gang aft agley' and
concluding with:

> Still, thou art blest, compar'd wi' *me*!
> The *present* only toucheth thee:
> But Och! I *backward* cast my e'e,
>   On prospects drear!
> An' *forward*, tho' I canna *see*,
> I *guess* an' *fear*![8]

There have been those who fault Burns for not having created an
oeuvre with a more distinctive moral tone, but to do so is to mis-
understand what Burns believed his function as poet and songwriter to be. His aim was to communicate to his fellow human
beings the beauty that he saw all around him, and how meaningful
his relationships with others could be.

Another poem in standard Habbie is 'To a Mountain-Daisie, On
turning one down, with the Plough, in April – 1786' in which
Burns's plough (that which will give him sustenance) is the cause
of disruption when he turns the daisy under. He addresses it:

> Wee, modest, crimson-tipped flow'r,
> Thou's met me in an evil hour;
> For I maun crush amang the stoure
>   Thy slender stem:[9]

Making a trio in the Kilmarnock edition is 'To a Louse, On Seeing
one on a Lady's Bonnet at Church' in which Burns hilariously
addresses the louse, telling it to 'Gae somewhere else and seek
your dinner,/... in some beggar's haffet squattle;/There ye may
creep, and sprawl, and sprattle,/Wi' ither kindred, jumping

cattle,/In shoals and nations',[10] where it will not be noticed among its numerous brethren. In this poem, however, Burns introduces a human warning to the young lady on whose bonnet the louse can be seen. He concludes:

O wad some Pow'r the giftie gie us
To see oursels as others see us!
It wad frae monie a blunder free us
        An' foolish notion:
What airs in dress an' gait wad lea'e us,
        And ev'n Devotion![11]

At about this time Burns was publicly admonished by his church for the sin of fornication, and one of the elders of the church was William Fisher, whose own character left much to be desired. 'Holy Willie's Prayer', which was not authorized for publication during the poet's lifetime, imaginatively follows Fisher after Burns had received more lenient treatment than desired by the elder. In this mock prayer Fisher addresses the fundamentalist Presbyterian God, who:

Sends ane to heaven and ten to hell,
        A' for thy glory!
And no for ony gude or ill
        They've done before thee.[12]

From this broad general statement of belief Holy Willie moves to the specific, asking that God's wrath be directed against Robert Aiken, Burns's friend and lawyer, to whom the poet dedicated 'The Cotter's Saturday Night'. Aiken had successfully defended the poet in the suit brought against him in the Presbytery of Ayr, and Holy Willie asks God to damn Aiken, and others who had sided with Burns, not only in the hereafter but also in the here and now. We note how the elder's mind constantly strays from faith to the concrete. Thus after calling down divine wrath upon Burns and his associates, Fisher ends:

But Lord, remember me and mine
Wi' mercies temporal and divine!
That I for grace and gear may shine,
        Excell'd by nane!
And a' the glory shall be thine!
        AMEN! AMEN![13]

From the way Holy Willie phrases his requests to the Almighty throughout the poem, it would appear as though earthly concerns were uppermost in his mind, and asking for divine intercession after death an afterthought. Burns's triumphant conclusion of the poem, which critics have claimed is the greatest short satire in the English language, makes Fisher seem almost condescending to God, when he concludes 'a' the glory shall be thine'.

Burns's Kilmarnock volume also contains another satire, 'The Twa Dogs', which compares a town dog, Caesar, who is very conscious of his superiority over Luath, his country cousin. The idea behind this poem goes back in Scottish poetry to Robert Henryson's 'The Two Mice' and others of his *Fables*, many of which, as Henryson admits, derive from Aesop. Although the country dog would appear to live the more rewarding life, Burns is clever enough to leave the discussion unresolved, by concluding the poem with these words:

> When up they gat, an' shook their lugs,
> Rejoic'd they were na *men* but *dogs*;
> An' each took off his several way,
> Resolv'd to meet some ither day.[14]

Written at the same time, although not published until the Edinburgh edition of 1787, is 'The Brigs of Ayr', a poem in which the Auld Brig and the New Brig exchange banter as did the two dogs. Built in 1232, the old bridge crossed the Ayr River at the town of that name, and by 1786 a new bridge was under construction to be completed two years later. Burns opens the poem on a personal note: 'The simple Bard, rough at the rustic plough,/Learning his tuneful trade from ev'ry bough'.[15] Burns introduces two spirits he chanced to overhear, the Auld and the New Brig, and then the poem shifts to a conversation between these two in which they contrast historical times with modern. The discussion ends when a fairy troop comes down the river. It should interest readers that two centuries later the Auld Brig is still standing and in use for pedestrians.

In eighteenth-century Scotland it was still common for people to practice medicine without having any formal training in the art, and this was the case of John Wilson, a schoolmaster at Tarbolton, who also operated a grocer's shop where he sold medicines and gave advice on people's illnesses. Burns's satire on Wilson is called 'Death and Doctor Hornbook', the name, of course, taken from the child's primer covered by a thin layer of horn, a teaching object still in use in eighteenth-century Scotland. Doctor Hornbook opens the poem thus:

> Some books are lies frae end to end,
> And some great lies were never penn'd:
> Ev'n Ministers they hae been kenn'd,
> In holy rapture,
> A rousing whid, at times, to vend,
> And nail't wi' Scripture.[16]

But Hornbook's tale, he assures his readers, 'Is just as true's the Deil's in hell'. He goes on to say, 'I was na fou, but just had plenty', when on his way home he met Death, whom he invited to sit and chat, after having been assured that Death meant him no harm. Death does not know the identity of Hornbook, and he begins his complaint that the good doctor is taking away all his trade:

> 'See, here's a scythe, and there's a dart,
> 'They hae pierc'd mony a gallant heart;
> 'But Doctor *Hornbook*, wi' his art
> 'And cursed skill,
> 'Has made them baith no worth a fart,
> 'Damn'd haet they'll kill!
>
> . . . .
>
> 'Whare I kill'd ane, a fair strae-death,
> 'By loss o' blood, or want o' breath,
> 'This night I'm free to tak my aith,
> 'That *Hornbook*'s skill
> Has clad a score i' their last claith,
> 'by drap and pill.[17]

Much of the poem is given to mocking the so-called remedies put forward by Wilson, but finally the effect is to chuckle at rather than to denigrate. Death is just about to tell his unknown listener what he intends to do to Hornbook when the church bell tolls the hour when spirits must depart, and Hornbook finishes his tale with the remark: 'I took the way that pleas'd mysel,/And sae did Death'.[18]

The subject of death leads us to another group of poems in the Burns canon – the elegy. These fall into two categories, the serious elegy and the mock elegy. The poet's elegy on his father is a major production of the earlier type; in it Robert details the fine qualities and high ideals of William, who died in 1784. Burns never quite got over the feeling that he had not lived up to this father's expectations, and we sense this in the elegy.

Turning to the mock elegy, we find Burns carrying on a long Scottish tradition of the dying words of a subject lamenting his or her earthly transgressions and warning the reader against making the same mistakes. In this tradition one thinks of the seventeenth-century 'Life and Death of the Piper of Kilbarchan', which has already been mentioned. In the eighteenth century we find Allan Ramsay's 'Lucky Spence's Last Advice' and Robert Fergusson's 'Elegy, On the Death of Mr David Gregory, late Professor of Mathematics in the University of St. Andrews'. Burns cleverly combines the dying words and the genuine elegy in a pair of poems, the first with the cumbersome title 'The Death and Dying Words of Poor Mailie, The Author's only Pet Yowe, An Unco Mournfu' Tale', which is followed immediately in the 1786 volume by 'Poor Mailie's Elegy'. The first poem finds Mailie addressing a herd boy with a message for Burns, in which she tells the poet how he should treat her two surviving lambs. Then we have the mock elegy which ends:

O, a' ye *Bards* on bonie Doon!
An' wha on Aire your chanters tune!
Come, join the melancholious croon
    O' *Robin*'s reed!
His heart will never get aboon!
    His *Mailie*'s dead.[19]

Like writers who reminded themselves of their own mortality by placing a skull on their writing table, Burns reminded the world of his by writing his own elegy in 1787, even making a play on his name in the title 'Elegy on the Death of Robert Ruisseau', bearing in mind that the word *burns* means a brook in Scots.

Another verse form which Burns borrowed from earlier Scottish writers was the rhyming epistle, five of which he published in the Kilmarnock volume. It was the custom for poets to exchange these verse letters; not infrequently these exchanges were called flytings, which consisted of highly stylized insults. In Scottish literature the best known of these occurred between the so-called Scottish Chaucerians William Dunbar and Walter Kennedy. The exchanges in a flyting took the form of good-natured banter rather than attack, because the participants were frequently friends. Not all fly-ting was an exchange between two people, as Kenneth Simpson points out.[20] In fact both 'The Twa Dogs' and 'The Brigs of Ayr' can be considered as flytings.

About halfway through the Kilmarnock volume, forming, as it were, the centerpiece of the collection, is 'The Cotter's Saturday Night'. The epigraph to the poem is a quotation from Thomas Gray's famous 'Elegy in a Country Churchyard', and one might say that Burns's poem is an expansion upon Gray's idea of the dignity of rural toil. In Burns we see the cotter and his older children come home from their various employments, to be met by the wife and small children. After a cheerful meal, the father leads the group in singing psalms and he reads the Bible aloud. The last three (of twenty-one) stanzas are devoted by the poet to extolling the virtues of his native land: 'From Scenes like these, old SCO-TIA'S grandeur springs,/That makes her lov'd at home, rever'd abroad'.[21] Burns then continues:

O SCOTIA! My dear, my native soil!
        For whom my warmest wish to Heaven is sent!
Long may thy hardy sons of *rustic toil*
        Be blest with health and peace and sweet content![22]

'The Cotter's Saturday Night' was one of Burns's most frequently anthologized poems throughout the nineteenth and earlier twenti-eth centuries, although today's reader may find the poet's idyllic picture of eighteenth-century life on a small farm rather strained. Certainly Burns's own experience as the son of a tenant farmer, and then one himself, bore scant resemblance to the life he pic-tured in the poem.

All of the poems mentioned so far were written by 1787. We must now move ahead to 1791 when Burns wrote one of the

world's greatest poems of diablerie, 'Tam o' Shanter'. Burns met
Captain Francis Grose in 1789 when he was in Scotland gathering
material and making drawings for his two-volume *Antiquities of
Scotland* (1789-1791). The poet convinced the antiquarian to include
a drawing of the ruined Kirk of Alloway, which Grose agreed to do
if Burns would write a poem on the subject. The poem and drawing
appeared in the second volume of the *Antiquities*.

In 'Tam o' Shanter' we follow Tam from his drunken market-day
revelries in Ayr when he rides home, past the ruined Kirk Alloway
where he beholds a devil's gathering in the churchyard. In a
drunken burst of enthusiasm he makes his presence known. In the
poem, Burns adopts several voices. We are warned, but Tam
ignores his wife Kate's advice:

> Whare sits our sulky sullen dame,
> Gathering her brows like gathering storm,
> Nursing her wrath to keep it warm.[23]

As Tam sits in the tavern enjoying himself, we are told that Care
itself:

> ...mad to see a man sae happy,
> E'en drown'd himsel amang the nappy[24]

and Tam's drunken elation is described thus:

> Kings may be blest, but *Tam* was glorious,
> O'er a' the ills o' life victorious![25]

Here the poem abruptly shifts from Scots to English in an eight-line
meditation on the transience of pleasure:

> But pleasures are like poppies spread,
> You seize the flower, its bloom is shed;
> Or like the snow falls in the river,
> A moment white – then melts for ever;
>
> ....
>
> Or like the rainbow's lovely form
> Evanishing amid the storm –[26]

This only passage in the poem in standard English serves as a dividing point – before it, Tam was comfortably seated in the tavern, after it he is outside. We are told that Tam was well mounted on his mare, Meg, and that he rode off, 'Despising wind, and rain, and fire',[27] because, do what they might, these three elements could not harm one who identified with the fourth element, the soil. As he approaches the haunted kirk, Tam has no fear because, 'Wi' usquabae, we'll face the devil!'[28] in a shift which allows Burns to identify with Tam through the use of the collective pronoun 'we'. The poet repeats this change of point of view when he, as narrator, says, 'Inspiring bold *John Barleycorn*!/What dangers thou canst make us scorn!'[29] as Tam views the cavorting of the dead. Unable to control his enthusiasm, Tam shouts out to a comely young witch, 'Weel done, Cutty-sark!',[30] whereupon the hellish legion takes off after Tam and Meg. But they have miscalculated the mettle of the mare. Devils cannot cross a running stream, and just as Cutty-sark was about to seize Tam, Meg made a mighty leap and all the witch got was the end of the horse's tail, leaving her with just a stub for the rest of her life. Burns concludes this splendid poem with these words of advice to anyone who reads his tale:

> Whene'er to drink you are inclin'd,
> Or cutty-sarks run in your mind,
> Think, ye may buy the joys o'er dear,
> Remember Tam o' Shanter's mare[31]

Burns is here, of course, indulging in a splendid irony. For what has been the price to Tam for his evening at the inn, the sight of Cutty-sark and the dance of the witches? The loss of his mare's tail! Isn't Burns subtly suggesting that the prophets of doom are wrong? We may be threatened by them, as Kate threatened Tam, but finally those who live life to its fullest are the richer in experience, although they may pay a trifling price for it. Read this way, 'Tam o' Shanter' forms a companion piece with Burns's celebration of low life in 'The Jolly Beggars'.

Mention has been made of James Johnson and *The Scots Musical Museum* and of Burns's enthusiastic collaboration with the editor. Of the 600 songs which appeared in the collection between 1787 and 1803 Burns supplied 171. He contributed to the project in three ways: he wrote lyrics for traditional Scottish airs which had none, he rewrote songs which existed in erotic or inferior form, and he collected traditional songs and music for Johnson. Not all the correspondence between the two has survived, so it is possible that Burns may have written, refurbished or collected even more than those we know about. The poet's last known letter to Johnson was published in vol. V of the *Museum*, and in the letter the poet wrote: 'Your Work is a great one... I will venture to prophesy, that in future ages your Publication will be the text book & standard of Scottish Song and Music'.[32] Burns was right; over two centuries later *The Scots Musical Museum* remains the most important collection in the field. It is no exaggeration to suggest that Robert Burns was the greatest songwriter in the English language.

With such a wealth of songs to choose from it will not be possible to comment even on all the great ones; what follows is discussion of only some of them. It was mentioned that Burns's earliest composition was a song. From 1787, when he became involved with *The Scots Musical Museum*, almost all of Burns's output was songs, with, of course, the major exception being 'Tam o' Shanter'. Although it is not known who was the heroine of Burns's song 'Mary Morison' it is universally recognized as a masterpiece, particularly admired by Scotland's greatest twentieth-century poet, Hugh MacDiarmid. There is a disturbing quality to the lines when the poet states, 'Yestreen when to the trembling string/The dance gaed through the lighted ha'.' Of the dancers he says:

Though this was fair, and that was braw,
        And yon the toast of a' the town,
I sigh'd, and said amang them a',
        'Ye are na Mary Morison'.[33]

Love was, of course, one of the principal topics of Burns's songs. He did write general love songs, but most of his best songs have a particular subject, although we are not now always able to identify the object of the poet's passion. Not unnaturally several songs are addressed to Jean Armour, who became his wife. One of the best loved of these is 'I love my Jean', written when Burns was preparing to bring her to Ellisland in 1788. The trip back to Mauchline was a long one and the poet, who was to set up house with her for the first time, felt the separation deeply. The song opens:

Of a' the airts the wind can blaw,
        I dearly like the West;
For there the bony Lassie lives,
        The Lassie I lo'e best:

. . . .

There's not a bony flower that springs
        By fountain, shaw, or green;
There's not a bony bird that sings
        But minds me o' my Jean.[34]

A love song addressed to the memory of Highland Mary was not written until November 1789, three years after her death. It opens:

Thou lingering Star with lessening ray
        That lovest to greet the early morn,
Again thou usherest in the day
        My Mary from my Soul was torn–

And it concludes:

My Mary, dear, departed Shade!
        Where is thy place of blissful rest!
Seest thou thy Lover lowly laid!
        Hearest thou the groans that rend his breast![35]

In December of that year Burns wrote to Mrs. Dunlop, to whom he had originally sent the song, discussing the possibility of a Hereafter, adding that in such a place he would, 'with speechless agony of rapture, again recognize my lost, my ever dear Mary'.[36]

    It will be noted that both of the above songs deal with absent love. Another such concerns the separation of Burns and Agnes M'Lehose. The couple had effectively parted when the poet left Edinburgh to begin farming at Ellisland in 1788. The poem begins:

Ae fond kiss, and then we sever;
Ae fareweel, and then forever!
Deep in heart-wrung tears I'll pledge thee,
Warring sighs and groans I'll wage thee.

. . . .

Had we never lov'd sae kindly,
Had we never lov'd sae blindly!
Never met – or never parted,
We had ne'er been broken-hearted.[37]

The song appeared in vol. IV of *The Scots Musical Museum* (1792) and it has been a popular favorite ever since. Sir Walter Scott is reputed to have said that it contained 'the essence of a thousand love tales'. Forty years after they parted, Clarinda wrote in her diary on the anniversary of their last meeting: 'This day I can never forget. Parted with Burns... never more to meet in this world. Oh, may we meet in Heaven!' By no means all of the poet's love songs are melancholic, however. 'Afton Water' is a good example of Burns combining a tender love song with a hymn in praise of the River Afton, for he was a great nature poet who frequently combined this love with some other emotion. The song in question begins:

Flow gently, sweet Afton, among thy green braes,
Flow gently, I'll sing thee a song in thy praise;
My Mary's asleep by thy murmuring stream,
Flow gently, sweet Afton, disturb not her dream.[38]

The poet then devotes another four stanzas to the Afton and Mary's relationship to it, with a concluding stanza which repeats almost verbatim the first. In a letter which contains this song, Burns speaks of his 'particular pleasure in those little pieces... [which introduce names and features] of rivers, lakes, or woodlands'.[39]

One of Burns's greatest songs, 'A red red Rose', which first appeared in 1794 in Peter Urbani's *Selections of Scots Songs*, is not addressed to any particular woman. It is one of the greatest achievements in the history of Scots or English songwriting. Of the 106 words in Kinsley's edition, only five have two syllables, one has three; all the others contain only one syllable. Furthermore, as is pointed out by T.F. Henderson, each of the four stanzas has been taken to a greater or lesser extent from one or more traditional songs or ballads.[40] Not one of the precursors cited by Henderson is in any way memorable, whereas every line of Burns's song is. 'A red red Rose' is an outstanding example of how Burns could take the dross of old songs and weave them into gold of his own. The song is so splendid that it should be cited in full:

O my Luve's like a red, red rose,
        That's newly sprung in June;
O my Luve's like the melodie
        That's sweetly play'd in tune. –

As fair art thou, my bonie lass,
        So deep in luve am I;
And I will love thee still, my Dear,
        Till a' the seas gang dry. –

Till a' the seas gan dry, my Dear,
        And the rocks melt wi' the sun:
I will love thee still, my Dear,
        While the sands o' life shall run. –

And fare thee weel, my only Luve!
        And fare thee weel, a while!
And I will come again, my Luve,
        Tho' it were ten thousand mile!–[41]

Bacchanalian effusions also figure large in Burns's repertoire. Among the best known of these, 'John Barleycorn', which the poet called a ballad, is based on an old song. In it the cereal is made human, and we follow it through its various stages until it becomes a liquor:

Then let us toast John Barleycorn,
        Each man a glass in hand;
And may his great posterity
        Ne'er fail in old Scotland![42]

Scottish nationalism was always a major concern of Burns, and his 'Scots Wha Hae', as it is now usually called, is one of the greatest of all Scottish patriotic songs. When first published in George Thomson's *Select Collection of Original Scotish Airs* in 1798 it bore the title 'Robert Bruce's Address to his Army at Bannockburn':

Scots, wha hae wi' Wallace bled,
Scots, wham Bruce has aften led,
Welcome to your gory bed,–
        Or to victorie.–

. . . .

Lay the proud Usurpers low!
Tyrants fall in every foe!
Liberty's in every blow!
          Let us Do – or Die!!![43]

The battle which this song celebrates saw Robert I (Robert the
Bruce) win an astonishing victory over the overwhelmingly superi-
or army of Edward II in 1314. The fight was commemorated by
John Barbour in *The Bruce* (1377) and also by Sir Walter Scott in
The Lord of the Isles. Burns was justifiably proud of the song, and
he sent copies of it to several friends. To Dr. Moore, some years
before he composed the song, Burns wrote, 'The first two books I
ever read in private, and which gave me more pleasure than any
two books I ever read again, were, the life of Hannibal and the
history of Sir William Wallace... the story of Wallace poured a
Scottish prejudice in my veins which will boil along there till the
flood-gates of life shut in eternal rest'.[44] Appropriately 'Scots Wha
Hae' has been called the 'Marseillaise' of Scotland.

'Love and Liberty' (also known as 'The Jolly Beggars') was written between 1784 and 1785. It is an extraordinary piece, set in a
Mauchline tavern, Poosie Nansie's. Tradition has it that Burns
dropped in late one evening and witnessed the singing and gaiety
of a group of wandering beggars. Each member of the group has
his or her song in the cantata. Here we find a representative group
of the dispossessed of Burns's world. The work ends with the
entire group singing:

See the smoking bowl before us,
          Mark our jovial, ragged ring!
Round and round take up the Chorus,
          And in raptures let us sing–

          Chorus
A fig for those by law protected!
          Liberty's a glorious feast!
Courts for Cowards were erected,
          Churches built to please the Priest.[45]

Burns had wished to publish the work in his 1787 Edinburgh edition, but was dissuaded from doing so. After this he set the work aside, and when asked about it by George Thomson in September 1793 he replied: 'I have forgot the Cantata you allude to, as I kept no copy... none of the songs pleased myself, except the last – something about,

'Courts for cowards were erected,
'Churches built to please the priest'.[46]

In the event the work was not published until 1799.

No assessment of the work of Burns would be complete if it ignored his erotic poems and songs. When he was living in Edinburgh, he was in the habit of frequenting a tavern in Anchor Close where a convivial group called the Crochallan Fencibles met. Among the members was William Smellie, founder of the club, printer of the poet's Edinburgh edition, and author and editor of the first edition of the *Encyclopaedia Britannica*. It would appear that Burns recited his bawdy poems to the group, and after his death many of the poems and songs as recited, not all by Burns, were published in a volume entitled *The Merry Muses of Caledonia; A Collection of Favourite Scots Songs, Ancient and Modern; Selected for Use of the Crochallan Fencibles* (1799).[47] Almost from the beginning there were attempts to deny that Burns had written any of the poems, but there are manuscript copies of several of them, and there are letters in which the poet included bawdy compositions, leaving no room for doubt as to his authorship. What distinguishes Burns's work in this field is that his productions are funny. Several are explicitly sexual, but they are not voyeuristic, they lead to laughter. It must also be said of Burns that while he gave the world a number of erotic poems, he also gave us purified versions of older bawdy songs. An example of this is the poem 'John Anderson my Jo', which existed in an indecent version as early as 1744, and which Burns transformed into the tender evocation of elderly love:

John Anderson, my jo, John
        We clamb the hill thegither;

. . . .

Now we maun totter down, John,
      And hand in hand we'll go;
And sleep thegither at the foot,
      John Anderson my Jo.[48]

I have left 'Auld Lang Syne', Robert Burns's great song of parting, for the last, although it was written by 1793. As with so many other songs, the poet doubtless found some of the words in earlier sources; Allan Ramsay had published in 1721 a song entitled 'The Kind Reception, To the Tune of Auld Lang Syne' which opens thus:

Should auld Acquaintance be forgot,
      Tho they return with Scars?
These are the noble Heroe's Lot,
      Obtain'd in glorious Wars.[49]

There is an even earlier version of the song in James Watson's *Choice Collection of Comic and Serious Scots Poems, Both Ancient and Modern*, where we find the following:

Should auld Acquaintance be forgot,
      And never thought upon,
The Flames of Love extinguished,
      And freely past and gone?[50]

Compare these to how Burns's song opens:

Should auld acquaintance be forgot
      And never brought to mind?
Should auld acquaintance be forgot,
      And auld lang syne!

      Chorus
For auld lang syne, my jo,
      For auld lang syne,
We'll tak a cup o' kindness yet
      For auld lang syne.[51]

Burns can have found only a phrase here and there in these earlier poems. In a letter of December 7, 1788, to Mrs. Dunlop he transcribed the song and added: 'Light be the turf on the breast of the heaven-inspired Poet who composed this glorious Fragment!'[52] This statement has caused some uncertainty among scholars: did the poet mean the fragments he had borrowed from earlier versions, or did he mean to suggest that all of the song was by another? He was vague, too, when he sent the song to George Thomson in September 1793: 'Auld lang syne' – The air is but mediocre; but the following song, the old Song of the olden times, & which has never been in print, nor even in manuscript, until I took it down from an old man's singing; is enough to recommend any air'.[53] I have also considered the possibility that Burns was being modest, and did not want to admit to having written what he knew was a masterpiece. Today the song is universally ascribed to Burns, and it has become what is probably the best-known non-political secular song in the world – sung throughout the English-speaking world, throughout much of Europe, in India, and elsewhere, particularly when people welcome in a new year.

It is difficult to praise Robert Burns too highly. R.W. Emerson, when gathered at the Boston Burns Club with others to celebrate the centenary of the poet's birth on January 25, 1859, had these words to say about the immortal Bard:

> ...as he was thus the poet of the poor, anxious, cheerful, working human-
> ity, so he had the language of low life. He grew up in a rural district,
> speaking a patois unintelligible to all but natives, but he has made that
> Lowland Scotch a Doric dialect of fame. It is the only example in history
> of a language made classic by the genius of a single man.[54]

Today there are several hundred Burns clubs throughout the world, and his birthday on January 25 is celebrated with as much fervor as is New Year's Day. His poems and songs have been trans-lated into most of the major languages, and for over two centuries his works have never been out of print. Each year tens upon tens of thousands of tourists visit the places where he lived: Alloway, Mount Oliphant, Lochlie, Mossgiel, Ellisland, and Dumfries. As a poet and as a man Robert Burns has captured the imagination and the love of admirers everywhere.

NOTES

[1] Robert Burns, *The Poems and Songs of Robert Burns*, edited by James Kinsley, 3 vols., Oxford: Clarendon Press, 1968, II, p. 657. Henceforth *Poems*.

[2] Robert Burns, *The Letters of Robert Burns*, 2nd edn., edited by G. Ross Roy, 2 vols., Oxford: Clarendon Press, 1985, II, pp. 381-382. Henceforth *Letters*.

[3] Robert Burns, *The Works of Robert Burns*, edited by William Scott Douglas, 6 vols., Edinburgh, 1877-1879, VI, p. 375. Henceforth *Douglas*.

[4] Robert Burns, *The Works*, cit., VI, p. 216.

[5] *Ibidem*.

[6] Robert Burns, *Letters*, cit., I, p. 137.

[7] *Ibidem*, p. 138.

[8] Robert Burns, *Poems*, cit., I, p. 128.

[9] *Ibidem*, p. 228.

[10] *Ibidem*, p. 193.

[11] *Ibidem*, p. 194.

[12] *Ibidem*, p. 74.

[13] *Ibidem*, p. 78.

[14] *Ibidem*, p. 145.

[15] *Ibidem*, p. 280.

[16] *Ibidem*, p. 79.

[17] *Ibidem*, p. 81 and p. 83.

[18] *Ibidem*, p. 84.

[19] *Ibidem*, p. 36.

[20] Kenneth Simpson, 'The Legacy of Flyting', *Studies in Scottish Literature*, vol. 26, 1991, pp. 504-514.

[21] Robert Burns, *Poems*, cit., I, p. 151.

[22] *Ibidem*.

[23] *Ibidem*, II, p. 557.

[24] *Ibidem*, II, p. 559.

[25] *Ibidem*.

[26] *Ibidem*.

[27] *Ibidem*.

[28] *Ibidem*, p. 560.

[29] *Ibidem*.

[30] *Ibidem*, p. 563.

[31] *Ibidem*, p. 564.

[32] Robert Burns, *Letters*, cit., II, pp. 381-382.

[33] Robert Burns, *Poems*, cit., I, p. 42.

[34] *Ibidem*, pp. 421-422.

[35] *Ibidem*, pp. 492-493.

[36] Robert Burns, *Letters*, cit., I, pp. 457-458.

[37] Robert Burns, *Poems*, cit., II, pp. 591-592.

[38] *Ibidem*, I, p. 461.

[39] Robert Burns, *Letters*, cit., I, p. 370.

[40] Robert Burns, *The Poetry of Robert Burns*, edited by W.E. Henley and T.F. Henderson, 4 vols., London, 1896-1897, III, pp. 402-406.

[41] Robert Burns, *Poems*, cit., II, p. 735.

[42] *Ibidem*, I, p. 31.

[43] *Ibidem*, II, pp. 707-708.

[44] Robert Burns, *Letters*, cit., I, pp. 135-136.

[45] Robert Burns, *Poems*, cit., I, pp. 207-208.

[46] Robert Burns, *Letters*, cit., II, p. 244.

[47] There are only two known copies of the original edition of this work: the Rosebery copy, on deposit at the National Library of Scotland, and a copy in the G. Ross Roy Collection at the University of South Carolina. In 1999 the University published a facsimile of the work, together with a short pamphlet about it which I wrote.

[48] Robert Burns, *Poems*, cit., II, p. 529.

[49] *The Works of Allan Ramsay*, edited by Burns Martin and J.W. Oliver, Scottish Text Society, 3rd Series, 19, 1945, p. 45.

[50] Part III, 1711. Attributed to Francis Sempill (c.1616-1682). For *A Choice Collection* see the edition edited by Harriet Harvey Wood, Scottish Text Society, 4th Series, 10, 1977, p. 71.

[51] Robert Burns, *Poems*, cit., I, p. 443.

[52] Robert Burns, *Letters*, cit., I, p. 345.

[53] *Ibidem*, II, p. 246.

[54] *Celebration of the Hundredth Anniversary of the Birth of Robert Burns, by the Boston Burns Club. January 25th 1859* (Boston, 1859), p. 37.

James Hogg

James Hogg, 'The Ettrick Shepherd', was born in Ettrickhall in the Scottish Borders, the second of four sons to tenant farmers Margaret Laidlaw and Robert Hogg. Due to his father's bankruptcy, the writer spent only six months at school, and was hired out aged seven to work as a cow herd; by the age of seventeen Hogg was a shepherd. He was fortunate in coming from a family of accomplished singers and storytellers; Hogg's grandfather, Will o' Phaup, transmitted much of his repertoire to his children, Margaret and William Laidlaw. Hogg read widely, too, using the libraries of his employers, the Laidlaws. He stresses an early identification with Scottish writing from Hamilton of Gilbertfield's version of Blind Harry's *The Wallace* (1722) to *The Gentle Shepherd* (1725).[1]

Hogg 'resolved to be a poet' after encountering Burns' work in 1797 and formed a literary society of shepherds. His first publication was a comic poem, 'The Mistakes of a Night', printed anonymously in *The Scots Magazine* of 1794. Hogg's later contributions to the periodicals, including *The Edinburgh Literary Journal, Chambers's Edinburgh Journal, The Quarterly Journal of Agriculture and Fraser's Magazine for Town and Country*, would be extensive. An early series of letters, too, following Burns' footsteps in trips to the Highlands, was published between 1802 and 1804 in *The Scots Magazine.*[2] Incidentally, during the 1832 visit of Hogg to London – where he was much more appreciated than in Scotland – Hogg brewed punch in Burns' punch bowl during a lavish dinner, on the 25th of January, for over two hundred people.

By 1800 Hogg was working with his father at Ettrickhouse, and in 1801 published the anonymous and popular song *The Patriot Lay of Donald McDonald* (1801). In 1801, too, Hogg's *Scottish*

Pastorals, Poems, Songs, etc. Mostly written in the dialect of the South shows him working skilfully within Scottish idioms, particularly in lyric styles. At this time, through the Laidlaws, Hogg's family became involved in Scott's project of collecting for *The Minstrelsy of the Scottish Border* (1802-1803). Famously, Hogg's mother disliked Scott's ballads: 'they were made for singing an' no for reading – they're nouther right spell'd nor right setten down'. Scott, who first met Hogg in 1802, assumed the role of quasi-patron although the relationship was, at times, ambivalent.[3] When the lease on Ettrickhouse expired in 1803, Hogg attempted to secure a lease in Harris but lost his savings. He spent a summer in Cumberland and then as a shepherd at Mitchell-Slack in Nithsdale. There, Hogg met Allan Cunningham, and the two writers formed a lasting friendship. In 1807 Hogg began to work as a land agent, and continued to do so, part time, until 1811.

In 1807 Hogg published his second volume of poetry, *The Mountain Bard* (several pieces had been published in journals like *The Scots Magazine*). There is an Ossianic and sentimental flavour to this, with parodic moments. In the same year, Hogg published *The Shepherd's Guide: being a Practical Treatise on the Diseases of Sheep* (1807), which won a prize from the Highland Society. Hogg earned £300 from his publications, and took the farms of Locherben, with Adam Brydon, and Cofardine in Dumfriesshire. By late 1809 he was in debt.

In February 1810 Hogg set off for Edinburgh, intending to write full time. His friend John Grieve (a hatter) offered useful contacts (including Hogg's future brother-in-law James Gray, a teacher at the High School) and Hogg became involved in an Edinburgh debating society, the Forum. On 1 September 1810, Hogg published the first number of a short-lived satirical journal, *The Spy*, drawing on models such as *The Spectator*. While initially it sold well, Hogg offended his audience in issues 3 and 4, and the final issue ran on 24th August 1811. His next poetry collection, *The Forest Minstrel* (1810), presented Hogg as the leading poet of Ettrick, in a Borders version of the Ossianic group. Like Ramsay and Burns, Hogg champions 'national music', shunning 'English songs' and 'Italian tirlie-whirlies' whilst maintaining 'the most scrupulous delicacy'.[4]

In 1813, Hogg made his literary breakthrough with the long narrative poem *The Queen's Wake*. Set on Mary Queen of Scots return to Scotland in 1561, it describes a poetry contest lasting for three nights. The best known items include 'The Witch of Fife', a rollicking account of a witch's night raid to Carlisle, and her husband's capture by the bishop's men. In Hogg's original version the old man was burnt at the stake. Scott, however, persuaded Hogg to save him: the wife rescues the husband and a moral is drawn:

> May ever ilke man in the land of Fyfe,
> > Read what drinkeris dree;
> And nevir curse his puir auld wife,
> > Rychte wicked altho she be.

'Kilmeny' is the most highly finished part of *The Wake*. The title character is a composite creation, as enigmatic as the fairy lady of 'Tam Lin' (Child 39), but 'pure as pure could be'. On one level, with its sombre Highland shepherd bard, Drummond of Ern, the poem reworks 'Thomas the Rhymer' (chapter 37). Like Thomas, Kilmeny has emblematic visions. He saw the narrow path of righteousness and broad path of wickedness. Kilmeny sees the 'stream of life' and Scotland's future: the demise of Mary Queen of Scots; the civil wars; the coming of Napoleon. Like Thomas, Kilmeny is seven years in the Otherworld and when she returns, like him, speaks, 'words of wonder, and words of truth'. Christian elements mix with tradition and with the 'land of vision', the metaphysical realm of Kilmeny's self-discovery. Reviews were mixed: *The Edinburgh Review*, for instance, admired 'original genius' but wished Hogg, 'could be persuaded to put a little more thought and matter in it – to make his images a little more select'. However, in terms of Hogg's poetical career, *The Wake* was a significant publication, which won Hogg attention from the *Literati* North and South of the Border (he corresponded with Byron and with Southey, and spent time with Wordsworth in the Lake District in 1814).[5]

In 1815, due to the wishes of the Duchess of Buccleuch (who died in 1814), Hogg was granted the farm of Altrive Lake, on Yarrow, for a nominal rent. In the same year he published *The Pilgrims of the Sun*, dedicated to Byron. The first edition consisted

solely of 'Pilgrims of the Sun' and 'Superstition'. However, from the
1822 *Poetical Works* onwards, in Hogg's lifetime, 'The Pilgrims',
'Connel of Dee' and 'Superstition' appear together, as parts of an
extended, and supernatural, narrative. The pilgrim, Mary Lee from
Carelha in Yarrow (the site of 'Tam Lin' (Child 39)) is similar to
Kilmeny. Accompanied by an angelic 'wight' in a white robe, she
makes a celestial journey, realising that all faiths are equally
respected by God, and achieving a new understanding of the relatively lowly position the earth holds. Hogg makes use of an eclectic range of sources here, including Dante's *Divina Commedia* (Cary's
complete blank verse translation was published in 1814, with parts
appearing in 1805 and 1806) and *The Pilgrim's Progress*. There are
similarities of outlook, too, to Blake's 'Jerusalem' and perhaps Allan
Cunningham – who featured Blake in *Lives of the Most Eminent
British Painters, Sculptors and Architects* (1829-1833) – introduced
Hogg to the then obscure writer's work. Astronomy, too, fascinated
Hogg, and the 1822 edition of *The Pilgrims* includes 'Verses to the
Comet of 1811', based on 'Stanzas Addressed to a Comet' in the
Edinburgh Magazine of 1819 and celebrating 'The Great Comet' of
1811 which was thought to foretell the fall of Napoleon. It is possi-
ble, too, that Hogg alludes to the anticipated solar eclipse of 1816.
Hogg probably draws, too, on the 1771 edition of *Encyclopaedia
Britannica*, using the contemporary theory of plural worlds by
analogy. There are traces, too, of the notions of heavenly order
expressed in Laplace's *Mécanique Céleste* (1799-1822) and of a
Newtonian 'motioned universe'. Another source is *Revelations* 21:
10, where an angel escorts the spirit of St John, 'to a great and high
mountain, and shewed me that great city, the holy Jerusalem'.
Reactions were mixed. Shrewdly, *The Augustan Review* observed:
'the author is said... to have been a shepherd; and... to possess little learning... he is not classical; but neither is he unlearned'. The
Scots Magazine admired the 'bolder character' of *The Pilgrims*, but
wished Hogg would stick to 'the mythology of his own country'.
Later critics have been dismissive. Batho reviews its textual history
(Murray's hostility, Byron persuading him to publish) and dismisses
The Pilgrims as a stylistic 'sampler'. Gifford comments, 'Hogg is no
thinker... playing about in other poets' styles, using in turn the
manner of Scott, Pope and Milton'. More recently, Gifford acknowl-

edged validity to Nelson Smith's verdict on the 'ambitious' *The Pilgrims*. Groves thinks the poem is an analogy of travel through the realms of Milton, Dryden and Pope.[6]

Hogg constantly sought new models, as can be seen in his parodic and experimental works. The bravura *Poetic Mirror* (1816) is a collection of imitations, including affectionate tributes to Byron and Scott, followed by less respectful parodies of Wordsworth, Hogg himself, Southey and Coleridge, and forthright satire on John Wilson. 'The Gude Grey Katt' pokes fun at Hogg's own style, taking off Hogg's recurrent theme of a virgin's magical flight; it ends with the Katt plunging the cleric who attacks its shape-changing abilities into hell. Although published anonymously, Hogg's unmistakable style meant that the book's authorship was recognised and, wryly, *The British Lady's Magazine* (1816) observed that, 'there possibly never existed, at one time, a set of bards more assailable either by serious or burlesque imitations'. Modern critics are divided on the value of *The Poetic Mirror* though they recognise key items. Gifford dislikes the 'irritating pseudo-Scots' of the 'Gude Grey Katt' and the revelation of the Katt's identity. Groves indicates the importance of 'The Gude Grey Katt' as it 'represents the imagination of James Hogg'. Antony Hasler has described the 'ingenious lies' of the text as crucial to the formation of Hogg's ambivalent creative personae. Certainly it allowed the writer to experiment in a wide range of styles, while infusing the results with his distinctive literary accent. Hogg's highly developed capacity for experimentation, and for self-satire, influenced his later tale of a supernatural journey, 'The Russiadde: A Fragment of an Ancient Epic Poem, supposed to have been written by Gilbert Hume, a Sutor of Selkirk'; this attacks the romantic notion of visionary poet as prophet through satire. Hogg adopts entirely different experimental techniques for *A Queer Book* (1832), reverting to the ballad and lyric forms of his earlier career, and subtly distorting these genres. Peter Garside points out that while 'queer' in English indicates strangeness, in Scots it carries connotations of wittiness and comedy.[7]

Also in 1816, Hogg published his long narrative poem, *Mador of the Moor*. Hogg postures here as a 'nursling of the wild, the Mountain Bard' and 'Nature's simple bard'. Set in the fourteenth century, *Mador* tells the story of a strong-willed rustic, Ila Moore, who becomes pregnant by an itinerant minstrel, Mador. When she traces her vanished lover, she discovers he is the King of Scotland. They marry and Mador acknowledges his son. *The British Critic* admired its 'dignified simplicity... which Burns himself scarce attained' forgiving 'occasional vulgarities'. Moreover, the reviewer noted similarities with classical literature, while denying the possibility of a Shepherd knowing such material: 'one would really have thought that the Ettrick shepherd had translated Simonides; but there is no plagiarism here, it is the voice of nature'. *The Scots Magazine* admired 'original... thought' and 'Scottish feelings' but thought the success of *The Queen's Wake* had led Hogg beyond 'the limits of his powers'. Later critics, like Thomson, found it morally distasteful. Gifford considers it to be 'in the worst Hogg vein... he repeats the snigger of Ramsay'. Recently, the strong heroine has been praised for questioning gender stereotypes and this judgement has some force, though it neglects folktale precedents like 'Rashiecoat', Scotland's Cinderella (AT 510). Similarly strong female leads feature in the ambitious *Queen Hynde* (1825) which reverses the plot of Fingal into a tale of heroic Irish assistance for the Scots, with Iliadic resonances and similarities to Macpherson's earlier piece, *The Highlander* as well as material from Mallet's *Northern Antiquities* (1770).[8]

From 1817 onward, Hogg was involved in establishing Blackwood's *Edinburgh Magazine*. He contributed a sizeable quantity of prose and poetry to the new journal, including the controversial and satirical 'Translation from an ancient Chaldee Manuscript' – extensively retouched by John Wilson and John Gibson Lockhart – in issue 2 (1817) and the 'Shepherd's Calendar' series which ran from issue 13 (1823) to issue 24 (1828); the latter is a comprehensive survey of the characteristic natural and supernatural experiences in Borders' agricultural life. More damagingly, Hogg was featured in the 'Noctes Ambrosianae' sketches which ran between 1822 and 1835, largely the work of 'Christopher North' (John Wilson). Lockhart's highly condescending description, in Peter's *Letters to His Kinsfolk* (1819), offered a prototype for this image. In August 1821 of Blackwood's, with respect to *The Mountain Bard*, his poetic talents were savagely assaulted; in

December 'Maginn' (Morgan O'Doherty) ridiculed Hogg's supposed alcoholism. But on the other hand, in the February 1819 issue Hogg was compared, as a lesser poet, with Burns and given the title of 'the poet laureate of the Court of Faery'. Just as Burns was seen as natural at the plough but ill-suited to the parlour, though, so the Shepherd is presented as ill mannered, bucktoothed and hirstute: too coarse to fit in with the Maga set. Hogg was aware of being pilloried. In 1825 he defined his feelings for Wilson to Blackwood as: 'a mixture of terror, admiration and jealousy, just such a sentiment as one deil might be supposed to have of another'. The 'Noctes', being widely read, did real damage to Hogg's reputation. As William Tennant sympathetically wrote to Hogg: 'I see you in Blackwood, fighting and reaping a harvest of beautiful black eyes from the fists of Professor John Wilson'.[9]

In 1818 Hogg published *The Brownie of Bodsbeck; and other Tales*, in two volumes and three parts: 'The Brownie of Bodsbeck', 'The Woolgather' (first published in 1811 as 'The Country Laird') – a tale of romance and rumour – and 'The Hunt of Eildon' which treats real supernatural shape-changing. There is also a dedication piece 'Verses Addressed to the Right Honourable Lady Anne Scott of Buccleuch' (the daughter of the Duke of Buccleuch), which presents Anne as pure and Christian, in the vein of Kilmeny. Later editions break up this set into stand-alone tales, destroying the writer's integrated text and representing it as a more conventional romantic novel by isolating its consitutent parts. 'The Brownie' itself is a powerful story, shaped from oral and written sources relating to the late seventeenth century 'Killing Times'. The elusive hero, John Brown, hides out on Chapelhope farm with his broken band of followers. He is based on, and was originally named after, John Balfour of Burlie although the name was changed due to Scott's non-complimentary use of Burlie in *Old Mortality* (1818). The plot revolves around the interpretation of Burlie's presence on the farm as a manifestation of its supernatural 'brownie', and the subsequent persecution of the farmer, Laidlaw, and his family, for sheltering renegade Covenanters. Hogg's sources include written and oral texts, from theological diatribes, to supernatural traditions of the brownie as 'an unearthly thing' and Ettrick legends of the cruel acts practised by Bloody Clavers, John Graham of Claverhouse, and his royalist troops. *The British Critic*, while admiring the remarkable tales, questioned Hogg's use of Ettrick tradition: 'he has given himself no trouble about the truth' and exhibited 'bad taste'.[10] Hogg, however, is engaging in stylistic experimentation here, blending genres from the historical novel after Scott to Gothic-scale horror, love stories and oral story cycles. He returned to the covenanting theme in his later novel, *Tales of the Wars of Montrose* (1835); closely based on oral history this is, perhaps, more mature in its historical attitude, but the storyline is less captivating than that of *The Brownie*.

Hogg's next major project, commissioned by Colonel David Stewart of Garth of the Highland Society of London, was *The Jacobite Relics of Scotland; being the Songs, Airs, and Legends, of the Adherents to the House of Stuart* (1819-1821). This two volume set shows Hogg's empathy with Jacobites, linked to a keen awareness of cultural repression and deprivation in the Highlands. Although the Society had suggested representing the Hanoverians, there are few Whig songs; Hogg attributed the disproportion to Scottish sympathies. The material is arranged chronologically: volume I is songs from before Sherriffmuir (1715); II relates to the 1745 Uprising and its aftermath. Some items were from oral tradition, some from manuscripts, and others from works like Johnson's *Scots Musical Museum* (1787-1803) and Cromek's *Remains of Nithsdale and Galloway Song* (1810). *The Relics*, like the *Minstrelsy*, utilised composite texts and Hogg used his familiarity with oral traditions, verbal and musical, to advantage. He included 'skeletons' of airs, drawing on his knowledge of the violin (like Burns before him) and aided by William Stenhouse (the Edinburgh accountant who would edit the music in later editions of Johnson's Musical Museum) and claimed that the airs could be harmonised for piano by 'any composer or professional player'. Appealing to Ossianic interests, as well as the post-Scott enthusiasm for the Highlands, Hogg distinguished Jacobite song from ballads and lyrics as: 'the unmarked effusions of a bold and primitive race'. Although not a fluent Gaelic speaker, Hogg had Highland correspondents like Peter Buchan make prose versions in English, which he then versified. The Jacobites, in this context, become latter-day noble savages (implying Hogg's fitness, perhaps, as the Ettrick Shepherd, to remember their Cause). Most of *The Relics* are traditional, but Hogg could ascribe 'anon' to add interest to his own, modern, material, exploiting his status as an authority on oral tradition, as Donaldson and Batho have observed. Contemporary reactions were mixed. Scott classed *The Relics* as 'a curious book'. Jeffrey, in the *Edinburgh Review*, identified 'absurd principles' in *The Relics* such as 'speculative Jacobitism' – fostering the Cause without risk – and condemned its 'coarse and gross taste'. Nevertheless, *The Relics* left a lasting impression on the Scottish song canon and Hogg helped to rework the Highlander's image from ruffian to heroic soldier and his criteria permeated the subsequent Jacobite canon.[11]

In April 1820 Hogg married his long-standing sweeetheart, Margaret Phillips, the younger daughter of a farmer in Annandale, twenty years younger than himself. In 1821 he took a nine year lease on Mount Benger, which caused him some difficulty due to the high level of rent. Although he had turned down an invitation to George IV's coronation (it clashed with St Boswell's fair), in 1822 Hogg published *The Royal Jubilee*, a double-edged tribute to the King on his notorious visit to Edinburgh of that year. A play with songs (probably never performed), this is a patronage request writ large, but it has an uneasiness of tone, especially in its Britishness. Contemporaries found it absurd: 'he is evidently slightly insane through the whole poem'. The *dramatis personae* consists of Scottish types, vying to welcome George to Edinburgh: a Queen of the Fairies with Jacobite sympathies, a Genius of the Ocean, an Ossianic Genius of the Gael, a Covenanting Genius of the West and the Genius of Holyrood. As well as overtones of *Midsummer Night's Dream*, there is a hint of the chaotic *Twelfth Night*, and Shakespeare's fantasy had been performed in Edinburgh in January 1816.[12] Rifts among the subjects are (at least superficially) healed by Archy Campbell, the Highland policeman, but the spirits go off in different directions, suggesting a fragmented Scottish identity (and perhaps the jostling of the *Literati* for precedence during the actual visit).

Also in 1822, Hogg published the four volume *The Poetical Works of James Hogg* which covers his lyric and ballad-style pieces comprehensively. In the same year, too, he produced *The Three Perils of Man: or, War, Women and Witchcraft*, an often hilarious, and sometimes supernatural, novel and a splendid example of Hogg's storytelling abilities at their best. As Gifford says: 'The Three Perils of Man represents the burgeoning of his deep interest in that other class of the supernatural, the world of "diablerie" and demonology'. This was followed by a companion novel, *The Three Perils of Woman; or Love, Leasing, and Jealousy, a Series of Domestic Scottish Tales* (1823). This consists of three parts: a section flirting with the style of contemporary novels of manners; a convoluted tale dealing with the deceits in marriage affecting Richard Rickleton, who had appeared in the first part, and a Jacobite tale. This, too, is a fine work, with mixed attitudes towards the natural and supernatural worlds, exemplified by the experiences of the heroine of the first piece, Gatty Bell, who falls into peril during a three-year coma produced by her over-zealous prayers.[13]

Hogg's most complex work, however, is *The Private Memoirs and Confessions of a Justified Sinner* (1824). André Gide drew attention to its religious and moral dimensions, as well as its interest for 'psychologists and artists, and above all surrealists who are so particularly drawn by the demoniac in every shape' and *The Confessions*, undoubtedly, is Hogg's masterpiece.[14] Ambiguity and obfuscation are prevalent throughout this book. There are, for instance, several accounts of the main events: one by its 'editor' – itself in two parts as his narrative and his final comments – one by the 'sinner' of the title, as well as reported eyewitness accounts of central events from possibly unreliable witnesses like Arabella Calvert. The dual narrative undermines the reader's sense of security with the text. Dramatically set in the Old Town of Edinburgh and, at crucial times, on Arthur's Seat, as well as in a resonant Borders' landscape (in physical and moral senses), it starts with an unwilling marriage and ends with murder, spiritual torment, and suicide. There are wonderfully believable character sketches, from the elderly but rapacious laird of Dalcastle, George Colwan, to his humane mistress to his overly precious wife and mother of two boys, the Glasgow Baillie's daughter Raby Orde. Her pompous pastor the Rev Mr Wringhim is possibly the father of the eponymous 'Sinner'.

On one level, this is a tale of unadulterated evil, focussed on a

devil who is, in his shape-changing and seductive form, close to
that of oral tradition. Equally, it is a tale of over-blown religious
bigotry and the misshaping of the notion of the Elect into the concept of those, beyond Free Will, who can do anything without sin-
ning. Yet again, it can be read as a startlingly modern study of a literally divided self represented, on one hand, by the fratricidal
brother Robert Wringhim and his heartier sibling George Colwan,
and on another by Wringhim's relationship with the Satanic
Gilmartin. Here, for instance, is Wringhim's first encounter with the
central figure of Gilmartin (perhaps the devil, perhaps his id, perhaps a Russian exile, or perhaps a figment of the imagination):

> I felt a sort of invisible power that drew me towards him, something like
> the force of enchantment, which I could not resist... That stranger youth
> and I approached each other in silence, and slowly, with our eyes fixed
> on each other's eyes... What was my astonishment, on perceiving that he
> was the same being as myself!... This singular being read my thoughts in
> my looks, anticipating the very words that I was going to utter.

The novel is at once structurally sophisticated, at times hugely
humorous and at others genuinely terrifying; a *tour de force* which
is at once original and distinctively Scottish, with echoes of 'Tam O'
Shanter' as well as of oral traditions. There are possible debts, too,
to Hoffman's *Die Elixiere des Teufels* which was translated by R.P.
Gillies and published in the same month as the *Confessions* in this
translation, in June 1824. Hogg, though, goes far beyond his models. As Gifford says: 'in suspending his account of these moral
actions between two bases of judgement Hogg has expressed a situation still of crucial importance and confusion... in a story which
still never fails to create unease and wonder'.[15]

Other notable work includes *A Border Garland* (1819), which
has a chapbook flavour, and includes a series of fine lyrics about
natural and supernatural love which are often set, here, to Hogg's
own melodies, indicating an unusual ability to explore traditional
conventions and innovate in music as well as in words (even
Burns, as far as is known, did not regularly make his own tunes).
The 1831 *Songs* selection includes items from previous collections,
anthologies and periodicals. The tone is overwhelmingly lyric and
pastoral, with many lugubrious items as well as humorous pieces.
Hogg's songs, too, have been set by composers including

Beethoven and Haydn and recorded, more recently, by the McCalmans on *The Ettrick Shepherd* (1980).[16] *Familiar Anecdotes of Sir Walter Scott* (published in New York and England as *The Domestic Manners and Private Life of Sir Walter Scott* in 1834) is an entertaining and humorous account which is highly revealing of the two writers' ambivalent relationship. *A Series of Lay Sermons on Good Principles and Good Breeding* was also published in 1834. Here Hogg postures as a country gentleman; offering (often tongue-in-cheek) advice to his family and friends.

Hogg was long stereotyped as merely 'the Ettrick Shepherd': a poetical genius with no intellectual depth. Bowdelerised Victorian editions, such as that by Thomas Thomson, prevented his work from being critically assessed but, more recently, Hogg's work has undergone a thorough reassessment. George Saintsbury was among the earliest to recognise the *Confessions* worth (although he suspected John Gibson Lockhart was the author). Works like George Douglas' *James Hogg* (1899) and Edith Batho's *The Ettrick Shepherd* (1927) began a considered re-evaluation of Hogg's work, and T.E. Welby's unexpurgated edition of *The Private Memoirs and Confessions of a Justified Sinner* (1927) made possible André Gide's influential preface to the 1947 edition of the *Confessions*. John Carey's 1969 edition of the *Confessions* continued Hogg's re-evaluation. The critical work of Douglas Gifford, David Groves and Douglas Mack, along with respectful modern editions such as those of the Stirling/South Carolina Research Edition of the *Collected Works of James Hogg* have allowed Hogg to finally achieve his rightful status as an innovative Scottish writer of international rank.[17]

NOTES

[1] Autobiographical information on Hogg is drawn from 'Memoir of the Author's Life', first published in James Hogg, *The Mountain Bard; consisting of Ballads and Songs, founded on Facts and Legendary Tales*, Edinburgh: A. Constable, 1807, revised in the expanded edition, Edinburgh: Oliver & Boyd, 1821, and expanded for *Altrive Tales*, London: J. Cochrane and Co., 1832, with additional material from

Hogg's 'Reminiscences of Former Days. My First Interview with Allan Cunningham', *The Edinburgh Literary Journal*, vol. 1, 1828-1829, pp. 374-375 and 'Reminiscences of Former Days: My First Interview with Sir Walter Scott', *The Edinburgh Literary Journal*, vol. 2, 1829, pp. 51-52. These show Hogg's developing literary persona: see Silvia Mergenthal, *James Hogg: Selbstbild und Bild*, Frankfurt am Main: Peter Lang, 1989. On Hogg's family see E.E. Petrie, 'Odd Characters: Traditional Informants in James Hogg's Family', *Scottish Literary Journal*, vol. 110, 1983, pp. 30-41 and 'Further Particulars in the Life of the Ettrick Shepherd', *The Scots Magazine*, vol. 67, 1805, pp. 501-503. See also Mrs. [Mary Gray] Garden, *Memorials of James Hogg: The Ettrick Shepherd*, Paisley: A. Gardner, 1885, and George Douglas, *James Hogg*, Edinburgh: Oliphant, Anderson and Ferrier, 1899. Modern critical biographies include Edith Batho, *The Ettrick Shepherd* (1927), rpt, New York: Greenwood Press, 1969; Louis Simpson, *James Hogg: A Critical Study*, Edinburgh: Oliver & Boyd, 1962; Douglas Gifford, *James Hogg*, Edinburgh: The Ramsay Head Press, 1976; and David Groves, *James Hogg: The Growth of a Writer*, Edinburgh: Scottish Academic Press, 1988. See too the journal *Studies in Hogg and his World*. A.L. Strout's *The Life and Letters of James Hogg*, Lubbock, Texas: Texas Tech. Press, 1946, appeared as the first volume of a projected two; the edited letters will shortly appear in the Stirling/South Carolina edition of the *Complete Works of James Hogg*, Edinburgh: Edinburgh University Press, edited by Gillian Hughes.

[2] See Gillian Hughes, 'James Hogg's Fiction and the Periodicals', unpublished PhD thesis (University of Edinburgh, 1981). The 'Tours' are reprinted in James Hogg, *Highland Tours: The Ettrick Shepherd's Travels in the Scottish Highlands and Western Isles in 1802, 1803 and 1804*, edited by W.F. Laughlan, Hawick, Roxburghshire: Byways, 1981.

[3] Hogg's comments about Burns are not in his 1807 or 1821 'Memoirs' but are in the 1832 version, p. 11ff. See James Hogg, *Scottish Pastorals: Poems, Songs, etc. Mostly Written in the Dialect of the South, 1801*, edited by Elaine Petrie, Stirling: Stirling University Press, 1988. See Valentina Bold, '"Neither right spelt nor right setten doun": Child, Scott and the Hogg family ballads', in Ted Cowan ed., *The Ballad in Scottish History*, East Linton: Tuckwell Press, 2000, pp. 116-141.

[4] James Hogg, *The Forest Minstrel*, Edinburgh and London: A. Constable and Co., 1810, pp. vii-ix.

[5] See Douglas Gifford, *op. cit.*, p. 43. 'The Queen's Wake', review, *The Edinburgh Review*, vol. 24, 1814-1815, p. 62.

[6] James Hogg, *The Pilgrims of the Sun: A Poem*, London: Murray, 1815. 'Connel of Dee' first appeared in James Hogg, *Winter Evening Tales*, 2 vols., Edinburgh: Oliver & Boyd, 1820, II, pp. 204-222. *The Poetical Works of James Hogg*, 4 vols., Edinburgh: A. Constable and Co., 1822, includes 'The Pilgrims of the Sun' along with 'The Haunted Glen', 'The Field of Waterloo', 'Connel of Dee' and 'Superstition', all vol. II, pp. 1-127, 179-228, 281-323, 115-149 and 151-166. See James Hogg, 'Stanzas addressed to a Comet', *Edinburgh Magazine*, vol. 5, July 1819, p. 30. See Gary W. Kronk, *Cometography*, vol. 2, unpublished, 1996, quoted HYPERLINK http://comets.amsmeteors.org/comets/1811.html; and HYPERLINK http://comets.amsmeteors.org/educate/comintro.html; R.J.M. Olson et al., 'The 1816 Solar Eclipse and Comet 1811 in John Linnell's Astronomical Album', *Journal for the History of Astronomy*, vol. 23, 1992, pp. 121-133. 'The Pilgrims of the Sun', review, *The Augustan Review*, vol. 1, May 1815, pp. 30-31. 'The Pilgrims of the Sun', review, *The Scots Magazine*, vol. 16, Dec 1814, pp. 930, 932. Edith Batho, *op. cit.*, pp. 75-76, 144-146. Douglas Gifford, *op. cit.*, p. 62; Douglas Gifford, 'James Hogg by Nelson Smith... James Hogg at Home by Norah Parr... James Hogg "Highland Tours", edited by William F. Laughlan', review, *Scottish Literary Journal*, supplement, no. 17, Winter 1982, pp. 84-89. Nelson Smith, *James Hogg*, Boston: Twayne, 1980, p. 133. David Groves, *op. cit.*, pp. 59-60.

[7] On the textual history, see Hogg's 'Memoir of the Author's Life', in *The Mountain Bard*, Edinburgh: A. Constable, 1821, pp. lvii-lx. James Hogg, *The Poetic Mirror*, London and Edinburgh: Longman; Ballantyne, 1816. David Groves ed., *James Hogg: Poetic Mirrors*, Scottish Studies 11, Frankfurt um Main: Peter Lang, 1990: this is the 1816 *Poetic Mirror* and the 'New Poetic Mirror', published in the *Edinburgh Literary Journal* (1829-1831). 'The Poetic Mirror', review, *The British Lady's Magazine*, vol. 4, 1816, pp. 381-387. Douglas Gifford, *James Hogg*, cit., pp. 47-48; David Groves, *James Hogg* (1988), cit., p. 77; A.J. Hasler, 'Ingenious Lies: The Poetic Mirror in Context', *Papers given at the Second James Hogg Society Conference, Edinburgh (1985)*, edited by Gillian Hughes, Aberdeen: Association for Scottish Literary Studies, 1988, pp. 79-96. James Hogg, 'The Russiadde', in *The Poetical Works*, 4 vols., Edinburgh and London: Constable; Hurst, Robison & Co., 1822, III, pp. 295-359. See reviews cited, *James Hogg: A Queer Book*, 1832, edited by P.D. Garside, The Stirling/South Carolina Research Edition of the *Collected Works of James Hogg*, 3, Edinburgh: Edinburgh University Press, 1995, pp. xi-xii.

[8] 'Mador of the Moor', review Art. VII., *The British Critic*, vol. 7, 1817, pp. 97-100. 'Mador of the Moor', review, *The Scots Magazine*, vol. 78, June 1816, pp. 448-452. James Hogg, *The Works of the Ettrick Shepherd*, 2 vols., edited by Thomas Thomson, new edition, London: Blackie and Son, 1865, I, pp. 104-105. Douglas Gifford, *James Hogg*, cit., p. 6. J.E. Barcus, 'When beauty gives command, all mankind must obey!': Gender Roles in Hogg's Mador of the Moor', *Studies in Hogg and his World*, no. 6, 1995, pp. 33-49. James Hogg, *Queen Hynde: A Poem*, in *Six Books*, London and Edinburgh: Longman; Blackwood, 1825. James Macpherson, *The Highlander*, Edinburgh: Ruddiman, 1758.

[9] The 'Noctes Ambrosianae' sketches are collected in John Wilson ed., *Noctes Ambrosianae*, 4 vols., Edinburgh: Blackwood & Sons, 1863, and reprinted as *Tavern Sages: Selections from the Noctes Ambrosianae*, edited by J.H. Alexander, Aberdeen: Association for Scottish Literary Studies, 1992. J.G. Lockhart, *Peter's Letters to His Kinsfolk*, 1819, reprinted and edited by William Ruddick, Edinburgh: Scottish Academic Press, 1977. See 'Autograph Poems, Letters, etc. James Hogg', NLS MS 2245, f. 150.

[10] *The British Critic*, vol. X, October 1818, p. 418.

[11] On Hogg's sources and techniques see 'Small Collections', NLS MS 3925 and *Jacobite Relics*, passim. See William Donaldson, *The Jacobite Song*, Aberdeen: Aberdeen University Press, 1988, pp. 100-107. Edith Batho, *op. cit.*, pp. 38-43. *Scott Letters*, VI, 1819-1821, p. 69; 'The Jacobite Relics of Scotland, being the Songs, Airs, and legends, of the Adherents to the House of Stuart. Collected and Illustrated by James Hogg, Author of the Queen's Wake, etc.', VIII, pp. 444. 'Edinburgh 1819', review Art VII, *Edinburgh Review*, vol. 34, August 1820, pp. 148-149.

[12] See James Hogg, *The Royal Jubilee*, 1822, edited by Valentina Bold, facsimile, and Valentina Bold, 'The Royal Jubilee: James Hogg and the House of Hanover', *Studies in Hogg and his World*, V, 1994, pp. 102-151 and pp. 1-19. September 1822, 'Hogg's Royal Jubilee, etc.', Blackwood's *Edinburgh Magazine*, p. 349. See the *Edinburgh Evening Courant*, January 4 and 11, 1816.

[13] Douglas Gifford, *James Hogg*, cit., p. 102; see Valentina Bold 'Traditional Narrative Elements in The Three Perils of Woman', *Studies in Hogg and his World*, III, 1992, pp. 42-56.

[14] André Gide, 'Introduction', in James Hogg, *The Private Memoirs and Confessions of a Justified Sinner*, London: Cresset Press, 1947, p. ix.

[15] Douglas Gifford, *James Hogg*, cit., p. 181.

[16] The McCalmans, *The Ettrick Shepherd*, London: Greenwich Village, 1980, GVR 209.

[17] See *The Works of the Ettrick Shepherd*, edited by Thomas Thomson, 2 vols., London: Blackie and Son, 1865. *The Collected Essays and Papers of George Saintsbury, 1875-1920*, London and Toronto: J.M. Dent & Sons, I, 1923, pp. 26, 31, 42. George Douglas, *James Hogg*, Edinburgh: Oliphant, Anderson and Ferrier, 1899; Edith Batho, *The Ettrick Shepherd* (1927), reprinted New York: Greenwood Press, 1969. James Hogg, *The Private Memoirs and Confessions of a Justified Sinner*, edited by T.E. Welby, London: A.M. Philpot, 1924; André Gide, 'Introduction' to James Hogg, *The Private Memoirs and Confessions of a Justified Sinner*, translated by Dorothy Bussy, London: Cresset Press, 1947. James Hogg, *The Private Memoirs and Confessions of a Justified Sinner*, edited by John Carey, Oxford: Oxford University Press, 1969. Valentina Bold, *Nature's Making: James Hogg and the Autodidacts*, East Linton: Tuckwell, 2004.

G. ROSS ROY

The Scottish-North-American Diaspora: Nineteenth-Century Poets Across the Atlantic

The outpouring of emigrants from Scotland to the United States during the nineteenth century brought a number of poets and versifiers to a new country, where they hoped to prosper. In colonial times there had been, of course, numerous Scottish settlers: bankers, teachers, bakers, farm labourers, and above all clergymen, because there was no seminary to train shepherds for the flocks until the founding of Princeton Theological Seminary in 1812, but even after this many congregations preferred a Scottish-trained cleric. Frequently a Scot would establish himself in America and then send home for workers or apprentices. Thus the first printer in the colony of South Carolina, a Scot named Peter Timothy, recruited all of his workers in Glasgow. Even the language persisted in the new land, where many people born in it spoke only the Doric until they went to school; a mid-nineteenth-century traveler in South Carolina was surprised to find that a Gaelic-speaking plantation owner, far from dropping his native tongue, had taught it to his house slaves.

Emigrants to the United States, or to the colonies at an earlier period, kept their Scottishness alive in the new country. Members of a village or a clan frequently settled close to where others with the same background had already established themselves. Social bonds were close and the Scottish community looked after any who fell upon hard times. During the nineteenth century several newspapers were founded by Scots to serve immigrants to the United States, although they also stressed the fact that they were all Americans, too.

Alexander Wilson (1766-1813) is today principally known as the father of American ornithology, forerunner of the more famous John Audubon. Born in Paisley, he was a weaver and a packman before emigrating to America in 1794. Wilson's first brush with the law had come in 1790 when he published an anonymous broadside attack on a Paisley silk manufacturer entitled 'The Hollander, or Light Weight', a poem on the not uncommon practice of shop owners to find trifling flaws in weavers' output and pay them far less than the agreed rate. Wilson's poem was quite popular and the manufacturer took action with the result that for a harmless satire Wilson was charged with criminal libel and incitement to unrest, although for reasons unknown Wilson did not stand trial.

But the poet was not through with the law. In 1792 he foolishly sent to William Sharp, owner of Long Mills in Paisley, a copy of his poem 'The Shark: or Lang Mills Detected' with the threat of publishing it unless Sharp paid him five pounds. Wilson was tried and jailed. Quite apart from Wilson's blackmail, the poem appeared at a time when the government was ill-disposed to tolerate calls for industrial reform.

Wilson did not confine his radical ideas to poetry. In 1793 he was associated with the Friends of the People, and in January 1794 we find him in jail for being 'concerned in framing and industriously circulating an advertisement addressed to "The Friends of Liberty and Reform."' Wilson was granted bail, but he realized that there was no place for him in Scotland and in May 1794 he left for America where a new life awaited him.[1]

Our major concern is, of course, with Wilson after he arrived in the United States. Combining his interest in ornithology with the writing of verse, he set out on foot from Philadelphia to Niagara Falls, and from this trip there emerged a long poem, 'The Foresters'. As a naturalist, Wilson commented on the many things which were new to him in this sparsely settled territory:

> Shrill, wildly issuing from a neighbouring height,
> The wolf's deep howlings pierce the ear of night;
> From the dark swamp he calls his skulking crew,
> Their nightly scenes of slaughter to renew...[2]

Like many immigrants of the time, Wilson disliked the Indians (the expression 'The only good Indian is a dead Indian' long predated John Wayne) and he writes approvingly of how the Indians had been driven out of the territory in 1799, making room for 'the

enterprise of our active and industrious settlers'.[3] As with all early
travellers to Niagara Falls, Wilson found them overwhelming:

> 'Midst dazzling foam and whirling storms of snow,
> While the whole monstrous mass, and country round,
> Shook us with horror at the o'erwhelming sound!'[4]

As one comes to expect in reading nineteenth-century Scottish
poets, emigrant or not, there is the almost obligatory poem on
Robert Burns, and Wilson's is neither better nor worse than most of
them. His is entitled 'Ode, for the Birth-Day of our Immortal
Scottish Poet' which, we are informed, was 'set to music by a bacchanalian club'. He does choose two of Burns's best satires for
mention:

> Hail blest *Ordination*! all hail *Holy Fair*!
> Ye glorious effusions! ye thrice sacred pair![5]

He had not lost his sense of humor, as we notice in his 'To the
Famishing Bard, From a Brother Skeleton', but he had learned his
lesson in Scotland and he refrained from pillorying public figures.
More typical of his adopted country are poems which chronicle
daily life. 'Verses Occasioned by Seeing Two Men Sawing Timber
in the Open Field, in Defiance of a Furious Storm' reminds the
reader that lightning quite frequently used to (and still does) kill
people who do not take precautions: 'My friends, for G-d sake!
Quit your wark... Anither blast/Like that, and a' yer sawing's past!'[6]

    While he had become more cautious in this new land, Wilson
certainly did not abandon politics. In 1801 he addressed a group in
Milestown, Pennsylvania, on the topic 'The Power and Value of
Natural Liberty' and he wrote a song 'Jefferson and Liberty: A
Patriotic Song' with the chorus:

> Rejoice! Columbia's sons, rejoice,
>   To tyrants never bend the knee,
> But join, with heart, and soul, and voice,
>   For Jefferson and Liberty.[7]

The poem concludes on an optimistic note:

> From Georgia to Lake Champlain,
>   From seas to Mississippi's shore,

Ye sons of freedom loud proclaim,
   The reign of terror is no more.[8]

Considering Wilson's support for Thomas Paine's *Rights of Man* and the early ideals of the French Revolution, and in view of the direction that revolution had later taken, Wilson's phrase 'reign of terror' applied to the political situation in America is hyperbolic overkill.

One of the most interesting groups in the canon consists of five poems which originally appeared in Wilson's *American Ornithology*, each poem devoted to a bird, to which the poet-naturalist prefixed a note on that bird. For instance, we are told in 'The Humming-Bird' that it is

> One of the few [birds] that are universally beloved; and, amid the sweet dewy serenity of a summer's morning, his appearance among the arbours of honeysuckle, and beds of flowers, is truly interesting.[9]

Given that Wilson, as did others, regularly shot birds which he wished to study, and that several species were extinguished because they fed on crops, domestic fowl, or livestock, it is refreshing to find him singing the praises of a bird without reservation. Today Wilson's poetry is usually reduced to footnote status in a discussion of the man as ornithologist, but he did furnish an interesting picture of an evolving young country.

David Bruce (d. 1830), son of a Caithness farmer, emigrated to Maryland in 1784 and in 1787 he moved to western Pennsylvania, where, in 1801, he published *Poems Chiefly in the Scottish Dialect*. The poems had first appeared in the *Washington Telegraphe* [sic] under the pseudonym 'The Scots-Irishman', perhaps to excite the interest not only of Scots, but of the considerable population of Scots-Irish who peopled the mountainous regions in the western part of Atlantic coastal states. The title of Bruce's volume is, of course, precisely that used by Burns in his 1786 volume, and the influence does not end there either, for we find two poems on Burns in the collection. The first 'Verses to the Memory of Robert Burns', opens:

Soft may thy gentle Spirit rest,
   Sweet Poet of the plain!

Light lie the green turf on thy breast,
   Till it's illum'd again.[10]

The third line of the poem is very interesting, because when Burns
sent a copy of 'Auld Lang Syne' to his friend Mrs. Frances Dunlop,
without admitting to the authorship of the song, he wrote: 'Light be
the turf on the breast of the heaven-inspired Poet who composed
this glorious Fragment!'[11] The 'Verses' are written entirely in
English, but the following poem in the collection, 'Verses on
Reading the Poems of Robert Burns', is written in Doric. It opens
'Ah! winsome Rob, whare are ye now' and continues with suggested answers to that question. Included is:

Mayhaps (as your ain Ossian sings)
Ye now are flitting wi' the winds,
   Light-sitting on a cloud:[12]

This is an intriguing passage because many early editions of
James Macpherson's epic were illustrated with engravings of the
bard Ossian depicted riding on a cloud; Bruce is here referring
to an iconography which would surely have been familiar to
Burns. Bruce continues: 'Whare'er ye be, whate'r's your fate,/I
trust ye're in a happy state... A'beit ye was *nae Saint*'. The work
then draws images from the poems by Burns, as when Bruce
writes:

L--d Robert, had ye liv'd but here,
Ye'd faund *Hornbooks* anow' asteer,
   Wha'd want your needfu' lesson!
We'er a' owre-run wi' siccan gear,
Ance ane can bleed a horse or mare,
   He sets up for Physician![13]

Not only does the poet display a good knowledge of Burns, but he
finds, on American soil, all of the types who are so humorously
satirized by Burns on Scottish soil.
   Not to be outdone in his poems to a national figure of the old
land, Bruce also includes two poems to a national figure of the
new, George Washington. The first of these immediately follows
the 'Verses' on reading Burns – 'Verses on General Washington
Retiring from Public Life'. In the second poem, 'Elegiac Verses to

the Memory of George Washington', Bruce regrets that there is now no one to take up the position Washington so ably filled in America's greatest time of need:

Where's now the prudent, temp'rate chief,
    Whose steady virtues long were try'd,
His troubled country's sure relief,
    In war her shield, in peace her guide?[14]

Bruce had left one hard-drinking country to emigrate to another, and in his collection he devotes a section of seven poems to the 'Water of Life'. In 1794, we are told, there was a 'Whiskey Insurrection' in western Pennsylvania and this led to a flyting between Bruce and other anonymous poets, whose effusions also appear in Bruce's volume. His opening blast, entitled 'To Whiskey', reads:

Great Pow'r, that warms the heart and liver,
And puts the bluid a' in a fever,
If dull and heartless I am ever,
    A blast o' thee
Maks me as blyth, and brisk, and clever
    As ony bee.[15]

It will be noted that the poet uses Burns's favourite Standard Habbie stanza form. Bruce continues the flyting with 'To Aqua Vitae' which is appropriately meant to accompany the opening lines of Burns's 'Address to a Haggis':

Fair fa' ye, canty Aqua Vitae
Indeed ye've given's a dainty ditty,
Just like yoursel, sae blyth and witty.[16]

This incomplete exchange shows us that there were other Scots in the region who were practicing their poetic craft.

William Cant Sturoc (1822-1903) is a good example of the humble-born Scot who makes good politically in America, while at the same time retaining a close connection emotionally with the country of his origin. He was born in Arbroath to a laborer and in 1846 he emigrated to Montreal where he carried on the literary interests he had brought with him from Scotland, publishing verse in *The Literary Garland* of that city. He moved to New Hampshire four years later and lived there for the remainder of his life. He read law in the office of Edmund Burke, who had served in the cabinet of President James Polk. Sturoc was later elected to the state legislature, serving as a staunch Democrat. He was an able debator inside and outside the state house, but his greatest enjoyment came from reading and writing poetry which he contributed to publications both in Scotland and America. He settled by Lake Sunapee, calling himself the Bard of Sunapee, and singing the praises of the beauty of the lake in a poem of that name, written in later life:

> Once more, my muse! from rest of many a year,
>   Come forth again and sing, as oft of yore.
>
> Lake of my mountain home, loved Sunapee![17]

A New Hampshire periodical, *The Granite Monthly*, described Sturoc:

> he is the educated, hospitable, ardent Scotchman. The blood of Bruce and Wallace is in his veins, the fire of Burns and Scott in his brain. Next to his adopted country, he loves Scotland, and he has often breathed that affection in exquisite verse.[18]

Bearing witness to the influence of Burns, Sturoc's poem 'Mary' contains these lines: 'Burns hymn'd his Mary, when her soul had pass'd/Away from earth, and all its sin and sorrow'.[19] Another love song, 'Bonnie Mary Bruce', emphasizes the strength of his attachment to Scotland, and contains a further echo of Burns:

> I cross'd the briny deep to win
>   A fortune an' a name,
> An' bring the gowden burden back
>   To deck our lovin' hame;
> But tho' I wan baith name an' gear,
>   They're a' but little use;
> The cauld, cauld clay now wraps the form
>   O' bonnie Mary Bruce.[20]

I would suggest that Mary Bruce represents the lost homeland to Sturoc, absent forever but never forgotten. We find this theme repeated elsewhere, as in 'Song' where he has lost 'winsome Jenny' and others:

> For in my dreams, by day or night,
>   Tho' wealth and beauty bind me, O,
> I'm wafted far, owre sea an' land,
>   To friends I left behind me, O.[21]

Sturoc himself admitted to his abiding interest in his homeland. John D. Ross quotes him as saying of his poetry and country:

> The little fugitive crumbs which I have cast carelessly upon the waters have been received on both sides of the Atlantic with more favor than they really deserve, yet, though 'owre the seas an' far awa', I always take a warm and hearty interest in all that concerns Scotland.[22]

Not long before Ross published his study (1889) Sturoc, who had found happiness and repose on the shores of Lake Sunapee, could with the greatest of sincerity publish 'My Native Scottish Hills', which, though 'cold and bleak':

> Yet still my heart with fondest pride,
>   And deepest passion thrills,
> As, gazing round me, far and wide,
>   I miss my native hills!

He develops this theme for several lines, juxtaposing the beauties of his adoptive America and his original home, to conclude:

> Oh, may my resting place be found
>   Secure from all life's ills,
> Some cheerful spot of hallow'd ground
>   Among the Scottish hills.[23]

And so this Jeffersonian Democrat, as he was called by *The Manchester* [New Hampshire] *Daily Mirror and American*, who had prospered financially and politically in America, remained emotionally tied to the Scotland he had left more than half a lifetime earlier.

James Kennedy (1848-1922) was born in Carsegownie, Forfarshire (now Angus), and moved to Dundee to become a machinist apprentice. Here he 'became interested in the agitation then in progress for the bettering of the agricultural classes in Scotland, and was soon known as one of the most active promot-

ers of the cause'.[24] He emigrated to New York in 1869. In one way
Kennedy is the best integrated poet to be discussed in this essay,
as even the title of his volume, *The Complete Scottish and
American Poems*,[25] attests, but his association with his new land
did not end there. He felt that Scots and English (or American)
should be completely interchangeable in poetry, and so we find
'Robert Burns' written in standard English, followed immediately in
his collection by 'In Brooklyn' in broad Scots. A passage from the
first poem reads:

> He sang the Freeman's song that breathes
>   Of Nature's universal plan;
> He wove the garland that enwreathes
>   The native dignity of Man.[26]

whereas Brooklyn natives are described:

> The freckfu' fowk are braw an' weel
>   That mak' their hames in yon town,
> An' ilka bodie's real genteel
>   Ye chance to meet in yon town.[27]

The penultimate line of the latter poem combines a Scottish and
American, but not English, use of the word 'real' as an adverb.

   One of the most interesting poems in Kennedy's collection is
'The Highlanders in Tennessee', which chronicles the exploits during the Civil War of the 79th Highlanders, of New York City, which
was attached to the New York State Militia – in all 1,374 men
served until May 1864, during which time 190 were killed or died
of wounds or disease, and 747 were discharged because of
wounds or sickness. The regiment's battles included some of the
most hotly contested in the war, and the poem is important as a
picture of Scots fighting in the Union Army as a distinct unit, even
wearing Highland dress. Kennedy describes the exploits of the
79th Highlanders in two other poems dealing with the regiment's
actions in South Carolina in April and June 1862. 'The Two
Brothers' recounts the true story of William and Robert Tofts, both
killed on June 16 at James Island. Although the Union side lost the
battle, the Charleston (South Carolina) *Mercury* wrote, 'It was left
to the... brave 79th Highlanders, to test... our Southern nerves...

Thank God! Lincoln has... only one 79th regiment'.[28] The long-standing battle between drinkers and temperance folk, mentioned already, was taken up by Kennedy, too. 'Whisky's Awa'!' is a delightful satiric treatment of the subject:

> What news is this? I speer fu' fain,
> Is this some joke o' th' printer's ain?
> Na, faith, it's truth that he's been say'n':
>   They've pass'd a law
> Through Pennsylvania, dale an' plain –
>   Whisky's awa'!
>
> . . . .
>
> If sultry weather should prevail,
> To slocken drouth nae ane need fail:
> There's caller cronk an' ginger ale,
>   Or, best o' a',
> In Susquehanna dip your pail –
>   Whisky's awa'![29]

Kennedy also has his tender side. In a poem whose very title evokes Scotland and Robert Burns, 'Bonnie Jean', Kennedy recalls his native corner and the woman he loves there, but alas! his reverie is not one of anticipated reunion, as was Burns's:

> O aft on fancy's fairy wing,
>   That wanders far and free,
> I come in bright imagining
>   Frae ower th' Atlantic sea.
> While mem'ry paints ilk leafy shaw,
>   Ilk meadow fair an' green;
> But aye serene aboon them a'
>   I mind on bonnie Jean.[30]

Every immigrant has left something of himself in his native country, and at times (especially times of crisis) will feel torn between two loyalties. Kennedy tackles this situation in a serio-comic poem, 'The Americanized Scot: or, Jem Wilson and the Queen', where he plays off Scottishness and Queen Victoria in representing a wider loyalty than that of the emigrant Scot to Scotland:

> Though he dwelt mony years in the wilds o' the West,

> Where the prairie spreads bonnie and green,
> He ne'er shook the auld yird frae his feet like the rest,
>   For Jem couldna gae back on the Queen![31]

The poem goes on in this vein for a few stanzas, when Jem finds that he has been left an inheritance, but learns that he cannot claim it unless he is a citizen of the United States:

> He ran an' he swore – on the Bible he swore –
>   Wi' a terrible gleam in his een, –
> Jem Wilson was subject to princes no more,
>   Renouncing forever the Queen! –[32]

Imagine the poor fellow's chagrin when he discovers that his inheritance is a ten-acre swamp! The over-righteous also come in for Kennedy's satire. Jock Wabster is 'minister-daft' and his only desire is:

> ...to hear a' the preachers – O that was his pride,
>   For an unco douce body was he.
> A pillar in Zion he'd been frae his youth,
>   An' deep draughts o' doctrine he'd quaffed...[33]

But after he had heard a few American preachers he came to his senses, and:

> Now doucely he plies his ain craft,
> An' on Sabbaths he reads owre the gude book at hame;
>   So he's nae langer minister-daft.[34]

Not unnaturally the outbreak of World War I brought very mixed emotions to a Scot living in a country that was not yet engaged in the conflict. A series of poems under the general title 'In the World War Time' depicts Kennedy's response. Three of them are distinctly Scottish: 'The Call of the War Pipe', 'Here's to the Highlands', and one which is perhaps closest to Kennedy's sense of pride in Scotland, which will play an important role:

> We hear of England's matchless might,
>   But let not Scotland's fame be hid –

....

Amid the battle's thunder crash
    None brighter gleams than Scotland's Shield,

In Flanders' fields, by Marne's red banks,
    Where'er the eager eye may turn,
There charge the Caledonian ranks,
    There shine the spears of Bannockburn![35]

Kennedy did not live long enough after World War I to write poems on the post-war period.

The diaspora of Scots moving to Canada was very different. In the first place, Canada was a colony of Britain from the taking of Quebec in 1759, and there was never any serious movement for independence as there had been south of the border. By the British North America Act of 1867 Canada was granted a large measure of freedom, but this was understood to be freedom within what had by then become the British Empire. Thus Scots searching for a better life were eager to move to Canada. In several parts of the country immigrants founded Scottish communities, some of them entirely Gaelic-speaking. The annals of the Hudson's Bay Company list many places with Scottish names: Forts Simpson, Davidson, Selkirk, the Mackenzie River. The clergy who came over to minister to their flocks had been trained in Scotland, and their successors were either Scots or Canadians trained in Scotland, because, unlike the Americans who had a seminary at Princeton, there was no similar institution in Canada until 1844.

In 1829 there appeared anonymously in *Blackwood's Magazine* a poem entitled 'Canadian Boat Song'. While the author of this beautiful song is still not known, a number of names have been proposed as its author: Sir Walter Scott, John Galt, James Hogg, John Wilson, John Gibson Lockhart and others. The sometimes forcible removal of crofters from the Highlands of Scotland began after the uprising of 1745, and was carried on through a large part of the nineteenth century as lords realized that they could make more money by raising sheep. The unnamed author of the 'Canadian Boat Song' had probably never visited Canada, but he captured admirably the pathos of those who had been expelled from their native land:

When the bold kindred, in the time long-vanish'd,

Conquer'd the soil and fortified the keep, –
No seer foretold the children would be banish'd,
   That a degenerate Lord might boast his sheep:
     Fair these broad meads – these hoary woods are grand;
     But we are exiles from our fathers' land.[36]

The 'Canadian Boat Song' became an immediate success and has remained popular ever since. R.L. Stevenson quoted it in his California book *The Silverado Squatters* (1883), and in 1885 the British statesman Joseph Chamberlain quoted it anent crofters to an audience in Inverness.

Evan M'Coll (1808-1898) was, perhaps appropriately, a Gaelic-speaker from the Lochfyne region, who had published in Scotland a volume of Gaelic poetry as well as one of Scots verse entitled *The Mountain Minstrel* (1836) which went through four editions. In Canada he wrote only in Scots; in fact little Gaelic poetry was written in either the United States or Canada, a fact which would bear investigation. One of M'Coll's poems is entitled 'The Highland Emigrant's Last Farewell', which set the tone for many such poems, heartfelt in its simplicity and sincerity:

Adieu my native land – adieu
   The banks of fair Lochfyne,
Where the first breath of life I drew,
   And would my last resign!
Swift sails the bark that wafteth me
   This night from thy loved strand:
O must it be my last of thee,
   My dear, dear Fatherland!

O Scotland! o'er the Atlantic roar,
   Though fated to depart,
Nor time nor space can e'er efface
   Thine image from my heart.
Come weal, come woe – till life's last throe,
   My Highland Home shall seem
An Eden bright in Fancy's light,
   A Heaven in Memory's dream![37]

We do not know why the poet was 'fated to depart', but it seems evident that he would much sooner be on the banks of Lochfyne. The poem ends with the lines: 'Farewell to thee – farewell to thee,/My dear, dear Fatherland!'

The most important Scottish poet to emigrate to Canada was Alexander McLachlan (1818-1896) who moved to Canada in 1840. 'The Emigrant' (1861) is an ambitious poem which contains an Introduction and seven books as follow: Leaving Home, The Journey, The Arrival, Cutting the First Tree, The Log Cabin, The Indian Battle and Donald Ban – this latter a hunter from the Highlands 'with the spirit of an ancient bard.'[38] As a result of this publication McLachlan was sent by the Canadian Government to Scotland to encourage other Scots to emigrate. While much of the poem could concern immigrants from any country, there are also specific mentions of Scotland in some sections. One subdivision of the poem is entitled 'Farewell, Caledonia!' in which each stanza concludes with a variant of 'the blue hills of Scotland I'll ne'er see again'.[39] Although he appears to have remained enthusiastic about his adoptive land, the poet admitted 'Much remains still to be told':

> Of the quacks, on spoil intent,
> That flock'd into our settlement –
> Of the swarms of public robbers,
> Speculators, and land jobbers –
> Of the sorry set of teachers,
> Of the bogus tribe of preachers,
> Of the host of herb physicians,
> And of cunning politicians.[40]

In a collection of poems entitled 'Scottish Portraits' we find 'John Fraser's Farewell to the Church of Scotland' in which the protagonist tells the reader that he has left the church of his forefathers because it no longer fulfills its mission:

> But tho' thou couldst teach man to suffer –
>   To suffer and even to die! –
> Yet poor human nature had longings
>   And wants that thou couldst not supply.[41]

Another church poem has a closer link to the reason why there were so many Scots to be found in Canada. 'John Tamson's Address to the Clergy in Scotland' is an ironic poem in which the speaker admonishes the 'Rev'rend gentlemen' of the Church of Scotland to attend to their duty; among those who should be addressed we find:

> Tell Sutherland's heich mighty duke,
>   Tell Athol, without fearing,
> The deevil keeps a black account
>   Against them for their clearing.[42]

In the poems dedicated to Canada and the Canadian scene there is a sense of well-being which is lacking in the poetry about Scotland. 'Young Canada or, Jack's as good's his Master' opens with the line 'I love this land of forest grand' and McLachlan goes on to tell the reader why:

> For here 'tis plain the heart and brain,
>   The very soul, grow vaster,
> Where men are free as they should be,
>   And Jack's as good's his master.[43]

McLachlan uses a well-known literary device about the difficulty of returning to earlier haunts when he writes:

> I winna gae back to my youthfu' haunts,
>   For they are nae langer fair:
> The spoiler has been in the glades sae green,
>   And sad are the changes there.[44]

And so the exile decides to keep the dream of his younger days rather than to be awakened from it.

We have briefly considered the poetry of some representative emigrant Scots who settled in America. Some prospered, some fared more modestly; some apparently longed for their motherland throughout their lives, some settled into the new country and wrote principally about it. No members of the clergy were mentioned in this essay, but several among those who settled here were poets, writing, as one would expect, mostly devotional verse which did not differ significantly from that being produced by colleagues who remained in Scotland. The emigrant ships also brought Scottish novelists who, like the poets, drew their subject matter from the old and the new. The poetry of Scottish-Americans always displays a hint of the divided self, a trait which was and is much to the fore in Calvinist Scotland, but from this tension sprang the creative impulse which inspired their best work.

Notes

[1] This information is taken from my article 'Scottish Poets and the French Revolution', *Etudes Ecossaises*, vol. 1, 1992, pp. 76-77.

[2] Alexander Wilson, *The Poetical Works* (Belfast, 1845), p. 255.

[3] *Ibidem*, p. 243.

[4] *Ibidem*, p. 276.

[5] *Ibidem*, p. 9.

[6] *Ibidem*, p. 94.

[7] *Ibidem*, p. 304.

[8] *Ibidem*, p. 305.

[9] *Ibidem*, p. 279.

[10] [David Bruce], *Poems Chiefly in the Scottish Dialect* (Washington [Pennsylvania], 1801), p. 27.

[11] *The Letters of Robert Burns*, 2nd edn., edited by G. Ross Roy, 2 vols., Oxford: Oxford University Press, 1985, I, p. 345. The letter was first printed in James Currie's edition of 1800, reprinted in Philadelphia in 1801, so that it is quite possible that Bruce saw the phrase there.

[12] David Bruce, *op. cit.*, p. 29

[13] *Ibidem*, p. 30.

[14] *Ibidem*, p. 119.

[15] *Ibidem*, p. 11.

[16] *Ibidem*, p. 15.

[17] J.D. Ross, *Scottish Poets in America, with Biographical and Critical Notices,* New York: Pagan & Ross, 1889, p. 61.

[18] D.H. Edwards ed., *Modern Scottish Poets*, 16 vols., Brechin: D.H. Edwards, 1880-1897, IV, p. 399. Henceforth Edwards.

[19] *Ibidem*, IV, p. 343.

[20] *Ibidem*, IV, p. 344.

[21] *Ibidem*, IV, p. 347.

[22] J.D. Ross, *op. cit.*, p. 63.

[23] D.H. Edwards, *op. cit.*, IV, pp. 347-348.

[24] J.D. Ross, *op. cit.*, p. 38.

[25] James Kennedy, *The Complete Scottish and American Poems,* New York: [s.n.], 1920, p. 183.

[26] *Ibidem*, p. 183.

[27] *Ibidem*, p. 185.

[28] *Ibidem*, p. 235.

29 *Ibidem*, pp. 40-41.

30 *Ibidem*, p. 92.

31 *Ibidem*, p. 147.

32 *Ibidem*, p. 149.

33 *Ibidem*, p. 118.

34 *Ibidem*, p. 119.

35 *Ibidem*, p. 199.

36 *Blackwood's Magazine*, vol. XXVI, Sept. 1829, p. 400.

37 E.H. Dewart ed., *Selections from Canadian Poets,* Montreal: J. Lovell, 1864, pp. 97-98.

38 *The Poetical Works of Alexander McLachlan,* Toronto: William Briggs, 1900, p. 210.

39 *Ibidem*, p. 221.

40 *Ibidem*, p. 256.

41 *Ibidem*, p. 388.

42 *Ibidem*, p. 396.

43 *Ibidem*, p. 208.

44 *Ibidem*, p. 104.

TONY VOSS

Thomas Pringle [1]

SCOTLAND

Thomas Pringle was born in 1789, the year of the French Revolution and died in 1834, the year of emancipation. He was born near Kelso, on Blakelaw, a farm held by his father, Robert. As a result either of Perthes' disease, a congenital condition, or of an accident in infancy, Thomas Pringle was lame and walked with crutches. His mother, Catherine Heatlie, of a Berwickshire farming family, died when Thomas, her third son, was barely six years old.

Blakelaw lay in the arable north of Roxburghshire rather than in the pastoral south. In 1798 'Pringle' was one of seven families who between them held two-thirds of the valuation of the whole county.[2] But Thomas was not of that ilk: his father paid 'ferm... a fixed yearly amount... as rent for land' (SND) to Andrew Wauchope, of Niddry. Since Robert Pringle held his land 'of some subject' rather than 'of the crown', he was not entitled 'to vote for the knight of the shire'.[3] On Blakelaw, beneath the farmer and his family there were 'cotters' and 'bondagers': the latter were women farm servants whose labour hired ploughmen were 'bound' to provide to the farmer, from their own families or by other means.

Thomas Pringle's disability meant that he was unlikely to work the land. He attended school in the parish of Linton, where the syllabus would have been religious knowledge and the three R's. In 1802 he entered the 'Latin' school in Kelso, which examined in 'Shorter catechism, Psalms, Passages of the Bible, knowledge of the Christian religion, Latin, grammar, reading and expounding the Classics'.[4] Here Pringle might have got to know Ruddiman's *Rudiments of the Latin Tongue* or an anthology like *A New Collection in Prose and Verse for the Use of Schools*. William Jerdan,

born in Kelso in 1782, described the school as a 'republic of letters'.[5]

In 1808, when Pringle enrolled in the University of Edinburgh,
what George Elder Davie called The Democratic Intellect must still
have been alive. The University relied heavily on lectures and on
the liveliness of student societies. The records show that Pringle
enrolled for Latin and Greek in 1805, Latin 2 in 1806 and Logic in
1808. He left no account of his studies and his friend Robert Story
wrote that 'His readings during the hours not engaged in the
preparation of the lessons of the day consisted chiefly in the belles
lettres of his mother tongue'.[6] The University Library holds manuscript notes taken by John Borthwick, a contemporary of Pringle's,
in the lectures on Moral Philosophy given by Dugald Stewart in
1806 and 1807. The idealism and confidence, not to mention the
schema of 'universal history', of the Scottish Enlightenment can still
be heard in Stewart's rhetoric:

> From the circumstances which are now exhibited upon the earth, it is
> probable that men will never suffer so much again from the tyranny of
> despots... Men in general are more enlightened than they were, and the
> communications which have taken place between different nations and
> climates will tend to convey the atmosphere of liberty from one country
> to another. – The press, the palladium of the freedom of the people and
> the powerful restrainer of the grasping of regal prerogatives will if it
> remain free [which in some country or other it always will be] form the
> irresistible protector of the comforts of the people. The sacred spark of
> LIBERTY will be always kept alive, and, fanned by the fostering breezes
> which are wafted by the leaves which grow from the press, will kindle
> the flame of liberty over the surface of the globe. – These political con-
> vulsions which are presently disturbing the peace of Europe, and which
> seem not yet to have spent their force will probably terminate in a gener-
> al peace which has not hitherto been equalled by any thing, but the fabu-
> lous ideas of the antients concerning the golden age.[7]

Thus Pringle might have come into contact with 'the tradition of
distinctive Scottish universalism'.[8] There is no record that Pringle
was a member of the Dialectical Society, but during his years at the
University, two of its perennial topics, straight out of enlightenment
debate were: 'Is the savage or the civilized state most happy?' and
'Does luxury tend to promote the improvement or decline of
nations?' Pringle did make use of the library. Perhaps significantly

his first recorded borrowing is *The Mysteries of Udolpho*, but he went on to the *Odyssey*, with Pope's translation, when he was enrolled for Greek. Among the poets he chose Cook's *Tasso* and Shenstone's *Works*. Among historians and philosophers he seems to have favoured particularly James Beattie, whose *Rome*, *Truth* and *Essays* he borrowed.

In religious persuasion Pringle's family identified with the Secession (Associate Presbytery) Church, and the poet himself 'set great store by a man's religious standpoint'.[9] As a student he both worshipped in private with friends and made close connections with clergymen. His theological conservatism, which did not prevent him being a theatregoer, blended with liberal political ideas. Pringle combined a strong sense of 'spiritual life based on the more experimental apprehension of the Gospel' with 'the democratic spirit that was still a power in the religious, if not in the political sphere in Scotland'.[10]

Pringle had left the University without a degree by January 1809, when he began work in the General Register Office as a clerk. He was responsible for the transcription and abridgement, from original records, of retours, documents written in Latin relating to legal procedures to do with inheritance, transcription and collation of parliamentary records, the checking of printer's proofs and the compilation of errata. Pringle was to stay in this job, on and off, for ten years.

As a student Pringle had founded a club which met weekly to discuss the members' poetry. In 1811 he and Robert Story published *The Institute: a Heroic Poem*, mocking the literary and debating Philomathic Society. In 1816 Pringle contributed several songs to *Albyn's Anthology*, edited by Alexander Campbell, and in the same year his 'Epistle to Mr. R.S.' was published anonymously by James Hogg in the *Poetic Mirror*, a collection of parodies of the work of living British poets.

In 1817 Pringle left the General Register Office, to become joint editor of *The Edinburgh Monthly Magazine*, in which he published, among other things, articles on Scottish Gypsies. These included material given to Pringle by Sir Walter Scott, whom Pringle had met while on Register Office work in Berwickshire. The *EMM* soon became *Blackwood's Magazine* and after a dispute with the new owners, in which Pringle suffered personally and showed both his impulsiveness and his sense of principle, he resigned, continuing as joint editor of *Constable's Edinburgh Magazine* and as editor of the *Edinburgh Star*, a bi-weekly liberal newspaper. Perhaps on the strength of these positions, on 19th July 1817, Pringle married Margaret, the daughter of William Brown, an East Lothian farmer.

But in 1819, in which year appeared his first volume of poems, *The Autumnal Excursion: or, Sketches in Teviotdale, with other Poems*, Pringle resigned his editorial posts and returned to the General Register Office. By 21st September, when he composed 'The Emigrant's Farewell' ('Our native land, our native vale...'), Pringle had decided to emigrate. With the help of Scott, Pringle and his family and servants were given a place in the Government's assisted emigration scheme to the Eastern Province of the Cape of Good Hope. The party, known in South Africa as 'The Scottish Party', sailed from Gravesend on 18th February 1820, and settled on their allotted land in the Baviaanskloof, which they named Glen-Lynden.

The Pringle party had left Scotland in the year of the 'Scottish insurrection', a movement for franchise reform and equal rights, a product of late eighteenth-century radicalism (and perhaps emergent nationalism) and a response to political suppression and economic exploitation, which was put down with execution, transportation and imprisonment.

SOUTH AFRICA

Pringle had never intended to settle as a farmer at the Cape, but as leader of the party and for other reasons, he stayed at Glen-Lynden for two years, during which time the Scottish Party's land increased from 100 acres per household to about 20,000 acres all told, largely as a result of Pringle's negotiations with the Government. The colonists adapted to the cattle economy of the indigenous people they displaced: recalling an earlier Scotland of drovers and reivers. At one point Pringle, the farmer's son, could think of himself, not without irony, as a laird. Many of the 1820 Settlers had suffered drought, dearth, crop diseases and strife with the indigenous African peoples, but the Scottish party prospered.

In October 1822, Thomas Pringle moved with his wife and her sister to Cape Town, where he was appointed sub-librarian of the Government Library. In the next year at Pringle's invitation, John Fairbairn came to the Cape, and together the two friends set up a school, which was soon flourishing.

After initially rejecting the idea, the Governor, Lord Charles Somerset eventually gave permission, subject to restrictions, for the publication of a journal. In January 1824 Pringle and Fairbairn assumed joint editorship of the *South African Commercial Advertiser* and two months later appeared the first number of the *South African Journal*, to be published every two months, alternately in English and Dutch. The Reverend Abraham Faure was the Dutch editor.

The *Advertiser* was soon in trouble. The Governor took exception to reports on a libel case against himself: Pringle and Fairbairn resigned and Greig discontinued publication. Shortly afterwards the Fiscal informed Pringle of the Government's dis-pleasure at apparently radical tendencies in the second number of the *Journal*. In a characteristic combination of principle and impulse, Pringle and Fairbairn discontinued the *Journal* and Pringle resigned his post at the library. Their school declined as a result of official disapproval. Pringle gave evidence to the two Commissioners who had been sent to the Cape by the Colonial Office to enquire into the administration of Somerset.

Pringle set out to return to the Eastern Cape in October 1824. On the way, in a fall from his horse, Pringle injured his leg and was obliged to remain at Genadendal, a Moravian mission station, for two months. Pringle spent most of 1825 in the Eastern Cape, and in June of that year he had an important meeting, in Graaff-Reinet, with Sir Andries Stockenstrom, a colonial official of progressive and humanitarian views, Dr. John Phillip, Secretary of the London Missionary Society at the Cape, and James Read, missionary.

In the last two years of his stay at the Cape, Pringle had written many poems, some of which were only published some time later. In 1824, as secretary of the Society or the Relief of Distressed Settlers he had published, in London, *Some Account of the Present State of the English Settlers in Albany, South Africa*. On 16th April 1826 Pringle, Margaret and her sister Janet sailed from Cape Town for London. He was deep in debt and hoped to gain redress. Before leaving South Africa Pringle wrote the first of a number of 'Letters from South Africa', which is dated 5th January 1826: under the title 'Slavery' it appeared in the *New Monthly Magazine and Literary Journal*, then edited by Thomas Campbell, the Scottish poet, to whom Pringle had earlier addressed a sonnet, on 17th October 1826.

LONDON

In London, Pringle set about applying for compensation for the losses he believed he had suffered as a result of official prejudice. Partly because he was no longer at the Cape, no longer a settler, he was unsuccessful. But in 1827 he became Secretary of the Anti-Slavery Society and was appointed editor of the literary annual *Friendship's Garland*. He held both posts until 1834: in that year the Emancipation Act was passed and the Anti-Slavery Society became the Aborigines' Protection Society. Pringle planned to return to South Africa, where he hoped to be appointed to a magistracy.

During his residence in London, Pringle published his poetry and journalism, in his own and other annuals, in anti-Slavery and other journals, while he was responsible for almost all of the Society's publications and for other aspects of its work. He also prepared the manuscripts of other writers for publication. In 1828 his poems were collected in *Ephemerides: or, Occasional Poems written in Scotland and South Africa*. In 1831 he edited and wrote a supplement to *The History of Mary Prince, a West Indian Slave*. And in 1834 first appeared Pringle's *African Sketches*, in two parts: *Poems Illustrative of South Africa* (an enlargement of part two of *Ephemerides*) and a prose *Narrative of a Residence in South Africa*.

On the 27th of June 1834 Pringle published and signed the Anti-Slavery Society's announcement of the Act of Abolition. The next day he fell ill and was diagnosed with consumption. His departure for South Africa was delayed. Pringle died on 5th December 1834 and was buried in Bunhill Fields.

SOUTH AFRICAN POET

Although Pringle spent less than six of his 45 years in South Africa, the trajectory of his life and the nature of his intervention there have given him a distinctive place in that country's ideological and cultural expression. The South African social formation has changed radically in the past decade. No longer is the country, politically speaking at least, under the hegemony of its settler, or historically recent immigrant minority. It is risky in such circumstances to predict the continuance of any literary canon, especially one so new as that of 'South African Literature in English'.

Soon after his departure from South Africa and even before his death Pringle was imaginatively identified with the South African landscape. He had himself named, or re-named, the land, but he had also taken up as a poetic resource the indigenous names and languages of the country. On 16th May Robert Godlonton published in the *Graham's Town Journal* a sketch describing a visit to the Baviaans River district, where the Pringles had settled:

> It was, perhaps, a lucky incident, that Fortune should, in one of her vagaries, transmit from the shores of Scotia to this part of the Colony, one of those enigmatical bipeds yclept a Poet; the consequence is, that it has almost attained the rank and celebrity of classic ground.[11]

Godlonton goes on to punctuate his account of his journey with quotations from poems by Pringle which accommodate indigenous toponymy to the diction of picturesque and sublime.

Godlonton, a settler apologist, who had had some differences with Pringle, the philanthropist spokesman, goes on to discuss the 'sober realities' (as opposed to 'fanciful images') of frontier politics, such as 'Caffer depredations'. At this point he makes no reference to Pringle's poems, 'The Caffer Commando' or 'Makanna's Gathering' perhaps (both first published in 1827), which were sympathetic to the indigenous people and critical of the settlers.

In 1885 L.H. Meurant remembered Pringle for having 'fought the battle for the freedom of the South Africa press'.[12] The poet's treatment of other 'sober realities' of South African history and society was largely ignored. Pringle's name was sustained for a long time in South Africa as the poet of the named (and appropriated) landscape or the lofty liberal idealist.

After Pringle's death the *Narrative* continued to appear at intervals until 1858. Individual South African poems were anthologized

there (and 'Afar in the Desert' was widely circulated), but the
Poems were not re-published until 1881 (in London and Cape
Town), in the period of the Anglo-Zulu War, the British Annexation
of the Transvaal, the first War of Independence and the first moves
towards South African 'confederation'. In 1902, at the time of the
South African War (the second War of Independence) the Abbey
Press of Edinburgh published *African Sketches: Poems* by Thomas
Pringle, whose introduction argued that these were 'poems fully as
descriptive of the South Africa of to-day as of his day of 1820'. In
1912, two years after Union, the year before the Natives' Land Act,
appeared William Hay's *Thomas Pringle: His Life, Times and
Poems*, published by Juta in Cape Town. Hay, whose edition had
been suggested by and was dedicated to Thomas Muir,
Superintendent-General of Education in the Cape Province, wrote
that Pringle the poet 'merits the particular esteem of South Africans
because... he found books in our running brooks, sermons in Cape
stones, and God in all things'. In 1970 Robert Wahl edited *Poems
Illustrative of South Africa* (the first part of *African Sketches*), published in Cape Town by Struik. Wahl's precision and scholarship
recognized that Pringle, who had for a century been 'regarded as
the "father of South African poetry"' was now a fit subject for South
African academic study: his 'assimilation of local idiom', (quoting
Lewin Robinson), his 'imaginative acceptance of the new country'
and his acute consciousness of the dilemmas of the colonial frontier encounter meant that in the history of South African literature
Pringle would 'always be remembered as a highly significant and
interesting pioneer'.[13] The most recent edition of Pringle, *African
Poems*, was published in 1989 to mark the bi-centenary of the
poet's birth. The editors Michael Chapman and Ernest Pereira,
while building on the work of Wahl, question Pringle's fatherhood,
but find an important place for his poetry in South African literature, more and more dominated by black writers, in a tradition of
protest writing:

> The problems he wrestled with – racial conflict, political oppression and
> censorship, economic exploitation – are equally relevant to-day.[14]

As he had been in Scotland, within South Africa Pringle can be
read as a regional poet. But his close identification with the Eastern

Cape does not mean that he cannot be assimilated to a South African national consciousness. In *Southern African Literatures* Michael Chapman argues that the complexities of South African history made the Eastern Cape the first location of Afrikaner, Black (Xhosa) and English South African identity as responses to modernity.[15]

Recent South African academic criticism of Pringle has explored the variety of his poetic and rhetorical response to the country, the contradictions of his settler/philanthropist identity, the extent to which his Scottish education and experience fitted him for his South African achievement, and the ambiguities of his encounter with the indigenous peoples of the country.[16]

'Scottish Poet' (DNB)

That Pringle is a South African poet does not mean that he is not still also (or at least has not been) a Scottish. Dual citizenship is available at a price, perhaps with varying terms of validity.

Pringle held his pastoral place in the album of Scottish poetry through the nineteenth century. In 1866 Alexander Whitelaw's *The Book of Scottish Song* includes 'The Emigrant's Farewell', 'Maid of My Heart', 'O the Ewe-bughting's bonnie' and 'Love's Constancy'. *The Edinburgh Book of Scottish Verse* edited by W. Macneile Dixon in 1910 holds on to 'The Emigrant's Farewell' and 'O the Ewe-bughtin's bonnie', which latter in the next year Sir George Douglas, Bart., included in *The Book of Scottish Poetry* together with 'The Nameless Stream' and 'A Farewell to the Borderland'. Pringle does not appear in Tom Scott's *Penguin Book of Scottish Verse* (1970), whereas Allan Cunningham (1784-1842), with whom Pringle collaborated in London, does.

In Millar's *Literary History of Scotland* (1903) Pringle is remembered as the editor of the *Edinburgh Monthly Magazine*,[17] whereas *Scottish Poetry: A Critical Survey* mentions 'The Ewe-Buchtin' as one of the 'chance reminiscences' of Burns, 'not all equally choice'. In 1909 J.B. Leishman had already devoted a chapter to 'Thomas Pringle, the African Poet'.[18]

Despite his entry in *The Macmillan Companion to Scottish Literature*, and Angus Calder's canny plea (published in a South African journal in 1982), I think Pringle has disappeared from all

but the most scholarly repositories of Scottish poetry. Wherever
Pringle's reputation were to lodge, it would ever be that of a minor
poet, but what he wrote before he left Scotland suffers inhibitions
from which his later experience liberated him.

Pringle's Scottish *oeuvre* includes nothing to challenge the
Romantic, picturesque, modest, tasteful, genteel standards of late
18th and early 19th century British verse. *The Institute* (1811), the
mock-heroic satire on 'the Polymathic Society', of which Pringle
was joint author with his friend Story is already characteristic. Each
of the four cantos carries epigraphs from Roman writers or Milton
and is peppered with allusion to or quotation from Cowper,
Goldsmith, Gray, Horace, Milton and Scott. The iambic pentameter
couplets are occasionally varied with triplets and alexandrines. The
narrative is explicitly (knowingly?) located in Edinburgh and the
vocabulary is Standard English with admixture of Scots ('caddie',
'ruff', 'scroggy'). The poem closes with an ostensibly ironic prophecy
of the enlightenment to be brought by the Institute, strangely pre-
figuring Pringle's later career:

> ...I sing a prophet's song,
> In awful strain which mortal never heard,
> How doors of future ages are unbarr'd!
> How th' INSTITUTE with sweet, heart-cheering tone
> Shall wake the Negro, 'neath the fiery Zone...
> Thro' island, country-town, and inland firth,
> On shepherds, fishers, smugglers, gipseys, hinds...

Pringle's reputation as a poet when he left Scotland depended
largely on *The Autumnal Excursion* which, begun in 1811 as
'Paterna Rura' (land of my fathers?), was first published in James
Hogg's *Poetic Mirror* in 1816, under the title 'An Epistle to Mr. R—
S— ', addressed to Robert Story. The *Poetic Mirror* was a collection
of parodies, all by Hogg himself except for Pringle's, of the eminent poets of the time. Pringle's was in the manner of Scott,
approved by the great unknown himself, and others, and read as
addressed to the poet laureate, Southey.

The *Excursion*, reminiscent of John Leyden's *Scenes of Infancy*,
is an imaginary and sentimental account of Pringle's return to the
Teviotdale of his childhood and youth, evoking the region's
scenery, history and legend. The poem's contrast of childhood and

maturity, past and present, derives strength from Wordsworth and
from Pringle's forthright confrontation of his own losses and disap-
pointments. The poem remains sentimental, however, because it
deals with past and future and makes less engagement with any
present, except perhaps in its picture of how 'improvement' had
changed rural Scotland. It has been argued that the poem gives
evidence that Pringle was already considering emigration at this
time: as in this passage, which is also characteristic in its evocation
of freedom:

>—Oh, ne'er shall he, whose ardent prime
>Was foster'd in the freeman's clime,
>Though doom'd to seek a distant strand,
>Forget his glorious native land –
>Forget – 'mid far Columbia's groves,
>Those sacred scenes of youthful loves.

In the first published version of the poem for 'far Columbia's'
Pringle had written 'Brahma's blood-stained': in a presentation
copy preserved in South Africa, Pringle deleted 'Columbia's' and
inscribed 'Algoa's' in ink above it.

    In this context, the political reference of freedom has no com-
munity and no vision: seeming merely to add to the chorus echoing *Wallace* and *Brus*. So this ostensibly patriotic reference to
Scotland is to a legendary past rather than to a political present.
The poem has all the antiquarianism and sentimentality that limits
Pringle to-day to the heritage sub-culture rather than admitting him
to the central poetic continuity. In fact Pringle's self-figuration as
emigrant, pilgrim or wanderer recurs throughout his Scottish verses,
as if they can find no future for the poet in their immediate
rhetorical situation. I would argue, indeed, that these poems
embody a poetics of frustration. Their visions of the future, personal or political, are vague, and their trajectories are circular.
Significantly, perhaps, one of Pringle's first published pieces, with
which he received help from Scott, was on the Scottish gypsies,
and even before his departure from Scotland he illustrates Auden's
diagnosis of the urban middle class as 'an orphan class, with no
fixed residence, capable of snobbery in both directions. From class
insecurity it has developed the family unit as a defence'.[19]

    In 1852, less than twenty years after his death, Pringle was

acknowledged in a series of lectures given at the Edinburgh
Philosophical Association on the poets 'of the past half-century', as
the author of both *The Autumnal Excursion* and *African Sketches*.
The speaker, D.M. Moir, who wrote for and edited *Blackwood's*,
granted Pringle scholarship, elegance and 'a certain racy vigour
occasionally amounting to power', but saw and expressed clearly
the relation between the two spheres in which Pringle's imagination had operated:

> His verses naturally fall into two sections, – those relating to the scenery
> and traditions, the sentiments and associations of his native Scotland; and
> those composed among the far-stretching wilds beyond the Cape, where
> the elephant comes down to drink at the cane-marshes and where the
> fox-chase is exchanged for the lion-hunt. For eloquence, elevation, and
> purity of style it would be difficult to point out many things in the octo-
> syllabic measure, superior to the *Autumnal Excursion*, descriptive of
> Teviotdale, and of the pastoral and pure associations by which it is linked
> to the mind of boyhood; and several of his songs and sonnets breathe
> alike of the fire and tenderness which hovered over the Border districts
> from the days of the old 'Flowers of the Forest' and 'Johnny Armstrong',
> down to those of Scott and Leyden; but his *African Sketches* are mature
> in thought and power; and, besides, are more striking, both from the
> novelty of the situations depicted, and the imposing grandeur of the
> scenery described. The finest of these are 'The Bechuana Boy', which
> unites Doric simplicity with classic finish; and the verses, 'Afar in the
> Desert', whose strange wild music is said to have possessed a charm of
> fascination even for the ear and heart of Coleridge.[20]

Pringle's colonial situations gave his poetry the appeal of novelty
in the market, and his settings appealed to current tastes for the
sublime, but, as Moir recognizes, the African poems are 'mature in
thought and power'. Perhaps the date of Moir's lectures, 1852, is
significant: in 1854 the Cape Colony was granted representative
government, which was a kind of imperial acknowledgement of
what Pringle had apprehended: that a colony can be a society, not
simply a reservoir of experience or raw material for metropolitan
consumption.

The achievement of Pringle's African poetry was built, however,
on the literary and imaginative foundations he had laid in Scotland.
If South Africa made Pringle a mature poet in thought and power,
it was the Scotland of his emotional experience, education, social

class and political persuasion that enabled him to take advantage of his re-location, where his non-conformist faith may have helped to align him against the Anglican establishment.

Pringle sits firmly 'in that tradition of Scottish eclecticism where creative writing, anthologizing, and editing are closely related'.[21] By 1820 Pringle had published antiquarian research, criticism and poetry, under his own name and anonymously. He had edited journals and a newspaper. His poetry included heroic couplets, octosyllabic couplets, sonnets, ballad measure and a variety of stanzaic verse. He devised words for traditional airs and for tunes composed by his sister Mary. He cobbled stanzas on to traditional and literary ballads. *Poeta nascitur, non fit* no doubt applied to Pringle but he was fitted for this calling by his late Enlightenment education, which gave him access to the rational, if idealistic, vision of human progress which is exemplified in Dugald Stewart's concern with 'the formation as well as the advancement of political society'.[22] After he left Scotland, Pringle continued his eclectic career as a jobbing writer: in South Africa he became in addition a farmer, a teacher, a secretary and an activist.

Pringle's Borders origins kept him in touch with what was still vital in an oral tradition. He tends to use certain terms, 'the Oppressor', 'Freedom', 'Oppression', 'Tyrant', 'Tyranny', in ways which recall W.J. Ong's remarks on 'clichés in many low-technology developing cultures'. These may 'strike high literates as mindless' but Ong sees them as 'residual formulary thought processes'.[23] This residual orality in Pringle's cultural constitution made sympathetic connections in South Africa. Certainly the 'border ballad' which Pringle made literary use of in 'The Forester of the Neutral Ground' developed, as Ong argues, 'on the edge of orality'.[24] Pringle's use of epithetic formulae eventually effected for him 'obligatory stabilization':[25] after his South African experience it signalled his acceptance of a code by which he claimed a place in the liberal humanitarian, evangelical, emancipationist discursive community.

Pringle's psychological make-up and socio-economic position, made it difficult for him to exploit the cynical opportunities of post-war Edinburgh, and in South Africa he would suffer again. But his colonial experience gave him the opportunity to look ironically on his own contradictory situation, as in 'The Emigrant's Cabin'. He was sympathetic to the indigenous people and yet took up arms to defend his party's land against those people from whom it had been taken by imperial expansion. Although he was sympathetic to the settlers, he sided, in the course of his South African sojourn, with the missionaries and philanthropists and in the Emancipation programme Pringle found a cause in which to unite and direct all his energies.

COLONIAL POET

Pringle identified strongly with his native land. Scots was spoken in his family circle. About his posthumous poetic reputation, he hoped to leave behind him something that 'his countrymen would not willingly let die' and he seems to have thought of those coun-trymen as Scots. In South Africa he identified with his own Scotch party and he argued with others that South Africa needed Scots rather than English settlers. His *Account of the Present State of the English Settlers in Albany, South Africa* reprints, from the *Morning Chronicle* of 12th July 1823, a letter which concludes:

> Certainly brother Sawney is the man best fitted for progressing in all countries and climates. Send, therefore, Scotch (and especially Highlanders), to people and defend the ceded Caffer territory. Of manu-facturers, pin makers, and fringe embroiders (sic), you have already sacri-ficed enough on the sour grass plains of Albany.[26]

Yet in his poetry Pringle's self-figuration is often contradictory: Briton, English, Scots, white. In South African encounters he must be one of the 'Amanglezi' (the English: 'The Emigrant's Cabin') or 'Englishman' ('The Forester of the Neutral Ground'). 'The Forester' addresses Pringle as 'Dear Stranger, from England the free', but in 'The Caffer Commando', Pringle is part of England 'in her tyran-nous mood'.

So the question of whether Pringle is a Scottish or a South African poet is not really a question at all. He is a colonial poet, in a category which aligns Pringle with a number of Scottish contem-poraries whose work is made distinctive by their involvement in the colonial enterprise. Thomas Campbell (1777-1844), to whom Pringle dedicated an early sonnet, and who published Pringle's first 'Letter from South Africa' (on 'Slavery'), had North American inter-

ests and wrote *Gertrude of Wyoming* in the same Spenserian stanzas that Pringle used for 'The Emigrants'. John Leyden (1775-1811),
born in Denholm, near Kelso, who is invoked as 'adventurous
Leyden' in 'The Emigrants' and shares with Pringle 'Teviot's Border
tongue' ('The Exile's Lament'), was the author of *Scenes of Infancy:
Descriptive of Teviotdale* (1808), a poem whose idyllic pastoralism
gives a moving picture of the social and economic change consequent on 'improvement' in Pringle's native county and must have
been a model for *The Autumnal Excursion.* Leyden had also compiled a two-volume *Historical Account of Discoveries and Travels
in Africa* (1799), and considered the idea of African exploration
himself, but made his name as an orientalist and linguist. John Galt
(1779-1839) spent three years in Canada; his novel *Annals of the
Parish* (1821), set in his native Ayrshire, gives an account of
Scottish parochial life c. 1760-1810 which reflects very much what
the history of Pringle's Roxburghshire childhood and youth must
have been like.[27] Alexander Campbell (fl.c.1800), the editor of
Albyn's Anthology, in which Pringle's words for music first
appeared, was the author of *The Grampians Desolate*, the subject
of which is the internal colonization of the Scottish Highlands. Less
well known is John Marjoribanks (fl. 1790s), who came from
Coldstream, east of Kelso, where some of his poems were published, had served as an officer in the West Indies, and wrote
Slavery, an Essay in Verse (1791). Simply as Scots, these post-Union
writers were in a colonial and provincial relationship with England.
James Thomson (1700-1746), whose *The Seasons* is recalled in *The
Autumnal Excursion*, also wrote 'Rule, Britannia' and is a striking
example of the colonized Scot.

   These were among the Scots whom the Union had admitted to,
or enlisted into 'the English Empire, which by 1800 was invariably
known as the British Empire'.[28] For Pringle, at least, this was an
ambiguous allegiance, but in his emigration to South Africa the
poet entered on a narrative that richly realized his Borders,
Enlightenment and Evangelical hcritage.

   On the Eastern Cape frontier Pringle found a horse-borne cattle
culture that recalled the history of the Scottish borders. 'The
Forester of the Neutral Ground' accommodates the energies of
class and race to a ballad narrative which maintained its topicality

in South Africa for nearly two hundred years. The narrative also figures the poet himself in a powerfully ironic position which nonetheless imagines terms in which the injustices of the present can be resolved in the future:

> Then tell me, dear Stranger, from England the free,
> What good tidings bring'st thou for Arend Plessie?
> Shall the edict of Mercy be sent forth at last,
> To break the harsh fetters of Colour and Caste?

In the Cape Colony Pringle lived along a frontier which recalled *The Autumnal Excursion*:

> That frontier edge, which erst defied
> The invaders' march, the oppressor's pride...

There, as a child, he had waged a 'bloodless Border war'. In South Africa the frontier was bloody enough and in 'Makanna's Gathering' Pringle evoked in the present what in Scotland he had recall'd from the past:

> The marshall'd bands; the battle plain;
> The Border slogan's pealing shout;
> The shock, the tumult, and the rout... (*The Autumnal Excursion*)

Pringle's sympathy for the indigenous people of South Africa, to judge from Dugald Stewart's lectures on Moral Philosophy, was encouraged by his Enlightenment education. Something of the difference between Pringle's Scottish and his South African imagination can be gauged from a comparison between his poem 'The Lament of the Captive Lady' and his description of the Xhosa woman he met at the Bethelsdorp Mission Station within a few days of his arrival in the Eastern Cape.[29]

A number of Pringle's South African poems use the conventions of dramatic monologue to give voice to African people. The most defiant of these are 'The Song of the Wild Bushman' and 'Makanna's Gathering'. The hunter-gatherer San (whom Pringle identified with Scott's 'people of the mist') contemplates a guerilla war against proletarianization: Makanna urges the Xhosa to a direct challenge, since the alternatives are 'To conquer or be slaves'. Of other poems in this mode 'The Brown Hunter's Song' is an idyllic evocation (with Biblical overtones) of a pastoral setting remote from colonial intrusion; speakers in 'The Captive of Camalu' and 'The Ghona Woman's Lullaby' are Christian converts and thus both reconciled to captivity and identified with Pringle himself. Pringle reserves the octosyllabic couplet for 'ethnographic' studies of 'The Coranna' and 'The Kosa' (also considered in isolation from colonial contact), and for 'Evening Rambles', a displaced re-run of the *Excursion*, which features third-person portraits of two servants (presumably Pringle's own): the 'brown herder', a Khoi, who 'born the white man's servile thrall, Knows that he cannot lower fall'; and 'the stout neat-herd', another version of 'The Bechuana Boy': 'A naked homeless exile he – But not debased by Slavery'. In South Africa, then, Pringle had sophisticated his poetic range to figure different relations of power and servitude in different rhetorical and prosodic ways.

Pringle's six years in South Africa were a dynamic passage. It seems that only after his meeting with Philip, Read and Stockenstrom did Pringle reach the focus on slavery which issued in his letter on the subject and thus led to his eight-year tenure of the Secretaryship of the Anti-Slavery Society. But by the time the *African Sketches* were published, in 1834, the year of the poet's death, his work had become predominantly a function of two forces: his colonial experience and the Anti-Slavery movement. From the opening poem 'The Bechuana Boy', a tale of post-abolition slave trading, even, in a sense, a 'slave narrative', to the final sonnet, 'To Oppression', the South African poems are aimed against slavery. The argument that slavery debases both exploiter and exploited is an aspect of 'The Slave Dealer': in a recognized genre of abolitionist/emancipationist verse, one of its predecessors being Southey's 'The Sailor who had served in the Slave Trade' (1789), Pringle's particular addition is the evangelical ending. A 'Wanderer' returns home, after the ill course of his life, to die, and confesses to his mother that he once whipped a negress slave to death. This portrait of frenzy and guilty fear is Pringle's particular case of the general psychology of violent exploitation outlined in his sonnet 'Slavery'.

In Pringle's poems, then, slavery is the extreme of servitude, but he is also concerned with both political and economic servitude: a number of poems ('A Noon-day Dream', 'A Common Character' and 'Oppression') deal with tyranny and despotism in terms which seem to recall Lord Charles Somerset, and give new substance to Pringle's references to freedom and southern treachery in his earlier poems. 'The Cape of Storms' distinguishes 'the servile' from 'the slave', perhaps recalling Pringle's Enlightenment inheritance, particularly Adam Ferguson's *History of Civil Society* (1767), whose Sixth Part is 'Of Corruption and Political Slavery'.

In the Kelso newspapers of his youth, and in the Morebattle library (founded in 1797), of which his father was a member, Pringle might have read of the debates, petitions and memorials leading up to the abolition of the slave trade in 1807, the year in which he left the University. The emancipation movement only regathered its humanitarian momentum by 1823, with the formation of the Anti-Slavery Association and Buxton's first parliamentary motion for the extinction of British colonial slavery. Before his colonial experience, Pringle seems to have shown no interest in the movement, but after clashing with the colonial order, his work becomes a kind of displacement of Blake's triple vision of Britain's second (i.e. African) Empire: for Blake the Elect were England, the Reprobate, France and that which remained, the Redeemable (the 'third world'). For Pringle the emancipationist movement constituted the Elect, the Reprobate were the colonial hierarchy, slave-owners and 'Oppressors': and the Redeemable were the slaves themselves, the Africans and the potentially converted readers of his poems: 'In such a scheme that Third World is to be appropriated to the missionary zeal of an Elected design'.[30]

CONCLUSION
Pringle remains a minor Scottish-born early nineteenth-century poet, who never returned to Scotland to live after he left in 1820. Does this view of his work make any claim to return him to Scottish poetry in the century after MacDiarmid's Scottish Renaissance? Do the compromises of his colonial situation, to which he was hoping to return at the time of his death in 1834, bear any traces of a defining 'Caledonian antysyzygy'?

The tensions and ambiguities of Pringle's allegiances are evident in a letter written in the last year of his life, contemplating a future beyond emancipation:

> If I could procure some public employment in London, which would admit of my devoting a portion of my time to the service of the cause of humanity, in which I consider myself solemnly enlisted for life, I would of course prefer remaining at home. But if that cannot be obtained in England, I am willing to return again to South Africa which, next to my native country, has the strongest claim upon me both of duty and affection.[31]

In London? At home? In England? South Africa? My native country? After 1820 he never considered settling in Scotland again, and here it sounds as though Pringle hoped that in South Africa he could maintain a respectable livelihood, serve 'the cause of humanity' and retain his identity as a Scot, a Scot of the diaspora. It is at least possible to argue that as a South African poet Pringle was a more Scottish poet than he had been in Scotland.

Consider that the identity of Scottish poetry moves along a spectrum between the absolute caricature of 'the complacent parochial Scot who cannot see past London ideas and standards' and the 'expansive and outward-looking'.[32] For many readers the latter is exemplified in the programme and the achievement of MacDiarmid, tending always towards 'the point "whaur extremes meet" – extremes of politics, language, culture and sensibility'.[33] From this jostling or assimilation of contraries, in which the provincial encounters the international, Scotland emerges as 'a country made of antitheses and contrasts'.[34] Thus translation is a crucial element: translation within, into and out of the literature. But 'the tradition of Scottish eclecticism'[35] depends also on 'the historical habit',[36] on a continuous editorial process and an accretion of 'exotic elements of vocabulary'.[37] Considered specifically as a function of the relationship between Scotland and English, Scottish literature may be 'a subversive element within a system supporting the hegemony of the colonizer's language'.[38]

This template fits snugly on the work of modern poets. It suits Yeats's 'whole "philosophy" of intersecting gyres' and 'the eclecticism of Modernist cultural assembly'.[39] Marco Fazzini has recently argued for a further convergence that enables him fruitfully to read 'contemporary Scottish poetry and hybridity' as a post-colonial phenomenon. How do such readings help us to approach Thomas Pringle? Two further quotations may help. Marco Fazzini quotes Cairns Craig:

> The liberation of the voice into the varieties of accent and dialect and alternative languages which the collapse of the English literary imperium made possible has provided Scottish writers with renewed energies deriving from the actual linguistic possibilities of their situation.[40]

And Fazzini describes the imaginative manoeuvring of Douglas Dunn as emanating from 'a creative encounter between colonizer and colonized, tradition and renovation, culture and barbarity, that uncertain border where an "inner emigré" can fight against an old idea of class struggle and cultural alienation'.[41] Thus, within the complex of contradictions a 'prominent feature' is 'social consciousness... the way in which [Scottish literature] often reflects the contemporary scene and the impact of history and change on the nation as a whole'.[42]

Pringle's poetry can be read as a late ripple of the 'almost immediate cultural reaction' to the Union of 1707.[43] He settled on the colonial frontier not after 'the collapse of the English literary imperium' but at the moment of its triumphant initiation in Africa. Yet even at its apogee the imperium was not absolute: an industrializing economy had to accommodate to pre-capitalist, cattle-centred cultures: the railway to the horse-borne: English common law to Roman-Dutch and African custom. Pringle extended his vocabulary from English, Scots and Latin to include Cape Dutch and Xhosa. His work of editorship and translation amplified the voices of Boer settlers, a Bechuana slave and a founding Xhosa poet who was a convert to Christianity. Pringle devised a flexible rhetoric for varieties of ethnic identity and the colonial categories of class and caste. He re-located the traditions of border ballad and war-song to a new frontier. Pringle was both subversive and progressive in the context of his time. One could argue that his fiction (verse) challenged while his reportage (prose) promoted the imperial version of modernity. In *African Sketches* he even effected a kind of 'Modernist cultural assembly' in the combination of 'Poems Illustrative of South Africa', a prose 'Narrative of a Residence' and the historiography and antiquarianism of his extensive 'Notes'.

Pringle had to revise his notions of culture and barbarity (his own and others'). And in South Africa he found his commitment to the campaign against slavery, which together with his Christianity fulfilled for him a kind of universal vision, and led to the addition of the vocabulary of West Indian slaves to his exotic word-hoard. Finally, Pringle's South African intervention survived him into an international and inter-linguistic exchange, beyond anything attained by his work before 1820.[44]

None of this can resolve the compromises and contradictions of Pringle's status, but it may enable us to acknowledge that Pringle can still be read for significance beyond South Africa. Perhaps he remained an issue-driven, journalistic poet because he never achieved an individual enabling myth, and was for too long weighed down by the demands of respectability and security.

NOTES

[1] I should like to thank Marco Fazzini for his encouragement and his help in the preparation of this paper. I have used some earlier published and unpublished work of my own. For Pringle's biography I have relied on Jane Meiring, *Thomas Pringle: His Life and Times*, Cape Town and Amsterdam: Balkema, 1968; Patricia Morris, *A Documentary Account of the Life of Thomas Pringle (1789-1834)*, Ph.D. Dissertation, University of London, 1982; and Leith Ritchie, *Poetical Works of Thomas Pringle with a Sketch of his Life*, London: Moxon, 1838.

[2] Robert Douglas, *General View of the Agriculture of the Counties of Roxburghshire and Selkirk*, Edinburgh and London: G. Nicoll, 1798, p. 17.

[3] *Ibidem*, p. 21.

[4] James Smith, *History of Kelso Grammar School*, Kelso: Tweedside Physical and Antiquarian Society, 1909, p. 70.

[5] William Jerdan, *Autobiography*, 4 vols., London: Arthur Hall Virtue and Co., 1852, I, p. 20.

[6] See Thomas Pringle, *Narrative of a Residence in South Africa*, edited by A.M. Lewin Robinson, Cape Town: Struik, 1966, p. xxv.

[7] Edinburgh University Lectures (Ms Notes): Moral Philosophy, by Prof. Dugald Stewart, 1806-1807. Taken by John Borthwick, pp. 415, 417-419.

[8] G.E. Davie, 'Discussion', in J.N. Wolfe ed., *Government and*

Nationalism in Scotland: An Enquiry by Members of the University of Edinburgh, Edinburgh: Edinburgh University Press, 1969, p. 205.

[9] Patricia Morris, *op. cit.*, p. 5.

[10] James Mackinnon, *The Social and Industrial History of Scotland*, London: Blackie and Son Ltd., 1921, p. 47.

[11] L.H. Meurant, *Sixty Years Ago Cape Town*, African Conoisseurs Press, 1885 (Reprint 1963), p. 96.

[12] *Ibidem*, p. 8.

[13] All quotations are from Robert Wahl, *Poems Illustrative of South Africa*, Cape Town: Struik, 1970, pp. xi, xvi, xviii, xxvi.

[14] See *African Poems of Thomas Pringle*, edited by Michael Chapman and Ernest Pereira, Pietermaritzburg: Killie Campbell Africana Library, University of Natal Press, 1989, p. xii.

[15] Michael Chapman, *Southern African Literatures*, London and New York: Longman, 1996, pp. 87-116.

[16] See Damian Shaw, 'Thomas Pringle's "Bushmen": Images in Flesh and Blood', *English in Africa*, vol. 25, no. 2, 1998, pp. 37-61; Matthew Shum, 'Thomas Pringle and the "Xhosa"', *English in Africa*, vol. 27, no. 2, 2000, pp. 1-28; Dirk Klopper, 'Politics of the Pastoral: The Poetry of Thomas Pringle', *English in Africa,* vol. 17, no. 1, 1990, pp. 21-59; Michael Chapman and Ernest Pereira, *op. cit.*; and Tony Voss, 'Thomas Pringle and the Image of the "Bushmen"', *English in Africa*, vol. 9, no. 1, 1982, pp. 15-28; Tony Voss, 'The Education of Thomas Pringle: 1789-1807', Pretoria: HSRC (Report on Research), 1988; Tony Voss, 'Thomas Pringle and the Dialogue of South African Servitude', *English in Africa*, vol. 17, no. 1, 1990, pp. 61-81. I thank Matthew Shum for showing me his unpublished paper '"A dark, deceitful and disorderly race": Thomas Pringle's "Notices Concerning the Scottish Gypsies"', which explores the proto-racism and aestethic romanticism which complicated Pringle's attitudes to the indigenous peoples of South Africa.

[17] J.H. Millar, *A Literary History of Scotland*, London: T. Fisher Unwin, 1903, p. 501.

[18] J.B. Leishman, *A Son of Knox and Other Studies Antiquarian and Biographical*, Glasgow: Maclehose, 1909, pp. 43-62.

[19] W.H. Auden, *The English Auden*, edited by Edward Mendelson, London: Faber & Faber, 1977, pp. 299-300.
See also the following statement: 'I would like to suggest that instead of "middle-class" or "bourgeois" as a definition of Nationalism, we substitute "literate" class. This helps in Scotland, where much of our landward peasantry achieved literacy early in our history'. A.R. Turnbull,

'Discussion', in J.N. Wolfe ed., *op. cit.*, p. 202.

[20] D.M. Moir, *Sketches of the Poetical Literature of the Past Half-Century in Six Lectures delivered at the Edinburgh Philosophical Association*, Edinburgh and London: Blackwood, 1852, pp. 286-287.

[21] Robert Crawford, *Devolving English Literature*, Oxford: Clarendon Press, 1992, p. 258.

[22] (Dugald Stewart), Edinburgh University Lectures, p. 297.

[23] W.J. Ong, *Orality and Literacy: the Technology of the Word*, London: Methuen, p. 38.

[24] *Ibidem*, p. 159.

[25] *Ibidem*, p. 39.

[26] Thomas Pringle, *Some Account of the Present State of the English Settlers in Albany, South Africa*, London; Underwood/Edinburgh: Oliver & Boyd, 1824, p. 108.

[27] In 1819 John Galt contributed the first essay under the title 'The Scotchman in London' to *Blackwood's*.

[28] See Allan Marnie, 'Good-Bye to the U.K.?', *TLS*, no. 4819, 11.8.1995, (pp. 7-8) p. 7.

[29] Thomas Pringle, *Narrative of a Residence in South Africa* (1834), edited by R.A.M. Lewin, Cape Town: Struik, 1996.

[30] J.J. McGann, *Social Values and Poetic Arts: The Historical Judgment of Literary Work*, Cambridge, Mass.: Harvard University Press, 1988, p. 235.

[31] Quoted in Jane Meiring, *op. cit.*, p. 151.

[32] D.D. Muirson, 'Nationalism as expressed in Scottish Literature', in J.N. Wolfe, *op. cit.*, p. 196.

[33] Robert Crawford, *op. cit.*, p. 251.

[34] Marco Fazzini, *Crossings: Essays on Contemporary Scottish Poetry and Hybridity*, Venezia: Supernova, 2000, p. 10.

[35] Robert Crawford, *op. cit.*, p. 258.

[36] *Ibidem*, p. 257, quoting George Gregory Smith.

[37] *Ibidem*, p. 255.

[38] Marco Fazzini, *op. cit.*, p. 28.

[39] Robert Crawford, *op. cit.*, p. 254.

[40] Marco Fazzini, *op. cit.*, p. 28.

[41] *Ibidem*, p. 10.

[42] D.D. Muirson, *op. cit.*, p. 190.

[43] *Ibidem*, p. 192.

[44] 'Afar in the Desert' was widely re-printed and translated. More par-

ticularly the German Romantic Freiligrath made some use of Pringle's poems (see Richard Pachaly, *Thomas Pringle und Ferdinand Freiligrath* Freiberg: Hochschule, 1879). I.M. Shklyazh, the author of *Thomas Pringle UrzhnoAfrikanskii Demokrat* (Thomas Pringle a South African Democrat [Moskva: Hayka, 1985]) based his work partly on 'a book collection put together in the late 18th – early 19th century by the Russian noble Vorontsov family and now in the library of Odessa State University. These works [include] those by Pringle himself and his friends and contemporaries...' (see Shklyazh, 'Preface', in *op. cit.*).

MARGARET LENTA

Lady Anne Barnard's Autobiographical Texts: An Author Effaced

Lady Anne Lindsay, born in Fife in 1750, and after her marriage Lady Anne Barnard, was the eldest of the eleven children of the impoverished fifth Earl of Balcarres. She had a remarkable life by any standards, full of the kind of achievements which were rare for women of any class. In the present day the fact that she recorded and theorised her life at length seems as important as any of the actions and relationships that she describes. In doing so she demonstrates that the legal and social constraints which were intended to keep virtuous women passive and confined to the family did not constitute an absolute barrier to achievement, nor to movement from one social group to another. At the same time she gives an account of the problems and opposition which a woman must encounter if her ambitions exceed those thought proper for her gender group.

Forced in her youth into the understanding that the lifestyle represented by the older generation of her ancient family, the Lindsays of Balcarres, was no longer viable, Lady Anne refused to accept the social down-grading which would have been implied by marriage to a rich merchant and moved to England. She understood that she was part of a movement of able and energetic young Scots to England in order to achieve the greater material success that was possible in London. James Boswell and her friend and suitor Henry Dundas, the political associate of Pitt and eventually Secretary of State for War, were two famous participants in this movement, though both of these remained firmly based in Scotland.

Lady Anne's efforts to establish herself as a member of the governing class of the United Kingdom are perhaps the most important subject of her writings, and the struggles she records are distinctively those of a woman who must avoid the censure of a society which makes it almost impossible for her to be seen to act on her own behalf. It is not clear to what extent she understood as a girl and a young woman the larger meaning of her acts: the rejection of unattractive suitors may have been a simple act of personal choice, and her move to London a longing to leave an unhappy home. Equally, the years of economic struggle in London may have been understood at the time as forced upon her, and without other motives. The elderly woman, however, who, looking back on the decisions and actions of her youth, wrote of the events of her life as a whole process, knew that she had transformed her life by her own acts.

In her old age, from about 1815 onwards, she embarked on the task of selecting from and rewriting the records which remained from her life. Although only two years of her unrevised diaries survive,[1] it seems likely that she had kept such diaries for most of her life. From these frank and informal records she compiled two major memoirs: the first, which remains unpublished, an account of her life in Scotland and England from her birth in 1750 until her old age, and the second, a travel journal of the years 1797-1798,[2] part of the period which she spent with her husband at the Cape of Good Hope. The revised account of her life in Scotland and England consists of six quarto volumes, beautifully recopied from her own revisions and copiously illustrated with engravings of her own drawings and engraved portraits by other artists of the people whom she discusses. The travel journal, which was published for the first time in 1995 as *The Cape Journals of Lady Anne Barnard 1797-1798*, consists of three volumes in the same format, again illustrated by Lady Anne herself, this time with pictures of the peoples and scenes of the Cape and its hinterland. A practising poet all her life, she wrote the poem which has been well known ever since, 'Auld Robin Grey', when she was an unmarried girl at Balcarres in 1771.

In the space of this essay, I cannot discuss the writings which deal with the Barnards' life at the Cape further than to say of them that they offer the most detailed and lively account extant of life in the Cape Colony during the First British Occupation (1795-1803). Lady Anne says of the Cape at the end of vol. IV of her memoir 'it was *there* (in Africa) – I spent the *happiest* years of my life', and it seems clear that this was because in Cape Town she had both the public position and the private influence which allowed her to use her talents to the fullest. The six-volume memoir of her life in Scotland and England, on which I shall focus here, is very different, and reflects a struggle which was rarely successful in small matters – Lady Anne never became really wealthy, nor achieved the marriage and public position in England for which she hoped as a young woman. Nevertheless, in her old age, she understands that she has made a transition of which she is proud.

In the memoir, though the most important subject is herself, she looks outward from the difficulties of her personal life to the societies of southern Scotland in the period 1750-1773 and London in the period 1773-1797 and 1802-1824, when the memoir ends, and supplies vivid accounts of all that she perceives. She understands fully the life to which she would have been restricted had she stayed in Scotland, and contends that it was necessarily unacceptable to a woman of her energies, talents and family history.

In the preamble to this memoir, which is dated 1822, she explains that seven years earlier she gave up her carriage and horses, converting them into 'transcribers' 'portrait painters' 'bookbinders' who would assist her in the conversion of her papers into volumes which the younger members of the family would enjoy reading. She recalls, early in the memoir, her father's maxim that a person who leaves no trace of his mind behind him fails society and his Maker and has 'existed in vain'.[3] Yet, with an ambivalence which is always characteristic of her, she has, early in the process of revision, obscured the nature of her memoir and disguised it as a fiction by giving 'Feigned names to Real characters – delicacy to contemporaries was my motive – I have outlived almost the whole and caution ceases to be necessary'.[4] She refers to herself as Louisa, her sister Margaret becomes Hortensia, the Lindsay family the St Aubins and Henry Dundas, Ludlow.[5] She frequently expresses her fear of being thought presumptuous or egotistical in producing memoirs and thereby claiming for her life a public significance which should only belong to a man. The first pages of the memoir, in fact, are full of contradictions, in which Lady Anne alternately asserts her belief that her life has been significant, and that it may well remain so even after her death, and her fear that her necessarily amateur productions may be treated with contempt. An injunction against publication is combined with an address to her family and friends, and this combination seems to summarise the ambivalence which she feels: 'family and friends', in her case make up a large enough group of critics for any amateur author to fear, or alternatively, a sufficiently large readership to gratify her.

The work, she claims, may be read 'as a story only',[6] and I have argued elsewhere that Lady Anne derived her forms and understanding of many of the events of her life from eighteenth century novelists, especially Richardson.[7] More important here is her wish to represent her personal history as a chapter in the long history of a great family, at her birth depressed and poor in the aftermath of the Jacobite rebellions of 1715 and 1745. The constraints of class and nationality are combined in Lady Anne's account with those of gender: her brothers, sent off to school as children and to suitable professions as adolescents, no doubt had parallel tales of struggles to tell, but her story is that of a young woman of her class who must re-establish herself by her own efforts.

Her elderly father told her, she says, the family history, and though what she recounts of it is brief and selective, it is typically lively. She writes of a Lindsay who witnessed James II in his saintly old age at St Germain, pardoning both his usurping daughters; one of his grooms, David Lloyd, who waited behind him at supper '...left the room in wrath, but put in his head to say in a loud tone "B– ches both... by God'.[8] This story, though there is no doubt that Lady Anne enjoys it for its own sake, has relevance to her account of her own life, in which she is to establish that her family has a right to the position in which she and her siblings have re-established it, of important servants of the British crown and trusted counsellors of monarchs. In terms of this intention, she depicts her father as learned, philosophical, an affectionate parent – but belonging to the past which his children were to leave behind. Succeeding his childless brother as Earl when he was already, in the view of his time, an elderly man, he lived on an income of £ 600 per year at Balcarres, where, she says, 'the old Library of Books... had made Chymists and Philosophers of all the Moths in the Castle'. She tells us that he 'argued everything... but he concluded every subject with the Beauty and wrongs of the Fair Mary

Queen of Scots and the Base Union of the Two Crowns...'.[9] Lady
Anne never identifies her father's views as mistaken, but she states
her opinion several times in the memoir that the 1707 Act of
Union, which made Scotland and England politically one country,
was to the advantage of both, and more importantly, she depicts
herself as forming part of a wave of able Scots who in her day
established themselves in the political life of the united British
Isles.

In her admirable work *Britons: Forging the Nation 1707-1837*,
Linda Colley writes of the rapid recovery of Scotland after the dev-
astation of 1745, and the fact that 'its economy expanded after the
1750s at a faster rate than ever before, in some respects at a faster
rate than the English economy'.[10] No doubt this was the case, but
the truth, as Colley admits, was that conditions in Scotland relative
to those in England remained for many years such that the ambitious and intelligent continued to believe that their opportunities in
Scotland were poor, and to make their way to England. During
Lady Anne's childhood, for example, the comparative poverty of
the Lindsay family confined them to Balcarres, which she realised
was a beautiful place, but felt as restricting: 'the sea girt in the
landscape all around in a semicircular form, and as it was there but
fourteen miles in breadth, the opposite shore on a clear day
seemed to invite those who were tired of t'other side to pay it a
visit – an invitation which I have often wished to accept'.[11]

Later, writing of the eighteenth-century severity with which her
mother governed the family, Lady Anne says, 'though our prison
was a cheerful one, yet still it was a prison'.[12] At this stage of her
life she longs to go to Edinburgh, which represents for her and her
beloved sister Margaret an escape from the petty squabbles of their
home. There is clearly much family anxiety concerning the girls'
marital prospects, since their dowries must be tiny and the families
into which they will be expected to marry are likely to be as needy
as the Lindsays. When Lady Anne receives her first proposal, significantly, from an elderly merchant who 'has frequently been
deranged in his intellects',[13] Lady Balcarres tells her 'you are not
very young... you are past sixteen... you are not what can be called
Handsome... you have got a blemish too [a small scar from
measles]... six hundred pounds is all you have to trust to'. Lady

Anne nevertheless refuses him.

Lord Balcarres, to whom his daughters are always 'my fair princesses', dies when Anne is seventeen and enjoying her first visit to Edinburgh as a young adult. The funeral, she says, was additionally affecting from 'the great number of young children' of whom the youngest was 'still in the arms of his nurse'.[14] After the death of her father Lady Anne records a series of incidents centring on the need for her and her sister Margaret to provide for themselves by marrying: their suitors include an attractive but impoverished younger son, a 'double-dealing' Count from the Low Countries, a young peer who cannot make up his mind which of the Lindsay sisters he prefers, and a sinister middle aged man whom she calls Sowerby, who has only one arm, and is lacking two fingers from that. Sowerby is a nabob, reputed to be very rich, but determined not to surrender control of a penny of his wealth, even to marry an earl's daughter. This part of the memoir is pervaded by a terrifying atmosphere of subterfuge and bullying, in which young women in their teens, unable to understand their mother's motives, their suitors or themselves, are under pressure to take responsibility for choices which will determine their lives. Lady Balcarres, whom the elderly Lady Anne who is revising the memoir understands was under great economic pressure, reproaches her daughters with their 'immoderate love of dissipation, which she said made us justly regarded as girls who were not likely to make good wives'.[15] If they do not marry soon, she warns them, they must realise that 'goods which stick so long on the market plainly proved themselves to be unsaleable'.[16] The girls are sixteen and eighteen at the time.

Colley writes of Edinburgh New Town, with its beautiful squares and broad streets, designed by James Craig in 1767 as 'a celebration of *British* patriotism, and an assertion of Scotland's and the city's importance in the Union'.[17] The portrait of Edinburgh in the late 1760s which Lady Anne offers is very different: it renders her sense that the city has ceased to be a capital; the promising young men have gone south to London and she and Lady Margaret are required to find husbands who will satisfy their family in a small provincial society: 'the fortunes of private families are small, rarely exceeding from £ 500 to £ 1000 pr annum, carriages are little used, except on particular occasions, Sedan chairs entirely supplying their place; ...of a morning neither the one nor the other are used... the young Woman of Fashion hops it along the street in a Morning in her Pattens without a Servant...'[18] But Colley's description of the reviving Scotland of Lady Anne's maturity does not contradict Lady Anne's descriptions; rather, it explains the influences which shaped Lady Anne's decisions and the movement of which she was part. 'Scots had been going south in search of greater opportunities for centuries, but not in such numbers, and rarely with the advantage – as now – of having fellow countrymen sufficiently highly placed to act as influential patrons'.[19] From this new and favourable situation, Lady Anne and her siblings were to benefit greatly.

Eventually Lady Margaret agrees to marry the rich financier Fordyce, on the grounds that she does not hate him, and moves to London. After her departure, Lady Anne's family, especially her maternal uncles, try to force her to agree to marry Sowerby, who, it is clear, will be a domestic tyrant. Lady Balcarres is angry because she cannot force Sowerby into appropriate settlements on his prospective wife; Sowerby himself threatens Lady Anne that he will revenge himself on her after their marriage for her family's treatment of him. Finally Lady Margaret writes begging her to come to London: 'come to my sisterly bosom and repose all thy griefs with me'.[20]

At this point (about 1773, though exact dates are not given) the first volume ends, and the second opens with Lady Anne and her sister in London. The point has been made however, through Lady Balcarres's sense of her daughters as burdensome and her inability to find suitable husbands for them in Scotland, and through the girls' own inability to make their way into a lifestyle acceptable to them, that the move to England was justified. Though the memoir is probably the fullest account in its period of a single woman's successful passage from one social group to another, there are events and processes which it omits, probably because the concept of a woman's performing them independently would have been unacceptable to Lady Anne's envisaged readers. We hear nothing of how what was presumably a visit to a sister was eventually extended to permanent residence, and not very much of how Lady Anne's small income (the interest on a capital sum of £ 600) is extended to cover her needs. We are told of her delight in London life: though Mr Fordyce, Lady Margaret's husband, is a coarse, eccentric bore, he cannot spoil the two young women's pleasure: 'the black broth of Sparta (for I dare not say the sheeps heads of Scotland) seclusion and correction... to which we had been accustomed in our youth made ensuing existence so full of Luxury to us that every little pleasure was joy'.[21]

At the beginning of volume 2, she asserts at once her loyalty to the British royal family and her right to acceptance into aristocratic circles with an account of her presentation to Queen Charlotte 'who was at that time reckoned to be the plainest and best beloved young Queen in Europe... of winning manners and whose only fault was that she set her faithful subjects a sneezing when they saluted her, by the quantity of snuff she took'.[22] This combination of loyalty and the humour which proceeds from unbiased perception becomes typical of Lady Anne's attitude to the royal family: much later, she comments on the Prince of Wales 'I suspected he would rather be the hero of a novel than the greatest general in the field or Prince in Europe'.[23]

Lady Anne and Lady Margaret, known as the Lindsay sisters, enjoy the position of political hostesses in London for twenty years. Though she has now left Scotland as a permanent place of residence behind her, Lady Anne is clear that she has joined a group, not exclusively Scots, but in which Scots are important: ''Twas the taste of the times to Hate us... to Envy us, but not to despise us... When we looked around there is no doubt that most of the Great offices of state were then filled by the Scotch'.[24] There is, she realises, a role acceptable to a Scots woman of her class available to her in London. But despite her pleasure in social success, she knows that a woman must marry in order to secure her position, and that her poverty will make a suitable marriage difficult: 'tho' I pleased, I had nothing for my Lovers to pay their debts with, or to appropriate to younger children'.[25]

There are indications that Lady Anne is growing richer, if only in the social opportunities which she receives, though as I have commented, we hear little that is explicit about her finances. Her financier friend Williamson invests her money for her,[26] and she has pleasure in decorating and furnishing a house.[27] In her surviving Cape diaries she writes of deriving income from letting houses in London, and we may guess that she began by taking over leases on houses and subletting them when she had refurbished them. At any rate, she is able to lend money to an admirer who is in financial difficulties, and who seems to be on the verge of proposing to her. He does not do so; she is not rich enough.

The memoir records Lady Anne's growing friendship with the Prince of Wales, as well her critical but affectionate relationship with Mrs Fitzherbert, whom she depicts as beautiful, but very silly. 'It was in our Box at the Opera the Prince of Wales first beheld her', Lady Anne comments, and adds, 'I feard the Situation would require a mind of more firmness and I may add Genius to get through it Honorably and upon High Grounds'.[28] Henry Dundas, who had taken his seat as a Member of Parliament at Westminster in 1775[29] and whose wife had left him in 1778, becomes an habitué of Lady Anne's house. She records her ambivalent feelings about him:

> 'tho he was not in mixed company a brilliant man, nor a comfortable one in a tete à tete for other reasons, in a trio he was excellent, he had none of the trick of his trade about him... what he could tell, he told freely to those he thought well of, and his conversation was not only great in its subjects and interesting in its nature, but luminous by the brightness and force of this thoughts...
>
> [Margaret] and I often regretted when he left us that all was sullied and spoiled to us in his company by the coarseness and want of delicacy in his manners...[30]

It is in this period too that Lady Anne meets William Windham, a rising politician known to his friends as 'Weathercock Windham' because of his fluctuating feelings. She is obviously attracted to him, and describes him as 'Apollo Belvedere bent by illness'.[31] He too is drawn to her, but at the same time determined not to commit himself to a marriage; her impression is that he wishes to punish her for the attraction he feels towards her. It is interesting to see that Lady Anne can recognise, though perhaps only in retrospect, an innate perversity in Windham, but cannot see that it is her enterprise and independence of spirit that frightens him. She goes so far to as to buy a house in Grosvenor Square, because it has a slant view of Windham's door.

In the midst of this period of fascination with Windham, Dundas begins to pay her marked attention, and her sister Margaret advises her to put Windham out of her thoughts 'and be candid about [Dundas], who is more estimable, tho' less engaging'.[32] To marry Dundas, the close friend and political associate of Pitt, would be to marry into the kind of public life which Lady Anne has always desired. Yet she finds Dundas personally unattractive, largely because she associates him with the unhappy days when she was a bullied and desperate young woman in Balcarres and Edinburgh. She is invited to a terrifying dinner at his house to meet his daughters, where she finds herself surrounded by 'hostile eyes'. 'After a heavy evening I went home, my spirits fatigued by the day and my ears grated with the Scotch dialect in all its purity, to which I had not been lately accustomed'.[33]

Dundas's conversation is always represented by Lady Anne as exaggeratedly Scottish: elsewhere in her writings she admits that she herself retained her accent all her life, but her sense of Dundas seems to be that he is unalterably part of a lifestyle which she has left. She records his speech when she is about to leave, against his wishes, for France: '"O" said he, after a pause, "how your sister and you gain on a Maun the mair and mair he kens of you, your *Loavliness* is in your favour, but your *Conversation* and your Judgement and your letters and your *Fauncy* mak's ye sic a fund and sae necessary to the Maun that is once fond of you that how am I to do without you now, my daulie?'[34]

Lady Anne does not finally reject Dundas at this point, but she lingers in Paris, where Windham is staying, though her friends advise her to give up hope of him. He cannot refrain from spending long periods with her – 'I was birds-lime (it was not said in compliment) – there was no getting away from me'.[35] What seems more important than this profitless attachment is a letter of advice which she claims to have received in this period from an old friend of Edinburgh days. I have already suggested that the memoir draws heavily on the forms of the novel established by Richardson and his imitators: it is hard in this case to read the letter as anything other than her own musings on her future, cast into a mode which the epistolary novel had made customary. The advice it contains is that she should not marry 'a Scotchman': 'Women are not prized in that country for their best qualities, they must be humble and not able, and the ornamental part is reckoned as only tending to *mischief*... your Husband and every connection of his will be jealous of you for what they will pre-suppose you think of them and in spite of all your good nature you will be ill used and baited when you grow old as I well remember you were at the beginning of your life...'[36]

On the advice of all her friends, she finally detaches herself from Windham and returns to London, where she finds that Dundas has become engaged to be married to Lady Jane Hope, the wealthy (and according to Lady Anne, very dull) elder sister of the Earl of Hopetoun. At this point, close to the end of vol. 4, it is clear that Lady Anne's life has reached a crisis: she is forty-two years old, and it seems unlikely that she will now make the kind of marriage, to a man in public life, for which she has hoped. Andrew Barnard, a retired soldier on half pay, himself in difficulties, both professional and financial, begs her to marry him. She records his frankness: he is in debt, his father, the Bishop of Killaloe, wishes him to return to active soldiering or to marry a disagreeable widow with £3500 per year. He asks on his knees if there is a chance that Lady Anne will accept him. She replies: 'I will throw aside all my Systems... I will stand the World's smile... and if a very Inferior fortune to what she offers will make you happy, I am yours... Infinitely too old for you... Infinitely *too poor* for you... perhaps not wholly suited to you... perhaps at present *not happy*... but if I can make you happier than you are I will try to do so'.[37]

There is great family rejoicing at this marriage, and much quotation from letters in the memoir, but Lady Anne does not forget to record the turbulent affairs of the Prince of Wales in the period: he falls in love with Lady Jersey, decides to leave Mrs Fitzherbert, but finds that rumours of a secret marriage with the latter, who is a Catholic, have caused fear in the country that he may force on it a Catholic queen. To allay these, he is obliged to marry his cousin Princess Caroline of Brunswick, whom he detests and finds most unattractive. Lady Anne (whom the Prince of Wales calls 'Sister Anne') is his confidante in much of this marital manoeuvring, and the point is again made that she is able to play an important, though a female, role in the affairs of state.

The memoir breaks for the five years which Lady Anne spends at the Cape of Good Hope, which are recorded in *The Cape Journals of Lady Anne Barnard, 1797-1798*, and in *The Cape Diaries of Lady Anne Barnard, 1799-1800*. Vols. V and VI, which record Lady Anne's life after her return from the Cape, focus less strongly on her personal affairs and more on events in London society and the progress of her family, especially after the death of Andrew Barnard, which took place at the Cape in 1807; he had returned there in 1806 as the adviser of the new British governor, Lord Caledon. The Lindsay family is now prospering, and has achieved the position and in the cases of some of its members, the property which marks them as members of the governing group. Lady Anne takes pleasure, as she did in her youth, in being the confidante of politicians and of the Prince of Wales, and she is able to demonstrate that she has been part of this family movement back to power and prominence. She ends her story with the death of her beloved sister Margaret who has remarried happily, and rejoices in the fact that she is able to care for her in her last days: 'the [Anne] of all her life'.[38]

Despite Lady Anne's intention to break off at this point, events are too much for her: she restarts with an account of the Battle of Waterloo and follows this with the sad story of the Princess Charlotte's confinement and the death of her baby son and herself. Lady Anne sees the princess, neglected and disliked all her life by her parents, brought up by worldly and insincere women, as the victim of her family quarrels. 'Not an apple Woman wheeling her barrow in the street but wished She had been near the Princess to have taken more care of her', she writes.[39]

Even in her old age, which she records in the last volume of the memoir, Lady Anne is typically eloquent and lively. She writes: '...when I am alone, I am not above five and twenty', and remains fascinated by what is going on in public life. She visits the Duke of Kent and meets the baby Victoria, who, she comments, 'perfectly resembled Grandpapa'.[40] After the death of George III, she is an amused spectator of the riots in support of the rights of the Queen, George IV's long estranged and understandably unfaithful wife. An old man is forced by the mob to cheer for the Queen: 'Here goes, my boys... huzah for Queen Caroline and may all your wives and daughters be like her'.[41]

She takes great pleasure in George IV's visit to Scotland in 1822, and sees it, as indeed it was, as a reconciliation between Scotland and the royal house of Hanover. But the memoir ends both sadly and symbolically, with the suppression of a small edition of the poems written by Lady Anne, Lady Margaret, and their much younger sister, Lady Hardwick. Lady Hardwick's husband is prominent in public life, and does not wish his wife's writings to appear. Despite the pleas of Sir Walter Scott, who has become Lady Anne's friend, the volume is not allowed to be sold. Lady Anne pays for and takes all fifty copies printed.

The incident epitomises the fate of Lady Anne's literary output: a prolific and, as I hope I have shown, a lively and perceptive writer, she renders in her autobiographical texts a woman's account of the important events which took place during her life, yet that account was not generally available until the end of the twentieth century – and in the case of her memoir, is still unpublished. It seems to me to be an important part of the history of Scottish women writers that she was compelled to suppress her poetry, and was made to feel that her memoir and travel journal must be restricted to an audience of family and close friends. Equally important, of course, is the fact that the respect of her distinguished family for the writings of its ancestors caused her autobiographical work to be preserved in the forms into which she had recast it. When, in 1901, the first of her writings appeared in print, the volume *South Africa a Century Ago: Letters Written from the Cape of Good Hope*,[42] they were the letters written by Lady Anne to Henry Dundas, giving him an account of affairs at the Cape. In his introduction Wilkins calls Lady Anne 'one of the best-known figures in the literary and social world of her day. Her fascinating personality is all too little known'.[43] The facts that she was well-known in her day, and so completely forgotten after it, make an important point: the conventions of her time and long after made sure that her reputation did not survive her, and that her work remained unavailable.

In 1924, more letters, most of them from Lady Anne to the first British governor, Lord Macartney, who returned to London at the end of 1798, were published with much commentary and interpretation by Dorothea Fairbridge under the title *Lady Anne Barnard*

at the Cape of Good Hope.[44] In 1973 the letters from the Cape to
Dundas together with a few others were re-edited by A.M. Lewin
Robinson and published as *The Letters of Lady Anne Barnard to
Henry Dundas.*[45] The editor has shown much greater respect for
the text than did Wilkins, who often combines two letters into one,
or omits passages without indicating what he has done.
Nevertheless the focus of the work is on the information which the
letters supply on a period of Cape history, rather than on their
uniqueness as a woman's detailed and knowledgeable account.
Not until 1995 did the revised Cape journals appear, under the title
of *The Cape Journals of Lady Anne Barnard, 1797-1798.* They
were followed in 1999 by *The Cape Diaries of Lady Anne Barnard,
1799-1800, vols. I and II* and these three volumes have allowed for
an understanding of Lady Anne's literary achievements and the dis-
advantages under which she worked. Since the *Journals* are a
revised work and the *Diaries* completely unrevised, the reader can
see what topics and opinions, now seen as of great interest, Lady
Anne suppressed in the revised work as inappropriate for a
woman who presented her work even to her family. Her letters,
especially those to Henry Dundas, are shown to be very considered productions, in which the purpose of informing him about
Cape affairs is carefully combined with explanation and justification of her husband's official actions. The memoir of Lady Anne's
life in Scotland and England, as I have said, remains unpublished,
and a chapter in the history of Scottish women therefore remains
unavailable to the reading public.

NOTES

[1] See Lady Anne Barnard, *The Cape Diaries of Lady Anne Barnard,
1799-1800*, 2 vols., edited by Margaret Lenta and Basil Le Cordeur,
Cape Town: Van Riebeeck Society, 1999.
[2] See Lady Anne Barnard, *The Cape Journals of Lady Anne Barnard,
1797-1798*, edited by A.M. Lewin Robinson with Margaret Lenta and
Dorothy Driver, Cape Town: Van Riebeeck Society, 1995.
[3] See Lady Anne Barnard, *Memoirs*, 1.1, hereafter cited as *Memoirs*.
Since the six-volume memoir of Lady Anne's life in Scotland and

England remains at the present time unpublished, volume and page numbers refer to the handwritten quarto volumes in the possession of the Earl of Crawford.

[4] *Memoirs*, 1, Preamble.

[5] In this essay the true names of the persons referred to in the memoir have been used to avoid confusion.

[6] *Memoirs*, 1.4.

[7] Margaret Lenta, 'The Shape of a Woman's Life: Lady Anne Barnard's Memoir', *Literator*, vol. 14, no. 3, 1993, pp. 101-115.

[8] *Memoirs*, 1.16.

[9] *Ibidem*, 1.22.

[10] Linda Colley, *Britons: Forging the Nation 1707-1837*, London: Vintage, 1996, p. 128.

[11] *Memoirs*, 1.36.

[12] *Ibidem*, 1.37.

[13] *Ibidem*, 1.53.

[14] *Ibidem*, 1.63.

[15] *Ibidem*, 1.146.

[16] *Ibidem*.

[17] Linda Colley, *op. cit.*, p. 128.

[18] *Memoirs*, 1.196.

[19] Linda Colley, *op. cit.*, pp. 129-130.

[20] *Memoirs*, 1.247.

[21] *Ibidem*, 2.8.

[22] *Ibidem*, 2.5.

[23] *Ibidem*, 3.56.

[24] *Ibidem*, 2.38.

[25] *Ibidem*, 2.206.

[26] *Ibidem*, 2.242.

[27] *Ibidem*, 2.264.

[28] *Ibidem*, 3.103.

[29] Michael Fry, *The Dundas Despotism*, Edinburgh: Edinburgh University Press, 1992, p. 54.

[30] *Memoirs*, 3.92.

[31] *Ibidem*, 3.100.

[32] *Ibidem*, 3.180.

[33] *Ibidem*, 3.181.

[34] *Ibidem*, 4.186.

[35] *Ibidem*, 4.220.

[36] *Ibidem*, 4.223.

[37] *Ibidem*, 4.278.

[38] *Ibidem*, 5.46.

[39] *Ibidem*, 5.75.

[40] ie, George III.

[41] *Memoirs*, 6.8.

[42] See Lady Anne Barnard, *South Africa a Century Ago: Letters Written from the Cape of Good Hope (1797-1801)*, edited by W.H. Wilkins, London: Smith, Elder and Co., 1901.

[43] W.H. Wilkins, 'Introduction' to Lady Anne Barnard, *South Africa a Century Ago*, cit., p. ix.

[44] See Dorothea Fairbridge, *Lady Anne Barnard at the Cape of Good Hope, 1797-1802*, Oxford: Clarendon Press, 1924.

[45] Lady Anne Barnard, *The Letters of Lady Anne Barnard to Henry Dundas*, edited by A.M. Lewis Robinson, Cape Town: Balkema, 1973.

PAM PERKINS

Women Writers in Early
Nineteenth-Century Edinburgh

Matthew Lewis was, according to at least one account, deeply dismayed when he heard that his acquaintance Susan Ferrier was trying her hand at fiction. 'I wish she would let such idle nonsense
alone,' he exclaimed, 'for however great a respect I may entertain
for her talents (which I do), I tremble lest she should fail in this
bookmaking, and as a rule I have an aversion, a pity, and contempt for all female scribblers. The needle, not the pen, is the
instrument they should handle, and the only one they ever use
dexterously'.[1]

This professed dislike of 'female scribbl[ing]' is familiar to any
reader of eighteenth- or early nineteenth-century British literature,
and it is tempting, when reading accounts of late Enlightenment
and Romantic-era Scotland, to see prejudices against women writers as being particularly entrenched in that society. The early nineteenth-century lawyer and man-of-letters Henry Cockburn thought
it matter for congratulatory comment that '[f]or a small place, where
literature sticks out, Edinburgh has never been much encumbered
by professed literary ladies.'[2] Nearly a century later, Henry Grey
Graham concluded the brief discussion of women writers in his
history of eighteenth-century Scottish literature with the observation that '[w]hen Englishwomen were writing their Scottish sisters
were quietly writing songs' – a state of affairs that he seemed to
find highly commendable.[3] Yet Edinburgh during the age of Scott,
Blackwood's, and *The Edinburgh Review* was not entirely hostile to
women's writing; nor despite the comments of Cockburn, Graham,
and others, were women writers limiting themselves to songs and
seeking desperately to maintain anonymity.[4] On the contrary, a
number of women were able to establish themselves as active and

influential participants in Edinburgh literary society, moving well beyond any decorously or conventionally 'feminine' literary world.

Susan Ferrier (1782-1854) is a case in point. She was neither a prolific writer, nor one inclined to experiment with form or genre, publishing only three novels in thirteen years (*Marriage* [1818], *Inheritance* [1824], and *Destiny* [1831]). Even so, the novels themselves provide evidence of the range of Ferrier's literary and cultural interests. When beginning work on *Marriage*, the most popular and successful of the three, Ferrier deprecatingly described her subject as 'the sudden transition of a high-bred English beauty, who thinks she can sacrifice all for love, to an uncomfortable solitary Highland dwelling among tall red-haired sisters and grim-faced aunts'.[5] This synopsis merits attention: low-key as it sounds, what Ferrier sketches here is in effect a merger of two then-popular genres, the domestic novel and the national tale. This was not necessarily an original move; her contemporary Mary Brunton had in already attempted something similar in her 1814 *Discipline*, although Brunton's fictional world lacks the comedy of Ferrier's. Yet Ferrier's novel encompasses far more than the clash between the values of a vain, spoilt Englishwoman and those of the contentedly ignorant, if well-meaning, Highlanders among whom she tries to live. *Marriage* satirizes a number of contemporary fads and fancies; its targets include everything from bluestockingism to the taste for vaguely oriental interior decoration. Ferrier might, in other words, have been writing domestic fiction, but her novels, particularly *Marriage*, with its wide-ranging satiric targets, explore a world beyond that of the quiet, private lives of marriageable young women.

Nor did Ferrier, despite her clear and strong desire for privacy, limit herself and her writing to a strictly domestic world. On the contrary, she began her career as a novelist by collaborating, for her own amusement, on writing fiction with her friend Charlotte Clavering. That sort of private literary exchange is not remarkable in itself, but Clavering's relatives, both by blood and marriage, included other women writers, at least one of whom, Lady Charlotte Bury, was shown parts of *Marriage* while the novel was in progress and while Bury was launching her own career as a novelist.[6] Granted, Bury is a very minor writer, but in her, Ferrier had not only another author as a reader but also an acquaintance who knew everybody in Edinburgh literary circles. Whether or not such social contacts helped stimulate her interest in writing and publishing, it is worth noting that Ferrier knew not just minor writers such as Bury but the major literary figures of the day, including Scott and William Blackwood, her eventual publisher. At the very least, she thus began her career with far more ready access to mainstream literary culture than did some more famous women novelists, such as Jane Austen or, a generation later, Charlotte Brontë. Women writers in the abstract might not have been particularly admired in late Enlightenment Edinburgh, but Ferrier's case indicates that the small, relatively interconnected social world of Scottish writers at that period might have provided quiet opportunity as well as more overt discouragement.

Granted, it is difficult to make any strong case for the importance of women to the Edinburgh literary scene on the strength of Ferrier's work alone. Although she was suspected of literary interests, as the Lewis anecdote makes clear, she refused to acknowledge authorship until relatively late in her career. '[A]nswer impertinent interrogatories by saying that as I don't acknowledge it, nobody else has a right to say it's mine, that is surely no untruth,' she wrote sharply to her sister following the publication of *Inheritance*, adding 'I could not bear the fuss of authorism'.[7] While the necessity of answering such 'interrogatories' in the first place might undercut some of Ferrier's claims about how well the secret of her authorship had been kept, it seems clear enough that she had no desire for wide public recognition. Yet there were other women authors in Edinburgh around that time who chose to publish under their own names and who built themselves solid literary reputations and careers. In particular, Anne Grant (1755-1838) and Elizabeth Hamilton (1756-1816), although neither is as well known today as Ferrier, were then nationally recognized writers who established a firm place for themselves in literary Edinburgh – so much so that despite his general dislike of literary women, Cockburn singled them out as noteworthy exceptions to the usual failings of bluestockings.

That exemption might seem particularly surprising in Hamilton's case, as her literary interests were even more varied than Ferrier's, and while she also published three novels (*Translations of the Letters of a Hindoo Rajah* [1796], *Memoirs of Modern Philosophers* [1800], and *The Cottagers of Glenburnie* [1808]), the titles alone indicate the very considerable distance of her work from the stereotypically feminine world of domestic fiction. The first two books – a reinvention of Montesquieu's *Lettres Persanes* for 1790s Britain and a comic attack on Godwinian radicalism that, notwithstanding its general conservatism, incorporates some praise of Mary Wollstonecraft – fit more comfortably with the political fiction popular in England at the end of the eighteenth century than with any particularly Scottish tradition, and that is the context in which they are usually discussed.[8] (Hamilton, born to a Scottish father in Ireland and raised from early childhood in Scotland, was in fact living in England and mingling with some members of the Godwin circle during her first years as a published writer.) Yet much of her other writing belongs in a distinctively Scottish intellectual tradition. Her work on educational theory, a subject that preoccupied her throughout her career, owes as much to Archibald Alison, Lord Kames, and Dugald Stewart as to John Locke; an attempt at writing classical history in her 1804 *Memoirs of Agrippina, Wife of Germanicus,* is imbued with the educational and historiographic theories of the Scottish Enlightenment.[9] *Cottagers of Glenburnie,* with its critical view of what the novel presents as backward and unhygenic Highland culture also fits in comfortably with a widespread early nineteenth-century fascination – in both Scotland and England – with what was seen as a remote and dying culture. Although Hamilton was no Highlander (she was raised near Stirling) she was sufficiently influential in her presentation of that world to win a polite public tribute from Sir Walter Scott at the end of *Waverley,* and to earn Ferrier's more private commendation. 'Have you been introduced to the McLarty family yet?' Ferrier asked Charlotte Clavering in an 1808 letter, alluding to Hamilton's central characters. 'I think they are the most exquisite family group imaginable'.[10] It is not surprising that the chaotic disorder of the Maclarty (to use Hamilton's spelling) family life would appeal to Ferrier's sense of humour; the lazy, slovenly Highland family whose refrain, 'I canna be fashed,' became something of a catchphrase among the book's many admirers, anticipates Ferrier's own uncouth but comically self-satisfied Highlanders.

Hamilton's novel invites a different kind of reading than Ferrier's, however, in part simply because Hamilton chose to publish under her own name, building upon what was, by 1808, her established popularity as a writer on moral and educational subjects. The novel was reviewed favourably by Francis Jeffrey, perhaps the most feared critic of his day, and one who was not noted for exercising the sort of condescendingly chivalric forbearance towards women authors that at least some critics of the time claimed to employ. (His harshness about Joanna Baillie, considered by some of her contemporaries to be the greatest dramatist since Shakespeare, caused particular offence.) Nor would this notice by the very self-consciously intellectual *Edinburgh Review* of what is, in many ways, a variation on the conventional domestic novel have surprised contemporaries. If anything, it was rather belated, as Hamilton was a sufficiently well-established figure for Jeffrey to have been considering a review of her work as early as 1804.[11]

Even if her greatest success came through her work in the conventionally feminine genre of the novel, Hamilton thus clearly saw herself, and was seen by her contemporaries, as working in the wider intellectual milieu of the Edinburgh Enlightenment. Her correspondence makes this point clear, even without additional evidence from the reviews. When preparing, for example, her *Series of Popular Essays* (2 vols., 1813), which is by far the most ambitiously philosophic of her works, she sought the advice and criticism of readers such as Archibald Alison, author of a popular and influential study of concepts of taste, and Macvey Napier, Jeffrey's successor as editor of *The Edinburgh Review*. When Napier sent what was apparently a thorough, critical, but very sympathetic response to the first essay, Hamilton proclaimed in her effusively grateful reply that, thanks to his help and encouragement, 'my flagging courage is revived, and my spirits raised to such a pitch, that even should Jeffrey open all his batteries against me, I shall stand the charge without dismay.'[12] Both the reliance upon Napier's judgment and the playful defiance of Jeffrey's give a clear indication of Hamilton's idea of her own audience: she was writing for educated, professional men, as well as for intellectually serious women, and, as such, she was implicitly claiming a place for herself in the

mainstream of the Edinburgh literary Enlightenment rather than
decorously remaining on the fringes.

Given that literary history has tended to see the main achievement of early nineteenth-century Scottish literature to be its fiction
– Scott's, pre-eminently, but also, to varying degrees, Hogg's,
Ferrier's, and Galt's – it might seem somewhat perverse to make
claims for Hamilton's significance by placing her work in the context of that of such contemporaries as Alison, Jeffrey, and Stewart,
rather than reading her against Scott, as indeed Scott himself invites
us to do by his note at the end of *Waverley*. The point is that
Hamilton was able to make a place for herself not just as a novelist
but also as a participant in what her contemporaries saw as one of
the most important intellectual movements of the day. Even if the
more conventional *Cottagers of Glenburnie* was and has remained
Hamilton's most successful work, the other writing is no less vital
to an understanding of both Hamilton herself and the role of
women in the Edinburgh Enlightenment. The rather simplistic –
and, for that matter, decidedly punitive – morality underlying
Cottagers might seem naïve at best to twenty-first century readers,
but Hamilton's non-fiction makes clear that the novel does not represent anything approaching her most sophisticated work on education and morality. Instead, it is an attempt to make at least some
of her ideas on those subjects accessible to a wide, popular audience. As such, when read against the essays, it indicates not
Hamilton's conventionality as a thinker but rather her willingness
to experiment with style and genre in order to make her theories
as widely appealing as possible.

Admittedly, Hamilton's interest in philosophical theories of the
mind is unusual among women writers of her day, but even so,
she was not the only woman to lay claim to serious attention from
the thinkers of the Edinburgh Enlightenment. Anne Grant, an exact
contemporary of Hamilton's, who, like Hamilton, settled in
Edinburgh as an adult after having already had some success as a
writer, did so as well, although in a very different manner. Grant,
born in Glasgow and raised in America, had lived in the Highlands
from the age of seventeen until she was widowed in 1801, and it
was this lived knowledge of Highland culture that became the
basis of her literary career. Her first book was a modestly success-

ful collection of poetry (1803) published by subscription and under her own name, in which Grant compiled and, with the help of George Thomson (famous at the time for his work with Burns), revised and edited poems that she had written and sent to friends during her thirty years in Fort Augustus and Laggan. Many of the poems are more or less light-hearted occasional verses – an invitation to an oyster supper, reflections on a wall blocking access to a beautiful walk, tributes to friends – but the book's centrepiece, *The Highlanders*, is neither playful nor frivolous. In five books of heroic couplets, Grant undertakes to describe Highland scenery, traditional Highland culture, the second Jacobite uprising and the escape of C.E. Stuart, and the political impact, on both the Highlands and Britain in general, of the disintegration of Highland social structure in the face of the Clearances and emigration. It is by any standards an ambitious piece of work, even if reviewers at the time were not certain that it was fully successful. (The *Anti-Jacobin Review*, which gave the volume one of the longest and most enthusiastic notices, thought that *The Highlanders* deserved 'warm approbation,' but nonetheless pointed out what it considered slips in grammar, rhyme, and metre.[13])

The themes and arguments that Grant sketched out in that poem preoccupied her for much of the rest of her literary career, and in two later works, *Letters from the Mountain* (1806) and *Essays on the Superstitions of the Highlanders* (1811), she returned to the concerns of her poem, reworking them in autobiography and in what might almost be called ethnographic essays. In doing so, she earned herself both literary success and public recognition as something of an expert on what was, thanks to figures as different as Samuel Johnson, James Macpherson, and Walter Scott, a region and culture that readers across Britain were finding increasingly fascinating. Grant never made any claim to the sort of scholarly mastery of her subject that Hamilton pursued; even in her essays, she insists that she is merely relaying lived experience. Such experience, however, gave her work claims to the attention of the Edinburgh intellectuals who were then busily theorizing the relationships between 'primitive' and 'modern' cultures. Indeed, Grant's shrewd representation of herself as being simultaneously an insider and an outsider in both Highland and Lowland society enabled her to claim a unique vantage point on both, one that enabled her to translate, so to speak, Highland culture for a Lowland and English readership in a way that (she insisted) no Highlander would and no non-Highlander could. As such, she was working somewhere between the relatively conventional feminine decorum represented by Ferrier, who chose to publish only novels and to maintain as much privacy and anonymity as was possible in a small, gossipy literary world, and Hamilton, who directly challenged comparison with the pre-eminent figures of literary and scholarly Edinburgh. When Francis Jeffrey reviewed Grant, several years after he reviewed Hamilton (and, as Grant indignantly suggested to friends, several years later than he should have, given the success of her books), he seemed to accept this view of her work. Her writing contains 'reflections that may be called original,' he argues, because even though many of those reflections 'have long been familiar to all who live within the precincts of literature or study,' they seem, in Grant's case, to have 'been honestly worked out of her own experience and meditation.'[14] Her work, in other words, runs parallel to that of those dedicated to 'literature or study,' as while it overlaps in content, it is the result not of study but rather of artlessly feminine openness to the world.

The work of these three writers by no means encompasses the full range of literature being published by early nineteenth-century Scotswomen. They and their contemporaries produced a body of writing ranging from the demurely sentimental, much-anthologised songs of Lady Nairne (1766-1845) to the novels, educational theory, and angry political journalism of Christian Johnstone (1781-1857). Yet both the connections among and differences in the work of Ferrier, Grant, and Hamilton, all of whom were living in Edinburgh at the same time, meeting each other socially and reading each other's work,[15] indicate something of the range and complexity of Scottish women's writing of this period. Far from being isolated by public scorn of 'bluestockings' or confined to traditionally feminine modes or genres, early nineteenth-century Scottish women had just as much opportunity to write 'dramas and histories and treatises' – not to mention metaphysics, educational theory and cultural politics – as did their English counterparts, and any literary history of late Enlightenment and Romantic Edinburgh would be incomplete without some recognition of their presence and achievements.

NOTES

1 Quoted in J.A. Doyle ed., *Memoir and Correspondence of Susan Ferrier 1782-1854*, London: Eveleigh Nash & Gray Son, 1929, p. 136. The original source of this anecdote is Lady Charlotte Bury's *Diary of a Lady in Waiting*, which, as Bury was a friend of Lewis, might provide a hint of how Lewis heard this rumour.

2 Henry Cockburn, *Memorials of his Time. 1856*, Edinburgh: T.N. Foulis, 1909, p. 268.

3 Henry Grey Graham, *Scottish Men of Letters in the Eighteenth Century*, London: A. & C. Black, 1908, p. 354.

4 The song writers were, of course, important in their own right, although there is no room to discuss them in this essay. For an analysis of their work, see Kirsteen McCue, 'Women and Song, 1750-1850', in Douglas Gifford and Dorothy McMillan eds., *History of Scottish Women's Writing*, Edinburgh: Edinburgh University Press, 1997, pp. 58-70.

5 *Memoir and Correspondence of Susan Ferrier*, cit., p. 76.

6 Lady Charlotte Bury was Clavering's maternal aunt. Clavering's mother-in-law, Eliza Fletcher, was a literary hostess who published a collection of blank verse drama (*Edward and Elidure*, 1825), and one of Fletcher's daughters eventually also wrote a novel (*Concealment*, 1837). Another, more tenuous connection with literary women was Clavering's long-time friendship with Joan Glassell, an aunt by marriage who had been raised by Anne Grant.

7 *Memoir and Correspondence of Susan Ferrier*, cit., p. 178.

8 What critical discussion there is of Hamilton has tended to focus on this aspect of her work. See, in particular, Gary Kelly's *Women, Writing, and Revolution 1790-1827*, Oxford: Clarendon, 1993. Balachandra Rajan has analysed Hamilton's first novel in the context of Romantic Orientalism in *Under Western Eyes: India from Milton to Macaulay*, Durham: Duke University Press, 1999.

9 See Mark Salber Phillips, *Society and Sentiment: Genres of Historical Writing in Britain, 1740-1820*, New Haven: Princeton University Press,

2000, pp. 115-122, on this aspect of Hamilton's work.

[10] *Memoir and Correspondence of Susan Ferrier*, cit., p. 55.

[11] In an 1804 letter to Francis Horner, Jeffrey writes 'Betty's book has not reached me yet. I mean to be merciful, if I touch her at all. To say the truth, I am sick of abusing.' The letter is quoted in Henry Cockburn's *Life of Lord Jeffrey*, 2 vols., Edinburgh: A. & C. Black, 1852, I, p. 163; Cockburn identifies 'Betty' as 'Miss Hamilton'. The work in question would probably have been *Agrippina*.

[12] British Library, Add. Mss. 34611, f. 21.

[13] Review of Mrs. Grant's *Poems, Anti-Jacobin Review*, no. 16, 1803, p. 107.

[14] Francis Jeffrey, review of *Essays on the Superstitions of the Highlanders, The Edinburgh Review*, vol. 18, August 1811, p. 481.

[15] With one obvious exception: Hamilton died before Ferrier published anything. But Grant and Ferrier, like Grant and Hamilton, certainly read each other, and Ferrier admired Hamilton.

Tom Hubbard

George Gordon Byron, Scotland and Europe: An Antithetical Mind

I declare a personal interest. During my university career I have studied and taught in several countries, and on two occasions my temporary homes have been a few minutes' walk from the child-hood haunts of major Romantic artists. I was a student at Aberdeen, where Byron grew up between 1792 and 1798; I was a temporary lecturer at Grenoble, staying at the semi-rural suburb of Meylan where Berlioz often visited N. Marmion, his maternal grandfather. At those locations Byron and Berlioz first experienced sexual love – the earliest stages of pilgrimages leading, in both cases, to contradictory forces of anguished idealism and acerbic cynicism. Berlioz eloquently demonstrated his share in the pan-European enthusiasm for Walter Scott and George Byron, and underscored (subconsciously?) the affinity between these two writers when he used the same theme in his *Rob Roy* overture and his *Harold en Italie* symphony. In his *Mémoirs* (1870) he described the latter as an attempt to evoke the pilgrimages and memories of 'une sorte de rêveur mélancolique dans le genre du Childe-Harold de Byron'.[1]

Such a sensibility makes it impossible, in my view, to regard Byron mainly within the canon and context of the *English* Romantics, with whom he was scarcely in solidarity: granted, there was personal friendship with Shelley, but he was hostile to what he considered Keats's 'mental masturbation';[2] moreover, he regard-ed Wordsworth's politics as unforgivably apostate and his poetry as risibly bathetic. The Scottish writer P.H. Scott has neatly described Byron as 'England's Scottish poet',[3] but perhaps 'Europe's Scottish poet' would be more to the point, while taking into account Burns and Scott as only two of several strong competitors for the title.

However, I'm not particularly interested in playing that game and would rather advance the proposition that Byron was a north European writer who dramatically impacted on the literature – and much else – of the whole continent. In the decades after 1815, with the fall of Napoleon and the subsequent hegemony of vindictively reactionary régimes, Byron appealed to cultures which had come late to Romanticism and which experienced both a yearning for personal and political 'liberty' and a near-despair that such was barely achievable in the present (or indeed any) climate. Byron maintained the charismatic role of 'committed' writer-activist – together with, in almost existential equipoise, the persona of witty hedonist. The hilarious British TV comedy series, *Blackadder*, has a spoof Lord Byron who is scorned as a *poseur* always 'swanning off to Italy, just to get laid'. More seriously, Professor Andrew Rutherford offers this defence: 'Yet even while devoting himself to debauchery and poetry, he was acutely conscious of Austria's domination of northern Italy; and as time went on he stressed the degradation more than the delightfulness of modern Venice, the shamefulness of Italy's political subjection'.[4] This led to his final appearance, as his own Byronic hero, on the other side of the Adriatic and death at Missolonghi in 1824, aged 36.

'Oh those scoundrel sovereigns!' exclaimed Byron in his journal entry for February 19, 1821. 'Let us but see them beaten – let the Neapolitans but have the pluck of the Dutch of old, or the Spaniards of now, or of the German protestants, the Scotch presbyterians, the Swiss under Tell, or the Greeks under Themistocles – *all* small and solitary nations (except the Spaniards and German Lutherans), and there is yet a resurrection for Italy, and a hope for the world'.[5] Readers of *English Bards and Scotch Reviewers* (1808) and *The Curse of Minerva* (1812) might have been surprised at such an ardent tribute to the particular 'small and solitary nation' of the Scotch presbyterians. In the latter of these two satires Byron had denounced Scotland as 'a land of meanness, sophistry and mist'.[6] A more familiar retraction of his anti-Scottishness appears in *Don Juan* (1823-1824), where he warmly acknowledges that he is 'half a Scot by birth, and bred/A whole one, and my heart flies to my head'.[7] His early grounding in Aberdeen Calvinism is widely regarded as an essential ingredient in the doom-laden protagonists of his narrative and dramatic poems such as *Lara* (1814), *Childe Harold's Pilgrimage* (1812-1818), *Manfred* (1817) and *Cain* (1821); 'predestination' is a pervasive *leitmotiv* in Byron, massively countered by the rebellious, will-to-power determination of his heroes. *Cain* is perhaps the boldest instance: Byron takes a primal tale from the Old Testament of his Scottish upbringing and transforms it into an almost proto-Nietzschean tract, where an *Übermensch* – albeit a deeply troubled one – challenges the slave morality of his pious brother, with tragic consequences.

Byron's Calvinist legacy was a matter of sensibility rather than of dogma. His generous-mindedness was revolted at the notion of eternal Hell-fire and brimstone: 'A *material* resurrection seems strange and even absurd except for purposes of punishment – and all punishment which is to *revenge* rather than *correct* – must be *morally wrong* – and *when* the *World is at an end* – what moral or warning purpose *can* eternal tortures answer?'[8] That could serve as a gloss on *Cain*, as well as on his lesser-known drama of the Flood, *Heaven and Earth* (1823). Angus Calder, a leading Byron scholar, has argued for a reading of the poet in terms of 'secularised Calvinism'. He cites the representation of Bonnivard, in *The Prisoner of Chillon* (1816), not as Christian Calvinist martyr as such; Byron, claims Calder, rather 'abstracts the Calvinist conception of the soul as utterly alone – the Prisoner is a type of Everyman. He confronts his own loneliness in relation to the material universe which, in Byron's cosmology, has replaced God as the aloof presence dominating human fate. [...] Time, matter, mock human enterprise'.[9]

Childe Harold holds not dissimilar views when he visits Bonnivard's locus – Lake Leman/Geneva and its Alpine setting – but for him the scene means transcendence rather than self-abnegation:

> I live not in myself, but I become
> Portion of that around me; and to me
> High mountains are a feeling, but the hum
> Of human cities torture [...][10]

For Harold (and Byron), the Genevan Rousseau, with his solitary wanderings and detestation of 'civilisation', suggests something more affirmative than a Genevan-Aberdonian Calvin. However we can still deploy Angus Calder's helpful 'secularised Calvinism', for it relates very much to a Scottish elementalism. During the Aberdeen years, Byron vacationed near the Grampian mountain of Lochin y Gair (Lochnagar), the subject of one of his earliest lyrics. Here he delights in a terrible beauty, 'Though cataracts foam 'stead of smooth-flowing fountains', infinitely preferable to the 'tame and domestic' landscape of England.[11] The violent clash of rock and water appeals to a Scottish sensibility attracted to stark extremes, nourished as it has been on Calvinist oppositions of the saved and the damned, as against the bland moderation prevailing south of the border.

To such forbidding notions we shall return, but it is well to emphasise the more immediately benign aspects of Byron's Scottish inheritance. He frequently recorded his delight in the works of Scott, whom he called 'the Ariosto of the North', and from Ravenna in 1820 he praised the 'rough, but *racy* – and welcome' tales of James Hogg, the 'Ettrick Shepherd'.[12] It was fashionable, across Europe, to invoke Scott, Macpherson/Ossian, Burns *et al.*, and indeed like so many of his continental peers Byron produced the almost obligatory imitations of Ossianic lore. However, owing to his early initiation in the folksong and balladry of north-east Scotland, Byron was privileged to be able to draw from sources deeper and more authentic than those generally available to his non-Scottish contemporaries. From north-east song grew his early lyrics, and to north-east song they have returned. The Harrow-educated aristocrat has not only derived from, but added to, a rich popular tradition; in Aberdeenshire Byron is not only studied, but *sung*. He shares with the Ayrshireman Burns, and with the Borderers Scott and Hogg, the ability to weave the ballad- and story-telling strands into the wider fabric of European culture; Byron's verse tales at once draw on the example of Scott and encourage poets across the continent to reunite poetry to narrative. The perennially close relationship, in Scotland, between 'folk' materials and 'high art', has set a powerful example to the rest of Europe, and Byron is a key player in the process.

The composer Ronald Stevenson (b. 1928) was, like Byron, born in England but found nurture in his ancestral Scotland; in the

1950s, he studied at the Accademia di Santa Cecilia in Rome and is a world authority on the music and thought of Ferruccio Busoni. He is well placed, as a musician steeped in Scottish music and poetry, to address himself to Byron's prosody. In a virtuoso essay, 'Byron as Lyricist: the Poet and the Musicians', Stevenson both recounts Byron's impact on European composers and analyses forensically the poet's use of the 'ee' sound so pervasive in Aberdeenshire pronunciation of Scots and English (e.g. 'name' and 'fame' pronounced 'neem' and 'feem'):

> What is the emotional significance of that 'ee' sound? Well, it's a very *closed* sound. It's the sound of a sneer. Maybe a sneer that can curl into a smile, but still a sneer. It is the cipher of the Luciferic in Byron. It is *worlds* away from the *open* sound of Blake's poetry, which is full of the 'ah' sounds of wonderment, the sounds of glad day (to borrow the title of one of his designs).[13]

To revert, then, to the darker note: Aberdeen folklore could yield material as menacing as Calvinistic judgment. In *Don Juan* Byron paid nostalgic tribute to 'The Dee, the Don, Balgounie's brig's *black wall*' adding a footnote explaining that the Brig [Bridge] of Balgounie, north of the old city, was the locus of a grim legend told in song: 'Brig of Balgounie, *black's* your *wa'*,/Wi' a wife's *ae son*, and a mear's *ae foal*,/Doun ye shall fa'!' [Bridge of Balgounie, black is your wall,/With a wife's only son, and a mare's only foal,/Down you shall fall!].[14] As his own mother's only son, the boy Byron would have enjoyed a delicious terror at the parapet; a mother's only son myself, I used to cross that bridge daily, at night. I might be excused if I find Byron's Brig more chilling than the more famous Brig o' Doon in Burns's supernatural verse-tale, *Tam O' Shanter.*

As more than hinted earlier, the Scots have a penchant for what Robert Louis Stevenson called 'black happiness', the Jekyll-and-Hyde meeting of extreme opposites. 'What an antithetical mind!' wrote Byron of Burns; '– tenderness, roughness – delicacy, coarseness – sentiment, sensuality – soaring and grovelling – dirt and deity – all mixed up in that compound of inspired clay!'[15] Exactly a week earlier he said as much about himself, if more jocularly : '[...] I can't read it [his journal] over; – and God knows what contradictions it may contain. If I am sincere with myself (but I fear one lies more to one's self than to anyone else), every page should confute, refute, and utterly abjure its predecessor'.[16] In the personality of his Lara, the eponymous hero of a verse-tale, 'inexplicably mix'd appear'd/Much to be loved and hated, sought and fear'd'; that even more intellectual brooder, Manfred, is only too conscious of his own, and mankind's, troubled compound of dirt and deity, 'contending with low wants and lofty will'.[17]

I suggest that Byron's 'antithetical mind' creates a rendezvous for Europe's geocultural polarities. Goethe may have recognised this when, in *Faust*, Part 2 (1832), he presents the Byronic young poet, Euphorion, as the son of Faust and Helen: the union of the Teutonic and the Mediterranean, of north and south. (Goethe and Byron influenced each other; Ronald Stevenson has pointed out that the opening lines of *The Bride of Abydos* echo Goethe's northman's tribute to Italy – 'Kennst du das Land, wo die Zitronen blühn?').[18]

Such sympathetic synthesis may imply a prior antithesis, where the cultures clash. In *Don Juan* Byron mocks British (north European?) prudishness in contrast to the sexual freedom enjoyed 'where the climate's sultry',[19] and Bernard Blackstone has claimed that Canto 4 of *Childe Harold's Pilgrimage*, with its celebration of Italian luminosity, counterpoints the previous canto and its 'Teutonic oppressiveness' of ruined castles overlooking the Rhine.[20] Yet surely there is no shortage of Rhine-wine hedonism in Canto 3, nor of tragic solemnity in Canto 4? Earlier in the same poem, right at the beginning of Harold's grand tour, Byron presents Cintra, the hilltop town north-west of Lisbon, as a 'glorious Eden', whose 'variegated maze of mount and glen' appears to be a desirable alternative to the memory of 'Sin's long labyrinth' which had so oppressed Harold in his father's hall back on 'Albion's isle' (Canto 1, stanzas 18 and 5 respectively). Writing to his mother on August 11, 1809, the young Byron expands rhapsodically on his discovery of Cintra: '[...] perhaps in every respect the most delightful [village] in Europe'; here, at the outset of his career, he offers a radiant reconciliation of the polar opposites: 'It [Cintra and the immediate hinterland] unites in itself all the wildness of the Western Highlands with the verdure of the South of France'.[21]

However, Byron's most sustained example of the north-south

synthesis is *The Island*, a neglected narrative poem, neglected, that is, until Angus Calder devoted an essay to it as part of a collection marking the poet's bicentenary.[22] The story is an imaginative development of events following the Mutiny on the Bounty, played out on a Polynesian island between a Scottish sailor and his native lover:

> Both children of the isles, though distant far;
> Both born beneath a sea-presiding star;
> Both nourish'd amidst nature's native scenes,
> Loved to the last, whatever intervenes
> Between us and our childhood's sympathy,
> Which still reverts to what first caught the eye.
> He who first met the Highlands' swelling blue
> Will love each peak that shows a kindred hue,
> Hail in each crag a friend's familiar face,
> And clasp the mountain in his mind's embrace.
> Long have I roamed through lands which are not mine,
> Adored the Alp, and loved the Apennine,
> Revered Parnassus, and beheld the steep
> Jove's Ida and Olympus crown the deep;
> But 'twas not all long ages' love, nor all
> *Their* nature held me in their thrilling thrall;
> The infant rapture still survived the boy,
> And Loch-na-gar with Ida look'd o'er Troy,
> Mix'd Celtic memories with the Phrygian mount,
> And Highland linns with Castalie's clear fount.[23]

Such an affinity, both likely and unlikely, looks forward to Robert Louis Stevenson's rediscovery of his Scottishness in Samoa: he and his Polynesian hosts would discover points of contact between their cultures as they exchanged their respective folktales of warlocks, devils and damnation.[24] When Byron means 'south', however, he usually means 'Mediterranean' and it may not be idle speculation to regard his broodings on Scottish-Calvinist predestination as possibly reinforced by Latin-Levantine fatalism: the Italian *che sarà, sarà*, the Roman Stoics whom he invokes in his *Detached Thoughts* ('a Soul which drags a Carcase'),[25] or even submission to Allah in the Turkish tales.

It is in *Don Juan*, though, that all four poles of Europe are brought together, where the north-south synthesis is further merged with that of east-west. That is to say, south-west meets north-east Europe in the person of Juan himself, as 'Our gay Russ Spaniard' (Canto 13, stanza 53), who has been in the service of Catherine the Great – in more ways than one. (The line 'Madrid's and Moscow's climes were of a piece' [Canto 10, stanza 30], resonates playfully as we learn of Juan's progress under the Tsaritsa's skirts). We have come far, or perhaps not so far, from May Gray's seduction of the pre-adolescent Byron in Aberdeen.

Kierkegaard once remarked that the three great European archetypes were Faust, Don Juan/Giovanni, and the Wandering Jew. Byron rings the changes on them all. Coleridge contemplated, then abandoned, a Faustian play based on the legend of the Scottish 'wizard'-polymath Michael Scot: Byron, however, rose to the challenge in *Manfred*, which Nietzsche actually preferred to *Faust* – Manfred, after all, refuses to be the slave of those spirits who have served him. It was a simultaneously defiant and resigned Byron who, in terms of almost Fausto-Manfredian amplitude (plus considerable hormonal overdrive), defended his *Don Juan* as the work-in-progress of someone who had seen and done it all:

> – it may be profligate – but is it not *life*, is it not the *thing*? – Could any man have written it – who has not lived in the world? – and tooled in a post-chaise? in a hackney coach? in a Gondola? against a wall? in a court carriage? in a vis a vis? – on a table? – and under it? [...] I had such projects for the Don – but the *Cant* is so much stronger than the *Cunt* – now a days, – that the benefit of experience in a man who had well weighed the worth of both monosyllables – must be lost to despairing posterity.[26]

Still, he persisted. His Don Juan, a relatively unreflective young man of physical action, is notably less existentialist than Mozart's Don Giovanni, whom Kierkegaard regarded as one who failed to make the leap of faith out of the 'aesthetic' stage of existence and towards the ethical and spiritual stages. But Byron's hero, if he lacks the self-consciousness of Mozart's, is all the more *sexy*stentialist.

As for the Wandering Jew, doomed to roam forever, he is for Byron that primal Old Testament figure, Cain, and in his own person Byron is the Wandering Scot or at least half-Scot, taking his black-caped amble (and sometimes stumble) across Europe. For all

his admiration of Hogg, he criticised him for his stay-at-home tendencies, lamenting that so many 'Scotch and Lake troubadours are
spoilt by living in little circles and petty societies'.[27] All Byron's fictional heroes are wanderers, and while he himself had scant desire
to return alive or dead to his native land, he could take on the persona of those who yearned for home: 'An exile, saddest of all pris-
oners/Who has the whole world for a dungeon strong,/Seas,
mountains, and the horizon's verge for bars [...]' (*The Prophecy of
Dante*, Canto 4, ll. 131-133).[28] The archetype modulated into the
Superfluous Man, Byron's legacy to the Russians: Pushkin's lan-
guidly westernised Onegin; Dostoevsky's basement-dwelling
monologuists and idealistic murderers; Goncharov's lazy Oblomov;
Turgenev's love-lorn Slavs at German spas. Dumas's Count of
Monte Cristo identifies with Manfred, Lara, and Werner; he has
made himself a prodigious scholar – of dark arts and sciences –
who, from his Mediterranean bases, plots the vengeance which he
believes God has 'predestined' him to carry out on those who once
wronged him.[29] Monte Cristo echoes Byron's utterance that though
'my mother was Scotch – and my name and my family are both
Norman – [...] as for myself *I am of no Country*'.[30]

Yet he is of many countries. Or at least his works are. *The
Bibliography of Scottish Literature in Translation* (BOSLIT) records
hundreds of translations into most of the languages of Europe;
even the most minor poems appear in, for example, Romanian and
Serbo-Croat.[31] Five years before Missolonghi, he fantasised about a
somewhat more subdued departure: '[...] "*implora pace*". I hope,
whoever may survive me and shall see me put in the foreigners'
burying-Ground at the Lido – within the fortress by the Adriatic –
will see those two words and no more put over me [...]'[32] What
could be further from the predestined tumble, from a dark old
bridge, into the Aberdonian abyss?

NOTES

[1] Hector Berlioz, *Mémoirs*, 2 vols., Paris: Garnier-Flammarion, 1969, I,
p. 298.

[2] References are to Lord Byron, *The Complete Poetical Works*, edited by J.J. McGann, 7 vols., Oxford: Clarendon Press, 1980-1993, here-after cited as J.J. McGann, *op. cit.*, and Byron's *Letters and Journals*, edited by L.A. Marchand, 12 vols., London: John Murray, 1973-1982, hereafter cited as L.A. Marchand, *op. cit.* There are a number of Byron or Byron-related websites, most notably: HYPERLINK http://www.cas.astate.edu/engphil/gallery/Byronq.html.
In order to avoid a clutter of unnecessary endnotes, quotations from the major long poems, easily accessible in many editions, are on occasion cited in the body of the essay by canto and stanza; however, I have given the J.J. McGann citations for quotations from the lesser known poems, as follows. See Byron, letter to John Murray (November 9, 1820), in L.A. Marchand, *op. cit.*, VII, p. 225.

[3] Paul Scott, 'England's Scottish Poet', *The Sunday Mail Story of Scotland*, no. 28, Glasgow: Maxwell Magazine Publishing, 1988, p. 780-781.

[4] Andrew Rutherford, 'Lord Byron: Citizen of the World', *Nea Estia*, (Athens), 1974, pp. 881-882.

[5] L.A. Marchand, *op. cit.*, VIII, p. 48.

[6] J.J. McGann, *op. cit.*, I, p. 325.

[7] J.J. McGann, *op. cit.*, V, p. 442.

[8] L.A. Marchand, *op. cit.*, IX, p. 45.

[9] Angus Calder, 'Byron and Scotland', *Cencrastus*, no. 15, New Year 1984, (pp. 21-24) p. 23.

[10] J.J. McGann, *op. cit.*, II, p. 103.

[11] Byron, 'Lachin Y Gair', in J.J. McGann, *op. cit.*, I, pp. 103-104.

[12] Byron, letter to John Murray (October 12, 1820), in L.A. Marchand, *op. cit.*, VII, p. 200.

[13] Ronald Stevenson, quoted in *Byron, Wrath and Rhyme*, London: Vision Press, 1983, (pp. 78-93) p. 83.

[14] J.J. McGann, *op. cit.*, V, p. 442 and p. 743 note 139.

[15] Byron, journal entry of December 13, 1813, in L.A. Marchand, *op. cit.*, III, p. 239.

[16] *Ibidem*, December 6, 1813, p. 233.

[17] J.J. McGann, *op. cit.*, III, p. 224 (*Lara*); IV, p. 63 (*Manfred*).

[18] Ronald Stevenson, *op. cit.*, p. 85.

[19] J.J. McGann, *op. cit.*, V, p. 29.

[20] Bernard Blackstone, *Byron. 1: Lyric and Romance*, Harlow: Longman, 1970, p. 32.

21 L.A. Marchand, *op. cit.*, I, p. 218.

22 Angus Calder, '"The Island": Scotland, Greece and Romantic Savagery', in *Byron and Scotland: Radical or Dandy?*, Edinburgh: Edinburgh University Press, 1989, pp. 132-150.

23 J.J. McGann, *op. cit.*, VII, p. 44.

24 See my 'North and South in the Writings of Robert Louis Stevenson', *The AnaChronist*, Budapest: Department of English Studies, Eötvös: Loránd University, 1997, pp. 59-70. The paper was originally read at the Universities of Trento and Bergamo in January 1996.

25 L.A. Marchand, *op. cit.*, IX, p. 45.

26 Byron, letter to Douglas Kinnaird (October 26, 1819), in L.A. Marchand, *op. cit.*, VI, p. 232.

27 Byron, letter to Thomas Moore (August 3, 1814), in L.A. Marchand, *op. cit.*, IV, p. 152.

28 J.J. McGann, *op. cit.*, IV, p. 238.

29 See Antonio Candido, *On Literature and Society*, translated, edited and introduced by H.S. Becker, Princeton: Princeton University Press, 1995, p. 7ff.

30 Byron, letter to Count Alfred d'Orsay (April 22, 1823), in L.A. Marchand, *op. cit.*, X, p. 156 [My italics].

31 BOSLIT can be consulted at HYPERLINK http://boslit.nls.uk.

32 Byron, letter to John Murray (June 7, 1819), in L.A. Marchand, *op. cit.*, VI, p. 149.

CRISTINA OSSATO

Thomas Carlyle's Myth of Order in 'An Occasional Discourse on the Nigger Question': Re-clothing 'The Guardian's Life and Duties'[1]

Zwei Seelen wohnen, ach! In meiner Brust
Die eine will sich von der andern trennen;
Die eine hält in derber Liebeslust
Sich an die Welt mit klammernden Organen;
Die andre hebt gewaltsam sich vom Dust
Zu den Gefilden hoher Ahnen.
W.J. Goethe, *Faust*

EDITORIAL DIFFICULTIES: 'PECULIAR VIEWS OF THE RIGHTS OF NEGROES [...] IN THESE EMANCIPATED EPOCHS OF THE HUMAN MIND'[2]

Similar to *Sartor Resartus* in style and content, an 'Occasional Discourse on the Nigger Question' came out in *Frazer's Magazine* in December 1849 and reprinted as a separate pamphlet in 1853. A preface by a fictional Editor introduces an 'Occasional Discourse' by an unknown Speaker, duly reported by the 'Absconded Reporter', Dr. Phelim m'Quirk, a notorious scoundrel, suddenly missing, and offered by his 'respectable, unfortunate landlady, desirous to make-up part of her losses in this way'. This 'Article', which contains 'peculiar views of the Rights of the Negroes [...] in these emancipated epochs of the human mind' is accepted for publication 'at a cheap market-rate', but the Editor firmly underlines his clear intention of withdrawing from 'the strange doctrines and notions shadowed forth in it'.[3]

Likewise in *Sartor Resartus*, the unknown Editor – 'Who or what such Editor may be, must remain conjectural, and even insignificant' – decides to translate and edit Teufelsdröckh's *Die Kleider, Ihr*

Werden und Wirken, a 'Volume on Clothes', with the purpose of 'bring[ing] [...] order [...] out of this Chaos' and spreading Teufesldröckh's philosophy of clothes in the British soil, but with the resolute warning: 'be it nowise apprehended, that any personal connexion of ours with Teufelsdröckh, Heuschrecke, or this Philosophy of Clothes, can pervert our judgment, or sway us to extenuate or exaggerate'.[4]

The emphasis on the seriousness with which initially both Editors want to detach themselves from the ideas and opinions of the Speaker and the Professor, together with the device of blurring the origins of the source of those written materials, is a significant clue to Carlyle's use of jeanpaulian humour and schlegelian romantic irony: any 'eminence' of the Speaker of 'genial capability' of the Professor is laughed and scoffed at (a syneddochic deflating or levelling of all dichotomies) and at the same time appreciated and looked up to (a syneddochic support or fostering of their views).[5] In other words, Carlyle uses this tone of apparent seriousness, moderation and modesty, as Jean Paul would define irony, together with a highly figurative language, because they represent the best weapon to introduce and open up a holistic debate over the impossibility of reaching ultimate (linguistic) truths or interpretations:

> We will not go deep into the question here about the Negro's rights. We will give a single glance into it, and see for one thing, how complex it is.[6]

> So that Teufelsdröckh's public History were not done, then, or reduced to an even, unromantic tenor: nay, perhaps the better part thereof were only beginning?[7]

APRONS: 'EXETER-HALL PHILANTHROPY AND THE DISMAL SCIENCE [...] OF BLACK EMACIPATION'[8]

The fictional lecture delivered to the 'UNIVERSAL ABOLITION-OF-PAIN ASSOCIATION' ('no time or place assigned')[9] starts with the Speaker's address to his 'PHILANTHROPIC FRIENDS'. With a slashing irony and poignant parody, Carlyle turns on one of those metaphorical 'Aprons',[10] the Exeter Hall philanthropists, both because they have given money to Jamaica overlooking the English and Irish poor,[11] and because, at bottom, lower classes and orders cannot be reformed or improved with responsibility.[12] He himself recognizes, in opposition to the signs of the times, that his ideas are 'in dissent with from all the world; in black contradiction, deep as the bases of my life, to all philanthropic, emancipatory, constitutional, and other anarchic revolutionary jargon'.[13] As if to corroborate Carlyle's personal views, the Speaker says:

> Sunk in deep froth-oceans of 'Benevolence', 'Fraternity', 'Emancipation-principle', 'Christian Philanthropy', and other most amiable-looking, but most baseless, and in the end baleful and all bewildering jargon – sad product of a sceptical Eighteenth Century, and of poor human hearts left destitute of any earnest guidance, and disbelieving that there ever was any, Christian or Heathen, and reduced to believe in rose pink Sentimentalism alone, and to cultivate the same under its Christian, Antichristian, Broad-brimmed, Brutus-headed, and other forms – has not the human species gone strange roads, during that period?[14]

Of course, Carlyle also tries to balance the Speaker's invective with the aversion of some people in the audience.[15] Nonetheless, it is clear how the West Indies' shortage of labour and the consequent rotting of sugar plantations is due to neglect and lack of compliance with 'the eternal law of Nature': 'That you should cut the ligature, and say, "He has made us equal", would be saying a palpable falsity, big with hideous ruin for all concerned in it.'[16] 'The idle Black man' in the West Indies 'must be compelled' 'to do what the work the Maker has intended by the making of him for this world!'[17]

Here, the Speaker seems to start from two different premises. First, the black race is inferior to the white race, and as such must be guided in its deeds (defence of the institution of slavery).[18] Second, the Bible allows the white man to lead the black man, a religious explanation to a natural fact.[19] Looking into the Bible, and more specifically, into the episode of Noah and his Sons (Shem, Ham, Japheth) there is a telling reference to Noah's curse of Ham and his offspring because of Ham's careless behaviour towards him. The very fact that Shem and Japheth help Noah get dressed and cover his nakedness while Ham overlooks it, gives them the moral and divine right to be guardians of their irresponsible brother, whose genealogy, geographically speaking, corresponds to the north of Africa, Egypt, Arabia, Ethiopia.

When Carlyle, again, in his essay 'Shooting Niagara: and After?' (1867) says that 'The Almighty Maker has appointed him [the black man] to be a Servant'[20] and when he refers to the Civil War in America and affirms that though 'the Americans are powerful [...] they can not make two men equal when the universe has determined that they are and shall be unequal',[21] it seems that he avails himself of this biblical episode to strengthen his ideas on racial differences.

It is also true, as Douglas Lorimer affirms, that at the time Victorians had an image of the Negro as 'the photographic negative of the Anglo-Saxon'.[22] In other words, it was easier for them to create the myth of British uniqueness through opposition: white vs. black, superiority vs. inferiority. In this sense, Caroline Reitz, talks about Carlyle's strategy of 'othering violence', that is attributing violence elsewhere (in this specific case, the black man) in order to realize the concept of British heroism.[23]

However, although Carlyle's continuous invectives fuel the 'emergent discourses of anthropology and racial science'[24] and indirectly nourish the notion of biological black inferiority held by the new pseudo-science of phrenology and David Hume's 'National Character' (1755),[25] it is difficult to pin down his writings with just one label: racialist. Critics themselves have held different opinions as to Carlyle's standpoint. For example, while Ian Campbell, J.R. Ward, E.W. Said, Iva G. Jones, Jude Nixon, P.T. Park, Simon Heffer, Denis Judd suggest Carlyle's complex racialism,[26] others, like David Daiches, T.C. Richardson, Caroline Reitz, Carol Collins, A.L. Le Quesne do not perceive so much an either/or situation.[27] They are more prone to consider Carlyle's ambiguous attitude towards life, as a sign of his paradoxical racial, racist and/or non-racist statements. Another critic instead, Gillian Workman, thinks that Carlyle's language to describe the Negro is 'more a rhetorical device than an expression of racial disgust: a disastrous artistic miscalculation, rather than a revelation of his uncontrolled racism.'[28]

I think that Carlyle's writings reveal his 'UNION and DIVISION'[29] attitude toward racialism, since race for him is a pretext to endorse a hierarchic structure of society, moulded on the platonic three-step cognitive scale,[30] where we are all slaves, or rather, servants (independently of the colour of the skin). In other words, Carlyle's objective is not the definition of the supremacy of one race over the other, but the enactment of an efficient model of order and productivity:

> And I incessantly pray Heaven, all men, the whitest alike the blackest, the richest and the poorest, in other regions of the world, had attained precisely the same right, the divine right of being compelled (if 'permitted' will not answer) to do what work they are appointed for, and not go idle another minute, in a life which is so short, and where idleness so soon runs to putrescence! Alas, we had then a perfect world; and the Millennium, and true 'Organisation of Labour', and reign of complete blessedness, for all workers and men, had then arrived – which in these our own poor districts of the Planet, as well lament to know, it is very far from having yet done.[31]

> There is properly but one slavery in the world. One slavery, in which all other slaveries and miseries that afflict the earth are included; compared with which the worst West-Indian, white or black, or yellow slaveries are a small matter. One slavery over which the very gods weep. [...] The slavery of Wisdom to Folly.[32]

My point, therefore, is that Carlyle is both racist (in the perspective of an unsystematic, generalized comparison of races) and non-racist (in the perspective of an economic-socio-political order). He is racist when he compares the idleness of a white man with that of a black man and the former is excused ('poor soul'), because of the 'epochs', while the latter is regarded as intolerable, with the consequence of blaming the black man's lazy and lascivious nature for the ruin of West Indian sugar-estates. The emancipated blacks become the receptacles of Jamaican economic depression.[33] He is non-racist when he recognizes that if both white and black men suffer from the same 'enemy' – idleness – then they must be delivered from it, in order to fulfil the common end of their being on earth (work) and maintain an efficient economic, social and political structure:[34]

> Frightful things are continually told us of Negro slavery, of the hardships, bodily and spiritual, suffered by slaves. Much exaggerated, and mere exceptional cases, say opponents. Exceptional cases, I answer; yes, and universal ones! On the whole, hardships, and even oppressions and injustices are not unknown in this world; I myself have suffered such, and

have you not? It is said, Man, of whatever colour, is born to such, even as the sparks fly upwards. For in fact labour, and this is properly what we call hardship, misery, etc. (meaning mere ugly labour not yet done), labour is not joyous but grievous; and we have a good deal of it to do among us here. We have, simply, to carry the whole world and its businesses upon our backs, we poor united Human Species; to carry it, and shove it forward, from day to day, somehow or other, among us, or else be ground to powder under it, one and all.[35]

THE EVERLASTING YEA: 'WE HAVE SIMPLY, TO CARRY THE WHOLE WORLD AND ITS BUSINESSES UPON OUR BACKS, WE POOR UNITED HUMAN SPECIES'

If *Sartor Resartus* can be considered a re-tailoring of Plato's myth of the cave which is narrated in the *Republic*,[36] it is interesting to see how Carlyle develops Plato's political theories (expounded in the same book) in 'An Occasional Discourse on the Nigger Question'.

According to Plato, the state should be governed by philosophers (guardians) and his explanation is based on the construction of the human body. Since it consists of three parts, the head, the chest, the abdomen and for each of these three parts there is a corresponding faculty of the soul (respectively: reason, passion/will and desire/appetite) with a purpose (wisdom, courage and self-discipline), then Plato imagines a State built up exactly like the tripartite structure of the human body: as the individual is balanced or 'virtuous' when his three parts function together, so the State is perfect when its members (guardians, auxiliaries and labourers) work efficiently together. Just as the head governs the body, so the philosophers (guardians) must rule the society.[37]

Carlyle, then, seeing the turmoil and the economic slump in the West Indies (and at home), falls back on the Greek philosopher – 'Amicus Plato'[38] – to try to find a solution to those thorny problems and, as a matter of fact, he confidently turns race issues into moral qualities, slavery into servantship, happiness into execution of one's job or actualisation of one's own station, wages and proprietorship into manfulness ('rights' into 'mights').[39]

Basically, Carlyle repeats what he previously affirmed in *Past and Present* (1843), that is, only through an 'Aristocracy of Talent', which means 'the Wisest', can Britain hope to solve all the problems engendered by the emancipation of slaves in the British West Indies, the dramatic high rate of Irish poverty and waste of land, the industrial revolution (the replacement of workers with new machinery and mass-production) and the rising birth rate. From *Sartor Resartus* (1833-34/1836) through *Chartism* (1839) and onward with *On Heroes, Hero-Worship and the Heroic in History* (1841), 'An Occasional Discourse on the Nigger Question' (1849), *Latter-Day Pamphlets* (1850) to 'Shooting Niagara: And After?' (1867), he reveals his scepticism of democracy ('Democracy [...] means despair of finding any Heroes to govern you'),[40] free-trade ('all this Mammom-Gospel, of supply-and-demand, Competition, Laissez-faire, [...] begins to be one of the shabbiest Gospels ever preached; or altogether, the shabbiest'),[41] electoral suffrage ('In Rome and Athens, as elsewhere, if we look practically, we shall find that it was not by loud voting and debating of many, but by wise insight and ordering of a few that the work was done. So is it ever, so will it ever be')[42] because they run against the principle of a divine hierarchic order: 'Cosmos is not Chaos',[43] 'The Universe itself is a Monarchy and Hierarchy',[44] 'the Universe is but one vast Symbol of God'.[45]

In *Latter-Day Pamphlets* he sums up his belief in order, when he maintains that 'Historically speaking, [...] there was no Nation that could subsist upon Democracy' and that the American democratic experiment, though apparently working, is far from 'a Model Republic, or a model anything, the wise among themselves know too well that there is nothing to be said'.[46] When Carlyle affirms that the true commander and king is 'he who knows for himself the divine Appointments of this Universe' because Wisdom means 'Valour and heroic Nobleness',[47] then he clearly re-echoes Plato's guardians who 'not only have the intelligence and the competence for the job, but also have to care for the community'. As such, this category 'which is naturally the least numerous, is the one which inherently possesses the only branch of knowledge which deserved to be called wisdom'.[48]

When Plato goes on qualifying the moral qualities of the auxiliaries (courage) and the labourers (self-discipline), and recommends the fulfilment of one's role in each category without wishing a disrupting interchange of roles (especially for the guardians), Carlyle mirrors this moral degree scale in the 'Mastership' and 'Servantship' concept, which 'in these days [...] is fallen sadly out of joint'.[49] Since 'every human relation' is naturally based on a principle of 'master and servant' and in his times it is overlooked (especially in the relationship between the black man and the white man) – 'No man reverences another' – then, 'not the West Indies alone, but Europe generally, is nearing the Niagara Falls'.[50]

What Carlyle is mostly concerned and worried about, is the general neglect of this 'sacred Hierarchy',[51] where 'all men are called upon to do what is in their power': 'To do competent work, to labour honestly according to the ability given them; for that and for no other purpose was each one sent into this world'.[52]

Earlier in *Past and Present* he better clarifies this ideal tripartite structure with government and enlightened aristocracy as the guardians ('The Wiser'), intellectuals and bourgeoisie as auxiliaries ('The Braver'), and workers as labourers ('He obeys those whom he esteems better than himself').[53] Though Carlyle admits the interchangeability of guardians and auxiliaries he denies the interchangeability with lower classes. Abhorring 'nomadism' in human relations as being 'prohibitory of any good whatsoever' and on the contrary, advocating 'permanency' as being the source of happiness – 'Happy he who has found a master'[54] – he argues that birth in a lower class means a right and a duty to obey those who have been born their masters. Black people, therefore, who are no longer slaves, have to understand that, anyhow, their position is that of servantship (like that of British 'Workers' to their 'noble' 'Captains of Industry')[55] and that a request of higher wages is not the solution to their dissatisfaction. The only solution is the acceptance of their role in society.[56]

Since the relationship between master and servant is the sound foundation of a thriving society, its recognition is the only 'conceivable deliverance from Tyranny and Slavery'.[57] Turning slavery into servantship, and levelling all men's status under the principle of work, Carlyle thus succeeds in having his racist and non-racist ideas co-exist. When Plato says that if 'each of the three classes [...] performs its proper functions and does its own job in the community, then this is morality and makes the community a moral one',[58] Carlyle himself uses this moral stance to turn a racial problem into an ethical, and consequently a socio-political one. And again, when Plato warns that 'children, women, slaves experience the greatest quantity and variety of forms of desire, pleasure and pain',[59] and as such they must learn self-discipline to check the nature of those passions and be able not to be overwhelmed by them (as reason governs appetite), Carlyle similarly inveighs against the death of the soul in the black man (his idleness and rebellion) which accounts for the present chaos, or 'wide-coiled monstrosities'[60] – 'Do I, then, hate the Negro? No; except when the soul is killed out of him'[61] – and against the 'enfranchised White Women', 'who instead of learning to work and to obey, learned to give warning, [...] took the "freedom" to serve the Devil with their faculties, instead of serving God or man'.[62]

However, as to women, it must be pointed out that while Plato grants them the same powers of reasoning as men's, provided they get the same training and are exempt from child upbringing and housekeeping, Carlyle instead maintains that women without a master become 'Distressed' and 'cannot so much as live', as is the example of those 'thirty-thousand Distressed Needlewomen' who go on complaining about their miserable plight, but forget that 'he or she that will not work, and in the anger of the gods cannot be compelled to work, shall die!'.[63] In a letter to Jane Welsh, a few months before their marriage, he says: 'The man should bear the rule in the house and not the Woman. This is an eternal axiom, the Law of Nature'. In other words, Carlyle again prefers to solve the relationship' between the two sexes in terms of master and servant, or again in religious terms of divine submission, as God's words to Eve suggest: 'I will greatly multiply your sorrow and your conception; In pain you shall bring forth children; Your desire shall be for your husband, And he shall rule over you'. 'A woman shall not wear anything that pertains to a man, nor shall a man put on a woman's garment, for all who do so are an abomination to the LORD your God'.

Though apparently this law of general hierarchization seems painful and wrong, Carlyle affirms that this is the only conceivable form of Happiness – 'All "happy" enough; that is to say, all working according to the faculty they have got, making a little more divine this Earth which the gods have given them' – since, besides the biblical injunctions – 'there is no other happiness for man but rejoicing in his own works, for that is his heritage' – Plato's tripartite structure of the mind (reason, passion/will, desire/appetite) points out that 'when the whole mind accepts the leadership of the philosophical part, and there's no internal conflict, then each part can do its own job and be moral in everything it does, and in particular can enjoy its own pleasures, and thus reap as much benefit and truth from pleasure as is possible for it'.[64]

Plato's belief in the attainment of the utmost degree of happiness when the reason governs the passions/will and desires/appetites (in order to be happy, one must be moral, since happiness and morality increase and decrease together), is reworked by Carlyle in his defence of self-mastery and accomplishment of one's duties. The black man therefore, together with the white man, should co-operate for the economic, i.e. moral, re-birth of the West Indies, without heeding the supply-and-demand principle, which would only foster black immigration.[65]

Since morality, in the sense of accomplishment of one's work and duty, is Carlyle's objective in his 'ideal community', then the problem of people's rights, wages and proprietorship is turned into people's 'mights'. Starting from the idea that 'the glory of a workman, still more of a master-workman, That he does his work well, ought to be his most precious possession',[66] Carlyle comes to the conclusion that 'might and right [...] are ever in the long-run one and the same'.[67] The concept of manfulness corresponds to self-actualization through work and as such, it abolishes any question as to 'the right of property': 'this question is abstruse enough'.[68] Carlyle thinks that people should stop regarding land in terms of material, personal possession since 'we have no Property in our very Bodies, but only an accidental Possession and Life-rent'.[69] Since the 'one perfect eternal proprietor is the Maker who created them: the temporary better or worse proprietor', the black man's rage against the white man's temporary property of the West Indian lands is irrational and groundless.

Again, Carlyle justifies the black man's subordinate position through a religious explanation. The white man becomes, therefore, the fittest temporary proprietor: when the European white man first saw the West Indian islands, 'they were as if not yet created – their noble elements of cinnamon, sugar, coffee, pepper black and grey, lying all asleep [were] waiting the white enchanter [...] [to] say to them, Awake!'.[70] However, if Carlyle here admits the white man's temporary ownership of those lands with his 'beneficent whip', Plato instead in the *Republic* warns the guardians and auxiliaries against the possession of private property. It could become a ground for personal corruption, a way of jeopardizing the good of the collectivity, an erosion of their own integrity: 'In the first place, none of them is to have any private property, except what is absolutely indispensable. [...] These precepts will guarantee not only their own integrity, but also the integrity of the community which is in their safe keeping'.[71]

It is clear, then, that Carlyle adjusts the platonic ban of private property of the guiding class to his own times: not its banishment, because it is not so much the cause of the West Indian Islands' economic collapse as the black man's indolence and emancipation, but the idea of its temporal possession, in order to support and boost the British imperialist policy, which in carlylean terms, sounds as the divine mission of making these Islands prosper economically and morally: 'The West Indies grow pine-apples, and sweet fruits and spices; we hope they will one day grow beautiful Heroic human Lives too, which is surely the ultimate object they were made for'.[72]

ORGANIC FILAMENTS: 'BEFORE THE WEST INDIES COULD GROW A PUMPKIN FOR ANY NEGRO, HOW MUCH EUROPEAN HEROISM HAD TO SPEND ITSELF IN OBSCURE BATTLE'[73]

Starting with the premise that the universe is a sacred hierarchy and that some men have been born wiser than others, and that the latter are appointed to rule the weakest, as Plato exemplifies with the metaphor of the ship,[74] it is logical that Carlyle, for whom 'there is no problem with the idea of national character' (Scottish or English),[75] ends up supporting British Imperialism.

Already in 'Chartism' (1839) he evinces his imperialist ideas through the anonymous Author of *Geschichte der Teutschen Sippschaft* (not yet translated into English), in 'Chapter on the Eras of England'.[76] Using the same structure pattern as *Sartor Resartus* where Teufelsdröckh claims that the mythus of Christian religion is worn-out and needs to be replaced by a new one, that of Natural Supernaturalism (goethian pantheism), here Carlyle has the narrator report 'instructive' extracts from this unknown German professor's book, and though apparently detached from him, the narrator becomes a maieutic tool to spread these ideas and let them be appreciated: 'the Author of this strange untranslated Work, whom we think we recognize to be an old acquaintance'.[77]

In 'The Nigger Question', Carlyle goes on emphasizing the bravery of the British conquerors in the West Indian Islands – 'heroic white men, worthy to be called old Saxons, browned with a mahogany tint in those new climate and conditions'[78] – and after listing their names, he maintains that that heroism shows the imprint of Oliver Cromwell, the 'hero as king' who brought about the English control over Scotland (1650-51) and Ireland (1649-50). Later in 'Shooting Niagara: And After?' Carlyle openly stands up for governor Eyre's repression of the blacks' uprising in 1865, confirming the fact that throughout his life his imperialist convictions do not wear off, and are indeed strengthened by the evidence of so many 'profligate Niggers and Mulattoes'.

Considering his belief in British imperialism and a hierarchic political model which treads on racial differences to make it work paradoxically in moral terms, it is not surprising that Carlyle's hero has often been regarded as a totalitarian dictator. However, keeping in mind that Carlyle's inspiration is Plato's community and Plato's ideal guardian is not a dictator since he warps the collective good for his own sake[79] but a 'benevolent ruler', then we come to the conclusion that similarly, Carlyle's hero has to be a wise and brave white man, who 'with [a] beneficent whip', 'best hitherto can educe from said lands the beneficent gifts the Maker endowed them with; or which is but another definition of the same person, he who leads hitherto the manfulest life on that bit of soil, doing, better than another yet found can do, the Eternal Purpose and Supreme Will there'.[80]

Of course, the fact that Carlyle was read by the Nazis, such as Goebbels[81] demonstrates how difficult the realization of this oligarchy of enlightened rulers was, and instead how easy it was to turn his moral authoritarianism into political totalitarianism, as Bertrand Russell pointed out tracing the intellectual and moral consequences of Romanticism and German idealism proceeding 'by logical stages, through Fichte, Byron, Carlyle and Nietzsche, into Hitler.[82] And again, how arduous it was to defend human dignity, the cause of the poor and working classes, with the belief (devoid of any definite racial ideology of human behaviour or cultural characteristics biologically, genetically determined) in black inferiority.[83]

The very fact that Carlyle expounded his theories in a fictional form, through an unknown Speaker (as a literary man) and not in a political tract (as a politician), underlines this ambiguity, blurring this 'unaswearable question':[84] was Carlyle's passion for the Greek culture, Plato's ideal community, motivated by a utopian dream to be somewhat put forward against any destructive, chaotic, heterotopian nightmares (the failure of reform governments and universal suffragists to redress the social dire straights of Victorian England and its colonies), in tune with the Greek revival widely expressed in Scottish and English architecture by W.H. Playfair or H.W. Inwood? Or instead, did this proposal of a political tripartite hierarchic system subtly hide and reveal Carlyle's fear and failure of confronting the dark side of himself, consequently projected onto the black man? In junghian psychology: was all this hierarchic discourse a Janus-faced, unconscious way to conceal the fear of recognizing his shadow, the evil aspects of his personality, the impossibility of coming to terms with the whole of himself?[85]

Carlyle's strict education which banned the emotional side in virtue of a rational, disciplined control over events summed up in his father's axiom that 'man was created to work, not to speculate, or feel, or dream'[86] was certainly a fertile ground in this sense, if it is true, as modern psychologists say, that often adults who exert strict models of authoritarianism were compelled to repress their emotions as a child, and as such, they only learned a stifling sense of duty, which is a sterile ground to make love grow but a fertile land to nourish feelings of guilt and grudge.[87]

(Un)fortunately, as the Editor of *Sartor Resartus* said, 'We stand in a region of conjectures' and as such 'No firm arch, overspanning the Impassable with paved highway, could [I] construct; only, as was said, some zig-zag series of rafts floating tumultuously thereon.'

NOTES

[1] See Plato, *Republic,* translated by Robin Waterfield, Oxford: Oxford University Press, 1993, pp. 114-132.

[2] Thomas Carlyle, 'The Nigger Question', in *Critical and Miscellaneous Essays,* London: Chapman & Hall, 1899, IV, p. 348. Abbreviated form: NQ.

[3] Thomas Carlyle, NQ, p. 348.

[4] Thomas Carlyle, *Sartor Resartus: The Life and Opinions of Herr Teufelsdröckh,* London: Chapman & Hall, 1896, Book I, ch. ii, p. 9, p. 20, pp. 26-27. Abbreviated form: SR. As to Carlyle's elevated notion of the Editor's task, see D.J. Trela, 'Carlyle's Editorial Theory and Practice in Oliver Cromwell's Letters and Speeches', *English Language Notes,* vol. 29, no. 2, December 1991, pp. 58-65.

[5] As to a reading of *Sartor Resartus* as a gradual approval-definition of the philosophy of clothes, i.e. the principle of union-division between (extra)textual signifier and signified, see Cristina Ossato, *Sartor Resartus, ovvero la creazione di un Nuovo Mito,* Alessandria: Edizioni dell'Orso, 2001.

[6] Thomas Carlyle, NQ, p. 373.

[7] Thomas Carlyle, SR, Book III, ch. xii, p. 237.

[8] Thomas Carlyle, NQ, p. 354.

[9] *Ibidem,* p. 348.

[10] Thomas Carlyle, SR, Book I, ch. vi, pp. 33-34.

[11] See Carlyle's letter to J.S. Mill, 21 March, 1833. See also, J.R. Ward, 'Carlyle and the "Nigger Question"', *The Carlyle Society Papers,* no. 2, 1988-1989, pp. 1-31. Aileen Christianson, 'On the Writing of the "Occasional Discourse on the Negro Question"', *The Carlyle Newsletter,* no. 2, March 1980, pp. 13-19.

[12] Thomas Carlyle, NQ, p. 362.

[13] Cit. in Simon Heffer, *Moral Desperado: A Life of Thomas Carlyle,* London: Phoenix Giant, 1995, p. 274.

[14] Thomas Carlyle, NQ, p. 351.

[15] *Ibidem,* p. 354.

[16] *Ibidem,* p. 371.

[17] *Ibidem,* pp. 356-357.

[18] See Len Gougeon, 'Emerson, Carlyle and the Civil War', *The New England Quarterly,* vol. 62, no. 3, September 1989, pp. 403-423.

[19] See also Ian Campbell, 'Carlyle and the Negro Question Again',

Criticism: A Quarterly for Literature and the Arts, vol. 13, no. 3, summer 1971, pp. 279-290.

[20] Thomas Carlyle, 'Shooting Niagara: And After?', in *Critical and Miscellaneous Essays,* cit., V, p. 5.

[21] Moncure Conway, 'Thomas Carlyle', *Harper's New Monthly Magazine,* May 1881, p. 908.

[22] Douglas Lorimer, *Color, Class and the Victorians,* Leicester (England): Leicester University Press, 1978, p. 11.

[23] Caroline Reitz, 'Beneath Barking and Froth: Carlyle and the Othering of Violence', *Carlyle Studies Annual,* special issue, vol. 17, 1997, pp. 7-21.

[24] Tim Watson maintains that Carlyle's support of Governor E.J. Eyre in the Morant Bay Rebellion (1865) laid the foundations for the 1860s anthropological construction of race and class. See Tim Watson's 'Jamaica, Genealogy, George Eliot: Inheriting the Empire after Morant Bay', *JOUVERT,* vol. 1, no. 1, 1997, pp. 1-27.

[25] J.R. Ward, *op. cit.,* p. 21.

[26] See Ian Campbell, *op. cit.*; J.R. Ward, *op. cit.*; E.W. Said, *Culture and Imperialism,* London: Vintage, 1994, pp. 116-133; E.W. Said, *Orientalism: Western Conceptions of the Orient,* Harmondsworth: Penguin, 1995, p. 152; Iva G. Jones, 'Trollope, Carlyle and Mill of the Negro: An Episode in the History of Ideas', *The Journal of Negro History,* vol. 52, no. 3, 1967, pp. 185-199; Jude Nixon, 'Racialism and the Politics of Emancipation in Carlyle's "Occasional Discourse on the Nigger Question"', *Carlyle Studies Annual,* vol. 16, 1996, pp. 89-108; P.T. Park, 'Thomas Carlyle and the Jews', *Journal of European Studies,* vol. 20, no. 77, March 1990, pp. 1-21; Simon Heffer, *Moral Desperado: A Life of Thomas Carlyle,* cit., p. 246 and pp. 274-286; Denis Judd, *Empire: The British Imperial Experience, from 1765 to the Present,* cit., pp. 82-91.

[27] David Daiches, 'Carlyle: The Paradox Considered', *Lecture delivered to the Carlyle Society of Edinburgh (session 1980-1981) as part of the Carlyle Centenary Conference at the University of Edinburgh,* February 1981; first published as *The Thomas Green Lecture,* 6, pp. 365-383. T.C. Richardson, 'Carlyle and the Scottish Tradition of the Double', in W. Horst Drescher ed., *Thomas Carlyle 1981: Papers Given at the International Thomas Carlyle Centenary Symposium,* Frankfurt am Main: Peter Lang, 1983, pp. 351-363; Caroline Reitz, 'Beneath Barking and Froth', cit.; A.L. Le Quesne, 'Carlyle', in *Victorian Thinkers,* Oxford: Oxford University Press, 1993.

[28] Gillian Workman, 'Thomas Carlyle and the Governor Eyre Controversy: An Account with some New Material', *Victorian Studies,* vol. 18, no. 1, 1974, pp. 77-102.

[29] The principle of co-existence of opposites which is the kernel of the philosophy of clothes is best expressed in chapter X of SR with the definition of the link between the Spirit and the Body.

[30] See Cristina Ossato, '*Sartor Resartus,* or Re-tailoring Plato's Myth of the Cave', *Rivista di Studi Vittoriani,* vol. 5, January 1998, pp. 89-108.

[31] Thomas Carlyle, NQ, p. 357.

[32] *Ibidem,* pp. 360-361.

[33] *Ibidem,* p. 356.

[34] *Ibidem,* p. 355.

[35] *Ibidem,* pp. 358-359.

[36] See my already mentioned *Sartor Resartus, ovvero la creazione di un Nuovo Mito.*

[37] Plato, *Republic,* cit., pp. 114-132 and pp. 190-226.

[38] Thomas Carlyle, SR, Book I, ch. ii, p. 9. A later reference to Carlyle's re-reading in Plato (July 1856) is in *Reminiscences,* edited by K.J. Fielding and Ian Campbell, Oxford: Oxford University Press, 1997, p. 159.

[39] Thomas Carlyle, NQ, pp. 361-362.

[40] Thomas Carlyle, *Past and Present,* London: Chapman & Hall, 1897, p. 215. Abbreviated form: PP.

[41] *Ibidem,* p. 183.

[42] Thomas Carlyle, 'Chartism', in *Critical and Miscellaneous Essays,* cit., pp. 158-159.

[43] Thomas Carlyle, NQ, p. 363.

[44] Thomas Carlyle, *Latter-Day Pamphlets,* London: Chapman & Hall, 1898, p. 21. Abbreviated form: LP.

[45] Thomas Carlyle, SR, Book III, ch. iii, p. 175.

[46] Thomas Carlyle, LP, pp. 18-19.

[47] *Ibidem,* p. 32 and p. 34.

[48] Plato, *Republic,* cit., p. 116 and p. 135.

[49] Thomas Carlyle, NQ, p. 362.

[50] *Ibidem,* p. 368 and p. 354.

[51] Thomas Carlyle, SR, Book II, ch. x, p. 159.

[52] Thomas Carlyle, NQ, p. 355.

[53] Cristina Ossato, 'Thomas Carlyle's Cosmology: Between Visual Art

and Literature', *Rivista di Studi Vittoriani,* vol. 7, no. 13, January 2002, pp. 27-43.

[54] Thomas Carlyle, NQ, pp. 367-368.

[55] Thomas Carlyle, PP, p. 271.

[56] Thomas Carlyle, NQ, p. 379 and p. 352.

[57] *Ibidem,* p. 362.

[58] Plato, *Republic,* cit., p. 140.

[59] *Ibidem,* p. 138.

[60] Thomas Carlyle, NQ, p. 354.

[61] *Ibidem,* p. 357.

[62] *Ibidem,* p. 366.

[63] *Ibidem,* pp. 366-367.

[64] Plato, *Republic,* cit., p. 336.

[65] Thomas Carlyle, NQ, p. 378.

[66] Thomas Carlyle, 'Shooting Niagara: And After?', in *Critical and Miscellaneous Essays,* cit., V, p. 35.

[67] Thomas Carlyle, 'Chartism', in *Critical and Miscellaneous Essays,* cit., IV, p. 147.

[68] Thomas Carlyle, NQ, p. 373.

[69] Thomas Carlyle, SR, p. 160.

[70] Thomas Carlyle, NQ, p. 374.

[71] Plato, *Republic,* cit., pp. 120-123.

[72] Thomas Carlyle, NQ, p. 376.

[73] *Ibidem.*

[74] See Plato's *Republic,* cit., p. 208 and Carlyle's re-working of the same idea in LP, p. 16.

[75] Ian Campbell, 'The Scottishness of Carlyle', *Carlyle Studies Annual,* no. 17, 1997, p. 77.

[76] Thomas Carlyle, 'Chartism', in *Critical and Miscellaneous Essays,* cit., IV, pp. 174-175.

[77] *Ibidem.*

[78] Thomas Carlyle, NQ, p. 377.

[79] Plato, *Republic,* cit. pp. 302-319.

[80] Thomas Carlyle, NQ, pp. 374-376.

[81] As to Carlyle's influence on the myth of the Great Man in Germany and Goebbels's preference for Carlyle's *Frederick the Great,* see Alan Steinweis, 'Hitler and Carlyle's "Historical Greatness"', *History Today,* vol. 45, no. 6, June 1995, pp. 33-38.

[82] Bertrand Russell, *A History of Western Philosophy*, New York: Simon and Schuster, 1945, p. 642. See also I.P. Mckeehan, 'Carlyle, Hitler and Emerson: A Comparison of Political Theories', *University of Colorado Studies,* vol. 2, no. 1, May 1943, pp. 1-29.

[83] As to Carlyle's ambivalent attitude toward the Jews, a combination of both reverence for the Biblical Hebrews and contempt for their being 'mere dealers in money, gold, jewels', see P.T. Park, 'Thomas Carlyle and the Jews', cit., pp. 1-21.

[84] Thomas Carlyle, SR, Book I, ch. viii, p. 41.

[85] 'The shadow is a moral problem that challenges the whole ego personality [...]. To become conscious of it involves recognizing the dark aspects of the personality as present and real. This act is the essential condition for any kind of self-knowledge, and therefore, as a rule, meets with considerable resistance'. C.G. Jung, *Aion: Researches into the Phenomenology of the Self,* translated by R.F.C. Hull, London: Routledge & Kegan Paul, 1959, p. 8.

[86] Thomas Carlyle, *Reminiscences*, cit., p. 8.

[87] Nazi soldiers, for example, represent the extreme case of a warped education that imparted harshness and repression of feelings. Hebrews came to embody all those emotions they had to shun in the name of duty, efficiency and racial perfection (empathy, sympathy, tears, compassion, fear, despair etc.): ignoring their own psychological inner split, they found an apparently easier, but always ineffective way out, by projecting their inner conflict onto the Hebrews who therefore were overloaded with the Nazis' unrecognised, abhorred passions. See Alice Miller, *La persecuzione del bambino: le radici della violenza*, Torino: Bollati Boringhieri, 1997, p. 70.

VALENTINA POGGI

Walter Scott the Novelist: History in the Bones

At the Scott Exhibition, Edinburgh Festival

(I)

He will outlast us, churning out his books,
advocate and historian, his prose
earning him Abbotsford and its borrowed gates,
its cheap mementoes from the land he made.
Walking the room together in this merciless
galaxy of manuscripts and notes
I am exhausted by such energy.
I hold your hand for guidance. Over your brow
the greenlight falls from tall and narrow windows.
His style is ignorant of this tenderness,
the vulnerable angle of your body
below the Raeburn with its steady gaze.

(II)

It was all in his life, not in his books
'Oh I am dying, take me home to Scotland
where I can breathe though that breath were my last.'
He limped through an Edinburgh being made anew.
He worked his way through debts, past a dead wife.
My dear, we love each other in our weakness
as he with white grave face diminishing through
stroke after stroke down to the unpaid room.
We know what we are but know not what we will be.
I tremble in this factory of books.
What love he must have lost to write so much.[1]

These lines by Iain Crichton Smith (1928-1998) express the personal response of a fellow Scottish writer to Walter Scott, but can also be seen as summing up the critical debate on the latter. Like many of Scott's young protagonists from the eponymous hero of *Waverley* onward, Smith's judgment wavers between praise and reservation, admiration and dismissal: Scott 'will outlast' the whole band of contemporary Scottish writers, his prodigious 'energy' having created a 'galaxy' of writings which, taken all together, 'made' Scotland a 'land', giving it 'a local habitation and a name' in Europe's collective imagination. All the same, such energy appears 'merciless' because it was governed – as verbs like 'churning/earning/borrowed' forcibly suggest – by a yearning after economic and social success. The impulse that produced the Waverley novels was basically materialistic, and it is no wonder that they should represent the first outstanding example of literary mass production, the triumph of an enterprising commercial spirit that turned literary works into goods for mass consumption.

A consequence of this tireless urge to write is a style denounced as 'ignorant of tenderness': implying that Scott's language and approach to characterization lack the subtlety and depth that come from the ability to value and preserve, in oneself and in others, that feminine element without which (at least to Smith's mind) neither art nor human life in general is complete. 'Past a dead wife' hints that Scott's later years were far less marked by regret for his lost companion than by his preoccupation with writing. (Indeed when his partner James Ballantyne was left a widower Scott showed only moderate sympathy).[2] He had to write, of course, in order to pay off debts incurred largely owing to his inadequate management of a threefold position as author, secret partner in a printing, and in a publishing concern. But writing had also become a personal obsession; a way, perhaps, to make up for what life had not given him? The cryptic conclusion of the poem – 'What love he must have lost to write so much' – could suggest either that Scott sought in writing an outlet for frustrated love, or that he had sacrificed all other affections to the creative urge.

Whichever Smith intended, the second hypothesis appears the more probable. The thwarted youthful love for Wilhemina Belsches is not accorded by 20th century biographers the romantic import

that Lockhart's *Life* ascribed to it. Donald Carswell and lately an
openly unsympathetic John Sutherland see the young Scott as far
keener on getting admittance into a higher social sphere where to
find scope for his budding poetic talent, than ready to fall truly and
deeply in love.[3] As Alexander Welsh convincingly argues, when
Scott deals with the love interest in his poems and novels he is
consistently in favour of restraint, sooner than release of that passion;[4] nor can this be interpreted as the outcome of a bitter lesson
painfully learned, since the agony of renunciation or loss is seldom
more perceptible than the protagonists' consciousness of the wisdom of self-control. Waverley quitting his suit to Flora McIvor, Julia
Mannering deferring to her father in the matter of Brown-Bertram,
the frigid couples in *The Antiquary*, *The Black Dwarf*, *A Legend of
Montrose*, cannot be said to claim any warm response from the
reader; even the tears of Henry Morton in *Old Mortality* and of
Frank Osbaldistone in *Rob Roy* are not quite heartrending. Love
and marriage appear in Scott, more than for their own sake, as
essential to the structuring of his plots: Henry's jealousy of Edith,
when he thinks her in love with Evandale, makes his bold defiance
of the Royalists more plausible than it would else appear, considering his moderation in politics and religion; Diana Vernon's sense
and candour make the reader like her as a person rather than look
at her as an erotic object. Her role with regard to Frank
Osbaldistone remains that of intriguing mystery and benevolent
deus-ex-machina. Both these novels dismiss the final union of
hero and heroine in vague or nonchalant fashion. However, when
the strength of love oversteps the limits of morality or prudence
the lovers are sure to come to grief: Effie and her seducer in *The
Heart of Midlothian* enjoy no real happiness even when married,
rich and respected; he is finally brought back to the scene of his
crimes to undergo all the pains of guilt, remorse and fear, to be
killed at last by his own unknown bastard son; she will spend her
last days in a convent, which to Scott was a fate worse than death.
In *The Bride of Lammermuir* Lucy Ashton and Edgar Ravenswood,
though guiltless of sexual indiscretion, are doomed to a tragic end
by political contrasts, family feuds and ancestral curses.

The main impulse and central theme of Scott's writing is not,
then, the dilemma between passion and reason, honour, or duty. If

his heroes are in two minds about some momentous issue, or hesitate between two models of behaviour (paradigmatically identified in *Waverley* with Colonel Talbot and Fergus MacIvor, in *Old Mortality* with Claverhouse and Burleigh), it is because Scott himself was two men at once: a lover of the past and a believer in the present, striving toward a necessary and arduous compromise between the one and the other, a prudent Briton and a passionate Scot, poised between nostalgia for the Jacobite lost cause and loyalty to the House of Hanover, regretting an independent Scotland and approving the Union.[5]

Another aspect to this dualism is his interest on one hand in antiquarian pursuits and historical documents, and on the other in the recovery of traditional folk material such as what he collected for his first important work, *The Minstrelsy of the Scottish Border*. Today the student of folklore is annoyed by Scott's inclination (later indulged in the novels, where he loved to insert pseudo translations from imaginary ancient ballads) to tamper with, and sometimes adulterate his sources; but this should be seen as an expression of his urge to appropriate the past, to strive for what today we would call 'full immersion' in it. Not for him the aloofness of the scholarly historian: while an effort towards impartiality was implicit in his being, as already said, 'in two minds', that very balance could only be achieved by imaginatively re-experiencing the atmosphere, feelings, manners and situations of ages gone by, so as to represent them in terms accessible to the imagination of his contemporaries.

Memory and imagination are co-essential to Scott's historical approach; but more than the memory of written histories pored over in the study, it was that of stories heard as a child from familiar figures who had played a part in them, or learned the facts from those who had. Those stories concerned principally the attempt by the young Pretender Charles Edward Stuart, in 1745-1746, to recover the throne lost by his grandfather James II (VII for Scotland). Scott's childish imagination invested those vicarious memories with a glow that decades could not quench; long before he came to resurrect them in *Waverley*, that glow proved powerful to light up farther recesses in the tunnel of the past. The fatal defeat of James IV at Flodden evoked in *Marmion*, James V's

Highland roaming in *The Lady of the Lake*, with their glimpses of grandly wild scenery and arcaic manners took by storm the readers of the dawning Romantic age. The sobriquet 'Wizard of the North' bestowed on Scott shows that he was indeed making Scotland alive with the charm of the picturesque and timeless: still, rather as a thrilling place for tourists to explore than as a three-dimensional reality. It took the success of another lame Scot, who could boast a lordship, a genius for amatory adventures and self-dramatization, a greater mastery of old and new verse forms, to help Scott find his true medium in narrative prose. Afterwards, in the course of half a dozen years he practically created, single-handed, a new narrative genre: the historical novel.

The fluctuating fortune of this genre (lately revived by famous best-sellers) should not blind us to the fact that Scott, besides making Scotland and Scottish things fashionable, was more effective than Richardson and Fielding had been in rendering the novel intellectually prestigious, as well as popular. It was largely thanks to him if novel-writing (and novel-reading) came to be associated with higher pursuits like historiography and the analysis of complex political, religious and national issues. For, without alienating the sympathy of readers eager for action, sentiment and local colour, the Waverley novels were allowed to justify the interest of people like church ministers, University professors and literary pundits such as Francis Jeffrey of the *Edinburgh Review*.

Of course the historical novel could never have come into existence merely owing to the lucky concurrence of someone's childhood memories, lively imagination, fluent pen and strenuous activity (genius apart, which some will allow, others deny Scott to have possessed). The rise of this genre was equally due to the circumstance that its creator was a Scot living in the wake of the extraordinary cultural revival that goes under the name of Scottish Enlightenment. In the latter half of the 18th century a number of Scottish philosophers, historians, agrarian improvers, economists and divines had devoted their energies to the analysis and appraisal of facts that were changing the ways of mankind and the face of the world. Especially in their own part of the world (whether they considered it as Scotland robbed of its nationhood, or as North Britain), changes belatedly following those in the South

and therefore all the more rapid and striking, compelled the educated mind to muse on the effects of the passing of time, on the
progress from primitive to civilized societies, and on the loss and
gain consequently experienced by different social groups. At the
most impressionable age Scott had lived in the country and lis-
tened to tales of past turmoil and heroism. His adolescence and
youth were spent in a city where David Hume and Adam Smith,
Boswell and Lord Kames, William Robertson and Adam Ferguson
had been debating and writing on ethics and aesthetics, law and
economy, natural science, history and religion.[6] This does not
mean that his knowledge about such themes was as deep and spe-
cialized as theirs; but that was the atmosphere he breathed, the
humus out of which the Waverley novels grew.

'The Waverley novels': the comprehensive definition appearing
in most histories of English literature is misleading because it tends
to make us forget that they were neither planned as a sequence
nor as, one and all, historical. In the first decade of his career as a
novelist Scott was clearly experimenting different approaches to
the art of fiction as well as to the problems of recreating the past.
In the introductory chapter of *Waverley* (1814) he directs the reader's expectations away from the familiar clichés of gothic and sentimental novel, displaying a Fielding-like awareness of the novelty
of his attempt. But in the next two books, *Guy Mannering* (1815)
and *The Antiquary* (1816), while clearly intending to exploit the
huge success of *Waverley* he starts in *medias res*, sets his plots in
periods gradually closer to his time, and capitalizes on adventure,
suspense and crime rather than on historical events or characters.
What these two novels share with *Waverley* is the emphasis on
Scottish manners, more or less explicitly compared, favourably or
unfavourably, with the English lifestyle. Scott's assertion, that he
took courage to publish *Waverley* from the example of Maria
Edgeworth's Irish novels, is rightly seen by Bushnell[7] not as an
affectation of modesty, but as evidence of his awareness that the
faithful rendering of the manners of a social group in a given place
and time, whether or not associated with mention of specific historical events, was a fit aim for the serious writer; it showed history
in the making, an endless balancing of permanence and change.
The farmers, gipsies and smugglers in *Guy Mannering*, the old

beggar and the fisherman's family in *The Antiquary*, are perceived and described as elements of a socio-cultural structure already gone or fast disappearing, which in turn was rooted in values and traditions of the distant past. At the end of *The Antiquary* Scott considered the cycle opened by *Waverley* complete. The year it appeared, 1816, saw also the first of the Series *Tales of my Landlord*: its framework, meant to preserve and at the same time bridge the gap between present and past, reveals Scott's new sense of the possibilities and demands of the genre.

The events narrated in the three Series belonged to periods beyond living man's memory: the 1679-1689 decade in *Old Mortality*, the Porteous riot of 1736 in *The Heart of Midlothian*, a time either shortly before or after the Union of 1707 in *The Bride of Lammermuir*, the mid-seventeenth century in *A Legend of Montrose*. Scott encapsulated this sequel in a frame implying the transmission of the original narratives by a plurality of mediators: the humble people, not professional historians, who told them to Patie Pattison, the consumptive school-usher that loved to hear true stories and record them in writing; Patie's executor, the schoolmaster Jedediah Cleishbotham, who took to himself all the merit for the publication of those writings; the landlord of the inn to whom, as willing listener and liberal dispenser of drink, Cleishbotham inscribed the narratives themselves. This Chinese-box structure is certainly part of the game at hide-and-seek the Great Unknown loved to practise, but at another level it expresses his deep insight into what today is called 'reader-reception', and the mental processes a writer can activate and negotiate. The historical events, seen as if through the wrong end of a telescope thanks to this multiple perspective, become at once more distant and more vivid than if they were conveyed by the already familiar device of the retrieved manuscript. The frame and the introductory chapter of each novel make us hear, so to speak, 'la rumeur des distances traversées'; and while we are being ferried over to the distant shore of the past we are not allowed to forget the *terra firma* of the present, nor the relation of similarity and difference, or cause and effect, that one bears to the other.

Such a relation emerges at its clearest and strongest in the *Tales of my Landlord* mentioned above, as well as in two novels outside the series: *Rob Roy* (1818), where a first-person narrator takes us from London to Northumberland to Scotland on the eve of the first Jacobite rising; *Redgauntlet* (1824), based on an imaginary abortive plan for a third rising, and presenting by a combination of letter-writing, diary, and omniscient narration, the attitudes of high, middling and low people to the dream of putting back the clock of history.

Scott's achievement in these novels is the creation of a world that, though unlike the one his (especially non-Scottish) readers were familiar with, still could (and can) be recognized as real; a world that envelops and crowds in on us with the fullness and depth of its detailed reconstruction of everyday life as lived in kitchen, shop, street, field, market, church, prison; in gossip, courting and quarrelling; while at the same time it vibrates with the tension caused by conflicts on a large scale, dissension and insecurity, danger and impending catastrophe. The characters on whom the plots hinge are not influenced only by their impulses or their immediate milieu, but feel the pressure of a wider and more complex social structure whose prevailing tendencies inevitably affect their lot for better or worse. In gothic and sentimental novels the plight of hero or heroine is usually caused by a villain. Here it is the consequence of some malaise in the body politic of which even the most insignificant members may be instruments or victims. In *Old Mortality* Morton's involvement with the Covenanters is due not so much to his having met with, and sheltered, the murderer of Bishop Sharpe, as to old Mause's shrill assertion of her Presbyterian faith before the Royalist troopers. As a result Morton will twice find himself waiting for execution, twice be rescued and in turn rescue his saviour; change from prisoner to soldier and back to prisoner, and finally quit the scene and go on exile for ten years. Neither of the contending parties can have his full moral support. The scene where Morton, in impotent anguish, watches MacBriar, one of the Covenanters who had been about to kill him, undergo torture by the Privy Council, symbolizes the plight of the moderate in times of civil strife, while it completes for the protagonist the circle of events begun with the old peasant woman's ill-timed outburst. After all, even the Mauses of this world (be they exasperating or heroic, as Scott and his Presbyterian critics respec-

tively found them)[8] fan the fire of radicalism, in despite of easygo-
ing fellows like Mause's son Cuddy. Both high and low, in short,
make history and influence the destiny of each other, though the
low are not always rewarded either with the crown of martyrdom
or of fame.

Scott rescues the humble from obscurity not by making them
'save the situation', as do youngsters in the *Treasure Island* kind of
novel, but by making his imagined world alive with their clamours
or silences, their fears or quiet satisfactions, passive resistence or
active benevolence. In *The Heart of Midlothian* Reuben Butler and
Jeanie Deans, in different ways, are shown resisting the tide of
public passion that tries to engulf them. Reuben is physically swept
along with the silent, sullen crowd on its way to the Tolbooth
prison, where he must act as chaplain at the execution of Porteous,
the 'enemy of the people' unjustly reprieved by the government.
Scott describes the prison-breaking expedition with its ominous
echoes of the Bastille, and the people's pent-up rage for justice,
with true epic restraint (Manzoni must have appreciated the French
translation of the novel, *La prison d'Edinburgh*, and remembered it
when he wrote about Renzo in Milan, just as the 'oste della Luna
Piena' talking to his wife reminds one of Niel Blane and his daughter in chapter 4 of *Old Mortality*). Butler's generous but useless
pleading with the crowd again shows the defeat of sense and moderation when passion guides political action: the rioters want
revenge for the fellow citizens killed by Porteous after the execution of a smuggler, who for them was no criminal but a gallant
rebel against the 'foreign' English government; the crowd's leader
Robertson wishes, besides, to offer his lover Effie Deans, under
trial for infanticide, an occasion to escape. Public and private
motives conspire to interfere with individual freedoms and moral
choices. Jeanie, Effie's sister and Butler's betrothed, finds that
according to popular feeling she should exculpate Effie by declaring in court that her sister had revealed her pregnancy to her. She
refuses to commit perjury in a memorable trial scene, and instead
sets out for London to ask for a royal pardon, just at the critical
moment when the Queen is enraged with the people of Edinburgh
after the Porteous riots. Jeanie reaches London against many odds
(her adventures on the road mark a temporary shift from the mode

of historical realism to that of romance), and the Duke of Argyle, the chief Scottish nobleman at Court, sees in her modest pride, firmness, truthfulness and faith in a justice tempered with mercy, an epitome of national virtues. By helping her to find grace with the Queen he himself recovers a better footing with the latter. For once, private and political motives converge for good.

The Heart of Midlothian is the most optimistic of Scott's mature works. In the prolonged aftermath of this climax (about one fifth of the whole novel) he laid himself open to criticism by an inclination to apportion rewards and punishments, and to indulge in the pathetic (the interesting madwoman Madge Wildfire dies singing, like a swan or like a character in an opera). To his credit however is the making Jeanie, now the Reverend Butler's wife in a comfortable Highland manse, feel a momentary pang of jealousy on realizing that her once dishonoured sister has become a fashionable lady, admired by that same Duke who is Jeanie's benefactor. By such subtle touches Scott prevents his heroine appearing too perfect. His predilection for her may have been partly due to the fact that in Jeanie he had shown the more humane aspects of his father's Presbyterian faith, which he had relinquished in favour of the Episcopalian but was still ready to celebrate, as having brought about the triumph of the Protestant Reformation in Scotland.

Nevertheless when, immediately after the success of *Ivanhoe* in 1820, he went back to Scottish themes and invented a new mediating frame for his history of the Reformation, he failed signally. In *The Monastery* an ubiquitous banshee is quite absurdly purported to cause, by some colorful magic in a subterranean grotto, the hero's simultaneous mental growth and conversion to Protestantism. In *The Abbot* the tenuous eponymous character practically disappears behind the figures of Mary Stuart on the eve of her ill-omened flight to England, and of her two young devotees, also predestined to a facile conversion. Failure apart, these novels confirm that with *Ivanhoe* Scott had turned a new leaf, going to history rather for the colorful pageant or backdrop of romance than for those not too remote processes of change whose after-effects could still be felt in the present. To gauge the difference between the two modes one has just to put *Redgauntlet* (1824), his last plunge into the bracing current of memory

enlivened with imagination and into the Scotland of sixty years
before, alive with smugglers and sailors, fisheries and law-courts,
belated Jacobites and canny Quakers, side by side with *The
Talisman*, published in 1825. In *Redgauntlet* the sense of time is
closely linked to that of place, while historical change is made palpable both by the reference to the ancestral curse on the family
and by the contrasting economic structures of nearly contiguous
communities; in *The Talisman* the Oriental setting is peopled with
the quasi-mythical figures of Coeur-de-Lion and Saladin, and the
stock-types of preux chavalier, villainous Templar, Machiavellian,
virtuous damsel and capricious lady; the plot is thick with disguis-
es, improbable coincidences, recurrent mutual rescuings. Although
cliché situations (the lost and found heir) and stocktypes (prosy,
testy old men and petulant interfering servants) are to be found
also in the Scottish novels, along with plot-structures alien to modern narratology, their recreation of a living past makes the reader
forget such strictures. But in most novels written after 1819 we
enter rather a *tableau vivant* than a world in its own right. Long
before the financial crash that from 1826 made writing a necessity,
and despite the painstaking research on which he based his
English and French stories Scott, more than interrogating history,
was producing escapist literature: a good read and little more.

Yet today many think of him mainly as the author of that kind
of novel. Outside Scotland, certainly in Italy, he is the author of
Ivanhoe, not of *Waverley* and *Old Mortality*. This may be due to
the fact that in translation much is lost of the racy Scots of his
lower-class characters, which in the original is a stumbling block
even for students of English. But whoever overcomes the difficulty
will become aware of Scott's true greatness, and of what Manzoni
would have been the first to acknowledge he had received from him.

NOTES

[1] Iain Crichton Smith, *Selected Poems,* Manchester: Carcanet, 1985, pp.
86-87.
[2] Compare *The Journal of Sir Walter Scott, 1829-32*, edited by W.M.
Parker, Edinburgh: Oliver & Boyd, 1946, pp. 20-21 and p. 24.

[3] Donald Carswell, *Sir Walter. A Four-Part Study in Biography,* London: J. Murray, 1930, pp. 13-20; John Sutherland, *The Life of Walter Scott,* Oxford: Blackwell, 1997, pp. 51-58.

[4] Alexander Welsh, *The Hero of the Waverley Novels,* New Haven: Yale University Press, 1963, passim.

[5] Compare David Daiches, *Literary Essays,* Edinburgh: Oliver & Boyd, 1956 pp. 94-95; D.D. Devlin, *The Author of Waverley,* London: Macmillan, 1971, p. 48; Alexander Welsh, *op. cit.,* and R.C. Gordon, *Under Which King? A Study of the Scottish Waverly Novel,* Edinburgh: Oliver & Boyd, 1969, *passim.*

[6] Compare John McQueen, *The Rise of the Historical Novel,* Edinburgh: Scottish Academic Press, 1989, Chapter I.

[7] N.S. Bushnell, 'Walter Scott's Advent as Novelist of Manners', *Studies in Scottish Literature* vol. 1, no. 1, 1963, pp. 15-34.

[8] Compare Beth Dickson, 'Sir Walter Scott and the Limits of Toleration', *Scottish Literary Journal,* vol. 18, no. 2, 1991, pp. 46-62.

VALENTINA POGGI

The Quaint Old World of John Galt

John Galt was born in 1779 in Irvine, a small town in the South West of Scotland not far from Glasgow. He travelled far and wide, both in the Mediterranean countries and in Canada where he founded the town of Guelph; spent many years in London trying to set up in business, and wrote many potboilers; but his best fiction is set in Scottish villages, and is rich with Scottish idioms and the rhythms of spoken Scots. His lifetime more or less coincided with that of Walter Scott; and he found his true vein in the early 1820s, when the Waverley novels had created a market for Scottish stories. Literary fashions often breed a host of gregarious writers eager to exploit the newly-discovered mine, and some thought Galt one such: Hazlitt, who admired Scott's novels while disliking their author, could not stomach the 'small talk' of Galt's middle-class characters. Francis Jeffrey while praising Galt's Scottish novels could not see his originality; he thought Galt tried to imitate Scott in the province of humour rather than that of romance. But Coleridge, though he acknowledged Scott's wider thematic and stylistic range, appreciated Galt as the master of pseudo-autobiography, a first-person narrative through whose account of facts and characters the reader is made to perceive truths unsuspected by the narrator himself.[1]

Galt's picture of Scottish life is rather complementary than indebted to Scott's. His protagonists live in villages and small towns of the West Country, instead of the Highlands or Edinburgh, and he deals preferably with the recent past or even the present; what is more, his cast of mind is that of the social historian rather than the imaginative re-creator of crucial deeds in the past. He depicts the humdrum goings-on of small communities or families, keeping climactic national and international events (like the

American and French revolutions) in the background, yet never lets us forget the role they have, in the long run, in shaping individual lives. Political and religious conflicts, scientific discoveries, industrial and economic innovations are the causes of the day-to-day cultural evolution he likes to focus on: the barely perceptible steps forward whose significance can be grasped only when aged people come to realize how much the world has changed since the time of their youth.

Galt's typical setting, the village where everybody knows everybody else and every piece of news is food for gossip, recalls Jane Austen's 'two-inches bit of ivory' and the kind of idyll George Eliot was to paint in *Silas Marner*. But what for them was the background was for him the main subject: he analysed the microcosm in process of change with the mind of a sociologist, when sociology was in its pioneering stage. He draws our attention, for instance, to developments in the means of transport: the opening of new roads, streets being paved and lit up, coaches hired for private use, whereas previously a coach was the privilege of the very rich; and consequently information and communication made easier and more general: the spread of a taste for literature, even the habit of reading newspapers, among people who formerly read, besides the Bible, only religious tracts or traditional ballads and tales, and heard of national and international events in a vague, belated form. Other foci of interest are agricultural improvements and developing tertiary trades: with shops opening where retail selling had been transacted by pedlars, or at fairs and on market-day; the introduction of foreign goods and crafts, and the consequent changes in diet, clothes, housing.

But Galt is not a mere statistician or sociologist. His 'theoretical histories', as he called his Scottish novels, were 'a kind of history that allowed for the play of imagination'.[2] He is fully alive to the quirks of character, the peculiarities of manners and locality. Though interested in changing mental habits and modes of feeling, in the new relationship being established between individual and community, he does not try to show all that through emblematic characters destined to accomplish crucial choices. He builds up a myriad of figures, of which many are humorous sketches, but others are fully realized round characters. Among these are the narra-

tors of his pseudo-autobiographies, at once the recorders and subjects of the process of change: Mr Balwhidder the minister of
Dalmailing, whose *Annals of the Parish* chronicle fifty years of
local history covering the whole of George III's reign, from 1760 to
1810; Mr Pawkie in *The Provost*, who is the Mayor of Gudetown for
nearly as long a period; Mr Jobbry, who in *The Member* sits in
Parliament for about a dozen years before the Reform Bill of 1832.
Each of them looks keenly at the world scrutinising 'the signs of
the times', but also responds to the changes he records, and his
growth as a character is no less interesting than the transformation
of yesterday's world into that of today. Through their limited,
biased viewpoints, Galt highlights the movement of history without
expressing too much enthusiasm for the modern age, nor whole-
sale regret for the past. Irony tempered with tolerance and sympathy is the mark of his world-view. By adopting a narrative persona
either naive or partially blinded by self-love he establishes an
ambiguous perspective, preventing the reader from pronouncing
too rashly for tradition *vs* innovation, orthodoxy *vs* unorthodoxy,
conservatism *vs* radicalism or vice versa. Often, though, we sense
that the author gets closer to the narrator when the latter proves
able to accept the course of history if only because that is the way
his neighbour is going. At the end of *Annals of the Parish*
Balwhidder expresses his faith in man and progress in Biblical language that shows him firmly rooted in the past as well as hopeful
about the future:

> the progress of learning and education has been wonderful [...] and with
> it has come a spirit of greater liberality than the world knew before,
> bringing men of adverse principles and doctrines into a more human
> communication with each other; showing that it is by the mollifying influ-
> ence of knowledge the time will pass, when the tiger of papistry shall lie
> down with the lamb of reformation, and the vultures of prelacy be as
> harmless as the presbyterian dove; when the independents, the anabap-
> tists, and every other order and denomination of Christians, not forgetting
> those poor wee wrens of the Lord, the burghers and antiburghers [two
> secessionist wings of the Presbyterian church] will pick from the hand of
> patronage, and dread no more.[3]

Even more confident is the Provost, who prides himself on having
introduced a better system of management in public affairs; though

it boils down to this, that instead of downright bribery and barefaced corruption he has used more circumspection, more 'judicious stratagems'; he has certainly acted in order to make his town more modern and better organized, and in so doing occasions have not been wanting for him to feather his own nest by those means for which today's Italians have coined the term *tangentopoli*. Less complacent is the eponymous character of *The Member* – a small nabob who, coming home from India, bought a seat in Parliament to be able to help his relatives to lucrative jobs – when he records the ideas of a young schoolmaster (probably the mouthpiece of Galt himself) arguing thus:

> the great properties have had their day; they are the relics of the feudal system [...] That system is in principle overthrown, and [...] it will be succeeded by one [...] that will gradually bring on an equalisation of condition.

The conservative M.P. is dismayed, but neither loses his poise nor vents his spleen in sterile anathemas:

> grieved I was that men of his degree could talk so glibly on subjects that puzzle the highest heads in the land [...] His sentiments, however, remain with me; and I cannot get the better of what he propounded about the feudal system being at an end [...] I concluded that a time was fast coming in which prudent and elderly men ought to quit the public arena, and leave it clear to the younger and the bolder. It was this conversation which in great measure led me to think of retiring from Parliament.[4]

For all the difference among these charaters in temper and moral integrity, they share a view of socio-cultural change as irreversible. Galt was no superficial regionalist bent on idyllizing the past. It was rather his awareness of the radicality of historical evolution that made him wish to register the obsolete and obsolescent customs of his part of the country; not as mere curiosities, like flies caught in amber, or like the toad in the stone the finding of which Balwhidder records as one of the memorable events of 1769 in his parish. Quaint and old-fashioned as his characters' fashions and mental habits may appear, through them we see the values and anti-values, passions and delusions, virtues and failings of mankind at work. And far from serving up provincial narrow-mindedness for the complacent mockery of enlightened readers, his sketches are underpinned by the consciousness that the provincial mind merely gives a less dignified version of the pretences and prejudices to be found in the most cosmopolitan milieu.

Narrow-mindedness is often associated in Galt's fiction with Presbyterian bigotry. Although he reacted to Scott's portrayal of the Covenanters in *Old Mortality* with a sustained vindication of their rights and dignity in the historical novel *Ringan Gilhaize* (1824), sectarianism in the moderate 19th century seemed to him rather ludicrous than heroic. His first Scottish novel (an earlier one, *The Majolo*, had been set in Sardinia) was *The Ayrshire Legatees* (1821), two thirds of which consist in the letters written by the Reverend Pringle's family, in London to cash a legacy from a rich Indian uncle, to their friends in the West Country; the rest presents the comments of the latter, assembled to hear them read. The most prominent in the group is Mrs Glibbans, whose name suggests loquaciousness and whose eloquence is ever at the service of religious orthodoxy. This 'worthy pillar of the Relief Kirk' is concerned lest her Minister's family be led astray in 'prelatic' London, and horrified on learning that, on a Sunday night, the Pringles barely escaped the sinful pleasure of hearing 'a Mozart' played on the harp:

'What think you, Mr Snodgrass', said the spirit-stricken lady, 'what think you of this dining out on the Lord's day – this playing on the harp; the carnal Mozarting of that ungodly family, with whom the corrupt nature of our friends has been chambered?' The minister was at some loss for an answer, and hesitated; but Miss Mally relieved him from his embarrassment, by remarking that 'the harp was a holy instrument', which somewhat troubled the settled orthodoxy of Mrs Glibbans's visage. 'Had it been an organ' said Mr Snodgrass drily, 'there might have been, perhaps, more reason to doubt; but, as Miss Mally justly remarks, the harp has been in use from the days of King David in the performance of sacred music, together with the psalter and the cymbal.' The wrath of the polemical Deborah was somewhat appeased by this explanation, and she enquired in a more diffident tone whether a Mozart was not a metrical paraphrase of the song of Moses after the overthrow of the Egyptians in the Red Sea...[5]

Along with heresy and the breaking of the Sabbath, sexual misdemeanour was the capital offence in the eyes of true-bred Presbyterians. As late as the end of the 18th century in small towns the customary way of dealing with that was the so-called stool of repentance or 'cutty stool': the erring couple (or the woman alone, if she refused to reveal the man's name) had to stand in church in full sight of the congregation while the preacher, from the pulpit, reproached and exhorted them to penitence. *Annals of the Parish* describes one such occasion when the behaviour of the man who had got a girl with child amusingly reveals the growing discontent with the humiliating practice:

> We had the girl summoned [...] and made her confess that the father was Nichol Snipe, Lord Glencairn's gamekeeper; and both her and Nichol were obligated to stand in the Kirk; but Nichol was a graceless reprobate, for he came with two coats, one buttoned behind him, and another buttoned before him, and two wigs of my lord's, lent him by the valet-de-chambre; the one over his face, and the other in the right way; and he stood with his face to the church wall. When I saw him from the pulpit, I said to him, 'Nichol, you must turn your face towards me!' At the which, he turned about to be sure, but there he presented the same show as his back. I was confounded, and did not know what to say, but cried out with a voice of anger, 'Nichol, Nichol! if you had been all back, you wouldna hae been there this day;' which had such an effect on the whole congregation, that the poor fellow suffered afterwards more derision, than if I had rebuked him in the manner prescribed by the session.[6]

This occurs early in *The Annals*, in 1764; forty years later the minister relates how the practice came to be discontinued:

> In conformity with the altered fashions of the age, the session came to an understanding with me, that we should not inflict the common church censures for such as made themselves liable to them; but we did not formally promulge our resolutions, wishing as long as possible to keep the deterring rod over the heads of the young and thoughtless. Our motive, on the one hand, was the disregard of the manufacturers of Cayenneville, who were an irreligious people; and on the other, a desire to preserve the ancient and wholesome admonitory and censorian jurisdiction of the ministers and elders. We therefore laid it down as a rule to ourselves that, in case of trasngression on the part of the inhabitants of the new district of Cayenneville, we should submit them rigorously to a fine; but that for the farming-lads, we would put it to their option to pay the fine, or stand in the kirk.[7]

Manufacturers *vs* farming-lads, paying of fine *vs* being shamed in front of the community, disregard *vs* acceptance of religious cen-

sure: there is still a contrast, but the hint about 'the altered fashions' suggests the minister knows that, eventually, even country
lads will adopt the outlook and behaviour of the factory workers,
at least in matters of private life. *The Ayrshire Legatees* shows that
around 1820 sexual trangressors were still summoned before the
elders, but in an informal discreet way, mostly aiming to bring
about a marriage when possible. Reverend Pringle from London
asks his substitute Mr Snodgrass to try and persuade Tam to marry
Meg so that their child can be 'admitted to church privileges', i.e.,
christened. This done, a benevolent elder suggests they sweeten
the pill to the reluctant father by paying for ceremony and chris-
tening-frock. Snodgrass agrees, quoting the Gospel command to
welcome the stranger, feed the hungry and clothe the naked. But
strait-laced and close-fisted Mr Craig objects:

> 'It's very true and sound what Mr Snodgrass has observed; but Tam
> Glen's child is neither a stranger, nor hungry, nor naked, but a sturdy
> brat, that has been running alone for more that six weeks.' 'Ah!' said Mr
> Snodgrass, familiarly, 'I fear, Mr Craig, you're a Malthusian in your heart.'
> The sanctimonious elder was thunder-struck at the word. Of many a vari-
> ous shade and modification of sectarianism he had heard, but the
> Malthusian heresy was new to his ears, and awful to his conscience; and
> he begged Mr Snodgrass to tell him in what it chiefly consisted [...] Mr
> Snodgrass seized with avidity the opportunity [...] we should do injustice
> to the philosophy of Malthus, if we suppressed the observation which Mr
> Daff made at the conclusion. 'God save us!' said the good-natured elder,
> 'if it's true that we breed faster then the Lord provides for us, we must
> drown the poor folks' babies like kittens.' 'Na, na!' exclaimed Mr Craig,
> 'you're all out, neighbour .– I see now the utility of church censures [...]
> the stool of repentance [...] is doubtless a Malthusian institution.'[8]

Besides Mr Craig's moralism and ignorance of contemporary issues,
Galt here exposes the wish of the ruling classes to repress the natural urges of the poor under colour of religious or scientific
motives, but in fact as a way to enforce a deeper discrimination
between social orders. That the 'carnality' of the poor and ignorant
is of a different cast from that of well-to-do righteous people,
becomes evident when it turns out that Mr Craig himself has
entered an 'irregular marriage' with his housekeeper. Mrs Glibbans
is outraged: 'a man so gifted wi' the power of the Spirit, as I hae
often had a delightful experience! [...] She shouldna be spairt. Nae

doubt, the fault lies with her.'[9] Incensed against the low-born woman, she voices the antifeminist double standard in sexual matters. But she, too, has desires to satisfy, as appears when the newly married wife dies in childbirth:

> She was taken, as Mrs Glibbans observed on the occasion, from the earthly arms of her husband, to the spiritual bosom of Abraham, Isaac and Jacob, which was far better. But the baby survived; so that, what with getting a nurse, and the burial [...] Mr Craig declared that he could not do without Mrs Glibbans; and she, with all that christianity by which she was so zealously distinguished, sent for her daughter, and took up her abode with him, till it would please Him, without whom there is no comfort, to wipe the eyes of the pious elder. In a word, she stayed so long that a rumour began to spread that Mr Craig would need a wife to look after his bairn; and that Mrs Glibbands was destined to supply the desideratum.[10]

It was probably owing to his frank allusions to homely facts like 'birth and copulation and death' that Galt was taxed with vulgarity by the more genteel Scott, Lockhart, Susan Ferrier. His works were often pruned, and in the case of *The Last of the Lairds* shamelessly mutilated, to please an age that was already prudish long before Victoria. No romancer, but an honest observer of human mores in real times and places, how could Galt ignore that sexual passion is not the exclusive province of the young and fair? or that, on the other hand, in real life love has to contend with other drives such as pride and avarice?

The protagonist of *The Entail*, perhaps his masterpiece, is a man obsessed by the thought that his ancestors had lost their estate, who disinherits his first born son (causing his premature death) in order to entail a larger property on the mentally retarded second son, whom the maternal grandfather has already made his heir. This tale of sordid feelings and belated repentance nevertheless teems with life, thanks to figures at once repulsive and attractive, like 'the Leddy', the protagonist's wife (a favourite with Byron), and her son Wattie, the 'natural' in whom foolishness and occasional shrewdness, soft-heartedness and malice are strangely but convincingly mixed. If in *Annals* Meg Gaffaw, comical in life and pathetic in death, owed something to Madge Wildfire of *The Heart of Midlothian*, Wattie is far more credible than the Davie Gellatly of

Waverley. These characters, of course, have no chance against the cool logic of modern times. The industrialist Mr Cayenne wants to let the dogs loose on poor Meg, who has fallen unaccountably in love with his daughter's appointed husband. Claud's astute youngest son George has Wattie certified *non compŏs mentis* and succeeds to the property. Only with the third generation will the heir of the firstborn recover the inheritance, thanks to the old Leddy's pride in her knowledge of legal matters.

Another born loser is the hero of *The Last of the Lairds*: besides being a 'natural', he is a remnant of feudal days, and he is done out of his lands by Mr Rupee, the representative of those Scots who, having done well in India (sometimes by extortionate methods), on their return could buy landed estates from lairds who had been unable to catch up with the changed agricultural and economic system. Galt has a dry laugh at the opulent nabob, whose villa is the emblem of bad taste and an outrage against the Scottish landscape:

> The lodges at the gate were built in the style of pagodas [...] The court of offices were in the purest style of classic architecture [...] The [...] mansion of the Burrah Sahib, was a splendid compilation of whatever had been elegant in antique, curious in gothic, or gorgeous in Oriental architecture. It was a volume of elegant extracts...

The narrator is shown into a room one entire end of which is occupied with a picture representing a tiger hunt:

> in the background an enormous tiger almost as big as a Kilkenny cat was returning into the jungle with a delicate, dandyish officer of the governor's guard in his mouth.[11]

The blithe megalomania of the nabob does not label him as a fool or villain, however. Galt hardly ever makes a character totally detestable (apart perhaps from certain lawyers). Not only is he thoroughly alien to the snobbery often manifested by Scott and Lockhart, but he can always steer clear of melodrama as well as of sentimentalism, thanks to his capacity to light up, side by side, mean and likeable aspects of ordinary people. The nabob is a parvenu and a tiresome talker and a keen unscrupulous businessman, but not so dishonest as to defraud an orphan boy of his rights; Mrs Soorocks is an insufferable busybody, but also a person of incredible vitality who does help her neighbours, as well as torment them with her indiscretions; the laird is a meanly-spirited body, yet he has moments of simple pathos; for example when, just after hearing the news of his imminent ruin, he questions all the assumptions of the new world, that rejects him and his like as fossils from the past:

As he walked along the dank unmowed grass, he paused suddenly, and stooping forward, he pulled a rose.
'It's my ain yet', said he with a smile, as he turned round and smelling it, held it out toward me.
'It has grown in my forefathers' land', he added, 'I got the slip from Castlesemple Gardens – I set it myself – I made the hole for it with my ain very finger – I watered it with the china jug that was my father's punch porringer, as I hae heard my kind mother say – and what can be a man's ain, if that bush and bud be na mine?'
Then he moved some four or five paces, and tearing the flower into pieces he scattered the petals around...[12]

An impossible dream of 'natural' rights, where a man's property is just what he brings to blossom with his own hands, hovers for a moment in the air like a question, and then is scattered like the petals of that rose. Progress must go on, the 'survival of the fittest' way. That was the lesson Galt had read in the history of his country; but this did not prevent his keeping a tender spot in his heart for the quaint old ways of the old world.

NOTES

[1] A.J. Ashley, 'Coleridge on Galt', *TLS*, 27 September 1930, p. 757.
[2] K.A. Costain, 'The Community of Man: Galt and Eighteenth-Century Scottish Realism', *Scottish Literary Journal,* vol. 8, no. 1, 1981, p. 17.
[3] John Galt, *Annals of the Parish*, edited by James Kinsley, Oxford: Oxford University Press, 1986, pp. 204-205.
[4] John Galt, *The Member*, edited by Ian Gordon, Edinburgh: Scottish Academy, 1975, pp. 117-118.
[5] John Galt, *The Ayrshire Legatees*, Edinburgh: James Thin, 1978, p. 55.
[6] John Galt, *Annals*, cit., pp. 29-30.
[7] *Ibidem*, p. 183.

[8] John Galt, *Ayrshire Legatees*, cit., pp. 43-44.

[9] *Ibidem*, p. 80.

[10] *Ibidem*, pp. 132-133.

[11] John Galt, *The Last of the Lairds*, edited by Ian Gordon, Edinburgh: 1976, pp. 64-66.

[12] *Ibidem*.

RICHARD AMBROSINI

R.L. Stevenson as Theorist and Popular Author: The Art of Writing and the Pleasure of Reading [1]

Robert Louis Stevenson owes his enduring popularity to *Treasure Island* (1883) and *Dr. Jekyll and Mr. Hyde*. Reprinted over and over again, and adapted for the cinema or the television, these two works have ended up subsuming within the categories of children's literature or the horror-story *de auteur* a literary output which fills over thirty volumes. The bracing adventure tale and the tortured investigation into the double in man, moreover, have proved too difficult to reconcile within one single artistic project. As a result, the existence itself of such a project has been denied altogether – and the many questions raised by the pleasure Stevenson's fiction continues to induce, over one hundred years after they were written, left unanswered.

The view that a writer who purports to entertain his readers must by definition be oblivious of any theoretical concerns is a legacy of the twentieth century.[2] The critical status of authors such as Virginia Woolf, Joseph Conrad, or James Joyce remains undisputed precisely because they are credited with having contributed to transform the novel into a theoretically informed artistic artifact. Nobody would even dream of claiming today that they are 'popular' – an adjective which comes natural instead, when we think of Stevenson.[3] And yet, it is interesting that Conrad himself once wrote: 'When it comes to popularity I stand much nearer the public mind than Stevenson, who was super-literary; a conscious virtuoso of style'.[4] He is right. Absolutely nothing in Stevenson's upbringing and early career suggests that he could ever seek popularity. Scion of a distinguished Edinburgh dynasty of engineers, throughout his life he remained a true-blood Tory, and when in his mid-twenties he 'came into his fantastic critical and popular prominence',[5] the celebrity he attained was marked by definite class connotations. His first travel book, *An Inland Voyage* (1878), was adopted at Eton for translations from English into Latin, and a society at Oxford chose the same slim volume as 'the "best specimen of the writing of English of this century"'.[6] This success, however, left him dissatisfied. And this because he 'longed to be something more than the darling of a literary set', what he called being 'a literary cherub – a head and a pair of wings, with nothing to sit down upon'.[7] *Treasure Island* seemed to give him the chance to break free from this artificial position, but the story appealed only to an élite of readers, among whom was the Prime Minister, William Gladstone. When the American painter, J.S. Sargent wrote to Stevenson to tell him that Gladstone '[talked] all the time about *Treasure Island*', he was almost annoyed, and replied: 'he would do better to attend the imperial affairs of England'.[8] And when another of his friends passed on the same piece of literary gossip to him, he commented: 'As for respecting... that fatuous rabble of burgesses called "the public", God save us from such irreligion; that way lies disgrace and dishonour. There must be something wrong in me, or I would not be popular'.[9] Little did he know at the time what it meant to be popular: one week later, *Dr. Jekyll and Mr. Hyde* appeared, and sold 40,000 copies in the first few months – a huge number, for him, but nothing for a truly popular author. Propelled by this success, the following year he arrived in the United States, where he was lionized by the popular press. He fled to a log cabin in upstate New York, close to the Canadian border, and was naive enough to torture himself over what he felt were the 'princely sums' he was being offered by American publishers. In fact, his American agent later confessed in his memoirs that for any established American author those sums would have been nothing but 'peanuts'.[10]

Obviously, we need to clarify what we mean by 'popular' before applying it to Stevenson, and a good way to start is to look up the word in the *Oxford English Dictionary*. Here are the main definitions: 'Plebeian; Adapted to the understanding, tastes, or means of ordinary people; Designed to gain the favour of the common people; favourite, acceptable, pleasing.' Leaving aside the horribly condescending tone of these dictionary entries, we find in them terms which can contribute to an understanding of Stevenson's life and works: 'pleasing', of course, but also 'designed to gain the favour of the common people'. His artistic project evolved from an investigation into the correlation between the pleasure he himself derived from creating a work of art, and the pleasure he could induce in the reader. When he became a novelist, it was the aesthetic and ethical implications of the creation of pleasure which motivated his search for a fiction of universal effectiveness. And we do not need to check the *Oxford Dictionary* to know that 'universal' includes, in addition to the British Prime Minister, the 'common people' – and children.

In Stevenson's numerous collections of essays, as well as in the eight volumes of his collected letters, we find a plurality of statements on art and literature, which reflects the variety of his narrative production. One particular definition of 'theory' can be found in a letter to Henry James written from Samoa in which Stevenson informs his friend about his difficulties in giving a representation of the South Seas. Imagine, he tells him, writing a book, while continually revising one's opinions. Very soon, he fears,

> I shall have no opinions left. And without an opinion, how to string artistically vast accumulations of fact? Darwin said no one could observe without a theory; I suppose he was right, 'tis a fine point of metaphysic; but I will take my oath, no man can write without one – at least the way he would like to.[11]

After a century in which so many artists have invoked every sort of dogma, political creed, or intellectual fashion to justify their works, it is refreshing to find an author who claims that theory is needed to write 'the way he would like to'. But more importantly, this formulation captures the key note of a life characterized by a search for an ever greater freedom of expression, in France, America and the Pacific. Let's forget the romantic myth built around Stevenson's travels. His first long stay in France coincided with the first exhibition of the Impressionist painters; he lived for long periods in the United States at the beginning and the end of the 1880s, at a time when mass circulation newspapers – at the peak of their power to define public reality – were creating the new structure of celebrity and fame which made possible the forty-year love affair between America and that other master stylist cum popular author, Mark

Twain.[12] In the South Seas, Stevenson witnessed the effects of European colonization, and reacted by taking considerable personal risks to defend the Islanders' rights – something few other white men did, let alone literary purveyors of exotic stories. Stevenson lived through all these experiences, always searching, always testing and extending his art. And in doing so, rather than building one theory he reformulated over and over again concepts he had developed early on, during his literary apprenticeship.

The continuity underlying Stevenson's whole corpus can be viewed only by setting the few of his narrative works which are still read today within the context of his entire fictional and non-fictional production. His essays and letters, in particular, can help set up a perspective on his entire literary career – which covered a span of twenty one years, even though only the second half, after *Treasure Island*, is usually taken into consideration. He himself was the first to complain about this elision, but knew that there was nothing to do about it, because, as he wrote, 'I am well aware that my paymaster, the great public, regards what else I have written with indifference, if not aversion'; just the same, he felt the need to remind his readers that *Treasure Island*, 'was far, indeed, from being my first book, for I am not a novelist alone.'[13]

The question to be asked, then, is what were the dynamics which led Stevenson from being a celebrated essayist to becoming not simply a 'novelist', but a manipulator of sub-genres derived from popular literature – and later the creator of fictional and non-fictional works impossible to classify? Once these dynamics are uncovered, a certain set of theories emerge, which guided the essay-writing of the first half of his career and were reformulated once new experiences forced him to question the social composition of his ideal readership.

The first intimations of the artistic project which guided Stevenson's entire work can be found in the letters to his cousin, Bob, a promising young painter. Starting around 1868, when he was eighteen years old, Stevenson developed his early theories on writing, understandably out of comparisons between painting and literature. The theoretical premises of this particular view of writing found an ideal audience in the summer of 1873, when he met Sidney Colvin, one of the best known art critics of his time,

Professor of Fine Arts at Cambridge, and a friend of John Ruskin, Sir Edward Burne-Jones, and D.G. Rossetti. Colvin was instrumental in launching Stevenson on a literary career, introducing him into the London literary set, and helping him publish his first essay, 'Roads'. A few weeks later, Stevenson was 'ordered South' to recover from a nervous breakdown and various physical ailments, and left for Menton, at the time, 'the capital of the Riviera... for English invalids'.[14] Colvin joined him there for two long stays, between December 1873 and March 1874. We do not know what the twenty-three year old Scottish youth and the Cambridge Professor of Fine Arts talked about. What is certain, is that starting from that period we find in Stevenson's letters references to a new and very personal theory of literature.

The most illuminating document from this period is a letter in which Stevenson tells his mentor about the difficulties he is encountering in trying to apply to a short story the abstract principles of 'the realistic movement of the age'. The convention adopted, he explains, is so difficult, that 'I have to put out much that pleases me... without producing commensurate power of giving pleasure in the accomplished work'. There was however an alternative to 'realism' – and as a matter of fact he himself had hit upon it years before, when with his cousin Bob they had discussed about how to recreate a certain scene, through different media, words or colors. He then gives three examples of how he would use the interplay of lights and shadows, or describe stairs and doors only when someone is descending or passing through them: every detail, he writes, must be functional to keeping the reader's attention focused on 'the essential interest of the situation'.[15] His apprenticeship over, on the brink of his chosen profession, we find that his aim is to clearly capture a scene with a painter's eye, without having to conform to any dogmatic notion of realism – and at the same time bearing in mind that the pleasure felt by an artist in the act of creation must be transmuted into the pleasure of its receptor.

He is confident enough to end the letter by declaring: 'That is the best example of my theory that I can give'.[16] But as is often the case with Stevenson, his 'theory' was also influenced by stimuli he found in the culture he lived in at the time. In reacting to new ideas, he transformed them into principles which then guided his writing. After leaving the Riviera, on his way back to Scotland he stopped in Paris in the very same days when the first Impressionist exhibition was inaugurated. He did not visit it, but he most probably heard about it from Bob, who was living there at the time. And a few months later he used the adjective 'impressional' in his essay 'An Autumn Effect' to describe a natural scene, which he compares to 'a clever French landscape', as well as to 'a Japanese picture' (XXII, p. 112).

A first indication of the direction in which his 'theory' developed – guiding his metamorphosis from essayist to novelist – emerged in an essay, 'Notes on the Movements of Young Children', in which he argues that children's play exemplifies a beauty that turns 'upon consideration not really aesthetic', as well as 'an impulsive truth... that shows throughout all imperfection' (XXII, p. 98). (The same, of course, could be said about Impressionist paintings.) On July 15, 1874, in a letter to Colvin he explained that 'Notes' – together with his first essay, 'Roads' – marked the beginning of a project 'which dates from early at Mentone', when he envisaged a series of essays whose purpose was to stimulate 'a friendlier and more thoughtful way of looking about one', – without necessarily feeling, 'bound to drag about Art every time to make it suitable'.[17] The outline of this project becomes clearer in a third essay, 'On the Enjoyment of Unpleasant Places', which six weeks later he described as a sequel to the other two, conceived as 'a word in season as to aesthetic contentment and a hint to the careless to look around them for disregarded pleasures'. These three essays already made an interesting start to a personal aesthetic theory, and he announced that he would soon have ready 'a little budget of little papers all with this intention before them, call it ethical or aesthetic as you will.... Twelve or twenty such Essays... put together in a little book... Essays on the Enjoyment of the World: by Robert Louis Stevenson'.[18] The 'little book' never materialized. But the young writer's ethically founded refusal of all aesthetic conventions inspired him to create a literary prose both elegant and free of any explicit moral burden, through which he portrayed his reaction to nature and human life in his essays and travel books of the 1870s.

Later in his career, while he was revising *Treasure Island*,

Stevenson was consulted by a young painter who had sought his advice on how to become an artist. He replied: 'for any art think less of what pays, first of what pleases... Progress in art is made by learning to enjoy'.[19] He knew what he was talking about. His own 'progress in art' had evolved through continuous reformulations of the aesthetic and ethical implications of his wanting to instruct his readers in new ways to 'enjoy the world'. These reformulations had eventually become a theory about how to create pleasure through reading – and it was according to this theory that he was revising his pirate story for an adult readership. This 'progress' involved a number of risks for an upper-class writer like Stevenson, who had to adopt psychological strategies and narrative techniques derived from the sub-genres of popular literature in order to induce in the readers of his own class the pleasure-creating effect he aimed at. If he went ahead, and combined his artistic prose with sensational plots, it was in response to moral imperatives implicit in a second reference to a personal 'theory' that we find one month after the announcement of the twelve-essay project. One day in London, he wrote to a friend that after leaving her,

> I found an organ grinder in Russell Square playing to a child; and the simple fact that there was a child listening to him, that he was giving this pleasure, entitled him according to my theory, as you know, to some money; so I put some coppers on the ledge of his organ, without so much as looking at him.[20]

What is striking about this scene is that it contains all the evidence repeatedly invoked to build a case against Stevenson, the author who betrayed his artistic vocation writing stories for boys, only to make money. How different the scene appears, however, once the elements of a theory of pleasure begin to emerge. What has been mistaken for a commodification of Stevenson's art was in fact the result of his ethically-motivated openness toward the challenges posed by the publishing market. But he never allowed the market to dictate his ideals in writing. Though he may have been influenced by the desire to entertain, this does not mean that he compromised the artistic and moral integrity which guided his attempts to reach out to a wider public.

It was a shift in his notion of an author's responsibility towards his readers that prompted him to invest with a new significance his

notion of 'creating pleasure.' This happened as a consequence of
the most formative experience of his life: his trip to the United
States in the summer of 1879, when he left Edinburgh to rescue
Fanny, the American woman he had met in France, who had been
forced by her husband to return to California. It was not going to
be a holiday on the French Riviera. He could not count on his
father's money, and had to travel in the steerage of an emigrant
ship. (He never recovered from this voyage and the continental
crossing aboard an emigrant train: his tuberculosis was diagnosed
for the first time in San Francisco, and ever after he led the life of a
chronic invalid.)

This voyage marked for Stevenson an exit from his previous
social sphere. In the *Amateur Emigrant*, the book he wrote about
this experience, he recorded his discovery of the 'Labouring
mankind', of their misery and their nobility, which, he wrote, 'I had
never represented... livingly to my imagination' (XV, pp. 11-12).
One episode, in particular, reveals how the transatlantic crossing
marked a turning point in the implications of 'creating pleasure.'
One day, as he entered the steerage, he saw that a

> white-faced Orpheus was cheerily playing to an audience of white-faced
> women. It was as much as he could do to play, and some of his hearers
> were scarce able to sit; yet they had crawled from their bunks at the first
> experimental flourish, and found better than medicine in the music...
> Humanly speaking, it is a more important matter to play the fiddle, even
> badly, than to write huge works upon recondite subjects. What could Mr.
> Darwin have done for these sick women? But this fellow scraped away;
> and the world was positively a better place for all who heard him. (XV,
> pp. 20-21)

Colvin and his other London friends were scandalized by the 'lurk-
ing subversive classlessness'[21] of *Amateur Emigrant*, and tried in
every way to discourage him from writing it. But he not only went
ahead, he also claimed, to his friends W.E. Henley, that after writing on contemporary life, 'all [my] past work is nothing to me... I
am only beginning to see my method'.[22] And to Colvin he
announced that once *The Emigrant* was finished, 'I'll stick to stories... I know I shall do better work than ever I have done before...
My sympathies and interests are changed. There shall be no more
books of travel for me. I care for nothing but the moral and the

dramatic, not a jot for the picturesque or the beautiful, other than about people'.[23] What he meant by 'caring about people' becomes clear in a letter written a few days later to a Scottish Professor of Education:

> When I suffer in mind, stories are my refuge; I take them like opium; and I consider one who writes them as a sort of doctor of the mind. And frankly... it is not Shakespeare we take to, when we are in a hot corner; nor, certainly, George Eliot – no, nor even Balzac. It is... Old Dumas, or the Arabian Nights, or the best of Walter Scott. It is stories we want, not the high poetic function which represents the world... We want incident, interest, action.[24]

Rather than writing to show to the reader how to look at the world to extract pleasure from it, from now on he would have struggled to create fictional worlds which would give pleasure to flesh and blood human beings he respects, and with whom he shares both sufferings and pleasures.

It is no coincidence that Stevenson began his first novel only after living in America. (He returned to Europe on August 17, 1880, and by August 25, 1881 he was already working on *Treasure Island*.) This breakthrough was not only a consequence of his discovering that the 'Unknown Public'[25] of the consumers of popular literature were not an anonymous mass, but individuals with common needs and aspirations. It was his having witnessed in the U.S. the growing power of the nascent mass media that made it impossible for him to return to a condition in which, as he wrote in a letter, 'we all live in a clique, buy each other's books and like each other's books; and the great, gaunt, gray, gaping public snaps its big fingers and reads Talmage and Tupper'.[26]

The American lesson prompted him, early in 1881, to write an essay – 'The Morality of the Profession of Letters' – in which we find a moral urgency unknown up to that moment in his public voice. In these days of daily papers, he writes: 'The total of a nation's reading... greatly modifies the total of the nation's speech; and the speech and reading, taken together, form the efficient educational medium of youth'. Whether we seek to please or to instruct, he adds, it is a moral duty for all practitioners of 'the art of words' to contrast the 'incalculable influence for ill' and the 'public falsehood' represented by journalism. The 'American reporter or the Parisian chroniquer', are not for him 'so much baser' than English journalists, but are much more dangerous: it is because they are 'so much more readable' that 'their evil is done more effectively, in America for the masses, in [France] for the few that care to read'. The remedy he has to offer is contained in his injunction to choose, for one's stories, only facts which are 'eternally more necessary than others... [and]... more interesting to the natural mind of man' (XXII, pp. 278-281) – endowed, that is, with an effectiveness which transcends class and age.

Four months later, in August 1881, while spending the summer in a cottage in the Highlands, Stevenson wrote to Henley to announce that he was working on the story which then became *Treasure Island*. This must certainly have been a 'progress in art', since he declares: 'It's awful fun boy's stories, you just indulge the pleasure of your heart, that's all'. The story – we learn from this letter – was not addressed to boys: he had a particular publisher in mind, ideally suited for the project, and provokes his friend, by asking: 'would you be surprised to hear, in this connection, the name of *Routledge*?'[27] – at the time a by-word for literary mass-production, following the great success of their 'Railway Library', a series of cheap reprints aimed at commuters.

The story of how the pirate story intended for Routledge was first conceived has often been told, but is worth recalling, in this context. One morning, in the cottage, to entertain his bored twelve-year old stepson, Stevenson drew the map of an island in watercolors. The painted image ignited his own fancy, and he started adding names to mountains, beaches and coves. There is no need to invoke comparisons between painting and writing to describe what was happening: in watching an ideal locus for adventure taking shape, he was transforming the game into an experiment in how to communicate, to an audience, 'the pleasure of your heart'. The otherwise fastidious author, started writing a chapter a day, using his stepson as a guinea-pig (it was the kid who decreed: 'No women in the story'!.[28] In the evening, the entire family met around the fireplace, and his father, a redoubtable sixty-three-year-old engineer, was 'caught at once with all the romance and childishness of his original nature' (II, p. xv). The result of this experiment was a tale in which the author, resorting to his own experience as a reader – and drawing on the lessons of his American experience – tried to reach out to a mass-readership, after the immediate enthusiastic participatory response of the flesh-and-blood audience he had available in the cottage in the Highlands. (Unfortunately, a few weeks later the circle of readers was joined by a flesh-and-blood critic, the first of a long series who classified *Treasure Island* as a 'boys' tale'. If the pirate story was sent to 'Young Folks' – and not to Routledge – it was because this critic heard the writer reading a chapter to the congregated family, and – transforming the game into reality – offered to bring the fifteen chapters written so far to the juvenile paper's editor, who was a friend of his.)

Whatever intention the author had when he began the story in August 1881, the text as we know it today was published in book form two years later, on November 14, 1883, after a long revision. Fortunately, we can retrace what the author had in mind in preparing the version intended for an adult readership. In the very same days in which he committed himself to proceed with the revision of *Treasure Island*, he was asked to write an essay;[29] thus, he had an opportunity to explain to the public of his essays, travel books, and first short stories why he had adopted a particular sub-genre for his first novel. In this essay, 'A Gossip on Romance', we find many of the themes and ideas formulated in the 1870s. And significantly, in underlining the continuity between his earlier works and his first experiment with the novel-form, Stevenson gave particular emphasis to the way in which his former theory of pleasure had become in the meanwhile a reading-model. 'Gossip' opens with a description of what the act of reading should be like:

> In anything fit to be called by the name of reading the process itself should be absorbing and voluptuous; we should gloat over a book, be rapt clean out of ourselves, and rise from the perusal, our mind filled with the busiest, kaleidoscopic dances of images, incapable of sleep or continuous thought. The words, if the book be eloquent, should run thenceforward in our ears like the noise of breakers, and the story, if it be a story, repeat itself in a thousand coloured pictures to the eye. It was for this last pleasure that we read so closely, and loved our books so dearly, in the bright, troubled period of boyhood. (XIII, p. 327)

The kaleidoscopic dances of images, the thousand colored pictures: this description of the act of reading constitutes an historical document of the creative tension felt by an artist who could not count on special effects, computer-created images. He only had words available, and to allow the reader to escape from reality, and travel in fantasy, identifying with a projected image of oneself, indeed they had to resonate in the ear like the noise of breakers.

Starting from this description of the reading process, Stevenson unravels a complex argument which leads him to postulate a reader-response psychology built around mechanisms based on the pleasure of reading. The great creative writers, he claims, are those who show us 'the realisation and the apotheosis of the day-dreams of common men' (XIII, p. 332). These day-dreams have nothing to do with the 'self-fulfilling stories of the pulp magazines'; rather, they are 'bridges between experience and desire'.[30] The difference lies, as usual in Stevenson, in the quality of the writing, which he describes – characteristically – as the 'pictorial or picture-making romance... [which is] not only the highest art possible in words, but the highest art of all, since it combines the greatest mass and diversity of the elements of truth and pleasure' (XIII, p. 335). But he is not thinking of the Impressionist writing of his essays. He is invoking what is for him the fundamental premise for creating an universal effect through words: the creation of 'epoch-making scenes' – such as, 'Crusoe recoiling from the footprint, Achilles shouting over against the Trojans, Ulysses bending the great bow'. Each one of these scenes, 'has been printed on the mind's eye forever', because it has 'put the last mark of truth upon a story [filling] up, at one blow, our capacity for sympathetic pleasure'. Time, he adds, cannot 'efface or weaken the impression' (XIII, p. 332). This, he concludes, is 'the highest and hardest thing to do in words', but once accomplished it 'equally delights the schoolboy and the sage, and makes, in its own right, the quality of epics' (XIII, p. 333). This is the word he was driving at.

'A Gossip on Romance' is crucial to an understanding of both Stevenson the theorist and the 'popular author'. Critics who have tried to assess his ideas on literature have recognized its importance, along with that of another essay, 'A Humble Remonstrance', which he wrote after *Treasure Island* was published to defend his use of a sub-genre associated with juvenile fiction. Since

Stevenson's name is most readily associated with adventures for boys, however, these two essays have been construed as being the sum total of Stevenson's theoretical thinking – and as profound as the psychology of a pasteboard pirate. We ought to reject this view, which has become a caricature when one particular phrase from 'Gossip' has been cited to put a seal on Stevenson's reputation as a children's writer: 'Fiction is to the grown man what play is to the child'. As a matter of fact, this comparison is only the beginning of a sentence which then proceeds to explain that only in fiction the grown man, 'changes the atmosphere and tenor of his life; and when the game so chimes with his fancy that he can join in it with all his heart, when it pleases him with every turn, when he loves to recall it and dwells upon the recollection with entire delight, fiction is called romance' (XIII, p. 340). Once set in the context of an argument culminating in the invocation of 'epics', the fiction/play comparison means in fact that fiction can express all its evocative power only if it touches something ancestral, common to all humanity. The reading-model set forth in 'Gossip' was founded on a pleasure which was 'infantile' only in the sense of primordial.

The repeated qualifications he offers in 'Gossip' of what he means by 'romance' constitute a vindication of how successful he had been in applying to a narrative in prose the theories which up to that point had guided his essay-writing. The pride he could feel in having accomplished this transition can be fully understood if we return to the winter of 1874, when in Menton Stevenson conceived the project of twelve essays on 'the Enjoyment of the World'. In those very same months, he was also articulating the rudiments of ideas which would later become his theory of fiction. It is a striking confirmation of the continuity underlying his artistic project, to find that in a book-review written in those months, he argued that the short-story form was in fact nothing else than a post-Darwinian version of classical fable. Even more importantly, in his essay on 'the movements of young children' the children's play is not only offered as an example of a beauty free from conventions but is also described as a 'reminiscence of primitive festivals and the Golden Ages' (XXII, p. 98). If child psychology was instrumental in advancing a model for an adult reader's response to literature, it was because it could explain how to bring new life to myths, by reaching down to the deepest, atavistic components of narrative.

These may appear to be hints and elliptical suggestions, but in fact they are indications of Stevenson's view of the potentialities implicit in narrative fiction. He gave to this view definite theoretical connotations when while staying in Menton he was offered an opportunity to address, for the first time, a public of intellectuals and literati. Victor Hugo's latest novel, *Ninety Three*, had just appeared, and Stevenson was asked to review it for the prestigious 'Cornhill Magazine'. As it turned out, however, only eleven out of the twenty eight pages of the essay he wrote, 'Victor Hugo's Romances', deal with the French master's works. The others are devoted instead to suggesting possible further developments for the nineteenth-century novel – developments which happen to coincide with what Stevenson proposed to realize himself. (To what extent he hijacked the review to voice his own ideas, is revealed when he makes quite clear that if it was up to him he would have chosen an American champion of the romance, Nathaniel Hawthorne.) The essay begins, by outlining a transnational history of the novel, alternative to the English line linking Henry Fielding to the Victorian 'novel with a purpose'. The purpose of this personal genealogy is to demonstrate that romance had progressed from Scott to Hugo following an ever-increasing artistic self-awareness; and as to what the next step may be, this Stevenson makes clear by choosing for the essay's epigraph a passage in which Victor Hugo envisages a future in which, 'After the picturesque but prosaic novel of Walter Scott, another kind of novel remains to be created... picturesque but poetic, real but ideal, true but grandiose, which will set Walter Scott alongside Homer'.[31]

Having announced, in his first literary essay, that he is the ideal candidate as Sir Walter Scott's successor, the twenty-three-year old who had so far published only one essay switches to the first person to address directly his readers. He begins by suggesting that literary criticism has until then found great difficulties in defining the 'artistic result of a romance, what is left upon the memory by any really powerful and artistic novel'. And – of course – he invokes a comparison between painting and writing to overcome these difficulties, describing this artistic result as an 'impression'. He then declares: 'in the present study... I propose chiefly... to throw in relief... this idea which underlies and issues from a romance, this something which it is the function of that form of art to create, this epical value' (XIV, pp. 25-26). In reading 'Victor Hugo's Romance', one understands why in 'A Gossip on Romance' Stevenson argued that the 'impression' created through 'epoch-making scenes' can contribute to fiction 'the quality of epics'. And when we think that in the earlier essay he had also specified, 'epical value is not to be found... in every so-called novel', we find an explanation for the crucial choice which marked his entire career: he wrote adventurous romances, rather than realistic psychological novels, because he was convinced this was the most elevated path toward artistic expression in prose narrative.[32] If Stevenson became a 'popular author,' it was because – given the cultural and historical conditions of his times – this was the only way open to him to reach the universal source of every literary form, and develop the myth-making potentials of fiction.

This is why we should not become defensive when we are told that Stevenson does not belong among the 'great English novelists.' He was the first to feel he was not only a 'novelist': he was more than that, he was a polygraphic craftsman of words; and even less did he consider himself 'English,' having adopted as forefathers a Scotsman (Scott), a Frenchman (Hugo), and an American (Hawthorne); and, finally, he did all he could to avoid becoming 'great,' experimenting with the sub-genres of popular literature, contaminating his pure prose with sensational plots – and thus contradicting that hierarchy of literary forms which later critics have taught us to considered as 'natural.'

One year before he died, Stevenson started writing an essay in which he went back to when, in his childhood, he first discovered the power of words – which dawned on him, in listening to his nurse recite aloud, with her strong Scottish accent, the Bible and the Psalms. The pleasure he derived from words, however, was unconscious: he followed whatever was read to him, listening for 'news of the great vacant world upon whose edge [he] stood', eager, he recalls, 'for delightful plots that I might re-enact in play' (XXII, p. 440). As it is already obvious, Stevenson is retracing here the steps which led him to construct his own artistic identity. The next step came when he passed 'from hearing literature to reading it' – for him, 'a kind of second weaning'. He is thinking of a particular spot in time: an evening, when alone in the woods he pulled out a book of fairy tales; 'the shock of that pleasure', he writes, 'I have never since forgot, and if my mind serves me to the last, I never shall; for it was then that I knew I loved reading' (XXII, p. 441).

The essay remained unfinished, and we do not know what conclusion Stevenson would have reached, given his stated intention to investigate, 'by what hints and premonitions, the consciousness of the man's art dawns first upon the child' (XXII, p. 436). A possible indication is provided however by the verse from a short poem by Horace contained in title – 'Random Memories: Rosa Quo Locorum'. It is a revealing choice. In the poem, the Latin poet imagines he is sitting under a bower in a vineyard. He orders only some wine, and enjoins the youth who is serving him not to embellish the table in the fashion of the Persians, with wreaths of intertwined lime tree boughs: there is no use, he adds, to go in search for the places where the tardy rose blossoms – the '*rosa quo locorum/Sera moretur*' [*Odes*, I.xxxviii. 3-4]). Set at the end of his first book of *Odes*, this scene signals Horace's leave-taking from his readers, in which he reaffirms his love for simple things as well as his fidelity to the Muse who has inspired him to sing not of weighty matters but of convivial banquets and fleeting passions.

It was not a Muse who inspired Stevenson to treat apparently 'simple' matters: it was a personal poetics of fiction, which led him to test the universality of his own pleasure of reading by drawing on his experience as a sickly child whose longing for life could find an outlet only in reading Scott, *The Arabian Nights* and Dumas. In doing so, he who was the most elegant stylist of his times, broke every conventional notion of literary decorum. But it was worth doing, because the modern myths he thus created have endured, as popular and resonant of meanings as ever. Indeed, simple epics.

Horace's 'simple' poetry was cherished by Caesar Augustus, who in any case could count on Virgil to have his family's origin traced back to Homer. Nineteen centuries later, William Gladstone carried upon his shoulders the weight of an even larger dominion, and had enough writers more than willing to praise him. And yet, he was happy to take one night away from the cares of the British Empire, and enjoy *Treasure Island*. Two thousand years have been enough to get rid of senseless comparisons between Horace and Virgil. Let's hope that Robert Louis Stevenson will not have to wait so long.

Notes

1 From *Robert Louis Stevenson Reconsidered: New Critical Perspective*. Copyright 2003 W.B. Jones Jr., by permission of McFarland & Company, Inc., Box 611, Jefferson, NC 28640. www.mcfarlandpub.com

2 See Jeremy Hawthorn, *A Concise Glossary of Contemporary Literary Theory*, London: Arnold, 1998 (3rd ed.), p. 175: 'The attitude of literary critics towards pleasure can perhaps be compared to that of [Marxists] towards sartorial fashion: during the present century they seem never to have been quite sure whether or not they approve of it, but on the balance they do not. Freud's *pleasure principle* dominated the new-born infant, but in the maturing or mature individual was placed under the sway of the *reality principle*, regaining its sway only in fantasy or day-dreaming'.

3 The *MLA Bibliography* lists, for the years 1963-2000, 384 entries on R.L.S, 6552 on Joyce, 3193 on Conrad, and 2747 on Woolf. How crucial for a writer's status is the perception of his or her being also a theoretician is amply illustrated by the number of essays dedicated to Umberto Eco since the publication of *Il nome della rosa* (1980): 430, that is fifty more than those written on Stevenson in forty years.

4 Frederick Karl and Laurence Davies eds., *The Collected Letters of Joseph Conrad*, Cambridge: Cambridge University Press, 1986*, V, p. 257.

5 Travis R. Merritt, 'Taste, Opinion, and Theory in the Rise of Victorian Prose Stylism', in George Levine and William Madden eds., *The Art of Victorian Prose*, New York: Oxford University Press, 1968, p. 27.

6 Paul Maixner ed., *Robert Louis Stevenson: The Critical Heritage*, London: Routledge and Kegan Paul, 1981, p. 8.

7 Quoted in Bradford A. Booth and Ernst Mehew eds., *The Letters of Robert Louis Stevenson*, New Haven, CT, and London: Yale University

Press, 1995, III, p. 278, note 11.

[8] *Ibidem*, V, p. 49.

[9] *Ibidem*, V, p. 171.

[10] Frank McLynn, *Robert Louis Stevenson: A Biography*, London: Hutchinson, 1993, p. 281.

[11] Bradford A. Booth and Ernst Mehew eds., *The Letters of Robert Louis Stevenson*, cit., VII, pp. 65-66.

[12] Emory Elliott (general editor), *Columbia Literary History of the United States*, New York: Columbia University Press, p. 633.

[13] Robert Louis Stevenson, 'My First Book – "Treasure Island"', in *The Thistle Edition of the Works of Robert Louis Stevenson*, New York: Charles Scribner's Sons, 1924, II, p. ix. All quotations from Stevenson's work are from this edition.

[14] William Pemble, *The Mediterranean Passion: Victorian and Edwardians in the South*, Oxford: Oxford University Press, 1987, pp. 86-87.

[15] Valerie Shaw, in *The Short Story: A Critical Introduction*, London: Longman, 1983, p. 35, points out how Stevenson employed these three principles in his first short story, 'A Lodging for the Night'.

[16] Bradford A. Booth and Ernst Mehew eds., *The Letters of Robert Louis Stevenson*, cit., I, pp. 476-477.

[17] *Ibidem*, II, p. 32.

[18] *Ibidem*, II, p. 43.

[19] *Ibidem*, III, p. 333.

[20] *Ibidem*, II, pp. 59-60.

[21] Frank McLynn, *op. cit.*, p. 165.

[22] Bradford A. Booth and Ernst Mehew eds., *The Letters of Robert Louis Stevenson*, cit., III, pp. 55-56.

[23] *Ibidem*, III, pp. 59-60.

[24] *Ibidem*, III, pp. 61-62.

[25] Wilkie Collins, 'The Unknown Public', 'Household Worlds', XVIII (August 21, 1858), p. 222. Cfr. Peter Keating, *The Haunted Study A Social History of the English Novel 1875-1914*, London: Fontana, 1989, pp. 401-402.

[26] Bradford A. Booth and Ernst Mehew eds., *The Letters of Robert Louis Stevenson*, cit., III, p. 297. Talmage and Tupper were, respectively, the compiler of a book of commonplaces entitled *Proverbial Philosophy* (1838-1842) and a popular American preacher.

[27] *Ibidem*, II, pp. 244-245.

[28] *Ibidem*, III, p. 225.

[29] *Ibidem*, III, pp. 276-279.

[30] David Daiches, *Robert Louis Stevenson: A Revaluation*, Norfolk, CT: New Direction Books, 1947, p. 26.

[31] 'Après le roman pittoresque mais prosaïque de Walter Scott il restera un autre roman à créer, plus beau et plus complet encore selon nous. C'est le roman, à la fois drame et epopée, pittoresque mais poétique, réel mais idéal, vrai mais grand, qui enchâssera Walter Scott dans Homère' (XIV, 17).

[32] Once in the South Seas, when he adopted a realistic mode of writing to portray the colonial scene of the Pacific, Stevenson found new motivations for defining his work as 'epic'. On December 5, 1892, Stevenson wrote to Henry James – his one-time opponent in the 1884 romance-realism *querelle* – that, 'You don't know what news is, nor what politics, nor what the life of man, till you see it on so small a scale and with your own liberty on the board for stake. I would not have missed it for much. And anxious friends beg me to stay at home and study human nature in Brompton drawing-rooms! And anyway you know that such is not my talent. I could never be induced to take the faintest interest in Brompton *qua* Brompton or a drawing-room *qua* a drawing-room. I am an Epick Writer with a k to it, but without the necessary genius' (*The Letters of Robert Louis Stevenson*, cit., VII, p. 449).

GIOIA ANGELETTI

John Davidson:
'The Great Poet is Always a Man Apart' [1]

In his review of G.G. Smith's *Scottish Literature: Character and Influence* (1919), T.S. Eliot seems to question the very existence of Scottish Literature by underlining, on the one hand, its lack of a continuing tradition based on a unified language and, on the other, the longstanding, incisive influence exerted on it by English literature. In particular, he identifies three stages in the development of a hypothetical Scottish literature:

> The first part of the history of Scottish literature is a part of the history of English literature when English was several dialects; the second part is a part of the history of English literature when English was two dialects – English and Scots; the third part is something quite different – it is the history of a provincial literature. [2]

The third part refers to the eighteenth-century Scottish Enlightenment and vernacular tradition, both centred in Edinburgh – the provincial capital, in Eliot's words. But sooner or later, he adds, 'the important men turn to the metropolis', which is an indirect allusion to what happened to many eminent Scottish writers in the following century. In the nineteenth century, John Davidson, James Thomson ('B.V.'), Thomas Carlyle, and R.L. Stevenson, among others, felt the magnetic attraction of the centre and thus left the Scottish province. Without directly referring to these 19th-century exiles, in his review Eliot unconsciously raises a crucial postcolonial question: in what sense and with what consequences can the provincial be incorporated into the central and metropolitan traditions?

John Davidson's literary achievement and his cultural and individual identity offer the reader of Scottish literature essential clues to an understanding of the predicament of Scottish writers in the

nineteenth century, when Anglicisation was a cultural phenomenon that they had to confront, either rejecting or embracing it. The
issues at stake were often much more complex than the language
question pointed out by Eliot – the split between Scots and English
as literary languages, and the gradual subjugation of the former by
the latter. The nineteenth-century convergence of literary and artistic forces on the British capital and the increasing sense that
Scotland was becoming a provincial place ruined by parochialism
gave rise to an identity problem experienced tragically by several
writers. The central dilemma was whether to restore this shattered
identity by rescuing the idea of a Scottish tradition – certainly fragmented, as Eliot suggests, but still lively and productive, as the
neglected poet James Young Geddes proved in provincial Dundee
– or to turn to the metropolitan and cosmopolitan tradition of
English literature. Both Davidson and Thomson, unlike Geddes,
chose the latter 'solution'.

Davidson moved to London in 1889, after spending his first thirty two years in Scotland. Strongly influenced as a young boy by his
father, a strict Evangelical minister, he gradually manifested an
independent and rebellious spirit in the context of all the varied
work roles he took on: the factory worker and the analyst's assistant in Greenock, the Glasgow clerk, and the schoolmaster in the
Glasgow area. He despised all these jobs equally, yet also learned
a lot from them, not least a deep understanding of the condition of
the social underdog, a figure who would recur frequently in his
best poetry. Although in London Davidson became a hack journalist for the most fashionable and prestigious journals, including *The
Yellow Book*, he lived as a perpetual outcast, despising both 'the
dour philistinism of Scotland and the fashionable languor of
London'.[3] The figure of the outsider, the wanderer and the hermit
are constant *topoi* of his works, from earlier poems, such as
'Thoreau' (*In a Music-Hall and Other Poems*, 1891) and 'The
Loafer' (*Ballads and Songs*, 1894), to his later long dramatic monologues – 'The Testament of a Man Forbid' (1901), for example,
begins with the key-statement 'Mankind has cast me out'.[4]

That Davidson was essentially 'a lad apairt',[5] a social and cultural outsider, both within the prevailing contemporary Scottish tradition – namely Kailyard Scotland – and the English cultural estab-

lishment is already evident in his works written before moving to London. If both the novel *The North Wall* (1885) and *Bruce: a Drama* (1886) clearly evince Davidson's early indebtedness to Scottish romance and the national epic tradition, though subject to his parodic revisions, in *Smith: A Tragic Farce* (1888) he endows the eponymous Byronic hero with a strong autobiographical element which looks ahead to his later tragic anti-heroes. Smith is Davidson's alter-ego essentially because he is a provincial genius who cannot and will not come to terms with the gentility of the establishment. He is a social misfit who fails to build a bridge between contemplative and active life-styles, and, unable to cope with this dilemma and the ensuing disruptive dualism of mind and body, he decides, unlike Hamlet, 'to take arms against a sea of troubles,/And by opposing end them'.

Smith is the first of the suicidal anti-heroes of Davidson's works. All of them inevitably lead one to investigate the causes of Davidson's own suicide on 23 March 1909 while he was supposedly recovering his health in Penzance, Cornwall. Both his poetic treatment of the suicide theme and his philosophical reflections upon it seem to confirm that there is a strong link between his ultimate tragic decision and his condition of exile, or, as Eliot defined himself, of 'Resident Alien' in English society.[6] In many of his poems, from the 'The Loafer' (1894) to 'The Testament of John Davidson' (1908), Davidson's idea of suicide is informed by Schopenhauer's conception of Will and by Ibsen's notion that morality arises naturally from the human spirit. Like the unorthodox preacher in Thomson's *The City of Dreadful Night* (1874), Davidson's *dramatis personae* are the spokesmen of the same motto – 'End it when you will'.[7] His alter ego par excellence, the protagonist of 'The Testament of John Davidson', sublimates in poetical words this tragic sense of the end:

> My feet are heavy now, but on I go,
>   My head erect beneath the tragic years.
> The way is steep, but I would have it so;
>   And dusty, but I lay the dust with tears,
> Though none can see me weep: alone I climb
> The rugged path that leads me out of time.[8]

Choosing to die was for Davidson both a manifestation of man's powerful self-consciousness and, in MacDiarmid's words, a way of escaping 'the horrible humility of mediocrity' which he had to endure in the estranging London establishment.[9] Davidson committed suicide because, as he wrote in the prefatory note to his last collection of poems, he felt 'The time ha[d] come to make an end':[10] after delivering his last idiosyncratic materialist credo in 'The Testament of John Davidson', he probably thought his mission on earth was accomplished. There is a disturbing megalomaniac and egotistical component in the later Davidson – especially in the series of the 'Testaments', his long narrative and dramatic monologues (1901-1908) – which becomes more acceptable if one associates it with his frustrations and his sense of displacement in the world.

Davidson embodied his claustrophobic sense of entrapment in the figure of the persecuted stag in the ballad 'A Runnable Stag' (*Holiday and Other Poems*, 1906). The magnificent, semi-mythical stag running away from the hunters during a chase, whose movement is impressively reproduced by the poem's galloping rhythm, is an image of the poet haunted by a society which tries to suffocate his artistic freedom by imposing its own codes. The final suicide of the stag – a sublime death in the sea – is the dramatisation of Davidson's own desire to find a way-out and escape from social and cultural restrictions, whereas in previous poems he expressed, though not without angst, his need of being accepted by the literati – as in the dramatic monologue of 'Ayrshire Jock' (*In a Music-Hall and Other Poems*, 1891). He continued to waver between these two opposite tendencies: a readiness to resist a dominant Anglocentricity and a yearning for literary success to defy the charge of provincialism hanging over the contemporary Scottish writing. An earlier personification of this tension is the character of John Baliol in the ballad 'John Baliol at Strathcathro' (*In a Music-Hall and Other Poems*, 1891). A kind of Scottish version of Richard II, Baliol resigns his Scottish crown to King Edward I but not his dignity and honesty – symbolically, he is the poet who respects and partly submits to the dominant English culture without abasing himself and his individual art.

Davidson's best works can be interpreted by means of a devolutionary reading which must take into account both his provincial origins and his writing from within the cultural centre without being totally integrated into it. As Kenneth Millard has demonstrated, this complex position of cultural ex-centricity was shared by many *fin-de-siècle* and modernist writers.[11] Davidson's, Conrad's, Eliot's, and Pound's 'otherness' from the English tradition was of a peculiar kind. More than they probably realised, they represented a provincial challenge to Anglocentricity by employing the English language and tradition while simultaneously challenging their cultural dominance (even the later MacDiarmid may be seen in this light). Thus Davidson's Scottishness was the essential 'foreign element', as Millard suggests,[12] enabling him to look at contemporary England with ironic *Verfremdung*, and to construct a subtle critique of its geographical, cultural and political assumptions.

Any analysis of Davidson's ambiguous relationship with England and the English literary tradition cannot leave aside what he himself saw as 'the adamantine axis of the universe', that is, irony.[13] Irony is taken by Davidson in its Fichtian philosophical meaning to justify his own contradictoriness and antithetical outlook, which of course also anticipates MacDiarmid's idea of 'antisyzygy' or conjunction of opposites. It is from this ironic stance that Davidson can, on the one hand, write that 'Socialism is the decadence of Feudalism [...] only a bad smell',[14] and, on the other hand, compose some of the most representative examples of what one may define as demotic and democratic poetry (like 'Thirty Bob a Week'). It is therefore through the filter of irony that one must read Davidson's 'Letter to the Peers Temporal of the United Kingdom of Great Britain and Ireland', the odd bombastic dedication to 'The Testament of John Davidson'.

From a postcolonial perspective, the letter is a piece of colonial history and a document addressing the questions of 'marginality', cultural imperialism and hybridity. Davidson wears the mask of the English imperialist to talk about three crucial contemporary sociopolitical questions: Ireland's independence, the Labour Question, and the Woman Question. As Thomson in *The City of Dreadful Night* speaks the language of Calvinism in order to subvert it, likewise one may see Davidson's identification with the English imperialist as an ironic device to attack the supporters of the imperial cause on their own cultural grounds. On the other hand, one can-

not disregard Davidson's opposite urge to see himself as a mouthpiece of the idea of Britishness in order to overcome his own
sense of ex-centricity. This ambivalent attitude also emerges in the
poem 'The Crystal Palace' (*Fleet Street and Other Poems*, 1908):
apparently he glorifies British imperialism through the image of the
exhibition centre, the 'Victorian temple of commercialism',[15] but
subtly he denounces the semantic void and the fragmented reality
of industrial Britain – a meaningless *bric-à-brac* of soulless things.

Perhaps one may connect Davidson's image of Scotland integrated into Britain with MacDiarmid's later appeal for a Scottish literature absorbing aspects from other cultures to become a world-liter-
ature overcoming its provincial status. Davidson's later works
should be read in this light; in them the poetic language itself
becomes an amalgam of heterogeneous jargons and 'foreign' elements. Yet the idea of Britishness as a way of looking at Scotland
from a broader perspective is already expressed in earlier poems.
The best example is 'A Ballad in Blank Verse of the Making of a
Poem' (*Ballads and Songs*, 1894).

Defying the conventions of the traditional ballad, Davidson not
only adopts free verse, but he also puts himself and his experience
as a creative artist at the centre of the poem, though camouflaged
as a third-person narrator. The figure of the novice artist who
rejects his father's Calvinism and all systematised creeds to cling to
the only belief that man is, in Wordsworth's words, 'the whole
compass of the universe', is the dramatic projection of Davidson's
own rebellion against his Scottish roots, and his family's
Evangelicalism. Nevertheless, despite this obvious rejection of the
past, he cannot suppress his opposing nostalgia for '[...] a town/Far
in the North, where time could take his ease,/And Change hold
holiday; where Old and New/Weltered upon the border of the
world'.[16] From a later passage – one of Davidson's best examples
of urban poetry – it becomes clear that the town here mentioned is
Greenock, where his family moved when John was two years old.
Yet from the very beginning of the poem Davidson seems to be
thinking of his nation as the northern part of a country that he
does not name but depicts as a mythical image of Britain – or even
of the whole universe. In other words, by seeing Greenock, but
especially Scotland, as part of a supranational dimension, Davidson

intends to juxtapose the local with the cosmic, the particular with the universal, and thus assert his anti-provincial vision of Scotland.

'A Ballad in Blank Verse' anticipates the all-embracing outlook that Davidson assumes in his 'Testaments', in particular in 'The Testament of John Davidson', in which his individual experience of a Scottish exile merges with the universal experience of Everyman, and Scotland's historical identity emerges from an ahistorical and mythical dimension – the many references to mythology are not only an anticipation of the modernists' mythic method, but they also testify to the poet's grand plan to write 'a new poetry [...], a new cosmogony, a new habitation for the imagination of men'.[17] In 'A Ballad in Blank Verse' Davidson sees himself as the microcosm embodying the unity-in-diversity of the macrocosm and his country almost as a non-geographical space.

In the 'Testament' the urge to overcome Scotland's cultural and geographical marginality becomes even more compelling. The use of an encyclopaedic style, a 'sparky eclecticism of styles and vocabularies', as Crawford defines it,[18] mingling the low and the high, the scientific and the poetic, and his antisyzygical amalgam of Christian and pagan imagery, real and surreal situations go beyond the yoking of opposites that Gregory Smith identified as the essence of Scottish literature. They look forward to Eliot's conception of the poet's mind and art as a fusion of contraries – beginnings and ends, East and West, savage and civilised. They also anticipate Morgan's negotiation between the local and the global epitomised in *From Glasgow to Saturn* (1973) and Dunn's anti-parochial vision in 'Here and There', where he says, 'So spin the globe: Tayport is Trebizond'.[19]

Davidson's opera omnia shows that the older he got the more urgent his need of acceptance from the literary establishment became. This helps one to condone the strongly jingoistic and imperialistic ideas that make some facets of his late work rather unpalatable to the reader.

In the poetry after 1905, when Nietzsche, Darwin and scientific materialism became central to his philosophical outlook, Davidson juxtaposed the idea of power embodied by imperial Britain with the images of the Superman and the fittest of the species. The ideas of Matter as the central principle of the universe and of Man as master of his fate were embraced by Davidson as means of filling in the void left by his repudiation of Christianity. These philosophical precepts apparently contradict his earlier refusal to submit to any systematised creed. In fact, rather than a coherent system of thought, they form a diverse amalgam of ideas taken from Schopenhauer, Nietzsche, Ernst Haeckel and even Wordsworth. Nonetheless, one cannot disregard his earlier critique of unquestionable theories (for example in 'Thirty Bob a Week') and his general ironic bent. Despite their apparent self-assertiveness, Davidson's megalomaniac alter-egos – especially the 'testators', these modern 'unacknowledged legislators of the world' – always betray an obsessive self-consciousness which does not make them very convincing.

An early example of the half-ironic treatment of the imperialist theme is to be found in 'St. George's Day' (*A Second Series of Street Eclogues*, 1896), one of Davidson's 'urban' eclogues. His bittersweet attitude towards the whole imperial issue emerges from one character's observation that 'there is no England now', because the imperial expansion led to a redefinition of English geographical and cultural identity after the incorporation of the colonies – 'Unwieldy limbs that lack a soul'.[20] One cannot help perceiving a pessimistic feeling behind this metaphor: the colonial machine is seen as an assemblage of awkward, disjointed cogs lacking a central motive power.

Thus Davidson seems to be questioning the unifying power of the centre on its periphery, and the absolute globalising energy of the dominant culture. At least this is what Menzies believes, but Menzies is only one of the author's *dramatis personae*. In a typically Victorian manner, Davidson could not help allowing his 'two voices' to emerge, and he dramatised this inner division by setting Menzies' democratic spirit against Basil's totalitarian and anglocentric views. So 'English' is for Basil a blanket term, Bruce and Wallace are 'mighty northern Englishmen' (l. 146), and the unifying principle – the 'mighty soul' (l. 165) – of the empire is 'the soul of English speech and thought' (l. 166). The 'Word', rather than the 'sword' (l. 221), of England is according to Basil the means of conquering the world. MacDiarmid also saw the English language as a powerful colonising force, and indeed he regretted that Davidson ignored 'the far greater suitability of Scots for the expression of his ideas than English could ever afford'.[21]

In fact, Davidson revealed an anxiety about language in one of his best dramatic monologues: 'Ayrshire Jock' (*In a Music-Hall and Other Poems*, 1891). The protagonist is the poet's dramatic double: even if he lives in Glasgow, he experiences internal exile. From his drinking habits one deduces that his literary efforts are not a source of gratification but frustration, because he is a Scot compelled to write in English to receive those 'kind letters from professors'[22] and publish his work. Jock personifies Davidson's dilemmas and psychological tensions in his relationship with his Scottish roots, in particular with his native language. Through John Auld he expresses his indignation against those who persist in writing in a doggerel Scotch only to perform a hackneyed imitation of Burns:

> They drink, and write their senseless rhymes,
> Tagged echoes of the lad of Kyle,
> In mongrel Scotch: didactic times
> In Englishing our Scottish style
> Have yet but scotched it: in a while
> Our bonny dialects may fade hence:
> And who will dare to coin a smile
> At those who grieve for their decadence? (ll. 73-80)

Auld/Davidson criticises those who write in an impure Scotch, in a hybrid language which has lost its essence and meaning. Hence, after admitting that 'Whisky and Burns made [him] a poet' (l. 64), he declares that his models are English and that he rhymes in English. Yet there is no self-confidence and conviction in his voice, but only the resigned tone of a frustrated artist who had to curb his 'very loftiest ambition' (l. 104) to live by his pen. His forced allegiance to the English tradition is in sharp contrast to his vision of the past rural tradition his youth was steeped in. The antithesis of past and present is expressed metaphorically by the opposition between the 'naked windows' (without shutters) of his Glasgow garret (l. 35) and the 'sea-green shutters' of the family cottage (l. 40), a Kailyard image which inevitably reminds us of G.D. Brown's anti-Kailyard novel, *The House with the Green Shutters* (1901). In fact, Davidson indirectly criticises the Kailyard mode by having his character shun the ghosts of the past - '[...] I'll turn my back;/I would not see my boyhood's days' (ll. 41-42). This kind of behaviour clearly reflects the poet's own ambivalent relationship with his national origins: on the one hand, he felt he had to break free from a restrictive Scottishness; on the other, he felt guilty about such an act of rejection, and, consequently, he could never totally rid himself of his haunting Scottishness.

Most of what may be called Davidson's poetry of the underdog, the social recluse and outcast, is marked by similar cultural and psychological tensions. Behind the surface structure of these texts there is always a subtext with specific social, moral and political targets. From a postcolonial perspective, one may say that some of these texts explore cultural differences and questions of economic and political power. A conspicuous example here is 'Thirty Bob a Week' (*The Yellow Book*, 1894). This dramatic monologue was praised by T.S. Eliot because in it 'Davidson freed himself completely from the poetic diction of English verse of his time' by adopting a colloquial style and revealing 'a good many dingy urban images'.[23] There is no denying the fact that the use of idiomatic English and of a conventionally non-poetic diction is one of the most striking peculiarities of this poem.

Nevertheless, what also deserves attention is the embedded critique of the contemporary work ethic and social injustice through its analysis of the complex relationship between the protagonist clerk and his social superiors. The poems subtext is also an attack on Victorian hypocrisy and obsession with duty, two moral attitudes ironically personified by the clerk who every single day dutifully participates in 'the daily dull official round' and then in the evening returns to his poor dingy house and feels his suppressed anger personified by an inner 'god-almighty devil [...]/Who would like to shout and whistle in the street,/And squelch the passers flat against the wall'.[24] By means of a dark humorous language, he sets himself against a Mr Silver-tongue who embodies power and the establishment. Yet his bitter feelings are not merely those of a man who is aware of being exploited by a privileged class, since Davidson's clerk, like Eliot's Prufrock or MacDiarmid's A Drunk Man after him, is a very complex character: he is an ordinary victim of society but he also questions and analyses his situation from an unusual philosophic and speculative standpoint. The clerk's tor-

tuous conjectures about his condition even challenge the preconceived idea of power and authority.

On the one hand, he gives voice to Davidson's scientific materialism: in an intricate harangue he tries to say that he must accept
his lot because all life is scientifically predestined and thus he cannot escape his predicament of being 'bossed', while 'it's just the
power of some to be boss' (l. 9). On the other hand, he seems to
suggest that real power consists in enduring his predestined plight
stoically - '[...] the difficultest job a man can do,/Is to come it brave
and meek with thirty bob a week' (ll. 88-89). At the end of the
poem the clerk seems to have found a reason to carry on living,
that is, the strength of his moral firmness and dignity allows him to
accept a Social Darwinian view of life, or scientific and social
determinism, while, at the same time – albeit contradicting himself
– he suggests that individuals are what they are because they want
to be that way: 'I woke because I thought the time had
come;/Beyond my will there was no other cause' (ll. 73-74).

Throughout his work Davidson shows that contradiction is not a
risk but a condition of being. In fact he even has one of his characters say that 'it appears everywhere from the highest to the lowest
– heaven, hell – husband, wife – day, night' and that 'the universe
is simply a contradiction in terms'.[25] This idea is connected with
his Blakean belief that there cannot be progress in life without
accepting contraries. Hence the multiple voice and the protean
point of view in his eclogues or in poems like 'In a Music-Hall' (*In
a Music-Hall and Other Poems*, 1891), while in 'Thirty Bob a Week'
the opposite forces of good and evil within the protagonist's
schizophrenic identity are personified by the 'god-almighty devil'
(45) and 'the sort of simpleton' (line 50). The strict interdependence
between good and evil is also one of the themes of another poem
with a strong critical subtext: 'A Ballad of a Nun' (*The Yellow Book*,
1894).

The story of the nun who leaves the secluded convent world to
reach the city and experience sexual life is only a pretext for the
author to express his moral acceptance of what Victorian society
and religion consistently condemned as sinful and unbecoming,
especially for a woman. Hence he represents the nun first undergoing an apparent downward journey into the heart of darkness

(in the city she has sex with a stranger), and secondly embarking on a quest to regain her self-esteem (eventually she is accepted back into the convent by the Virgin). The ultimate message of this unconventional ballad is that the nun's physical experience was a necessary step towards a deeper understanding of spiritual life. Anticipating MacDiarmid, Davidson here seems to suggest that 'man's spreit is wi' his ingangs twined/In ways that he can ne'er unwind'.[26] Like Blake's Thel, the nun discovers her sexual life far from her familiar world and finally returns to it with a broader knowledge of herself and humanity. The underlying social critique concerns the hypocritical morality of Victorian British society and the bigotry of many religious people. Of course he subtly attacks his father's strict Calvinist ethics and, more generally, any fanatical creed, but he also gives voice to his repudiation of the conventional Victorian image of woman as the angel in the house. His nun is another Lady of Shallot, but, contrary to Tennyson, Davidson does not sentence her to death, because her decision to plunge into life is the process whereby she reaches perfection. Through her physical experience, the nun also becomes the vehicle of Davidson's conception of pain as a basic human state, a theme which he will exploit to an extreme degree in 'The Testament of a Vivisector' (1901) – this poem, like H.G. Wells' *The Island of Dr. Moreau* (1896), dramatises the consequences of evolution and the progress of Victorian science.

Davidson's conceptions of irony and of the yoking of opposites risks being simplistically linked with Gregory Smith's definition of the Caledonian antisyzygy which MacDiarmid would later exploit and adapt to his own needs. One may certainly agree with Norman MacCaig that 'a characteristic of the Scot [is] a large capacity for containing in himself elements that contradict each other',[27] but 'antisyzygy' can in fact be found in any literature because it goes beyond the Calvinist dualistic model and the hackneyed Dr Jekyll-Mr Hyde figure. As a matter of fact, the polarities, contradictions and paradoxes which typify the themes, the structure and the style of Davidson's works are the most anti-parochial and modern aspects of his literary output. They not only establish a link with other non-Scottish Victorian writers, such as A.H. Clough, but they also look forward to later developments in world literature, represented by universal writers such as Lawrence, Eliot, Pound, Joyce, and Woolf, among others.

MacDiarmid set Davidson against a Scottish literary background characterised by 'pseudo-pastoral rubbish about an Arcadian life which had no relation to the facts at all',[28] because both his use of a colloquial language and his handling of urban themes make of him a precursor of modernist concerns, a 'proto-Modernist', in Dunn's words.[29] Though originally a provincial writer, from his 1889 move to London Davidson came to develop a style and themes which grant him a place within and beyond European literature. For example, if the prevalent voice in his poetry of the underdog looks back to the subversive idiom of eighteenth-century Scottish vernacular poetry and forward to MacDiarmid's and Goodsir Smith's poems, the multivocalism and the encyclopaedic style of his eclogues, his 'Testaments' and later poems such as 'The Crystal Palace' link him with Clough's polyphony of voices and use of idiolects – for example in *The Bothie of Tober-na-Vuolich* (1849) –, and also with Pound's and Joyce's multilinguism. Likewise, Davidson's eclectic style, his urge for a 'poetry of fact' and of a marriage between poetry and science immediately call to our mind Carlyle's hybrid genres and MacDiarmid's notion of world-language in his long catalogue-poems. Yet Davidson's multifariousness and eccentricity of motifs, forms and styles – the antisyzygy between real and surreal, fact and fiction, literature and science, his 'tendency to slip suddenly from beauty to absurdity'[30] – also link him with Whitman's eclecticism and with the shifting heterogeneous styles of much contemporary poetry.

Although it is undeniable that Davidson could never free himself totally from 'the roots that clutch', to borrow Henry James's expression,[31] and in particular from his Calvinistic background, throughout his life he struggled to overcome his provincial status and cultural difference by means of his eclectic writing and philosophical outlook. Even if his copious production includes imaginative failures, his best works – some of his demotic urban poems, of his ballads and eclogues and of his last blank-verse medley poems – paved the way for later literary developments not exclusively in Scotland. Two decades before the Scottish Renaissance, Davidson introduced into Scottish literature new energies which would allow it to overcome its provincial state; hence what Watson said *à propos* of MacDiarmid's achievement in the 1920s throws light on the essential pioneering role played by Davidson's 'new poetry':

> the modernistic and expressionist dynamic which [he] introduced to Scottish life and literature [...] was absolutely crucial to the reconstruction of a healthy culture which could find a place in the twentieth century without assuming exclusively monological linguistic and cultural rights, and without always looking backwards to the bens and the glens of a romanticised and static past.[32]

In Davidson's case, these new energies and 'dynamic' essentially consist of the introduction into poetry of conventionally prosaic themes, and the simultaneous use of a colloquial style and scientific jargon to produce an encyclopaedic kind of poetry. For all these reasons John Davidson and other late-nineteenth-century Scottish writers whose work displays similar aspects – like James Thomson ('B.V.') – should no longer be marginalised by the British canon as provincial and minor. They lived as outsiders throughout their lives and undoubtedly their work, as a reflection of their complex condition of exile, is hardly classifiable according to any specific Scottish or English tradition, but from a broader perspective – be it British, European or international – their achievement cannot be neglected.

NOTES

[1] John Davidson, 'On Poetry', in *The Poems of John Davidson*, edited by Andrew Turnbull, Edinburgh and London: Scottish Academic Press, 1973, II, (pp. 531-538) p. 534. All references to Davidson's poems are taken from this edition and will be given after quotations in the text, apart from the very first reference.
[2] T.S. Eliot, 'Was There a Scottish Literature?', *The Athenaeum*, 1 August 1919, (pp. 680-681) p. 681.
[3] Tom Hubbard, 'Irony and Enthusiasm: the Fiction of John Davidson', *Scottish Literary Journal,* vol. 11, 1984, (pp. 71-82) p. 75.
[4] 'The Testament of a Man Forbid', in *The Poems of John Davidson*, cit., II, pp. 329-334 (l. 1).

[5] See Tom Hubbard, 'John Davidson: A Lad Apairt', *Chapman*, vol. 40, 1985, pp. 34-38.

[6] See Robert Crawford, *Devolving English Literature*, Oxford: Clarendon Press, 1992, p. 220.

[7] James Thomson, *The City of Dreadful Night*, edited by Edwin Morgan, Edinburgh: Canongate, 1993, p. 57.

[8] 'The Testament of John Davidson', in *The Poems of John Davidson*, cit., II, (pp. 377-427) p. 427.

[9] Hugh MacDiarmid, 'John Davidson. Influences and Influence', in *John Davidson: A Selection of His Poems*, edited by Maurice Lindsay, London: Hutchinson, 1961, (pp. 47-54) p. 52.

[10] See John Sloan, *John Davidson: First of the Moderns*, Oxford: Clarendon Press, 1995, pp. 279-281.

[11] Kenneth Millard, 'John Davidson: Scottish Versus English', in *Edwardian Poetry*, Oxford: Clarendon Press, 1991, pp. 131-154.

[12] *Ibidem*, p. 131.

[13] John Davidson, 'Letters to the Editor. Irony', *Speaker*, 22 April 1899, p. 455.

[14] See Maurice Lindsay ed., *op. cit.*, p. 34.

[15] 'The Crystal Palace', in *The Poems of John Davidson*, cit., II, pp. 426-433 (l. 14).

[16] 'A Ballad in Blank Verse', in *The Poems of John Davidson*, cit., II, pp. 293-302 (ll. 2-5).

[17] John Davidson, *God and Mammon. A Trilogy. The Triumph of Mammon*, London: E. Grant Richards, 1907, p. 167.

[18] Robert Crawford, *op. cit.*, p. 249.

[19] Douglas Dunn, 'Here and There', in *Northlight*, London: Faber & Faber, 1988, pp. 26-27 (l. 11).

[20] John Davidson, 'St. George's Day', in *The Poems of John Davidson*, cit., I, pp. 222-229 (ll. 101 and 160).

[21] Hugh MacDiarmid, 'John Davidson. Influences and Influence', cit., p. 47.

[22] 'Ayrshire Jock', in *The Poems of John Davidson*, cit., I, pp. 11-14 (l. 88).

[23] T.S. Eliot, 'Preface', in *John Davidson: A Selection of His Poems*, cit., unnumbered page.

[24] 'Thirty Bob a Week', in *The Poems of John Davidson*, cit., I, pp. 63-65 (ll. 16 and 45-47).

[25] John Davidson, *The Great Men and A Practical Novelist,* London: Wardand Downey Limited, 1891, p. 4.

[26] Hugh MacDiarmid, *A Drunk Man Looks at the Thistle*, edited by Kenneth Buthlay, Edinburgh: Scottish Academic Press, 1987 (ll. 585-586).

[27] Norman MacCaig, 'A Note on the Author', in Hugh MacDiarmid, *Scottish Eccentrics*, Manchester: Carcanet, 1993, (pp. vii-xii) p. vii.

[28] Hugh MacDiarmid, 'John Davidson. Influence and Influences', cit., p. 51.

[29] Douglas Dunn, 'Language and Liberty', in Douglas Dunn ed., *The Faber Book of Twentieth-Century Scottish Poetry*, London and Boston: Faber & Faber, 1992, (pp. xvii-xlvi) p. xvii.

[30] Aldous Huxley, 'John Davidson', in *The English Poets*, edited by T.H. Ward, London: Macmillan, 1887-1918, V, (pp. 573-575) p. 574.

[31] Henry James, *The Ambassadors*, Harmondsworth: Penguin, 1973, pp. 165-166.

[32] Roderick Watson, 'Dialectics of "Voice" and "Place": Literature in Scots and English from 1700', in *Scotland: A Concise Cultural History*, edited by P.H. Scott, Edinburgh and London: Mainstream Publishing, 1993, (pp. 99-125) p. 120.

GIOIA ANGELETTI

James Thomson ('B.V.'):
The Predicament of a Scot in London

I wish to draw into clear light the facts (*sic*) that, in two moods of two several hours not a day asunder, a man's relations to the most serious problems of life may be, and often are, essentially opposite; that the one may burn with *hope and faith*, and the other lour black with *doubt and despair*; and that there is no possibility of conciliating (philosophically) this antagonism, since the two are mutually unintelligible.[1] (my italics).

The above quote contradicts those critics who reductively nick-name James Thomson ('B.V.')[2] the 'Laureate of pessimism' and interpret his work accordingly. Thomson is a poet of doubt and despair as well as of hope and faith; not only did he hope and believe before plunging into pessimism and nihilistic materialism, but he paradoxically retained a few evanescent signs of quasi optimism till the very end. As his biographer Charles Vachot observed: '[...] jamais en lui le désespoir ne régna longtemps sans conteste: sa vie intérieure est faite de la lutte, ou de l'alternance, de ce dés-espoir avec un goût obstiné de la vie; son oeuvre est le dialogue toujours rebondissant de la douleur et de la joie'.[3] Therefore, despite the general opinion, it is this pervasive dialogue between pain and joy, darkness and light, rather than utter gloom that per-meates Thomson's *opera omnia*, though the shadows often became overwhelming for him. After all, he admitted himself 'that the truth of midnight does not exclude the truth of noonday, though one's nature may lead him to dwell in the former rather than in the latter'.[4]

The dialectic of light and darkness imbuing Thomson's poetry from his juvenilia to his more mature works explains why Thomson's moral and religious *Weltanschauung* never coincided with a stable system of beliefs, since even his rejection of orthodox

Christianity was paralleled by a sense of moral anxiety and intellectual distress that prevented him from embracing a definite and incontrovertible atheistic philosophy.[5] In one of his juvenile poems Thomson gives voice to the tension between opposite moods at the centre of his life and poetry:

> Striving to sing glad songs, I but attain
> Wild discords sadder than Grief's saddest tone [...]
> My mirth can laugh and talk, but cannot sing;
> My grief finds harmonies in everything.[6]

These lines were written as early as 1860, yet the spiritual dichotomy here described accompanied Thomson throughout his life, even after he had reached the most pessimistic conclusions. Seeing himself as a perpetual wanderer, victim of an existential curse and constantly haunted by a sense of guilt, he never experienced the support and solidarity of a family, although he never denied the centrality of sympathy and kindness in his tormented existence.[7]

If it is true that, on the one hand, a growing sense of disenchantment with the world as well as personal tragic experiences[8] led him to withdraw more and more into himself and assume a pessimistic stance, on the other hand, his satirical essays included in such volumes as *Essays and Phantasies* (1881) and *Satires and Profanities* (1884) testify to his constant interest in the social, political and moral issues of the time. Like other Victorian intellectuals, he felt a moral urge to see the present state of things changed, but a self-torturing anxiety and sense of guilt sentenced him to a condition of perennial estrangement and wandering – 'When travelling about I always find myself immensely better than when confined to one place', wrote Thomson in the *Secular Review* in 1882.[9] His hostility to certain aspects of Victorian society determined his condition of social misfit, or, as Meeker says, of 'a Bohemian in the very respectable Mid-Victorian period', enduring that he remained eccentric and displaced within both the Scottish and the English cultural establishments.[10] This radical and sceptical spirit coexisted with an abiding fear of losing completely his foothold on reality, a pre-existentialist 'Angst' that Thomson recorded in the following diary entry dated Sunday, November 4, 1869: 'I felt myself like one who having climbed half-way up a long rope [...], cuts off all beneath his feet; he must climb on and can never touch the old earth again without a fatal fall'.[11] Hence Thomson could not escape the reality defined by the pandemonium of the Victorian city by retreating into some private sphere of his own. Nor could he, like his friend Bradlaugh, find consolation in a single-minded commitment to a fixed rationalist ideology: he always backed away from any notion of absolute philosophical systems.[12]

Thomson escapes monolithic categorizations, his works standing eccentrically on the borderline between different, at times antithetical, traditions, while his liminal condition of a Scot physically and psychologically exiled in London informs his whole literary output.[13] Quoting George Herbert, he believed that man can be 'some twenty several men at least/Each several hour', which explains why he admired the protean poetic genius of his fellow countryman James Hogg, on whom he wrote an essay,[14] and Byron's eccentric verse and temper. Like his models, he also was, to borrow Vachot's words, 'Homme des extrêmes, nul plus que lui n'est prompt à passer de l'un à l'autre'.[15]

Despite the wide variety of themes and forms, the three phases into which Thomson's literary output can be divided – his apprenticeship years (1842-1860), his mature phase (1860-1874) and his later years (1874-1881) – are marked by two crucial concerns: first, a problematic and conflicting relationship with God, which he continued to confront even when he turned to atheism; secondly, a tormented introspective analysis of his own predicament in the world, of his angst-provoking response to the cultural and economic changes of modern society, and to the problem of how to relate to other people in a mechanistic universe, in particular within the urban wasteland he perceived in London. Inevitably these two concerns appear at the centre of the work that gained him fame in the literary world, the long poem *The City of Dreadful Night* (1874), and it is on them that the present essay intends to focus. As with other important aspects of the work, it is not always easy to assess them in unequivocal ways, since the poem does not only describe a labyrinthine city but is itself a labyrinthine text, open to multiple interpretations and a variety of critical approaches.[16]

In ironic contrast with Thomson's nihilism in the early Seventies, *The City* does not exclude God; on the contrary the language of

the poem is fraught with echoes of and allusions to Him, to His
Word, and thus to Christianity and Calvinism, which it is the
author's ultimate aim to subvert or overturn. Thomson's obsessive
insistence in the poem that the modern world is bereft of love in
all its forms points to his distressing recognition of the problems
inherent in living and dying in a world deprived of any form of
divinely reassuring meaning. As a matter of fact, *The City of
Dreadful Night* is one of the most significant – albeit ironic – literary testimonies to the Victorian concern with eschatology. In particular, by the 1860s many Victorians had ceased to believe in the
physical and geographical existence of hell and, consequently,
were questioning the theory of damnation. However, the language
traditionally associated with the place of eternal sin and punishment continued to provide Victorian writers, including the sceptic
and agnostic, with a vocabulary with which to describe painful
spiritual experiences in *this* world, in particular the urban *inferno*
(as in Dickens's, Gaskell's, Gissing's and Oliphant's fiction, among
others) and the spiritual *inferno*, or the representation of a loveless
world (as, for example, in George Meredith's sonnet sequence
Modern Love). The 'religious' language in *The City of Dreadful
Night* is an intertextual discourse encompassing aspects of both
types of hell. The numberless echoes of and allusions to the
Scriptures or other texts loaded with religious meanings are for the
most part subject to a parodic or satirical overturning whereby they
become means of attacking Christian orthodoxy and the whole
ecclesiastic apparatus.

This is the main intent lying behind the recurrent repetition of
number 3 and its multiples, starting from the very structure of the
poem (21 sections, excluding the Proem) and involving many
episodes, narrative patterns and prosodic forms. Thomson did not
experiment with *terza rima*, but the use of ternary rhythms (especially the sextet) and the pervasive echoes of Dante's *Inferno* are
an obvious tribute to the Italian model, starting from the first of the
three epigraphs prefaced to the poem.[17] However, Thomson's version of 'hell on earth' (or of the earth *sub specie aeternitatis*) is so
idiosyncratic and at times so self-contradictory that it cannot be
identified with any specific condition; it is a hybrid world whose
dwellers seem to resist all strict categorizations, since they include

both beastly figures like the crawling creature in Section XVIII and innocent, angelic beings like the 'woman with a red lamp' in Section IV and the mourned 'Lady of the images' in Section X. Dantesque echoes recur in the topographic description of the city, in the Limbo state of the citizens, removed 'from Heaven and Earth and Hell' (VI, l. 57), doomed to an 'insufferable inane' (VI, l. 24), or *taedium vitae*, and in the image of the River of the Suicides in Section XIX, but all this intertextual material is often subject to a parodic revision to convey unorthodox messages that have nothing to do with Dante's eschatological vision and anagogic intent. The inhabitants of the City do not even have that little morsel of hope they should throw into 'Pandora's box' (VI, l. 37) by the gate of Hell if they want to enter that 'positive eternity of pain' (VI, l. 23) preferable to their existential *ennui*. In other words, they cannot even obey the imperative: 'Leave hope behind all ye who enter here' (VI, l. 21). Thomson often plays with this kind of paradox and grotesque situation, in a way that looks forward to the characters and atmospheres of the theatre of the absurd.

There are moments though when irony and dark humour are replaced by purely horrific effects and a more shocking sense of angst, as in Section IV, where the wandering spirit, one of Thomson's alter egos, amidst a wasteland full of dangers and threats, confronts his own double, or what he calls his 'corpse-like' (IV, l. 100) self going away with a woman who is holding her own bleeding heart in her hand. Meanwhile he sees from a distance his other self staring at the couple, deprived of all illusions and hopes, and finally left alone on the shore. This disquieting scene is not only a parody of Christ's temptations in the desert as described in Matthew 4:1-11, Mark 1: 10-13, and Luke 4: 1-13. Nor is the woman 'with a red lamp in her hand' (IV, l. 64) only a secularised version of a typical iconographical representation of Christ, as, for example, in W.H. Hunt's painting 'The Light of the World' (1851-1853). First, the Biblical hypotexts offer Thomson an expedient to introduce the theme of perseverance and stoic fortitude recurring in several parts of the poem and culminating in the final climactic representation of Melencolia, the imperturbable statue of the City. Secondly, the Biblical echoes are used ironically to depict a humankind which has lost religious hope and whose apparent sources of consolation are in fact causes of distress and mental schizophrenia. Many Victorian poems illustrate the disintegration of the human spirit, but few of them manage to do so through such vivid, plastic images and effective dramatic strategies.

All the allusions to the Bible in the poem are stripped of their sacred significance and applied to a reality which seems to hold the form but not the content of certain aspects of Christianity. Hence the presence in the city of preachers who use the rhetoric of Calvinism to deny its crucial tenets, as in Section XIV. Here the narrator is an unconventional sermonizer, a bizarre hybrid between a Calvinist preacher, with 'steadfast and intolerable eyes' (XIV, l. 19), a 'great sad voice deep and full' (XIV, l. 24), and the Carlylean Victorian sage addressing an anti-Christian homily to the astounded congregation gathered inside the city cathedral. The preacher participates in the general self-dramatisation of the poem, whereby the wanderers and miserable inhabitants of the City are poetic mirrors of the author himself, or projections of his spiritual dilemmas and metaphysical conundrums. In this case, the sermon becomes the vehicle of Thomson's atheistic thought, summed up in the minister's words 'There is no God' (XIV, l. 40), 'this little life is all we must endure' (XIV, l. 49), 'I find Necessity Supreme;/With infinite Mystery, abysmal, dark' (XIV, ll. 75-76), and, to justify suicide, '[…] if you would not this poor life fulfil/Lo, you are free to end it when you will' (XIV, ll. 82-83). The anti-Gospel is also the expression of the poet's materialist creed, a crucial testimony of the religious crisis of those years, which led Thomson, as well as his fellow countryman and contemporary writer John Davidson, to embrace, albeit sadly, Darwinism and a sort of secularised Antinomianism, whereby the 'elect' are not those chosen by God but simply the fittest in the struggle for life:

> All substance lives and struggles evermore
> Through countless shapes continually at war,
>   By countless interactions interknit:
> If one is born a certain day on earth,
> All times and forces tended to that birth,
>   Not all the world could change or hinder it. (XIV, ll. 67-72)

However, unlike Davidson, Thomson did not conceive of suicide as the ultimate rebellion against God. As the anonymous critic of

The Spectator wrote in 1889:

> [Thomson] admitted fully and repeatedly that the logical outcome of all
> his philosophy was suicide, [...], but maintained that for him personally
> there was a deterring reason. He was a poet; [...] he could not bear to
> cease to sing. [...] He would not, he said, make an end, because he felt
> the impulse to sing; and all his song was protest, useless and feeble
> unless addressed, consciously or unconsciously, to Something that could
> hear.[18]

The thought that someone might hear his 'songs in the desert', as
he calls them in the 1878 poem 'I Had a Love',[19] helped him to
face the darkness, but, unfortunately, not to win the battle against
his alcoholic addiction.

Section XIV ends with the image of the 'shadowy congregation'
(XIV, l. 89) left to brood on the alternative between endurance and
suicide, a dilemma cropping up again in Section XIX, where the
'River of the Suicides' (XIX, l. 4) is an echo of the forest of the suicides in *Inferno*, Canto XIII. *The City of Dreadful Night* recurrently
presents this wavering between the vision of a meaningless world,
of 'aeons of slow pain' (XIII, l. 30) which legitimise suicide, and
the necessity to endure stoically, because, if life is but '[...] one
night after all:/What matters one brief night of dreary pain?' (XIX,
ll. 29-30). This tension between the sad acceptance of a cruel destiny
and rebelliousness against it can sometimes result in rage against
Fate or, paradoxically, against that very God that the narrator continuously denies.

In Section VIII, for example, the external narrator overhears the
conversation between two anonymous characters who, like the
protagonist of an earlier poem entitled 'Polycrates on Waterloo
Bridge' (1865), talk to each other while staring at the river flowing
under them. One of them is a disenchanted believer blaspheming
against God, the other an atheist denying the existence of any
supreme Being in the universe, be it 'God or Fiend' (VIII, l. 33).
The two opposite views are drawn up facing each other in a dramatic confrontation, or what, in Arnold's words, may be defined as
a 'dialogue of the mind with itself'. The blasphemous character
inveighing against God may be the young Thomson enraged by
the Creator of a disgraceful world, here confronted by the mature
Thomson, a Nietzschean disciple who expounds his atheistic doc-

trine and mechanistic philosophy in a cold and detached tone. Like
the characters in Section XII, all 'isolated units' (XII, l. 1) convinced
that nothing exists except the 'real night' of the city, the atheist is a
member of a 'sad Fraternity' (Proem, l. 36) who have 'no God
above them/To sanctify and glorify and love them' (Proem, ll. 20-
21), and who prefer to face the 'real night' rather than fall victims
of useless illusions of a happier afterlife.

It is to deny the existence of God and of any divine purpose in
the universe that Thomson borrows two quotations from the Italian
poet Giacomo Leopardi as prelude to the pessimistic philosophy
expounded in the whole poem.[20] The first epigraph introduces the
theme of the purposelessness and spiritual emptiness of life which
emerges in several sections,[21] whereas the second one focuses on
the idea that death, or 'Dateless oblivion and divine repose' (XIII, l.
42), as Thomson defines it, is the ultimate resort, the 'One anodyne
for torture and despair' (I, l. 80), even if it is followed only by the
black abyss of nothingness.[22] Thomson shares with Leopardi the
idea that nature is a cheat and indifferent to man; with sardonic
irony he observes,

> [...] men regard with passionate awe and yearning
> The mighty marching and the golden burning,
>   And think the heavens respond to what they feel. (XVII, ll. 5-7)

Unlike Blake, Thomson denies that 'everything that lives is holy',
that there is a divine essence behind the majestic appearance of the
universe. On the contrary, he admits that 'The spheres eternal are a
grand illusion,/The empyrean is a void abyss' (XVII, ll. 27-28).

The same sense of spiritual emptiness is conveyed by the gaze
of the sphinx in Section XX, whose vision, says the first-person
narrator, is 'of infinite void space' (XX, l. 48). This is one of the
most iconographic episodes of the poem, describing the dramatic
confrontation between a colossal 'couchant sphinx in shadow to
the breast' (XX, l. 9) – symbolising blind necessity – and, opposite to
her, an armed angel 'standing in the moonlight clear' (XX, l. 10) –
possibly an image of man. The gradual disintegration of the angel
under the 'solemn trance-like look' of the sphinx (XX, l. 18) – he
loses first his wings, secondly his sword and thirdly his head – till he
becomes a heap of broken stones is a representation the Victorian

man's spiritual fragmentation in front of pitiless and harsh Necessity. There is no possible panacea for the inhabitants of the City; when they look into the 'tenebrous regard' (XXI, l. 63) of Melencolia, that 'bronze colossus of a winged Woman' (XXI, l. 6) who is also their Patroness, they can only read:

> The sense that every struggle brings defeat
>   Because Fate holds no prize to crown success;
> That all the oracles are dumb or cheat
>   Because they have no secret to express;
> That none can pierce the vast blank veil uncertain
> Because there is no light beyond the curtain;
>   That all is vanity and nothingness. (XXI, ll. 64-70)

It is the same message that the minister launched from the pulpit in Section XIV:

> I find no hint throughout the Universe
> Of good or ill, of blessing or of curse;
>   I find alone Necessity Supreme;
> With infinite Mystery, abysmal, dark,
> Unlighted ever by the faintest spark
>   For us the flitting shadows of a dream (XIV, ll. 73-78)

The only faint value surviving the gloom is Melencolia's 'indomitable will' (XXI, l. 52) and 'iron endurance' (XXI, l. 82) in front of 'the dreadful mysteries of Time' (XXI, l. 46); she cannot provide her subjects with a solution to their dilemmas but only prove that at least they are bound by their 'old despair' to form a melancholy brotherhood.

'The city of dreadful night' is both a *topos* symbolically standing for any modern urban space, and, to borrow Leonard's expression, a 'place of the mind', an imaginary landscape onto which the poet has projected his own angst, fear and sense of displacement. However original and innovative in its blend of physical and metaphysical aspects, realistic and fantastic descriptions, Thomson's poem is in line with a long tradition including the Biblical Jerusalem, Ezekiel's prophecies, Dante's *Inferno*, several Romantic and Victorian works, Eliot's *The Wasteland*,[23] and contemporary works such as, among others, Roy Fisher's *The City* and Calvino's *Invisible Cities*. There are certainly similarities between Thomson's representation and the city described as 'Hell on earth' by other Victorian writers.[24] Nonetheless, rather than a fictional image of the real dreadful life of the Victorian city, Thomson's city is like a nightmare from which one cannot wake, a surreal combination of disturbing experiences into which the author translates his own states of mind, feelings and thoughts.

Before *The City of Dreadful Night* Thomson wrote two works that look forward to it: the long poem *The Doom of a City* (1857) and the De Quinceyan prose fantasy 'A Lady of Sorrow', which was first published in *The National Reformer* in 1867 and was then included in *Essays and Phantasies* (1867).

The former describes the journey (clearly symbolic) of an insomniac wanderer through and then beyond the labyrinthine topography of a city in an urge to 'dare the desert sea'[25] and, like the Tennysonian Ulysses, face the 'unknown awful realm where broods Eternity' (p. 13, l. 25). Eventually, though, he returns to the city, a London described as a modern Sodom, affected by a claustrophobic, sepulchral atmosphere, and inhabited by 'peopling corpses' (p. 13, l. 31), similarly living in 'a dark dead dearth/Of soulless silence yawned in dreadful mystery' (p. 23, ll. 138-139). In other words, an earlier version of the 'city of dreadful night', characterised by the same spiritual paralysis, the same dramatic contrast between real life and dreams, and similar human relations (if they exist at all). However, whereas the narrator of the 1874 poem roves through and around the city without ever leaving it, in the earlier work the pilgrim abandons the lugubrious place and defies the open sea alone. Similarly, in 'A Lady of Sorrow', the hero/anti-hero, roaming around London in the company of a mysterious figure (Sorrow) disguised now as an Angel, now as a Siren, encounters men who look like shadows subjected to a Sphinx in the desert of Life, the personification of pitiless Fate, of a 'God petrified' or 'the dumb, blind, soulless deification of Matter' (p. 314). The city is described as 'a vast Metropolis which was become as a vast Necropolis' (p. 314), a maze of interminable streets, a 'mournful desert' through which the wanderer can at least detect some 'tokens of brotherhood' (p. 315).

Critics have read the poem in different ways. According to Roden Noel it is '[...] the note rather of a powerful idiosyncrasy afflicted to the verge of madness than the note of an impersonal world sorrow';[26] Lance St. John Butler sees it as 'a drug-addict's view of London by night' [27] and Peter Quennell as the representation of '[...] a sort of nightmare London [...] seen through the eyes of a drunken army-schoolmaster as he wandered back to the Pimlico slum in which he lodged'.[28] However plausible some of these interpretations may be, they all seem to ignore the fact that Thomson had a specific audience in mind when he composed it. From the beginning of the poem he makes it clear that he is not writing just for himself but for all those who are victims of 'dolorous mysteries' (Proem, l. 37), disillusioned wanderers, like himself, 'who may have thought themselves peculiar and outcast'[29]. However, in a letter to his friend Dobell, Thomson admitted that the poem 'is so alien from common thought and feeling [...] that scarcely any readers would care for it'.[30] In fact, instead of providing the readers with a source of comfort to confront their metaphysical dilemmas, he can only project in front of their eyes a world of spiritual darkness in which the only chance of survival coincides with stoic endurance and acceptance of the 'dreadful night'. Or their last resort may be the consoling thought that other people share the same doom. This common realisation is defined by Sharpe as a 'collective consciousness':[31] at least the 'sad Fraternity' (Proem, l. 36) is comforted by the fact that they are not the only ones to 'dree' the same 'weird' (V, l. 25) and endure the 'dolorous mysteries' (Proem, l. 37).

In two letters written respectively to George Eliot and to his sister-in-law Julia, Thomson described the poem as 'the outcome of much sleepless hypochondria', 'written under evil inspiration of insomnia', a trouble he had to confront till the end of his days.[32] Indeed the narrator is also the insomniac protagonist of a journey through the city labyrinth, a 'City [...] of Night, but not of Sleep' (I, l. 71), '[...] of Night; perchance of Death,/But certainly of Night' (I, l. 1). The city architecture and surrounding landscape form a grotesque picture made out of the juxtaposition of disparate elements: the general atmosphere is one of numbed silence but now and then odd sounds can be heard; the city is wrapped by deep darkness but the street-lamps are lit up; it looks like a desert, although some people walk through the bare streets; like a real city it includes piers, bridges, and causeways but is strangely surrounded by waste marshes, savannahs, savage woods and 'A trackless wilderness' (I, l. 32). In other words, as Foakes suggests, 'the remote and the familiar, the imaginary and the actual are united'.[33] Even if the physical, structural components of the city present an ordinary shape, they seem to have lost their usual function, reduced as they are to fragments of a void, almost dehumanising universe. Even the ruins of this city have lost all romantic association and have become objective correlatives of an irrefutable sense of fragmentation, loss and nemesis. As for most Victorian writers, the ruin here is an image of death rather than of a continuing relationship between past and present.

The inhabitants are imprisoned inside their mansions, which are 'dark and still as Tombs' (I, l. 45), so that the city looks like a necropolis, or, as the anonymous critic of *The Academy* pointed out, as 'an edifice of black marble'.[34] The few people the narrator encounters have 'worn faces that look deaf and blind/Like tragic masks of stone' (I, l. 52). They are anonymous, sleepless victims of *ennui*, which makes them walk heads down or stop in a pondering posture, thus anticipating the attitude of their Patroness Melencolia. This grand statue overlooking the City embodies the only possibility of surviving within it, or suggests the attitude required in order to confront 'the dreadful mysteries of Time' (XXI, l. 46). Thomson drew the image of the 'winged Woman' (XXI, l. 6) from Albrecht Dürer's engraving *Melencolia I* (1514), and had already provided earlier versions of the same icon in the petrified Sage of *The Doom of a City* and the colossal statue in 'A Lady of Sorrow'. The critic P.C. Noel-Bentley, after describing the 'city of dreadful night' as a reversed Jerusalem in which the basic symbols of divinity have lost their significance, remarks:

> In such a world Melencolia symbolizes the only existence that is possible. She sits, a parody of the divine female figure (Beatrice or Mary), high over the City on a plateau (itself a parody of the Biblical mountain) surrounded by symbols of isolation, her instruments.[35]

In spite of her awareness that empirical speculation will not allow man to penetrate the 'dreadful mysteries of Time', Melencolia keeps on using her scientific tools because it is her inexorable moral duty to do so, so that 'her sorrow shall be turned to labour' (XXI, l. 54) until death: 'Baffled and beaten back she works on still,/Weary and sick of soul she works the more,/Sustained by her indomitable will.' (XXI, ll. 50-52). The author's underlying message is to emulate Melencolia, embrace her self-awareness, fellowship, and sober contemplation as ethical principles necessary to survive in a world where materialism and science are undermining the foundations of morality and religion.

Between 1881 and 1882, just a few months before dying, Thomson wrote a few love poems, all included in the posthumous volume *A Voice from the Nile and Other Poems* (1884). It is as if, aware of his forthcoming death, he intended to prove to himself and his readers he was still capable of perceiving the sense of harmony in the world, even if the other, opposed sense of chaos and anxiety was the more prevalent. As one of his *noms de plume* suggests – 'Crepusculus' – he did not live in the 'dreadful night' of the city from beginning to end but was sometimes comforted by the interplay of light and shade, the experience of liminal states that prevented him from plunging into utter darkness. Till the end Thomson continued to believe in love and friendship, and to appreciate the refreshing effect of a walk in the countryside, though his ultimate wish was to find repose in the 'solemn sanctity of death'.[36]

Unfortunately he reached that repose tragically, as a consequence of a slow self-destruction through dipsomania. For a long time his name and work were neglected and forgotten, like the speaking voice in one of his poems, 'He cried out through the night' but received 'No answering light,/No syllabled sound' in return, 'His voice in its might/Rang forth far and far,/And then like a star/Dwindled from sense/In the Immense'.[37] Luckily Edwin Morgan's recent edition of his masterpiece has not only brought both name and work back into the light but also acknowledged Thomson's influence on later writers.[38] Since then *The City of Dreadful Night* has continued to fascinate, bewilder, and stimulate critical attention, but wider recognition is still required to validate its author's poetic stature and also valorise the work of those who have started to listen to voices once consigned to the desert of non-canonical Victorian writing.[39]

NOTES

[1] James Thomson, 'Sympathy', in *Essays and Phantasies*, London: Reeves and Turner, 1881, (pp. 228-249) p. 242.

[2] 'Bysshe Vanolis', one of his pseudonyms derived from the anagrams of Shelley and Novalis, two poets he read from his early youth.

[3] Charles Vachot, *James Thomson*, Paris: Didier, 1964, p. 133.

[4] Letter to George Eliot, 20 June 1874. Cfr. Charles Vachot, *op. cit.*, p. 193.

[5] Thomson was brought up in Port Glasgow in a fervent religious household, rooted in the principles of Evangelicalism imparted by his pietistic mother. This religious faith remained unshaken and supported him throughout his school years in London and at Chelsea, at least until 1851, when he was transferred to Ballincollig in Ireland to work as army schoolmaster. Two main events here marked the beginning of his estrangement from orthodoxy: his friendship with Charles Bradlaugh, the social reformer and anti-status-quo advocate of radicalism who became the proprietor of *The National Reformer*, and his first experience of love with Matilda Weller, the daughter of a sergeant. The influence of Bradlaugh's charismatic personality and the untimely death of the young Matilda first triggered Thomson's religious crisis. The strong appeal of Bradlaugh's free thinking was then combined with a melancholy perception of the fugitiveness of human life and a weaker and weaker belief in the afterlife.

[6] 'Two Sonnets', in *Vane's Story, Weddah and Om-el-Bonain, and Other Poems*, London: Reeves and Turner, 1881, (pp. 165-166) p. 166. After the first full quotation, all subsequent quotations from Thomson's poems will be indicated within brackets in the text, as long as the source of the quotation is clear.

[7] In one of his notes Thomson wrote that 'great goodness – that is, sympathy – is as rare as the intense and comprehensive imagination', Bodleian Library, MS.Don.e.43, fol. 3.

[8] In 1840 his sister died of measles contracted from him, two years later he lost his mother. In 1853 he was struck by the tragic news of his beloved's death, the young woman Matilda Weller. Another cause of suffering was his brother's mental illness, a source of financial and psychological troubles for the whole family.

[9] Letter to an anonymous addressee, *Secular Review*, 15 July 1882, p. 249.

[10] Edward Meeker, *The Life and Poetry of James Thomson ('B.V.')*, New Haven: Yale University Press; London: Humphrey Milford; Oxford:

Oxford University Press, 1917, p. 5.

[11] Cfr. K.H. Byron, *The Pessimism of James Thomson (B. V.) in Relation to His Time*, London: Mouton & Co.; Paris: The Hague, 1965, pp. 146-147.

[12] See 'On the Worth of Metaphysical Systems', in *Essays and Phantasies*, cit., pp. 296-302.

[13] Thomson settled in London in 1862 and lived there till his death caused by dipsomania in 1882.

[14] 'James Hogg, the Ettrick Shepherd', in *Biographical and Critical Studies*, London: Reeves and Turner, 1896, pp. 398-436.

[15] Charles Vachot, *op. cit.*, p. 413.

[16] *The City* is a poem 'whaur extremes meet', to use Hugh MacDiarmid's phrase, characterised by ambiguities and allowing clashing readings. So, if to some the poem may seem an expression of utter gloom and despair, to others it can even convey that peculiar kind of philosophical consolation that Thomson himself stresses in the Proem by calling attention to the cathartic power of art and the meaning of human fellowship. The poem is double even in its form, interweaving two main types of sections. On the one hand, there are the Proem and the eleven odd-numbered sections, descriptive and philosophical in content, all written in the present tense and in the same stanza form (ABABCCB); on the other hand, there are the ten even-numbered narrative sections on what the wanderer saw and experienced in the city, written in the past tense and characterised by different metres. The alternating pattern of philosophical and narrative sections accounts for the medley of poetic modes and the vast genre variety, including descriptions made by a homodiegetic or a heterodiegetic narrator, gothic tales, philosophical dialogues, and radical sermons, all representing different stages in the *dramatis persona*'s journey into his heart of darkness. According to some critics, there are two different intermingled poems in *The City of Dreadful Night*, coinciding with the two phases of composition (the first in 1870 and the second between 1873 and 1874). In 1870, Thomson created the embryo of the poem: a trilogy of short allegorical narratives about a wanderer in search of clues to the mysterious meaning of life. Later on he joined the three pieces together and entitled the new poem *The City of Night*. Between January and October 1870, he composed eleven sections which became sections II, XVIII, XX, I, V, XI, VII, IV, X, VI, and III in the final version of the poem. After a three-year pause, Thomson resumed the composition adding the sections finally numbered VIII – thematically

linked with the last two 1870 sections (VI and III), all concerning the human Fellowship shared by the city dwellers. All the sections composed after it (XIX, IX, the Proem, XII, XIV, XVII, XV, XVI, XIII, XXI) focus not so much on the narrator's preoccupation with his own destiny as on the vision of a community of individuals sharing the same tragic condition – the 'sad Fraternity' (Proem, l. 36). According to Schaefer '[...] the 1873 city is no longer symbolic of a state of mind, a realm of personal grief, of individual suffering which cannot communicate; the poem now deals with a universal situation that concerns all mankind [...]' (cfr. W.D. Thesing, *The London Muse, Victorian Responses to the City,* Athens, Georgia: University of Georgia Press, 1982, p. 143). For all these information cfr.: W.D. Schaefer, *James Thomson (B. V.): Beyond 'The City',* Berkeley and Los Angeles: University of California Press, 1965; W. Sharpe, 'Learning to Read *The City',* *Victorian Poetry,* vol. 22, 1984, pp. 65-84; and W.D. Thesing, *op. cit.* – in particular here the 'Introduction', pp. xv-xviii, and 'Romantic Versions of the City', pp. 133-146.

[17] This is the famous inscription on the door of Hell: 'Per me si va nella città dolente' (*Inferno,* III, l. 1). Thomson's interest in Dante crops up in a 1872 letter to W.M. Rossetti, in which he says that the two books he took with him to America were the Globe Shakespeare, Pickering's Dante and Cary's translation of the *Divine Comedy.* Cfr. *Poems and Some Letters of James Thomson,* edited by Anne Ridler, London: Centaur Press, 1963, p. 244.

[18] Anon, 'Why James Thomson did not kill himself', *Spectator,* 23 March 1889, pp. 394-395.

[19] For some obscure reason, Thomson did not want Dobell to publish the poem in the 1880 volume *The City of Dreadful Night and Other Poems,* so the only available version is to be found in Ridler's edition under the more general title 'Lines, 1878', pp. 205-208:

> 'Songs in the Desert! Songs of husky breath,
> And undivine Despair;
> Songs that are dirges, but for Life not Death,
> Songs that infect the air
> Have sweetened bitterly my food and wine,
> The heart corroded and the Dead Sea brine.' (ll. 37-42)

[20] For an analysis of the literary relationship between Leopardi and Thomson see my article 'Two Cities of Dreadful Night: James Thomson ('B.V.')'s London and Giacomo Leopardi's Recanati', *La Questione Romantica,* no. 3, ('Orrore e Terrore'), 1997, pp. 155-167. Thomson's

translation of Leopardi's letters and tales were collected and edited by
Bertram Dobell under the title *Essays, Dialogues and Thoughts of
Giacomo Leopardi. Translated by James Thomson (B. V.)* (1905).

[21]   Poi di tanto adoprar, di tanti moti
        D'ogni celeste, ogni terrena cosa,
        Girando senza posa,
        Per tornar sempre là donde son mosse;
        Uso alcuno, alcun frutto
        Indovinar non so.
        ('Canto notturno di un pastore errante dell'Asia', ll. 93-98)

This is Morgan's prose translation: 'Then out of such endless working,
so many movements of everything in heaven and earth, revolving
incessantly, only to return to the point from which they were moved:
from all this I can imagine neither purpose nor gain' (note ii, p. 73).

[22]   Sola nel mondo eterna, a cui si volve
        Ogni creata cosa,
        In te, morte, si posa
        Nostra ignuda natura;
        Lieta no, ma sicura
        Dell'antico dolor [...]
        Però ch'esser beato
        Nega ai mortali e nega a' morti il fato.
        (from 'Coro dei monti', a poem from 'Dialogo di Federico
        Ruysch e delle sue mummie', in *Operette Morali*, ll. 1-6, 31-32)

Morgan translates thus: 'Eternal alone in the world, receiver of all created things, in you, death, our naked being comes to rest; joyful no,
but safe from the age-old pain [...] For happiness is denied by fate to
the living and denied to the dead' (note iii, pp. 73-74).

[23] For a study of the relationships between Eliot and Thomson see
Robert Crawford, 'James Thomson and T.S. Eliot', *Victorian Poetry*, vol.
23, 1985, pp. 23-41, and by the same author the chapter 'City' in *The
Savage and the City in the Work of T.S. Eliot*, Oxford: Clarendon Press,
1987, pp. 35-60. Eliot himself observed that two authors in particular
influenced him in his formative years, 'the author of *The City of
Dreadful Night*, and the author of *Thirty Bob a Week*'. See T.S. Eliot,
'Preface', in *John Davidson. A Selection of His Poems*, edited by
Maurice Lindsay, London: Hutchinson & Co., 1961, unnumbered pages.

[24] See, for example, Arnold's 'Kensington Gardens' and Tennyson's *In
Memoriam* or *The Idylls of the King*, Dickens's novels and Carlyle's
Latter-Day Pamphlets.

[25] *The Doom of a City*, in Anne Ridler ed., *op. cit.*, (pp. 12-54) p. 13, (l. 14).

[26] Roden Noel, 'James Thomson', in A.H. Miles ed., *The Poets and the Poetry of the Century*, London: Hutchinson & Co., 1899, (pp. 627-638) p. 637.

[27] Lance St. John Butler, *Victorian Doubt. Literary and Cultural Discourses*, New York; London; Toronto; Sydney; Tokyo; Singapore: Harvester Wheatsheaf, 1990, p. 47.

[28] Peter Quennell, 'A Victorian Pessimist. Review of *The City of Dreadful Night and Other Poems*. With a Preface by Henry S. Salt', *New Statesman and Nation*, vol. 4, 1932, (pp. 235-236) p. 236.

[29] 'Saying of Sigvat', in *Essays and Phantasies*, cit., (pp. 213-219) p. 214.

[30] Letter to Dobell, quoted in Anne Ridler ed., *op. cit.*, p. xxx.

[31] W. Sharpe, *op. cit.*, p. 67.

[32] Letter to George Eliot, quoted by Edwin Morgan in his 'Introduction' to *The City of Dreadful Night*, *op. cit.*, p. 14. One of his last poems recording the effects of long sleepless nights is 'Insomnia' (*A Voice from the Nile and Other Poems*), which contains several echoes of *The City of Dreadful Night*.

[33] R.A. Foakes, 'The Vanity of Rhetoric. Matthew Arnold's Poetry in James Thomson's *The City of Dreadful Night*', in *The Romantic Assertion. A Study in the Language of Nineteenth Century Poetry*, London: Metheun & Co., 1958, (pp. 149-179) p. 173.

[34] Anon., 'Academy Portraits. James Thomson', *The Academy*, vol. 3, December 1898, p. 384.

[35] P.C. Noel-Bentley, '"Fronting the Dreadful Mysteries of Time": Dürer's *Melencholia* in Thomson's *City of Dreadful Night*', *Victorian Poetry*, vol. 12, 1974, (pp. 193-203) p. 198.

[36] 'The Sleeper', in *A Voice from the Nile*, London: Reeves and Turner, 1884, (pp. 62-65) p. 65.

[37] 'Night', in Anne Ridler, *op. cit.*, p. 133, (ll. 19-21 and ll. 14-18).

[38] Edwin Morgan, Introduction to *The City of Dreadful Night*, *op. cit.*, p. 7. Morgan sees echoes of the poem in Eliot's *The Waste Land*, in Jack London's *The People of the Abyss* (1903) – where London East End is called 'the City of Dreadful Monotony'– and John Rechy's *City of Night* (1963).

[39] See, for example, the Italian translation of *The City of Dreadful Night* by Liliana Losi and Mili Romano, *James Thomson. La Città della terribile notte*, a cura di Mili Romano, Rimini: Panozzo Editore, 2000.

COLIN MILTON

Scots as a Literary Medium 1870-2000:
'I saw a rose come loupin oot'

In the opening line of 'The Ballad of the Crucified Rose' from *A Drunk Man Looks at the Thistle*, the speaker is surprised by the sudden appearance of a spectacular rose blossom on a thistle, a 'camsteerie plant', which for centuries has only produced 'pin-heid flooers'. The image does less than justice to the long and distinguished history of writing in Scots but is, nevertheless, appropriate for the flowering of vernacular writing in the twentieth century in the face of the powerful standardising and anglicising tendencies of the age. The modern revival of the vernacular as a literary medium has its roots in the later decades of the nineteenth century, and is part of a broad cultural renewal which is more complex, more continuous with previous cultural developments, and less unambiguously connected with political nationalism than the 'Scottish Renaissance', that polemical construct devised by C.M. Grieve and his allies to promote their own distinctive cultural vision. In lowland Scots, the renaissance has produced the finest body of vernacular work since the eighteenth century, and also a wealth of translations and versions in Scots of texts from other languages. In the final phase of the period under review, vernacular drama has been of particular importance; indeed, in the words of one well-qualified observer 'the greatest quantity and variety of Scots-medium writing since 1945 has been in dramatic writing...'[1]

During the period, the Scots and Gaelic traditions found fresh sources of inspiration and energy, and grew in new directions, particularly in poetry and drama. Prose and prose fiction, especially the novel (often seen as the master genre of contemporary literature), however, have not flourished to the same degree, though William Donaldson has salvaged lively vernacular writing, journalistic and fictional, from newspaper files, [2] which demonstrates that, from the second half of the nineteenth century, Scots was developing as a medium for dealing with topical issues and contemporary life generally. The material appeared in publications which circulated locally and had a predominantly working- or lower middle-class, Scots-speaking readership; naturally they employed (in Donaldson's phrase) a 'speech-based' medium, based on current local Scots.

The development of a vernacular prose capable of dealing with modern life virtually ceased, however, at the end of the century, when new communications technologies and changed business conditions made titles less local in circulation and appeal. In the twentieth century, non-dramatic prose wholly in Scots has been rare, though interest in Scots as a prose medium has grown in recent decades, and it has been used increasingly, particularly for short stories. The resumption of a modern Scots prose tradition was encouraged by the coming of radio in the inter-war years and by developments in the Scottish theatre between the 1940s and 1960s. Early radio broadcasting was strongly local in character, with a considerable appetite for material reflecting vernacular culture, while from the 1950s, Scots became an important medium both for original drama and for dramatic translation. The two traditions come together in the work of Robert McLellan, mainly known as a dramatist, whose *Linmill Stories* [3] were broadcast between 1960 and 1965. Drawing on the time McLellan spent as a boy on his grandparents' fruit farm in Renfrewshire, the stories use a local and (near) contemporary Scots in contrast to generalised and archaising vernacular used in the historical dramas for which McLellan is best known. More recently, the writers included in collections like James Robertson's 1994 anthology, *A Tongue in Yer Heid*, [4] show a decided continuity with the Victorian pioneers discussed by Donaldson. They employ a 'speech-based' idiom which draws on contemporary spoken Scots in its many regional and social varieties; tales by Sandy Fenton and Sheena Blackhall use the 'traditional' rural Scots of the North-East while those by, for instance, Irvine Welsh, Janet Paisley and Alison Kermack, use the urban demotic of the Central Belt. The steady change in attitudes to the dialects of urban, industrial Scotland and the resulting development of contemporary urban Scots as a flexible prose medium over the last forty years has made possible Matthew Fitt's extraordinary *But n Ben A-Go-Go* (2000), a dystopian fantasy set in a grim future Scotland transformed by catastrophic climate change, an AIDS-like epidemic, and the development of a parallel virtual-reality universe. With narrative as well as dialogue in Scots, it uses an invented idiom constructed out of the urban vernaculars of the Central Belt crossed with elements of more traditional and literary Scots, with an admixture of terms from contemporary science and technology in the international language of these fields – English. The resulting composite idiom mixes the familiar and the strange in a way entirely appropriate to the bizarrely altered Scotland in which the story is set:

> Inverdisney Timeshare Penitentiary kythed throu the banks o tropical haar like a muckle sleekit Atlantic-gaun liner.
> The bleck een o solar panels thirled tae its side were as regular as port-holes. The dour smoke-gless command centre on tap o the white struc-ture could easy hae been mistaen for a brig. An its three braid cylindrical antennae rived the skyline like masts redd up against a lang ocean voy-age.[5]

The reader is drawn into a compelling narrative, part quest for ori-gins, part chase thriller, willingly accepting the challenge presented by the language for the sake of the extraordinary cityscapes, land-scapes and cyberscapes which it allows Fitt to create.

The finest Scottish novel of the last decades of the nineteenth century, William Alexander's *Johnny Gibb of Gushetneuk* (1871),[6] derives from Donaldson's 'newspaper' tradition. First published as a serial in the liberal *Aberdeen Free Press* in 1869-70, it employs the familiar combination of standard English narrative and Scots dia-logue – but in a way which reflects the fact that its original audi-ence was a local, largely Scots-speaking one. The principal charac-ters are Scots speaking, and use the distinctive Aberdeenshire dialect. The result is that Scots is central to the novel's meaning and effect to a degree unusual in late-nineteenth-century Scottish fiction; indeed, one key chapter, 'Johnny Gibb discusses the situa-tion', is almost entirely in the vernacular. The subjects discussed in it: the relations between landlord and tenant, labour and owner-ship, contemporary community interest and historic property rights, illustrate the rich expressive capacities of Scots. In the 1920s, C.M. Grieve was to argue that Scots had lost its ability to express 'significant intellection' when it ceased to be the speech of the educated; Johnny's meditation, however, shows Aberdeenshire Scots serving as an effective vehicle for such intellection – and there is nothing 'kailyard' in the passage, which is a forceful contribution to a fierce contemporary debate over the rights of crofters and small farmers. The lairds' entitlement to rent is questioned, and the labour theory of value vigorously propounded:

> I'm weel seer that it was never the arreengement o' Providence that the man that tills the grun an' spen's the strength o' 's days upon't sud be at the merciement o' a man that never laid a han' till't, nor hardly wair'd a shillin' upon't, to bid 'im bide or gyang.

The solution is a radical political one, rooted in the democratic religious tradition which Johnny represents:

> We're taul that the 'earth is for the use o' all: the king 'imsel' is served by the field.' The government o' the countra sud tak' the thing i' their nain han' an' see richt deen; an' the best teetle to the grun sud be the man's willin'ness to lawbour't, and grow corn an' cattle for the susteenance o' man.[7]

The novel is set in 1843, the year of the Disruption, in which the Church of Scotland split over the right of landowners to impose ministers on congregations; for Alexander this was a turning point in the struggle between inherited privilege and the rights of the common man. But *Johnny Gibb* is not only, or even primarily, a historical novel; the real focus is on the land struggles of the 1860s and 1870s which led ultimately to the passing of the crofting legislation of the following decade – and, of course, on the continuing struggle for a juster society.

At the end of the nineteenth century, the consensus among the Scottish *literati* was that both the vernacular literary tradition and lowland Scots itself were dying; T.F. Henderson's judgement that Burns had been the last important writer to work in Scots, his successors mere 'twinkling lights' serving only 'to disclose the darkness of the all-encompassing night',[8] was echoed by J.H. Millar, for whom most recent verse had 'the air of a more or less – and generally a less – skilful imitation of Burns.'[9] Burns cast a long shadow, and the more conventionally 'literary' among his nineteenth-century successors found it impossible to escape his influence. The Scots used by the great vernacular poets of the eighteenth century had drawn its vitality from the spoken language of the time, but in the hands of later imitators, it became a vapid book-Scots, cut off from the living dialects, and increasingly stereotyped and archaic. As a result, it gradually lost its linguistic energy and ability to deal with contemporary concerns. So when Scots re-emerged as a significant literary medium in the mid-nineteenth century, it was not so much a *revived* literary Scots as a *reinvented* literary Scots.

This reinvention was not, however, a single or simple process. In its initial phase, from the last decades of the nineteenth century to the 1920s, the dominant impulse was to bring literary Scots back into close association with current *spoken* Scots in its various varieties; progressive writers created a literary language which was speech-based and therefore recognisably regional. From the 1920s, young writers, strongly influenced by the theories of C.M Grieve and the astonishing early Scots lyrics of his poetic *alter ego*, 'Hugh MacDiarmid', adopted a 'synthetic' approach, combining elements from different periods and regions in an attempt to recreate a 'full canon of Scots'.

The development of a speech-based written vernacular in all the main dialect areas of lowland Scotland in the second half of the nineteenth century was the result of a number of converging developments: the new popular press created a market for vernacular writing, while the period also saw the beginning of the scholarly study of dialects, prompted by the recognition that 'colloquial, so-called illiterate forms of speech [are] as important to the science of comparative historical philology as the study of dead and existing literate languages.....'.[10] Dialect and other non-standard forms became important in the literature of the period, particularly in prose fiction, as younger writers from Kipling to Synge sought to reconnect the language of literature once more with contemporary spoken English in all its varieties.

There were threats as well as encouraging developments. The Education (Scotland) Act of 1872 established universal, compulsory, rate-supported elementary education, and while the extension of educational opportunity and the drive to improve the quality of schooling met with general approval, there were also fears that local identity would be eroded, and a standardised (and anglicised) 'national' culture and speech substituted for Scotland's diverse traditions and dialects. One early twentieth-century editor of *Johnny Gibb* remarked that in it

> The Doric is... at its raciest, caught just in time before the Education Act of 1872 began to take effect. The dialect will not die yet awhile, but there is little doubt that under a compulsory English education its purity and breadth of vocabulary are already on the wane.[11]

Contemporary anxiety about the future of vernacular culture found definitive expression in Charles Murray's 'The Whistle'. Published originally in 1905, it headed Murray's revised *Hamewith* collection of 1909,[12] quickly becoming his best-known piece, learned and recited by schoolchildren throughout Scotland – ironically, since it presents the school as the enemy of the culture of home and locality. In his tale of a herd-lad and the home-made whistle on which he plays traditional tunes, Murray created a powerful symbol: during the summer the lad delights the community with his 'rants sae lively, schottisches, reels an' jigs'. Returning to school in winter, his whistle is confiscated and burnt by the master. The official curriculum has no place for his talent, or respect for the tradition he represents. Considered realistically, the destruction of the whistle cannot be final; after all the boy could make a new whistle as easily as he made the old – but on the symbolic level, the poem resonated strongly with contemporary fears that a standardising and anglicising education would erode local cultural identities rapidly and completely.

While 'The Whistle' seemed to endorse the pessimism about the future of vernacular culture in an age of mass education, the impact it made showed, paradoxically, the continuing vitality of Scots as an expressive medium, and demonstrated that vernacular writing had a future. In the second half of the nineteenth century, then, increased knowledge of Scottish dialects, and a new respect for dialects in general, helped fuel a determination to preserve and develop the vernacular as a medium of expression. Even the anglicising influence of the classroom was not wholly negative; in juxtaposing Scots and English in the lives of pupils, it helped them recognise, by contrast, the features of their own dialect; it is no coincidence that the creators of the modern vernacular literature of the North-East – Violet Jacob, Mary Symon, Charles Murray and Marion Angus – were born in the 1860s and belonged to the first generation to be exposed to the new system of schooling.

Scots did not disappear, of course, and in the decade or so between *Hamewith* and his 1920 collection, *In the Country Places*,[13] Murray had come to realise that formal education was less powerful than he had thought when ranged against other informal kinds. 'It Wasna His Wyte' also centres on a schoolboy, but the focus is on his slow and reluctant journey to school through the countryside sights, sounds and encounters which constitute his *real* education, with the school almost an irrelevance. The adult recollection of similar journeys which concludes the poem suggests that this is true for many Scots (the richly idiomatic vernacular used underlines the superficiality of classroom 'anglicisation'):

> It's thirty year, said ye, it's forty or mair,
> Sin' last we were licket at squeel;
> The dominie's deid an' forgotten for lang,
> An' a' oor book learnin' as weel.
> The size o' a park – wi' the gushets left oot –
> We'll guess geyan near, I daur say;
> Or the wecht o' a stot, but we wouldna gyang far
> Gin we tried noo the coontin' in 'Gray'

Even in the first half of the nineteenth century, vernacular Scots was not 'dying' either as a spoken tongue or as a medium of creative expression, nor was it used exclusively in pallid imitations of Burns. Poets like the Aberdonian William Thom, whose *Rhymes and Recollections of a Handloom Weaver* appeared in 1844,[14] and Janet Hamilton,[15] from Langloan, Coatbridge, who contributed to Cassel's *Working Man's Friend* from 1849, used the current Scots of their respective regions to describe, at first hand, the impact of the huge changes of the time on working people.

Often, too, communities had expressive resources invisible to literary intellectuals: the Highlands had their township bards, and many smaller Scots-speaking communities had a vigorous tradition of vernacular verse, story- and song-making. It was such a tradition in the North-East which produced, between 1830 and 1880, the

'bothy ballads, or 'ploughmen's songs'.[16] Vigorous, earthy and sardonic, they paint a vivid picture of the lives of farm workers at a
time of rapid agricultural change. North-East vernacular enthusiast
J.M. Bulloch pointed out in 1918 that composing verse in the local
variety of Scots was an established tradition in the area:

> The art of writing verse in the vernacular has always been popular in our
> 'corner', but for a long period it was considered rather 'vulgar', and, with
> a few exceptions, unliterary. Only a small portion of it ever reached the
> status of book form.[17]

This kind of verse was regarded as 'vulgar' and 'unliterary' because
it circulated mainly in oral form and used a Scots close to the current speech of ordinary people rather than a literary idiom. Literary
works which used a 'speech-based' Scots were drawing on a 'living
language' with 'all the power of assimilation which belongs to life',
and so included 'words which might shock a literary purist in "classic" Scots.'[18] In the literary world of late-nineteenth-century Britain,
'sub-literary' language of this kind could only became respectable
through the patronage of an established literary figure and, according to Bulloch, it was only when 'Stevenson took it in hand' that
this kind of writing became 'a literary and successful venture'.[19]

   Stevenson's main contribution to vernacular poetry is the sixteen
poems which make up Book II of his 1887 collection, *Underwoods*.
The slightness of his output is not surprising: like many of his contemporaries, he was convinced that Scots could not survive much
longer, and that his ambition to 'have my hour as a native Maker'
was 'an ambition… of the heart rather than of the head, so restricted is it in prospect of endurance...' The sentimental appeal of Scots
was not the only reason for Stevenson's vernacular experiments,
however; dialect was fashionable in literature and in the wryly
humorous note to the Scots poems in *Underwoods*,[20] Stevenson
professes to be following the fashion while mocking its extreme
forms. The obsession with the accurate representation of non-standard speech means that 'in every novel the letters of the alphabet
are tortured… to commemorate shades of mispronunciation.' So,
while emphasising that his own verse is rooted in the sounds,
rhythms and intonations of the Scots he grew up with, he rejects
narrow ideas of dialect 'purity':

> I am from the Lothians myself; it is there I heard the language spoken about my childhood; and it is in the drawling Lothian voice that I repeat it to myself. Let the precisians call my speech that of the Lothians. And if it be not pure, alas! what matters it?

The 'impurities' in Stevenson's Lothian Scots are lexical borrowings – 'if I had ever heard a good word, I used it without shame', he says, 'not caring if it hailed from Lauderdale or Angus, from the Mearns or Galloway.' His remark has been taken as anticipating the idea of a 'synthetic' Scots, created from the resources of different periods and regional forms of the vernacular, but it is hardly a linguistic programme even in embryo; it stems not from ideology but from a curiosity about language, and a delight in its variety and idiosyncrasy natural to the writer. And Stevenson's note, with its 'Table of Common Scottish Vowel Sounds' and observations on the orthography of Scots, is clearly designed to allow the English reader in particular to translate what is on the printed page into sounds, and thus 'hear' the 'drawling Lothian voice' of the poems – most of which are dramatic monologues.

In most respects, indeed, Stevenson's view of the vernacular was contrary to that held by Grieve and his Renaissance allies. In his (premature) lament for Scots, for instance, it is clear that he does not think of it as a single thing; indeed he values it highly because it is 'malleable', existing in a number of distinct forms, each rooted in different local circumstances and histories:

> The day draws near when this illustrious and malleable tongue shall be quite forgotten: and Burns's Ayrshire, and Dr Macdonald's Aberdeen-awa', and Scott's brave, metropolitan utterance will be all equally the ghosts of speech.

For Stevenson, the modern vernacular tradition is heteroglossic rather than unitary, its varieties differing to such an extent that Scots from outside his own locality sounds alien: confessing as an Edinburgh man to 'a friendly feeling for the tongue of Fergusson and Sir Walter', Stevenson adds, 'Burns has always sounded in my ear like something partly foreign'. Here, as the reference to Fergusson indicates, the foreignness of Burns's language is a matter of distance in space rather than distance in time. However Scots is a democracy of dialects; the preference for Edinburgh Scots is personal, the result of early exposure and has nothing to do with the innate superiority of the 'brave, metropolitan utterance' to other varieties. This sense (and celebration) of the variety of Scots is what makes the prospect of its loss especially regrettable: when the vernacular disappears it will mean the end of many modes of expression, not just one. The contrast with Grieve's dismissal of the current varieties of Scots as debased and fragmentary survivals of a complete and canonical 'language' is marked.[21] And though Stevenson has been linked with Burns, Ramsay and Fergusson as a pioneer of a supra-regional standard, he himself saw the Scots of both Burns and Fergusson as recognisably regional in character. In fact, it is not because he anticipated synthetic Scots that Stevenson is important to the vernacular poetic tradition, but because his use of Lothian dialect helped bring literary respectability to writing in regional varieties of Scots, which had been regarded till then as 'sub-literary.'

At first sight, Stevenson belongs firmly among the Burns imitators; the Burns-stanza is used for eleven of the sixteen *Underwoods* poems, and 'Scotch drink and Scotch religion' are recurrent themes. The echoes of Burns link the late eighteenth and late nineteenth centuries, but their main function is to show how much has changed in the intervening time. The speakers of several poems – 'A Lowden Sabbath Morn', 'Embro Hie Kirk', 'The Scotsman's Return from Abroad' and 'Late in the nicht...' – belong to the familiar category of the 'unco guid', seeing themselves as members of the elect, and display the complacency, self-righteousness and rancour of Burns's Holy Willie. But what they represent is no longer powerful; the godly have been reduced to 'A score or twa/Auld wives wi' mutches an' a hoast'. Even where the doctrines of Calvinism are still preached, they have lost their power: the sermon which concludes 'A Lowden Sabbath Morn' is soporific rather than terrifying:

> Bethankit! what a bonny creed!
> What mair would ony Christian need?-
> The braw words rumm'le ower his heid,
>   Not steer the sleeper;
> And in their restin' graves, the deid
>   Sleep aye the deeper.

Against this dogmatic slumber, Stevenson set the energising ideas
of the time: evolution as a ruling principle; a Godless, but perhaps
populated, universe; natural laws which are indifferent to human
interests; a vastly extended sense of time and space – in short, a
scientific perspective has replaced a religious one. The vast new
timescales linked with geology and cosmology form the background to 'The Maker to Posterity' and explain its comic tone;
imagining the fate of his Scots poems in a remote future when the
tongue has long ceased to be spoken and all knowledge of it lost,
the speaker first succumbs to a kind of sentimental regret familiar
in Scottish poetry ('Few spak it than, an' noo there's nane./My puir
auld sangs lie a' their lane,/Their sense, that aince was braw an'
plain,/Tint a'thegether'). But plangency gives way to a comically
triumphant warning to future poets that their work will not last
even as long; living late in time, the final collapse of the universe
will overtake their creations – and themselves. In place of the
grandeur and terror of the Christian end of time, with mankind
centre-stage at the Last Judgement, Stevenson makes humanity the
victim of a cosmic accident. The departure of the last human
beings is comically humiliating and undignified; with 'the hale
planet's guts... dung/About [their] ears', they fly through space 'sair
gruppin' to a spar/Or whammled wi' some bleezin' star.' Though
comic, this vision is rooted in the new scientific world-view:
insignificant and ephemeral, we inhabit a universe which is full of
vast forces and utterly indifferent to our needs and purposes.

In the standard accounts of the prehistory of the Scottish
Renaissance, Stevenson's name is linked with that of Perthshire-
born James Logie Robertson, whose versions of Horace in Scots
appeared in the *Scotsman* from 1881. Their popularity was an indication both of the widespread interest in dialect writing at the time
and of the appeal for the classically-educated of the interplay
between the Scots poems and the Latin originals. Their success led
to their appearance in book form in 1885 as *Horace in
Homespun*;[22] subtitled 'Sketches of Scottish Life and Character
among the Ochils'. Spoken by a vernacular *persona*, 'Hugh
Haliburton', a Perthshire shepherd, the Scots was based on Logie
Robertson's own 'mother tongue and native speech', though influenced by literature. To the modern reader, it is the poems based

on first-hand observation of rural life which are most satisfying –
'Packie's Return', for instance – with the packman starting on his
rounds now that the roads are clear of snow, and springtime tasks
beginning again. 'The Tinklers' is unusual in its emphasis on the
discomforts of the travelling life (in the period, the gangrel is usually presented positively, as the embodiment of freedom and native
traditions in an increasingly regulated society). A vivid portrait of
man and wife trudging in the pouring rain, it has a sardonic,
Hardyesque quality, hinting at a story not fully revealed:

> On sic a day wha tak's the gate?
> The tinkler an' his tousie mate;
> He foremost, wi' a nose o flint,
> She sour an' sulky, yards ahint.
>
> . . . .
>
> Her man an' maister stalks in front,
> Silent mair than a tinkler's wont;
> His wife an' warkshop there ahint him, –
> This day he caresna if he tint them.

Like Stevenson, Logie Robertson was interested in science; as a student at the University of Edinburgh he had won prizes ranging
from the Rhetoric Medal to the Murchison Prize in Geology, and
the latter discipline is drawn on for a poem which not only anticipates MacDiarmid's poetic use of scientific ideas but even employs
the later poet's 'cosmic' viewpoint. 'The White Winter' transposes
into a modern scientific framework a Latin original (the second
Ode of Horace's third Book), which is a prayer to the gods to end
the tempestuous weather sent as a punishment; the speaker of
Logie Robertson's poem considers whether the present cold is
merely seasonal or represents the beginning of a new Ice Age, an
idea which draws on the theory set out in James Geikie's *The
Great Ice Age and its Relation to the Antiquity of Man* (1874) that
glacial and interglacial periods alternate. Like 'The Maker to
Posterity', the poem invokes the extended timescale of contemporary science and the insignificance of human history in comparison: in 'centuries gane,/When human cretur' there was nane', the
earth has travelled 'In ages auld/Thro' regions o' the frigid air,/Past

kennin' cauld.' The universe was not created for human beings, and 'What aince has been may happen twice', with the speaker's apocalyptic (but in its use of a familiar folk-song formula, oddly homely) vision of the icy past returning and all life being wiped out:

> There lay the continents array'd,
> Like corpses o' the lately dead,
> In a cauld sheet,
> Wi icebergs sittin' at their head
> An' at their feet!

Logie Robertson spent his professional life as a schoolmaster in Edinburgh, but retained a life-long interest in rural affairs. He was aware that there were major changes going on in his native country-side during the 1870s and 1880s (in 1888-89, he contributed a series of articles to W.E. Henley's *Scots Observer* under the general title 'The Revolution in the Rural Districts'), but these are only rarely reflected in his Scots poems which for the most part use situations and characters from rural life as a basis for moralising reflections or general truths. There are references to rural depopulation, to enclosure, to the erosion of the rights of cottars and to the attractions of emigration, but evidently Logie Robertson did not think poetry an appropriate medium for topical concerns. They are explored instead in the prose of his *Observer* articles. In them he uses another vernacular *persona*, Gibbie Doss, a wanderer who has returned to his near-derelict home and has been reduced to stone-breaking to make a living. Gibbie uses forceful Scots to argue that it is changes in the countryside rather than the attractions of the city which have depopulated rural areas, in particular 'the muckle-farm system', which has forced out the small cultivator.

If his direct contribution to the revival of vernacular verse was modest, Logie Robertson played an important part in helping to create the conditions which made the achievements of MacDiarmid and his Renaissance allies possible. He helped to make the vernacular tradition available to his contemporaries in accessible form through his popular editions of Ramsay and Burns; and in 1895, he published a selection from William Dunbar, the late-Medieval makar who became the main Scottish Renaissance symbol of an alternative to the Burns tradition. Logie Robertson's *Dunbar* is 'adapted for Modern Readers', and illustrates some of the constraints facing a late-Victorian editor who wanted to make early Scottish literature available to a wide public. To make Dunbar linguistically accessible and morally acceptable to the general reader, Logie Robertson excluded some of the poet's best work on the grounds of 'coarseness', and robbed much of the rest of its character by 'translating' it into Burnsian Scots or English. Nevertheless the edition was part of a life-long effort to promote interest in, and increase knowledge of, Scottish literary and cultural traditions among his contemporaries. Despite their shared belief that lowland Scots was in retreat as a result of anglicising pressures, and would survive only as a 'book-tongue', Logie Robertson and Stevenson helped to ensure the continuity of the vernacular verse tradition, and create the conditions for its renewed flowering in the following century.

Openness to experience, and a habit of plain, even blunt speaking is a characteristic of the Scottish tradition, but as Logie Robertson's censoring of Dunbar indicates, by the late nineteenth century such frankness and inclusiveness was unacceptable, at least in publications aimed at a general readership. However it continued to find vigorous expression in the oral tradition and in works derived from it. Writing to fellow-poet David Rorie in 1925, Charles Murray referred to some North-East songs he had sent to the collector, J.B. Duncan many years before as '"roch" [rough or coarse] to a degree', reflecting the fact that 'we are pretty plain spoken as a race.' Murray's father Peter, carpenter and land-steward, was steeped in local musical and verse-making traditions and, as his son put it, 'has done a bit of rhyming in his time too pointed to be printed'.[23] As ideas of refinement and propriety came to dominate cultural discourse in the late nineteenth century, it became more and more difficult for the pointed to get printed. Many late nineteenth and early twentieth-century critics were unhappy about the candour of the vernacular tradition. The Scots poems in Stevenson's *Underwoods* caused the *Atheneum* reviewer to remark uneasily that in Scots 'a man may venture upon freedom of expression which is denied the chaster Southern muse'.[24] In an address to an English Association meeting in 1912, J.C. Smith was more frankly disapproving, quoting George Saintsbury's claim that 'Literary Scots at all times… admitted a coarseness of actual language which is rarely paralleled in literary English'; he added: 'The charge unhappily is just; but you will not expect me to illustrate it.'[25] In this climate, writers with conventional literary ambitions avoided anything likely to shock publishers or the 'respectable' reader. The oral tradition was very different; Gavin Greig, the great song collector of the early twentieth century, observed that 'folksong has been able to deal with many situations that literary song would hardly dare to touch; with the result that the humbler minstrelsy covers a vastly wider area of human experience.'[26] It is clear from the material collected by scholars of the folk tradition from William Motherwell to Hamish Henderson that what is true of folksong is true of folk-culture generally: all human life is there.

Charles Murray, regarded by most of his contemporaries as the most important vernacular poet of the first decades of the twentieth century, had close and direct connections with the oral tradition of his native Aberdeenshire through his father. This, and his intimate knowledge of Ramsay, Fergusson and Burns, allowed Murray to create a Scots poetry which contemporaries saw as bringing to maturity the work of Stevenson and Logie Robertson. Murray acknowledged the importance of his eighteenth century predecessors but did not copy their language or forms (he rarely uses the Burns stanza, for instance); instead, like them, he created a flexible and expressive poetic language from the Scots he heard around him as he grew up. His literary language was rooted in the life of a community in which physical work and the spoken word were central, and his poetry grows out of the way in which people in such a community characteristically deal with experience – through the particular, personal and anecdotal. It is a social poetry, its accessibility and strong speech-based rhythms making it ideal for public performance – 'For recitation at soirée or smoker there was nothing like it', as one of MacDiarmid's admirers patronisingly phrased it.[27]

It is difficult now to understand the excitement which *Hamewith* aroused on its appearance; to anyone familiar with MacDiarmid's radical approach to Scots, and his technical and thematic audacity, his predecessor's work is bound to seem conven-

tional by comparison. But Murray's first published poem, 'The
Antiquary', appeared in 1889 in Henley's *Scots Observer*, 'a weekly
magazine… intended as a contribution to the Scottish literary
revival'.[28] Unionist and imperialist politically, the *Observer* was,
nevertheless, 'advanced' in literary sympathies, printing Henley's
own highly individual poems and work by Stevenson, Logie
Robertson, Andrew Lang, Yeats – and Kipling, whose 'Barrack-
Room Ballads' created an immediate sensation when they began to
appear in February 1890. In other words when he began to publish, Murray was a literary progressive; in particular, his use of a
poetic language based on the current spoken Scots of a region
sparsely represented in the canon aligned him with those who
were trying to reconnect literature with the energies of popular
speech, and bring new voices into it. *Hamewith*, a collection of
(mostly) Scots poems was first published in Aberdeen in 1900 and
attracted mostly local attention, but the expanded edition of 1909,
brought out by the London- and Edinburgh-based firm of
Constable and Co was a sensational success, despite the dense
Aberdeenshire Scots of many of the poems. *Hamewith* established
Murray overnight as Scotland's best-known vernacular poet, and
looking back even allies of Grieve recognised that he had 'brought
a new province into Scottish poetry – Buchan', and in a language
new to most south of Scotland readers – for, as Robert Bain
remarked grudgingly 'the fascination of the unknown dialect considerably helped the vogue of the poet'.[29]

Murray was largely a poet of rural life, but there is nothing of
the kailyard in his work. Murray's countryside is dynamic, full of
activity – and also of tensions and conflicts; it is undergoing rapid
and fundamental change. In 'Jeames', the cultivator and the
leisured class are in conflict: the small tenant farmer curses his
sporting landlord for the damage done by the laird's 'birds an'
bawds' [hares]. 'The Packman' chronicles the rise of the pedlar,
who starting with only the pack on his back and his own energy,
becomes the local shopowner and banker. As he rises, the gentry
fall, and his daughter marries 'a strappin' (and cash-strapped)
'Deeside laird.' We learn from the gravedigger in 'A Green Yule'
that, with the death of the landowner, his widow will be at the
mercy of the shrewd 'hame-drauchted' factor, and the estate will

soon be on the market. In these poems, the landed gentry, once the masters, have lost their energy and sense of purpose, and new, rising groups are taking their place. The process is presented positively, though with a recognition that there are gains and losses involved – the packman, once a key figure in the transmission of the ballads, songs and lore of the community, cannot bear to be reminded of his beginnings now that he is settled and respectable.

Hamewith illustrated the expressive possibilities of North-East Doric, and demonstrated that both the dialect and the distinctive life of the region could capture the interest of a wide audience; above all, perhaps, it showed that Scots did not need to be confined to the comic or sentimental. It strongly influenced the vernacular poetry of the next decade or so, much of the best of which was produced by writers from the North-East like Violet Jacob, Mary Symon, David Rorie, Marion Angus and Helen Cruickshank. Violet Jacob's career shows the influence of Murray's success; her first publication was a comic poem in Scots, while her first 'serious' collection, *Verses* (1905), is entirely in English. However in her second and third volumes, most of the work is in Scots, and the regional roots of the language used are clear from the titles – *Songs of Angus* (1915) and *More Songs of Angus* (1918).[30] In the note to *Poems Scots and English* (1917), John Buchan stressed that his Scots was not a book-tongue, but based on the speech of 'the hill country of the Lowlands, from the Cheviots to Galloway', which I could always speak... more easily than I could write...'[31]

Even C.M. Grieve – who was to attack Murray – and North-East Scots – quite viciously ('anything more corrupt... would be difficult to find in any dialect of any tongue'[32] was his comment on Murray's dialect) – recognised the importance of the North-East to the development of vernacular writing in the first two decades of the twentieth century, referring in July 1925 to 'what may be termed the North-East Revival'. Some months earlier, in a letter to Herbert Grierson, he had even associated himself with it, speaking of 'the Scottish succession in which I am fain to have a part – Hugh Haliburton, Charles Murray, Mrs Violet Jacob and others...'.[33] Initially, however, he had repudiated that succession. On his return from war service in 1919, Grieve had rejected Scots as a medium, feeling with the majority of critics and literary men at the time that it lacked the resources to deal with contemporary life. So in 1921 for instance, he argued that, for the contemporary Scottish writer, English was 'an immensely superior medium of expression', and Scots only 'a backwater of the true river of Scottish national expression' with, at best, a marginal literary role as the 'preserve of the *tour de force* and the *jeu d'esprit*.'[34] If this view of Scots belongs to the elegiac tradition of Millar and Henderson, it also recognises – in conceding that it can still be a vehicle for the '*tour de force* and the *jeu d'esprit*' – the renewed energy and technical enterprise which Stevenson and others in the recent 'Scottish succession' had brought to the tradition.

Grieve's rejection of Scots in the years immediately after the Great War is, however, surprising for Scots had shown itself capable of dealing truthfully and movingly with that cataclysmic event. The quality of the best vernacular war poetry was recognised during and immediately after the war itself, but it has scarcely featured in the post-1960s revival of interest in Great War literature – partly because it is in Scots, and partly because it was written by civilians and is usually about civilian experience. In a tradition which has usually privileged poetry written by combatants, and accepted the jaundiced view of civilian attitudes expressed by soldier-poets like Owen and Sassoon, war poetry written by non-combatants has tended to be dismissed as naïve at best, and callously jingoistic at worst. The consequence has been the almost complete exclusion from the war canon of two important kinds of civilian war experience: that of the generation too old to fight, but whose sons and grandsons went to war, and that of women, whose husbands, sweethearts – and children – did so.

Some of the finest work of MacDiarmid's vernacular predecessors, Murray, Violet Jacob and Mary Symon among them, deals with the war, and it was the character of the vernacular literary tradition itself and the fact that their poetic language was based on current spoken Scots, that is responsible for its high quality. The Scottish literary tradition at its best has always maintained close links with oral and popular culture; as a result it was less influenced than the mainstream English tradition by late-Victorian demands for 'refinement', and so was better adapted to expressing the realities of war experience. Scots poets could also draw on a native ballad and song tradition in which battles, feuds, murders and other violent and atrocious events are presented with exceptional power. By drawing on traditional techniques – rapid pace, lack of overt emotion or moralising, concentration on the physical rather than the psychological – the Scots poets of the early twentieth century were able to create exceptionally moving war poetry. And because Scots itself had been, for several centuries, the medium of ordinary people rather than intellectuals, it was rooted in the physical and the particular; if, as Grieve charged, it lacked the resources for 'significant intellection', it nevertheless had the power to deal profoundly and memorably with experience by means of the local and specific. In fact it approached the ideal of Hemingway's lieutenant Frederic Henry in *A Farewell to Arms* who, repelled by the exalted euphemisms of patriotic rhetoric, wishes for a language entirely composed of particulars:

> There were many words that you could not stand to hear and finally only the names of places had dignity. Certain numbers were the same way and certain dates and these with the names of the places were all you could say and have them mean anything. Abstract words such as glory, honour, courage, or hallow were obscene beside the concrete names of villages, and numbers of roads, the names of rivers, the numbers of regiments and dates.

The Great War was widely seen as an expression of a 'Prussianism' which aimed to impose on the whole of Europe the militarised and authoritarian order which Prussia had established within Germany itself. As the use of Scots and the maintenance of other aspects of vernacular culture could be seen as conscious acts of resistance in the face of the anglicising, standardising and homogenising tendencies of the age, so too they could be seen as expressions of resistance to equivalent, but far more alien and malevolent forces, operating internationally. It is not surprising in an age when Britain's multi-racial, multi-cultural Empire was at the height of its development that the strength of 'British' culture should be seen as rooted in diversity – of the mother country, with its several historic 'nations', as well as of the wider Empire. The claim that the dynamism of Britain was linked with creative tensions within the country, and the cultural and ethnic mixture of its peoples, was an important element in wartime propaganda and helps to explain why, in the period, vernacular poetry, often in quite dense Scots, appeared in London publications ranging from the sober *Times* – Charles Murray's 'A Sough o' War' appeared there in November 1914 – to the popular *Graphic*, in which Mary Symon's 'After Neuve Chapelle' appeared in April 1915. At this historical moment then, choosing to write in vernacular Scots was often a conscious expression of *British* patriotism:

> ...all movements that make for the expression of national sentiment and idiosyncrasy are in the ascendant, largely as a protest against the tendencies to road-roller everything and everybody to a dead level and to 'standardise' life. This is not a reversion to particularism. It is a simple recognition of the fact that the life of the whole is dependent on the life of the part; and it is a useful check to the movement which has made Germany attempt to establish one general scheme of Kultur – that is to say a civilisation of her own making.[35]

The lessons of the folk tradition can be seen clearly in Charles Murray's 1916 song-like lyric 'When Will the War Be By?', which focuses on the anxiety and grief of loved ones left behind. The poem challenges the claim of the soldier-poets that civilian life continued unaffected by the conflict and that those at home rarely thought of the men at the front. Murray's poem reflects more accurately than these notions the intimate connection between home front and battlefront in what was, after all, a war of mass citizen armies and total mobilisation which blurred the distinction between civilian and soldier, combatant and non-combatant. Its two short stanzas present the situation of a girl left behind, moving from her loneliness and anxiety to her anguish at learning of her lover's death. The central motif is the form of folk-divination in which petals are pulled from a flower, here used by the girl to determine when the war might end:

> 'This year, neist year, sometime, never,
> When will the war be by?'

In the second stanza the list of possibilities undergoes a sinister change as the family look at the newspaper, which carries reports of the fighting and also the latest casualty lists – 'Weel, wounded, missin', deid' loads the possibilities three to one against survival, so the end of the poem comes as no surprise:

A lass raxed oot for the list to read –
'Weel, wounded, missin', deid';
An' the war was by for twa.

Murray offers no consolation: there is no indication that the lad's death has helped the national cause to prevail and no suggestion of an afterlife in which the lovers may, in time, be reunited. Instead we are left with the stark fact of loss and grief, made the more poignant by the youth of the couple.

If 'When Will The War Be By' deals with the moment of loss; Violet Jacob's 'The Field by the Lirk o' the Hill', from the same year, deals with its long-term consequences. Spoken by an elderly mother who has lost her only son, there is a hint that she thinks the death worthwhile ('Prood maun ye lie/Prood did ye gang'); however the main emphasis is on the continuing pain of living with the knowledge that he will never return. And the poem suggests that the loss is not just of one individual, but of an entire way of life – those who would have continued the life and work of the community, ensuring its fertility in every sense, will never return:

The yaird's a' weed
And the fairm's a' still –
Wha'll sow the seed
I' the field by the lirk o' the hill.

These poems were written before general disillusionment is supposed to have set in – that is they predate the Somme battles in summer 1916. Mary Symon's 'The Glen's Muster-Roll',[36] a powerful elegy for a war-hit community, was published as early as February of that year. In it, a country dominie reads the names on the school honour-roll, noting the fate of each former pupil and remembering their schooldays. The poem illustrates how closely the war was followed by those who remained at home: it has a density and particularity of reference unusual in the Great War canon though, surprisingly, reverses are emphasised rather than victories. Opening with a confident patriotic swing, there is an accumulating sense of loss as deaths are recalled. The poem ends with a consequence of war even more difficult to confront than death in battle; Robbie, the most gifted of the dominie's pupils has survived the fighting, but returned hopelessly damaged in mind and body. In the face of

this living reminder of the effects of war, the adult and official justi-
fications seem slick and shallow, and the dominie is left without
consolation:

> '...where's the nimble nostrum, the dogma fair an' fine
> To still the ruggin' heart I hae for you, oh, Loon o Mine?'

In the last stanza, the dead and wounded return to the schoolroom
for something which is part-tribunal, part ghostly last lesson. Now
the pupils are the questioners, and the master, once the confident
representative of authority has no answers:

> '...as I sit a vision comes: Ye're troopin' in aince mair,
> Ye're back fae Aisne an' Marne an' Meuse, Ypres an' Festubert;
> Ye're back on weary bleedin' feet – you, you that danced an' ran –
> For every lauchin' loon I kent I see a hell-scarred man.
> Not mine but yours to question now! You lift unhappy eyes –
> Ah, Maister, tell's fat a' this means.' And I ye thocht sae wise
> Maun answer wi' the bairn words ye said tae me langsyne:
> I dinna ken, I dinna ken. Fa does, oh Loons o' Mine?'

It is not only the master who can find no justification for the events
which have sent the boys to 'the hell where youth and laughter
go'; 'fa [who] does?' effectively dismisses the official case for the
war as well; *no-one* knows. All 'answers' and even the adult language, the political rhetoric, in which such answers are couched,
are rejected in the end. Only the 'bairn words' expressing ignorance and helplessness are left, and in a moving change of role,
the authority figure is transformed into an ignorant schoolboy.

   The title of Charles Murray's post-war volume, *In the Country
Places* (1920)[37] suggests a retreat from the troubled post-war world
into rural nostalgia, but the sardonically humorous 'Gin I Was God'
offers a radical view of the significance of the war. The speaker
outlines how he would respond if he were God and had just
learned about this most recent outbreak of human wickedness and
destructiveness. Bored with the incessant angelic praise he (or,
rather, He) has wandered 'To some clood-edge' where he can
'Look ower an' watch hoo things were gyaun aneth'. Seeing
with horror 'hoo men I'd made mysel'/Had startit in to pooshan,
sheet an' fell,/To reive an' rape, an' fairly mak' a hell/O my
braw birlin' Earth', he is furious and retracting the promise not

to send a second Flood:

> '...or they'd time to lench a second ark,
> Tak' back my word an' sen' anither spate,
> Droon oot the hale hypothec, dicht the sklate,
> Own my mistak', an', aince I'd cleared the brod,
> Start a'thing ower again...'.

The reference to 'pooshan' (poison gas, first used by the Germans at Ypres in 1915), and to the scale of the destruction, which is making a hell of the *whole* world, links the poem firmly to the Great War, and to the chemical weapons first used in it. But, strikingly, it is 'men' in general who are guilty, not just the Hun; our vaunted civilisation as a whole is guilty, not a particular people. This sardonic God's-eye view of the human record, echoed in some of MacDiarmid's early poems, appears again in Murray's striking version of Horace's *Carmina* 1, 34, with its audacious concluding images of the break-up of the great European land empires in military defeat and revolution:

> But noo the Kaiser and his Kings are skirtin' fae the lan';
> They seen got youkie roon the chouks when God put tee a han';
> An Fortune like an aeroplane comes loopin' doon the blue,
> An' kills a Czar to place in pooer some raggit Russian Jew.

These expressions of the effect of the Great War seem truer from a twenty-first century perspective, than the 'progressive' responses of the time. Of course neither Murray's speaker nor MacDiarmid's can simply be identified with the poet, but the anger, disgust and sense of foreboding in the work of the older poet now seem a more appropriate response to the age of the dictators than celebrations of Lenin or the Cheka.

In the autumn of 1922, C.M. Grieve, journalist, polemicist, author of poetry and prose in English, and scourge of the contemporary vernacular movement, found himself writing poetry in Scots. Grieve himself described how it came to happen, and printed the two short poems which were his first vernacular compositions, in his regular 'Scottish Books and Bookmen' column in the *Dunfermline Press* for 30 September – though he was not entirely frank about the circumstances in which they were written, attributing the poems, 'The Watergaw' and 'The Blaward and the Skelly', to a visiting 'friend' who had become interested in Sir James Wilson's *Lowland Scotch as Spoken in the Lower Stathearn District of Perthshire* (1915). Though a scholarly monograph seems an unlikely source of poetic inspiration, Grieve's 'friend' found it stimulating, and 'passed over to me the two sets of verses which I have pleasure in reproducing here.' Grieve added, 'They serve a useful purpose, I think, in rescuing from oblivion and restoring to literary use, forgotten words that have a descriptive potency otherwise unobtainable.' He went on to suggest that the friend's poems were not mere philological curiosities, but had 'some genuine poetic merit too.'[38] In the original account, the 'friend' was not named, but when the more interesting of the two poems, 'The Watergaw', was reprinted shortly after in Grieve's own *Scottish Chapbook*, it was attributed to 'Hugh MacDiarmid', who had already contributed a number of English poems to that publication.

After the appearance of 'The Watergaw', Scots poems by 'Hugh MacDiarmid' began to appear regularly in the *Chapbook* and elsewhere, and for a time the fiction was maintained that Grieve and MacDiarmid were different persons – though with feelings of mutual regard. Grieve's vehement attacks on the contemporary vernacular movement spearheaded by the Burns Federation, and his repeated assertions of the superiority of English, lie behind his initial reluctance to claim his first Scots poems as his own. But his failure to acknowledge paternity was not merely a tactic to avoid charges of inconsistency; it reflected something more profound. The invention of 'Hugh MacDiarmid' registered his own surprise and puzzlement at what he found himself doing; in relation to the views to which he was consciously committed, it must have indeed seemed as if someone else was responsible for the poetry. Even after he began writing in Scots, Grieve continued to attack the campaign to promote the language; so, in November 1922, two months after the appearance of his first lyrics, again in the *Dunfermline Press*, he was claiming that 'Vernacularists are engaged in a futile and stupid endeavour to put back the clock... The main stream of Scottish literature must be that in which the vital pre-occupations of the nation are most effectively presented. The Doric is utterly incapable of any such task.'[39] The inconsistency is more apparent than real, however; the fact is that Grieve

could not know, when he began to write poetry in Scots, how far
the vernacular would be able to serve his expressive needs or how
long-lived his vernacular self would be. The conclusion to his original *Dunfermline Press* article – 'a Scotsman may waste his time in
many a worse way than in giving a new lease of life to ancient
words by means of verses such as these' – suggests that initially he
saw writing in the vernacular as little more than an antiquarian
pastime. The fact is that when Grieve 'discovered' Scots, he had no
ready-made theory about its potentialities; Grieve the critic and
theorist found out what Scots was capable of by responding to the
growing body of work which the creative self (soon to be named
'Hugh MacDiarmid') was producing. The process was, inevitably, a
tentative and exploratory one. The unplanned and unexpected discovery of the poetic possibilities of Scots coloured Grieve's subsequent thinking about language and the business of creating and
responding to poetry, convincing him that 'the act of poetry [is] the
reverse of what it is usually thought to be; not an idea gradually
shaping itself in words, but deriving entirely from words...' He
adds, significantly, that it was 'in this way that I wrote all the best
of my Scots poems.'[40]

So Grieve discovered himself as a Scots poet not through
rethinking his view of the vernacular, but through responding
despite his strong intellectual convictions to particular Scots words
and phrases. His conclusion was that the language itself had
evoked a response below conscious level which swept aside his
conscious beliefs and set him to work with more energy and originality than he had shown before. The words and phrases recorded
by Wilson (and in sources like Jamieson's *Dictionary*[41]) owed their
subversive effect to their physical character, their sounds and
rhythms, which had a 'meaning' and effect more profound than
mere semantics; they proved that 'It's soon, no' sense, that faddoms
the herts o' men.' What happened had more than individual significance, moreover; through his encounter with Scots, particularly
with older Scots, Grieve felt that something latent in himself, hitherto overlaid by alien linguistic and cultural influences, had been
liberated and was demanding expression.

Grieve's 'conversion' made him sharply aware of the importance
of the physical as against the intellectual dimension of language,

particularly for the kind of lyric poetry which he now found himself writing, and it demonstrated that whatever its limitations as a medium for 'intellection', the vernacular possessed other kinds of power in abundance. With this insight came a sense of the limitations of rationality and conscious awareness; in MacDiarmid's work their pretensions are frequently ironised, not least through the use of Scots itself, which is not usually the language of intellectual activity. The need to keep the arrogance of intellect in check and thus remain open to creative promptings from other areas of the psyche, is a major theme of MacDiarmid's greatest Scots poem *A Drunk Man Looks at the Thistle* in which the narrator laughs

...to see my crazy little brain
– And ither folks – tak'n' itsel' seriously

He asks to be saved from the arrogance of intellect, using a vivid metaphor to illustrate the relationship between the intellect and the unconscious:

Like standin' water in a pocket o'
Impervious clay I pray I'll never be,
Cut aff and self-sufficient, but let reenge
Heichts o' the lift and benmaist deeps o' sea.

Grieve disagreed strongly with contemporary vernacular enthusiasts about the nature and value of the contemporary regional dialects. For the vernacularists, as for Stevenson, the variety of Scots reflected the diversity of Scotland itself, each dialect mirroring the history and character of its region. For Grieve, the existence of regional dialects was evidence of the 'disintegrated' state of Scottish culture; they were the fragmentary and decayed remains of what had once been a unitary language. Grieve failed to recognise that dialects are coherent and systematic structures rooted in the linguistic history of a particular area – indeed, he insisted that dialect differences were no more than 'local abnormalities', rooted in 'illiteracy or misunderstanding'. As a result, he was convinced that the vernacular tradition could not be reinvigorated using current Scots. And since non-standard spoken varieties of a language are characteristically used by the 'lower' social classes who lack extended education, they have, inevitably, a 'very circumscribed expressive range' and 'low literary values'. In sum, contemporary spoken Scots is no more than the sum of an unsystematic collection of errors, misunderstandings and 'colloquialisms' (there is an echo in this last of the familiar idea that though 'historic' Scots is linguistically respectable, contemporary Scots is only a kind of 'slang').

This view of non-standard language varieties is familiar enough. Rooted in snobbish assumptions about the relationship between class, education and linguistic competence, it is based on popular usage in which 'the terms dialect and language are... opposed to each other', with 'Forms of speech with no corresponding written form, or those used by uneducated people'... [being] labeled "dialects" and contrasted with the true "languages" of the literate and educated.'[42] Though serious scholars like Sir James Murray had abandoned such notions before the end of the nineteenth century, they remained powerful, particularly in Scottish schools, till recently. As a result, in most classrooms, current Scots was forbidden, though Scots in historical or aesthetic contexts (the reading and reciting of verse or the singing of songs) was accepted and even encouraged.

In fact Grieve's attack on the defenders of the current dialects was as much political as linguistic; enthusiasm for local language and culture seemed to him divisive in its emphasis on differences *within* Scotland as against the (as he thought) more significant differences between Scotland and England. Since the most prominent vernacular activists were the 'successful London Scots' of the London Burns Club and its Vernacular Circle, it must follow that their campaign was a unionist project, aimed at perpetuating 'old divisions and differences' and thus retarding the nascent movement towards independence; those involved in

> the movement headed by the Burns Federation... have committed themselves merely to an attempt to perpetuate the debased dialects still more or less current and disavowed any intention of recreating the national language *in toto.*[43]

Their aim is an 'absurdly fractional' one, and if they succeed Scots will remain in the kailyard. To be capable once again of addressing the 'full range of poetic purpose', it is necessary to reconstitute it

from elements drawn from different regions and periods. Thus
Grieve is scathing about the suggestions for developing a modern
written Scots made by Sir James Wilson:

> Sir James suggests as the basis of rendering the dialect the actual pronun-
> ciation of old people who have spoken it all their lives in daily converse.
> This is… to 'found' on decayed and corrupt forms, and is moreover to
> make the most plebeian and illiterate usage the criterion. You will no
> more get good broad Scots that way than you could get a good literary
> medium of English from the colloquialisms of a group of Cockneys or
> Westmoreland farm-servants.

To get a better foundation for a modern literary Scots, it would be
necessary, Grieve argued, to go back a very long way, for 'the only
way to avoid that partition of the Scots language into dialects
which is an aspect of its degeneration is to go back to the idioms,
vocabulary etc of Dunbar and Henryson and the other old
Makars.'[44] So by 1925 or so, Grieve had concluded that the vernacularists were mistaken not so much in looking to the past as in not
looking back far enough, to a time when a 'full canon of Scots'
was available.

In emphasising the constructed and historical nature of the language required by the contemporary Scots writer, with its sources
in scholarly works like Jamieson's *Dictionary* and the poetry of the
Makars, Grieve was implying, conveniently, that the literary man
had little to learn from his native Scots-speaking contemporaries.
The programme for remaking the canon of Scots outlined in 'A
Theory of Scots Letters', is entirely consistent with this: the creation
of a 'synthetic Scots' capable of addressing 'the full range of poetic
purpose' is largely a matter of recovering materials from the past of
the language, rather than from the present dialects. The emphasis
is on the old, the forgotten, the disregarded – Jamieson's dictionary, for instance, reveals a '*vis comica*' that lies bound 'by desue-
tude and misappreciation in the recesses of the Doric', and earlier
Scots contains a 'vast unutilised mass of lapsed observation made
by minds whose attitudes to experience and imaginative tendencies were quite different from any possible to Englishmen and
anglicised Scots today'. But, conveniently, it was just these 'attitudes to experience and imaginative tendencies' which would be
required tomorrow, for

...the whole unrealised genius of the Scots Vernacular has brilliantly fore-casted... tendencies which are only now emerging in European life and literature, and which must unquestionably have a very important bearing upon the future of human culture and civilisation.[45]

Scots is a once and future language; vigorously physical, but sensitive to the subtlest psychological and emotional effects; capable of expressing contrary things in the same phrase or even word – in short, the ideal vehicle for literary modernism as defined by Eliot and Pound in the early decades of the twentieth century. Indeed, Grieve's claim that Scots is perfectly adapted for 'advanced' literary purposes depends on the application to the cultural history of Scotland of Eliot's influential idea of a 'dissociation of sensibility' – a psychic division – dated to the seventeenth century, in which sensation and thought, formerly integrated, split apart. Eliot traced the process to the effects of the Reformation. In that context, the apparent tragedy of Scots, its failure to develop beyond the six-teenth century, will turn out to be a source of strength. For in the historical vernacular, Grieve claims, sensation, feeling and thought are still bound inextricably together.

This emphasis on the need to return for inspiration to the remote past, when a 'canonical' Scots embodied a national *weltan-schauung* utterly different from that of the English (thus bringing about a return of the repressed) was central to Grieve's thinking about Scots from the time of his first experiments. His *Dunfermline Press* commentary on the language of his first Scots lyrics empha-sises that the words and phrases used by the poetical 'friend' are 'obsolete', 'unused', 'forgotten'; they are 'ancient words' rescued from 'oblivion' and given 'a new lease of life'. Summing up the effects of Grieve's encounter with Sir James Wilson's book, Duncan Glen says 'thus did an interest in archaic words prompt C.M. Grieve or 'Hugh MacDiarmid' to write in Scots.'[46] But, Wilson's monograph was a product of just that interest in and affection for the kind of Scots which Grieve had dismissed as 'plebian and illit-erate'; the *current* speech, that is, of ordinary country people. And Wilson makes it quite clear in his introductory note that his main interest is not historical, but in the living dialect:

I have not attempted to give the history of the words, but have contented myself with giving a true account... of the words, grammar and idioms actually used by the best living speakers of the local dialect within the area.[47]

Wilson's book appeared in 1915, only seven years before Grieve's first vernacular experiments; the field-work on which it was based takes the dialect back a few more years – and doubtless the 'best living speakers' were older members of the speech-community – nevertheless, far from being 'obsolete' or 'forgotten', the words, phrases and idioms recorded by Wilson were current in Strathearn only a decade or so before 'The Watergaw' and 'The Blaward and the Skelly' were written. And if Grieve's emphasis is on assembling a 'synthetic' Scots from materials quarried from the distant past of the language, MacDiarmid's most effective poetry draws mainly on its current resources. The narrative voice of *A Drunk Man Looks at the Thistle*, for instance, is clearly based on contemporary spoken Scots, and even the extraordinary lyric passages in that poem are less notable for their lexical strangeness than for their metrical virtuosity and the use of Scots to create a powerfully oblique symbolist poetry reminiscent of the great European masters. Conversely, MacDiarmid's Scots does not resemble the pastiche Middle Scots which Lewis Spence was experimenting with in the mid-1920s, nor is it like the archaising and 'synthetic' Scots employed by Sidney Goodsir Smith in the 1930s and 1940s.

The fact is that it was contemporary rural speech, as recorded in Wilson's book, which turned Grieve into MacDiarmid: the titles of both his first Scots poems come from it; 'blaward' (the cornflower) and 'skelly' (the charlock) are only a few lines apart in Wilson's list of trees and plants; 'watergaw' appears on the same page as 'onding' and 'yow-trummle', 'chitter' is in the glossary, while the saying which begins the second stanza of 'The Watergaw' is slightly adapted from one in Wilson's list of proverbs and sayings – 'there's nae reek ee laverock's hoose the nicht'. 'Hugh MacDiarmid' came into existence through Grieve's encounter with the speech of (in his own phrase) 'mere hinds and chawbacons.'

The irrelevance of Grieve's theories to MacDiarmid's best work is hardly surprising; regional dialects are not deteriorated fragments of a once integrated 'language'; they are coherent, evolving and, of course, interacting systems. As such, they are much more than lexical warehouses to be raided for 'vivid' words and phrases. The same can be said, of course, of the vernacular in its various historic phases. The fact that the linguistic materials to be synthesised in a programme like Grieve's are all Scots of one sort or another does not necessarily mean that they can be combined effectively, even in poetic discourse. Indeed, in poetry and drama especially, with their close links with the spoken word, 'sayability' is an important issue, and sets limits to linguistic eclecticism; there are significant differences, after all, between the current dialects, and between past and present stages of the language, in sound, stress and cadence, so that effective borrowing across geographical or histori-cal space requires a finely-tuned poetic ear. MacDiarmid had that ear, but Grieve, mistakenly convinced that most of the differences between dialects were either linguistically trivial or the result of error and corruption, failed to recognise its importance.

The fact is, however, that the most durable of the poetry pro-duced by MacDiarmid's 'Renaissance' followers is not that which follows Grieve's prescriptions, but that which has firm roots in the grammar and syntax of particular regional varieties of Scots. As George Bruce points out, this was true even of MacDiarmid's own literary language:

> [his] synthetic Scots, as it unhappily has been called, was based on a Scots that he himself spoke, and which he heard all about him on the Borders... Hence in all his poetry in Scots the language had authority, no matter how much vocabulary he may have added by consulting literary sources for Scots words.

Commenting on the work of MacDiarmid's successors and imita-tors, Bruce contrasts those like William Soutar whose mother-tongue knowledge of the language allowed them to create a credi-ble literary Scots with 'those who had not used the tongue in their youth'. When these latter 'turned to Lallans (or Scots) in admiration of MacDiarmid and deliberately thickened their Scots, the poem frequently rang false...'[48] Soutar himself criticised some of his younger contemporaries in the same terms – among them Sydney Goodsir Smith; for him 'the chief fault of all the younger school' of vernacular poets was that 'many of the words have not passed through the blood and the imagination', with the result that 'they remain counters and are often set in the wrong context.'[49]

Soutar's Scots, in contrast, is firmly based on the Perthshire speech which was his mother tongue. This firm linguistic basis allowed him to extend and develop his native dialect, turning it into a flexible and expressive poetic medium. As his biographer says: 'It was because the main stream of his literary vocabulary sprang, directly and copiously, from his own talk that Soutar could allow words from other sources to flow into it without muddying the current. The current ran so strongly that all extraneous contributions were swept along in the tide.'[50] Soutar came from a background in which the cultural and religious traditions of lowland Scotland were unusually strong; his parents belonged to an 'Auld Licht' congregation and the household was Scots-speaking. And unusually for a young man from a comfortably-off family, he spent almost all his short adult life in the parental home; after war service and university, he became bedridden in 1930 at the age of 32, and lived with his parents till his death in 1943. This continuing immersion in a Scots-speaking milieu helps to explain Soutar's complaint that 'English is *not* natural to me; and I use it "consciously", even in conversation; it is always something of an effort to me to find my words; and not uncommonly I labour as if I were speaking in a foreign language.'[51] As for most Scots, however, English was the 'natural' medium for *written* expression, and Soutar's first poetic attempts were in that language.

Soutar's first contact with Grieve in May 1922, was followed by the publication of three (English) poems in the last issue of the latter's *Northern Numbers* and, over the next year or so, the Perthshire poet became increasingly interested in the cultural renaissance which Grieve was promoting – and in playing a part in it. Initially, this did not mean using Scots as a literary medium: after all, till his own 'discovery' of Scots in the autumn of 1922 (and for some time afterwards) Grieve insisted that the forward-looking Scottish writer must use English, a view Soutar shared at first. His earliest compositions in Scots date from September 1923 – a year after Grieve's *Dunfermline Press* poems appeared – his interest in the vernacular tradition having been stimulated by reading the old Scots ballads for the first time in the summer of that year, and by the strong impression made by some of the Scots lyrics by 'Hugh MacDiarmid' which had been appearing in Grieve's *Scottish Chapbook* since October 1922; these, together with the Doric triolets, 'Spring' and 'Winter' in Murray's *In the Country Places*, prompted his first venture into Scots – four 'Triolets in the Doric'.

These first experiments were small-scale because Soutar believed that contemporary Scots lacked the resources for major poetry; his comment on MacDiarmid's first collection of lyrics in 1925 was 'Good work, Christopher my lad – but the big things which Scotsmen have to do yet in literature must be done in English'[52] ('yet' looks forward, however, to a time when Scots will be capable of more). By 1928 Soutar had accepted that for Scots to become again the vehicle for major literature, it would be necessary to extend its resources. However he recognised more clearly than Grieve that the new literary language would have to appeal not just to a small coterie of literary nationalists but to the Scottish public at large. He recognised, too, that the best way to begin to develop the language was to aim at the young, whose linguistic habits and attitudes were still malleable; in a 1928 essay, he argued that the hope for the renaissance lay 'in the future… when a generation has grown up who are familiar with this synthetic language and have gathered around it these associations which breathe life into the bones of words.'[53] In a 1931 letter to Grieve, he put it more poetically:

> If the Doric is to come back alive, it will come on a cock-horse. How are you going to get it into the schools otherwise?… I fancy, the best beginning would be in bairn-rhymes of six or eight lines which contain no more than one or two uncommon words… we should thereby begin a sort of vaccination with the Doric; the children will grow up with it in their blood – they would have a vocabulary to build on.[54]

Ironically, this harks back to the Vernacular Circle strategy attacked by Grieve. The Circle, too, had emphasised the need to get Scots 'into the schools' and particularly into early education. In 1925, Soutar had read *The Scottish Tongue*,[55] the published version of some of the lectures delivered to the Circle early in their campaign. It included the text of a lecture given in January 1921 by Sir William Craigie, future editor of the *Dictionary of the Older Scottish Tongue*, outlining a programme for Scots modeled on initiatives in Norway, Friesland and the Faroes. For Craigie, 'school-teaching and school-books' were the `first requirements for a successful 'revival' of Scots, a first step towards the creation of a full modern

CoLIN MILTON

vernacular literature, in which all the genres, including the long poem, drama and prose fiction, would be represented.

The Scottish Tongue had a significant influence on Soutar, crystallizing his ambition to join the native tradition – after reading it he expressed the hope 'that I shall come under the plaidie of the old Makars some day.'[56] Personal ambition and cultural programme came together in his 1933 volume of Scots poems for children, *Seeds in the Wind*, the title referring to the hope, expressed more directly in 'The Thistle' that the poems will help Scots to spread:

> Blaw, wind, blaw
> The thistle's head awa:
> For ilka head ye whup in the air
> The yird will lift a hunner, or mair,
> Doun in the lair o' yon sheuch be the shaw.

The fact that two of Soutar's three volumes of Scots poetry were aimed at children – *Seeds in the Wind* was followed in 1937 by *Riddles in Scots*, with *Poems in Scots*, his only 'adult' volume appearing in 1935 – shows how far Soutar's view of how best to develop Scots differed from Grieve's. The younger poet felt that, given the present state and situation of the vernacular, it would be a considerable time before Scots was capable of giving full expression to contemporary experience. The young were the most promising audience because for almost all children in lowland Scotland, then as now, the culture of neighbourhood and playground was a predominantly vernacular one. Soutar's two volumes for children take their inspiration from this lively communal culture, with its juxtaposition of the topical and the traditional, and combination of ritual solemnity with extravagant, grotesque or subversive humour. The mainly short poems employ forms appropriate to a juvenile audience – nursery rhyme, chant, singing game, riddle – but the overall effect of a collection like *Seeds in the Wind* is substantial even for the adult reader, for, in the words of one contemporary reviewer, while the 'form is, in the conventional sense, minor, his issues and preoccupations are major.'[57] In presenting the world as a child might see it – as a place of mystery and wonder, joy and terror – many of the poems challenge the habitual responses and stale perceptions of adulthood; these celebrations of the *childlike* are complemented by poems which expose much adult behaviour as *childish*.

Though Soutar disagreed strongly with Grieve's élitism, arguing that poetry could only make a contribution to general cultural renewal if it was grounded in the experience of ordinary people and accessible to them, his own practice was influenced by the older poet's idea that current Scots needed to be radically extended. So despite being a mother-tongue Scots speaker, Soutar 'worked for years to widen the range of his Scots vocabulary';[58] he kept notebooks in which he recorded Scots words and, between 1932 and 1936, worked systematically, word by word, through Chambers' *Scots Dialect Dictionary*. However it was the native-speaker's secure and unselfconscious command of idiom, which allowed him to recognise which 'new' material was capable of assimilation and absorb it into his personal poetic language. Such a process has little in common with the systematic construction of a 'synthetic Scots' on Grieve's model, as the Edinburgh poet Robert Garioch stressed in a passage which, unusually, uses Scots for discursive prose:

> ... when A first ettled ti write poetry in what A fondly imagined ti be ma ain Edinburgh dialect, that is, in the very mainner in whilk the words form thirsels within ma heid, or iver they are sorted up to suit the conversational tone o braw leddies in a drawinroom, ir that o drucken cairters in a pub... A fund masel maistly sneered it iz yit anither synthetic Scots; an iz yit anither synthetic Scot A hae been generally lauched at iver eftir. I wad therefore like ti say a word ir twa anent ma Edinburgh dialect in particular, an the Scottish tongue generally. Noo it hiz aye appeared ti me thit, gin ony Scottish speech wud be true an naiteral-like, it maun follow the same development in the individual iz ony ither language ir dialect whatsoiver... This process... begins in oor early childhood, when we first begin ti parrot the soons spoken bi the folks roon aboot iz. The foond o oor tongue, therefore, is accent: the wee bairn stammers oot his smaw speech in the accent o his ain fireside: the accent that will bide in his speech till his voice is heard nae mair. The words thirsels hae less import than the accent in whilk they are spoken... [In] the later development o the speech o ony individual whaw gaes aboot a bit an reads onything that he may git a haid o, involves the assimilation o aw kinds o words an phrases, ivery yin o whilk, hooiver, is pronounced mair ir less in his ain local accent.[59]

Garioch makes conspicuous use of pronunciation spellings which

reflect the sounds and stress-patterns of his own dialect to show
the absurdity of the charge that his Scots is 'synthetic'. His emphasis on 'accent' as 'the foond [foundation] o oor tongue' underlines
the importance of an idiomatic spoken Scots as a basis for the literary 'voice', and his point about our flexible (but not unlimited)
ability to 'assimilate' new material to our own 'local accent', illuminates both his own practice and that of Soutar. Drawing on the
resources of contemporary urban Scots and on a vernacular tradition in which poetry was, characteristically, part of the life of the
community, Garioch created a poetic persona 'essentially social:
informal, humorous, entertaining, melancholy' in sharp contrast to
that adopted by MacDiarmid, 'always separate, alone with a peculiar and intense vision of the cosmos.'[60] Nevertheless, without
MacDiarmid's demonstration of the potential of Scots for a genuinely contemporary poetry, it is unlikely that Garioch would have
made it his main medium; and his long, meditative poem, 'The
Muir', clearly shows the influence of MacDiarmid's belief that for
Scots to become a genuinely contemporary medium, it would have
to engage with the radical implications of modern science for
human beliefs and values.

Both Soutar and Garioch use a poetic language grounded in
the language they grew up speaking; their fellow renaissance
poet Sydney Goodsir Smith, once seen as the most significant
vernacular presence of the period from the 1940s to the 1960s
lacked this early immersion. In retrospect, Goodsir Smith seems
to have owed his reputation more to the fact that his poetic idiom
represents the most thoroughgoing attempt to follow Grieve's
ideas for a reconstituted 'canon of the vernacular', in particular
in its substantial borrowings from historic Scots, than to the
intrinsic merit of his poetry. The orthography of his most praised
work, the lyric sequence *Under the Eildon Tree*[61] (1948, revised
1954) harks back to the Scots of the makars, but draws eclectically
on words and idioms from different periods in an attempt to create
– with only sporadic success – a vernacular idiom flexible enough
to accomodate contemporary experience in all its diversity.
Goodsir Smith also puzzles the reader by his habit of inventing
'Scots' spellings for words which the vernacular shares with standard English. The intention, of course, is to make Scots *look* more

consistently different from English than it actually is – a tactic which related to the fact that many lines in the *Eildon Tree* lyrics were clearly conceived in standard English and then 'translated'. Considering Goodsir Smith's reputation just after his death in 1975, and the failure of his work to attract the widespread appreciation which he felt it deserved, MacDiarmid conceded that 'the main reason was the language in which Sydney wrote', adding:

> This was a language he invented and which no one else ever wrote or spoke or could conceivably have done.[62]

Goodsir Smith succeeds best when his language draws on the energy and rhythms of contemporary colloquial Scots as in 'The Grace of God and the Meth-Drinker'. The speaker's affectionate-abusive address to an old drunk seen in the street combines the demotic of the city streets with Scots tradition of flyting in a powerful comment on the situation of the marginalised and outcast. However, for all its local felicities and gestures towards the contemporary, Goodsir Smith's poetic idiom is essentially a pastiche 'historic' Scots; concocted largely from literary sources, it never comes convincingly to life.

The fact is that, from the 1950s, Scots was no longer the main medium of younger generation of Scottish poets. As Robin Fulton remarks of the period, 'it is incontrovertible that the bulk of the most important Scottish poetry has been written in English',[63] adducing Edwin Morgan, Iain Crichton Smith, Norman MacCaig, George Bruce and George Mackay Brown and others. Some younger poets – notably Alex Scott and Alastair Mackie – continued to use Scots as their primary medium, but it is significant that both were native speakers from the North-East, where a distinctive local Scots continued to be very strong and which had a well-established and sophisticated tradition of dialect writing. As a result they brought fresh resources to the literary language which MacDiarmid had developed. Derrick McClure's summary of Scott's achievement can stand for both:

> In view of the strength of the North-East's local literary tradition, and the very considerable differences between the languages of this and of the 'national' literature – which... derives its grammar and phonology principally from the dialects of the Eastern Lowlands – it might be expected

that a linguistic merger between the two forms would be particularly unlikely. This, however, has been achieved to a considerable extent in the poetic idiolect of Alexander Scott; and is one of the reasons for the distinctiveness of his voice among the many outstanding poets of the Scots Renaissance. Scott's native-speaker fluency in the North-eastern speech of his childhood, and his upbringing in a community where the 'Doric' – as it is universally called – is freely used for all purposes among most sections of society... ensures that the Scots of his poetry (and prose) is firmly rooted in the rhythms and idioms of colloquial speech...[64]

MacDiarmid's fundamental aim – to recreate an independent, confident Scottish literary tradition – continued to inspire Scottish writers in the period after the Second World War, but his particular prescriptions, linked as they were with the uncompromising élitism of the modernist movement, ceased to command assent. Younger writers were also less convinced that the expression of a contemporary Scottish sensibility required the use of Scots (MacDiarmid himself had largely abandoned the vernacular after the 1930s, after all, without thereby compromising his Scottishness). From the late 1940s, the most vigorous and inventive Scots is found not in the 'high' literary tradition revitalised by MacDiarmid but in two art-forms which are generally more accessible and popular in character – song and drama. The topical songs of the folk-revival in the 1950s and 1960s drew most often on the urban vernacular of Glasgow and its environs. Writers and singers like Hamish Henderson, Matt McGinn, Morris Blythman ('Thurso Berwick') and Ewan McColl thought of themselves as continuing a tradition which gave expression to the experience of the common people in work and leisure, war and peace, struggle and protest. The writing and performing of new songs proceeded alongside the collecting and recording of Scotland's song heritage, both Scots and Gaelic, the aim being to reconnect ordinary people with traditions weakened by the commercialisation of popular entertainment and thereby bring into being a song culture capable of reflecting contemporary life. Hamish Henderson in particular believed that the most effective way to create a popular poetry was through song; writing to *The Scotsman* on 13 January 1960, for instance, he said:

... in the long run it is the folksong revival which offers the best hope for a genuine popular poetry, a poetry which, when it gathers strength, will make many of the raucous booths of Tin Pan Alley shut up shop. Our own poets, in particular, will feel a real thrill of liberation when they realize that the primary question facing them is not so much one of language as one of idiom; realize, too, that all resources of a folk-poetry of unrivalled beauty and power are there at their elbow, to help and sustain them...[65]

The folk revival was linked with the politics of the early Cold War years, in particular with the distinctive amalgam of socialist, nationalist and republican ideas called into being by such things as the appearance in Scotland after the coronation in 1952 of post-boxes labelled E II R (Elizabeth I had not been queen of Scotland), the stationing of American Polaris nuclear submarines at the Holy Loch in the early 1960s, and the terminal decline of the heavy industries on which Scotland's economy was disproportionately dependent. Even sectarian songs and tunes reflecting the Catholic-Protestant antagonism of west-central Scotland were appropriated to the new purposes – the jaunty melody of the best-known Orange, monarchist and unionist anthem, 'The Sash My Father Wore', for instance, was borrowed for the lively Scottish republican song entitled 'The Coronation Coronach'.[66] Using the urban vernacular of Glasgow, Scotland's greatest industrial city, the song irreverently surveys the members of British royal family in the verses, while the refrain reiterates the determination to 'mak oor land republican/In a Scottish break-away'. Jim MacLean's 'NAB for Royalty' (appropriately to the tune of 'The Deil's awa wi the Exciseman') sardonically presents the royal family as beneficiaries of the welfare state (NAB is the National Assistance Board, the body then responsible for administering state benefits). The song ironically reverses the common charge that welfare benefits go to the 'undeserving poor'; the royal family are, clearly, the undeserving rich:

There lives a family in the land
The famous royal crew, man;
They willna work, they willna want –
They're livin on the B'roo, man!
[B'roo = bureau, the Employment Bureau, now the Department of Health and Social Security]

These and songs like them use contemporary urban language and settings, but draw on a old radical tradition, most strongly associated with great cities, of republican songs and verses which mock monarchy and lampoon royal personages.

Many of the best songs associated with the anti-nuclear protests of the time also owe their effectiveness to their use of Glasgow dialect, a variety of Scots often disparaged (even the introduction to the *Scottish National Dictionary* describes the speech of 'the industrial area near Glasgow' as 'hopelessly corrupt'), but described by one of its recent chroniclers as 'rich' and 'vital', giving expression to 'the robust and irreverant humour, resilience and abhorrence of pretension'[67] of Glaswegians themselves. As well as using the language of industrial west-central Scotland, the songs use its landscapes, and draw their imagery from the history and life of the area. The very funny 'The Glesca Eskimos' illustrates the characteristics of the genre; an injudicious reference to anti-nuclear demonstrators as 'eskimos' by an American submarine commander prompted the song, which brilliantly develops the conceit that the activists are indeed eskimos, and on the hunt for the Captain himself, wittily transformed into a kind of West of Scotland Moby Dick. Like several of the protest songs of the time, the 'The Glesca Eskimos' draws on a street-song tradition of mockery and defiance largely associated with childhood, but in the Glasgow area also with sectarian organisations and their songs, bands and marches. The swaggering air to which 'The Glesca Eskimos' is set is usually associated with the American Civil War song, 'Marching through Georgia' (used here with conscious irony *against* American claims to be defending the freedom of the West) but it is also the tune of a sectarian Protestant song, 'The Brigton Billy Boys' and the song – again with conscious irony – plays on the reputation of Glasgow and its region for gang-based sectarian and criminal violence; it transposes the locally admired persona of 'the hard man' into a political context, and employs the local euphemisms for street violence:

> We've been in mony a rammy, lads, we've been in mony a tear,
> We've sortit oot this kind afore, we'll sort them onywhere,
> O, get your harpoons ready – he's comin up for air
>   We are the Glesca Eskimos.

Even the squalor often associated with industrial areas is pressed into service for comic effect – the first threat to the arrogant captain is to 'coup him doon the stank' (upend him into the street drain) because being 'Up tae the neck in sludge an sewage fairly stops yuir swank.' The squalor extends to political and economic life, as reflected in the splendidly politically incorrect chase episode in the second verse:

> It's in an oot, an up an doon, an on an aff the piers,
> There's cooncillors, collaborators, pimps an profiteers –
> The hairies jouk the polis, an the polis jouk the queers...

Here, while the 'hairies' (generically young women; here prostitutes attracted by the naval presence) dodge the police, the police themselves attempt to avoid the gay men at the scene – the hunters becoming the hunted.

Hamish Henderson, the dominant presence in Scottish folklore studies for much of the second half of the twentieth century, was the chief link between a still vibrant tradition of popular ballad and song and the new generation of singers and song-writers. From the nineteen fifties, he worked untiringly to spread knowledge of vernacular song and a sense of its value as a historical resource and as a continuing active tradition (a 'carrying stream'). Challenging traditional definitions, he argued that songs of modern urban and industrial life, of contemporary war and politics, were as worthy of attention as Child ballads and the lyric song tradition. Several of his own best-known songs draw on a distinct body of contemporary oral material, soldiers' songs, and like their models, 'The 51st Highland Division's Farewell to Sicily' or 'The Ballad of the D-Day Dodgers' use contemporary colloquial Scots and sardonic humour to convey the anti-heroic stoicism of the common soldier. His most famous lyric, 'The Freedom Come-All-Ye, is a political song written for the anti-nuclear campaigners of the 1960s; however the fact that it is directed at exploitation, militarism and racism generally has allowed it to transcend its immediate occasion (appropriately it is set to a fine pipe tune, 'The Bloody Fields of Flanders', which takes its title from the defining conflict of the twentieth century – the Great War).[68] Henderson himself described it as being written in a regional variety of the vernacular, the Perthshire Scots, which was the language of his childhood.

The body of material discussed here represents one of the first widespread efforts to use the urban dialect of Glasgow and its environs for 'serious' creative purposes. Significantly, however, none of the songs referred to is included in recent anthologies of Scottish poetry. This is not entirely the fault of the editors: the fact that songs come with music complicates judgements about their literary quality, and the fact that the best songs are comic and topical has also worked against their inclusion in the canon, which tends to privilege the 'serious', 'timeless' – and tuneless.

The retreat of modernism accelerated after 1945. Regarded by those on the victorious Allied side as a 'people's war', victory created a sense among writers and artists that they could and should learn from popular traditions, and that an art in touch with these could contribute to social change, making life better for all. In particular, attitudes to the speech of urban working class people began to change; up to then, it was often heavily stigmatised, being seen as, at best, a *patios* and at worst as a crude, impoverished and error-filled *failure* of articulacy. Unrepentant modernists like MacDiarmid, however, continued to attack the new cultural attitudes; in two celebrated 'flytings' with Hamish Henderson and other correspondents in the columns of the *Scotsman* and the *Weekly Scotsman* in 1959-60 and 1964,[69] the veteran Communist caricatured their absurd enthusiasm for the working classes:

> Mr Henderson… seems to find his ideal man in the 'muckle sumph', and to wish to scrap all learning and all literature as hitherto defined in favour of the boring doggrel of analphabetic and ineducable farm-labourers, tinkers and the like. Personally I continue to think Dante, for example, or Goethe greater poets – and more creditable specimens of homo sapiens – than McGonagall or the authors of any – and all – of the 'folksongs' Mr Henderson and his colleagues so assiduously collect. I do not envy the task of whoever may ultimately have to go through the great mass of indiscriminate tape-recordings accumulated by the School of Scottish Studies in order to find any elements of real value. Looking for a needle in a haystack will be a far easier job. Such collecting is a waste of time and money.[70]

As usual, MacDiarmid was out to provoke, but 'analphabetic' and 'ineducable' suggest that, like many highly literate and print-fixated individuals, he genuinely could not grasp the fact that 'literacy' is not a necessary condition for creative expression, and that high art can be both created and communicated without it. Despite MacDiarmid's sardonic caricature of the folk revival, he himself was one of its inspirers; as Alec Finlay says of the revival in his 'Afterword' to Hamish Henderson's selected letters, it 'extends the cultural project MacDiarmid had begun in the 1920s.' But there was a crucial difference: the poet's separatism and quasi-racial emphasis on a return, via a 'reconstructed' unitary Scots to a Celtic or even pre-Celtic Scotland, was rejected in favour of highlighting contemporary conditions and 'the material realities of the Scottish voice in all its distinctive variations and languages'.[71]

A 'literary' Scots based on spoken, particularly urban working-class vernacular became important even earlier, however, in another genre – drama. Developments in drama were not, however, completely independent of those in folk-song; the song revival and theatre were directly connected, for instance, through the involvement of Joan Littlewood and Ewan McColl in both, and late-night ceilidhs followed their Theatre Workshop productions in Edinburgh between 1948 and 1953. Later companies in the same radical tradition, like 7:84 were to draw on traditional music and song as dramatic resources in plays *like The Cheviot, the Stag and the Black, Black Oil* (1976), as well as developing the tradition in specially written topical political lyrics.

Bill Finlay has spoken of '... a resurgence of original dramatic writing in Scots that was initiated in the 1940s and 1950s but has flowered particularly strongly since 1970.' In the resurgence, he adds, 'it is probably Scots speech that is the most fundamental influence.'[72] The beginnings of the renewal of vernacular drama lie in the pioneering 1945 production by Glasgow Unity Theatre of Gorky's *The Lower Depths.* Described by Findlay as 'the first instance of an urban Scots version of a foreign stage classic', the production was given 'in the idiom of the actors without any attempt by them to become "Russian"'. It is a mark of the situation in the arts at the end of the Second World War that on the plays' transfer to London after its initial local success it was greeted with great enthusiasm – and, unexpectedly, the actor's Glasgow Scots was hailed as one of the attractions of the production. One press report quoted the producer's own reaction – '"Apparently", Mr Mitchell remarked smiling, "our ugly monotonous Glasgow accent that we were so afraid of became to the ears of the Sassenach a beautiful, euphonious, rhythmical speech!"'[73]

As with poetry, however, many supporters of national cultural revival and of the vernacular tradition – particularly those of the older generation – did not approve of the use of urban working-class speech in literature. For the dramatist Robert Kemp writing in 1954, for instance, the demotic of the industrial areas was a 'music-hall pronunciation of Scots', the 'by-product of industrialisation and slums', in contrast to 'country speech [which] is the finest speech and holds in it a sense of natural aristocracy. There is nothing slip-shod or vulgar about it.'[74] However, in rejecting the modern ver-nacular of Scotland's industrial areas, Kemp and those who thought like him were, in effect, refusing to listen to the majority of ordi-nary Scots, and denying themselves the chance to deal directly with current economic, social and political issues. They could explore the present situation of Scotland only indirectly, through historical settings and subjects – for only that way could they 'deploy [their] preferred variety of Scots, with its combination of non-urban and literary qualities.'[75] Much of the historical drama thus produced looks back to an imaginary era of linguistic unity – or near unity – in lowland Scotland, the linguistic homogeneity being used to suggest that whatever their differences in rank, the characters share a common outlook and values.

Such portrayals of Scottish life did not engage, however, with the experience of the industrial working class of Scotland's cities; in the words of one of the slum-dwellers in Unity Theatre's greatest hit of the 1940s, *The Gorbals Story*:

> Scotland doesna mean much tae Glesca folk... yon pictures they print on boxes o shortbread – big blue hills and coos that need a hair cut.[76]

The stereotypical symbols of Scottishness represent a romanticised rural milieu; the Gorbals tenement-dwellers belong to a very differ-ent Scotland, and many are immigrants – a baker from the high-lands, a labourer and his family from rural Ireland, a pedlar from India. To represent their experience, a literature which exploits 'the material realities of the Scottish voice in all its distinctive variations and languages' is needed.

The new generation of playwrights used the language of work-ing-class people in their portrayals of working-class life. The cen-tral part played by Unity Theatre in creating this new drama is hardly surprising; originally founded by working people for work-ing people, one of the company's main aims was to remedy the failure of earlier Scottish companies to present plays about working class experience. However as well as its concern with class, Unity had a 'national' agenda – it was 'by policy a native theatre, deliber-ately rejecting the accent of the London West End stage and searching for an independent technique which, far from trying to root out and replace the local speech and characteristics of its artists, seeks to present them on stage as effectively as possible.' As Findlay puts it: 'harnessing the peculiarities of Scots speech – and Glasgow working class speech in particular – was central to Unity's pro-Scottish policy.'[77]

The success of *The Lower Depths* brought commissions for a clutch of new plays about working-class life in modern Scotland, Ena Lamont Stewart's *Starched Aprons* (1945) and *Men Should Weep* (1947), Robert McLeish's *The Gorbals Story* (1946), George Munro's *Gold in His Boots* (1947), and Benedick Scott's *The Lambs of God* (1948) among them. The result was that a vigorous drama 'engaging with the realities of urban working class life and doing so in an urban demotic Scots',[78] had grown up by the 1960s and 1970s. The enthusiastic audiences in the latter decade for playwrights like Stewart Conn, Bill Bryden, Roddy McMillan and John Byrne included many who were not 'traditional' theatre-goers, because their plays, set in the present or recent past of industrial west Scotland, addressed current social, economic and political issues in powerful and accessible ways. Roddy McMillan's *The Bevellers* (1974), for instance, portrays working lives and workplace relationships, rare subjects in drama. It follows the first (and last) day of a new apprentice in a small workshop devoted to the dying craft of glass-engraving. The senior craftsman, Bob, proud of his skills outlines the history of the craft, praising earlier generations of workmen for their ability to maintain high standards despite poverty and discrimination:

The trade wis maistly centred up roon aboot Cowcaddens. Lots o

Irishmen in it, tae. Hard men – hard drinkers, a lot o them. Piece-work-
ers, and no often steady work. Used tae wait in the pub tae a few jobs
came in and go intae the shop when the gaffer sent fur them... Some o
these jobs they had in the oul' days wid have ruptured ye. Every man
saw the job right through – start tae finish – and they had tae be fast at
the game. There wis plenty o men tae step intae their shoes if they wer-
nae.

But the craft drains the life of the men who practise it even as they
create beautiful things, and the ghost-like survivor Alex warns the
apprentice 'Don't stey at it... Get intae the sun an' the fresh air'
because once the trade 'gets intae ye... it's very hard tae make the
break.' He adds:

Ah'm no sayin there urnae some lovely things aboot this trade, but it's a
in the end-product, like. A bit o figure-work or a good – a beautiful mirror – well bevelled an' set – will staun against anythin' in any craft. Ah've
seen work by some o the oul' fullas that wid bring wee needles intae the
corners o yur eyes it wis that lovely...[79]

While the play is a lament for the passing of craft-skills, it also
underlines the high price often exacted from those who exercise
them. More importantly, though, these passages challenge two of
MacDiarmid's élitist claims: that the ordinary man is a 'muckle
sumph', inarticulate and aesthetically undeveloped; and that 'high
art' is the only really worthwhile activity.

Vernacular drama and the folksong movement helped change
attitudes to the 'gutter dialect' of Scotland's greatest industrial city,
so that by the 1970s, Glasgow speech had become 'an area of
experiment and a badge of pride'[80] in, for instance, the poetry of
Tom Leonard and the fiction of James Kelman. More radical even
than the dramatists and song-writers in their approach to working-
class speech, Leonard and Kelman both insist on the primacy of
the spoken, and on authenticity – as Irvine Welsh does for the
speech of Edinburgh 'schemies' in his 1993 novel *Trainspotting*.
They therefore include in their work the tabu words and phrases
which express the frustration and violence generated by the conditions in which the poor, marginalised and excluded have to live.
Such recent writing presents a radical challenge to another of
MacDiarmid's central convictions: that the main task of the modern
vernacular writer is to help assemble a 'full canon of Scots' from

the historical and current dialects which are its disintegrated elements, thus creating a medium capable of giving expression to all kinds of experience. For, as Tom Leonard has pointed out,[81] different language varieties reflect the contrasting and even conflicting experiences and interests of different social groups; the creation (or imposition) of a 'standard' is a way of concealing this by denying full (or any) validity to the experience embodied in the 'non-standard' speech.

In today's Scotland – with a current poster campaign funded by the Scottish Executive urging Scots to recognise that we live in 'One Scotland' with 'Many Cultures' – Grieve's quasi-racial nationalism looks increasingly irrelevant (of course MacDiarmid the poet had a more comprehensive understanding of experience and wider sympathies than Grieve the ideologue). The new multi-culturalism has implications for Scots itself: for, as James Robertson has said in the context of recent vernacular writing: 'Narrow definitions [of Scots] based on ideas of "pure dialect", or where the Doric or Lallans is set up against "debased", "gutter" or "urban patois" Scots, do nothing to strengthen people's confidence in their own way of speaking and thinking'. He adds: 'In my view there is no such thing as *the* Scottish voice.' The collection bears out his claim in the range of 'voices' heard in it – from the 'traditional' rural Scots of the Northeast to the working class vernacular of Scotland's cities, and from Stanley Robertson's retelling of 'The Wishing Well', a traditional tale from traveler tradition, to Irvine Welsh's bleak 'A Soft Touch', a violence- and profanity-filled tale set in an Edinburgh housing scheme, which is, nevertheless, a love story.[82] Here at the beginning of the new millennium and a new era in Scottish political life are displayed, at last, 'the material realities of the Scottish voice' in many, if not all of its 'distinctive variations and languages.'

NOTES

[1] Bill Findlay, 'Motivation and Method in Scots Translations, Versions and Adaptations of Plays from the Historic Repertoire of Continental European Drama', unpublished PhD thesis, Queen Margaret University College, Edinburgh, 2000, p. 10.

[2] William Donaldson, *The Language of the People: Scots Prose from the Victorian Revival,* Aberdeen: Aberdeen University Press, 1989.

[3] Robert McLellan, *Linmill Stories,* Edinburgh: Canongate, 1990.

[4] James Robertson ed., *A Tongue in Yer Heid: a Selection of the Best Contemporary Short Stories in Scots,* Edinburgh: B and W Publishing, 1994.

[5] Matthew Fitt, *But n Ben A-Go-Go,* Edinburgh: Luath Press, 2000, p. 20.

[6] William Alexander, *Johnny Gibb of Gushetneuk,* Aberdeen: Walker, 1871.

[7] *Ibidem,* chapter XLIV, 'Johnny Considers the Situation'.

[8] T.F. Henderson, *Scottish Vernacular Literature: a Succinct History,* Edinburgh: David Nutt, 1898, p. 458.

[9] J.H. Millar, *A Literary History of Scotland,* London: Union, 1903, p. 679.

[10] K.M.E. Murray, *Caught in the Web of Words: James Murray and the Oxford English Dictionary,* London: Yale University Press, 1978, p. 74.

[11] Alexander Mackie, 'Introduction and Appreciation', in William Alexander, *Johnny Gibb of Gushetneuk,* Edinburgh: Douglas and Foulis, 1951, p. xxi.

[12] Charles Murray, *Hamewith* (Aberdeen: Wyllie, 1900), London: Constable and Company, 1909.

[13] Charles Murray, *In the Country Places,* London: Constable and Company, 1920.

[14] William Thom, *Rhymes and Recollections of a Hand-Loom Weaver,* London: Smith, 1844.

[15] Janet Hamilton, *Poems, Sketches and Essays,* Glasgow: Murray, 1885.

[16] The most comprehensive gathering of these songs is to be found in P.A. Hall ed., *The Greig-Duncan Folk Song Collection,* Aberdeen: Aberdeen University Press, III, 1987.

[17] J.M. Bulloch, 'Introduction' to John Mitchell's *Bydand,* Aberdeen: Bon-Accord Press, 1918, p. vi.

[18] *Ibidem,* p. v.

[19] *Ibidem,* p. vi.

[20] Janet Adams Smith ed., *Robert Louis Stevenson: Collected Poems,* London: Hart-Davis, 1971, pp. 486-488.

[21] See, for instance, the reference in a letter by C.M. Grieve in the *Scottish Educational Journal* of 18 September, 1925 to current spoken Scots as consisting of 'decayed and corrupt forms' and as exemplifying

'plebeian and illiterate usage'. In Grieve's article 'The New Movement in Vernacular Poetry: Lewis Spence; Marion Angus' published in the issue of 27 November, 1925, he refers to 'the debased dialects still more or less current'. These disparaging references are typical of what Grieve had to say about current spoken Scots, in all its varieties in the 1920s. They can be found – with many similar comments – in the reprint of Grieve's *Scottish Educational Journal* articles published as *Contemporary Scottish Studies*, Edinburgh: Scottish Educational Journal, 1976, p. 38 and p. 61.

[22] 'Hugh Haliburton' (James Logie Robertson), *Horace in Homespun*, Edinburgh: W. Paterson, 1886.

[23] Charles Murray, letter to David Rorie, 21 December 1925, LO 928, archive collection A12 (*David Rorie Collection*, Reference and Local Studies Department, Aberdeen Central Library).

[24] Joseph Knight, review of R.L. Stevenson's *Underwoods*, *Atheneum*, 10 September 1887, pp. 333-334.

[25] J.C. Smith, 'Some Characteristics of Scottish Literature', *English Association Leaflet no. 22*, London: English Association, 1912.

[26] Gavin Greig, 'The Traditional Minstrelsy of the North-East of Scotland', in Stephen Miller ed., *The Subject of Folksong: Collected Writings on Scottish Folksong*, Onchan, Isle of Man: Chiollagh Books, 2000, (pp. 109-118) p. 116.

[27] George Kitchin, 'The Modern Makars', in James Kinsley ed., *Scottish Poetry: a Critical Survey*, London: Cassell, 1955, p. 256.

[28] Charles Carrington, *Rudyard Kipling: His Life and Work*, London: Macmillan, 1955, p. 153.

[29] Robert Bain, 'Scottish Poetry of Today', *Burns Chronicle*, second series, I, 1926, p. 49.

[30] Violet Jacob, *Songs of Angus*, London: John Marray, 1915, and *More Songs of Angus*, London: Country Life, 1918.

[31] John Buchan, *Poems: Scots and English*, London: Nelson, 1953, p. 7.

[32] C.M. Grieve, *Contemporary Scottish Studies*, cit., p. 7.

[33] C.M. Grieve to Herbert Grierson, 30 April, 1925. See *The Letters of Hugh MacDiarmid*, edited by Alan Bold, London: Hamish Hamilton, 1984, p. 307.

[34] C.M. Grieve, 'A Scotsman Looks at his World', *Dunfermline Press*, 25 November 1922, p. 6.

[35] J.M. Bulloch, *op. cit.*, pp. vi-vii.

[36] See Mary Symon, *Deveron Days*, Aberdeen: D. Wyllie, 1933.

[37] Charles Murray, *In the Country Places*, London: Constable and Company, 1920.

[38] C.M. Grieve, 'Scottish Books and Bookmen', *Dunfermline Press*, 30 September 1922, p. 7.

[39] C.M. Grieve, 'A Scotsman Looks at His World', *Dunfermline Press*, 25 November 1922, p. 6.

[40] Hugh MacDiarmid, *Lucky Poet*, London: Methuen, 1943, p. xiii.

[41] John Jamieson, *An Etymological Dictionary of the Scottish Language*, 2 vols., Edinburgh, 1808; *Supplement to the Etymological Dictionary of the Scottish Language*, 2 vols., Edinburgh, 1825. Both published by subscription.

[42] K.M. Petyt, *The Study of Dialect*, London: Deutsch, 1980, p. 11.

[43] C.M. Grieve, 'The New Movement in Vernacular Poetry: Lewis Spence; Marion Angus', in *Contemporary Scottish Studies*, cit., p. 61.

[44] *Ibidem*, p. 38.

[45] C.M. Grieve, 'A Theory of Scots Letters', in Alan Bold ed., *The Thistle Rises: An Anthology of Poetry and Prose by Hugh MacDiarmid*, London: Hamish Hamilton, 1984, (pp. 125-141) p. 131.

[46] Duncan Glen, *Hugh MacDiarmid and the Scottish Renaissance*, Edinburgh: Chambers, 1964, p. 76.

[47] Sir James Wilson, *Lowland Scotch as Spoken in the Lower Strathearn District of Perthshire*, London: Oxford University Press, 1915, pp. 3-4.

[48] George Bruce, 'The Scottish Literary Revival', in George Bruce ed., *The Scottish Literary Revival: An Anthology of Twentieth Century Poetry*, London: Collier-Macmillan, 1968, (pp. 1-8) pp. 3-4.

[49] William Soutar, *Diaries of a Dying Man*, Edinburgh: Canongate, 1991, p. 149.

[50] Alexander Scott, *Still Life: William Soutar 1898-1943*, London: Chambers, 1958, p. 135.

[51] William Soutar, *Diaries*, cit., p. 92.

[52] Quoted in Alexander Scott, *Still Life*, cit., p. 57.

[53] *Ibidem*, p. 60.

[54] *Ibidem*, p. 116.

[55] W.A. Craigie, John Buchan, Peter Giles, J.M. Bulloch, *The Scottish Tongue: A Series of Lectures on the Vernacular Language of Lowland Scotland*, London: Cassell, 1924.

[56] Quoted in Alexander Scott, *Still Life*, cit., p. 56.

[57] *Ibidem*, p. 121.

[58] *Ibidem*, p. 135.

[59] Quoted in Manfred Görlach, *A Textual History of Scots*, Heidelberg: Winter, 2002, p. 253.

[60] Robin Fulton, *Contemporary Scottish Poetry: Individuals and Contexts*, Loanhead, Midlothian: Macdonald, 1974, p. 161.

[61] Sydney Goodsir Smith, *Under the Eildon Tree: a Poem in XXIV Elegies*, Edinburgh: np, 1948; rev. ed. London: G.B. Serif, 1954.

[62] Hugh MacDiarmid, 'Sydney', in *For Sydney Goodsir Smith*, Loanhead, Midlothian: Macdonald, 1975, (pp. 43-46) p. 43.

[63] Robin Fulton, *op. cit.*, p. 154.

[64] J.D. McClure, 'The Poetic Language of Alexander Scott', in David Hewitt ed., *Northern Visions*, East Linton: Tuckwell, 1995, (pp. 110-129) pp. 111-112.

[65] Alec Finlay ed., *The Armstrong Nose: Selected Letters of Hamish Henderson*, Edinburgh: Polygon, 1996, p. 96.

[66] Words for Scottish republican and anti-Polaris songs from descriptive notes included with *Ding Dong Dollar: Anti-Polaris and Scottish Republican Songs*, Folkways Records FD 5444, 1962.

[67] Michael Munro, *The Patter: A Guide to Current Glasgow Usage*, Glasgow: Glasgow City Libraries, 1985, p. 4.

[68] Collected in Hamish Henderson, *Collected Poems and Songs*, edited by Raymond Ross, Edinburgh: Curly Snake Publishing, 2000.

[69] See Alec Finlay, *op. cit.*, pp. 79-100 and pp. 117-141.

[70] *Ibidem*, p. 97.

[71] *Ibidem*, p. 333.

[72] Bill Findlay, 'Motivation and Method...', cit., p. 11.

[73] *Ibidem*, p. 36.

[74] *Ibidem*, p. 70.

[75] *Ibidem*, p. 73.

[76] Robert McLeish, *The Gorbals Story*, Edinburgh: 7:84 Publications, 1985, pp. 21-22.

[77] Bill Findlay, *op. cit.*, p. 36.

[78] *Ibidem*, p. 38.

[79] Roddy McMillan, *The Bevellers*, Edinburgh: Southside, 1974, p. 22 and p. 44.

[80] Edwin Morgan, 'Glasgow Speech in Recent Scottish Literature', in J.D. McClure ed., *Scotland and the Lowland Tongue*, Aberdeen: Aberdeen University Press, 1983, (pp. 195-208) p. 199.

[81] See Tom Leonard, 'The Locust Tree in Flower, and Why It Had Difficulty Flowering in Britain', in *Intimate Voices 1965-1983*,

Newcastle upon Tyne: Galloping Dog Press, 1984, pp. 95-102.
[82] James Robertson ed., *A Tongue in Yer Heid*, cit., pp. 16-23 and pp. 183-191.

ALAN RIACH

The Scottish Renaissance

The Scottish Renaissance is the term now applied to the literary and cultural regeneration of Scotland initiated by Hugh MacDiarmid (C.M. Grieve) in the 1920s. More precisely, the term might be located in what happened between the first appearance of MacDiarmid's lyric poetry in Scots in 1922 and the publication of a series of controversial and iconoclastic essays by C.M. Grieve, *Contemporary Scottish Studies*, in *The Scottish Educational Journal* from 1925-1927. Grieve/MacDiarmid, as poet, critic and cultural revolutionary, effected an assault upon the intellectual and emotional conventions of his era. He took hold of the pillars of the Scottish literary and cultural establishment and did the job of Samson.

On 4 December 1925, Grieve wrote: 'A certain type of critic is apt to say that the movement so far has consisted only of propaganda – only "of the posters" – that the actual work has still to be done. This is a mistake. The Scottish Renaissance has taken place. The fruits will appear in due course. Earlier or later – it does not alter the fact. For the Scottish Renaissance has been a propaganda of ideas and their enunciation has been all that was necessary.'[1]

The 'ideas' were essentially to end the reliance upon sentimental, stereotypical representations of Scotland that had become common through the late 19th century and to bring modern Scottish culture into alignment with the most advanced European thought and avant-garde artistic techniques. Grieve attacked and destroyed as many existing preconceptions responsible for the *status quo* as he could, in religious, political, and social terms and on every other front.

On 5 February 1926, he specified some of these ideas more closely: 'From the Renaissance point of view... it is utterly wrong to make the term "Scottish" synonymous with any fixed literary forms or to attempt to confine it. The Scottish Renaissance movement sets out to do all that it possibly can to increase the number of Scots who are vitally interested in literature and cultural issues; to counter the academic or merely professional tendencies which fossilise the intellectual interests of most well-educated people even; and, above all, to stimulate actual art-production to a maximum.'[2]

As Grieve's notoriety spread, he began to be more widely read. His columns were followed from week to week as if they were a cliff-hanging cinema serial. The essays were published as a book in 1926: *Contemporary Scottish Studies* is a landmark in modern Scottish literature.[3]

The Scottish Renaissance proposed an almost total demolition of Scotland's cultural identity as it had come to be accepted through the nineteenth century. On 25 June 1926, MacDiarmid described Scotland as 'a country that has been at a literary standstill for the best part of a century so far as the production of work of European consequence is concerned'. In his view, with the rise of the British Empire, two things had happened to Scotland: it became invisible, and it became internationally recognisable in stereotypes and caricatures.

It became invisible in the sense that many of its major artists, composers and writers were exiled from their own national identity and became bulwarks of the British establishment, while an incalculable number of Scots became both the victims and the perpetrators of Empire itself. They and their country became dissolved in the great imperial project. Thomas Carlyle in his lectures *On Heroes and Hero-Worship* (1841), refers to Samuel Johnson as his countryman – an Englishman. Further down the line, when Field Marshall Montgomery spoke in the Royal Albert Hall on 23 October 1946 to an enormous reunion of El Alamein veterans, he subsumed Irish, Welsh and Scots in the patriotic declaration: 'We are all Englishmen here!'

But at the same time, throughout the world, Scots were becoming recognised in stereotypical ways. Perhaps the best example is one of the most famous photographs ever taken: of John Brown, standing just to the left of Queen Victoria (who is on horseback). When it was made into a postcard, in 1863, its first year of issue, it sold over 13,000 copies and was sent all over the world. The image of John Brown presents the features that were to hold sway (and in some respects, still do): a dour, serious expression suggests the conscience and determination of the set of his character, staring straight at the camera: a direct man, it would seem, without subtlety or humour. The seriousness, to us, seems at odds with and yet part of his self-important costume: the bonnet, the kilt and the outlandish sporran. Above all, he is standing before the mounted monarch – clearly, he is in her service, at her command, a man who, if called upon, can be counted on not to reason why, but to do as he's told, and die. MacDiarmid recognised that this attitude had led directly to the First World War. He considered that war to be the ultimate consequence of imperialism and thought of Scotland as one of Europe's small nations especially fit for post-war regeneration. The Scottish Renaissance movement was intended to effect that regeneration.

Crucial in the development of the movement was the role played by newspapers and little magazines: *The Scottish Chapbook* (1922-1923*), The Scottish Nation* (1923), *The Northern Review* (1924), *The Pictish Review* (1927-1928), *The Scots Independent* (1927-1933), *Scots Observer* (1927-1934*), The Modern Scot* (1931-1934) and *The Free Man* (1932-1935). MacDiarmid and other Scottish writers also contributed to London-based intellectual journals like *The New Age* and *New Britain* and to the more widely-distributed national press in Scotland.[4]

MacDiarmid also edited a series of three anthologies of Scottish poetry, *Northern Numbers*, in which an older and established generation of poets were published alongside their younger, more radical contemporaries.[5] The sentimentalism of Donald A. Mackenzie (1873-1936), Neil Munro (1864-1930) and Charles Murray (1864-1941) was ruthlessly exposed by the modernity of new poets of the Scottish Renaissance, such as John Ferguson, William Jeffrey, Muriel Stuart, Roderick Watson Kerr. For example, one of the poems by which Mackenzie was represented in the first series, 'Isle of My Heart', began in an unmistakable tone of nostalgic longing, its author fondly

>   dreaming
> Of the dear days that were,

On that jewel of an island
In the sweet Hebrides.

By contrast, John Ferguson was writing sonnets about unemployed
chorus-girls and music-hall comedians, bank accountants and the
inmates of a sanatorium, and Roderick Watson Kerr (known at that
time as 'the Scottish Siegfried Sassoon'), was writing bitterly of
urban squalor in a Christian Mission hall for the poor. The 'tea and
buns' supplied by pious philanthropists are 'quite fit for gentle
ladies' palates' but at 'twopence the lot' they 'cost the soul of any
of these ones –/The female things, I mean. Two pence? Ah,
yes,/That woman's body sells each night for less'.

This proto-feminist verse is reflected in the editorial policy of
the third and most radical of the three anthologies. Of twenty contributors, ten are women. No editor of Scottish poetry before or
since has done as much as Grieve/MacDiarmid to insist that the
voices of women should be heard to represent the nation.

The Scottish Renaissance movement has had an incalculable
long-term effect but it also arose in the aftermath of a distinct wave
of cultural expression which apparently ended with the shattering
climax of the First World War. This is the remarkable production of
work in art, music and cultural debate identified with the writers,
painters and composers of the late nineteenth century.

In music, late Victorian Scotland produced more than one generation of composers whose work attempted to express a distinctively Scottish dynamic. Alexander Campbell Mackenzie (1847-
1935), who knew Liszt, Greig and Paderewski and whose work
was highly praised by Elgar, produced a Burns Rhapsody (1881), a
Pibroch Suite for violin and orchestra (1889), a Scottish Piano
Concerto (1897) and numerous other pieces with emphatic Scottish
character. But finally the gravity pulled towards London.
Mackenzie's most famous concert overture runs spirited and
sprightly variations on a sailor's hornpipe and 'Rule Britannia'. It is
entitled 'Britannia' – not 'Caledonia' or 'Alba'. At one crucial level,
imperial Britain is the focus of its celebration (though it is not
merely a piece of jingoistic chauvinism or bombast).

A generation younger, Hamish MacCunn (1868-1916) was more
radically devoted to finding forms for the orchestra to express
Scottish identity. Border ballads inform the musical scenes depicted

in 'The Dowie Dens o' Yarrow' or 'The Lay of the Last Minstrel' and the Highlands are evoked by his most famous piece, 'Land of the Mountain and the Flood'. Eighteenth-century Edinburgh is the location of most of the 'Grand Opera' of 1894, *Jeanie Deans*, an extremely tight composition (much compressed from its source, Scott's *The Heart of Midlothian*). MacCunn saw himself as a composer for the new era, a musician of the future, combining the flair and flamboyance of Liszt with hard pragmatism, but he died in his 40s, in the middle of the First World War.

Neither of these composers (and there are others, most notably perhaps, William Wallace [1860-1940] and John Blackwood McEwan [1868-1948], with his 'Border Ballads', Solway Symphony and landscape-piece 'Hills o' Heather') can be located in a generic national movement of integrated political purpose. Mackenzie remained a paragon of the British capital's establishment. MacCunn, radical as he was, took the arch-conservative Walter Scott and (arguably) Scott's most conservative novel for his finest operatic text. Wallace's orchestral mastery in the tone poem on his namesake, *William Wallace* (1905), has more in common with the late Romantic tone poems of Richard Strauss, such *Ein Heldenleben* (*A Hero's Life*, 1889) or *Also Sprach Zarathustra* (1896) than with the expression of the ferocity of struggle and the primal scream in Stravinsky's *Rite of Spring* (1915); nevertheless, it was a far more sophisticated representation of national identity than the Victorian impulse to hero-worship which saw Lord Buchan's commissioning John Smith of Darnick to carve the red sandstone statue of Wallace erected overlooking the Tweed in 1814 or the Wallace monument at Stirling, of 1859-1869. McEwan, in his impressionist or post-impressionist idiom, is clearly attempting something in a line of descent from the landscape artists of Victorian Scotland, though he moves further into a distinctly twentieth-century idiom, while also sharing the deepening sense of Scottish identity intrinsic to the song-settings of F.G. Scott.[6]

The development of the tradition of landscape painting tells a similar story of a movement from conventional and comfortable depictions whose appeal was predictable (for example, the work of Tom Faed or Horatio McCulloch) to more radical, austere and self-consciously European work by William McTaggart in the 1890s, and later, the Scottish Colourists, S.J. Peploe, F.C.B. Caddell, Leslie Hunter and J.D. Fergusson. Most crucially, from the turn of the century to the outbreak of World War One, the Colourists developed coherent and startling techniques spurred by the work of Whistler, Cézanne, Van Gogh, Gaugain and Toulouse-Lautrec, and then Fauve and Cubist works by Matisse and Picasso. From Europe, they returned to Scotland with their own innovative work, among the first modern painters to be exhibited in Britain.[7]

In musical and artistic terms, the cultural production of Scotland was rich and varied in the late nineteenth and early twentieth centuries. But it was unco-ordinated. The different fields of creative endeavour were related and overlapped, but without a corresponding or effective political dimension. Consequently, the national expression of cultural diversity remained unfulfilled. In literature the story is even more disturbing.

Throughout the nineteenth century popular Scottish literature became increasingly incapable of dealing with growing industrialism in the cities or with the conditions of the Highlands. As a direct result of the Highland Clearances from about 1814 on, the vast diaspora of Scots around the world was a ready market for nostalgic images and stories of a home they'd never return to, and that, if it ever existed in the past, did so no longer. By the end of the century, a series of poetry anthologies known as the 'Whistle-Binkies' was providing sentimental verses derived from Burns's love-songs but lacking Burns's poignant charm, subtlety, animality or flair, while in prose the predominant school was that of the 'Kailyard' or vegetable-garden: home-grown tales of small-town Scottish life with patronising wisdom dispensed by the local minister. The romance novels of A.S. Swan and the 'Kailyard' stories of Ian Maclaren were essentially escapist fiction for readers at home and abroad. S.R. Crockett, writing sweet stories or boys' adventures, derived his vision of heroic deeds and domestic fidelities from a dilution of Walter Scott.

There was another side to the end of the nineteenth century, though. The poetry of John Davidson and James 'B.V.' Thomson revealed darker aspects of the Victorian psyche, urban degradation, the industrialised city, a world of alienation and despair. 'Mankind has cast me out' begins Davidson's 'Testament of a Man Forbid' and the haunting, nocturnal vision of Thomson's *City of Dreadful Night* has none of the 'Kailyard' pieties.[8] MacDiarmid's poem 'Of John Davidson' brings together individual loneliness and the universe of religious scepticism characteristic of the end of the nineteenth century: Davidson's suicide by drowning is remembered as 'A bullet-hole through a great scene's beauty,/God through the wrong end of a telescope.'[9]

In novels, the other side of small-town Scotland was exposed by the appalling psychological oppression and physical violence depicted in the brutal tragedies of G.D. Brown's *The House with the Green Shutters* and John Macdougall Hay's *Gillespie*. And while R.L. Stevenson was safely identified as a children's writer in *Treasure Island* and *Kidnapped*, he is more accurately a writer of childhood's end, as Jim Hawkins and David Balfour learn how to say goodbye to their colourful heroic mentors L.J. Silver and Alan Breck Stewart, and *Dr Jekyll and Mr Hyde* is an unremittingly adult fable, the 'most serious' work, in Henry James's words.[10]

But the world of Scottish literature in 1922 was aptly caricatured by MacDiarmid himself: like all other literatures, he said, it had been written 'almost exclusively by blasphemers, immoralists, dipsomaniacs, and madmen' – but, unlike most other literatures, it had been written *about* 'almost exclusively by ministers' – with the consequence that critical opinion had been neutralised.[11]

So the work of the Scottish Renaissance was not only to encourage literary production but also to revitalise the national cultural climate. One set of articles by MacDiarmid comprises 'A Theory of Scottish Letters' (1923) in which the Scots language was considered not as a pawky vernacular idiom for small-minded canniness and sentimentality but, somewhat hyperbolically, as 'the only language in Western Europe instinct with... uncanny spiritual and pathological perceptions'.[12] We have seen MacDiarmid's pioneering work in the essays of *Contemporary Scottish Studies* and the *Northern Numbers* anthologies. It should also be considered in the context of the work of his contemporaries, many of whom he befriended and encouraged. Among them, the major Scottish writers of the 1920s and 1930s with whom MacDiarmid shared close creative friendships were all men – Compton Mackenzie (1883-1974), Edwin Muir (1887-1959), Neil Gunn (1891-1973), William Soutar

(1898-1943), Lewis Grassic Gibbon (1901-1935), Fionn MacColla (1906-1975). Similarly masculine was the group of poets who, across more than one generation, developed their art in MacDiarmid's company, and who knew him, to a greater or lesser degree of intimacy, as a friend: Robert Garioch (1909-1981), Norman MacCaig (1910-1996), Sorley MacLean (1911-1996), Sydney Goodsir Smith (1915-1975), George Mackay Brown (1921-1996), Iain Crichton Smith (1928-1998) and Edwin Morgan (b. 1920). These writers collectively comprise the poetic *geist* of later twentieth-century Scottish literature after MacDiarmid's cultural revolution of the 1920s and alongside MacDiarmid's later career.

Central to that *geist* was the gravitational pull of Scotland as the ground in which literary and intellectual work could be earthed, and an opposition (often voiced, almost always implied) to Anglocentrism. However, in 1936, in *Scott and Scotland*, Edwin Muir argued against separate Scottish traditions in the modern world: 'Scotland can only create a national literature by writing in English' Muir said. To MacDiarmid, this was a betrayal of all he had achieved and hoped to do, a strangling of literary possibility and an obsequious surrender to English authority. MacDiarmid spurned Muir's friendship and alliance, and scorned his conclusions.[13]

MacDiarmid invented two slogans in the 1920s, to herald the intentions of the Scottish Renaissance movement and declare what he hoped it would achieve: 'Not Burns – Dunbar' was one. By this he intended to urge fellow poets and critics to abandon the debased tradition of Burns – the sentimental nationalism and Jacobite 'Stewartolotry' and the saccharine devotion to cosy domesticity sourced and enshrined in 'The Cottar's Saturday Night' (Burns's poem in which a poor farming family find weekly solace in Bible readings). He also wanted to reject the slow-witted comedy to which the Scots language had been reduced. The monopoly over Burns and vernacular Scots was jealously held by Vernacular Scots Societies and Burns Clubs throughout Scotland and internationally. The opposition was strong. When MacDiarmid's friend Catherine Carswell (1879-1946), wrote a new, serious, unintimidated biography of Burns (1930), she was sent a bullet in the post and told to desist. MacDiarmid championed a return to the linguistic vibrancy, political volatility and intellectual life of the late medieval poet William Dunbar.

The other slogan was: 'Not Traditions – Precedents!' He was recommending the rejection of anything that might straightjacket creativity and the strategic adoption of individual points of departure and cultural growth. Even MacDiarmid's recognition of Dunbar had a precedent in the 1890s, when Patrick Geddes paid similar homage to Allan Ramsay. Patrick Geddes (1854-1932), is known now as a polymath and radical innovator, biologist, town-planner, sociologist and teacher. For MacDiarmid, he was 'not only one of the greatest Scotsmen of the past century but in our entire history.' In 1895 and 1896, Geddes produced four issues of a review journal entitled *The Evergreen*, commemorating Allan Ramsay's *The Ever Green* of 1724, a collection 'of Scots Poems Wrote by the Ingenious before 1600'. The new journal appeared to London reviewers to be 'a counter-blast at the established reviews'. H.G. Wells remarked, 'It's bad from cover to cover and even the covers are bad' and this comment was quoted as publicity for the journal! But Geddes was able to entitle an essay in the 'Spring' issue of 1895, 'The Scots Renascence' and he described the possibility of improving the future for Edinburgh and its citizens – though he emphasised the possibility rather than the achievement. The precedent Geddes set was also a prophecy: 'One day noble traditions long forgot will rouse a mightier literature.' This sense of underdeveloped potential pushed towards the articulation of the cultural energies of which Scotland might be capable in the Renaissance of the 1920s. MacDiarmid referred to Geddes's hopes in the editorial of the first number of his magazine *The Scottish Chapbook* in 1922, picking up the thread.[14]

The Scottish Renaissance was primarily conceived as a literary movement, to be led by the example of the work of poets. However, MacDiarmid immediately included theatre and fiction in his vision. Experimental Scots theatre movements, working-class theatre, the Scottish National Players (in the 1920s) and Ewan MacColl and Joan Littlewood's Theatre Workshop (in the 1940s) were encouraged, alongside radical journalism and avant-garde novels such as the early work of Neil Gunn and the later achievement of Lewis Grassic Gibbon. The whole matter of Scotland's linguistic diversity required reconsideration and the superstructure of literary and cultural criticism demanded to be reinvented, rejecting conventions of realism and adapting to more disruptive forms of modernist aesthetics. In 1926, MacDiarmid recommended *Ulysses* and *The Waste Land* as the two works which will 'survive as the representative expressions of early 20th century life and thought in the English language.' Few of his Scottish contemporaries were so acute in their literary perceptions.

The Scottish Renaissance went further though. As we have seen, there were precedents to be taken up in music and art (especially painting), and MacDiarmid saw himself working closely in conjunction with the composer F.G. Scott and the artist William Johnstone. Johnstone referred to them as 'Three Borderers' setting out heroically, like the three musketeers, in his autobiography, *Points in Time*. Scott, Johnstone wrote, became greatly excited by the prospect of 'a Scottish Renaissance of the arts' and envisaged the three friends at the core of it, 'all having a revolutionary point of view', raising the standard of the arts. Johnstone insisted that Scott's musical settings of MacDiarmid's poems 'broke entirely new ground... It was the birth of a twentieth-century Scottish Renaissance.'[15] No British composer of the time is closer to Schoenberg than Scott. Scott and Johnstone were not the only significant figures of the period though; the composers Ronald Center (1913-1973) and Ronald Stevenson (b. 1928) and the painters William Crozier (1897-1930) and William McCance (1894-1970) deserve further study also.

A new writing of Scottish history was demanded, from a northern, rather than Anglocentric, perspective. By extension, the whole matter of education was at the heart of the effort of the Scottish Renaissance. The ultimate ideal was a regeneration of the cultural life of the nation, and the educational revolution that had to be effected to help bring this about was central to it. It was not until the 1990s that schoolchildren were officially encouraged to express themselves in the Scots tongue. The division between class-room English and playground Scots had broken down and the political imperative was pressing.

MacDiarmid was keen to credit the French critic and philosopher Denis Saurat with the invention of the term 'renaissance écossaise' but Saurat was only repeating MacDiarmid's use of the phrase in 1923. Kenneth Buthlay has noted that the 'infant mortality rate' in this Renaissance was high, and that one reason MacDiarmid used so many pseudonyms was simply to swell the ranks.[16] Other poets associated with the movement more or less closely (and sometimes whether they liked it or not) included Lewis Spence, Pittendrigh Macgillivray, Marion Angus, Muriel Stuart, Helen Burness Cruickshank, William Jeffrey and William Soutar. Of these, Soutar is the most substantial and enduring, and his work set an important precedent for later poets writing in Scots, including J.K. Annand, Robert Garioch and Sydney Goodsir Smith.

One of the most important long-term effects of the Scottish Renaissance has been the unprecedented overhaul of the nation's cultural identity, with new histories of Scottish literature, art, music and economic and social development offering new ways of comprehensively understanding a national culture, before, through and after its participation and near-extinction in the rise and fall of the British Empire. One of the most important concomitants of that has been the resurrection of works by a number of artists and writers which had been obscured even during the time of the Renaissance itself: the novels of Nan Shepherd and Catherine Carswell, or John Buchan's sister 'O. Douglas' for example. These explorations and rediscoveries coincide with academic and scholarly survey work and ongoing excavation (for example, William Donaldson's discovery of popular prose fiction in Victorian newspapers), but they also coincide with continuing creative energies, prodigious, innovative and internationally acclaimed. If, as T.M. Devine has said, the Scottish Renaissance 'failed to inspire any broader flowering of Scottish culture in the inter-war years'[17] then one must recognize that perhaps that is because its yeast has taken longer to ferment and fructify, and its forms are still evolving.

NOTES

[1] Hugh MacDiarmid, *Contemporary Scottish Studies*, edited by Alan Riach, Manchester: Carcanet Press, 1995, p. 210.
[2] *Ibidem*, pp. 264-265

[3] *Ibidem*, p. xii.

[4] Many of MacDiarmid's articles from these periodicals are collected in *The Raucle Tongue: Hitherto Uncollected Prose,* 3 vols., edited by Angus Calder, Glen Murray and Alan Riach, Manchester: Carcanet Press, 1996, 1997, 1998.

[5] C.M. Grieve ed., *Northern Numbers: Being Representative Selections From Certain Living Scottish Poets* (volumes 1 and 2, Edinburgh: T.N. Foulis, 1920-1921; volume 3, Montrose: C.M. Grieve, 1922).

[6] For a general overview see John Purser, *Scotland's Music: A History of the Traditional and Classical Music of Scotland from Earliest Times to the Present Day,* Edinburgh: Mainstream, 1992. As for the Scottish Renaissance music see the following discography: Composers: 1. Sir Alexander Campbell Mackenzie, Scottish Concerto, on *The Romantic Piano Concerto* – 19, Hyperion CDA67023; *Violin Concerto/Pibroch Suite,* Hyperion CDA66975; *Alexander Mackenzie* (includes Burns – Second Scottish Rhapsody), Hyperion CDA66764; Concert Overture: Britannia, on *Victorian Concert Overtures,* Hyperion CDA66515; 2. William Wallace: *Creation Symphony,* Hyperion CDA66987; *Symphonic Poems,* Hyperion CDA66848; 3. Hamish MacCunn, *Land of the Mountain and the Flood and other music* (includes extracts from *Jeanie Deans*), Hyperion CDA66815; 4. Sir John Blackwood McEwan, *Three Border Ballads,* CHANDOS CHAN9241; *A Solway Symphony,* CHANDOS CHAN9345. Collections: *Scotland's Music* (2 CDs), LINN CKD 008; *Essentially Scottish* (includes piano music by Mackenzie, MacCunn and others), KOCH/SCHWANN 3-1590-2H1. The booklet notes for many of these CDs are vitally informative and many were written by John Purser (see his book *Scotland's Music,* listed above). No CD exists of the music of the foremost composer of the Scottish Renaissance, F.G. Scott.

[7] For a general overview see Duncan MacMillan, *Scottish Art 1460-1990,* Edinburgh: Mainstream, 1990.

[8] John Davidson, 'The Testament of a Man Forbid', in *The Poems of John Davidson,* 2 vols., edited by Andrew Turnbull, Edinburgh and London: Scottish Academic Press, 1973, (pp. 329-334) p. 329.

[9] Hugh MacDiarmid, 'Of John Davidson', in *Selected Poems,* edited by Alan Riach and Michael Grieve, Harmondsworth: Penguin, 1994, p. 166.

[10] Cited in Marshall Walker, *Scottish Literature since 1707,* Harlow: Longman, 1996, p. 206.

[11] Hugh MacDiarmid, *Selected Prose,* edited by Alan Riach, Manchester: Carcanet Press, 1992, p. 3.

[12] *Ibidem*, p. 22.

[13] Edwin Muir, *Scott and Scotland: The Predicament of the Scottish Writer*, London: George Routledge and Sons Ltd., 1936, p. 178.

[14] See Philip Boardman, *The Worlds of Patrick Geddes: Biologist, Town planner, Re-educator, Peace-warrior*, London: Routledge & Kegan Paul, 1978, p. 152. And see also Hugh MacDiarmid, S*elected Prose*, edited by Alan Riach, cit., p. 6.

[15] William Johnstone, *Points in Time: An Autobiography*, London: Hutchinson, 1980, p. 72.

[16] Kenneth Buthlay, *Hugh MacDiarmid (C.M. Grieve)*, Edinburgh: Scottish Academic Press, 1982, p. 13.

[17] T.M. Devine, *The Scottish Nation 1700-2000*, London: Penguin Books, 1999, p. 321.

CHRISTOPHER WHYTE

Seeking for Continuities in MacDiarmid's Poetry: Overcoming Fragmentation

I

What is to be done with MacDiarmid, once the dustclouds of nationalist enthusiasm have finally settled? Few twentieth-century poets have been so conditioned, in their reception and appreciation, by their association with a political movement, and with the movement in cultural politics which led, in time, to the establishment of a Scottish literary canon (one whose validity was still, in the latter half of the twentieth century, open to question from the wider academic establishment). The increasingly disastrous nature of MacDiarmid's political affiliations, from defending the operations of the Soviet secret police in the early 1930s[1] to rejoining the Communist party in the wake of the 1956 Hungarian uprising,[2] should warn us against the dangers of reading his work through the prism of any unitary political, or national, commitment. More than a decade has passed since W.N. Herbert bemoaned the lack of a 'comprehensive analysis of any kind of so large and varied a corpus', earlier critics having largely 'confined themselves to the explication of the poet's principles, or the rejection of those principles because of their undisciplined or anti-establishment basis'.[3] Yet the task of establishing connections, of detecting shared concerns and parallel practices in different areas of what is undoubtedly a disparate body of work, is still far from completion. Indeed, the amount of critical attention devoted to MacDiarmid's poetry has if anything diminished in the years since Herbert voiced his complaint.

The distortions that nationalist criticism has tended to operate in the body of MacDiarmid's work are all too evident. The poet's earlier period, from the founding of the periodical *The Scottish Chapbook* in 1922 to the publication of *A Drunk Man Looks at the Thistle* in 1926 and the amalgamation of four separate formations in the National Party of Scotland in 1928,[4] has tended to be privileged at the expense of his subsequent production. The reasons for such a distortion are not far to seek. It is no easy matter, and may well be ill-advised, to try and disentangle MacDiarmid's programme for the revitalisation of Scottish literature, and of Scottish culture more generally, on a basis of independence from English influence and the English tradition, from his commitment to agitating and organising for political and legislative independence. At times it seems legitimate to ask whether the poetry was inspired by the programme, or whether the programme was developed so as to offer a context for MacDiarmid's poetic practice. In a setting like the Scottish one, where loyalty to either of the indigenous literary languages, Scots and Scottish Gaelic, has been noticeable for its weakness and even absence, MacDiarmid was paradoxically cast as the revivalist champion of the first. It inevitably followed that, as he gradually abandoned Scots for a range of experimental forms of English in the 1930s, the difficulties of reconciling such work with the role generally ascribed to him became insurmountable.

Achieving due recognition for both Scots and Gaelic was an integral part of the platform of the Scottish Renaissance Movement as originally formulated. At a distance of nearly eight decades, there can be no denying its effective failure in this area. One cannot but smile wrily at the legend, perhaps started by MacDiarmid himself, that he mislaid his lyric gift as a result of a fall from the upper deck of a motorbus in London.[5] What more exemplary punishment could there be, for a poet whose imagery and language (in tune with generalised contemporary perceptions of where the true Scotland could be found) were rural rather than urban, than falling victim to one of the latest monsters spawned by a technocratic society? And what more appropriate setting for that punishment than the imperial metropolis, for which he had unwisely and treacherously abandoned a settled if highly active existence in the Scottish provinces? MacDiarmid's move from Scots to English can more usefully be looked on as responding to a failure to gain any kind of institutional recognition for the stigmatised language. After all, poets cannot, *pace* Shelley, alter single-handed the course of either political or cultural history. Moreover, developments between 1928 and 1933 led the National Party of Scotland to purge its more radical, fundamentalist elements,[6] so that, as the Second World War approached, it offered a changed face to the world. MacDiarmid's explicit sympathies for the international Communist movement, and his idolising of Lenin as to all effects a second Christ, meant that he naturally fell foul of this process, just as his commitment to political and cultural separatism caused him to be disowned by the Communist party organisation.[7]

So, by as early as 1932 MacDiarmid had been ostracised, in terms of both nationalist activism and the cultural movement he initiated. For the nationalist canon, the authors who set the tone of the 1930s were William Soutar and Neil Gunn: a poet who owes as much, if not more, to English Georgian poetry and the prosody of the metrical psalms, as to either literary modernism or the ballad tradition; and a novelist whose idealisation of an integral Gaelic past can be shown to be bogus, underpinning a political and social philosophy no-one could define as radical.[8] This ostracisation had a geographical background (MacDiarmid took up residence in Whalsay, a small island in the Shetland archipelago, in May 1933, not abandoning it till he moved to Glasgow in January 1942, to undertake work in a munitions factory) as well as a personal one. The publication of a new volume of selected letters has cast a revealing light on the traumatic circumstances surrounding the break-up of his marriage and subsequent divorce, and which no doubt go some way to explaining the abuse of alcohol which came to characterise the poet.[9]

But worse (or better) was to come. In these conditions of isolation MacDiarmid entered upon what may be termed his third period, working at a series of ill-defined portmanteau poems, an open text or texts which achieved publication, in a form that need not be regarded as definitive, only in 1955.[10] The question of periodisation, in a different sense, leaps out. Is *In Memoriam James Joyce* to be assigned to the postwar period, at a stage when what would soon be defined as postmodernism was in the air, already distancing and, as it were, setting at an angle the achievements of literary modernism in the wake of a previous war? Or does it belong to the

1930s? Whatever solution is adopted, there is little doubt that, in spite or maybe thanks to his isolation, MacDiarmid moved from positions that can be termed modernist in the direction of post-modernism at a speed which his artistic solitude probably increased rather than impeding.

Although championed by figures such as Edwin Morgan or Alan Riach,[11] *In Memoriam James Joyce* continues to be an underread, even an unread text, impermeable to critical approaches inspired by nationalist commitment. Nationalist critics of the older stock simply do not know what to make of it. What remains of the present essay hints, within a limited space, at the necessity of overcoming the nefarious periodisation to which readings of MacDiarmid's poetry have all too often been subjected. Its strategy is to seek out continuities which will bind together works written across a period of several years, habits of mind and of poetic practice which argue that there are fundamental coherences in this enormous output, independent of the poet's political affiliations at the time of writing, and of any necessary implication with nationalist (or any other) ideology. The ultimate aim should be to rescue the full body of MacDiarmid's poetry from the segmentation and fragmentation to which it has been subjected, not because of its inherent flaws, but because of the incompleteness, partiality and inadequacy of so many of the hermeneutic tools brought to bear upon it.

II

> *Geh in der Verwandlung aus und ein.*
> Rainer Maria Rilke

The early lyrics written in Scots between 1922 and 1926, perhaps the only segment of MacDiarmid's work to have met with universal admiration, are far from being the impenetrable nuggets of verbal magic, the mysterious and ultimately inexplicable flashes of poetic genius they are all too often viewed as. A coherent and recurrent pattern underpins them, structured around the notion of liminality. Liminality indicates position on a threshold, at a passover point between two states often diametrically opposed, such as the animate and the inanimate, the living and the dead, the present and the absent. Movement across the threshold is rarely unidirectional. More often it becomes an oscillation, a wavering. The threshold itself may be a curtain, a door, even a tombstone, hinting tantalisingly at what lies beyond without, however, giving access to it. In terms of imagery, the stone and the child are again and again evoked in connection with liminality. Christian teaching, which offered (in its more traditional forms) the certainty of a resurrection of the flesh, with the dead literally rising from their graves, made of the gravestone (in MacDiarmid's imaginary) a sort of revolving door. The dead are not permanently dead, but destined to return to life at the end of human history, a point which is no less of a temporal threshold than the birth of Christ. Children, and especially infants, are liminal beings. It is easy for adults to remember a time when the children around them did not exist, and children are of their nature ephemeral, constantly changing, growing towards an adulthood which will divest them of the very qualities which made them children.

The lyric 'The Watergaw',[12] whose first publication in 1922 is often taken as marking the onset of the Scottish Renaissance, deploys the imagery of liminality in an explicit fashion. The look which so haunts the speaker was in the eyes of someone on the point of crossing the threshold between the living and the dead. The crucial preposition 'ayont' (meaning 'beyond') is referred here to a curtain of heavy rain on which the illusionistic rainbow of the title is projected. The lyric is situated at the turning point between day and night (the 'forenicht') and is permeated by movements of oscillation ('yow-trummle', 'chitterin'). The fire in the hearth which, at the beginning of the second stanza, has been allowed to die out in sign of mourning, has itself moved between being and nonbeing. And the insight adumbrated at the close of the lyric, the purport of the dying person's gaze, is only indicated, never made accessible, as if it, too, resided on the other side of a curtain that divides irreconcilable states of existence.

The movement from one state to another may be characterised by a collective rather than an individual catastrophe, such as the end of the world or the crucifixion of humanity's saviour.[13] It is characteristic of MacDiarmid's art at this juncture to deploy richly

Christian imagery for ends that are not Christian. In 'The Eemis Stane',[14] the link between stone and planet is essential. Do we not conceive of the planets as huge, rotating boulders, magically suspended in an abyss of nothingness? Here the world is like a stone teetering on the edge of a precipice, on the point of falling and, presumably, being shattered to smithereens. It 'wags' in the typical movement of oscillation. 'The Watergaw' had brought together the human and the inhuman, the sentient and the insentient, an optical illusion on a stormy night and the mute communication of someone about to die. 'The Eemis Stane' proceeds from the impersonal to the subjective, to 'eerie memories' whose movements are evoked by those of the stone. In the second stanza it becomes a tombstone or a monument, bearing a writing concealed by two veils or curtains, the work of 'fame' and 'history'. It is no more accessible (to the reader) than the insight at the close of 'The Watergaw'.

Planets traditionally bear the names of deities who themselves embody fundamental human drives and impulses, thereby establishing a powerful link between the animate and the inanimate. 'The Bonnie Broukit Bairn'[15] presents them as a group of adults engrossed in superficial conversation, unaware of the catastrophe threatening when the earth, the child, the liminal being they are neglecting, overwhelms them with its tears.

The notion of liminality makes it possible to tease out the underlying coherence of the four poem cycle 'Au Clair de la Lune',[16] included, like all the lyrics so far mentioned, in MacDiarmid's 1925 collection *Sangschaw*. Of its two epigraphs, the first repeats the association of the moon with yellow and with 'birdiness' set up in 'The Bonnie Broukit Bairn' ('The auld mune shak's [note the oscillation] her gowden feathers'), while the second aligns a further pair of opposing states with those already evoked, madness and sanity, as well as setting up a connection with the planets ('stars') justified by the associations of the word 'lunatic'.

The first poem, 'Prelude to Moon Music', presents the end of human history, of time as we conceive it ('Earth's littered wi' larochs o' Empires./Muckle nations are dust'), a threshold which is a kind of death, and which makes it possible for the Moon to summon a wondrous music from the chanter of death's bagpipes. In the second, 'Moonstruck', the world is set gyrating like a child's spinning top (so very like a speeded up planet). Though a bird of prey, and dark (a 'craw'), the moon is 'licht-lookin''. It has feathers of a 'caud gowd' which 'quhither' (quivering or trembling,[17] the oscillation again). Her prey is the speaker, and when she pounces on him, he is projected into an unprecedented world of sensation (insanity?) which makes irreconcilable opposites converge. The noise of the oceans is barely perceptible. Thunder resembles a tiny bell. And the movement of time, now that history is over, becomes itself a kind of oscillation, the backwards and forwards, zigzagging movement of a crazed insect:

> An' the roarin' o' oceans noo'
> Is peerieweerie to me:
> Thunner's a tinklin' bell: an' Time
> Whuds like a flee.

It would be possible to speak of the first poem of the sequence as 'before', the moment when the transformation is about to take place. The second presents the transformation itself, while the third deals with the consequences, the 'after'. The epigraph, taken from A.E. Housman, offers a backwards and forwards movement, across a threshold (the surface of the sea) and between opposing states (the human and the inhuman, being alive and being dead). It is possible that MacDiarmid intended it to be taken, in Darwinian terms, as referring to the evolution of the human race from amphibian creatures, making their way out of the sea onto solid land, and destined to retrace this path when humanity itself dies out. In terms of this poem's imagery, the threshold is the surface of the waters beneath which the earth glitters like a fossil, the relict of a distant past. It is a 'bare auld stane', with a bemusing choice of adjectives. Does 'bare' mean that once there was writing on it? And what precisely would a 'new' stone be like? A disembodied 'Thocht' (no longer human?), no longer capable of material perception, but gifted with 'keethin' sicht', would appear to be making the transition from one side to the other ('owre') of the 'wave'. Its golden colour links it to the moon, whose beams are oscillating, undulating ('kelter') in the firmament above.

Simpler and more traditional in its choice of imagery, the final
poem in the sequence is nonetheless coherent with the concerns
foregrounded hitherto. Diana, the virgin goddess with 'yellow hair'
brings together moon and 'yellowness', has the impersonal yet personalised nature of a planet, and is a huntress seeking her prey,
just like the moon in the second poem. It is possible that her vir-
ginal status keeps her teetering on a threshold she could, but will
never step over. There is movement across, as her hair flies out
'ayont' the storm, while she lifts her shining breasts '*oot owre* the
thunner-wa*'* (my italics). The third stanza foretells a further transformation, when the chaos to which thought is at present exposed
will terminate, yielding to a song with the power to soothe all
humanity's turbulence.

The consistencies, even the repetitions, are so striking, that one
can hardly question the existence of a structure, a system, even a
language, capable of bodying forth MacDiarmid's concerns at this
stage (and much later!) without subjecting them to the impoverish-
ment of direct statement. So powerful is the pattern of liminality
that it informs even explicitly 'borrowed' or 'derived' lyrics such as
'O Jesu Parvule'.[18] In its way this is a pastiche, a profoundly
Christian and even Catholic poem evoking that threshold (catastrophic?) period in Scottish history, the establishment of the
Protestant Reformation. The baby Christ is both God and man,
human and inhuman at one and the same time, his closest kin not
his mother but the planets ('a' the starnies an' he are sib'). He is, or
his mother would like him to be, on a threshold, between being
awake and falling asleep, but this is the very opposite of what the
'byspale', the wondrous, precocious, uncannily unchildlike child,
has in mind.

At least in its first half, 'Empty Vessel'[19] (taken from the next collection, *Penny Wheep*, which operates overall at a lesser level of
intensity than *Sangschaw*) is a 'found' poem, quoting 'Jenny
Nettles' a song in Allan Ramsay's *Tea-Table Miscellany* (1724-
1729).[20] Yet, as with 'O Jesu Parvule', MacDiarmid succeeds in rendering the already made, the pre-existing, consonant with his own
concerns. The first line has 'ayont', and a pile of stones (the 'cair-
ney'), while the third and fourth present the liminal being (the
'bairnie') which has just crossed the dividing line between oppos-

ing states (presence and absence). The first line of the second stanza introduces oscillation ('swing') (and one wonders if the mother in 'O Jesu Parvule' may have been rocking her marvellous baby to and fro) while the stanza, as a whole, sets up a parallelism between the animate and the inanimate. The bereft mother is compared to the forces propelling the planets in their orbits ('Wunds wi' warlds to swing') as well as to the light which illumines the world ('The licht that bends owre a' thing') with a haunting implication that, as in the first stanza, the focus of all this attention may be absent, that 'a' thing' may have vanished. The history of humanity, from this perspective, might already be a thing of the past.

III

MacDiarmid returns to analogous concerns, and draws on related patterns of imagery, at the culmination of *A Drunk Man Looks at the Thistle*, the long poem in Scots which he published in the same year as *Penny Wheep*. The passage in question runs to 252 tercets, each of the three lines having the same end rhyme. This is a considerable technical feat, and serves to highlight the crucial role of the passage within the poem as a whole. Its dominant image is borrowed from Yeats's *A Vision* (1925),[21] a further instance of MacDiarmid's magpie tendencies, though the tone of the passage is anything but Yeatsian. The earlier lyrics had concentrated on moments of transition, cataclysmic events which marked the beginning or the end of an epoch, and on an overall conception of history which went beyond the merely human, eager to embrace the history of non-being itself. The cycle evoked at the close of *A Drunk Man* is of 26,000 years, believed to mark the 'precession of the equinoxes' (Buthlay notes that 'the change in direction of the earth's axis as it turns round the axis of the ecliptic describes a complete cone approximately every 26,000 years').[22] Contemplation of time and history evokes planetary movements, and the speaker tosses the world (the planet earth?) into a pool as if it were no heavier than a pebble:

I've often thrawn the warld frae me
Into the Pool o' Space, to see

> The Circles o' Infinity,
>
> Or like a flat stane gar'd it skite,
> A Morse code message writ in licht
> That yet I couldna read aricht. (ll. 2443-2448)

This is a popular children's game in Scotland, and as the pebble dances across the surface of the water it appears to produce a script inaccessible to the speaker. The echoes of 'The Eemis Stane', where the letters on the stone were choked by moss and lichen, and of the unarticulated meaning at the end of 'The Watergaw', possibly clear to the speaker but hidden from the reader, are clear. The surface of the water, the location of this writing, is itself a liminal point. The overwhelming aspiration, as *A Drunk Man* nears its close, is towards a moving beyond, a leaping across, imaged as the movement from one planet, one luminary to another:

> By whatna cry o' mine oot-topped
> Sall be a' men ha'e sung and hoped
> When to a'e note they're telescoped? (ll. 2473-2475)

The background is an unbearable crushing, a compression which threatens to annihilate both consciousness and meaning. It is clear that the speaker has much more in mind than the simple possibility of space travel:

> But a' the music that mankind
> 'S made yet is to the Earth confined,
> Poo'erless to reach the general mind,
>
> Poo'erless to reach the neist star e'en,
> That as a pairt o'ts sel' is seen,
> And only men can tell between. (ll. 2485-2490)

The planet earth is viewed in mineral terms, our 'native speck o' grit' (l. 2493), and in this, the first and most important climax of the sequence of tercets, the notion of a threshold is made explicit. Foolhardy as it may be to attempt to paraphrase MacDiarmid's imagery here, it is as if the wheel which stands for planetary motion on the largest scale (for Yeats's Great Year 'in which the heavenly bodies were supposed to return to their original relative positions',[23] though it is also, probably, a gramophone record) could, were humanity to take the necessary step across the threshold, be absorbed into human consciousness. Human beings could then beget planets (thus also, it may be, new cycles, and a new kind of time and history):

> For gin the sun and mune at last
> Are as a neebor's lintel passed,
> The wheel'll tine its stature fast,
>
> And birl in time inside oor heids
> Till we can thraw oot conscious gleids
> That draw an answer to oor needs... (ll. 2497-2502)

The 'Au Clair de la Lune' sequence is never far away in this conception of epoch-making, cataclysmic transitions associated with changes in the nature of being. Planets would normally be thought of as inanimate entities yet, if the interpretation suggested above is accurate, the animate here gives birth to the inanimate still in a state of becoming (the planets are balls of fire, not yet cooled), making hard and fast distinctions between the two impossible.

Though the extracts quoted above move far beyond a specific concern with Scotland, *A Drunk Man Looks at the Thistle* repeatedly interrogates the nature of national belonging, reaching an agnostical conclusion. MacDiarmid's predicament as a Scottish poet is analogous to the struggle of a host of others whom he does not name yet cannot blame, despite their impotence:

> Nor blame I muckle, wham atour
> Earth's countries blaw, a pickle stour,
> To sort wha's grains they ha'e nae poo'er. (ll. 2530-2532)

IV

In the extended English language poem 'On a Raised Beach', first published in 1934 in *Stony Limits and Other Poems*,[24] though nationalist concerns have been left aside, or far behind, a pattern of imagery related to that of MacDiarmid's 1925 and 1926 volumes is clearly discernible. There, the stone which in its rounded form could be a planet had also appeared as a flattened slab, marking a tomb or covering a grave. One of its manifestations was as the stone rolled aside from the tomb of Christ at the moment of the resurrection (which marked, in Christian belief, a positive change in the status and potentiality of humanity as a whole). These associations are clear in 'Crowdieknowe'[25] which, for all its lighthearted tone, offers a powerful key to unlock the world of MacDiarmid's lyrics, and in a longer item imitated from the Russian of Dmitry Merezhkovsky, significantly entitled 'The Last Trump'[26] (both from *Sangschaw*). They persist in the later poem. 'On a Raised Beach' takes its title from the geological phenomenon which produced the stony plateau it describes. The speaker sees his listeners as thirsting for one of these to act as harbinger of a further resurrection:

> 'Ah!' you say, 'if only one of these stones would move
> – Were it only an inch – of its own accord.
>   This is the resurrection we await,
> – The stone rolled away from the tomb of the Lord'.[27]

Stretched out on the stones, it is as if the speaker were waiting for a shift, a cataclysm, a liminal moment ('Nothing has stirred/Since I lay down this morning an eternity ago/But one bird'.) The stones demand his attention because it is with them that 'the world began', and in proclaiming their superiority to 'anything *more recently born* than themselves' (my italics) he blurs the boundary between the animate and the inanimate, the human and the inhuman, in characteristic fashion. They fascinate him because, by concentrating on them, he feels able to dismiss 'All but all of evolution', to shoot backwards as the Housman epigraph to the third of the 'Au Clair de la Lune' lyrics had suggested. Indeed, he insists that 'They came so far out of the water and halted forever'. In the early lyrics, stones, planets and stars are closely linked, and in 'On a Raised Beach' we read that 'these stones are one with the stars'. The ethical preparedness the speaker urges on his listeners is in view of a future transition, 'Reasoned planning for the time when reason can no longer avail'. Though they seem motionless to us, the stones are possessed by an 'intense vibration'. Vibration, oscillation, shifting backwards and forwards had been the typical movement of the Scots lyrics, and it is in line with the generally negative role of the moon in MacDiarmid's poetry of that period that the stones should here be impervious to the oscillation the planet would induce, while at the same time themselves containing a very different kind of oscillation:

> The moon moves the waters backwards and forwards,
> But the stones cannot be lured an inch farther
> Either on this side of eternity or the other.[28]

The mention of another side to Eternity suggests a liminal situation. But it is hard to determine how far the poem envisages further transition, one more cataclysmic, transformational moment. The speaker loves the stones because they allow him to embrace two turning points ('I grasp one of them and I have in my grip/The beginning and the end of the world'). They embody the coming together of opposites that was so recurrent in the earlier poetry: 'I lift a stone; it is the meaning of life I clasp/Which is death, for that is the meaning of death'. He insists that 'not one stone will move,/Not the least of them, not a fraction of an inch'. If a man is to become 'at one with creation', it is essential that the stone which covers him should not be cast aside. And yet in the very act of stating this, the speaker lets slip that no stone can 'be hurled/Aside *yet* to let any of them come forth' (my italics), since 'slow as the stones the powers develop/To rise from the grave – to get a life worth having'. At this point, barely ten lines from the poem's close, it would seem that there may indeed be a further resurrection, one that will draw close at a speed dictated by the stones and in harmony with their rate of changing.

V

There is always a risk of simplification in any attempt to explicate a poem's meaning. The readings offered here do not aim to explicate, but rather to describe a poetic language, patterns of theme and imagery which continue across contrasting phases in MacDiarmid's writing. The contrasts are unmistakable in terms of language, of the deployment of poetic form, of the very notion of what constitutes poetry, as well as of the poet's developing and shifting ideological commitments in the course of his life. Yet the consistencies, if we are prepared to seek them out and pay attention to them, are equally unmistakable.

This essay proposes a *method* rather than offering hard and fast conclusions. Before ending, I would like to propose a further line of discussion which may be of assistance in highlighting the internal coherence of MacDiarmid's approach to poetry, throughout his extended career. A variety of critics have put forward a variety of defences against the imputation of plagiarism with regard to *In Memoriam James Joyce*. Sensitive to the relevance postmodern theory can have for our reading of the poem, Carl Freedman finds MacDiarmid's use of extensive quotation 'so extreme as to disable any supposed attempt at actual deception'. Rather it is a means of subverting 'the normal assumption that a given (stable) text stands in a relation of middle-class ownership to a given (stable) subject', of 'undermining... such notions as private property and stable personal identity'.[29] Cogent as they are, such defences betray a preoccupation with the ethical aspects of MacDiarmid's practice, one that has given most of his critics pause at one stage or another. For Alan Riach, '"Plagiarism" is too small a grenade to throw against a work like this', and he quotes the poet himself to the effect that 'The multiplicity of quotations, references and allusions must be completely understood' as 'they constitute the *language* in which [the poem] is written'.[30] At least since the appearance of seminal essays by Kenneth Buthlay,[31] however, it has been clear that the extent of quotation in *In Memoriam James Joyce* goes far beyond the acknowledged and even the perceptible. Is it essential, or even useful for the reader to know that a more ostensibly 'poetic' passage on the hues of autumn trees, which offers the reader a degree of relief from the unrelenting poetry of fact some 600 lines into the poem's first section,[32] has been lifted from an obscure novel of the 1920s? Any more than it is to know about the ballad borrowings in 'Empty Vessel', or the degree to which the 'Au Clair de la Lune' sequence is dependent on quotation from Jamieson's dictionary?[33] The point is not just that 'plagiarism' was a lifelong practice with MacDiarmid, as germane in its way to the celebrated early lyrics as it is to *In Memoriam James Joyce*. What matters is the question that inevitably follows from this, and our ability to answer it. What is the appropriate way to read this poetry? What elements can usefully be held within a reader's consciousness as he or she traces a path through or across it?[34] To go even further, what kind of *ideal reader* is implied by a text like *In Memoriam James Joyce*, given that every text, and not merely those which are startlingly innovative, holds within it an as it were subliminal blueprint for how and by whom it should be read? It is hard to conceive of any human reader possessing the kind of encyclopaedic consciousness MacDiarmid may have aspired to, but certainly fell far short of embodying. Who then can best explore, decode and enjoy this poetry? And what do we need to do if we are to resemble, within the limits of the possible, that adumbrated figure?

NOTES

[1] 'As necessary, and insignificant, as death/Wi' a' its agonies in the cosmos still/The Cheka's horrors are in their degree...' See Hugh MacDiarmid, 'First Hymn to Lenin', in *The Complete Poems of Hugh MacDiarmid*, 2 vols., edited by Michael Grieve and W.R. Aitken, London: Martin Brian & O'Keeffe, 1978 (reprinted Manchster: Carcanet, 1993), p. 298.

[2] For MacDiarmid's contradictory behaviour on this occasion, see Alan Bold, *MacDiarmid (Christopher Murray Grieve): A Critical Biography*, London: John Murray, 1988, pp. 409-410.

[3] W.N. Herbert, *To Circumjack Cencrastus: the Poetry and Prose of Hugh MacDiarmid*, Oxford: Clarendon Press, 1992, p. xiii and p. xi.

[4] Alan Bold, *op. cit.*, pp. 231ff.

[5] The incident is described in Alan Bold, *op. cit.*, p. 241.

[6] R.J. Finlay charts the internal divisions, which he sees as culminating in an 'inevitable showdown... at the annual conference of May, 1933' in 'The National Party of Scotland 1928-1933', chapter 2 of his *Independent and Free: Scottish Politics and the Origins of the Scottish National Party 1918-1945*, Edinburgh: John Donald, 1994.

[7] On May 19th 1933 MacDiarmid received a letter intimating 'that the NPS had no room for extremists' and communicating his expulsion from the party. He then applied for membership of the Communist Party of Great Britain, from which he was expelled for 'nationalist deviationism' in November 1936. See Alan Bold, *op. cit.*, pp. 289, 318, 343.

[8] See in this connection Christopher Whyte, 'Fishy Masculinities: Neil Gunn's The Silver Darlings', in Christopher Whyte ed., *Gendering the Nation: Studies in Modern Scottish Literature*, Edinburgh: Edinburgh University Press, 1995, pp. 49-68.

[9] Hugh MacDiarmid, *New Selected Letters*, edited by Dorian Grieve, O. D. Edwards and Alan Riach, Manchester: Carcanet, 2001.

[10] W.N. Herbert envisages a single project, *Mature Art*, 'a text tinkered with for forty years, which never saw light in any final, "authorized" form', and attempts to reconstruct it on the basis of 'a number of projects MacDiarmid was engaged with in the mid-1930s, which subsequently resurfaced in the 1950s and 1960s' (see W.N. Herbert, *op. cit.*, p. 157 and p. 165). See further his 'MacDiarmid: Mature Art', *Scottish Literary Journal*, vol. 15, no. 2, November 1988, pp. 24-37. Kenneth Buthlay, on the other hand, speaks of *The Kind of Poetry I Want* as 'the second volume of a work perpetually in progress... in reality the sequence was endless, its parts indefinitely permutable' (see Kenneth Buthlay, *Hugh MacDiarmid*, Edinburgh: Scottish Academic Press, 1982, p. 123).

[11] Riach is the author of the only monograph so far devoted to the later work, *Hugh MacDiarmid's Epic Poetry*, Edinburgh: Edinburgh University Press, 1991. By Edwin Morgan, see 'Jujitsu for the Educated', *Twentieth Century*, vol. 160, no. 955, September 1956; 'James Joyce and Hugh MacDiarmid' and 'MacDiarmid's Later Poetry against an International Background', in *Crossing the Border: Essays on Scottish Literature*, Manchester: Carcanet 1990, pp. 169-187 and 188-204; and 'Recycling, Mosaic and Collage', *Edinburgh Review*, vol. 93, no.1, 1995, pp. 149-166.

[12] *The Complete Poems of Hugh MacDiarmid*, cit., p. 17.

[13] 'The Innumerable Christ' (*The Complete Poems of Hugh MacDiarmid*, cit., p. 32) brings together, as turning points or thresholds, Christ's birth and crucifixion, multiplying these across a number of worlds or 'stars'. The poem deploys, in a fashion characteristic for these lyrics, both 'stars' and 'bairnies', as well as the crucial preposition "yont".

[14] *The Complete Poems of Hugh MacDiarmid*, cit., p. 27.

[15] *Ibidem*, p. 17.

[16] *Ibidem*, p. 23.

[17] In the glossary to *The Complete Poems* the word is explained as 'quiver'. MacDiarmid had, however, previously glossed it as 'beam', and Kenneth Buthlay derives it from 'quhidder' in Jamieson's *Etymological Dictionary of the Scottish Language*, meaning 'a slight and transient

indisposition'. See his 'Adventuring in Dictionaries', in Nancy Gish ed., *Hugh MacDiarmid: Man and Poet*, National Poetry Foundation, University of Maine and Edinburgh: Edinburgh University Press, 1992, pp. 147-169 (here p. 159).

[18] *The Complete Poems of Hugh MacDiarmid*, cit., p. 31.

[19] *Ibidem*, p. 66.

[20] See Kenneth Buthlay, *Hugh MacDiarmid*, cit., p. 21.

[21] See Hugh MacDiarmid, *A Drunk Man Looks at the Thistle*, annotated edition by Kenneth Buthlay, Edinburgh: Scottish Academic Press, 1987, p. 173. There are no line numbers in *The Complete Poems* text.

[22] *Ibidem*, p. 177.

[23] Kenneth Buthlay, *op. cit.*, p. 173.

[24] Now in *The Complete Poems I*, cit., pp. 422-433.

[25] *The Complete Poems of Hugh MacDiarmid*, cit., p. 27.

[26] *Ibidem*, p. 29.

[27] *The Complete Poems of Hugh MacDiarmid I*, cit., p. 432.

[28] *Ibidem*, p. 427.

[29] 'Beyond the Dialect of the Tribe: James Joyce, Hugh MacDiarmid and World Language', in *Hugh MacDiarmid: Man and Poet*, cit., pp. 253-273 (here p. 270).

[30] Alan Riach, *op. cit.*, p. 52.

[31] See 'Some Hints for Source-Hunters', *Scottish Literary Journal*, vol. 5, no. 2, December 1978, pp. 50-66, and 'The Ablach in the Gold Pavilion', *Scottish Literary Journal*, vol. 15, no. 2, 1988, pp. 39-57.

[32] See *The Complete Poems of Hugh MacDiarmid II*, cit., pp. 756-758.

[33] See Buthlay's 'Adventuring in Dictionaries', cit., pp. 156-161.

[34] Buthlay's listing, in *Hugh MacDiarmid*, of 'at least three counts' on which it matters for the reader to be aware of an original source is stimulating in this connection, but not conclusive (see p. 102).

The Place of Edwin Muir [1]

'One should appreciate, after all, the advantages of one's origin. Its worth lies in the power it gives one to detach oneself from the present moment'. This observation appears in Czeslaw Milosz's *Native Realm*, where it follows a passage describing his life in the Embassy of the People's Republic of Poland, during the years immediately after World War II:

> At many a reception in Washington or in Paris, where enthusiastic ladies would approach a Red with a delicious shiver, I felt that I was only half-present. Too many shadows enveloped me: the clanking of sabers, the rustling of Renaissance gowns, the fragrance of old houses full of animal hides, hunting arms, coaches, rusted armor; and this robbed what was going on around me of some of its reality. Generations of men tormented by the devil, fingering their rosary beads, winked at me with humor.

At around the same time as Milosz was sleepwalking through those receptions in Paris and Washington, Edwin Muir was serving as a representative with the British Council in Prague, in the hiatus before the Communist takeover of Czechoslovakia. Undoubtedly he too experienced a sensation of being only half-present, for such abstractedness was habitual with him and was often remarked upon during his lifetime. The ghosts of the forebears who winked at Muir would not have been fingering rosaries, but we can be sure that they too were 'tormented by the devil'. The creak of oars may have haunted him more than the clank of sabers; farm-carts rather than coaches may have rolled along his dream roads; but like Milosz, Muir was sustained in his roles as poet and bureaucrat by a place he carried inside himself, an original Orkney that was both a remembered origin and an imagined elsewhere.

Muir resembles Milosz in other ways. He was one of the few

English language poets of his time with an immediate sense of the traumas happening inside Europe during the 1930s and 1940s. It was as if the fall he personally experienced in the first decade of this century, when he moved from the traditional world of Orkney to the world of slums and wage-packets in Glasgow, sensitized him to terror. Marginal, vulnerable, with the solitary's antennae that are often so much finer than those of intellectuals in the swim, Muir was destined to become a kind of dual citizen of the imagination: he was fully at home within the insular traditions he had inherited (as an Orcadian, a Scot and an English-speaker), and yet he would also become a kind of ghostly blood-brother to the poetic progeny of Kafka (whom he and Willa Muir translated).

Muir crossed two thresholds: first, from a medieval if not neolithic Orkney he moved into the industrialized, individualized world of the twentieth century; and then from the relative security of his Scots and anglophone culture he entered the cosmopolitan and destabilizing world of Eastern Europe before and after the war. So to consider 'the place of Edwin Muir' is to consider the gift for bilocation which he developed, an ability to move from 'the story' to 'the fable', from the historical dimensions of his experience to the mythic significance it held for him; but the phrase will also lead us towards some consideration of where Muir stands in the history of modern poetry in English, of his 'place' as a poet who was D.H. Lawrence's junior by two years, T.S. Eliot's senior by one, and an exact contemporary of Rupert Brooke...

As a composer of English verse, Muir is obviously closer to the practice of Brooke than to that of Eliot. His lines derive from the iambic lines of Tennyson and Wordsworth, his pentameters keep the accent, and other aspects of his style reach back to the oral traditions of folk-song and the ballad. In fact, long before he spanned the European divide, Muir was already spanning the divide between the oral tradition of his native Orkney and the art poetry of the English language; and he speaks most surely as a poet when the resources of these two inheritances are brought fully into play.

However, the two modes can also work against each other in a way that was prefigured by the singing which Muir heard around him as a child. In *An Autobiography* he observes that the words and tunes of the old Orkney ballads were possessed without anxiety by the island's singers. The singing of the ballads was as much a self-forgetting as a performance, and this was in marked contrast to the rendering of the newer printed songs that came north from London. These would be self-consciously and deliberately enunciated, with a corresponding onset of uncertainty in the singer about the relationship which the essence of the song had to the fact of his or her own being.

In Muir's poetry, a similar uncertainty is observable in his many lapses into literary diction; poeticisms abound all through his career, and not just as a consequence of his not belonging to the school of modernism which went 'in fear of abstractions'. It is more the fact that Muir's life carried him from essentially pre-Gutenberg conditions into what was *de facto* the era of Marshall MacLuhan, with the result that his verse occasionally has the air of a man moving around in a slightly unfamiliar language. A lot of the poems betray a convalescent frailty of utterance. This can have to do with the low pressure of feeling surrounding a poem's occasion, or with the fact that certain themes and images get dulled through repeated treatment in the course of the *oeuvre*; but the impression of a man shaky on his verbal pins derives also from the poet's subliminal hesitancy between the oral culture that his ear was founded on and a more print-based idiom acquired by him later as a clerk, writer and administrator. For a complete realization of his potential as a poet, Muir has to dwell in those two places at the same time.

The simplest force and deepest gratitude are felt in *An Autobiography* when Muir remembers certain sensations of security or illumination or release which seemed to give access to a plane of being more extensive than his own personal existence, yet parallel to it and supportive of it. These memories are generally of a benign sort, as when he recollects what his first consciousness of life was like in the cradle: 'I was lying in some room watching a beam of slanting light in which dusty, bright motes slowly danced and turned, while a low murmuring went on somewhere, possibly the humming of flies'. After childhood, as he confesses a few lines further on, that sense of a slow unending dance, 'the sense of deep and solid peace' came back to him only in dreams. So, not unexpectedly, it is dream states that underlie and are induced by his most characteristic poems. Muir's level best involves access to a far-off, slightly somnambulist plane, and on these occasions the reader is gratified by the entranced atmosphere, if also a little unnnerved by the eerie placidity of it all; but his very best combines the lucent presence of such states with a simultaneous apprehension of menace.

Again, an early moment in *An Autobiography* suggests the nature of these more complex and commanding achievements. He tells how he felt terror on hearing of the death of a farmer who used to bring him sweets in his snuff-lined pockets, and then goes on:

> In a child's mind there is at moments a divination of a hidden tragedy taking place around him, that tragedy being the life he will not live for some years still, though it is there, invisible to him, already.

This apprehension of broken harmonies, of the entry of contradiction into life, is what we demand of the highest art, and we demand it in precisely the way it appears here – not as a great accumulation of negative data, not as an assault by the bad evidence, but as an intuited, endangering pressure of reality, a true weighing of things as they are dreaded against things as they are desired. The odd thing about Edwin Muir as a twentieth-century poet is that he had more than enough experience of his own to tilt the scales towards a negative reading of the human condition, yet could nevertheless maintain his innate, positive disposition. Critics have properly resisted him when the thrust of his poetic uplift took too little cognizance of the actual gravity of the lived conditions, but it must be acknowledged that without his habitual, muffled compounding of abstract joy and pondered sorrows, Muir could never have established the peculiar balance between substance and sonorousness which distinguishes his finest work.

To read a poem like 'Merlin', however, from his 1937 volume, *Journeys and Places*, is to find him working at what I have called his 'level best':

> O Merlin in your crystal cave
> Deep in the diamond of the day,
> Will there ever be a singer
> Whose music will smooth away

> The furrow drawn by Adam's finger
> Across the meadow and the wave?
> Or a runner who'll outrun
> Man's long shadow driving on,
> Break through the gate of memory
> And hang the apple on the tree?
> Will your magic ever show
> The sleeping bride shut in her bower,
> The day wreathed in its mound of snow
> And Time locked in his tower?

The needle on the scale trembles deliciously here. On one side, the balance inclines to wish-fulfilment of a kind that Walt Disney could film and market as something indistinguishable from his own brand of fantasy. All the elements of never-never land are there: magicians, bowers, brides, towers. Yet the usualness of these things is fleetingly renewed by the quality of the imagining. 'To hang the apple on the tree', for example, has an unexceptionable allegorical significance, but as a phrase it possesses a simplicity and unexpected clarity, the buoyancy and superficies of language-life which distinguish poetry. The same is true of the second line, 'Deep in the diamond of the day', and of the penultimate, 'The day wreathed in its mound of snow'. These incline the balance away from whimsical fantasy towards a more humanized and poignant note; so if the poem does not expose us to what Robert Frost called the 'desert places between stars', it does at least intimate a receptivity to 'the still, sad music of humanity'. And it does so by the liturgical, unhurriable procession of vowels in a line like 'Deep in the diamond of the day'.

The secure, lucid place imagined in the poem is surely related to another place where the young Muir once knelt at family prayers. The note of 'Merlin' seems to harmonize perfectly with the note which the boy's father struck on those occasions, described by Muir as 'a sort of mild chant'. In fact, the overall effect of 'Merlin' upon the reader is probably much the same as that experienced by the child-poet when he heard his father enunciate the following words which always held a special fascination for him: 'a house not made with hands, eternal in the heavens'.

Mild chants of houses not made with hands: from beginning to end Muir composed poems that could be so described. Poems with a steady metrical beat and a certain narcotic intonation. Poems like 'The Ring', 'The Window', 'The Toy Horse', 'Telemachus Remembers' – the list could be extended, but in these and similar poems Muir's early experience of security in the first good place, his susceptibility to the difference-eroding chant of the ballads, seems to have had a determining effect upon his poetic practice.

But it also has to be said that in these poems the order of art is rather too amiably imposed upon the disorders of experience. A pane of Tennysonian glass, such as intervened between the Lady of Shallott and the traffic on the road, keeps the thick-witted world at a remove. Not unexpectedly, there is even an unashamed echo of Tennyson in 'Telemachus Remembers':

> The weary loom, the weary loom,
> The task grown sick from morn to night,
> From year to year. The treadle's boom
> Made a low thunder in the room.
> The woven phantoms mazed her sight.

This is beguilingly skilful, and nobody is going to suggest that a poem of impeccable verbal order must necessarily misrepresent the complexities of living – a reading of 'The Combat' would suffice to give the lie to such an oversimple equation of perfect melody with spiritual or intellectual gullibility. Nevertheless, Muir's well earned faith in the immortality of the soul and his hard-won if high-placed perspective on personal and historical suffering come through in these poems as a shade too readily available. They dwell too calmly in the written place, within the imagined circle. They are of course a bonus of Muir's personal journey, poems to which he has every literary right. But they are Parnassian poems, understanding Parnassian according to Hopkins's famous definition in his letter to A.W.M. Baillie. For Hopkins, the term denoted a kind of poetry that was second to the poetry of inspiration:

> It can only be spoken by poets but it is not in the highest sense poetry... It is spoken *on and from* the level of the poet's mind, not, as in the other case, when the inspiration... raises him above himself.

One thinks here too of Auden's definition of inspiration as that which has occurred when a poet writes better than we could have reasonably expected. The poems by Muir just mentioned are not of this inspired sort. They do not do the whole work of art, they do not move a personal force through an artistic distance. Instead, they tread the force with stationary efficiency and produce a strain in the melodious rather than in the laborious sense of that word. They return us, in fact, to Eden; and as Peter Butter rightly insists, in his study of Muir, Eden as a destination is less poetically rewarding than Eden as a starting point. From there, the poetic imagination ventures most rewardingly outwards into fallen time; its project is most forceful and its achievements most bracing when it attempts a transitional perspective, when it stands with *only* 'one foot in Eden'. In the poem of that name, appropriately, Muir's music is a combination of primal song chant and the differentiated, alienated precisions of the modern world. The poem does propose a patient, generally accepting attitude to fallen reality, but its action is more strenuous than in the poems discussed so far, and its strain of sweetness is consequently more durable. There is a haulage job being done by the metre; it and the rhymes and the argument are dragging forward a positive meaning. And allied to this vitality is a bareness of diction which keeps the poem from indulging in longueurs or relishing its own effects:

> Yet still from Eden springs the root
> As clean as on the starting day.
> Time takes the foliage and the fruit
> And burns the archetypal leaf
> To shapes of terror and of grief
> Scattered along the winter way.
> But famished field and blackened tree
> Bear flowers in Eden never known.
> Blossoms of grief and charity
> Bloom in these darkened fields alone.
> What had Eden ever to say
> Of hope and faith and pity and love
> Until was buried all its day
> And memory found its treasure trove?
> Strange blessings never in Paradise
> Fall from these beclouded skies.

'One Foot in Eden' and other 'chant' poems such as 'The Annunciation' – the one beginning 'The angel and the girl are met' – and 'The Return of the Greeks' and 'The Child Dying' demonstrate the possibility of bringing off that most delicate and difficult of feats: writing a poem in which the good fairly wins a points-victory over its opposite. But then that feat is only worth while when the opposition is fairly admitted – as it is beginning to be in these works.

It could be said that one of Muir's strengths is a sense of proportion. This is a quality which Muir attributes in important measure to Robert Frost, in a review of the American poet which appeared in *The Listener* in 1943 (reprinted by Peter Butter in *The Truth of the Imagination*). What Muir writes of Frost we can fairly say of Muir himself:

> [He] is one of those poets who so evidently succeed in doing what they wish to do that they tempt everyone to point out their limitations. The limitation is so clearly there, as it is not in poets who undertake more than they can manage. But when one examines [his] limitation one finds that it rises from proportion, and that his proportion in turn is rooted in character. If he were to say more than he says, as people sometimes wish he would, it would destroy the balance of his view of life. As for the character itself, it has the soundness and natural distortion of growing things which have already grown sufficiently to posses a distinctive shape.

Muir, by the time he had started to write poetry in the 1920s, had also grown sufficiently to produce a distinctive shape. At that moment of beginning he could have declared what he declared in his last unfinished poem:

> I have been taught by dreams and fantasies
> Learned from the friendly and the darker phantoms
> And got great knowledge and courtesy from the dead
> Kinsmen and Kinswomen, ancestors and friends.

If there is an echo of Yeats's rhetoric in those lines, there is also a memory of Wordsworth's image of himself as an 'inmate of this active universe'. Indeed, Muir's career as a poet has about it something of Wordsworth's indeflectible purpose. For both of them, poetry was a necessary part on an effort at self-restoration and self-integration, an aspect of the attempt to align powers of the self with powers of the cosmos. Muir and Willa starting out in Czechoslovakia and Germany in the 1920s remind one of Dorothy

and William withdrawing to the south of England in the 1790s; and
the simplicity of Wordsworth's ballad poems of that time, in which
the greening of vegetation and the startle of birdsong are analogies
for the shoots of self-healing he was experiencing, such simplicity,
such mirroring of outer and inner things are typical of an early
Muir poem like 'October in Hellbrunn'. Of this and other poems
composed in Salzburg, Willa Muir says: 'they read like notes made
by a child-like melancholy observer'; and that they 'have an over-
tone of gentle sadness'. This is true, but I believe that 'October in
Hellbrunn' is of a higher poetic order than her affectionate references suggest:

> The near-drawn stone-smooth sky, closed in and grey,
>   Broods on the garden, and the turf is still.
> The dim lake shines, oppressed the fountains play
>   And shadowless weight lies on the wooded hill.
>
> The patient trees rise separate, as if deep
>   They listened dreaming through the hollow ground,
> Each in a single and divided sleep,
>   While few sad leaves fall heedless with no sound.
>
> The marble cherubs in the wavering lake
>   Stand up more still, as if they kept all there,
> The trees, the plots, in thrall. Their shadows make
>   The water clear and hollow as the air.
>
> The silent afternoon draws in, and dark
>   The trees rise now, grown heavier is the ground,
> And breaking through the silence of the park
>   Farther a hidden fountain flings its sound.

This park scene has become what Wordsworth called 'a prospect
of the mind'; the images inhabit in two places at one time. The
trees, for example, sleep 'a divided sleep' between earth and air,
and the cherubs standing in air are reflected in water. We are not
just dealing with a gentle evocation of literary melancholy; we
have entered a state of consciousness similar to that which Muir
recollected from childhood, when the child's mind divined 'a hidden tragedy taking place... the tragedy being the life he will not
live for some years still, though it is there, invisible to him,

already'. 'October in Hellbrunn', then, is certainly a poem of tran-
quil restoration, in that there is fullness and curativeness in the
thorough craft of its stanzas, but I would argue that it is also a
poem of the apprehensive and imperilled consciousness.

This is not to suggest that Edwin Muir had foreknowledge of
what the fate of Europe would be two decades later. But there was
already a place in him prepared for what did occur. When catastrophe came out of the borderlands of dread into the actual events of
history, Muir's poetic strength revealed itself: he was able to co-
ordinate the nightmare of history with that place in himself where
he had trembled with anticipation. The solitary boy who at the age
of 5 or 6 on the island of Wyre was filled with fear and wonder at
horses and herons was being prepared for the vocation of poetry.
The heron would come back in a dream, grey and shining, and
behind the stiff hedge of its unlikely tail feathers it would transform into a beast on four feet that were padded like a leopard's or
a tiger's. The rest of the dream story is given in *An Autobiography*:

> Then, confronting it in the field, there appeared an ancient, dirty, earth-
> coloured animal with a head like that of an old sheep or a mangy dog.
> Its eyes were soft and brown; it was alone against the splendid-tailed
> beast; yet it stood its ground and prepared to fight the danger coming
> towards it, whether that was death or merely humiliation and pain. From
> their look I could see that the two animals knew each other,... and that
> the dark, patient animal would always be defeated, and the bright, fierce
> animal would always win. I did not see the fight, but I knew it would be
> ruthless and shameful, with a meaning of some kind perhaps, but no
> comfort.

From that nugget of psychic matter Muir fashioned his poem 'The
Combat'. A poem with a meaning but no comfort, unless there is
comfort to be found in a disconsolate renewal of effort. 'The
Combat' can be read politically as a parable of the war against
Nazism or, more particularly and far less satisfactorily, about the
Battle of Britain. It can be read – maybe too trimly – within the
Christian idea of redemption through suffering. It can, at any rate,
be recognized as providing a completely satisfactory paradigm of
reality.

'The Combat' has something of the quality which Muir attributed
to the ballads. It belongs 'on the other side of the great plateau of

the eighteenth century, with its humanitarian passion and its great hopes for mankind'. It 'has no sentimental appeal' but operates 'on the level of tragic acceptance'. Its heraldic apparatus is animated by a strong rhythmic energy. Here Muir manages to do by rather abstract means what Keith Douglas managed by radically different means in a poem like 'Vergissmeinicht' – he manages to combine the contradictory demands of tough-mindedness and compassion:

> A while the place lay blank, forlorn,
> Drowsing as in relief from pain.
> The cricket chirped, the grating thorn
> Stirred, and a little sound was born.
> The champions took their posts again.
>
> And all began. The stealthy paw
> Slashed out and in. Could nothing save
> These rags and tatters from the claw?
> Nothing. And yet I never saw
> A beast so helpless and so brave.

What lifts this beyond Muir's 'level best' is its stamina as writing. Its spaciousness as parable is not gained at the expense of intensity. It almost possesses the 'rich, dark wintry magic' which the child Muir recognized in a sketch of Burns.

Wintriness, however, is not the natural weather of Muir's work. His typical music is fuller, more like the half-consoling roll-away of summer thunder, a music in tune with the 'deepening drumming' which hoofbeats make on the evening road in his poem 'The Horses'. 'The Horses' is another of his indisputable achievements, a poem in which the archaic scenario carries the burden of a modern predicament. Again, a late poem brings into focus an early premonition and combines it with the phantasmal recognitions of the adult living under atomic threat. Both his earlier poem (in quatrains) about the horses – published in 1925 – and the subsequent prose account of horses in *An Autobiography* are haunted by the old familiar sense of a consciousness undergoing experience which has not yet yielded up its meaning. But as Robert Frost correctly observes, poets are like giants 'always hurling experience ahead of us to pave the future against the day when we may want to strike a line of purpose across it from somewhere'. What happens in this third attempt is that the meaning has been yielded and the line of purpose struck, in earnest and with triumph.

'The Horses' appeared in Muir's 1956 collection, *One Foot in Eden*, but it was in his 1949 volume, *The Labyrinth*, that Muir's unfashionable and eccentric poetic ways had begun at last to be rewarded. His metaphysically projected imagination had kept him out of the political swim of 'Thirties' poetry. There seemed to be nothing up to date about him. But in the forties, and especially in *The Labyrinth*, we can watch the gratifying phenomenon of a solitary poetic endeavour being recognized as representative; or to put it less magniloquently, Muir's subject was by then everybody's subject.

Osip Mandelstam believed that the poet's function was to address 'the reader in posterity'. In other words, poetic imagination working at its most absorbed is always contributing to the evolution of an awareness that will have to evolve fully before the imagination's contribution can be fully appreciated. My point is this: since we are now more fully aware of the world that Muir knew, first as a co-translator of Kafka and Hermann Broch, and then as a result of his direct experience of Germany and Czechoslovakia before and after the war, we are also now in a better position to set his work in context. The worth of his origin in Orkney (to go back to Milosz's proposition) was that it contributed in part to his ability 'to detach himself from the present moment' of English literary culture in the 1930s and 1940s and to write a poetry recognizably akin to that written by his Eastern European juniors, those ironists and parablists and fabulists with whom anglophone readers have only recently become familiar through translation.

Still, Muir was not a Middle-European. He was first Orcadian, then Scottish, then a creature of the English literary tradition. And within that tradition, I would see him as an heir of the Wilfred Owen who wrote 'Strange Meeting', the Owen who combined a natural religious temperament with a wounded social conscience, the Owen who was working as a vicar's assistant in Dunsden at about the same time as Muir was going through the scandal of his labours in the bone factory in Greenock. Both men were seared by contact with poverty and both developed a rhetoric that was somnolent and elegiac, yet politically purposeful. If nothing in Muir's poetry corresponds to the awful documentary content in Owen's, his essential achievement nevertheless corresponds to the kind of thing Owen managed in poems such as 'Miners' and 'Strange Meeting' – poems which display a mixture of visionary breadth and particular social witness.

Both men succeed in giving expression to a sensibility that is deeply affected by Christianity and almost too susceptible to the appeal of passive suffering. It is for this reason that Muir's early period of Nietzchean 'hardness' is so important and likewise Owen's period of somewhat vindictive outrage and protest. These phases surely contributed to their fully empowered styles, for it is true, as Yeats says, that style is the equivalent of self-conquest in a writer. When, for example, they embrace the futility and moral beauty of the victim in poems as different as Owen's 'The Send-Off' and Muir's 'The Combat', they both do so with a proper indignation against a world that seems not only to condone but even to ordain such an arbitrary and cruel imbalance in the sharing out of pain. At such moments, both of them are wary of the pathos of weakness and the temptations of the martyr-complex, and the poems they write represent a victory over their innate tendencies towards resignation. So if technically, as a composer of lines, Muir did not cease to belong to the pre-modern world of Rupert Brooke, imaginatively he did cross 'The Bridge of Dread', both within himself and in the wider field of the times he lived through.

But you may well be wondering: 'Why all this about the English tradition in poetry? Is the place of Edwin Muir not in Scotland? What about the possibility of a Scottish literary tradition?' The fact of the matter is that my perspective on Muir is that of an Irish writer with a natural interest in such questions. I have therefore a deep curiosity about how such a one fits in – one, that is, Scottish by birth and attachment, English by language and cultural adaptation, but one who still managed to turn that common division to good creative account. And I would contend that Muir's Scottishness, assailable once upon a time for not displaying a sufficiently nationalist fervour or not sporting the correct ethnic regalia, now appears unassailable in the light of an older alliance between Scotland and Europe.

Muir's best poems open a path where there is free coming and going between the local conditions and the reality which is the dominant one of the age. They deal with matters of the sort that had haunted the English 'Thirties poets', but they do not employ the Thirties poets' topical political idiom or their rhetoric of concern. Muir's style and approach were all his own, indifferent to and undetermined by any perceived English/Scottish difference. By displaying little obvious anxiety about cultural domination from south of the border, by accepting with equanimity the poetic inheritance it bestowed and then walking a little dreamily to the one side, on into Europe, Muir became a figure whose legacy has not yet been fully appreciated. As the old sureties are leached from the vernacular cultures of Europe, east and west, and a permeability occurs, and a corresponding capacity for absorption develops behind their artistic and political borders, Muir's work will deserve more and more to be remembered and re-read.

NOTES

[1] This is an edited version of the Alexander Stone Lecture in Bibliophily delivered in November 1988 at the University of Glasgow. For further readings see the following books: Edwin Muir, *First Poems*, London: The Hogarth Press, 1925; Edwin Muir, *Journey and Places*, London: Faber and Faber, 1937; Edwin Muir, *The Labyrinth*, London: Faber and Faber, 1949; Edwin Muir, *An Autobiography*, London: The Hogarth Press, 1954; Edwin Muir, *One Foot in Eden*, London: Faber and Faber, 1956; Edwin Muir, *The Truth of the Imagination: Some Uncollected Reviews and Essays*, edited by Peter Butter, Aberdeen: Aberdeen University Press, 1988; Czeslaw Milosz, *Native Realm: A Search for Self-Definition*, Berkeley: University of California Press, 1981.

CARLA SASSI

James Leslie Mitchell/Lewis Grassic Gibbon: The Challenge of a Kaleidoscopic Identity

James Leslie Mitchell (1901-1935), journalist, novelist, essayist, best known by his pen-name – Lewis Grassic Gibbon – has stood as a 'monument' of Scottish twentieth-century literature as well as a leading representative of the so-called 'Renaissance' along with his contemporary Hugh MacDiarmid for the past fifty years or so. His best-known work – the trilogy set in his native Mearns, *A Scots Quair* – has achieved the status of a classic and has been re-printed several times by Scottish as well as by leading British publishers, since its first appearance in 1946.[1] The BBC productions of 1975, 1982 and 1983,[2] as well as a popular stage version presented at the Citizen's Theatre in Glasgow, for the Mayfest in 1993[3] have certainly contributed to moving both the work and its author to the centre of the Scottish canon.

However, notwithstanding the growing interest of critics and academics in Mitchell's work, and the publication of a number of translations of *A Scots Quair* and of *Sunset Song,*[4] it has to be acknowledged – sadly – that so far Mitchell has failed to catch the attention of a wide international audience – a fate shared by other 'Scottish Renaissance' representatives, with the notable exception of Hugh MacDiarmid. An extremely challenging writer and an intriguing character – as the present essay purposes to demonstrate – Mitchell is still relatively unknown outside the British Isles, particularly in Italy.[5] There are of course several reasons for this: the untimely death of the author when he had just started establishing himself as a writer and the Scottish 'accent' of his last and most famous works are just two among many factors which led to his long neglect by 'Southern British' critics and, as an inevitable consequence, also by scholars outside Britain. Conversely, in his home country, Mitchell has become more and more popular and has been gradually identified as the quintessentially Scottish novelist – the 'Mearns Chronicler'. Paradoxically, both perspectives, even though leading to very different evaluations of Mitchell's work, contribute towards his appreciation exclusively – or mainly – in terms of 'local interest' and thus to a stifling circumscription of the scope of his literary work.

Another notable obstacle to a wider re-evaluation of Mitchell is that he is indeed a 'difficult' writer: his 'eccentricity' and the subsequent difficulty at classifying his work within mainstream categories or ideologies is reinforced by the writer's deep anger and iconoclastic attitude – a 'ferocity of opinions'[6] that pervades, disquietingly, all his work. Mitchell was restless as a person and as an artist: the boundary dividing his life from his writing was often razor thin, allowing frequent overlapping and trespassing. In the course of his short life he impersonated a number of 'roles', without ever being entirely faithful to anyone. Beside the well-known distinction between James Leslie Mitchell, the English writer based in Welwyn Garden City (who wrote on a number of topics, including history, anthropology and archaeology) and his 'distant cousin', the Scottish novelist 'Lewis Grassic Gibbon',[7] he offered different and sometimes contradictory representations of his identity – a fact which inevitably puzzled or even deceived both critics and the public. Perhaps it is not surprising – in the political and cultural context of the early twentieth century – that Mitchell, born in a peasant community in north-eastern Scotland, at times strived to shed his Scottishness and to conform to the 'Southern standard', in accent as well as in 'manners', once he settled in England.[8] Certainly it appears more striking that – after the publication of *The Conquest of the Maya* (1934)[9] – he managed to make critics and reviewers believe that he had actually spent months of work excavating at archaeological sites in South America.[10] Mitchell proclaimed himself an Anarcho-Communist, and yet settled comfortably in a middle-class English 'garden city', bought a car and at times manifested a form of disgust (even though mixed with pity) at the proletarian masses who inhabited the slums of British cities.[11] He approached Scottish nationalism by contributing with Hugh MacDiarmid to a series of essays collected in *Scottish Scene, or the Intelligent Man's*

Guide to Albyn, and yet managed – within the same collection – to pen highly anti-nationalist statements.[12] These are just a few of the many 'contradictions' which can be gleaned from a reading of Mitchell's work and of his yet unpublished correspondence.[13]

The present essay identifies Mitchell's 'kaleidoscopic' perspective as a highly distinctive feature of his *Weltanschauung* and work, rather than as a negligible incongruity as it has sometimes been considered by critics. This approach provides a more unified and coherent assessment of Mitchell's work.[14]

James Leslie Mitchell grew up and spent the early part of his life in Arbuthnott, a small crofting village among the red-clay fields of the Mearns, in north-eastern Scotland. It is not incorrect to say that this rural district, in the year of Mitchell's birth – incidentally the same of Queen Victoria's death – was as distant from the 'centre' of the Empire as other 'remote' British colonies of the same period. The distance – measured in cultural and linguistic as well as economic terms – separating the native peasant community of the Mearns from London is conveyed effectively by Mitchell in *A Scots Quair*, a fascinating polyphonic 'counternarrative', that re-writes Scottish history from the point of view of the 'colonised' – the peasants of the rural districts and the workers of the industrialised towns. The language of the narration itself has famously been described as a 'Creole' – a mixture of English and Scots, which challenges the language of the centre and represents perhaps the most powerful act of appropriation (in post-colonial terms) in the trilogy. Interestingly – even though his commitment to a re-evaluation of Scots as a literary language is very strong – Mitchell does not wish to revert the course of history and does not pursue an ideal of linguistic purity. In fact he does not wish to restore 'authentic' (pre-Union) Scots, but rather he aims to exploit the full creative potential of the spoken language, as it had developed after three centuries of English cultural domination.

The prose of *A Scots Quair* represents in many ways an outstanding celebration of hybridity, not only of languages (Scots/English) but also of narrative modes and genres, with its suggestive combination of oral style, folk-narrative, allegory and harsh realism. The opening of *Sunset Song* (the first of the three novels) offers a persuasive example of this:

Kinraddie lands had been won by a Norman childe, Cospatric de Gondeshil, in the days of William the Lyon, when gryphons and suchlike beasts still roamed the Scots countryside and folk would waken in their beds and hear the children screaming, with a great wolf-beast, come through the hide window, tearing at their throats. In the den of Kinraddie one such beast had its lair and by day it lay about the woods and the stench of it was awful to smell all over the countryside, and at gloaming a shepherd would see it, with its great wings half-folded across the great belly of it and its head, like the head of a meikle cock, but with the ears of a lion, poked over a fir tree, watching. And it ate up sheep and men and women and was a fair terror, and the King had his heralds cry a reward to whatever knight would ride and end the mischieving of the beast.[15]

With *A Scots Quair* – as its ambitious title suggests[16] – Mitchell sought to define a new Scottish literary 'space' beyond the senti-mental tradition of the Kailyard, epitomised by Ian Maclaren's *Beside the Bonnie Brier Bush* (1894) and the realism of George Douglas Brown's *The House with the Green Shutters* (1901):

So that was Kinraddie that bleak winter of nineteen-eleven and the new minister, him they chose early next year, he was to say it was the Scots countryside itself, fathered between a kailyard and a bonny brier bush in the lee of a house with green shutters. And what he meant by that you could guess at yourself if you'd a mind for puzzles and dirt, there wasn't a house with green shutters in the whole of Kinraddie.[17]

If Kinraddie represents Scotland's new literary space, then the introductory chapter to *Sunset Song*, 'Prelude', can be considered as Mitchell's 'manifesto'. He had, however, little time to develop his project of 'reform': after *A Scots Quair* he started a new novel, which was to take the experiment further, but did not have the time to complete it. The manuscript of the projected novel (*The Speak of the Mearns*[18]) was published posthumously in 1982 and certainly, as all unfinished material printed without the consent of the writer, it leaves the question open as to what it would have actually become, had the author lived to complete it.

Mitchell returned (albeit through his fiction only) to his native land only after long period of voluntary exile: in Arbuthnott he had grown up as a rebel and a misfit (a role to which he would cling for the rest of his life) – a 'bookish' and sensitive boy in a crofting village where everyday living conditions were often demandingly hard. Mitchell both hated and loved the tight-closed community he was born to – an ancient and self-contained world ruled by the cycles of the land, with only a Kirk and a small school to provide an alternative to toilsome work in the fields. And yet, this apparently deprived background provided Mitchell with a formidable source of intellectual stimulation and of creative imagination, further enhanced – as we shall see – by his experience in the Middle East as a soldier in the British Army. His imagination had been struck – when he was just a boy – by the traces left by the past civilisations of his native region, and he developed an early awareness of the multi-faceted, multi-layered and unstable nature of his (as any other else) community's cultural identity – a notion which was to haunt his imagination for the rest of his life. The Neolithic standing stones, the Pictish inscriptions, the Roman remains and the Norman churches, are recurring images in Mitchell's Scottish fiction and stand as mementoes of the fleeting nature of cultures, of their inevitable succumbing to the overwhelming law of change – in the Mearns as elsewhere.

Change is an obsessive theme in Mitchell's fiction – a sense of fixity and wholeness can be recovered by his characters only temporarily, through their relation with the land. As Chris, in *A Scots Quair*, puts it – 'Nothing endures but the land':

> [...] she minded the Greek words of forgotten lessons, *Panta rei. Nothing endures.*
> And then a queer thought came to her there in the drooked fields, that nothing endured at all, nothing but the land [...]. Sea and sky and the folk who wrote and fought and were learnéd, teaching and saying and praying, they lasted but as a breath, a mist of fog in the hills, but the land was forever [...][19]

In this context, it is hardly surprising that Mitchell's (positive) heroes and heroines are often 'nomads'[20] – either moving in space, 'tinkers' (as Ewan in *Sunset Song*), or imaginary descendants of the ancient Picts,[21] or moving between cultures and languages – 'hybrids' as is Chris in the same trilogy. Mitchell espoused the eccentric and yet fascinating Diffusionist theories, propagated by G.E. Smith, which privileged the nomadic pattern of life against that of settled communities.[22] With Smith, Mitchell believed that the

'Golden Age' hunters had been free from the slavery of fixed beliefs and cyclical rituals introduced by agriculture and that they had roamed on the land, freely negotiating their identity with it. Diffusionism provided Mitchell with a powerful imaginative myth, which he developed in his work: his novels often focus on characters who defy the fixed pattern of life in settled communities – it is those who experience and accept change, and thus acknowledge the relativity of all cultural and ideological models and reach beyond the blind rigidity of their contemporaries' rules, that represent Mitchell's privileged point of view.

What most of all forged Mitchell's sensitivity and ideology – beside the historical landscape of the Mearns – was undoubtedly the tension between two 'worlds', two cultures and two languages. He certainly shared this experience with the majority of the writers and intellectuals representative of the so-called 'Renaissance', who – in the early twentieth century – staged the first systematic reaction after the Union against an overarching Englishness. Most of them came from rural Scotland, rather than from Lowland cities. Beside Mitchell, Hugh MacDiarmid (born in Langholm, Borders), Sorley MacLean (born in Raasay, Hebrides), Neil Gunn (born in Dunbeath, Caithness), to name but a few among the most established writers of this period, came from 'marginal' regions, where resistance against cultural homologation to the 'centre' had been strongest. If on one side the Mearns had provided Mitchell with a distinctive cultural imprinting – the Scots language, the folk oral tradition, a way of life which had remained almost unchanged for centuries – the school had offered him access to an entirely different world – the English language, the written word, 'modernity'. Two worlds that – in the early twentieth century – were perceived as mutually exclusive thus challenging Mitchell's attachment to his native culture and originating a heart-rending 'split', personified most painfully by Chris in *A Scots Quair*.

> [...] two Chrisses there were that fought for her heart and tormented her. [...] You saw their faces in firelight, father's and mother's and the neighbours', before the lamps lit up, tired and kind, faces dear and close to you, you wanted the words they'd known and used, forgotten in the far-off youngness of their lives, Scots words to tell to your heart, how they wrung it and held it, the toil of their days and unendingly their fight. And the next minute that passed from you, you were English, back to the

English words so sharp and clean and true – for a while, for a while, till they slid so smooth from your throat you knew they could never say anything that was worth the saying at all.[23]

Chris is an 'in-between', a 'hybrid' – terms which have been recently associated with the work of H.K. Bhabha,[24] to whose theories the present essay is partly indebted – and also, as a consequence, an outcast. Irrespective of where she stands – in her native Kinraddie (in *Sunset Song*), as well as in Segget, the mill town of *Cloud Howe*, or in Duncairn (in *Grey Granite*), 'the city which the inhabitants of the Mearns... have hitherto failed to build'[25] – she remains isolated, withdrawn, aloof. She is, at times, even slightly disagreeable in her awareness of being 'superior' to those who surround her. Chris is obviously endowed with a wider and deeper understanding than most characters in the trilogy, and she views people and events from what seems, from the very beginning, a privileged perspective. Chris is never 'one': while the central dichotomy in her personality is stressed in the text several times, we soon discover that she conceives of herself as of a 'prism' with several facets, most of them yet to be discovered. Her identity cannot be described in fixed terms as it continually changes, and a new side surfaces at each glance she gives at her reflected image on the mirror – one of the most recurrent among Chris's actions in the novel:

[...] and then she raised her head and saw herself in the long, old mirror of the parlour wall, and thought how she'd changed, it crept on you and you hardly noticed [...][26]

Mitchell's impatience with pre-defined roles, as well as at external rules, started early, when – at the age of 17 – he left school in order to train as a cub reporter for the Aberdeen *Press and Journal*, thus coming into contact with the grim reality of urban life in an industrial town and developing a sympathy for Anarcho-Communist ideals, which he nurtured to the end of his life. Mitchell enrolled in the Royal Army Service Corps as a soldier in 1919 and served for a period of three years, during which he was sent to the Middle East (Egypt, Palestine, Mesopotamia and Persia), a move he made certainly more out of despair and the need to earn a living than out of a real attraction for military life. What the narrator of *Stained Radiance* claims about John Garland's outlook on life in the Army could easily be extended to Mitchell:

> He hated the Air Force. Like ninety per cent of those in the ranks, he had enlisted under the compulsion of hunger and unemployment. His stomach had conscripted him more surely than any Man Power Act could have done. He had forgiven the Service the fact of its feeding him.[27]

The Middle East experience – yet largely unrecorded (most of the correspondence dating from this period was in fact burned by Mitchell's wife Ray[28]) – probably worked as a catalyst of the would-be writer's early experiences and impressions and helped him shape his imaginative myths. The encounter and clash between different cultures (Western and Eastern) in fact inspires his first literary effort, *Polychromata* – a series of twelve short stories published originally in *The Cornhill Magazine* between 1929 and 1930.[29] The meaning of the title is revealed at the very beginning of the first story:

> Many-coloured? It is one of the names of our little Cairo – Polychromata. She has many names, the Gift of the River, and nowhere do her colours flaunt as here, in the Khalig el Masri [...][30]

The kaleidoscopic, cosmopolitan reality of Cairo between the wars, and the equally magmatic and multi-layered history of the Middle East deeply impressed Mitchell, who dealt with them in two other works beside *Polychromata*: a second collection of short stories, *Persian Dawns and Egyptian Nights* (1932),[31] subdivided – as the title implies – to two separate cycles, and a novel, *The Lost Trumpet* (1932).[32] In all these works the movements of confrontation, exchange and antagonism among different cultures generate diverse outcomes: it is interesting to see, for example, how the characters who live at a cultural/linguistic crossroads, or uprooted emigrants/travellers – 'hybrids' – are often endowed with more wisdom and humanity than those who are identified with a single ethnic group or culture. As Zara and Rhizos, in 'Dieneke's Dream' (in the *Egyptian Nights* cycle), the young couple who tries to overcome the barrier of hatred dividing the Greek immigrant community from the Cairene one. The Egyptian girl and the Greek boy project for themselves a modern future of freedom and social justice and, unlike their neighbours, who deeply distrust and despise each other, they share their daily life and academic interests ('daily, almost, he and Zara, both students at the University, travelled into Cairo together [...]'[33]). Or as Anton Saloney, the intriguing narrator of *Polychromata* and a 'nomad' by profession: 'Professor of English literature in Kazan Gymnasium', he then becomes 'colonel in the army of Deniken' and sets 'to wander the world for the good of the proletarii [...]'.[34] Amima (in *Persian Dawns*) is another 'nomad' at heart who enjoys hunting by herself on the plains and mountains surrounding her native Arlarlu – a small border outpost, a crossroads and a passing place for Persians, Mongols, Circassians and Arabs.

It is necessary to stress that Mitchell's representation of the East can hardly be described as innovative, as it perpetuates many of the clichés and stereotypes typical of the colonial tradition: notwithstanding his genuine contempt for and resentment against imperialism and his criticism of Western traditional representations of the 'Orient', his outlook remains, in fact, biased. In 'Siwa Plays the Game', for example, the narrator sneers at the Romantic vision of the Orient offered by the English writer who has never been to Egypt,[35] but the 'realistic' picture of the Arab world offered as an alternative proves to be equally mannered as well as charged with racist overtones:

> For Arabs were neither hawk-nosed nor handsome! instead, they had generally the appearance of having been violently dropped upon their faces by careless nurses in their early youth. They were neither taciturn nor abstemious nor fanatic; instead, they behaved, as he told me, like drunken dock-labourers on a charabanc tour [...][36]

Even though Mitchell undoubtedly displays sympathy towards the natives (especially when identified with the oppressed and exploited class), the East remains on the whole a screen onto which he projects his ideas and a workshop where he gradually shapes his art and his vision – immensely valuable for that, and crucial in the understanding of his later 'Scottish fiction', and yet often disappointing as an 'alternative' representation of the Orient.

Mitchell is possibly the writer within the 'Scottish Renaissance' who questions the 'centre' most widely and powerfully: if on the one hand he subscribes to the nationalist project (for example with his contribution to *A Scottish Scene*[37]) and articulates a line of resistance against a pervasive anglocentrism, on the other hand he stages an idiosyncratic and yet highly interesting resistance to the discourse of the nation. Mitchell undoubtedly goes a long way in the re-evaluation and re-appropriation of Scottish culture and language, and yet, if nationalism is ostensibly an ideology of 'oneness', then his fiction undermines it by discouraging – almost systematically – a univocal definition of identity, as exemplified in his privileging of 'polyhedral' or 'hybrid' characters. His fiction continually points towards the heterogeneous roots of (national) identity and focuses on the exploration of relations and interactions between cultures, rather than on the attempt at defining it in fixed and monolithic terms. Mitchell's representation of the self as multiple deconstructs identity to show it as multi-layered: in *A Scots Quair*, in particular, the frequent narrative shifts from first to third-person narration and to free direct style challenge the distinction between subjectivity and objectivity. 'Difference' is therefore inscribed in his writing as fluidity – the action of change leads to a break-down of categories, to the flowing of one thing into another.

Writing, as he did, in the 1930s, Mitchell lacked the ideological tools to frame and voice his experience of 'in-betweenness': his anger, his iconoclastic attitude, the restlessness with which he switched 'roles' can also be explained on the grounds of his uneasiness with current political and cultural categories, and can be seen as an individual – yet highly valuable – attempt at transcending them.

NOTES

[1] Lewis Grassic Gibbon's *A Scots Quair* was first published by Jarrolds (London, 1946). The three novels had already been published separately by Jarrolds respectively as *Sunset Song* (1932), *Cloud Howe* (1933) and *Grey Granite* (1934). All references in this chapter are from the Pan Books edition (London, 1982). For further reading see W.K. Malcolm, *Critical Works on James Leslie Mitchell/Lewis Grassic Gibbon: A Bibliography*, Arbuthnott, Lewis Grassic Gibbon Centre Official Website. Available: http://www.grassicgibbon.com/criticalworks.htm.

The two main biographies are: I.S. Munro, *Leslie Mitchell: Lewis Grassic Gibbon,* Edinburgh: Oliver & Boyd, 1966; and M.J. McGrath, *James Leslie Mitchell (Lewis Grassic Gibbon): A Study in Politics and Philosophy in Relation to his Life and Work,* unpublished PhD thesis, University of Edinburgh 1983. Among the various books and articles see the following: Douglas Young, *Beyond the Sunset: A Study of James Leslie Mitchell (Lewis Grassic Gibbon),* Aberdeen: Impulse Publications, 1973; Angus Calder, 'A Mania for Self-Reliance: Grassic Gibbon's *A Scots Quair',* in Douglas Jefferson and Graham Martin eds., *The Uses of Fiction: Essays on the Modern Novel,* Milton Keynes: Open University Press, 1982, pp. 99-113; W.K. Malcolm, *A Blasphemer and Reformer: A Study of James Mitchell/Lewis Grassic Gibbon,* Aberdeen: Aberdeen University Press, 1984; Ian Campbell, *Gibbon,* Edinburgh: Scottish Academic Press, 1985; Thomas Crawford, 'The View from the North: Region and Nation in *The Silver Darlings* and *A Scots Quair',* in R.P. Draper ed., *The Literature of Region and Nation,* Basingstoke: Macmillan, 1989, pp.108-124; Uwe Zagratzky, *Libertäre und Utopische Tendenzen im Erzahlwerk James Leslie Mitchells (Lewis Grassic Gibbons),* Frankfurt am Main: Peter Lang, 1991; Jeremy Idle, 'Lewis Grassic Gibbon and the Urgency of the Modern', *Studies in Scottish Literature,* vol. 31, 1999, pp. 258-268; Margery Palmer McCulloch and S.M. Dunnigan eds., *A Flame in the Mearns – Lewis Grassic Gibbon: A Centenary Celebration,* Association for Scottish Literary Studies, Occasional Papers, no. 13, 2003.

[2] Respectively *Sunset Song* (1975), directed by Moira Armstrong (writing credits Bill Craig), *Cloud Howe* (1982) and *Grey Granite* (1983), both directed by Tom Cotter (writing credits Bill Craig).

[3] Directed by Tony Graham, first performed by TAG Theatre Company at the Crawfurd Theatre, Jordanhill, Glasgow, 1991; *Sunset Song* was subsequently revised for a larger cast.

[4] Notably in French (Paris, 1997), in German (Berlin, 1970-1974), in Hungarian (Budapest, 1960, 1964 and 1976) and in Slovak (Bratislava, 1977).

[5] Notwithstanding Valentina Poggi Ghigi's valuable contributions, notably her essay on 'Lewis Grassic Gibbon e il primato della terra', in Valentina Poggi Ghigi, *Voci da un paese lontano: il romanzo scozzese del Novecento,* Bologna: Il Mulino, 1992, pp. 49-71, and her translation of 'Forsaken' ('Abbandonato'), in Valentina Poggi ed., *Scozia controluce: racconti fantastici del '900,* Santarcangelo di Romagna: Fara Editore, 1995, pp. 15-27 and of 'Smeddlum' ('Fegato') in *TRATTI,*

Autumn 1996, pp. 53-61, Lewis Grassic Gibbon remains largely unknown to Italian scholars and readers. Significantly, the latest edition of a popular reference book, such as the *Enciclopedia della letteratura* (Milano: Garzanti, 1997), devotes brief descriptions of the work of Neil Gunn and Hugh MacDiarmid, but curiously fails to mention 'Lewis Grassic Gibbon'.

[6] Cf. Jeremy Idle, 'A Ferocity of Opinions', *Books in Scotland*, vol. 40, Winter 1991, pp. 6-7.

[7] Mitchell enjoyed the 'game' of keeping the two identities separate (even though the truth was soon revealed to his readers) and created a self-ironical fiction surrounding the two 'distant cousins' (as he labelled his 'literary selves'), going to the extent of claiming that – beside having distinct attitudes and interests – each would use his own personal typewriter, and each would pose differently for official photographs: Mitchell was the one in profile, Gibbon would face the camera and had a pipe in his mouth (Interview with Ray Mitchell, *Welwyn Times and Hatfield Advertiser*, 19th March 1976). It is obvious, from the synopses of the projects he was working at, shortly before his premature death, that Mitchell was not planning to shed either of his 'selves'.

[8] Cf. [Memories of Jean Baxter], Acc. 4760 (National Library of Scotland – Manuscripts and Rare Books Collections).

[9] James Leslie Mitchell, *The Conquest of the Maya,* London: Jarrolds, 1934.

[10] Ivor Brown's preface to the first edition of *A Scots Quair* (1946) takes Mitchell's report for true. The same preface was used by the successive publishers of the trilogy, thus perpetuating the 'lie' up to the 1982 Pan Books edition.

[11] Cf. Lewis Grassic Gibbon, 'Glasgow', in Lewis Grassic Gibbon and Hugh MacDiarmid, *Scottish Scene, or the Intelligent Man's Guide to Albyin,* London: Jarrolds, 1934, p. 30.

[12] Cf. Lewis Grassic Gibbon, 'Glasgow', cit., pp. 136-147.

[13] Most of Mitchell's correspondence is held by the National Library of Scotland. It is certainly to be regretted that an edition of his correspondence has not yet been made available to scholars.

[14] This is the (questionable) aim – in my opinion – underlying the recent 'homogenisation' of all Mitchell's literary output under the Scottish pseudonym 'Lewis Grassic Gibbon'. Such choice seems, in fact, not only to comply to market logic ('Gibbon' being the most popular of the 'two' writers), but also has ideological connotations.

[15] Lewis Grassic Gibbon, *Sunset Song,* in *A Scots Quair,* London: Pan

Books, 1982, p. 1.

[16] The title of the trilogy echoes – consciously, in all probability – *The Kingis Quair* (ca. 1424), the courtly Scots poem attributed to King James I. It is interesting to remember that this poem marks a milestone in the Scottish literary tradition – 'modernising' it through the influence of English and European models such as Chaucer, Gower and Boethius.

[17] Lewis Grassic Gibbon, *Sunset Song,* in *A Scots Quair,* cit., pp. 23-24.

[18] Lewis Grassic Gibbon, *The Speak of the Mearns,* Edinburgh: The Ramsay Head Press, 1982.

[19] Lewis Grassic Gibbon, *Sunset Song,* in *A Scots Quair,* cit., p. 117.

[20] Cf. Carla Sassi, 'Scottishness and the Nomadic Myth in Lewis Grassic Gibbon's Fiction', in Igor Navrátil and Robert Pynsent eds., *Appropriations and Impositions. National, Regional and Sexual Identity in Literature* (Proceedings of the 5th International Conference on the Literature of Region and Nation, Bratislava, Národné literárne centrum, 1997), pp. 94-100.

[21] I.e. those who – in Mitchell's vision – had preserved the characteristics of the first inhabitants of Scotland – the 'Golden Age hunters' described in 'The Antique Scene' as 'naked, cultureless, without religion or social organisation, shy hunters, courageous, happy, kindly...' (Lewis Grassic Gibbon and Hugh MacDiarmid, *Scottish Scene, or the Intelligent Man's Guide to Albyn,* cit., p. 20).

[22] Diffusionism – an anthropological theory which opposed Darwin's faith in progress – was introduced in Britain by an Australian Egyptologist, Grafton Elliot Smith (1871-1937), whose work Mitchell highly esteemed. According to Smith nomads, hunters and food-gatherers lived in a happy communal anarchy, with no laws, no religion, no externally imposed moral code until the accidental discovery of agriculture (in ancient Egypt) and its subsequent expansion all over the world. Like the French Encyclopaedists, the Diffusionists believed that man was naturally mild and that his progressive degeneration had been caused by civilisation; unlike them, they could make use of empirical evidence – thanks to the results of recent archaeological and ethnological studies – to support their theories.

[23] Lewis Grassic Gibbon, *Sunset Song,* in *A Scots Quair,* cit., p. 32.

[24] Both terms indicate the ambivalent and contradictory space where cultures are defined – it is this ambivalence which for Bhabha makes the claim to the 'purity' of cultures untenable. Cf. H.K. Bhabha ed., *Nation and Narration,* London: Routledge, 1990; and H.K. Bhabha,

The Location of Culture, London: Routledge, 1994.

[25] From the 'Cautionary Note' to *Grey Granite* in *A Scots Quair,* cit.

[26] Lewis Grassic Gibbon, *Sunset Song,* in *A Scots Quair,* cit., p. 140.

[27] James Leslie Mitchell, *Stained Radiance: A Fictionist's Prelude,* London: Jarrolds, 1930. The quotation is from the latest edition, Edinburgh: Polygon, 1993, p. 13.

[28] Cf. Notes by Ian Campbell, Acc. 9504 (National Library of Scotland – Manuscript and Rare Books Collections).

[29] The collection is available today for the first time in print in its original sequence in Valentina Bold ed., *Smeddum: A Lewis Grassic Gibbon Anthology,* Edinburgh: Polygon, 2001, pp. 203-419. The stories had been published, in a different order and with the addition of a thirteenth story – 'For Ten's Sake' – in James Leslie Mitchell, *The Calends of Cairo,* London: Jarrolds, 1931.

[30] 'Polychromata I: He Who Seeks', *The Cornhill* LXVII, 1929, pp. 97-107. The quotation is from Valentina Bold ed., *Smeddum. A Lewis Grassic Gibbon Anthology,* cit., p. 223.

[31] James Leslie Mitchell, *Persian Dawns, Egyptian Nights,* London: Jarrolds, 1932.

[32] James Leslie Mitchell, *The Lost Trumpet,* London: Jarrolds, 1932.

[33] The quotation is from James Leslie Mitchell, *Persian Dawns, Egyptian Nights,* Edinburgh: Polygon, 1997, p. 239.

[34] James Leslie Mitchell, 'Polychromata II: The Epic', *The Cornhill,* vol. LXVII, 1929, pp. 160-170. This quotation is from Valentina Bold ed., *Smeddum: A Lewis Grassic Gibbon Anthology,* cit., p. 237.

[35] James Leslie Mitchell, 'Siva Plays the Game', *T.P.'s and Cassell's Weekly,* 18th October 1924, pp. 849-850. This quotation is from James Leslie Mitchell, *Persian Dawns, Egyptian Nights,* cit., pp. 264-265.

[36] *Ibidem,* p. 265.

[37] Lewis Grassic Gibbon and Hugh MacDiarmid, *Scottish Scene, or the Intelligent Man's Guide to Albyn,* cit.

CHRISTOPHER WHYTE

The Poetry of Robert Garioch:
More Ambition than Reduction

The Scottish humanist Arthur Johnston, having been both a student
and a professor at the University of Heidelberg, and having written
passionately of the plight of the Elector Palatine and his family in
the period between accepting the Bohemian crown in 1619 and
the Battle of the White Mountain in 1620, returned to Aberdeen in
1622, after nearly twenty years on the teaching staff at the
Protestant University of Sedan, where Andrew Melville had been
among his colleagues. He was to spend the remainder of his life
between Scotland and London, and the grim realities of farming in
Aberdeenshire provide an often ruefully depicted background to
his Latin poems of these years.[1]

One poem, however, offers a more heartening and celebratory
picture. It adopts the persona of a local salmon fisher, who is
lamenting the, to him, senseless prohibition against catching fish
on a Sunday. The local minister is the addressee. In other words,
the poem falls into the delightfully termed category of the piscatorial eclogue, in which neither the care of flocks, nor the tilling of
the soil constitutes the principal focus, but instead reaping the harvest of the waters. More than three centuries later, Robert Garioch,
then approaching his seventieth year, was to translate the 'Fisher's
Apology' into Scots.[2]

In doing so, he followed in the footsteps of several outstanding
predecessors, each of whom had in turn faced the problem of
coming up with an acceptable vernacular equivalent for the elegiac
distichs of a classical original. The complexity of the task should
not be underestimated. No-one, even today, has a very precise
idea of just how classical languages sounded. What matters for the
computation of verse in Latin is the length of the vowels within

each foot, making possible a range of dizzying substitutions, liable to confuse anyone who is not an acknowledged expert. The contrast between long and short vowels in Latin is replaced in Romance and Germanic languages by a contrast between stressed and unstressed syllables, so that the metre of the translation reflects the original metre only through the loosest of analogies.

In Latin elegiac poetry, dactylic hexameters alternate with pentameters, forming pairs which explain the use of the term distich.[3] The practice of the German Romantic poet Friedrich Hölderlin can be described roughly as follows. All lines have six stresses, are made up of dactyls, trochees and iambs combined with a measure of freedom, and begin with a stressed syllable, so that an iamb cannot occur in initial position. In each distich, the first line ends in an unstressed, the second in a stressed syllable. Moreover, in the second, the third stressed syllable, preceding the caesura, is followed immediately by another stressed syllable, something that never happens in the first line.[4] The Catalan poet Carles Riba, in his celebrated *Elegies de Bierville*, written in exile in France in the wake of the final collapse of resistance to Franco, follows Hölderlin's example and, indeed, the influence of both Hölderlin and Rilke is evident in his work.[5] Garioch, dealing with a language which has no codified spelling, pronunciation or grammar, and whose social use is more or less exclusively dialectal, faced particular difficulties, which leave their trace in an occasional clumsiness or obfuscation of rhythm. These are the opening lines of his translation of Johnston's poem:

> Ceres' priest, ye Mysta, am I no to fish on a Sunday,
> > Whit fir dae ye mannace my nets, boden in fier of weir?
> There is ane dour enactment whilk thirls aa the Semites,
> > But no the likes of hiz; we are aa Japhet's bairns.[6]

Basically his pattern is the same as that of Hölderlin and Riba. But the characteristic rhythms of Scots frequently lead him to start lines with an iamb. And the elision in the first line between 'Mysta' and 'am' is awkward (though it does serve to highlight Garioch's playful pun, retaining Johnston's Latin 'Mysta' because it coincides with a form of address still used by Scottish children of school age to attract the attention of a passing adult).

As well as a delighted itemisation of the various ways in which salmon may be caught (with nets, or rod and line, using a cast-net or a kind of harpoon, and so on) the poem assembles a series of half joking arguments against the ban on Sunday fishing. A farmer's ploughing may safely be postponed till the next day, but the movements of fish are unpredictable, and the salmon, with sickening regularity, seem to congregate in unusually large numbers on a Sunday:

> Anither wechty maitter is that it's aye on the halie morning
>   The pools are maistly keepit fair hotteran wi fish.
> Whit fir duis Sunday offer sic hauls if it winnae let ye
>   Spreid nets? This kinna temptation jist maks gowks of folk.

Fishing is classified as a pastime by many, and therefore should not count as work; the steadfast devotion of his family will counterbalance this breach of the commandments; if the days of creation are justly reckoned, God rested on Saturday, not on Sunday. Many more arguments are cited in defence of the fisherman's views.

Why so much attention to the minutiae of versification, and to a poem which is, moreover, only a translation? If these questions are in the reader's mind, they are worth pausing over, resting, as they do, on assumptions which go some way towards explaining why Garioch's poetry has so far failed to achieve the kind of recognition it deserves. Common understanding of poetry in the British Isles continues to privilege the spontaneous outpouring of subjective feeling over engagement with difficulties which appear to be of a strictly impersonal nature. As a boy, Garioch had been one of the last people to play the piano to accompany silent movies in a local picture house.[7] His love of music persisted throughout his life, and he would have been familiar with the pleasure which is to be derived from seeing a virtuoso confront a significant technical challenge, carrying it off with aplomb, and without detriment to the expressive quality of the music.

Free verse, which should rightly be considered the most demanding of verse forms, since it requires an ability to generate a fresh metrical pattern for each line, tends today to be regarded as an artless format which neatly sidesteps issues of craftsmanship or professionality, apparently rendering them irrelevant. These assumptions give free verse a spurious democratic allure. And the expectation, a hangover from the aesthetics of the Romantic period, that texts should flaunt their originality, naturally shoves translated work into the second rank. It also blinds us to the intertextuality which is both an inescapable condition of all poetry and, potentially, one of the major sources for the pleasure we take in it. Unlike his contemporary and fellow Scots language poet Sydney Goodsir Smith, Garioch was not in any sense a modernist. If he recognised any kind of elite, it was one whose superiority could stand the public test of craftsmanship, and was the fruit of a long and patient apprenticeship. As for originality, despite his at times intensely critical attitude to MacDiarmid,[8] there may be more in common in the two poets' practice towards the end of their careers than meets the eye. Garioch's appropriation and re-elaboration of another man's work in the Belli sonnets, translated from the Roman dialect, which are the main achievement of his later years and perhaps of all his work, while much more explicit and apparently conventional in nature, is not so very different from the magpie habits which gave rise to *In Memoriam James Joyce.*[9]

The choice of an author to translate is rarely casual, or innocent, and, while Garioch may possibly have been alerted to the 17th century poet's work by MacDiarmid's enthusiastic championing of it in his autobiography *Lucky Poet*, and by the inclusion of an English prose version of the 'Fisher's Apology' in MacDiarmid's 1942 *Golden Treasure of Scottish Poetry*,[10] less contingent factors which could have drawn Garioch to Johnston are not far to seek. Johnston, like Garioch, was an Episcopalian, that is, he belonged to an occluded Scottish tradition, alien to Calvinism but no less Protestant, forming a significant strand in the complex confessional and political history of the nation. In a poem on the National Covenant, Johnston had exhorted his countrymen to beg forgiveness from their monarch Charles I.

Garioch's ironically titled sonnet 'And They Were Richt'[11] could be a latter day reflection of Johnston's piscatorial eclogue, dealing as it does with the forced termination of a lively debate, which had followed the 1962 production, during the Edinburgh Festival, of Catholic convert Fionn MacColla's controversial play about the

Reformation, *Ane Tryall of Hereticks*. Midnight had struck and the next day was Sunday. 'Wha daur debate religion on a Sunday?' the persona growls, with withering irony.

Translation plays a crucial role in the establishment and the refining of recently formed literary languages. At a time when poetry in Scots looked as if it had fallen irrevocably behind Scottish poetry in English, in terms of innovation and development, and when MacDiarmid's celebrated early lyrics seemed separated from the contemporary by an insurmountable barrier, Garioch worked stubbornly, and perhaps wrong-headedly, to standardise (and thus depersonalise) the literary medium he had evolved. He did this thanks to the twin strategies of filtering authoritative texts from the past through its prism, while also subjecting it to the acid test of metrical precision. That he should have attempted this indicates to what an extent he was struggling against the grain of his epoch, was, in a very real sense, an anachronism. The effect of a success-ful standardisation would, of course, have been to make the medi-um available for general use, just as translation served to wean it away from the tone and the preoccupations of any individual poet. Garioch's preferred spelling, very near to phonetic in its represen-tation of stressed vowel sounds, his eschewal of apostrophes and, for example, a detail such as his preferred interpretation of words like 'warld' as disyllable, or 'trauchlit' as a trisyllable (and see 'thirls' in the opening of 'A Fisher's Apology' above) are ample evidence of his intentions, and of how consistently he carried them out.

This is why any largescale attempt to interpret Garioch's poetry in terms of what is known as the 'reductive idiom' is doomed to be unsatisfactory. Readings of Scottish vernacular poetry along such lines can be traced back at least as far as David Craig's influential study *Scottish Literature and the Scottish People 1680-1830*, pub-lished in 1961. Craig believes that a 'sceptical, ironic downright-ness... came to be the standard idiom of Scottish poetry' and sug-gests that 'the peculiar Presbyterian frame of mind got an impulse from, and in turn singled out and reinforced, an existing national bent'. In his view, 'it came naturally to Burns' (and the same has been implied of Garioch) '...to write as one without a share in the full resources of wealth, goods, power, opportunity, or range of job available in his country' since, in Burns' time, 'a sense of being "on the outside" was inevitable for the poor man'.[12] The 'reductive idiom' imples the use of pithy, largely colloquial Scots to undermine and cut down to size people who are perceived to be getting above themselves, or straying unjustifiably beyond their proper and allotted sphere. The effect is of a double reification on the part of critics of the poetry. Unlike less stigmatised literary languages, Scots labours under the expectation that one should only write in Scots about the kind of topics people who might speak Scots habitually deal with and, moreover, using the tone and attitude that they might use. Garioch's sonnet 'Heard in the Cougate',[13] with its meticulous annotation of double initial consonants, along with throat clearings and expectorations, satirises such an attitude by pushing it, in rather manic fashion, to its limits:

'Whu's aa thae fflagpoles ffur in Princes Street?
Chwoich! Ptt! Hechyuch! Ab-boannie cairry-on.
Seez-owre the water. Whu' the deevil's thon
inaidie, heh?'

The concept of a 'reductive idiom' veers dangerously close to a national stereotype, a supposed detestation of artificiality, pretension and sophistication. And indeed, certain critics have not been above seeing this characteristic embodied in the Burns stanza, whose truncated fourth and sixth lines are supposed to bring the reader up short. The stanza in question, however, has its origins, as far as modern research has been able to pursue it, in the language of the medieval mystery plays, before that in the Provençal poetry of the King of Aquitaine, and ultimately, perhaps, in Latin hymnology of the Early Middle Ages.[14]

Garioch is not above using the 'reductive idiom' himself. The sonnet 'Did Ye See Me?'[15] ironises a public function involving both a dedication and a reception, which the speaker attended and at which he pronounced a discourse. The ironic distancing is evident in the rhyming words of the quatrains. All eight lines end in 'ioun', and Garioch's metrical pattern demands a comically antiquated pronunciation of these four letters, as two syllables:

I'll tell ye of ane great occasioun:
I tuke pairt in a graund receptioun.
Ye cannae hae the least perceptioun

hou pleased I was to get the invitatioun...

If we stress the second, as we are encouraged to, then the 'oun' rhyme recurs three times more in the sextet, with an effect of overkill appropriate to the pompous and ponderous nature of the ceremony. Yet even here the speaker's stance is not exactly that of a working man wearing, or clutching, his cloth cap. He has, after all, played a starring role in the cavortings, and bitterly regrets having worn formal graduate's dress, which made him all the more vulnerable to the derision of the bystanders, 'the keelies of the toun':

> We cudnae stop it: they just gaithert roun
> to mak sarcastic cracks and grin and stare.
> I wish I hadnae worn my M.A. goun.

Such examples, nonetheless, belie the general tendency of Garioch's poetry, which can be read as a determined and resilient struggle against the limitations imposed on his linguistic medium by social and cultural assumptions and restraints. This is, I think, the most useful way of reading 'The Percipient Swan'.[16] The poem is a monologue by a swan in the pond of a municipal park, confined both by its dimensions and because its wings have been clipped. Part of the creature's torment is that its spectators are as bored by the performance as it is. This is no normal swan. It has 'ideas and notions/and aibstract conceptions'. If it were virtuous, it would go mad. But it has a healthy core of rage and rebellion and is gathering its forces for a proverbial swansong of a rather unusual kind: 'my sang sall foretell/no my ain destruction;/I sall rhyme the end/of your hale stupid faction'. The pond and its confining dimensions can be read as standing for Scots language poetry and the narrowed focus of so many of its practitioners in Garioch's time. His avowed intention is to break out of these limitations and, in the process, disconcert and vanquish the kind of audience whose expectations have so irritated him.

The hugeness of Garioch's ambition is explicit in 'The Muir',[17] an extended poem of 511 lines inspired by the 1953 Reith Lectures and the poet's attempt to come to terms with concepts from the newly emerging field of quantum physics. Not content with such challenging subject matter, Garioch posed himself a technical challenge, too, and in doing so set resonating an intertextuality which also indicates how high his aims were. The entire poem is couched in pentameter lines rhyming *abab, bcbc, cdcd...* The trick of carrying one rhyme on into the next quatrain is not as innocent as may seem, because it sets up a teasing and musical instability in the reader's mind. How is that fifth rhyme to be understood? As beginning a new complement of four, or as completing a five rhyme pattern of *ababb?* Could the whole poem be read as consisting of five line units, where the last line of one also constitutes the first line of the following? What the metre does, in effect, is to lop the closing hexameter off a Spenserian stanza and then project what is left into infinity. The pattern, though, is not Spenserian. Garioch has taken it from the most ambitious narrative poem in Scots between Gavin Douglas's *Eneados* and *Hellenore* by the Angus poet Alexander Ross, namely *Roland Furious*, the compressed and selected version of Ariosto's *Orlando Furioso* prepared for James VI by John Stewart of Baldynneis in the 1580s.[18]

It is commoner, however, for Garioch to adopt a disguise which effectively conceals more ambitious agendas beneath a covering of what might be regarded as conventional, and acceptable, from a Scots language poet of his time. 'Sisyphus',[19] probably his most anthologised poem, is a case in point. It offers a striking example of what may with justification be described as a metrical pun. Generations of schoolchildren, and of first year university students, have been delighted by its bumpity bumpity rhythm, so appropriate for the description of a weighty stone rattling down a hillside full of outcrops and protuberances. It is just the kind of illustrative, well nigh pictorial auditory effect they have been taught to look for. But of course, they are misled. The prime purpose of metrical patterning in poetry is not to illustrate its subject matter or, indeed, to mirror any external ordering beyond itself. Garioch's poem is couched in dactylic hexameters of painstaking accuracy. His vernacular equivalent is indeed more rigid than the classical model on which it is based. The latter permitted substitutions of long syllables (not at the beginning of a foot, and not at all in the last foot) by two shorts. In Garioch's version, the first five feet all have three syllables, the sixth two, reflecting the two longs of the classical spondee:

Bumpity doun in the corrie gaed whuddran the pitiless whun stane.
Sisyphus, pechan and sweitan, disjaskit, forfeuchan and broun'd-aff,
sat on the heather a hanlawhile, houpan the Boss didna spy him,
seein the terms of his contract includit nae mention of tea-breaks...

The classical legend of Sisyphus's punishment in Hades is dressed
down for modern presentation. The incongruity is evident in the
vocabulary, where archaic Scots items such as 'disjaskit' and 'forfeuchan' rub shoulders with items shared with English, such as
'contract' or 'slipped discs'. However, not just the metrics, but also
the subject matter is double, functioning as an alibi, or a disguise.
It is easy enough to read the poem, with a wry smile, as a tongue
in cheek protest against the alienating work which provides the
modern labourer ('tea-breaks', 'cheese piece') or even schoolteacher ('his cheque at the month's end') with material security, in
exchange for collusion in its repetitive meaninglessness. But at a
deeper level, the preoccupation of 'Sisyphus' is with the difference
between alienated and unalienated labour. Since the prime
instance of the latter, for Garioch, is the making of poetry, his metrical punctiliousness, here and elsewhere, is as much an expression
of the poem's theme as an aspect of its form.

The two kinds of labour are set unmistakably side by side in
'Perfect'.[20] Again, the poem has an alibi. It can be read as in the
persona of a furniture maker whose daily labour has been mecha-
nised, so that now, instead of dealing directly with his raw material, wood, he merely pushes buttons on a machine:

I hae been Moved On wi the times.
I'm in chairge of a machine as big as our hous.
I set the haunnles on the dials, press a button.
Out comes, say, Honduras mahogany, shade nine.

The object produced is the same each time. It is, in fact, 'perfect',
and the speaker's horror at such identical perfection gives the
poem its title. At the close, he contrasts 'daft' (the positive term,
meaning 'obsessive' or 'possessed') and 'donnart' (the negative
term, meaning 'dehumanised' or 'moronic'), and admits to being
the former, but not the latter. Description of the tools of the trade
allows the persona to bring in an exciting range of exotic vocabulary, making the exercise of his craft seem all the more unnatural:

Wuid wants to bide the colour it started.
I stain it wi dragon's bluid or turmeric,
burnt sienna. Pernambuco wuid, burnt umber,
indigo, even, if I'm in the mood.

Given the associations of Scots with the past, with what is old-fashioned or has gone out of fashion, it is tempting to see the poem as
merely a rejection of modernity. But it is more fascinating to read it
as a championing of unalienated labour, the furniture maker's but
more crucially the poet's. Just as the wood resists and resents the
attempts to force it into a form it does not recognise ('I wark wi
naitur agen naitur'), so the poet's material, language, resists his
attempts to force it into a metrical pattern. Joseph Brodsky makes
the same point in perhaps exaggeratedly metaphysical terms:

> Lurking within the use of standard meters is, of course, the danger of
> mechanical speech, and every poet overcomes that danger in his own
> way, and the more difficult the process of overcoming, the more detailed
> – both for himself and for the reader – becomes the picture of a given
> psychological state... Form is even less separable from content in poetry
> than body is from soul, and what makes the body dear is precisely that it
> is mortal (in poetry the equivalent of death is mechanicalness of sound or
> the possibility of slipping into cliché).[21]

What is crucial is that the resistance should never fully be overcome, that the words and the rhythms of the language should
never entirely yield to the metrical grid being forced upon them.
The implication is that unalienated labour is process- rather than
product-oriented, and can never really finish. The object may
change. The dynamic nature of interaction with the material does
not. Having completed one table, or poem, the poet, or furniture
maker brings the same crazed intensity to his next task. The notion
of achieved perfection is profoundly foreign to such labour, and
the greatest enemy is an impatient customer: 'every job sent out
afore it's duin,/naethin-like perfect yet'. Earlier in the same essay,
which concerns the verse letter Marina Tsvetayeva penned to
Rainer Maria Rilke on receiving the news of his death, Brodsky
claims that

> ...the further a poet goes in his development, the greater – unintentional-
> ly – his demands on an audience, and the narrower that audience is. The

situation oftentimes ends with the reader becoming the author's projection, which scarcely coincides with any living creature at all. In those
instances, the poet directly addresses either the angels... or another poet
– especially one who is dead...[22]

As his contribution to a volume edited by Sydney Goodsir Smith to
mark the bicentenary of Robert Fergusson's death, Garioch came
up with, not a critical essay, but a verse letter, using the Burns
stanza or Standard Habbie, one of the favourite metres deployed
by the poets of the 18th century vernacular revival. It opens with a
forthright admission that Garioch experienced himself as an
anachronism. He ought to have lived in the 18th century, rather
than the 20th:

> Fergusson, tho twa-hunder year
> awa, your image is mair clear
> nor monie things that nou appear
>   in braid daylicht.
> What gars perspective turn sae queer?
>   What ails my sicht?[23]

The poem, which runs to 276 lines, is scattered with references to
Fergusson's poetry ('Daft Days' and 'Leith Races' in line 50, the pastoral elegy on William Wilkie in line 61, 'The Ghaists: a Kirkyard
Eclogue' in line 97 and Fergusson's planned but never completed
magnum opus, 'Auld Reikie', in line 121) and to the circumstances
of his life (his dreary employment as a kind of human photocopier,
his lively social life as a member of one of the city's clubs, his religious obsessions and his death in Bedlam).[24] Living at a time when
the dominant mode of Scots poetry was parodic and reflexive,
Fergusson, like Garioch, struggled to write serious, learned poetry
with a firm neoclassical base, of which 'The Farmer's Ingle', with
its debts in ideology and mood to Virgil's *Georgics*, is the prime
example. He even planned versions of the *Eclogues* and the
Georgics which could be set alongside Gavin Douglas's of the
Aeneid to provide a complete Virgil in Scots.

     More generally, what drew Garioch to Fergusson's poetry and to
his age was the notion of vernacular humanism, a combination of
classical, principally Latin learning and culture with a firmly colloquial deployment of the Scots tongue. Nothing could be further

from the assumption, in the latter part of the 20th century, that Scots should be characteristically the idiom of the marginalised, underprivileged in both social and political terms. The poem climaxes in a utopian vision of Garioch and Fergusson returning home from a pub crawl. In traditional fashion, neither can bear to climb the stairs to his home, so they go back and forth from one close to the other:

> To Warld's End Close frae Ramsay Lane
> we'd ding Auld Reekie's black rigg-bane.
> Whan Ne'er-gate's ten-hour bell had gane
>   that wadnae daunt us;
> I'd gie scotch-convoy back again
>   to Dawnie Douglas.[25]

Garioch has slipped imperceptibly from the simple past to the ambivalent imperfect or conditional tense, as if this were something he and the 18th century poet had done time and again. As if they were, in the truest sense of the word, contemporaries. And the illusion persists until they at last bid farewell in the chill morning air.

If Fergusson offered Garioch a much needed anchor in what was for him, under many aspects, an enviable past, his life and, specifically, his mental breakdown reflected crucially modern perplexities. In a passage running to seven stanzas, immediately preceding the poem's conclusion, the speaker comments that a contemporary poet has just as many causes as Fergusson had to fear losing his reason. This is the nightmarish side of the barely conceivable discoveries in experimental physics which had furnished the subject matter of 'The Muir':

> What gart ye break throu reason's ice?
> Compared wi ye, we're no sae wyce.
> Maybe we're yaised wi madness; vice
>   and lust for pouer
> bring furth some hellish new device
>   ilk ither hour.[26]

The paradoxical and creative nature of Garioch's superficially anachronistic stance is evident in the way he manages to lodge the preoccupations of the immediate postwar period, with Hiroshima and Nagasaki recent memories, in a tribute to his predecessor:

> Ye didna hae to fash your thoombs
> wi hydrogen or atom boombs,
> nor monie a nesty thocht that soums
>   aye in our heid
> and flegs us in our flimsie rooms...[27]

Impressive as both 'The Muir' and 'To Robert Fergusson' are, demonstrating as they do Garioch's mastery of the long poem at a period when it was regarded as among the most taxing tests for a modern poet, it is likely that his major achievement consists of the 120 sonnets he translated from the Roman dialect of Gioacchino Belli towards the end of his life.[28] Initially dependent on line for line versions, supplied by D.S. Carne-Ross (who commissioned the first six translations), then by Antonia Spadavecchia and finally, over a period of six years, by Antonia Stott,[29] Garioch became more and more capable of confronting these with the original text, even, on rare occasions, working directly from it before calling on his collaborator for assistance.

Here, too, there is a paradoxical dynamic of anachronism and modernity. Garioch himself felt at times that the Belli translations were a second-rate alternative to original work, a means of keeping his hand in when inspiration had begun to fail. A view of this kind would be in line with the dominant aesthetics of European poetry from the Romantic movement onwards, with their exasperated subjectivity and demand for originality at all costs. What could be new in replicating (to all appearances) the work of an arch-conservative which was moreover, in terms of the nation he belonged to, a linguistic backwater? Faced with a hermeneutic tradition still irresistibly drawn, in spite of all its protests to the contrary, to construct an underlying narrative, artistic when not explicitly biographical, for the work of any single poet, Garioch's Belli sonnets put up an opposition no less determined than MacDiarmid's in *In Memoriam James Joyce*. The poet, as living, irrepeatable, sentient being, was unavailable, absent without leave. His place appeared to have been taken by a brilliant and enthusiastic clerk, selecting, compiling and transcribing someone else's texts.

It is worth pausing to consider the innovative nature of the text Garioch produced. Had he lived longer, more sonnets would no doubt have been translated, each taking its place according to the number it carries in Belli's chronologically ordered sequence. In other words, a text in a process of continuous, open-ended augmentation and transformation. In line with the urge towards standardisation evident in almost all his Scots language poetry, Garioch was scrupulous about metrical regularity and rhyming. Indeed, rather as present-day music students set the task of harmonising a Bach chorale will often begin with the cadence to each phrase and work back from these, Garioch would appear to have started, in many cases, with the rhymes, working back to construct full lines 'behind them', as it were. Moreover, his approach was consistently 'foreignising'. He did not attempt to disguise or to 'Scotticise' Roman place or personal names, or to replace the references to Catholic piety and superstition with Calvinist references which would sit more appropriately with his linguistic medium. It is probable that the kind of audience which took such delight in Chaucer's extended versions from Boccaccio's Italian would reach a juster and more appropriate assessment of Garioch's achievement in the Belli sonnets than readers whose tastes have been formed by Eliot, Yeats, Larkin and Heaney. Yet it may be true in the end that, rather than lagging behind the 20th century in his poetical practice, Garioch was some way in advance of it.

In conclusion, our characterisation of Garioch's work may be usefully rounded off by comparing his work with that of his most distinguished contemporary among Scots language poets of the postwar years, Sydney Goodsir Smith (1915-1975).[30] Born in New Zealand of Scottish parents, and educated at an English public school, Goodsir Smith had little direct experience of Scots until well into his adult years. He constructed a highly artificial linguistic medium, borrowing freely from the work of the pre-Reformation makars, so that, whereas Garioch's Scots tends to self-effacement, towards a homogeneity which may well be utopical but is nevertheless eloquent of the urge to standardisation, Goodsir Smith's is more often than not a dazzlingly idiosyncratic hotch-potch. Garioch works to achieve a pliable medium which can lessen the perceived gap between speaking and writing and can serve, in time, other talents and other purposes than his own. What matters about Goodsir Smith's Scots is that it is unrepeatable, an emanation

of the outsized persona he created for himself. Take aw⌐
sona, and the medium itself crumbles, has no further purpⴲ

Where Garioch's links are to the eighteenth century and, ᴸ
that, to Scots-speaking Latin scholars of the seventeenth anᴑ ᴀx-
teenth century, Goodsir Smith has an explicit debt to modernism
and to the French 'decadent' poetry of Tristan Corbière and Jules
Laforgue.[31] While the two poets have in common a strong identification with the cityscape of Edinburgh, Goodsir Smith projects
himself as a vagabond, a *flâneur* in the Baudelairean mould, frequenting its pubs and prostitutes with stylish and unapologetic
extravagance. His finest achievement is probably a sequence of
twenty-four love lyrics entitled *Under the Eildon Tree*.[32] These may
well have a biographical basis, but they activate an eclectic range
of references to Classical and Celtic literatures, to Robert Henryson
and to Goodsir Smith's contemporaries. As epigraphs the sequence
carries a quotation from Gavin Douglas and another from Ezra
Pound's versions of Propertius. With its self-deprecation and
eschewal of any form of political or ethical commitment, the
sequence may well be a ribald riposte to Sorley MacLean's *Dàin do
Eimhir*.[33] Goodsir Smith's persona as debauchee and forlorn lover
overwhelms much of his poetry to the extent of sometimes getting
in the way of any sober (in every sense) evaluation of it, while
what can disorientate and perplex in Garioch's fundamentally more
complex work is its failure to offer any such persona as a vehicle,
as a hook for the reader to hang different poems on, fitting them
together into some kind of cohesion. While Goodsir Smith was
inspired and energised by his contacts with MacDiarmid and
MacLean, and with those elements in the programme of the
Scottish Renaissance Movement which were still alive and productive in the aftermath of war (and his version of Blok's 'The
Twelve'[34] indicates a clear wish to emulate his predecessors' desire
to engage with Russian poetry around the time of the Bolshevik
Revolution), Garioch was much more of a loner, physically isolated
as a schoolteacher in Kent until he took early retirement, and more
reliant on reading and on an imagined dialogue with poets of the
past than on any of his contemporaries.

In the end, though Goodsir Smith's work merits and demands
(and still awaits) thoroughgoing and meticulous annotation and

assessment, it is likely that Garioch's star will prove the brighter overall, thanks to the solidity and validity of the intertextual relationships he established and the cultural programme they imply, as well as to the paradoxical nature, suggested earlier in this essay, of his links to the past, also the source of his surprising modernity and his promise for the future.

NOTES

[1] For Arthur Johnston, see J.W.L. Adams, 'The Renaissance Poets (2): Latin', in James Kinsley ed., *Scottish Poetry: A Critical Survey*, London: Cassell 1955, pp. 68-98, and in particular pp. 89-94; Leicester Bradner, *Musae Anglicanae: A History of Anglo-Latin Poetry 1500-1925*, New York: MLA, 1940, Chapter VI: 'Scots in the Seventeenth Century', pp. 158-200, and in particular pp. 172-183; and T.D. Robb, 'Arthur Johnston in his Poems', *Scottish Historical Review*, vol. 10, 1913, pp. 287-298.

[2] Garioch's poems are here quoted from Robert Garioch, *Complete Poetical Works*, edited by Robin Fulton, Edinburgh: Macdonald Publishers, 1983. Page references are to this edition.

[3] See for example J.W. Halporn, Martin Ostwald and T.G. Rosenmeyer, *The Meters of Greek and Latin Poetry*, London: Methuen, 1963, pp. 10-13 and 67-72.

[4] Hölderlin's practice is analysed here strictly for the purposes of comparison with Garioch. In his essay 'Hölderlins Verskunst' (see *Friedrich Hölderlin: Studien*, Frankfurt am Main: Suhrkamp, 1987, pp. 82-109). Wolfgang Binder holds that, of the 64 possible realisations of his underlying pattern for the elegiac distich, Hölderlin restricts himself to four or at most five ('Hexameter und distichon', pp. 96ff.) For David Constantine 'a poem is an elegy if it is written in elegiac couplets (hexameter + pentameter), and this regardless of its subject matter'. He further notes that 'The classical elegiac couplet was never naturalized in English', and that Hölderlin's 'lines frequently transgress the rules and regulations which the rigorists devised'. (*Hölderlin*, Oxford: Clarendon Press, 1988, pp. 182-183).

[5] See Enric Sullà, *Una interpretació de les 'Elegies de Bierville' de Carles Riba*, Barcelona: Editorial Empúries, 1993, pp. 44-50 and, more generally, Manuel Balasch, *Carles Riba: la vessant alemanya del seu pensa-*

ment i de la seva obra, Barcelona: Edicions del Mall, 1987.

6 Robert Garioch, *Complete Poetical Works*, cit., p. 106.

7 See Garioch's essay 'Early Days in Edinburgh', in Maurice Lindsay ed., *As I Remember: Ten Scottish authors recall how writing began for them*, London: Robert Hale, 1979, pp. 45-58.

8 See, for example, a letter dated December 1st 1980 to J.B. Caird, where Garioch notes that 'MacCaig... *does seem* to be impressed by attributes of MacD[iarmid] that are not there at all, so far as I can see, or by his behaviour, that looks very like antics to me. In fact, I weary of that deflated windbag... in a major poet, I should expect to find a love and mastery of the sounds, meanings and influential/co-operative properties of words...' It is possible that Garioch also had MacDiarmid in mind when, in a letter to Alastair Mackie written at the end of the following month, he observes that 'more and more I see the value of the "mediocre", so much despised by certain great people whose value declines in my judgement by several degrees every year or even month'. Robin Fulton ed., *A Garioch Miscellany*, Edinburgh: Macdonald, 1986, pp. 96 and pp. 98-99.

9 For an extended study of the Belli sonnets see Christopher Whyte, 'Garioch and Belli', in Bill Findlay ed., *Frae Ither Tongues: Essays on Modern Translations into Scots*, Clevedon: Multilingual Matters, 2004, pp. 188-214.

10 MacDiarmid published an English prose version of 'A Fisher's Apology' by Arthur Johnston [sic] in his *Golden Treasury of Scottish Poetry*, London: Macmillan, 1946 (originally 1940), pp. 217-230, though he stated in his autobiography that 'with the collaboration of my friend George Elder Davie' he had 'translated ['A Fisher's Apology'] for the first time and turned [it] into English verse'. See Hugh MacDiarmid, *Lucky Poet*, edited by Alan Riach, Manchester: Carcanet, 1994, (originally 1943) p. 285.

11 Robert Garioch, *Complete Poetical Works*, cit., p. 84.

12 David Craig, *Scottish Literature and the Scottish People 1680-1830*, London: Chatto & Windus, 1961, pp. 76-77 and p. 80.

13 Robert Garioch, *Complete Poetical Works*, cit., p. 83.

14 Peter Zenzinger '"Habbie Simpson' and the Early Elegy Tradition', in Dietrich Strauss and H.W. Drescher eds., *Scottish Language and Literature: Medieval and Renaissance*, Frankfurt am Main: Peter Lang, 1986, pp. 481-496, and F.M. Chambers, *Old Provençal Versification*, Philadelphia: American Philosophical Society, 1985, pp. 24ff.

15 Robert Garioch, *Complete Poetical Works*, cit., p. 83.

[16] *Ibidem*, pp. 6-8.

[17] *Ibidem*, pp. 54-66.

[18] See Thomas Crockett ed., *Poems of John Stewart of Baldynneis*, vol. II (text), Edinburgh and London: William Blackwood for the Scottish Texts Society, 1913; also G.A. Dunlop, 'John Stewart of Baldynneis, the Scottish Desportes', *Scottish Historical Review*, vol. 12, 1915, pp. 303-310; M.P. McDiarmid, 'John Stewart of Baldynneis', *Scottish Historical Review*, vol. 29, 1950, pp. 52-63, and R.D.S. Jack, *The Italian Influence on Scottish Literature*, Edinburgh: Edinburgh University Press, 1972, pp. 125-140.

[19] Robert Garioch, *Complete Poetical Works*, cit., p. 28.

[20] *Ibidem*, pp. 40-41.

[21] Joseph Brodsky, *Less than One: Selected Essays*, Harmondsworth: Penguin Books, 1987, pp. 208-209.

[22] *Ibidem*, p. 200.

[23] Robert Garioch, *Complete Poetical Works*, cit., p. 18.

[24] See M.P. McDiarmid ed., *The Poems of Robert Fergusson*, Scottish Texts Society, 2 vols., Edinburgh and London: Blackwood, 1954-1956.

[25] Robert Garioch, *Complete Poetical Works*, cit., p. 24.

[26] *Ibidem*, p. 22.

[27] *Ibidem*, p. 23.

[28] *Ibidem*, pp. 215-280.

[29] Garioch's 'Letters to Antonia Scott' (in *A Garioch Miscellany*, cit., pp. 148-171) are a rich source of insights into his attitudes, feelings, and procedures while working on these translations.

[30] See Sydney Goodsir Smith, *Collected Poems*, with an introduction by John Calder, London: John Calder, 1975, the autobiographical letter to Maurice Lindsay printed as a *Saltire Self-Portrait*, and *For Sydney Goodsir Smith*, Loanhead: Macdonald, 1975 which, alongside essays by various hands, contains 'A Checklist of the Books and Pamphlets' by W.R. Aitken.

[31] See in this connection (in French) Christopher Whyte, 'Corbière, Laforgue et Goodsir Smith', in David Kinloch and Richard Price, sous la direction de *La Nouvelle Alliance: Influences francophones sur la littérature écossaise moderne*, Grenoble: ELLUG, Université Stendhal 2000, pp. 61-90.

[32] Originally 1948, published in a second, revised edition as *Under the Eildon Tree: a Poem in XXIV Elegies*, Edinburgh: Serif Books, 1954. Now in *Collected Poems*, cit., pp.147-187.

[33] See lines such as the following, from the fifth elegy, 'Slugabed': 'O, michtie Stalin in the Aist!/Could ye but see me nou,/The type, endpynt and final blume/O' decadent capitalistical thirldom...'.

[34] Sydney Goodsir Smith, 'The Twal', in *Collected Poems*, cit., pp.109-118. The Blok translation appeared as part of *Figs and Thistles*, Edinburgh: Oliver & Boyd, 1959.

ALAN RIACH

Norman MacCaig:
The Poetry of Experience

The year 2000 marked the 90th anniversary of the birth of Norman MacCaig. When he died, two days before the bicentenary of the death of Robert Burns in 1996, his timing was characteristically perfect. The well-laid plans for tartan clichés to celebrate Scotland's 'National Bard' in hackneyed hagiography were properly sidelined by the nation's immediate recognition that it had just lost one of its greatest poets. He is best known as a great love poet of the natural world, with wonderfully memorable poems about frogs, toads, birds, mountains and lochs. But there are two other major themes to which his poetry returns.

For MacCaig, the provisional nature of identity demands humility; to speak requires caution. He advises us to listen to his words carefully, for some of them are spoken 'not by me, but/by a man in my position' ('A man in my position'). In 'Centre of centres' he asks: 'How many geometries are there/with how many circles/to be a centre of?' He understands how 'Eyes change what they look at./Ears never stop making their multiple translations'. So he is a poet of decisive diffidence whose painterly immediacy is matched by philosophical speculation and leavened with wry humour:

If we lived in a world where bells
truly say 'ding-dong' and where 'moo'
is a rather neat thing
said by a cow,
I could believe you could believe
that these sounds I make in the air
and these shapes with which I blacken white paper
have some reference
to the thoughts in my mind
and the feelings in the thoughts.[1]

And he is a great elegist, free of sentimentalism or self-pity. The quiet elegies that dominate MacCaig's last books, *The Equal Skies* (1980), *A World of Difference* (1983) and *Voice-Over* (1988) are a magnificent series. In them, he leans towards 'the last certainty' like trees lean in the wind, 'tugging to get there, and thank God/I'm clogged with the world. It grips me,/I hold it' ('Journeys'). The resources of these poems of grief, loss and ageing are as absolutely limited as Beethoven's in the late quartets. Collectively they are one of the great achievements of modern poetry. But he is never merely solemn. In fact, his *Collected Poems* is one of the funniest books in the world. For example, in 'City Fog':

Even the Tollcross clock
looks glum, as if it knew
five past ten might as well be
ten past five.[2]

In 'Hogmanay' a cock fed oatmeal damped with whisky crows twelve times and falls on its beak, to be matched later by the man who fed it, falling, glass in hand, on his back – the images become surreally mingled in MacCaig's equally inebriated vision. In 'Notations of Ten Summer Minutes' odd happenings in a Highland village are almost arbitrarily noted down and chink and jingle against each other like gold coins in a pocket. MacCaig's happiness – it's not rapture, it is invariably attentive – is infectious. When you share a smile with him in these poems, it's a good thing.

His humour has a grim side too, like the 'homicidal hilarity/of a laugh in a ballad' ('Space travel'). In 'Orgy', ants eating doped bees discover 'that the innkeeper was the inn'. 'In a snug room' presents a sleek, self-satisfied and complacent man thinking of the flattering reference to him in the morning papers, the companionable lunch he's just enjoyed, the profitable deal he's just signed, the donation he's sent to his favourite charity, his 'true love' coming towards him in a taxi – 'And Nemesis slips two bullets/into her gun/in case she misses with the first one.' This humour is macabre and dark, but even here the startlement of a new perception immediately becomes the warmth of a concurrence of recognition.

The essential biographical facts suggest the disposition of MacCaig's character. He was born in Edinburgh in 1910. His father was a chemist, fastidiously Edwardian, neat and kindly; his mother came from the Isle of Harris in the outer Hebrides, spoke Gaelic and English but had never learned to read and write and played with language all the time. As a boy, MacCaig returned to her family home and experienced both the warmth of the community and the extreme austerity of the Calvinist Free Church, with its adamant rejection of song, drink and dance. Sustaining love and cold self-denial were both essential components of this culture, but summers in Scalpay also offered MacCaig a richly realized perception of the seasonal richness of a natural world of seascape, moor, rock and small fishing lochs with all their flora and fauna. This island world is close to the Highlands in which MacCaig spent many of his later summers, in Assynt, in the north-west of the Scottish mainland. Like Wallace Stevens, like Shakespeare, changing seasons and the cycle of the year are strengths he adheres to gainfully. In conversation in 1995, MacCaig talked of this part of the country as his favourite place: 'The landscape, walking through it, is just so beautiful, and the loch itself is so beautiful, and the fish in it are so big, that you don't get many at a time. In fact, sometimes you get none. [Laughter.] It's the most important place to me in the world, including Edinburgh... most important. I think of it every night, when my head drops on the pillow.'[3]

MacCaig is a poet of this place, of farms where 'A hen stares at nothing with one eye,/Then picks it up' ('Summer Farm'), where 'mice/Squeak small hosannahs all night long' and cows become 'Swagbellied Aphrodites, swinging/A silver slaver from each chin' ('Byre'). The world is made immediate through this richness of reference and metaphor: 'A Man I Agreed With' loves everything that accepts 'the unfailing hospitality of his five senses.' He would never insult a caterpillar by asking '*what do you mean?*'

It's a world of mountains that seem to change shape as you walk them, moving like music ('God was Mozart when he wrote Cul Mor' – 'Moment musical in Assynt'), a world of bell heather, stags and sparrows, the 'rubber-lipped' cod, basking shark, crickets, toads, frogs, puffins, Highland games, rowan trees, cormorants, eagles, where a kingfisher 'jewelling upstream' seems 'to leave a streak of itself behind it/in the bright air' ('Kingfisher'). A waterfall plunges into a ravine like 'coins into a stocking' ('Falls of Measach'). We might visit glens and corries, fishermen's pubs, hear of absentee landowners, meet crofters, poachers, fishermen, aunts, uncles and friends.

But the other location of MacCaig's poetry is almost equally important, and as he always approaches it with that same sly, gaunt and evaluating eye, it is equally freshly perceived. This is the city, Edinburgh, the ancient capital of Scotland, divided between the old town and the new. The old town is skewered by the Royal Mile (half kitsch, half history), running from the soaring Castle down to Holyrood Palace, surrounded by fabulously Gothic turret-ted tenements, bridges, twisting roads, tunnels and arches (and the imposing heights of Arthur's Seat and Salisbury Crags looming nearby). Across the railway tracks and Princes Street Gardens, the new town is precisely designed in classic eighteenth-century ele-gance, airy and open to the cold wind off the Forth and the plains of Fife beyond. Like a seam of gold through the frosty gentility of this side of the city runs Rose Street, a parallel to the old town's Royal Mile, an 'amber mile' of pubs frequented in the 1950s and 1960s by un-genteel drinkers and numerous writers to many of whom MacCaig, with his tall, angular frame and sardonic asides, momentary bursts of infectiously anarchic laughter, occasional *gravitas* and frequent wit, was a familiar and unfailingly friendly figure.

MacCaig went to school in Edinburgh and then to the university, where he read Classics, graduating in 1932. At university he met Isabel Munro, whom he described as 'an extraordinarily good dancer' and therefore a proper match for himself, 'a hot boy at the jigs'[4]. They married in 1940. He trained as a schoolteacher and worked in primary schools until his retirement. Visits to Italy and New York prompted their own poems and in the 1960s he became the first writer-in-residence at the University of Edinburgh and, in the 1970s, at the University of Stirling. Here his progress reports on students were classically brief, for example: 'A mouse. Not just a mouse – a quiet mouse.' His acerbity was respected. Many of his students and school pupils revered him.[5]

In his poetry, Edinburgh is no less central than the Highland landscapes of Lochinver. Here, the 'night tinkles like ice in glass-es./Leaves are glued to the pavement with frost' ('November night, Edinburgh'). In 'Out from a lecture', the High Street 'sits drinking' a

'swirling punch/Of buses, fruitshops, mackintoshes, windows'. In
'Edinburgh courtyard in July', 'Hot light is smeared as thick as
paint/On these ramshackle tenements.' In 'Cheese and wine party'
the poet pulls back from politely acquiescing in the chatter of academics to place himself in a more elemental world. The Meadows
(an Edinburgh parkland of fields) is an urban reminder of this
world, under a sky of 'nameless stars'. Similarly, 'An academic' is
described as 'the frog/who wouldn't a-wooing go', who tries to
'measure/lightning with a footrule' and to 'dismantle Juliet, Ahab,
Agamemnon/into a do-it-yourself kit/of semantic gestures.'
MacCaig wishes upon his learned friend 'a present of weather,
a/transfusion of pain.' The marvellous scathing comedy of this is
salutary: for MacCaig, no city sophistication or academic expertise
excuses a person from simple recognition of human fact. He is
never the alienated solipsist. His addiction to the sardonic is purify-
ing; he is warm but sharp, gentle but thorny.

MacCaig's politics are normally implicit. However, they are
direct enough in his treatment of the national tragedy of the
Highland Clearances in his longest poem 'A Man in Assynt' (from *A
Man in My Position*, 1969). Here he begins with the geological prehistory of north west Scotland but rapidly moves to the question of
ownership, the vexed relation between property and love:

> Who owns this landscape? –
> The millionaire who bought it or
> the poacher staggering downhill in the early morning
> with a deer on his back?[6]

The pragmatic urgencies of politics (crofters' rights, the evils of
absentee landlords) are set against elemental and almost abstract
ideas: 'Who possesses this landscape?/The man who bought it or/I
who am possessed by it?' MacCaig admits that these are 'False
questions' because 'this landscape is/masterless' – docile 'only to
the weather'. But the questions do not go away.

There are other Highland poems of pure, unalloyed anger
which employ traditional Gaelic forms in specific accord with their
subjects, such as 'Aunt Julia' (who cries out Gaelic questions to the
boy MacCaig who cannot understand her till it's too late to reply:
her language is lost, but not forgotten, in his English, her questions
are unanswered but reverberate in urgency); or 'Two Thieves'

(where the sea is a natural robber of the shore, but the Duke who
evicted his tenants and drove them to Canada and further shores,
is a robber for whom there is neither sympathy nor moral forgiveness). Both these poems move to explosive closing lines and
clinch on the matter of the loss of the Gaelic language (MacCaig's
mother's tongue). MacCaig understands the closeness in which personality and language are bound, not theoretically, but always
keeping in touch with the particular individual in the snowfields of
history. If MacCaig's subject in these poems makes him particularly
resistent to Anglocentric political convention, so, more generally,
do his poetic forms.

For example, one traditional Gaelic form is the praise-poem, in
which the poet celebrates in direct fashion, a boat, a dog, a man,
other poems, a road, a thorn bush. For MacCaig, the rejection of
irony in these poems never means a subtraction of wit. 'Praise of a
collie' describes the dog flowing 'through fences like a piece of
black wind'. 'Praise of a man' describes someone going through a
company 'like/a knifegrinder': the 'dull minds' scatter 'sparks of
themselves' and suddenly become 'razory', become 'useful.'

The shape of his career is clear enough. His first two books, *Far
Cry* (1943) and *The Inward Eye* (1946), were associated with the
'New Apocalypse' movement, a neo-romantic reaction to the overt-
ly politicised poetry of pylons and industrialism of Auden and
Spender for example. The 'New Apocalypse' writers (Dylan
Thomas, G.S. Fraser, J.F. Hendry and others) insisted on the signifi-
cance of the unconscious, the surreal, the predominance of
imagery and movement over form and reason. A friend of
MacCaig's borrowed, read and returned these first books with the
comment: 'And when are you going to give us the answers,
Norman?' MacCaig said it was the only criticism he ever found
valuable. He acted on it.[7]

Nearly ten years passed before *Riding Lights* (1955), the first
book he allowed to be republished in his *Collected Poems*. He
described the poems in the new book as the result of his 'long
haul towards lucidity'.[8] Another ten years followed in which relatively strict metrical forms shaped his poetry, then free verse began
to predominate with the 1966 volume *Surroundings*: that was
MacCaig's main formal mode thereafter. This sequence of events is

important but it's more important to note that the work MacCaig chose to preserve in his later collected editions is all poetry of experience – the earliest poems he acknowledged date from when he was in his mid-40s, well after Dante's mid-way point of life. That is exemplary.

In the 1950s and 1960s, MacCaig was generally accommodated by Anglocentric critics and anthologists such as Anthony Thwaite and A. Alvarez, but any overview of his poetry reveals its deeply national inclination. 'How Scottish are you?' an interviewer once asked him. 'Hundred per cent,' he replied.[9] But there is never any sense of chauvinistic nationalism in MacCaig. Everything is attached to a wider world of reference and delight. In 'Pibroch: The Harp Tree' he writes about classical bagpipe music as something whose formality, precision, crystalline colours and labyrinthine fugues would have delighted J.S. Bach and imagines Bach and a Pibroch made man-like enjoying a glass of Rhenish wine together. Only a Scottish imagination, perhaps, could have started with the brutish strength of a 'Brooklyn cop' and then caught the man's ironic as well as expansively comic aspects: 'Built like a gorilla, but less timid'. The senses of humour at work combine sideways comedy with gravity in a way that undercuts solemnity. In '19th floor nightmare, New York' a tremblingly sleepless big city party-goer rises from a bed of nightmares, pads across her hotel room and pulls back the curtain to look out – 'straight/into the left eye of King Kong'. That marvellous bathos combines an immediately accessible comedy with an ugly recognition: King Kong is the nightmare turned into reality, Fay Wray's worst dream come true, a fiction in a poem from a famous film; but he's also a metaphor for New York, a city (unlike Edinburgh) too large for MacCaig to scale in human terms. The sun comes up on Edinburgh, but Manhattan comes up on the sun ('Last night in New York'). MacCaig's sense of the big city is neither *angst*-ridden nor festive: his taking its measure qualifies his own identity and its. Although New York's 'uncivilised darkness/is shot at by a million lit windows', nevertheless, 'midnight is not/so easily defeated' ('Hotel room, 12th floor').

MacCaig's way of defeating midnight, or at least keeping it at bay, is by close attention to, and almost infinitely generous celebration of, the natural world. When he mentions a fulmar, it's not a reference to another kind of bird. These creatures are fixed in MacCaig's language, but despite the commonality of life ('winter, territory, greed' – 'Real life Christmas card') he never trusts words entirely. He wants to represent a non-verbal world responsibly, so he doesn't try to transmogrify the birds and animals into human caricatures. The caterpillar is more like a caterpillar, not like a man, through MacCaig's comparison of it standing erect and turning from side to side 'like a retired sea-captain/scanning horizons.'

There is a strong contrast here with Ted Hughes, whose 'Hawk Roosting' seems an allegory of one aspect of human nature, or whose 'Pike' seems like an underwater symbol of a prehistoric human subconscious that rises towards the poet. An instructive comparison between Hughes's monstrous pike and MacCaig's 'Basking Shark' clearly shows how richly weighted with human characteristics the pike is, whereas MacCaig's shark is precisely and limitedly itself: a 'roomsized monster with a matchbox brain'. Both water-creatures prompt similar human questions, but differently: Hughes's encounter with the pike ends on a sustained note of confrontation, the poet-fisherman and the fish both 'watching'; MacCaig's encounter with the shark is less melodramatic and the question it prompts is more laconic, troubled, wondering and isolating:

> So who's the monster? The thought made me grow pale
> For twenty seconds while, sail after sail,
> The tall fin slid away and then the tail.[10]

The question lingers shiveringly, partly because of the distinction between the physical presences of man and beast: their monstrous similarity is defined against their evident otherness, whereas Hughes is constantly edging human and animal qualities into a closer affinity. (Another good example would be to compare any of Hughes's *Crow* poems from 1972 with MacCaig's 'Solitary crow' from the 1968 volume *Rings on a Tree*). In fact, Hughes followed MacCaig's progress keenly, starting with the poems appearing in magazines in the 1950s: 'of all the UK poets then alive,' Hughes wrote in 1995, 'his was the only work in which I found stylistic clues for my own way forward. On top of that, I saw clues there for what I actually had to say.' Hughes also noted that MacCaig's influence on younger poets has been 'pervasive and positive. And it continues.'[11] MacCaig remarks in 'Names' that there are numbers of 'extraordinary little fish/with extraordinary names' which they don't know any more than he knows who named them. But in 'Limits' what troubles and frightens him is that

> our knowledge goes,
> so far as we know, only
> so far as we know.
>
> And I think, when molecules jump
> from one figuration to another
> they may not go hallelujahing into heaven
> or howling into hell,
> but
> water becomes ice.[12]

This is what keeps his sense of simple values keen. There is an assertive drive here, an impatience with self-expanding verbiage. Answering an academic question about the imaginative structure of one of his poems, he said: 'Oh, I think that kind of talk stinks the joint up, as Ellington said when they asked him if he was influenced by Debussy.'[13]

As Marshall Walker says, 'there is a tension in a MacCaig poem that comes from the sense that each word, each line has passed a rigorous test of validity in competition with the appeal to the poet of leaving the subject alone without interference from him. Impelled to use words, he remains suspicious of them: "the ones I use", he says, "often look at me/with a look that whispers, Liar" ("Ineducable me").'[14] Perhaps this helps to account for MacCaig's great friendship with MacDiarmid, similarly opposed to 'linguistic imperialism'. MacCaig's possibly apocryphal comment on his friend's ambitious fishing in the world's literary oceans reflects very happily back on himself: 'Let me see you catch anything yet', MacDiarmid alleged that MacCaig said to him, 'Big enough not to throw in again'.[15] His comic lament for Hugh MacDiarmid ('After his death' – although it was written years before the event) concludes:

> The government decreed that
> on the anniversary of his birth
> the people should observe
> two minutes pandemonium.[16]

The pleasure of this enhances the poignancy of his later (actual) elegy for MacDiarmid, 'Two thoughts of MacDiarmid in a quiet place', which ends:

> I gaze down into a pool, and a trout
> moves from the bright shallows,
> as MacDiarmid did,
> into a depth where my eyes see nothing.[17]

MacDiarmid died in 1978. Two years earlier, another close friend, A.K. MacLeod of Lochinver, had died. MacCaig's 'Poems for Angus' commemorate his friend but all the elegies of his last books reflect more widely on the nature of consolation and solitude. In 'Two friends' he refers to MacDiarmid and MacLeod together. The last word spoken by each of them was MacCaig's first name:

> My two friends
> had never met. But when they said
> that last word
> they spoke to each other.
>
> I am proud to have given them a language
> of one word, a narrow space
> in which, without knowing it,
> they met each other at last.[18]

In these elegies, the hurt in loss and the blessing in perception is equally strong. Their range of expression never allows them to stall, dull or droop into banality. The tone shifts. In 'Buzzard circling' the hunting bird is the centre of the landscape but contains within itself another centre, a place 'that will suck in/all circumferences.'

MacCaig's independence of thought and conviction afforded him the only universal subscription he endorsed, the only general pronouncement on the value of art and poetry he allowed himself to repeat: that it helps to maintain the only order worth keeping: 'Intellect and sensibility – the arts develop both. Poetry teaches man to do more than observe merely factual errors and measurable truths. It trains him to have a shrewd nose for the fake, the inflated, the imprecise and the dishonest... To have unexamined emotional responses is as immature, as dangerous, as to have unexamined beliefs.'[19]

The poetry of Norman MacCaig answers his own criteria. It is mavellously dependable: as necessary as a compass to co-ordinate the location of value and as reliable as single malt whisky to give you a taste of it. It does not profit from being read in bulk (he is most excellent in small doses – the opposite of Byron). But every one of his poems shows the virtue of spontaneity. Again and again they transform the incisiveness of perception into the pleasure of illumination. Their art is the permanence of miracles.

NOTES

[1] Norman MacCaig, *Collected Poems: A New Edition*, London: Chatto & Windus, 1990, p. 153.

[2] *Ibidem*, p. 375.

[3] Alan Riach, 'Norman MacCaig in Conversation' in *PN Review* 120, vol. 24, no. 4, 1998, (pp. 19-27) p. 26.

[4] Marjory McNeill, *Norman MacCaig: A Study of His Life and Work*, Edinburgh: Mercat Press, 1996, p. 10.

[5] *Ibidem*, p. 85.

[6] Norman MacCaig, *Collected Poems*, cit., p. 225.

[7] Norman MacCaig, 'My Way of It', *Chapman* 16, vol. 4, no. 4, Summer 1976, (pp. 3-7) p. 5.

[8] *Ibidem*.

[9] Christopher Carrell ed., *Seven Poets*, Glasgow: Third Eye Centre, 1981, p. 38.

[10] Norman MacCaig, *Collected Poems*, cit., p. 220.

[11] Ted Hughes, 'For Norman MacCaig' in *Norman MacCaig: A Celebration*, Edinburgh: Chapman Books, 1995 (4-page supplement, p. 1).

[12] Norman MacCaig, *Collected Poems*, cit., p. 211.

[13] Christopher Carrell ed., *Seven Poets*, cit., p. 36.

[14] Marshall Walker, *Scottish Literature Since 1707*, Harlow: Longman,

1996, p. 298.

[15] Hugh MacDiarmid, 'In Memoriam James Joyce', in *Complete Poems,* 2 vols., edited by Michael Grieve and W.R. Aitken, Manchester: Carcanet, 1993-1994, (pp. 735-889) p. 851.

[16] Norman MacCaig, *Collected Poems*, cit., p. 244.

[17] *Ibidem*, p. 400.

[18] *Ibidem*, p. 347.

[19] Norman MacCaig, 'My Way of It', cit. p. 7.

CHRISTOPHER WHYTE

The Gaelic Poetry of George Campbell Hay: Defence from Recent Strictures

With the publication in 2000 of a collected edition of Campbell Hay's poems and songs, meticulously and sensitively edited by Michel Byrne in a handsome two-volume set from Edinburgh University Press,[1] it might have been assumed that the reputation of this at least trilingual poet had been established beyond any reasonable doubt. A review of the edition by Meg Bateman, herself a Gaelic poet of some repute, suggests, however, that this is far from being the case.[2] Her strictures offer a useful point of departure for gauging, even within a relatively brief space, Hay's achievement, as well as his influence and standing with Gaelic poets from later generations.

Bateman finds the tone of Hay's poetry 'too exhortatory, or too near pastiche, lacking the irony and self-reflectivity of a contemporary voice'. And indeed, it is possible to argue that his mindset is closer to that of the late medieval and early Renaissance period than to the years between the two world wars, that he owes more to the abstract concepts of scholastic theology than to the haunting uncertainties of an Eliot or an Auden. At times he even makes explicit use of allegory, and it is characteristic of him to present the reader with an image whose appropriate interpretation is then suggested, either gradually or with the abruptness of a caption.

This kind of poem has proved highly influential with Hay's successors. Derick Thomson made it his own in the volumes preceding *An Rathad Cian* (The Far Road [1970]), which marks a new departure in his poetry, with the relation between vehicle and tenor becoming chronically unstable. The pattern continues to find favour with younger writers like Anne Frater or Rody Gorman. As early as *An Dealbh Briste* (The Broken Picture [1951]) Thomson had given it a peculiar twist by selecting as the poem's focus a contemporary object (in this case, a telephone kiosk) alien to the 'Gaelic world' and, as often as not, beyond the reach of the language itself. Both Bateman and Gorman enjoy bringing 'alien' elements such as goulash or a chip-pan into their poetry, and the use they make of windscreen wipers (the former preserves the English word, while the latter uses a Gaelic term) indicates that the *frisson* induced by attributing symbolic significance to such 'unpoetic' items is undiminished.[3]

Hay does no such thing. He avoids, in his imagery, wandering beyond the limits of the literary and the poetic. In 'Stoc is Failleanan' (Stump and Shoots, p. 220), a tree which has been felled,[4] and which nonetheless puts forth fresh green shoots the following spring, symbolises the potential for renewal inherent in the Gaelic language and its associated culture, despite apparent truncation:

> Ar cainnt 's ar cultar, car sealain
> ged rachadh an leagadh buileach,
> cuiridh am freumhan 's an seann stoc dhiubh
> failleanan snodhaich is duilleach.[5]

Here the last verse does indeed function as a caption appended to the image which has been presented. The technique can appear mechanical, and indeed, Hay's confessedly didactic purpose means that clarity is essential. Yet two observations can be made about the emergence of poems of this kind. On the one hand, they respond to the blocked development of the language (in social, scientific and technical terms) which had been a grim reality since at least the eighteenth century. Hay chooses to redeploy the traditional imagery, reviving as much as he feasibly can of its associated vocabulary, while proposing new meanings for it. This is, at least in part, a way of energising inherited or recovered material. On the other, such poems are a halfway house on the road to a poetry of philosophical speculation, clearly distasteful to Bateman, which disdains both subjective outpourings and diaristic annotation. A similar urge lies behind a not entirely successful experiment by Sorley MacLean, his 'Eadh is Féin is Sàr-Fhéin',[6] which similarly deploys elements of a Highland landscape, with the associated vocabulary, to evoke abstract psychoanalytic concepts. Among younger poets, only Fearghas MacFhionnlaigh has shown any tendency to follow MacLean and Hay in this direction, as evidenced in his long poem 'A' Mheanbh-Chuileag' (The Midge).[7] More will be said later about Hay's specifically philosophical mode.

The 'caption' type of poem is reasonably flexible. In 'Na Tuinn ris na Carraigean' (The Waves against the Rocks, p. 190) a series of philosophical interrogations, which constitute the main body of the poem, are framed by appearances of the relevant image, the sea beating upon the shore. The beginning of the final quatrain implies that national belonging is a limitation be overcome:

> Ciod e ma chruthaicheadh an talamh seo
> le cladaichean g'ar cròthadh?
> A mhuir, mo mhuir-sa, tha 'n speur rionnagach
> le gaothaibh saor ag ulfhairt òirnne![8]

Hay is more commonly identified with an explicit, even doctrinaire, nationalist commitment,[9] evident, for example, in 'Feachd a' Phrionnsa' (The Prince's Army, p. 209), which depicts the soldiers of Prince Charles Stewart's army about to cross the border with England, in the course of the Jacobite Rebellion of 1745. While unashamedly phallic, with its image of the blade which must be unsheathed after too long a slumber ("'s a liuthad bliadhna meirg' is dùsail/a mhaolaich i san truaill dhùinte'),[10] the poem's conclusion need not be interpreted exclusively or even primarily in military terms. Hay is remembering an army which sacrificed everything for a not unjust cause, and he exhorts his readers to a similar fidelity to perennially endangered values, though there may be scant hope of saving them. The core of the poem is its penultimate section, whose view of the human predicament is elegiac, modern and even existentialist in nature:

> Aon chuairt, aon chuairt gheibh sinn air thalamh
> a nochdadh an fhaghairt a th' annainn,
> a dheuchainn faobhar ar tapachd,
> a chosnadh cliù do 'r tìr no maslachd.[11]

It is as if the purpose of each human life were to offer a brief splash of colour against a background of unrelieved black, white and grey. The notion underpins one of Hay's most strikingly archaic poems, drawing on the notion of the Ship of Fools, 'Clann Adhaimh' (Adam's Clan, p. 183), with an 'Envoi' (or Ceangal) which reads as follows:

Siud i is brù air a siùil is 'deuchainn gach sgòid,
long àrsaidh le sunnd is sùrd is lèireadh air bòrd;
fàire làn rùn nach do rùisgeadh fo cheann a croinn spreòid,
is cop uisge a stiùrach a' dùnadh 's ga chall sa mhuir mhòir.[12]

The earlier part of the poem describes the ship as filled with a host of allegorical personifications, interestingly grouped in contrasting pairs. If this is pastiche of a kind, that need not be a weakness (though Bateman might look on it as such). In so far as Hay is struggling to reclaim a domain of abstract intellectual discussion for Gaelic poetry, and doing so, courageously, with minimal reference to Protestant or even Christian terminology, there is a rightness about his being drawn back to the late Middle Ages, as the most recent historical period in which Celtic language communities participated fully and on equal terms in scholarly discourse on the broader European front. Having said that, the world of this ship's voyage is not so different from the one which prompts the meaningless, unmotivated crimes of the hero of a novel by Albert Camus or Alexander Trocchi.

This is why Bateman's classification of poems like 'An t-Eòlas nach Chruthaich' or 'Prìosan dha fhèin an Duine' as 'versified sermons', 'over-worked and over-stated', which 'fail the numinous potential of poetry' is lacking in discernment. Hay's ontology is not beholden to established religion and has none of the dead weight of conventional thinking behind it. Even a poem like 'Is e Crìoch Àraidh' (p. 184), taking as its departure a phrase from the Presbyterian catechism, shows a relentless pessimism, even a Manicheanism, difficult to reconcile with religious orthodoxy. Its view of human life, indeed of the whole range of human activity, is unrelentingly bleak:[13]

Is deuchainn gheàrr ar beatha bhochd,
laimrig an aiseig null gar tìr.
A-bhos tha 'n t-olc 's na sìontan borb,
ach thall tha foirfeachd agus sìth.[14]

Appropriate ethical behaviour is, interestingly, spoken of in aesthetic terms, as if the rules leading to fulfilment of an artistic intention applied equally to the conduct of an individual human life:

> Cluich an t-ùrlar mall air tùs,
>   's gach roinn 'na dhèidh, le lùths nad chuir,
>   air Crùnluath bras do là cuir ceann,
>   till air an ùrlar mhall is sguir.[15]

The use of terms derived from classical bagpipe music allows Hay
to give his discourse the colouring of a specific place and culture.
Though Bateman claims that such poems operate through a 'syntax
of prose', their energy surely derives from the repeated collision
and explosion of opposites. The Maker's plan for human life, in 'Is
e Crìoch Araidh', is expressed in terms of such pairs ('a roinneas
gàire oirnn is deòir,/breith, bàs, breòiteachd, slàint' is lùths').[16] The
passengers on the ship of 'Clann Adhaimh' are similarly grouped
('Bròn, Aoibh, Aois is Òige, Sàr is Suarach'),[17] as is their environment ('Fo speur tha uair grianach, uair sgreunach,/– clais is cìrein –
fèath is doinnean...').[18]

  Both habit of mind and habit of expression, such pairing of
opposites is indicative. Hay does not conceive of identity or ideology in monolithic terms, but in terms of difference. He used the
Arab world and his experience of it to bring into focus his own
chosen, not allotted, cultural inheritance. Fortuitous as his
encounter with the Arab culture of North Africa was, a consequence of obligatory conscription in an army whose battles he had
little sympathy for, hindsight gives it the look of an inevitable stage
in Hay's poetic path, rather than merely an accident.[19]

  It is not surprising to see Bateman display such a lack of sympathy and even insight for Hay's achievements. Her own poetry is
unashamedly confessional in nature. The reader of her lyrics is
encouraged to construct an underpinning narrative in which a
female subject repeatedly comes to grief in an unfeeling and
unsympathetic world, the individual poems themselves like brief
sparks set flying by this grim collision. In the culminating poem VII
of his 'Dàin do Eimhir' sequence, MacLean engaged in philosophical questioning of a depth and seriousness to match Hay's own, yet
it is prompted and framed by a narrative of unsuccessful love and

placed in the mouth of the narrator. No such structures underpin Hay's poetry. It does not require the reader to construct an image of the speaker, identified more or less closely with the writer. Hay the man is, if you like, conspicuous by his absence from the poetry, as if he felt the need to point beyond his own, limited experience to issues of greater import for his readership.

His stance, at one and the same time vitalist and pessimistic, is more Nietzschean than Christian in origin. From a passage in a letter to his mother, concerning 'Prìosan da Fhèin an Duine?' (Man His Own Prison?, p. 174), it is clear that he saw how individual poems fitted together, and would have been distressed by Bateman's verdict:

> As you'll see, this poem, 'Atman' and 'Knowledge that Does Not Create' are really a group, and their ideas all lie in the same direction. But there's no harm in their being published separately, especially as there may be one or two more on this theme, or themes related to it. Let me know if it strikes you as *sermonising in tone* or not. It's impossible for me to tell, and *sermonising or moralising is a deadly trap to fall into.*[20]

Byrne assigns the poem to the end of November 1944, and notes the debt of its opening lines to an essay by Benedetto Croce Hay had read shortly before. The poem's philosophy is instinctual. Individual men and women, like animals, should follow the innermost promptings of their nature, as this is what it means to be alive. The parallel with animals indicates that this philosophy is moral only in the broadest sense. Far from being prose-like, 'Prìosan da Fhèin an Duine?' makes rich use of the vocalic assonance, in internal and final position, which Hay inherited from Gaelic tradition. The italicised vowels in the lines which follow should help to indicate the richness of his verbal melody:

Seall an t-amhsan clis 'na sh*ai*ghid
 o 'fh*ai*re fo na ne*òi*l,
's an t-eun a' luasgan air a shl*a*taig,
 a' cur a bhith air f*a*d 'na che*òl*.
Their gnìomh is guth gach cre*u*tair ruinn,
 ach *èi*steachd riu air ch*òi*r:
'Cha chuir ceann is cridh' air *iom*rall thu.
 Bi *iom*lan is bi be*ò*.'[21]

Even lines have the same stressed vowel in final position, while
the last stressed vowel in each odd line is echoed in the body of
the line that follows (a device known as 'aicill'). Repression is
anathema to such impulsive living. Is it an exaggeration to suggest
that in the third stanza Hay is seeking to body forth, in Gaelic, the
workings of neurosis and the personality structures formed as a
result?

> Ach nì e tric de 'bhuadhanna
> bròg chuagach fo 'shàil,
> cuid dhiubh fon chuip, gun srian riu,
> 's an dà thrian diubh 'nan tàmh.
> Bidh an cridhe 'na thìoran aimhreiteach,
> 's an ceann aige 'na thràill,
> no bidh an corr 'na phrìosanach
> 's an inntinn air 'na geàrd.[22]

The penultimate stanza reviles both conventional living and conventional morality, and reiterates Hay's imaging of right living as
intensely colourful, the opposite of customary, undifferentiated
grey.

   Bateman is willing to recognise 'an irrepressible, inventive musicality' in Hay's poetry, yet complains that it 'often leaves the subject matter far behind'. This implies an atomistic view of poetry,
with form and subject matter as distinct entities in need of being
adapted and calibred one to the other. Such an approach, of
course, rarely gives equal value to the two elements, but tends to
privilege subject matter, demanding that form act as its medium or
handmaiden. Hay, by contrast, has practised what one might call a
'subjectless poetry', focused on wellworn topics drawn from the
Gaelic tradition. If we are to appreciate them fully, we need to
attribute a measure of autonomy to formal aspects, allowing them
to transgress any too rigid boundary and become meaningful,
become 'subject matter' in themselves. Outstanding instances of
this kind of poem are 'Do Bheithe Bhòidheach' (To a Bonny Birch
Tree, p. 20) and 'Siubhal a' *Choire*' (The Voyaging of the *Corrie*, p.
8). To define such items merely in terms of their subject matter
would be reductive. Saying what they are 'about', respectively, a
birch tree and a sailing trip, tells us little or nothing 'about' them. If
we are to reach an adequate assessment of Hay's achievement,

then the balance between formal aspects and subject matter must be allowed to tip in both directions, when we do not decide that such distinctions are altogether irrelevant.

For 'Bisearta' (Bizerta, p. 176), Hay adapted a metre of Petrarchan origin referring it to a poem by Girolamo Savonarola.[23] Does the choice suggest a degree of identification, on Hay's part, with the preacher who so relentlessly castigated the faults of his society that eventually elements in it rose up murderously against him? The poem describes the unrelenting bombardment of the civil population of this Tunisian town, the speaker's detached stance precluding support for either of the warring parties. His sympathies and his passion are reserved for the pointless suffering of ordinary people ('Cò a-nochd a phàigheas/seann chìs àbhaisteach na fala cumant?').[24] The forces dictating his existence operate in such a profoundly inhuman way that Hay's very human sympathies can only isolate him from the society he is compelled to live in.

Hay's sympathy for and passionate identification with the Arab populations he moved among, through no decision of his own, indeed again his will, in the course of war service, are the obverse of his Scottish nationalism. They are surely sufficient to exonerate him from definitive charges of chauvinism. There is no space here to make extended observations on his most ambitious enterprise, 'Mochtàr is Dùghall' (Mokhtâr and Dougall, p. 105), the 'long unfinished narrative pocm' which runs to 1273 lines, occupying 57 pages in Byrne's edition. Begun shortly after Hay's move to Italy in June 1944, the poem had reached something like its present form by November 1946. Further progress was impeded by a break-down suffered in May or June 1946, which marked the onset of a mental instability the poet would never fully recover from.

While it may be inappropriate to draw conclusions from an incompleted project, the poem, as it has come down to us, prompts fascinating questions. Planned to place accounts of an Arab and a Gaelic soldier, and of their ancestry, side by side, it concentrates overwhelmingly on the Arab part. Would Hay have encountered insoluble difficulties when the time came to treat the Gaelic soldier in comparable detail? Did his 'appropriation of the foreign' release his poetic gifts in a way the attempt to 'speak' the culture he had chosen as his own (and which may have been even more of a construction) could never do? Was the intention of 'leapfrogging' over the alien culture into a longed for Gaelic 'authenticity' doomed to failure from the start? And should we therefore rejoice that 'Mochtàr is Dùghall' remained in a fragmentary state?

The poem as it stands opens up Gaelic writing, skilfully and convincingly, to a very different culture. This is one of two major aspects of Hay's achievement, neither of which is referred to by Bateman in her assessment. According to Ronald Black, 'Mochtàr is Dùghall' 'permanently broadened the range of Gaelic verse', ensuring that 'any kind of subject-matter was possible'.[25] The second is extremely pertinent to Bateman's own practice. Hay was not brought up as a Gaelic speaker. The language was not in regular use in Tarbert Loch Fyne, his father's native town, to which his mother returned when his father died in 1919, and where the small family spent summer holidays throughout his adolescence.[26] His success in mastering the language, and in producing work in it some of which, at least, is of the first rank, made it easier for future generations of learners, Bateman included, to do the same (although the distinction between 'native' and 'learner' poets continues to carry a certain weight in Scotland).

Perusers of Byrne's edition will note that Hay was productive in all three of Scotland's acknowledged languages for literature, yet his work in Gaelic should prove to be his most solid and lasting contribution. Until the necessary critical tools for confronting the work of a trilingual poet are at hand, it is essential that his Gaelic poetry, at least, should be assessed according to parameters which are both relevant and appropriate, and which serve to highlight Hay's distinctive combination of craftsmanship and polemics, of alienation and detached, yet piercing human sympathy.

NOTES

[1] George Campbell Hay, *Collected Poems and Songs*, 2 vols., edited by Michel Byrne, Edinburgh: Edinburgh University Press, 2000. In the treatment that follows, poems are page referenced for the first volume of this edition (henceforth simply Michel Byrne, *op. cit.*), which is the

source of all English translations of both titles and texts. A one-volume paperback edition has recently become available: Edinburgh: Edinburgh University Press, 2003.

[2] See *Scottish Studies Review*, vol. 2, no. 2, Autumn 2001, pp. 150-151.

[3] See further my note on Meg Bateman *Aotromachd agus Dàin Eile/Lightness and Other Poems*, Edinburgh: Polygon, 1997, and Rody Gorman *Fax and Other Poems*, Edinburgh: Polygon, 1997, in *Lines Review*, no. 141, June 1997.

[4] Hay had a specific tree or trees in mind, at Toll a'Cheiligh, the Bay of the Cockerel on the north side of East Loch Tarbert (Michel Byrne, *op. cit.*, II, pp. 162, 240).

[5] 'Our speech and our culture,/though they should be wholly cast down for a time,/their roots and their old stock/will put forth sappy shoots and leaves again'.

[6] 'Id, Ego and Super-Ego', first published in Norman MacCaig and Alexander Scott eds., *Contemporary Scottish Verse 1959-1969*, London: Calder & Boyars, 1970, pp. 160-162, now in Sorley MacLean/ Somhairle MacGill-Eain, *From Wood to Ridge/O Choille gu Bearradh*, Manchester: Carcanet and Edinburgh: Birlinn, 1999, pp. 242-244.

[7] Published as a separate volume by Gairm of Glasgow in 1981. English translation in *Cencrastus*, no. 10, Autumn 1982.

[8] *'What if this land has been created/to hem us in with its shores?/Sea, my sea, the starry sky/howls over us with its free winds!'*

[9] In Bateman's view, Hay 'envisages an independent, rural Scotland, peopled with the descendants of heroes', and she considers his 'equation of a specific land with a specific people with a prescribed set of inherited characteristics' to be 'problematic'.

[10] '...so many years of rusting and slumber/it has been growing blunt, set fast in its sheath...'

[11] 'One spell, one spell do we get on earth/to show the temper of the metal in us,/to test the edge of our courage,/to win fame for our country or shame'.

[12] 'There she goes with a curve on her sails, putting each sheet to the test,/an ancient ship with bustle and cheer and suffering aboard her;/a horizon full of secrets unrevealed under her bowsprit head,/and the foam of her wake closing and losing itself in the great sea astern'.

[13] Bateman puzzlingly speaks of Hay's poetry as 'inducing a sense of well-being and optimism about human nature'.

[14] 'Our poor life is but a short trial,/the jetty of the ferry across to our land./On this side are evil and the savage storms,/beyond are perfec-

tion and peace'.

15 'Play first the slow Urlar,/and after it each part with vigour in your cadences,/complete the headlong Crunluath of your days,/return to the slow Urlar and cease'.

16 'who shares out laughter and tears to us,/birth, death, sickliness, health and vigour'.

17 'Grief, Joy, Age and Youth, Eminent and Of-No-Account'.

18 'Under a sky now sunny, now lowering/– trough and crest – calm and tempest'.

19 Michel Byrne, *op. cit.*, II, pp. 25ff. details Hay's opposition to conscription, his time spent as a fugitive in the Kintyre hills before being apprehended in May 1942 and brought to trial, and his eventual enrolment in the Royal Army Ordinance Corps, which he took as 'an intentional slight'. An application to transfer to the Intelligence Corps was, not surprisingly, turned down.

20 Michel Byrne, *op. cit.*, II, p. 150 (my italics).

21 'See the gannet come as an arrow/from his watching under the clouds,/and the bird rocking on its branch,/putting all its being into its music./The actions and voices of every creature say to us,/if we would but listen to them rightly:/"Head and heart will not lead you astray./Be complete, and be alive"'.

22 'But often he makes of his qualities/a lopsided shoe under his heel,/some of them, unbridled, under the whip,/and two thirds of them in idleness./The heart may be a turbulent tyrant,/with the head under it, its thrall,/or the body may be a prisoner,/with the intellect standing over it on guard'.

23 Dated to November 1942 to May 1943 in Michel Byrne's note (*op. cit.*, II, p.151). It is regrettable that Byrne should have omitted, from his thoroughly admirable edition, the Gaelic renderings of seven Petrarch sonnets (originally published in *O Na Ceithir Àirdean* [in Gaelic with some English prose translations], Edinburgh and London: Oliver & Boyd, 1952 pp. 47-50) which surely constitute a major part of Hay's overall achievement. Where the Savonarola poem alternates seven and ten-line syllables (*settenari* and *decasillabi*), the syllable count in Hay's longer lines is more flexible. But he does introduce a characteristically Gaelic 'aicill' (see above) between the final stressed vowel in the short line and an internal vowel in the longer line which follows.

24 'Who to-night is paying/the old accustomed tax of common blood?'

25 See Ronald Black's 'Introduction' to *An Tuil: Duanaire Gàidhlig an*

20mb Ceud/Anthology of 20th Century Scottish Gaelic Verse,
Edinburgh: Polygon, 1999, p. xxxix.

[26] See the account under 'A Stey Brae an' Bonnie: a Short Biography',
in Michel Byrne, *op. cit.*, II, also 'George Campbell Hay: Bard of
Kintyre', in Angus Martin, *Kintyre: The Hidden Past*, Edinburgh: John
Donald, 1984, pp. 48-71.

COLIN MILTON

Dialects, Orality and the Poetry of Tom Leonard: In the Beginning Was the Sound

In 1983, the Glasgow-born poet Edwin Morgan reported that 'The acceptable emergence of Glasgow speech, both as an object of linguistic study and as a medium for serious writing, is recent.'[1] The general neglect of Glasgow speech by both scholars and writers during the most dynamic period of the city's growth is, as Morgan implies, surprising. After all, Glasgow has been Scotland's biggest city since the middle of the nineteenth century, and has played a central part in its transformation from a predominantly rural country to a modern industrial one. Since Glasgow is the dominant urban centre of the Central Belt in which four-fifths of the population of Scotland live, Derrick McClure's question, in his recent full-length study of twentieth-century poetry in Scots, seems a natural one: 'is it not at least a tenable position that the voice of Scotland is most truly heard in the speech of working-class Glaswegians rather than in the "synthetic Scots" of scholars and literati?'[2] The enquiry is prompted by the language of Tom Leonard's Glasgow dialect poems, which McClure rightly sees as 'profoundly subversive' of the central project of twentieth-century literary nationalism – the attempt by Hugh MacDiarmid and his allies to create (or recreate) a 'full canon' of literary Scots by drawing on the resources of different regions and different periods. Leonard, in contrast, is best known for his Glasgow dialect poems, which employ a written-down version of contemporary working-class Glasgow speech to comment on, among other things, language, class, culture, and social conditions.

Born in 1944, and brought up in Pollock, on Glasgow's southside, Leonard belongs by birth to the substantial Catholic minority in sectarian south-west Scotland. His influence on the Scottish liter-

ary scene over the last thirty years has been out of all proportion
to his modest output: his four full-length publications to date[3]
include an anthology and a biography, with only *Intimate Voices:
Selected Work 1965-1983* (1984) and *Reports from the Present*
(1995) containing the original poetry, essays and polemics which first
appeared in magazines and periodicals from the 1970s on. Though
very diverse, Leonard's work shares common characteristics: an
emphasis on the physical character of language, and on language
as an object in itself as well as a medium through which things are
expressed; on the inter-relations of language, class and power and
of the written and the spoken; on the defamiliarisation of linguistic
activities which we normally take for granted. Running through all
of it is a recognition that what is perceived as 'true', and 'real'
varies with historical, social and personal circumstances. It is this
which lies behind his consistent experimentation: new kinds of
subject matter, new forms and new means of expression – as well
as poems in Glasgow dialect, sound poetry and concrete poetry
have been among his enthusiasms – have always drawn Leonard.
His work is often 'unfinished', open-ended, inconclusive; the
sketch, the fragment, the outline, the doodle, are among his characteristic forms. Leonard first came to general attention with the
publication of *Six Glasgow Poems* in 1969;[4] though not the first
experiments in using Glasgow Scots as a 'serious' literary medium
(there are precedents in the social-realist drama of the 1940s and
1950s), his very radical approach in these short (sometimes very
short) poems to creating a written-down equivalent of working-
class Glasgow Scots aroused great interest. It was not simply his
formal innovations in themselves, however, which attracted
attention – his treatment of language was recognised as having
significant social and political implications, not least in relation to
the legacy of MacDiarmid and the Scottish Renaissance movement.
And the unsettling effect of the poems was reinforced by the
searching reflective and polemical pieces on language, class and
culture which began to appear in Scottish literary magazines.

Although he recognises the challenge Leonard's Glasgow dialect
poems present to the central ideas of the established vernacular
movement, McClure rejects the idea that the Glasgow voice in
them is the true voice of Scotland; indeed he denies that it is a

'voice' at all in any substantive sense, seeing it as no more than 'a patois', the speech 'of a people without a voice', in itself the mark not of literacy but of the 'rejection of literacy'. As a mere 'patois', and one created wholly out of 'rejection', its range of uses is necessarily limited – it cannot, McClure claims, 'express anything but an inarticulate protest'.[5] Edwin Morgan's judgement is radically different; Scotland's most distinguished living poet refers to the 'remarkable work of Tom Leonard' and to the new possibilities opened up by the publication of *Six Glasgow Poems*:

> His Glasgow-language poems, though usually quite short, bring together in highly concentrated form a number of separate interests: 'voice' and sound and the transcription of sound; sociolinguistic and political concern; poetic structure, and especially line-structure; and comedy from the playful to the ferocious.[6]

Morgan's emphasis on the virtuosity with which Leonard uses his dialect medium, and the range and diversity of issues explored through it contrasts sharply with McClure's reference to it as an impoverished patois. The latter's response shows the continuing influence of MacDiarmid's idea that modern Scots dialects are fragmentary and degenerate survivals of what was once a unified national language, and the persistence of what Morgan terms the 'long-ingrained attitudes – linguistic, social, aesthetic'[7] which stigmatised Glasgow speech, and discouraged linguistic or aesthetic interest in it till recent times. One of the ironies of Scottish literary history is that the long-ingrained attitudes in question – that Glasgow Scots is not really Scots at all, but a bastard speech, impoverished, crude and chaotic – have frequently been expressed by those like McClure who think of themselves as enthusiasts for the vernacular. The locus classicus is William Grant's introduction to the *Scottish National Dictionary*, in which that distinguished scholar of the Scots language describes Glasgow speech as 'hopelessly corrupt'[8] – the native vernacular having been contaminated by the speech of the 'Irish and foreign immigrants' who arrived in the area from the mid-nineteenth century. In a trenchant passage in an essay entitled 'On Reclaiming the Local', Leonard attacks the assumptions which lie behind such attitudes (and points to the destructive consequences which they can have):

It's in the reification of linguistic codes and their possession by dominant and powerful classes wherein lies real danger, now literally for the whole world. That reification will always contain as part of its mechanics the device to maintain the illusion that social conflict does not exist, or that such conflict as exists can be meaningfully recreated, and resolved, within its own perimeter. Self-expression outside that code becomes simply a mechanism of self-elimination. The dominant refuse to recognise that all language is an instrument of consciousness: instead, it is held as a symptom. Others don't 'have' a language – they 'are' it. In dismissing the language, one dismisses the existence of its users – or rather, one chooses to believe that they have dismissed themselves.[9]

The language on which Leonard's Glasgow poems draw does indeed represent a rejection of 'literacy' as McClure alleges, but the reasons for that rejection – and its consequences – can only be understood if the concept of literacy itself is subjected to critical examination. We have come to regard 'literate' and 'cultured' as virtually synonymous, and to believe that only the literate are capable of understanding and expressing themselves fully, so we need to remind ourselves that pre-literate societies (and non-literate communities in otherwise literate societies) are capable of creative feats if the highest order. Indeed, as David Buchan has pointed out, most of what is distinctive in the culture of lowland Scotland, and much that is finest in it, like the song-tradition, was created and transmitted through the oral, vernacular, tradition.[10] So, while McClure is certainly right to point to widespread working-class alienation from the kind of 'literacy' which the school system aims to impart, this is not just a contumacious rejection of opportunities for betterment. It is, rather, a reaction to the denial by teachers, schools and the official curriculum that working class experience (and vernacular culture generally) has any value. Since the Education (Scotland) Act of 1872 made elementary education compulsory for all, the aim of Scottish schooling has often seemed to be the elimination – or at best the marginalisation – of the culture and speech which the majority of ordinary Scots pupils bring into the classroom – and its replacement by a standardised, anglicised, middle-class identity.

The major education acts of the 1870s, which set out to standardise and harmonise school provision, caused alarm up and down Britain among those who valued local diversity and idiosyncrasy. In Scotland, the effort to enforce standard English as the sole medium of instruction was felt to be particularly threatening, since what was being attacked was not just a local or regional speech, but one which was felt to be, in all its varieties, a central expression of national consciousness. Scots was not usually banished from the classroom entirely, but it was pushed to the margins, becoming largely limited to specific 'aesthetic' or historical uses – like the learning by heart and recitation of vernacular poetry from the Ballads to Burns and Charles Murray. This token presence was not enough to allay the fear among cultural patriots that, within a generation or so, educational reform, in combination with other standardising pressures, would create a bland, homogeneous 'national' culture (and speech) across the whole of the British Isles.

It is hardly surprising, then, that from the last quarter of the nineteenth century, a recurrent theme in the work of Scottish writers conscious of the rich cultural traditions of lowland Scotland has been the clash between the vernacular culture which most pupils bring to school with them and an alien school ethos. The clash is not between education and ignorance, or between literacy and illiteracy, but between two contrasting kinds of culture, one locally based, orally transmitted and expressed in a local vernacular, the other determined centrally by the Scottish Education Department, promulgated by writing and print, and imparted through English. Many observers from the late nineteenth century on were pessimistic about the outcome of this *kulturkampf*; in the battle between pupil and teacher, community and state, the latter seemed bound to win. Charles Murray's poem 'The Whistle' is a landmark expression of these contemporary anxieties; originally published in Chambers's *Journal* in 1906, it became enormously popular after its appearance in the second (1909) edition of *Hamewith*.[11] The 'whistle' of the title is a home-made instrument made by a herd-lad with a natural musical bent; on it, to the delight of those around, and without any formal lessons, he plays the traditional music of the region. However when the lad returns to school after the summer, the master confiscates and burns the whistle: the official curriculum has no place for the boy's musical talent, and school and schoolmaster represent a ideology in which folk-music, and vernacular culture in general, are looked down on as outmoded and irrelevant. In the 1910s and 1920s, 'The Whistle' was popular, not just in Murray's native North-East, but throughout Scotland – even in non Scots-speaking areas, because it reflected widespread contemporary anxiety about the threat to vernacular culture posed by compulsory, standardised – and anglicised – schooling. Grassic Gibbon presents the same conflict in *Sunset Song*;[12] set in the North-East in the first decades of the twentieth century, Chris Guthrie, the heroine, is the daughter of a tenant farmer. Her teachers come of the same peasant stock, but have turned their backs on it, and parade their recently-acquired and precarious 'gentility'. They sneer at their rural pupils' lack of 'culture', and try to replace the children's Scots with English (the pupils retaliate by mocking their teachers' incompetent attempts to speak the standard).

While both 'The Whistle' and *Sunset Song* are set in rural communities where local dialect and culture have maintained much of their vigour and self-confidence, William McIlvanney's *Docherty*[13] depicts a world closer to Leonard's own experience of growing up in urban working-class community with a heavily stigmatised sociolect. Also set in the first half of the twentieth century, the novel traces the experience of a working-class family in urban, industrial west-central Scotland. Encouraged by a sympathetic elementary school teacher, Conn Docherty, a miner's son, thinks of continuing his education. However a confrontation with one of his secondary teachers disillusions him, and as a result he leaves school to work in the pit. Significantly, the clash between teacher and pupil centres on language; when the master, Pirrie, demands why two of the boys have been fighting, Conn answers, without thinking, in his own dialect, and not in the English which is the language of the classroom. Asked to repeat what he has said in 'proper' English (with unconscious irony, his teacher refers to it as 'the mother tongue') he replies in Scots again, this time deliberately. The master recognises the reply for what it is – a gesture of defiance which asserts the worth of Conn's community and speech against the values of the school. Ironically, like the schoolmasters in *Sunset Song*, Pirrie himself comes from a working-class background, and the violence of his reaction (Conn is soundly beaten for using his own dialect), is an expression of unacknowledged guilt and anger at himself for betraying his roots.

'The Whistle', *Sunset Song* and *Docherty* all emphasise the hostility of the school to dialect and to vernacular culture generally, presenting the pupils largely as victims. Tom Leonard's 'Poetry', in contrast, shows the victim striking back. In it, a Glasgow working-class speaker looks back on his experience in the English class. Through quasi-phonetic spelling, Leonard conveys the speaker's cruelly accurate mimicry of the teacher's mannered pronunciation. Here the ridicule which Chris Guthrie and her schoolmates directed at their snobbish teachers takes a more sophisticated form. The poem's emphasis on the phonetic dimension encourages reading aloud, emphasising the conventional association of poetry with a particular kind of voice – with 'received pronunciation'. At the same time, the poem makes clear that these sounds are inextricably associated with a particular kind of outlook and social position:

> the pee as in pulchritude
> oh pronounced ough
> as in bough
>
> the ee rather poised
> (pronounced ih as in wit)
> then a languid high tea...
>
> pause: then the coda –
> ray pronounced rih
> with the left eyebrow raised
> – what a gracious bouquet![14]

Here a nexus of material circumstances, attitudes and tastes is conveyed satirically through the references to, for instance, the leisured habit of late-afternoon high tea, the genteel aversion from anything that suggests intense feeling ('languid'), the stereotypical expression of sceptical connoisseurship ('left eyebrow raised'), and the dual reference to wine and flowers in 'gracious bouquet'. The voice which talks about poetry is, very clearly, a class voice and represents a way of life which is utterly remote from the speaker's. The cultural element of the school curriculum is also felt to be alien to the speaker's experience because the voice, and the way of life it evokes are, very recognisably, *English* and not Scots.

Leisure, social and cultural confidence, material comfort, 'good
taste', English as against Scots, are all associated here with 'culture'
and its appreciation (poetry stands for all the 'high' arts because it
has often been seen as their apotheosis), so it is hardly surprising
that the speaker concludes 'That was my education/– and nothing
to do with me'. This is not an assertion that 'canonical' poetry is
irrelevant to working-class readers (or English poetry to Scots readers); nor, as Leonard makes clear in one of his essays, is it a claim
that those who use received pronunciation are incapable of literary
understanding or insight. The point is that 'high' culture has usually
been mediated through this kind of confident, class-marked voice,
so that it has come to seem the 'natural' voice for it. This association is liable to make poetry or art or serious music seem irrelevant
or inaccessible to those who speak in other ways – and, of course,
it can be deliberately used to exclude them. There is anger in the
poem, but it is cleverly sublimated: Leonard deconstructs the pretensions to objectivity and universal validity of the 'RP' voice by
turning the characteristic stance and tone of 'cultured' discourse –
witty, poised, and analytical – against its own claims. The 'educated' voice implicitly claims authority, and is often unthinkingly
accepted as a neutral vehicle for the 'truth': to draw attention to its
characteristics is to uncover its lack of transparency, and lay bare
its historical and social roots. It is exposed as a class voice, reflecting the circumstances, interests, values – and limitations – of a particular social group.

The attitudes mocked in 'Poetry' are rooted in the idea that the
cultural dimension of the school curriculum is there to 'raise' the
cultural level of working-class pupils; the aim is to refine their
tastes and wean them away from coarse popular forms of entertainment. Many of Leonard's poems subvert conventional assumptions about the way in which cultural interests and social class are
linked, and attack traditional hierarchies of taste. In the fourth of a
sequence of poems entitled 'Unrelated Incidents', the speaker is
'sittn guzz-/lin a can/a newcastle/brown wotchn/scotsport hum-
/min thi furst/movement a/nielsens thurd/symphony – happy/iz
larry yi/might say'.[15] Here, a cliché notion of working-class male
pleasures – happiness is watching televised soccer, beer-can in
hand – is disrupted by the reference to the music of Carl Nielsen.

Nielsen's symphonies may belong to 'high' culture, but they are as much part of the speaker's life as Newcastle Brown Ale and Glasgow Celtic, and all three combine harmoniously to create a sense of intense happiness. The point here is that an enthusiasm for football is not something which has to be outgrown in the ascent to 'higher' forms of pleasure like symphonic music. Leonard's alternative is an inclusive conception of culture, in which symphonies and soccer are both recognised as 'arts'. 'Unrelated Incidents 4' ends with a virtuosic description-cum-celebration of a classic solo goal which illustrates the point; in a single sentence of twenty-three short lines, Leonard conveys the movements of the scorer in words, using pauses, line-breaks, changes of pace and variations in rhythm with breathtaking effect. Since, in the European tradition, poetry has been regarded as the most prestigious of literary genres, celebrating footballing skills in a poem implies that these skills are as much worth celebrating in the medium as those of (say) the painter, sculptor or composer. It is perhaps inevitable that in challenging cultural demarcations, exclusions and snobberies, and seeking for a more democratic conception of culture, Leonard looked to the United States rather than to England – or Scotland. His use of phonetically-rendered contemporary colloquial language as a poetic medium owes something to ee cummings' poetic transcriptions of American speech, while William Carlos Williams is generously acknowledged as an inspiration both in his 'presentation of voice as a fact', and in his democratic celebration in poetry of life's 'ordinary' pleasures. 'Jist ti Let Yi No', described as being 'from the American of Carlos Williams',[16] is a reworking of the American poet's apology for eating the peaches in the fridge; transposed into a west-of-Scotland working-class setting, it becomes a delighted recollection of the coolness and strong taste of 'thi speshlz' (the reference is to a popular strong lager, Carlsberg Special Brew).

The Glasgow dialect poems challenge what Leonard sees as a linguistic and aesthetic hegemony: the stance and voice of the dominant canonical tradition is one which marginalises other stances and other kinds of voice – particularly oppositional ones. Two flawed models of the relations between language varieties provide the implicit rationale for the marginalisation and stigmatisation of non-standard forms – the first centres on the contrast between completeness and incompleteness; the second on that between correctness and incorrectness. In the first, the relation between the standard and regional or social varieties is conceptualised as one between 'language' and 'dialect', with the former capable of encompassing the full range of human experience and the latter restricted to sectional or fragmentary perspectives. The second model holds that the standard form is the 'correct' form, and dialects deviations from it, resulting from ignorance or incompetence. In his many discussions of the history and present state of Scots, C.M. Grieve ('Hugh MacDiarmid') applied both models within a Scottish context. Contemporary Scots dialects were dismissed as both degenerate and fragmentary, the decayed remains of a once vigorous and complete national language. The task of reconstituting that language, by drawing on the Scots of all periods and all regions, was a task for the literary élite.

The sense that culture, and even 'reality' is a class possession is linked, in turn, with another fundamentally mistaken belief – that the written standard, the language of literature, is the written realisation of 'received pronunciation'. Leonard exposes the fallacy in a trenchant passage in an essay on William Carlos Williams:

When you have in a society on the one hand a standardised literary grammar (standardised spelling and standardised syntax) and on the other hand a standardised mode of pronunciation, the notion tends to get embedded in the consciousness of that society, that the one is part of the essence of the other. Prescriptive grammar, in other words, becomes the sound made flesh of prescriptive pronunciation. The tawdry little syllogism goes something like this: –

1. In speaking of reality, there is a standard correct mode of pronunciation.

2. In writing of reality, there is a standard correct mode of spelling and of syntax.

3. In reality, correct spelling and correct syntax are synonymous with correct pronunciation.

Putting it another way, if a piece of writing can't comfortably be read aloud in a 'correct' (Received Pronunciation) voice, then there must be something wrong with it. It's not valid.[17]

Laying bare the class basis of the spoken standard by exposing it as one dialect among many is linked with Leonard's attack on beliefs which he sees as pervasive in attitudes to language in class/bound Britain: one such belief is that 'received pronunciation', the speech of the privileged or their imitators, taught in the private sector of education, is the language of the 'true' and the 'real'. The belief has a quasi-rational basis in the association of received pronunciation with extended education, and its lack of connection with any particular locality. A particular class-based kind of speech thus comes to be associated with an informed and dispassionate outlook, free of the distortions of personal feeling, of class bias, or of provincial narrowness. Though weakening now, the idea that received pronunciation under its various names – BBC English, the Queen's English, public school English – imparts authority to what it expresses continues to be influential. The result is that what it expresses is often still accepted as 'the truth'. Not everyone is taken in, however. The Glasgow speaker in 'Unrelated Incidents 3', sensitive to what Leonard calls elsewhere the 'extra-semantic kinetics' of language, sardonically decodes the message to working-class listeners conveyed through the 'BBC English' of the newsreader:

thi reason
a talk wia
BBC accent
iz coz yi
widny wahnt
mi ti talk
aboot thi
trooth wia
voice lik
wanna yoo scruff...

...thirza right
way ti spell
ana right way
ti tok it. this
is me tokn yir
right way a
spellin. this
is ma trooth.
yooz doant no
thi trooth

yirsellz cawz
yi canny talk
right...[18]

Though 'this/is ma truth' seems like an admission by the voice of
authority that truth is relative, and that there are other possible
'truths' (so 'you', the working-class radio-listener might have a different but equally valid truth) it is important to realise that these
are not the newsreader's actual words, but a 'decoding' of them by
the Glasgow-speaking listener which reveals their true, but unstat-
ed, meaning. From an establishment point of view, there is no
alternative truth, and the role of the working class is simply to listen and accept what the 'official' voice says: 'yooz doant no/thi
trooth/yirsellz cawz/yi canny talk/right. this is/the six a
clock/nyooz. belt up'. The poem exposes what Leonard calls the
'reification of linguistic codes', revealing what that process is
designed to hide: that 'truth' is socially constructed, with class the
most important element in shaping it. And since it stigmatises alternative voices ('self-expression outside that code becomes simply a
mechanism of self-elimination') the reification of received pronunciation helps to 'maintain the illusion that social conflict does not
exist'.

Leonard's analysis of the relations between language, culture,
class and power clearly owes a good deal to Marxism – in addition
to reification, exploitation, class conflict, ideology and false consciousness are important concepts in his work. For instance, it is
because class conflict is fundamental to capitalist societies that the
language of working-class communities embodies a kind of reality
which is not simply different from 'official' reality, but opposed to
it. Again, if the voice of the less-privileged majority is not heard, it
is because indoctrination by schools and the media, has created a
false consciousness, leading many working-class people to see
their own speech as defective, and defer to the authority of the
standard. Leonard also shows how concepts central to the ideology
of contemporary western societies like 'culture' and 'justice' are
essentially class creations. 'Poetry' lays bare the class origins of a
cultural form often linked with the 'spiritual' and 'transcendental';
'justice' is demystified in the same way, appropriately in a poem
which uses its 'one dialect', standard English:

And their judges spoke with one dialect,
but the condemned spoke with many voices.

And the prisons were full of many voices,
but never the dialect of the judges.

And the judges said:
'No-one is above the Law.'[19]

As 'Poetry' suggests, the conventional definition of what it is to be 'cultured' reflects the circumstances, habits and interests of a particular social group, made up of those who are highly educated, confident and free of immediate material pressures. These conditions help to explain why 'disinterestedness' has often seemed the foundation of the truly cultured outlook; G.M. Young, for instance, saw it as one of the most important legacies of the Victorian age:

> The function of the nineteenth century was to disengage the disinterested intelligence, to release it from the entanglements of party and sect – one might almost add of sex – and to set it operating over the whole range of human life and circumstance.[20]

It was also, paradoxically, an important value for the dedicated communist and ardent nationalist C.M. Grieve. In his important essay, 'A Theory of Scots Letters', Grieve describes 'disinterestedness' as the 'master-problem' in relation to culture, adding: 'I venture to say that whoever has understood the meaning of "disinterestedness" is not far-off understanding the goal of human culture'. It is also the element which 'gives a recognisable, but hardly definable unity to the work of all true Scottish writers'.[21] For Leonard, however, the idea of escaping from 'entanglements' to some 'objective' stance is a delusion; for him, 'impersonal' is a more accurate term than 'disinterested' for the stance assumed by the cultured individual, which is decidedly not neutral in its effects:

> The trouble with asking humans to enact the impersonal is that they usually do so by objectifying the humans around them. The humans around them won't behave like objects, so the 'impersonal' diagnostician has to construct mechanistic models of these humans that turn them into the object they have refused to become. The models of depersonalisation are invariably linguistic, and thus at the heart of politics is language, at the heart of language is politics.[22]

Instead of recognising the complexity, variety and unfixed nature of the rest of humanity, the 'educated' viewpoint involves an essentialism which imposes a 'bogus unified "personality"' on other, less privileged social groups, and treats the experience of regions or localities not in their own language, but in a supra-regional standard; as Leonard puts it, the 'dominant value-system has been allowed to marginalise that which does not correspond to it, declaring it deviant and therefore invalid. It has been able to do so by the method of making the mode of expression of these dominant values literally synonymous with "objectivity". It is the mode of expression which counts: that device by which the persona is given the status of being detached, impersonal, above the battle'.[23] This kind of 'impersonality' has its equivalent in the art of poetry, taking the form of the

> ...patriarchal image of the poet as detached diagnostic judge [which] still dominates influential literary scenes – Separation is assumed – of the judging from the personal experience, of the poet/narrator from the beings who inhabit the world described. This is what is expected, this is what being a Real Poet is all about. The poet is a spectator at someone else's experience, be that someone else a he, a she, 'they', or the I of former (!) working-class days. This is to be 'objective', the professional tone, the invisible suit of office. The 'professional' exists through a language that acquits him of present personal involvement; he is in control, through his craft. The ardently opinionated, the ardent in all forms, the raisers of voices, the thumpers on the table, the swearers, the passionate, those who burst into tears – all these are absent.[24]

This standpoint is reflected in the 'usually patronising' presentation of non-standard speech in literature. Where 'a writer-narrator presents standard English, and a quoted character-persona presents something else' apostrophes are typically used to indicate 'by sign the prescriptive norm from which a "character" is "deviating."' The message to the reader is that

> The character can't talk proper words, so the writer-narrator indicates where there's bits missed out, so you can better understand. The apostrophes indicate a supposed deficiency which the reader, over the head of the persona, as it were, must supply. The personae are trapped within the closed value-system that denigrates their use of language, while the writer-narrator communicates with the reader over their heads.[25]

Leonard's advice on how to avoid such an effect illuminates his own practice as a dialect poet:

> ...any attempt to indicate specific speech sounds by secondary spelling codes must avoid layers of puns etc. that provide nudges and winks at the speakers expense: only by giving the speaker a consciousness that might include knowledge of these codes (ie. So the speaker may be at least partly the author) can this be valid. In this way the speaker can implicitly refer to the nature of the codes being used and the language to which it refers.[26]

For Leonard, the language of his own working-class community is just as much an 'instrument of consciousness' as the standard. The repository of the distinctive experiences, attitudes and values of those who speak it, it stands in no need of translation, commentary, or supplementation. It is an indispensable medium for any writer who wants to present working-class people on their own terms and unpatronisingly, but it also presents a formidable challenge because it is essentially something spoken rather than something written. And in working class communities, speech is more central to people's experience than writing or print, so in writing about such a community it is particularly important to create a medium which has a close relation to the spoken word. For Leonard himself, working-class by origin, but also, through education, belonging to the world of print and 'literature', using Glasgow speech is an important way of asserting a continuing connection with, and loyalty to, his own community. Conversely, his rejection of standard English as a medium for the poems which deal directly with working-class experience signals its inadequacy and inappropriateness for the task.

In his discussion of the literary uses of Glasgow speech, Morgan talks of the 'loving particularity'[27] which characterises successful literary depictions of dialect. Generally regarded as a slovenly patois until the 1970s, Glasgow speech rarely attracted respectful attention before then. From that decade, however, it became 'both an area of experiment and a badge of pride'. Writers who experimented with it had a common starting point – they 'wanted to claim that if you want to use urban dialect it is first of all necessary to listen, and in doing so, to find distinctions and subtleties which the usual (and sometimes mythical) stereotypes writers have drawn on in the past have blunted or overlaid or simply missed. Emphasis on what is actually spoken, rather than on what legend or popular belief or the music-hall may in part have substituted for it, leads to thoughts about spelling, about [the] "phonetic transcription of speech"...'[28] Morgan concedes that the attempt to transcribe every nuance of spoken pronunciation can go too far, but adds: 'there is clearly a value in calling attention to the realities of a speech that has never yet been fully described'.[29]

While there are established conventions for representing Scotland's 'traditional' dialects on the page, using a 'speech that has never yet been fully described' as a literary medium (and which is not closely related to the traditional forms), is much more of a challenge, and Leonard's solutions are, necessarily, radical ones. While most dialect writers content themselves with a few stereotypical features – local words and phrases, or phonetic or semi-phonetic spellings to indicate non-standard pronunciation – Leonard's spelling is more consistently phonetic, often ignoring word and phrase boundaries, and his line and 'stanza' divisions are designed to give a sense of the characteristic rhythms and sound patterns of Glasgow working-class speech. As a result, the poems are visually strange; likely at first to puzzle the reader, they only begin to make sense when read aloud. Some familiarity with the idioms and rhythms of Glasgow speech is needed to do this, but in Scotland at least this is not a barrier since west of Scotland accents are familiar from the broadcast media. And when the written 'score' is 'performed' in this way, the ingenuity, accuracy and appositeness of Leonard's notation becomes increasingly apparent: it is his respect for all 'living language' as a 'vehicle for consciousness' which lies behind Leonard's attentive listening and meticulous transcription. Though *Six Glasgow Poems* helped to change perceptions of Glasgow Scots and encourage writing in urban vernacular, the challenges Leonard faced in devising a sensitive and sophisticated notation for the speech of city are still not fully recognised: the most recent major anthology of Scottish poetry, for instance, describes his technique reductively as the 'use [of] phonetic misspellings to render working-class Glaswegian speech'.[30]

Leonard's respect for the Scots spoken by ordinary people, in all its varieties, is in marked contrast to the attitude of the cultural nationalists of the Scottish Renaissance (and some of their present-day heirs). The basic Renaissance position was set out, in a characteristically uncompromising way, by C.M. Grieve in an influential series of articles in the *Scottish Educational Journal* between 1925 and 1927; for Grieve, the existing Scots dialects are the 'corrupt' and 'debased' fragments of a once complete 'language'. Later Renaissance spokesmen like Douglas Young and Robert Kemp largely echoed Grieve's judgements, though they tended to make an exception of the traditional rural dialects. It was these activists who met in 1947 to codify the rules for the spelling of modern literary Scots which were set down in the 'Lallans Style Sheet'. Though it had (and still has) some influence, the appearance of the style-sheet did not resolve the problem of how to write down what is basically a spoken vernacular, and Leonard comments wryly on the attempt in a cartoon-cum-poem in *Intimate Voices*. A square in mid-page headed 'MAKAR'S SOCIETY' advertises

GRAN' MEETIN'
THE NICHT
TAE DECIDE THE
SPELLIN'
O' THIS POSTER

ADMISSION: THRITTY PEE
(A HEID)[31]

The self-contradictory message underlines the absurdity of the project which the poster advertises. It mocks the idea that the written has precedence over the spoken, that literary intellectuals can legislate for a spoken vernacular which belongs to the community of ordinary speakers and, taken along with the dialect poems in Leonard's volume, it implies that the basis of a vital contemporary poetry in Scots is not discussion between writers, but active participation in the life of the Scots-speaking commmunity.

Leonard's painstaking attempt to represent on the page the precise sounds and rhythms of one particular contemporary speech-variety, and thus to 'indicate the act of the individual speaker in the utterance' is an affirmation of the value of the spoken in all its physical, situational reality. That the care is lavished on a heavily stigmatised variety is an assertion that *every* speech-variety is worth

attention and respect; 'all living language is sacred' as Leonard
insists in an untitled poem which starts unpromisingly with the
speaker accepting what everyone has told him – 'right inuff/ma
language is disgraceful'.[32] A comic list of all those who have told
him this follows; they range from the predictable – 'ma maw'
(significantly not 'ma paw'), through the usual representatives of
the middle class – teacher, doctor, priest, boss – to entertainingly
eccentric individual examples, including 'sum wee smout thit
thoat ah hudny read chomsky' and 'a calvinistic communist thit
thoat ah wuz revisionist'. Even those on the Scottish literary
scene, whether traditionalist or avant-garde have been hostile:

  po-faced literati grimly kerryin thi burden a thi past tellt me
  po-faced literati grimly kerryin the burden a thi future tellt mi

The use of contemporary sociolect as a literary medium is bound
to create anxiety among those who need to believe in the stability
of the printed word and the objectivity of a standard language –
whether English or 'Lallans'. Class-marked, and inextricably linked
with a particular place and time, Leonard's Glasgow Scots constantly reminds the reader that language is essentially transactional, its
form and meaning conditioned by person, place and circumstance.
The voice in Leonard's dialect poems is not condemned just
because of the way it sounds, of course; other features of the
speaker's working class speech are also 'disgraceful', as the speaker's final dismissal of his critics (unapologetically) reveals:

  ach well
  fuck thi lohta thim

Leonard's use of taboo words here and elsewhere in his work is
considered and deliberate. One reason for including them, of
course, is authenticity; they are a normal part of the speech of
many, even most, working class males. The usual explanation for
their use among those who disapprove of them is that they are
symptoms of linguistic poverty caused by lack of education; those
who swear do so (it is often claimed) because they lack the vocabulary to express themselves 'properly'. However, as Leonard recognises, swearing is not necessarily evidence of a lack – or something
simply negative: the defiant 'fuck thi lohta thim' at the end of 'ma

language is disgraceful', for instance, shows the speaker rejecting that judgement (and continuing, defiantly, to use his 'disgraceful' language). We feel sympathetic because until this point he has been a victim, subject to attack from his early years and from all sides because of the way he expresses himself. His anger and defiance seem justifiable.

Often, as here, taboo words are a response to attack; they represent a refusal to accept stigmatisation. Generally they form part of what, in a parody of the technical and sanitising vocabulary of linguistics and other academic disciplines, Leonard calls the 'extra-semantic kinetics of the poor'. That these 'extra-semantic' items are not peripheral or dispensable features of working-class speech is illustrated appropriately enough through an exchange with 'a linguist',[33] a romantic exile from working class life who has become part of the academic world and now feels nostalgic for the concreteness and authenticity of working-class speech ('ah wish I could talk like you/ahv lost my accent'). It's not just a loss of accent, however, as the speaker's response makes clear – other important features have been lost in the move up the social scale:

> thi crux iz says ah
> shiftin ma register
> tay speak tay a linguist
>
> would you swear tay swerr
> and not abjure
> the extra-semantic kinetics
> uv the fuckin poor

Despite the regret at losing it, there can be no return to working-class speech in its fullness for the linguist, not simply because acquired middle-class inhibitions would make that difficult, but because the speech itself grows out of and is a (legitimate and understandable) response to particular social circumstances. Because 'bad language' reflects the conditions of life of the poor and powerless, and expresses their anger, and refusal to accept their lot, to clean up working-class speech is to distort it, removing the uncomfortable evidence of social conflict. So, in a savage review of Albert Mackie's *Talking Glasgow*, Leonard dismisses it as

Another of those 'warm-hearted' linguistic racist affairs, where all of 'us' good middle-class or ex-working-class folk can sit back and have a good laugh at how 'they' working-class Glaswegians talk... Not a 'fuck' or a 'cunt' will disturb the pleasant time to be had by the reader! As is usually the case with this sort of production, not listening accurately is the necessary precondition for perpetuating the various cosy myths! But if you don't treat language seriously, you don't treat people seriously. Nowhere will real linguistic aggression or anger show alongside the of-course-always-bowdlerised 'humour'; the natives here are not even allowed the luxury of getting restless.[34]

The innovative methods Leonard employs to represent Glasgow dialect in print underline the radical differences between the spoken and written word. By 'writing the spoken' in this way, he reminds us that they are very unlike one another, and subverts our usual unthinking sense that there is a close (and unproblematic) relationship between what we say and the conventional written forms – a sense likely to be particularly strong among the highly literate minority who read contemporary poetry. Also, in lending the spoken the authority of print, he challenges the old-established but still powerful idea that the written is primary, that it is somehow more 'real', and embodies a standard of correctness to which speech ought to conform. Using the (traditionally authoritative) written/literary as a medium for the spoken, hence ironising or subverting the former is, in fact, an important part of Leonard's aesthetico-political agenda; to do this is to vindicate the experiences of speakers and speech communities which are unliterary, and in which the spoken word, the oral, is central. But Leonard's technical innovations are not just there to remind us that the spoken and the written are two different things: what is represented in Leonard's Glasgow poems, after all, is a dialect (or sociolect), and this underlines another important truth about spoken language in Scotland (and the British Isles generally), that the mother-tongue of most people is not the spoken standard, but a local speech variety, rooted in a particular area, social group and time. And to employ a poetic language which looks radically unlike the usual language of literary texts, and which the experienced reader has to make a special effort to interpret, suggests that the values of the community whose language it is may also differ significantly from those of 'literary' people. The 'strangeness' of both form and content is part of a deliberate strategy of unsettling readers and challenging their assumptions. So the last poem in *Six Glasgow Poems,* provocatively entitled 'Good Style',[35] begins by mocking the reader who has struggled with Leonard's unconventional presentation:

helluva hard tay read theez init
stull
if yi canny unnirston thim jiss clear aff then
gawn
get tay fuck ootma road

It is the literary reader, accustomed to dealing easily with the printed word, and with an interest in contemporary poetry, who is being addressed here: even he will have trouble decoding these poems. And the speaker anticipates that such a reader may feel that grappling with the poem will not be worth the trouble; after all, how could this uncultivated working-class voice have anything significant to say to one of the educated? The ironic implication is that though education and culture are both associated with open-mindedness, conventional education, and conventional definitions of 'culture' often stop exploration rather than encouraging it. The speaker of a stigmatised dialect gleefully takes his revenge on the educated reader, at the same time putting him for the moment in the same position as those who find it 'helluva hard tay read' the standard because it is alien to their dialect. In 'Fathers and Sons', the last poem in *Intimate Voices*,[36] the speaker movingly recalls his reaction to his own father's difficulties with print:

I remember being ashamed of my father
when he whispered the words out loud
reading the newspaper

The father belongs to a generation of working class men for whom the spoken word is the main and natural medium of communication, with writing and print only of marginal importance; as a result he can only follow the printed word by turning it into utterance. A single generation separates the father struggling with the printed word and the son at ease with it and in it (in the second and third sections of the poem, the speaker is giving a poetry reading); the contrast between the two is a reminder that it is only recently that effective schooling and wider educational opportunities have been

available in working-class communities. However what appears to
be a change for the better also has less attractive consequences: a
better education inevitably creates a cultural and linguistic separation between the generations, and may also encourage children to
feel superior, and look down on their parents. Ironically, a member
of the speaker's audience suggests that the poet's use of 'phonetic
urban dialect' may be limiting ('"Don't you find/the use of a phonetic urban dialect/rather constrictive?"'), voicing exactly the doubt
about the expressive possibilities of working-class speech which
had given rise to the poet's original shame at his father's apparent
limitations; the choice of medium is at once an expiation of guilt, a
positive affirmation of the speaker's working-class origins, and a
demonstration of the literary viability of his speech-based medium.

   Several of the Glasgow dialect poems present this division
between working-class parents and ex-working-class children from
the other side, giving a shrewd parent's-eye view of education. If
the picture of the father spelling out words in the newspaper is a
figure of pathos, the father in 'The Qualification'[37] is the opposite;
sharply aware of his own situation and of the state of society, he
comments sardonically on both the manipulation of news by the
mass media, and the 'revolutionary' ideas of his university-attend-
ing son. In a society dominated by the printed word, in which
those expert in using it acquire power and privilege, those less
comfortable with it tend to be stigmatised as 'illiterate', and the
possibility that they might be as perceptive as the educated – or
more so – is rarely entertained. The belief that those who are not
highly literate are ignorant or unaware or stupid is, however, challenged in the poem: the speaker is no dupe – he can see through
the manipulative techniques of the media, and recognise their anti-
working-class bias:

   wurk aw yir life
   nuthnty show
   pit oanthi nyuze
   same awl drivl

   yoonyin bashn
   wurkir bashn

His student son's revolutionary rhetoric ('shood hearma

boay/sayzwi need gunz/an armd revalooshn/nuthn else wurks')
seems something positive at first: maybe the next generation will
not settle for the kind of life he has had to lead. However the
rhetoric is dismissed as just that – universities are, after all, centres
of talk, not action, devoted (to rephrase Marx) to the task of understanding the world rather than changing it:

> awright fur him thoa
> uppit thi yooni
> tok aw yi like therr
> that's whit its fur

The social dimension of Leonard's use of contemporary urban
working-class speech as a poetic medium is important; one of his
aims in the Glasgow dialect poems is to convey the experience of
working-class life in that city in the second half of the twentieth
century, using the language of the people who live there. Leonard
modifies the conventions of the written standard in radical ways so
that they reflect as closely and accurately as possible the characteristics of Glasgow speech; as a result of this 'making strange' the
reader is reminded continuously of the oral roots of what is on the
page. Of course Leonard is not the first to make use of a working-
class Glasgow voice – or voices – because though all his speakers
use Glasgow Scots, we are made aware that age and gender add
their own inflections. In the first of the 'Unrelated Incidents'
sequence,[38] he has a critic of his work say that as the 'langwij a/the
guhtr', Glasgow Scots is 'awright fur/funny stuff' but not for 'luv n
science/n thaht..'; for these, English 'thi langwij/a thi/intillect' is
needed. There is a long, and continuing tradition of employing
Glasgow Scots for 'funny stuff' – the characteristic combination of
sharp observation, profanity, mordant humour and baroque fantasy
to be heard in Glasgow's streets and pubs has, for instance, been
exploited on stage by comedians like Billy Connolly. Connolly's
brilliance as a performer has much to do with his own creative talents, of course, but he also draws on a long tradition: the speech
of Scotland's biggest city has been a medium for stage comedy at
least since the rise of working-class forms of theatre like music hall
and variety in the late nineteenth century. Leonard's reference to
this tradition in 'Unrelated Incidents 1' is not disapproving, nor is it

intended to imply that the comic is necessarily less significant than the 'serious' (much of his own Glasgow poetry is funny in a variety of ways) – it is the *restriction* of Scots to the comic, with the corollary that it is incapable of expressing serious emotions or serving as a vehicle for exploring ideas, that he rejects.

Bringing the voice of urban working-class experience fully and directly into literature is one of Leonard's aims, but it is not the only one. The emphasis on the spoken word in much of his best work is part of a wider philosophical interest in all forms of art which incorporate reminders of the temporal and relative dimensions of the 'truth' they present. On the front cover of Leonard's first collection, *Intimate Voices: Selected Work 1965-1983*, is a poem which takes its title/first line from the beginning of St John's gospel, 'in the beginning was the word' (reminding us that our Christian heritage has made we Europeans a people of the book, and made the authority of the written word fundamental to our culture). The line is then subjected to a series of transformations by which the spelling becomes increasingly phonetic; as a result, it moves closer and closer to a language which is spoken and local, till with the penultimate line it has become 'nthibiginninwuzthiwurd'. The last line, 'in the beginning was the sound', returns to the standard English of the first, but flatly contradicts the claim it makes: in tracing the (written) word back to its roots in sound, the poem has shown its falsity. Sound is primary, and speech is the fundamentally creative language-activity; despite its superior prestige in literate societies, writing is ultimately dependent, even parasitic, upon the spoken word.

For Leonard, language, along with the rest of man's cultural and 'spiritual' achievements, has its ultimate origins in the body and the material world, and not in a 'higher' spiritual realm. Western societies are now largely secular, but the centuries-old habit of stigmatising the physical remains deeply embedded, and even those who reject it consciously may still be in the grip of its influence. It is Leonard's recognition of this which lies behind his comment on the fact that, while interest in oral traditions has grown in recent years,

> those most concerned to emphasise the importance of what is now called 'orature' are often the people most hostile to any indication of oral pronunciation. There is literature, and there is the oral. But there must be no vestige of the fact of orality emphasised in the transcription. This would

be as it were to move to the viscous, the existential, away from the Word as thing in itself which is pronounced. To indicate the act of the individual speaker in the utterance is to 'debase' the word and to question the common reality of that to which it refers.[39]

This resistance to including in the written record of the oral any reminder of its ultimate origins in the physical activity of speech has its (unrecognised) roots in the disparagement of the physical, and in the illusion that human creativity has its origins in a pure, lucid and eternal realm, a 'spiritual' world of 'things in themselves'. In the context of linguistic change and variation, such beliefs have often found expression in support for standardisation and a prescriptive approach to language use. Throughout history, the rapidity of linguistic change has caused anxious observers to look to the establishment of standard forms as a way of 'ascertaining' and 'fixing' the language; the aim is to make it exact, copious and stable, capable of reflecting clear and distinct categories and enduring and substantive realities. Swift's 'A Proposal for Correcting, Improving and Ascertaining the English Tongue' of 1712 is one of the best-known expressions of this desire:

> ...what I have most at heart, is that some Method should be thought on for Ascertaining and Fixing our Language for ever, after such alterations are made in it as shall be thought requisite. For I am of Opinion, that it better a Language should not be wholly perfect, that that it should be perpetually changing; and that we must give over at one Time or other, or at length infallibly change for the worse...[40]

The 'normalisation' of the oral and dialectal cuts off an utterance from its specific location in time, place and individual experience, so that it is made to seem 'timeless' and 'objective'. An orthography which represents dialect forms and structures, on the other hand, acts as a reminder that language is shaped in fundamental ways by region, class and historical moment – thus challenging the idea of a stable tradition, common national culture and shared social experience. Leonard argues that the writer who draws on the spoken word has an obligation to include such indications; only in this way can he remind the reader of the true origins of utterance in 'the viscous, the existential', demystify the 'Word as thing in itself', and challenge the idea that the written word is stable, objective and authoritative.

Leonard's challenge to conventional assumptions about language is part of a wider radicalism which leads him to reject some of the central beliefs of the European Christian tradition. Several poems illustrate the damaging effects of beliefs inculcated by Christianity, in particular the feeling that body and spirit are opposed, and that spiritual development depends on the denial of the 'flesh'. Beliefs like this are shown as distorting the lives and relationships of many of Leonard's speakers. And though religious views in the Glasgow area are sharply polarised – immigration brought an intense traditional Catholicism with its roots in rural Ireland into contact with a strongly Calvinist kind of protestantism – for Leonard, in their effects on individual human lives, the two traditions are indistinguishable. Both are puritanical and sexually repressive, and those brought up in them have difficulty in coming to terms with their bodies and their sexuality. Often religious conditioning arrests emotional growth and distorts sexual development. The title of 'The Hardmen'[41] refers to a specifically west of Scotland male subculture of swagger, violence and criminal activity – which the poem begins by linking with the distorting effects of both religious traditions:

noa sumhn

see Calvinism
see Catholicism
shame a thi body
sex

The parallel phrases invite the reader to agree that 'shame a thi body/sex' is fundamental to both traditions – and the use of 'Calvinism', which resembles 'Catholicism' more closely than the generic 'Protestantism', reinforces the idea that the two traditions are the same in their essentials. The poem outlines their part in the aetiology of the 'hardman' role, dismantling the idea that it represents a powerful kind of independent maleness. The hardmen are stuck in a kind of permanent adolescence; 'stull tiedty thir muthirz', they cannot form relationships with women, and their lives revolve round drinking heavily ('bevvyin') and macho displays of toughness. They are so ill at ease with themselves that the most basic communication with others is difficult: 'eevnthi wey they

tok/stifflike yi no/no moovna muscle/cowboyz.' The last comparison, together with the use of the word 'bandits' in the fourth section, and the imagined desert location of the ending, are a
reminder of the world of the western movie, and the influence of
its strong silent heroes on generations of young urban males. The
idea of immaturity is reinforced: small boys of Leonard's generation
(and mine) played incessantly at Cowboys and Indians. Though it
is a world in which violence rather than sex is the dominant
impulse, the world of the western movies is, nevertheless a homo-
erotic one centring, like that of the hardmen, on 'adolescent' same-
sex relationships rather than on 'adult' relationships between men
and women. The Freudian idea that homosexuality is a result of
normal sexual development being arrested at a pre-adult stage is
implicit in the poem: the obsessive homophobia of the hardmen
('they aw hate queerz') and their exaggerated maleness, are symptoms of their own unacknowledged homosexuality, and appropriately the poem ends with a mock-solemn warning from the older
speaker to his young hearer:

geeyi a tip sun
fyirivir stucknthi dezirt
stuckwia Glasweejin
a hardman

noa sumhn
wotchyir bawz

'A Love Poem'[42] deals with an individual (and more representative)
case. The speaker reflects wryly on the way in which cultural and
religious influences complicate basic human feelings. In the
European tradition, love is linked with the romantic ideal, defined
(unpromisingly) as a 'yernin/fur thaht conceived az/uniquely innocent' based in 'thi self conceived az/uniquely guilty'. As if that were
not difficult enough, ideals of womanhood in working-class
Catholic communities are simultaneously restrictive and contradictory; recalling his 'dependence on ma maw/thi virgin mary/our
lady uv the sink', the speaker complains that 'ma idea a wum-
min/wuz screwed up fray birth'. The identification of mother and
Virgin denies female sexuality (the secularised equivalent is the
romantic idea of the beloved as 'uniquely innocent'), while 'our

lady uv the sink' ironically reflects the traditional religious view of women as being at their noblest when sacrificing themselves to family and domesticity. Women as independent, sexual beings do not figure in either the religious ideal of the feminine, or the romantic ideal derived from it. Exposed to confused and contradictory ideas about love and women from an early age, it is not surprising that the lover is unclear about his feelings and desires, and cannot express them. The conclusion of the poem has a kind of desperate comedy about it; the tongue-tied lover imagines himself hooked up to a lie-detector and subject to interrogation about whether 'ah really luv you' (the self, we remember, is 'conceived az/uniquely guilty'). But even in these circumstances, he cannot imagine making a direct avowal, and takes refuge – in characteristically male fashion – in a technological 'solution' to his emotional problem:

    wur sumdy tay ask me
    if ah really luv you

    an hooked me up
    tay a lie detector
     ahm really convinced

    thit thi graphic printout
    would scientifically prove
    thi quality uv ma emotion.

On the socio-political level, Leonard exposes the role of organised religion as a mechanism of social control, ironically contrasting the radical social origins of Christianity and its egalitarian message with what the churches have made of it. His frequent references to Catholic-Protestant antagonism in West-Central Scotland serve as a reminder of how religion has been used by politicians to keep the working-class divided and maintain an unjust and exploitative social system. His criticism of institutional Christianity is forcefully summed up in 'Feed Ma Lamz',[43] a contemporary Ten Commandments promulgated by a god who identifies himself in terms of the hierarchy of the industrial work-place ('Amyir gaffirz Gaffir. Hark!'), and who delivers his commands with the threatening jocularity of a factory overseer or army sergeant. The medium

for this contemporary Decalogue is strongly urban and demotic
using, for instance, rhyming slang ('thou shalt not steal' – colloquial-
ly 'no thieving' – becomes 'nay tea-leaven') and abbreviations from
world of crime and the courts: 'thou shalt not kill' does not figure
in Leonard's list, but is replaced by 'nay g.b.h.', which prohibits the
infliction of grievous bodily harm, the legal term for serious
assault, with the politically convenient qualification 'septina wawr'.
In form, 'Feed Ma Lamz' is a list of prohibitions, each beginning
with 'nay' (conveniently both a biblical negative and a phonetic
rendering of the Scots pronunciation of 'no'), emphasising the negative and repressive character of the morality of both Catholic and
Protestant traditions in Scotland. Inevitably, we read the list with
the original Commandments – and Christ's remark about false
teachers who give stones rather than bread to their hearers – in
mind, recognising it as a travesty of the original. In contrast to
Christianity with its message of universal love and brotherhood,
this creed is founded on division and exclusion; its first command-
ment is 'nay fornirz ur communists'. It aims to control behaviour
down to the smallest detail, forbidding any expression of dissent
through bad language or verbal defiance ('nay langwij/nay lip'),
and it separates joy from holiness ('nay laffn ina Sunday'). Despite
the contemporary voice, this is a revengeful and bloodthirsty Old
Testament god of prohibitions and threats of eternal damnation –
the poem ends with the ferocious humour of

> Stick way it
> -rahl burn thi lohta yiz.

Leonard does not attack the churches because he rejects the
Christian ethic, but because, in his view, they have done so: their
collusion with the rich and powerful and support for 'just' wars are
a betrayal of Christian values. His poems show moral goodness
and spiritual worth as things which are more likely to be found
among the oppressed and outcast than among the godly and
respectable. 'The Good Thief', the best-known of the original *Six
Glasgow Poems*[44] is his most memorable expression of this belief.
A reworking of the story of the two thieves crucified with Christ in
Luke 23: 39-43, it is spoken by the thief who recognises the injustice of Christ's punishment and who is rewarded by Our Lord with

the promise: 'Today shalt thou be with me in Paradise'. Set at the culminating moment of the Passion narrative, Luke's story lends strong emphasis to the New Testament idea of a latent spirituality which is to be found more often in lowly, the outcast, or even the criminal (the thief emphasises that he *is* a thief and not a victim of society), than in the privileged and educated. While the respectable Jews have called on Pilate to crucify Christ, the tormented victim of the law is able, even in his own last extremity, to recognise the divinity in Christ and testify to it. In the transposition from Golgotha to Glasgow, from the ancient Near East to contemporary Scotland, some of the miraculous details of the original story are 'normalised'; the darkness 'at the sixth hour' has no apocalyptic significance; it is merely the failing light of a Scottish winter afternoon. Leonard also changes the story considerably: there is no hint here of the light of Paradise. This thief is not eloquent, nor does he refer to his companion's innocence and divinity. The emphasis is on the human – the poem is an awkward, uneloquent expression of sympathy – showing a concern which appears more through the speaker's silence about his own suffering, and his steady attention to his fellow-victim, than through explicitly comforting words:

    heh jimmy
    yawright ih
    stull wayiz urryi
    ih

Impressive though this is, the limits of his compassion are also revealed:

    heh jimmy
    ma right insane yirra pape
    ma right insane yirwanny us jimmy
    see it nyir eyes
    wanny uz

Though the dialect-spelling of 'wanny uz' might suggest that 'uz' is everyone in the working class speech-community, it is clear that fellow-feeling extends only to a section of it – those who are Roman Catholics (the Christ-figure is identified as a 'pape', a papist). Sectarian divisions stand in the way of working-class unity, weakening efforts to change society; the working-class remain victims. With its references to 'thi GEMM' (the game), 'three a cloke' (the standard afternoon kick-off time) and 'thi lights', the end of the poem brings in the great urban working-class passion, professional soccer – a passion particularly strong in Glasgow, where even sport is divided along sectarian lines. At the end of the poem, the speaker looks at death with the stoical humour of a heroic-age warrior; his main regret in dying is missing the big match ('lookslik wirgonny miss thi gemm'). This both reveals how deep the passion for football runs in this community – it is almost a substitute religion – and underlines the fact that it is the pleasures of this life which matter to the speaker, not the prospect of heaven.

In the poem, crucifixion and criminality are, of course, metaphorical – the first refers to the effects of poverty on the human spirit, the second to the related fact that in both the subjective and objective circumstances of their lives it is as if the poor are suffering punishment for some serious offence. The same metaphor is employed in one of Leonard's shortest pieces: entitled 'Cold, Isn't It',[45] which alludes to another, earlier stage in the Passion story:

> wirraw init thigither missyz
> geezyir kross

This is Leonard's most condensed expression of his central vision. A male voice addressing a struggling, overburdened woman, it reaches across another of the divisions often reflected in Leonard's Glasgow poems, suggesting a possible new beginning in the relations between the sexes. The offer is individual, but the gesture originates in an idea of community ('wirraw init thigither'). In the first instance, the community is the working-class people of Glasgow, but the standard English of the title suggests that the difficulties and discomforts of life are experienced by everybody, even though some – women, the poor – have a particularly hard time of it. The allusion to Christ's words in Matthew 20: 19 – 'Thou shalt love thy neighbour as thyself' – is unmistakable: like Blake, another 'working-class' poet with a highly individual vision, Leonard combines fierce anti-clericalism and hostility to institutional religion, with a vision of community, solidarity and mutual aid which owes a great deal to the gospels.

608 COLIN MILTON

NOTES

[1] Edwin Morgan, 'Glasgow Speech in Recent Scottish Literature', in J.D. McClure ed., *Scotland and the Lowland Tongue*, Aberdeen: Aberdeen University Press, 1983, p. 195.

[2] J.D. McClure, *Language, Poetry and Nationhood: Scots as a Poetic Language from 1878 to the Present,* Phantassie, East Linton: Tuckwell, 2000, p. 172.

[3] *Intimate Voices: Selected Work 1965-1983*, Newcastle: Galloping Dog Press, 1984; *Radical Renfrew: Poetry From the French Revolution to the First World War by Poets Born or Sometime Resident in the County of Renfrewshire*, Edinburgh: Polygon, 1990; *Places of the Mind: the Life and Work of James Thomson* ('B.V.'), London: Jonathan Cape, 1992; *Reports from the Present: Selected Work 1982-1994*, London: Jonathan Cape, 1995.

[4] Tom Leonard, *Six Glasgow Poems*, Glasgow: Midnight Publications, 1969.

[5] J.D. McClure, *op. cit.*, pp. 172-173.

[6] Edwin Morgan, *op. cit.*, p. 205.

[7] *Ibidem*, p. 195.

[8] William Grant, 'Introduction', *Scottish National Dictionary*, Edinburgh: Scottish National Dictionary Association, 1931, I, p. xxvii.

[9] Tom Leonard, *Reports from the Present*, cit., p. 41.

[10] David Buchan, *Scottish Tradition: a Collection of Scottish Folk Literature*, London: Routledge, 1984, p. 13.

[11] Charles Murray, *Hamewith*, London: Constable & Co., 1909.

[12] Lewis Grassic Gibbon, *Sunset Song*, London: Jarrolds, 1932.

[13] William McIlvanney, *Docherty*, London: Allen & Unwin, 1975.

[14] Tom Leonard, *Intimate Voices*, cit., p. 36.

[15] *Ibidem*, p. 89.

[16] *Ibidem*, p. 37.

[17] *Ibidem*, pp. 95-96.

[18] *Ibidem*, p. 88.

[19] Tom Leonard, *Reports from the Present*, cit., p. 17.

[20] G.M. Young, *Victorian England: Portrait of an Age*, London: Oxford University Press, 1960, p. 186.

[21] C.M. Grieve ('Hugh MacDiarmid'), 'A Theory of Scots Letters', reprinted in *The Thistle Rises: An Anthology of Poetry and Prose by Hugh MacDiarmid*, edited by Alan Bold, London: Hamish Hamilton,

1984, pp. 125-141, and pp. 126-127.

[22] Tom Leonard, *Reports from the Present*, cit., pp. 35-36.

[23] *Ibidem*, p. 36.

[24] *Ibidem*, p. 34.

[25] *Ibidem*, p. 40.

[26] *Ibidem*, p. 40.

[27] Edwin Morgan, *op. cit.*, p. 197.

[28] *Ibidem*, p. 199.

[29] *Ibidem*, p. 201.

[30] Robert Crawford and Mick Imlah eds., *The New Penguin Book of Scottish Verse,* London: Penguin Books, 2000, p. 540.

[31] Tom Leonard, *Intimate Voices*, cit., p. 53.

[32] *Ibidem*, p. 120.

[33] *Ibidem*, p. 113.

[34] Quoted in Edwin Morgan, *op. cit.*, p. 206.

[35] Tom Leonard, *Intimate Voices*, cit., p. 14.

[36] *Ibidem*, p. 140.

[37] *Ibidem*, p. 50.

[38] *Ibidem*, p. 86.

[39] Tom Leonard, *Reports from the Present*, cit., p. 68.

[40] Jonathan Swift, 'A Proposal for Correcting, Improving and Ascertaining the English Language', in Tony Crowley ed., *Proper English? Readings in Language: History and Cultural Identity*, London: Routledge, 1991, pp. 30-41 and p. 37.

[41] Tom Leonard, *Intimate Voices*, cit., p. 58.

[42] *Ibidem*, p. 133.

[43] *Ibidem*, p. 46.

[44] *Ibidem*, p. 9.

[45] *Ibidem*, p. 11.

COLIN NICHOLSON

Edwin Morgan's Sonnets From Scotland*:*
Towards a Republican Poetics

Italy figures significantly (and variously) in Morgan's output, as it does historically in Scottish writing,[1] not least for its Renascence identification of rhymed, harmonious utterance as song; grounding a labile template in language and form for subsequent European lyricists. Since the inventor of this extensible instrument had been interested in the whole of Europe, Morgan comments, 'it is fitting that his influence should be widely felt, from Scotland to Cyprus, from Portugal to Hungary.' So when he uses Petrarch to frame urban dereliction as lived, twentieth-century experience, he is already shattering the 'glaze of the ideal' Petrarch laboured to effect.[2] Preserving its outline, 'Glasgow Sonnets' (1972) strips a Renascence practice of its conventional furniture, designing instead Scottish interiors to mobilise disruptive metre against high cultural assumption. But 'stalled lives never budge', and the last of ten city sonnets measures a 'they' against an 'us' to bring into focus tenement children in living conditions 'that use/their spirit to the bone':

>   and when they trudge
>   from closemouth to laundrette their steady shoes
>   carry a world that weighs us like a judge.[3]

In 'Glasgow Sonnets' the rhyme pattern carries a world whose rhythms weigh it like a judge. In *Sonnets From Scotland* (1984), Morgan re-invents the form, deploying an *abbacddcefgefg* pattern of his own devising to frame expeditions into strange places where free-floating, time-travelling speakers construct a space-time continuum for alternative takes on Scotland's imaginable pasts, presents and futures. Within and across this innovative schema of self-management, metaphorical land management can return to first princi-

ples: 'Immensities/are mind, not ice, as the bright straths
unfreeze.'[4] Extending Scottish particularities of territorial identification and cultural relationship, temporality is sequenced while occasion is both locally specific and differentially reconstructive, displaying the 'sense of a more intellectual attack, the apparently
more intense, troubled, and boldly speculative deploying of emotion' that Morgan finds elsewhere.[5] The first of the fifty-one poems
to be written for this project, 'The Solway Canal' identifies an engi-
neering possibility that would put clear blue water as the border
with England and is, Morgan comments: 'obviously, connected
with Scotland's identity and place, its reality or non-reality as a
nation.' The collection grew out of that and a need to address
more fully the impulse to self-government that seemingly crashed
in the Referendum of 1979, when a Scottish majority in favour of
devolutionary change failed to meet the 40% of the total poll set as
threshold by a Westminster Parliament:

> There was a sense of political numbness after that. I had been hoping
> that there would be an Assembly, and the sense of let-down was very
> strong. But despite that, or maybe even because of it, the 1980s have
> been a very prolific period for Scottish writing, both in the novel and in
> poetry. I felt impelled to write a lot in the eighties and this sequence was
> the first fruits of that.[6]

Interpellating the reconfigured cultural history and historical culture it projects, a flexible evolutionary frame for this serial act of
reinforcement, from first formation on the earth's crust to future
political republic, produces a sonnet-sequence like no other, dis-
tributed as a performative Scottish assemblage across time, and
developing an interactive force-field since described as a key work
of the post-Referendum period.[7]

   Spoken from the endless perspective of what might be Time
Lords, a strong sense of let down is the measure in the first poem's
earth science activation of extensible parameters, for post-referendum disappointment to find geological expression: 'Drumlins [long
whaleback mounds of glacial deposit] blue as/bruises were grated
off like nutmegs'. That is a large hurt and Morgan is anxious to put
it to use: 'Slate' exits on an emergent, surreal landscape impatiently
kicking its heels.[8] Later on the evolutionary scale, when what
might be a dolphin speaks 'Carboniferous', what would become

one of Glasgow's middle-class, residential districts, Bearsden, is still ocean. Flexing a textual archaeology suitable to his purposes, Morgan uses it to reconstitute fear of difference – "*Et in Arcadia,* said the shark,/*ego*" – and to measure the self-doubt signalled in the recent devolution vote:

> We feared instead the force that could inter
> such life and joy, in fossil clays, for apes
> and men to haul into their teeming heads.[9]

To disinter that promise, 'Post-Glacial' melts stalled movement into renewal:

>   when mild rains
> drive back the blizzards, a new world it is
> of grain that thrusts its frenzied spikes, and trees
> whose roots race under the stamped-out remains
> of nomad Grampian fires.[10]

Scotland's complicated linguistic inheritance identifies Argyle as the region where Ireland's mission to spread Celtic religion and language was begun in the middle of the sixth century. Columba had a biblically scripted Jesus (and an enchanted world) for his empowering text: in a window-opening association, 'In Argyle' finds on a beach there the skull of a Sumerian poet, and elegises him as the maker of the stone-carved cuneiform *Gilgamesh* epic about powerful Middle Eastern passions and a quest for immortality: 'Now he needs neither claws nor tongue to tell/of things undying. Hebridean light/fills the translucent bone-domes'.[11] Two millennia separate a figure of the same name who ruled in southern Mesopotamia and the version of *Gilgamesh* found at Nineveh and dateable to the middle of the sixth century BC. Morgan, whose version of this narrative of male bonding and loss recognises a hero 'immortal only in the words he left',[12] knows scripted transmission of origin and early record as an irreducible combination of narrative invention and memory, encrypting into myth (like the text and stories Columba came to read and tell) when they combine into reference-systems for evolving life-worlds. Since language fixes memory, speculative narration includes immortality signifiers as a function of grammar:

> Nothing brings
> the savage brain back to its empty shell,
> distracted by the shouts, the reefs, the night,
> fighting sleet to fix the tilt of his wings.[13]

In Morgan's reconstructive continuities, the skull 'watches west-ward still.' By pluralising the speaker of Hugh MacDiarmid's poem 'Perfect' and rewriting its first line, 'I found a pigeon's skull on the machair' as 'We found the poet's skull on the machair',[14] the sonnet mobilises other fables of invention. 'Perfect' led to a charge of pla-giarism being levelled against MacDiarmid:[15] in Morgan's handling it becomes one of the ways writing enters other writing; slippage embedded in crafted form, and an example of the legendary (what is read) speaking prior text. Myths of identity are just that, systems of collective self-recognition that delimit by pre-scribing possibility, and the skull-discoverer who speaks 'In Argyll' stretches locally scripted time for a rewriting as infinitive continuity – 'to fix the tilt of its wings' – of MacDiarmid's 'Perfect' closure.

In the sequence's analytic, Columba and Kentigern (traditionally Glasgow's first bishop), break off their 'Colloquy in Glaschu' in sur-prise at hearing a Highland fighter appropriating Latin song: their story is already developing in ways then unforeseen. Tangential and speculative relationship to scripted and imagined event, instan-tiated in alternative rhythms of measurement, bring into play some of the ways in which the measuring time of recorded event becomes a reality on account of the emergence of measurement itself – story becoming history as conventionally written and received. Energising the making of story in its own right (and trig-gering the sequence's epigraph about changing times being the hope of the people), 'Memento' includes the term for chalk circles that Brecht made famous, and postpones its verb until the penulti-mate line of its mission 'over the hills and far away to bring/over the hills and far away to mind'.[16] Reality as the clock ticks is radi-cally adjusted when 'The Ring of Brodgar' viewed through a 'timeprint' unearthed in a distant future brings into play the largest megalithic circle in Scotland; originally 60 stones (the tallest 4.5 metres) chopped out of rock by pre-Bronze-Age people then living on Orkney, carefully placed in possible relation to lunar or astral observation and evidently arranged according to specific measure-

ment. The standing stones of the Picts take us back to a now vanished precursor society and to early stirrings in a complex process
of kingdom-making by which, Michael Lynch reminds us, 'a cluster
of different peoples – Britons and even some Scandinavians as
well as Picts and Scots – came in the ninth and tenth centuries to
owe common allegiance to a single king, "of Scots"'.[17] 'If those
stones could speak' – is all an interlocutor has time to utter when
Morgan projects this initiating bricolage; interrupted for the
timeprint 'with truths to bring/into the freer ages' – to deliver grim
senses of living and dying among real people in a harsh time to a
construing audience, and left echoing sounds of the real to helpless listeners:

> A thin groan fought the wind that tugged the stones.
> It filled an auditorium with pain.
> Long was the sacrifice. Pity ran, hid.
> Once they heard the splintering of the bones
> they switched the playback off, in vain, in vain.[18]

Moving in and out of dateable event and speculative fiction, as
successful ideologies customarily do, the sequence weaves a variously connecting record in its own account. Around a 2,000 year
old yew tree in the graveyard at Fortingall in Fife, and a nearby
rectangular site defended by ditches, a legend developed identifying the site as Pontius Pilate's birth-place: 'They told us he sat here
beneath the yew/even in downpours; ate dog-scraps. Crows
flew/from prehistoric stone to stone all day'. In endless parody of
governing betrayal as an abdication of personal responsibility, as it
shifts orality into print, this apocryphal tale dramatises linguistic
cross-pollination – here figured as 'a Latin harsh with Aramaicisms'
– shaping a Scottish utterance, and satirising obsessive guilt:

> He crawled to the cattle-trough
> at dusk, jumbled the water till it sloshed
> and spilled into the hoof-mush with blue strands,
> slapped with useless despair each sodden cuff,
> and washed his hands, and watched his hands, and washed
> his hands, and watched his hands, and washed his hands.[19]

As Morgan generates alternative political sensibility, inherited
belief-systems and genealogies fabled or otherwise are up for

appropriation; and he scrutinises his own procedures. For Time
Lords recording earthly event from deep space, codes of representation articulating preferred productions of meaning are topic when
'The Mirror' refracts lived experience through speaking and script-
ing systems, and slippage is the order of the day: 'The multitudes
of the world cannot know/they are reflected there; like glass they
lie/in glass, shadows in shade'.[20] Lying in glass is nicely ambiguous
for breath that fades and language that mirrors its own production;
evanescent and renewable, delusive and of determining power.
Witness Tacitus in *Agricola*; part biography, part eulogy, part history of his father-in-law's conquests, translating into his own tongue
the Pictish King Calgacus – 'Do you imagine that the Romans' bravery in war matches their dissoluteness in time of peace? No! It is
our quarrels and disunion that have given them fame'. Scripted
utterance becomes differently extensible when 'they create a deso-
lation and call it peace' resonates a continuing emotional wilderness.[21] In answerable gesture, 'names as from outer space, names
without roots' are written out in 'The Picts', where an origin myth
based on a culture that has vanished as effectively as the blue dye
with which its warriors painted their bodies, retains imaginative
appeal: 'writers/like us regain mere pain on that blue road,/they
think honour comes with the endurance'.[22] In Morgan's scriptorium
the record shows endurance as a tested attribute. It needs to be: on
the distant threshold of the Gutenberg galaxy, 'Matthew Paris'
(1200-1259), in quotation marks to appropriate his putative utterance for Scottish verse, shows terms of description and points of
reference in early versions of Scotland's story developing within
perspectives and parameters centred elsewhere. Paris, whose
Historia Anglorum included Scottish territory, and for whom the
north 'is great and strange, a mouth of baleen [whale] filtering the
unknown', is left bemused if curious – but waiting to colonise textual space: 'their element, my margin, waits'.[23] He in turn forms a
thread in Morgan's firmly tethered, sometimes surreal and inven-
tively open-ended design; as does the Italian optimist who survived flying off the battlements 'At Stirling Castle, 1507'. Elliptical
and cross-fertilising connections inscribed in *Sonnets From
Scotland* are implicatory and provocative, as they accumulate a
ringing clarity of attitude. Morgan writes a permissive constitution

for subjectivity, while traceable histories unfold. Milton politicised the English sonnet in helpful ways and Morgan acknowledges the debt; but Puritan ethics are another matter. Reversing an assumed flow of influence, inverted commas insert the testimony of a Scottish theologian from the generation after Knox, an impeccable Calvinist, anti-Episcopalian propagandist and a 'strong sound sergeant of the creed', one 'Thomas Young, M.A. (St Andrews)' who taught the young Milton: 'He never understood predestination,/but then who does, within the English nation?'. Young's textualised memory redirects Miltonic phrasing towards present relevance: 'John could only ask how God was served/by those who neither stand nor wait, their ardour/rabid (he said) to expunge virtue's seed'.[24]

A religious history is also a political history that divided people in what sometimes broke out as civil war entailing brutal domestic effect. Aristocratic ruthlessness and the abuse of women are personalised in 'Lady Grange on St Kilda', whose death was announced in Edinburgh, 1731, and a mock funeral staged by her husband, then Lord Justice Clerk of Scotland, and brother of the 6th Earl of Mar, a leading figure in the 1715 rising. After threatening to expose continuing Jacobite activity, Rachel Chiesley was spirited away to offshore islands and kept incommunicado for the rest of her life: 'so strong/they thought I was and so I am'.[25] Resistance to locally determining power speaks its difference as a disclosure and refusal of male practice and preference that implicates monarchist politics in effectively negative ways. The textual body politic assembling here is as gapped and fissured as any other on offer; but if there is a structuring principle to *Sonnets From Scotland* other than its generalised temporal sequencing it is, as Cairns Craig recognised, prospective inclusiveness: 'assert[ing] the interactions rather than the oppositions of Scotland's divided linguistic inheritance… recovering the Scottish past as a *totality* rather than as a series of fragments, as an inner dialectic (and a dialogue of dialects).' Craig points out that by bringing into conversation together James Hutton, an Edinburgh geologist who recognised the igneous nature of rock formation and, in *A Theory of the Earth* (1785), helped lay the basis for modern geology, with his contemporary Robert Burns, Morgan's speculative fiction co-ordinates poetic Scots and rational English, sometimes held to be an operative division in Scottish culture since the eighteenth century.[26] In the interactive union of its transactions, 'Theory of the Earth' reconstitutes geologist as man of imagination and, in closing lines that nicely catch the vanishing of detail, reconstructs Burns's 'A Red, Red Rose' in the light of scientific discovery. Inclusion of Hutton's 'We find no vestige of a beginning,/no prospect of an end' stretches scripted temporality for them both; linking internally with the sequence's opening phrase 'There is no beginning', and perhaps sub-textually with De Quincey.[27] As well as a complex, evolving rootedness, real-time visitors to Morgan's home city bring into issue mobility, invention and adaptation; figured now as a Glasgow lad with the world all before him enlisting as cabin-boy's assistant and setting off for Arnheim with 'Poe in Glasgow'; now as a radically stoned 'De Quincey in Glasgow' (but at the time semi-permanently in another country of the mind), conjuring vengeful visions of a city graveyard known locally as the Necropolis:

> Its crowded tombs rise jostling, living, thronged
> With shadows, and the granite-bloodying glow
> Flares on the dripping bronze of a used kris.[28]

Different aspects of that shadow world strike G.M. Hopkins, 'melted/by bulk and warmth and unimposed rough grace', moving through 'Irish Glasgow' slums and troubling his Jesuit superiors by flirting with radical politics after witnessing the street-level effects of a nineteenth-century's jealous god: 'Industry's pauperism singed his creed'.[29] Together with De Quincey's melodrama (and each of the sonnets), a sensitive and repressed Englishman moving through an alien sound-world he finds non-threatening is both dialectally and dialogically engaged in Morgan's project. As, differently, is George Seferis gaily sniffing Greek air on a Scottish island: 'he thought the dancing sea, the larks, the boats/spoke out as clear as from Aegean throats'. Freely associating on Eigg, Seferis remembers reading about Walter Scott 'purloin[ing] a suffocated clansman's skull'; thinks of him as a 'tawdry Ulysses'; recalls that 'crowns of Scottish kings were sacred'; and by refusing the hierarchies they symbolised, enlists in the civil society of the sequence: 'who misses/them, peasants, slaves? Greeks too could shrug the cull'.[30]

Morgan is a real-world analyst: Seferis would not survive to speak on his island if the West of Scotland were targeted by nuclear weapons. Bringing home the possible consequences of so much annihilating hardware packed into small geographical space, and implicitly returning political self-determination as an urgent priority, blasted hopes reconfigure a serial apocalypse; projecting Jehovah the Destroyer as nuclear-armed male locating the region as 'The Target'; and life persisting in a distant future 'After Fallout'. The closing lines of 'A Golden Age' counsel resilience: 'in thistle days/a strengthened seed outlives the hardest blasts',[31] thereby individuating the 'millions of seeds' blown through a devastated Edinburgh in 'The Age of Heracleum'.[32] 'Computer Error: Neutron Strike' transforms the horn that stirred Columba and Kentigern into 'an automatic foghorn', whose light 'warned out to none below, and none above'.[33]

***

'Theory of the Earth' dramatises an operative conjunction between the English of the Enlightenment intellectual and the Scots of the ploughman poet.[34] When a slowly mobilising Glaswegian realises that his street-fighting friends are drunkenly incapable, 'Gangs' traces a subsequent development to deliver a clear understanding and bristling, street-wise refusal of contemporary governing priorities and their anodyne (and repressive) formulations by moving from threatening group to the etymology Burns knew, of 'gangs' as movement, journeyings: 'Ah'm oan ma tod. But they'll no take a len/a me, Ah'm no deid yet, or deif, or dumb'.[35] Which makes the poem's urgent demotic an energising location for the sequence's optimistic conspectus. In the public address of this explicitly political collection, activating speech opens 'The Ring of Brodgar'; and in 'Silva Caledonia' explorers lost in the legendary darkness of Scotland's primeval forests, hoping to hear native voices they have heard before, shape a parable for the present when they sense impending movement:

> up above, a sense of wings, of flight,
> of clattering, of calls through fog. Yet men,
> going about invisible concerns,

are here, and our immoderate delight
waits to see them, and hear them speak, again.[36]

In concert with the voices remembered here; with the conversation
overheard in 'Colloquy in Glaschu'; with the 'hoarse voice singing
come love watch with me[37] of folk-singer and song writer Matt
McGinn who died two years before the Referendum; with imps of
time leaping and vibrating across the universe like cosmic tam-
bourines in 'Travellers (1)';[38] and a broken-winged Angel in 'Post-
Referendum' who stirs to 'hear a meeting sing', 'Gangs' dramatises
a combative vitality for self-identifying sound-worlds in the face of
invasive – and subordinating – English discursive practice.

The divisions and self-divisions a complicating linguistic and
cultural inheritance has bequeathed as cultural mytheme to Scottish
self-scrutiny and its representations are entertainingly abolished
when 'Caledonian Antisyzygy' pushes sonnet to ludic limit in a
series of idiomatic jokes; transforming Scottish reference into
tabloid cant and television trash – 'Doctor knocks box talks./Claims
T.V. favours Grim Duo, Burke, Hare' – and listens instead for
responsive speech:

> – Right, join hands. Make sure the door is locked, or
> nothing will happen. – Dark yet? – Cover clocks.
> – Knock. – Listen! – Is there anybody there?[39]

Deriving playful possibility from prior text, '1983' includes limerick
to rewrite 'a parrot Edward Lear drew has just died' as the parrot's
testimony to Lear's exuberance. Listening to the 'infinitely various
waters' of Scotland's coast-line, 'A Place of Many Waters' bubbles a
plenitude 'true/as change is true'.[40] In refusal of pre-constituted fixity, and making story out of 'The Solway Canal' trope that separates Scotland at its English border, 'Outward Bound' (and *Sonnets
From Scotland* generally) reverses the political implosion of
'Inward Bound' by 'mov[ing] on pure sound' to stimulate recognitions in a responsive geography:

> Greenland twisted round to hear it, Key West
> whistled, waved, Lanzarote's ashy face
> cracked open with laughter. There was no ground
> of being, only being, sweetest and best.[41]

'A simulacrum, a dissolving view?' asks the following poem, whose tropic resourcefulness grounds experience against conceptual dominance:

> It seemed as solid as a terrier
> Shaking itself dry from a brisk black swim
> In the reservoir of Jupiter's grim
> Crimson trustless eye.[42]

Meanwhile structures of feeling, like the 'unforeseen reluctance' shared by departing visitors in the final poem, inscribe their certifying presence in uncertain medium: 'like a slate we could not clean/of characters, yet could not read, or write/our answers on, or smash, or take with us'.[43]

So *Sonnets From Scotland* earns its prospective celebrations. In the mirror of time, Glasgow imagined as a 'Clydegrad' of the future resists any pre-determined destination, even by free-floating signifiers that programme sameness as choice: 'where will they arrive/with all, boat, city, earth, like them, afloat?';[44] in answerably surreal projection, Scotland 'On Jupiter' chides the silence of political withdrawal at a time of possible movement:

> and if the land had launched its own life out
> among the echoes of inhuman air,
> its launchers were asleep, or had withdrawn,
> throwing their stick into a sea of doubt.[45]

Elsewhere stockades, schiltrons, spears and 'forced ranks' compose an embattled context for 'The Poet in the City' to derive from scavenging city gulls his dream of an existentialism without angst: 'of freedom with all guilts and fears unfelt';[46] and for 'After a Death'[47] to touch a personal candour of love and loss and memory of both. Further on in time 'The Coin' redeems the one that 'clattered at the end of its spin' to close 'Post-Referendum', by producing out of numismatic inscription a science-fiction parable of self-defining statehood: 'Respublica Scotorum'. Read by departing space visitors as sign of a temporary soundlessness, the date has been worn away because, our speaker realises as he climbs into his machine:

> as many fingers had gripped hard
> as hopes their silent race had lost or gained.

> The marshy scurf crept up to our machine,
> sucked at our boots. Yet nothing seemed ill-starred.
> And least of all the realm the coin contained.[48]

Imagining past futures and future pasts for these re-locations of
culture, as it garners a complex politics to represent a complex
phenomenon *Sonnets From Scotland* delivers a studiedly transhis-
torical and an habitually transcontextual project, charting a thereby
intertextually historicised republic. Bound to their titular theme by
going forth from specific place to multiply with a wit and will sufficient for any Old Testament advisor, these voices, visions and
appearances in an imagined community are the personalities and
events that constitute its evolving body politic. Colloquial register
and sophisticated rhetoric articulate an open society of individually
self-identifying and cross-referential language-use, and construct a
collective expectation. Guiding complicating syntax through conversational rhythms to keep the logically formal and the dynamical-
ly transfigurative in operational conjunction acts as technical guarantee for an inventive multiplicity of speaking and spoken subjects.
An unusual interplay of subjectivity, agency and time stages an historical society of powerful imaginers, and a reminder that the ability to imagine is itself close to the core of Morgan's meaning is to
the point.[49] Perhaps that is why the final sonnet issues a
'Summons' to political awakening. When time-travellers register
their reluctance to leave, the sequence echoes its other horns and
reconstructs conventional sonnet cycle topic:

> If it was love we felt, would it not keep,
> and travel where we travelled? Without fuss
> we lifted off, but as we checked and talked
> a far horn grew to break that people's sleep.[50]

NOTES

[1] See R.D.S. Jack, *The Italian Influence on Scottish Literature*,
Edinburgh: Edinburgh University Press, 1972, and *Scottish Literature's
Debt to Italy*, Edinburgh: Edinburgh University Press, 1986, pp. 49-54.
[2] Edwin Morgan, 'Fifty Renascence Love Poems', in *Collected*

Translations, Manchester: Carcanet, 1996, pp. 161-162.

3 Edwin Morgan, 'Glasgow Sonnets', in *Collected Poems*, Manchester: Carcanet, 1990, p. 292.

4 Edwin Morgan, *Sonnets From Scotland*, Glasgow: Mariscat Press, 1984, p. 11. For convenience hereafter referenced in the relevant pages of *Collected Poems*, p. 438.

5 Edwin Morgan, *Collected Translations*, cit., p. 160.

6 Edwin Morgan, interviewed in my *Poem, Purpose and Place*, Edinburgh: Polygon, 1992, p. 76.

7 Cairns Craig, *Out of History: Narrative Paradigms in Scottish and British Culture*, Edinburgh: Polygon, 1996, p. 201.

8 Edwin Morgan, *Collected Poems*, cit., p. 437.

9 *Ibidem*.

10 *Ibidem*, p. 438.

11 *Ibidem*.

12 Edwin Morgan, *Gilgamesh* (second version, 1997); unpublished typescript.

13 Edwin Morgan, *Collected Poems*, cit., p. 438.

14 *Ibidem*.

15 Hugh MacDiarmid, *Complete Poems*, edited by Michael Grieve and W.R. Aitken, Manchester: Carcanet, 1994, I, p. 573. See also the explanatory note on the facing page.

16 Edwin Morgan, *Collected Poems*, cit., p. 441.

17 Michael Lynch, *Scotland: A New History,* London, Pimlico, [1991] 1997, pp. 13-14.

18 Edwin Morgan, *Collected Poems*, cit., p. 438-439.

19 *Ibidem*, p. 439.

20 *Ibidem*, p. 440.

21 Tacitus, *The Agricola and The Germania*, translated by Harold Mattingly, rev. by S.A. Handford, Harmondsworth: Penguin, 1970, pp. 80-81.

22 Edwin Morgan, *Collected Poems*, cit., p. 440.

23 *Ibidem*, p. 441.

24 *Ibidem*, p. 442.

25 *Ibidem*.

26 Cairns Craig, *op. cit.*, p. 201.

27 Douglas Dunn, 'Morgan's Sonnets', in Robert Crawford and Hamish Whyte eds., *About Edwin Morgan*, Edinburgh: Edinburgh University Press, 1990, p. 79 and p. 83.

[28] Edwin Morgan, *Collected Poems*, cit., p. 444.

[29] *Ibidem*, p. 445.

[30] *Ibidem*, p. 448.

[31] *Ibidem*, p. 457.

[32] *Ibidem*, p. 453.

[33] *Ibidem*.

[34] Cairns Craig, *op. cit.*, pp. 201-202.

[35] Edwin Morgan, *Collected Poems*, cit., p. 449.

[36] *Ibidem*, p. 439.

[37] *Ibidem*, p. 448.

[38] *Ibidem*, p. 447.

[39] *Ibidem*.

[40] *Ibidem*, p. 450.

[41] *Ibidem*, p. 456.

[42] *Ibidem*.

[43] *Ibidem*, p. 457.

[44] *Ibidem*.

[45] *Ibidem*, p. 456.

[46] *Ibidem*, p. 451.

[47] *Ibidem*, p. 449.

[48] *Ibidem*, p. 455.

[49] Douglas Dunn, *op. cit.*, p. 83.

[50] Edwin Morgan, *Collected Poems*, cit., p. 457.

WILLIAM GILLIES

Sorley MacLean's Gaelic Oeuvre: Writing in a Dying Tongue

As the body of serious criticism of Sorley MacLean's work begins to build up, it becomes clear that his reputation as a major poet survives the passing of his great personality and presence. He was an European poet in his vision and his impact, but also a Gaelic poet who wrote in a minority language for a relatively tiny audience of educated Gaels. He is doubly owned: by the smaller circle of Gaelic-speakers who read him in Gaelic, and by his wider audience, who meet his poetry in English, French, German, Italian, Welsh or Irish translations. It would be wrong to suggest that he was unaware of, or unconcerned by the wider interest in his work, at least latterly. For as well as allowing others to translate them, he supplied his own translations of poems included in collections of his works.[1] But his decision to write in Gaelic was explicit and programmatic.[2]

The contributions to *Sorley MacLean: Critical Essays* represented a landmark in the establishment of a consensus as to why and how MacLean's poetry is important.[3] Some convergent perceptions emerged: he appeared to many as a Promethean figure who had allowed the Gaelic voice to speak with a new clarity to the European world and, simultaneously, brought the liberation and responsibility of modernism to Gaelic poetry. A murmur of unease was expressed, at the time when *Critical Essays* appeared, about the competence of non-Gaelic speakers (which included the editors and a number of contributors) to write about a Gaelic poet. This criticism was not wholly valid; but it could be recast as the proposition that most of the essays in this collection, like most critical writing about MacLean, 1. founded themselves on translations rather than on the Gaelic originals, 2. dealt with MacLean as a

Scottish or British or European poet, rather than as a Gaelic poet, and 3. concentrated on MacLean as a poet of ideas with little reference to the art, craft and original language of his poetry. Although the truth of this proposition is undeniable – and worrying – there were exceptions, most notably John MacInnes' 'Language, Metre and Diction in the Poetry of Sorley MacLean', a perceptive and authoritative exposition of the matrix of Gaelic poetic practice and understanding that MacLean had to come to terms with when he decided to write in Gaelic, and the nature of the transformation he wrought in so doing. In that essay and elsewhere MacInnes has stressed the importance of starting from the original Gaelic text and with the poet as a Gaelic poetic practitioner, and has faced up to the difficulty of providing a sufficient commentary to enable non-Gaelic readers to distinguish between the 'given' and the innovative elements.[4] We need more of this basic spade-work: both to pre-empt uncritical hero-worship and to satisfy current dissatisfaction with bare translations, even (or perhaps especially) when these are provided by the author.[5]

The present essay is intended as a further contribution to the de-mystificatory process. Since questions relating to MacLean's philosophy and politics are reasonably well covered by others and reasonably accessible through English versions of his poems, I shall concentrate mainly, though not exclusively, on matters of language and poetics, which have received less attention. I propose to approach the potentially problematic task of exegesis by focusing mainly on a single poem: the early work entitled 'A' Chorra-ghridheach' (The Heron), which I find revealing in regard to these practical questions.[6]

MacLean's key poetic attitudes and practices had been pretty completely worked out by the time of his earliest surviving works. His target audience of literate, educated Gaels had access to Gaelic literature through two main channels: an oral-local tradition, and one mediated by books and the teaching of school and University. The totality of this literature comprised: 1. the bardic poetry and ballads and tales of the old learned tradition; 2. the orally preserved remnants of an old vernacular ('popular' or 'sub-literary') song tradition; and 3. a merged stream of vernacular bardic poetry which flourished in the 'heroic age' of the Jacobite period and continued, although more dispersed and localised and attenuated, down to MacLean's own day. Although he argued passionately for 'the Old Songs' as the principal glory of Gaelic literature, and had harsh words for some of the more showy or sugary poetry that was praised by nineteenth-century critics and their followers in his own day, he was a self-conscious and indeed proud heir to this tradition in its entirety.[7] This was the literary tradition within which he, and his audience, would operate.

'A' chorra-ghridheach' was written when MacLean was still at University, in 1931 or 1932. In it, the poet is joined, at a moment of frustration and confused emotions, by a heron, which alights near him on a beach. The poet draws a contrast between the bird, which is focused and intent, and himself, seething with the doubts and confusions of the human world. Poet and bird are alike in their individuality, their isolation, and their drive to survival. They both survey the same scene. But while the heron's concentration is emotionless, undistracted, poised for the climactic moment of the kill, which promises temporary well-being through freedom from hunger, the poet's mind, as he seeks to comprehend everything from the beauty of his surroundings to the meaning of life, is cluttered and clouded by emotions and associative leaps triggered by competing desires and apprehensions.

I give now a fairly literal translation of the poem insofar as I understand the author's meaning. It is based on the latest text, i.e. that of the corrected edition of 'O Choille gu Bearradh', and is naturally indebted to MacLean's own translation.[8] I have aimed at a consistent degree of nearness to the Gaelic, where MacLean's version is more variable, and I have tried to minimise ambiguity and obscurity. I have taken certain liberties with the punctuation where I feel the flow of the poem demands this.[9] I have endeavoured to hint at the linguistic, rhythmical and metrical texture of the poem in a very general way, but make no great claims in that regard, given such complicating factors as the differing definition and function of rhyme and assonance in Gaelic and in English poetry:

1   A faint, yellow moon on the horizon,
     the heart of the land without a throb of laughter,
     a deathly chill pouring scorn
     on golden windows in a slow-moving sea.

2   It is not the feeble elegance of the moon,
or the cold beauty of the deep,
or the shore's idle surge-talk
that pervades my spirit tonight:

3   feebleness in engaging,
death-chill in life-force,
cowardice in the heart,
no belief in anything.

4   A head-bowed heron came,
landed on the high tide mark,
folded her wings closely
taking stock all around her,

5   alone beside the wave,
like an intelligence alone in the Universe,
her reason like man's reason,
earning a meal the limit of her intent...

6   (Volatile mind questing,
more restless flesh having returned,
unsteadiness and sleep without a glimmer,
music and delirium and an hour of rapture.

7   The hour of rapture is the bright time
that comes from the benighted brain of blindness,
a new day dawning on the sight,
a smile of better times in the deception.)

8   ...there on the bare stones of the shore,
beholding the oiliness of a waveless sea,
listening to the gurgle of the sea,
with brine rubbing over the stones,

9   by herself in the vastness of the Universe –
however numerous her scattered tribe –
and out of the gloom, bursting on her,
the thrust of the bright, blue god.

10   I am with you, yet alone,
beholding the coldness of the smooth linn,
hearing surge on shingle

breaking on the bare slabs of the world.

11 What is my thought beyond her thought?
    The loveliness of moon and restless sea,
    food and sleep and a dream,
    brain, flesh and temptation?

12 Her vision of rapture with one thrust
    coming in its season without holding back,
    without sorrow or doubt, only one thrill:
    the straight, unbending law of herons.

13 My vision, on a wretched enterprise,
    broken, twisted, with a sheen of temptation,
    blemished, with but one glimmer, joyless:
    a brain, a heart, and an unhappy love.

What, precisely, was novel about this poem, whose form and content is fairly typical of MacLean's output in the 1930s? I shall now try to isolate some features of the poem that may have contributed to the unsettling blend of familiarity and novelty that many educated Gaels have experienced on first making acquaintance with MacLean's poetry. The basic ploy of juxtaposing the author and a bird (or animal, or similar) is by no means unheard of in Gaelic poetry, which can furnish examples both before and after Burns's 'To a Fieldmouse' and Shelley's 'Ode to a Skylark': see, for instance, Domhnall Mac Fhionnlaigh's 'Òran na Comhachaig' (The Song of the Owl) from the sixteenth century, or Iain Mac Lachlainn's 'Don Chuthaig' (To the Cuckoo) from the nineteenth. But the way 'A' chorra-ghridheach' is developed contains some surprises from the Gaelic point of view.

   In the first place, Gaelic poetry is well used to the conceit that Nature reflects the poet's mood. To some extent, the old, powerful idea of the smiling land reflecting the righteous ruler (or the opposite) lies behind it. Thus the unlettered Duncan Bàn Macintyre (1724-1812) envisions his beloved Misty Corrie as ravaged and weed-choked as a result of his own expulsion and replacement as forester there. Equally, the highly literate William Ross (1762-1791) tells how 'the sweet harpers [i.e. the birds] will bow their heads in sorrow in the treetops' as they join him in lamenting the death of

Bonnie Prince Charlie in Rome in 1788.[10] But whereas the traditional Gaelic poets see themselves as inhabiting the same eco-system as the animals and birds, MacLean describes a disjunction between the heron, whose sense-data pertain solely to the world around her, and himself, with the sound of the surf breaking on 'the bare slabs of the world' in his ears.

Again, traditional Gaelic poetry utilises a specific motif in which the sadness of the poet is contrasted with the rejoicing of the birds. Sometimes this crystallises in an opposition between the immobility of the speaker and the freedom of the birds to soar away from a troubled predicament or to fly to a lover. But a motif of this sort exists largely as an unexplored trope in the Gaelic songs. It derives its vitality and poignancy from being part of the shared experience of the singer and the audience, and lacks the philosophical and psychological probing on the nature of perception (human and animal) contained in MacLean's poem.

Similarly, a well-known Ulster Irish song ascribed to the poet Cathal Buí Mac Giolla Ghunna is addressed to a bittern whose frozen body the poet encountered by an ice-covered loch. The poem is really about the poet's fondness for alcohol, and the thematic point is the paradoxical link between the two: the poet extends his sympathy to the bird for having died for the want of a drink; but his sympathy is limited by the fact that the bird has been misguided enough to die for the want of a drink of water. There is humorous contrast and epigrammatic force aplenty in the various versions of this popular song. But its motival 'died for thirst' theme is undeveloped; it remains as the point of the poem rather than becoming a starting point for something new. That preference for embellishing rather than developing a motif is a good illustration of the difference between most traditional and most modernist Gaelic poetry.[11]

On a different tack, Gaelic poetry is not without a sense of brooding melancholy, even comforting melancholy. (To some extent this is the legacy of Macpherson's 'Ossian', but there is a more deeply rooted strand too.) The sense of pessimism that flourished in nineteenth-century Gaelic poetry had a longer history. For the eighteenth century, William Ross speaks, in the poem already mentioned, of 'the deceptiveness of the world, how sad that all

flesh is prey to death'. And the seventeenth-century religious poetry contained in the Fernaig Manuscript contains echoes of an earlier sounding of the same note, in poems warning against the vanity
of this world.[12] But the traditional Gaelic examples lack the existentialist, atheistic basis that is implicit in MacLean's poem. By contrast, William Ross's poem concludes on a note of resignation: we
have to be content with what God has ordained.

In short, traditional Gaelic poetry in general lacks the explicit
analysis and psychological concern that are manifest in 'A' Chorra-
ghridheach'. It generally lacks the *difficulty* of language and allusion of MacLean's poem. Where the traditional poet seeks to
enhance communication by playing on the expected, the modern
poet, as here, demands engagement by subverting expectations.
The universality of MacLean's concern is palpable and contrasts
with the localism of most traditional Gaelic poetry. Finally, the
modernity of 'A' Chorra-ghridheach' lies in the densely packed
originality of his thought. Of course, the *degree* of the density and
originality sets the poem apart from much modern poetry too; but
it is the *fact* of their presence that makes it 'modern' as opposed to
'traditional'. To a Gaelic speaker used to the latter this represented
a different order of challenge from the difficulty, based on rich
vocabulary and allusive detail, in seventeenth-century poets like
Iain Lom and the Blind Harper, or from the different sort of difficulty found, say, in nineteenth-century religious poetry, with its
specialised vocabulary, highly-developed dialectic, and (to a latter-
day readership at least) daunting familiarity with the Bible. To
Gaels with a University education, or otherwise attuned to the
enterprise and intellectual apparatus of modernism in the arts,
MacLean's work came as a triumphant vindication of the power of
Gaelic to assimilate and adapt; to other Gaels, with expectations of
poetry that would be inclusive and poets who would come half-
way to meet their audience, the effect was more challenging, and
sometimes so challenging as to be off-putting. We should remember that the disjunction between 'high' and 'low' culture, with
which we are so familiar in English, was traditionally less clear-cut
in Gaelic. The elimination of the old Gaelic literary intelligentsia
had led to a greater degree of inclusiveness in the literary culture,
in which bards were expected to speak to and for 'the people'. To

break with that understanding was to inflict an unexpected blow.

The intellectual novelty of 'A' Chorra-ghridheach' was matched, in what seems to me to have been a deliberately consistent way, at other levels. To turn now to the dynamics of the poem, Gaelic literature shows a preference for the lyric over the narrative mode. In textual terms the 'old songs' that MacLean championed as a critic were largely dramatic monologues, with a few dialogues. The one notable exception was the heroic ballads; yet even in them there is a strong narratorial presence. At this level, 'A' Chorra-ghridheach' seems a very 'normal' Gaelic poem. It starts, indeed, pretty much like a traditional song, with an evocation of the time (moonrise) and place (the sea-shore), and a preliminary statement of what is on the poet's mind. Again, the device of stating what is *not* on his mind (verse 2) as a prelude to revealing what *is* (verse 3) is a very usual gambit in Gaelic poetry, from the learned court poetry to the anonymous folk songs. Yet there are some unexpected twists. For instance, while a traditional lyric can make leaps in space or time or speaker without explicit 'stage directions', it is not usual for narrative to be entangled with the monologue – unlike the Lowland Scots ballads, where the conventions permit this to take place regularly. So verse 4 comes as a shock. In the same way, the normal linear development of oral poetry is broken by what are essentially parentheses – verse 3 and, if my punctuation is correct, verses 6 and 7 – and especially by the apparent introduction of a companion at verse 10, which would surely have been included in the initial scene-setting in a traditional treatment.[13]

The same manipulation of the traditional expectations can be seen at work in the metrical construction of the poem. The fact that most traditional Gaelic poetry was either sung or chanted to musical accompaniment has dictated that it normally presents itself in identically shaped stanzas (though a musically complementary refrain is usual in some categories). Gaelic also makes constant use of rhymes between stressed vowels – to bridge a caesura in a line, to bind lines together, and to bind verses together. As one begins to read 'A' Chorra-ghridheach' aloud, or even to glance at it on the printed page, a very common traditional metrical form based on 4-line stanzas is immediately suggested. This occurs in vernacular stressed-metre poetry, as the vehicle for light songs, usually with line-endings *aaab*, where the *a*-rhyme holds the individual verse together and the *b*-rhyme is constant throughout all the verses and holds the whole poem together. Stanzas of four lines with end-rhyme were also the basis of most Classical Gaelic verse, whose basis was fixed syllable count and line cadences, with the rhyme-pattern *abab* commonest. Here, however, there was no rhyme carried through from verse to verse.[14] To read the first three verses of 'The Heron' prompts a mixture of reactions from a reader used to traditional Gaelic poetry. Here they are in Gaelic:[15]

1 Gealach fhann bhuidhe air f*àire*,
   cridhe 'n fhuinn gun phlosgadh *gàire*,
   aognuidheachd a' dèanamh *tàire*
   air uinneagan òir an cuan *snàgach*.

2 Cha ghrinneas anfhann na *gealaich*
   no maise fhuaraidh na *mara*
   no baoth-sgeulachd onfhaidh a' *chladaich*
   tha nochd a' drùdhadh air m'*aigne*.

3 Anfhannachd an *strì*
   aognuidheachd am *brìgh*,
   gealtachd anns a' *chrìdh*,
   gun chreideamh an aon *nì*.

In verses 1 and 2 the four disyllabic end-rhymes (italicised) are the first thing to strike one. They are long-*a* rhymes in verse 1 and short-*a* rhymes in verse 2.[16] This is a fairly unusual variant of the more usual *aaab* pattern. If identical rhyme were carried forward from verse to verse it would run the risk of monotony, and it tends to be used for special effect, e.g. in John MacCodrum's 'Moladh Chlann Domhnaill' (In Praise of Clan Donald), in which the poet commemorates his appointment as Sir James MacDonald's 'song-thrush' or official bard with a song that verges on a *tour de force*.[17] Again, William Ross's 'An Suaithneas Bàn' (The White Cockade) on the death of Bonnie Prince Charlie has the following chorus, where the insistent long-*a* end-rhyme, like the internal rhyme in the diphthong *ua*, may suggest the finality of the tolling bell or the solemnity of the funeral march:

Soraidh *bhuan* don t-*Suaith*neas *Bhàn*,

gu Là *Luain* cha *ghluais* on *bhàs*,
ghlac an *uaigh* an *Suaith*neas *Bàn*,
is leacan *fuar*aidh *tuaim* a *thàmh*.

[Farewell forever to the White Cockade
that will not stir till Judgement Day,
the grave has seized the White Cockade,
chilly flagstones are the tomb of its resting.]

The end-rhymes in the first verse of 'A' Chorra-ghridheach' similarly suggest that something solemn and portentous is coming up.
Verse 2, however, dispels any fears of a *tour de force*, by changing
the end-rhyme. As the poem proceeds and this practice continues,
the effect is to put a particular focus on each verse as a discrete
sense unit. Possibly, it stirs a memory of the Classical syllabic poetry, in which the same effect is noticeable to a Modern Gaelic reader. Verse 3, however, brings us up sharply with its abrupt change
of rhythm and cadence: the shorter lines with their closing mono-
syllables produce an insistent effect comparable to that in the chorus of 'An Suaithneas Bàn'.

A change of rhythm and metre like this is not unheard of in the
earlier Gaelic poetry. The eighteenth-century poets Duncan Bàn
Macintyre, Alexander MacDonald and Rob Donn Mackay all tried
their hand at poems which imitated the different *tempi* and phrase-
structure of the different movements of the *ceòl mòr* ('big music' or
'pibroch') of the bagpipe with its 'ground' and 'variations'. And
within the structural framework of the eight-line Gaelic 'big songs'
there are specimens with line endings in the pattern *ababcccb*.
Because of these precedents, we may feel that verse 3 is shaping
up to the pattern *cccb*.[18] But the expectation is thwarted with the
final hammer-blow.

The next group of verses, 5-8, involves a different sort of disjunction in terms of the structure of the poem. For verses 6 and 7
seem to be a parenthesis involving a break in sense between 5 and
6, and again between 7 and 8. MacLean keeps the disjunction
under control by imposing a more insistent level of continuity in
rhythm, on which it is necessary to dwell briefly now.

MacLean famously claimed a 'painful sensitivity' to rhythm,
which he explained as a sort of compensation for having no ear
for melody.[19] His critical writings provide ample testimony to his

sensitivity to poetic rhythm, which is also manifestly present in his own poetry. He himself seems to have believed that 'the most satisfactory basis' for Gaelic verse was a blend of the freedom from 'beat' that could be found in the syllabic verse of the Classical period, and the freedom from absolute syllabic regularity that characterised the post-Classical poetry. This discreetly disciplined quality, which MacLean praised in the older songs, was also a characteristic of his own compositions, including 'A' Chorra-ghridheach'. The first verse lays out the ground rules for a rhythmically consistent pattern of four stresses per line. Given that Gaelic words are stressed on the first syllable, it reads naturally (i.e. with normal speech rhythm and normal elisions of unstressed vowels) as follows:

Gealach fhann bhuidh(e) air fàire,	x - x x - x -
cridhe 'n fhuinn gun phlosgadh gàire,	x - x - x - x -
aognuidheachd a' dèanamh tàire	x - - - x - x -
(ai)r uinneagan òir an cuan snàgach.	(-) x - - x - x x -

Given the underlying accentual pattern of x - x - x - x -, jingle is avoided by the omission of a short syllable after 'fhann' in line 1, which also contrives to steer a tight course between 'fhann-bhuidhe' (faint-yellow) and 'fhann', 'buidhe' ('faint (moon), yellow (on the horizon)'). Line 2 is 'regular'. In line 3, 'aognuidheachd' has the shape x - -, but the '-eachd' is in a position that can be musically prominent and the ear is led by a process of rationalisation to analyse the line as one with a musical dimension.[20] In line 4, the variety obtained by the 'extra' short syllable in 'uinneagan' and the 'missing' short syllable after 'cuan' may be suggestive of the quick movement of the panes of reflected moonlight produced by the slow movement of the smooth sea.[21] It is worth stressing the singability of this verse beside its readability: it could be sung to the tune of MacCodrum's 'Smeòrach Chlann Domhnaill' (Song-thrush of Clan Donald) without doing violence to traditional Gaelic singing practices, and it can be read out without doing any violence to natural Gaelic speech rhythms. This, I take it, is the 'tight rope' which the modern poet walks, according to MacLean: steering a course between the tyranny of metre and the formlessness of 'chopped prose'.[22]

To return to verses 5-8, we may say that MacLean, having set up the metrical parameters of the poem in verse 1, immediately began to extend these by introducing adventurous and unexpected effects in verse 2 (where he is listing some of the topics that are *not* on his mind), verse 3 (where the metre actually changes to match the interjected quality of the verse), and verse 4 (where the shift in mode from lyric to narrative may have acted as the trigger for a barer, less rhythmical verse). By contrast, verses 5-8 are more 'singable', like verse 1. It may not be too much to suggest that the metrical smoothness of these verses is intended to provide continuity and help the reader or hearer to transcend the sense-breaks which frame the parenthesis in verses 6-7, and keep the picture of the heron from fragmenting during the 'aside' on the psychology of the kill. One more example must suffice. In verse 10 the *aaaa* rhyme-pattern is broken for the first time, becoming *aabb*. Partly, as we have suggested (note 13), this was to enable the echo of the traditional *'s mi 'nam ònar* to be incorporated; but it is surely also there to chime with the sense-break, as we take on board the presence of the poet's hitherto unsuspected companion.

Similar intentions and effects can be glimpsed in MacLean's rhetoric and diction, confirming the conclusions of John MacInnes referred to above. Thus in 'A' Chorra-ghridheach' we have noted the traditional rhetorical device of listing rejected alternatives before coming to 'the thing that is *really* on my mind'. Another sort of repetition which is likewise favoured in traditional Gaelic verse is glimpsed in the parenthetical verses 6 and 7, where 'tràth mire' (hour of rapture), having been introduced at the end of verse 6, is repeated with elaboration in verse 7. I take it that MacLean's use of traditional sign-posting like this is intended to produce a familiar, reassuring counterpoint to the ideas he is loosing on us, which flout traditional expectations and are difficult and profound in themselves.

Similarly, MacLean's choice of words is eclectic and his use of words shows a readiness to bend and strain Gaelic to the limits. As MacInnes has pointed out, MacLean's practice follows that of the traditional poet in being supra-dialectal, and in his pleasure in careful and accurate usage, right down to correctness in case endings. At the same time, however, and in contradistinction to the traditional poet, MacLean quarries and pillages words and meanings

SORLEY MACLEAN'S GAELIC OEUVRE

and nuances from all the sources available to him: local-dialectal, biblical-theological, and earlier literary sources, and ends up creating his own diction *de novo*.[23] This can be seen as an escape, a refusal to be contained; it implies an attitude to language, and more particularly to literary language. He did not have to go so far as MacDiarmid did, nor would it have been in his nature to be so cavalier with the traditions of a living language; but he did need to create a little distance between his usage and what had gone before.

This sort of analysis can be done with useful results, it seems to me, on any of MacLean's poems. It does not capture everything that is important, of course; but it nevertheless seems to respond to part of the poet's agenda, and to tie in with the assumptions and prescriptions he reveals in his critical writings. It can hardly be neglected by critics. That it yields such consistent results is part of the justification for believing it was an integral part of his programme, however unself-consciously or inadvertently it made its contribution to the whole composition he was working on at a given moment. The fact that the cumulative effect of all these choices – poetical, literary, linguistic – is so harmonious and seamless is part of what Iain Crichton Smith called the 'miracle' of Sorley MacLean's poetry.

NOTES

[1] Some of the poems in *Dàin do Eimhir agus Dàin Eile*, Glasgow: William MacLellan, 1943, were provided with English translations in a section entitled 'Versions of Selected Poems' (pp. 97-103). See also *Four Points of a Saltire*, edited by Tom Scott, Edinburgh: Reprographia, 1970; *Reothairt is Contraigh/Spring Tide and Neap Tide*, Edinburgh: Canongate, 1977; *O Choille gu Bearradh/From Wood to Ridge* (corrected edition), Manchester/Edinburgh: Carcanet, 1999.

[2] Sorley MacLean, *O Choille gu Bearradh*, cit., p. xiv.

[3] Edited by R.J. Ross and Joy Hendry, Edinburgh: Scottish Academic Press, 1986. There is a useful bibliography of MacLean criticism in Ronald Black ed., *An Tuil: Anthology of Twentieth-century Scottish Gaelic Verse*, Edinburgh: Polygon, 2000, pp. 767-68.

[4] See also, on the language of theology and religious debate in MacLean's work, 'A Radically Traditional Voice: Sorley MacLean and the Evangelical Background', *Cencrastus*, vol. 7, Winter 1981-1982, pp. 14-17.

[5] The contextualisation of MacLean's *Dàin do Eimhir* has lately been dramatically enriched by the publication of *Dàin do Eimhir/Poems to Eimhir*, edited by Christopher Whyte, Glasgow: The Association for Scottish Literary Studies, 2002.

[6] See *Dàin do Eimhir*, cit., pp. 73-74, and pp. 102-103. In subsequent collections the originals and translations are printed *en face*: see *Four Points of a Saltire*, cit., pp. 114-116; *Reothairt is Contraigh*, cit., pp. 2-5; *O Choille gu Bearradh*, cit., pp. 2-5.

[7] MacLean's essays on Gaelic poetry, collected in *Ris a' Bruthaich: The Criticism and Prose Writings of Sorley MacLean*, Stornoway: Acair, 1985, provide an extended and illuminating commentary on his thinking on literature; compare William Gillies, 'The Poet as Critic', in R.J. Ross and Joy Hendry eds., *op. cit.*, pp. 185-200.

[8] There are some minor differences between the translation in *Dàin do Eimhir* and that in the subsequent collections. Note that since *corra-ghridheach* is a feminine noun in Gaelic, MacLean refers to the heron as 'she'. I have done the same.

[9] The circumstances of the publication of the original edition of *Dàin do Eimhir* left a legacy of unfinished business in this respect. When I worked with MacLean on the text of *Reothairt is Contraigh* he was almost invariably amenable to editorial suggestions of this sort.

[10] Angus MacLeod ed., *The Songs of Duncan Ban Macintyre*, Edinburgh: Oliver & Boyd, 1952, pp. 174-183; J.L. Campbell ed., *Highland Songs of the Forty-Five*, revised edition, Edinburgh: Scottish Academic Press, 1984, pp. 286-291.

[11] Even the famous Old Irish poem 'The Scholar and his Cat' (for which see, e.g., Gerard Murphy, *Early Irish Lyrics*, Oxford: Oxford University Press, 1956, pp. 2-3), which may have been known to MacLean from his Celtic classes when he composed 'A' chorra-ghrid-heach', exercises its wit at the 'first position'.

[12] See, for example, the poems by Donnchadh Mac Raoiridh and Murchadh MacCoinnich printed in Roderick Watson ed., *The Poetry of Scotland*, Edinburgh: Edinburgh University Press, 1995, pp. 212-217.

[13] The intention to shock is underlined by the echo of a traditional opening formula in *'s mi 'nam ònar*: compare the well-known ceilidh song 'Air m'uilinn 's mi 'nam ònar' '(Resting) on my elbow, all alone...'.

The 'you' addressed in verse 10 has usually, I think, been taken as referring to the heron. (The switch from third to second person is not unknown in the 'Old Songs', though it is not as ubiquitous as in the Scots ballads.) I tentatively associate verse 10 with the reference to an unhappy love in verse 13: the poet's fate is to be physically with his unnamed companion, but in all other respects isolated.

[14] There are other differences: e.g. vernacular rhymes are simple vowel rhymes, while the Classical rhymes also require strict relationships between the consonants following the rhyme-bearing stressed vowel. For a summary of the rules see William Gillies, 'Gaelic: The Classical Tradition', in R.D.S. Jack ed., *The History of Scottish Literature: Vol. 1: Origins to 1660*, Aberdeen: Aberdeen University Press, 1988, pp. 251-252. For fuller details see Eleanor Knott, *Irish Classical Poetry*, Dublin: Colm O Lochlainn, 1957. There is as yet no recommendable treatment of the vernacular metrics.

[15] The text and layout are as in *O Choille gu Bearradh*; the italics are mine.

[16] There is apparently a further level of manipulation. Gaelic verse uses rhyme more freely than English does, but the test for rhyme is looser. In verse 1 the 'perfect' rhymes between 'fàire', 'gàire' and 'tàire' go beyond the normal requirements of Gaelic metre and suggest that the *aaaa* rhyme-scheme is 'really' *aaab*. Any aural expectation thus raised is dashed in verse 2, however, where if one listens out for more than the 'normal' *aaaa* effect the patterning works quite differently, pairing 'gealaich' with 'cladaich' and 'mara' with 'aigne' (i.e. *abab*). This mixed aural bombardment puts maximum focus on the booming *aaaa* rhyme in verse 3.

[17] See William Matheson ed., *The Songs of John MacCodrum*, Edinburgh: Oliver & Boyd, 1938, pp. 44-49.

[18] To the present writer, reading verse 3 always suggests the second half of the first verse of Duncan Ban Macintyre's 'Moladh Beinn Dobhrain' (The Praise of Ben Doran): 'Munadh fada *réidh*/cuilidh 'm faighte *féidh*/soilleireachd an t-*sléibh*/bha mi sònrachadh', for which see Angus MacLeod, *op. cit.*, p. 196, ll. 2770-2773.

[19] Sorley MacLean, *Ris a' Bruthaich*, cit., p. 8.

[20] Similarly, in the favourite traditional song line 'cianalas a' tighinn air m'aire' ('homesickness coming into my mind'), the accentual pattern is x - x- x - x -. The word cianalas is x - - in speech, but with the help of the melody of the song fulfils the x - x requirement by being 'long + short + musically (i.e. tonally) prominent'.

[21] The bracketed vowels in lines 1 and 4 are to be elided as in normal speech.

[22] See Sorley MacLean, *Ris a' Bhruthaich*, cit., p. 13.

[23] See R.J. Ross and Joy Hendry eds., *op. cit.*, p. 145 and p. 152.

IAN MACDONALD

The Poetry of Derick Thomson

This poet is called Ruaraidh MacThòmais in Scottish Gaelic, and his poetry is in Gaelic, but it is likely that most readers of this essay will have to depend on the translations provided. It is a truism that much can be lost in translation, but it must be said again here, when two languages as unlike each other as Gaelic and English are involved (even if they have been cheek-by-jowl for well over a millennium). In the best poetry the medium is always part of the message, and while the lexical meaning can be transmitted to a greater or lesser extent, the richness of rhyme and rhythm is less likely to be preserved in translation. Similarly with cultural resonances and allusions.

There are well over 300 items in the canon of Derick Thomson's poetry, but its bibliography is unusually straightforward. Up to 1982 his work is to be found in four collections, with none having any poem in common. They are *An Dealbh Briste* (1951), *Eadar Samhradh is Foghar* (1967), *An Rathad Cian* (1970) and *Saorsa agus an Iolaire* (1977). In 1982 he published *Creachadh na Clàrsaich: Plundering the Harp*, 'Collected Poems 1940-1980', of which he wrote in his Preface:

> This book is much closer to being Collected Poems than it is to Selected Poems. There are various omissions, about twenty in all, from previously published collections... Various recent poems belonging to the category of work in progress, and any poem dating after May 1980, are not included either.

All of the first four books except *An Rathad Cian* had included *some* English translations, printed at the end of the book and mostly in prose, but nearly all the poems in *Creachadh na Clàrsaich* are accompanied by parallel translation. The book is still available and is the most convenient access to most of Thomson's work, as the first four collections are all out of print.

Creachadh na Clàrsaich has been followed by two more recent collections, *Smeur an Dòchais* (1991) and *Meall Garbh* (1995), both of which have parallel translation throughout. Since these most recent volumes have appeared, Thomson has written a good number of poems which remain uncollected – over 3,000 lines in all.[1]

*　*　*

It will be clear from the foregoing that Thomson's creative drive has lasted into old age, but that energy and that achievement is characteristic of him. His activities have been many and varied, but all his work has involved the Gaelic language which he has spoken since infancy in his native Lewis, the largest island in the chain that forms the Outer Hebrides, also known as the Western Isles, off the west of Scotland.

Thomson was born here in 1921, the younger of two sons of teachers (his father was also a poet), and soon showed himself as academically accomplished. An outstanding school career was followed by a successful Degree course at the University of Aberdeen, although that was disrupted by the Second World War, during which he served in the RAF. He eventually graduated with distinction in 1947, having decided on an academic career, and gained additional qualifications at the University of Cambridge and at the University College of Wales in Bangor. University appointments at Edinburgh, Glasgow and Aberdeen followed, and between 1963 and 1991 he was Professor of Celtic at Glasgow, retiring from the Chair there at the age of seventy.

Another fine Gaelic poet, the late George Campbell Hay, has described Derick Thomson as 'the man who has done more for Scottish Gaelic than any man living'.[2] His achievements have included outstanding scholarly research – particularly, although not exclusively, the charting and assessment of poetry in Gaelic, on which he has written a definitive work; a great deal of editing and publishing, both of books and journals; and the fostering of the Gaelic language in many other ways, whether through initiatives such as the setting up of the Historical Dictionary of Scottish Gaelic and the Gaelic Books Council, or through decades of influence on generations of students (he was a gifted teacher), or through working on panels or committees and producing much PR via both the spoken and the written word.

The extraordinary range of his achievements has been recognised by Fellowships and honorary Degrees, by the award of the first Ossian Prize (in 1974) and by a *Festschrift* in the form of a special issue of the academic journal *Scottish Gaelic Studies* published from the Department of Celtic of his *Alma Mater* in 1996.[3] The Dedication in that volume provides a useful summary of his life and work, and is followed by a list of his publications up to 1992.

*   *   *

Thomson has published short stories, but poetry is, above everything, his chosen creative medium, and Gaelic poetry at that. Not that there was no choice involved as to the language: bilingual from a very early age, he wrote poetry in English too, but he has said that while he was still a young man he made a conscious choice to write only in Gaelic.

His first collection was *An Dealbh Briste* (The Broken Picture), published in 1951, and the perception of this book is still that it is primarily a book of love poems. In one of these, 'N E Seo an Dàn Deireannach Dhutsa?' (Is This the Final Poem for You?), the poet refers to the loved one as 'prime cause of poems for me', and of the 48 poems, more than half are love poems.

They chart the course of a failed love, and at times the utterance is heartfelt and intense, as in the last lines of the poem just mentioned:

Cha dèan mi dàn deireannach no [dàn toisich dhut...	I shall not make final or first poem [for you...
ach aona dhàn fhada...	but one long poem, that...
a mhaireas gu sìorraidh	will last for ever
làn molaidh is mil-bhriathran...	full of praise and honey words...

Generally, the treatment is bleaker, as in the third section of 'Ròghadal, 1943' (Rodel, 1943):

| Fann, airtneulach, bàsmhor, | Wan, grieving, mortal, |

a' sìoladh troimh ghainmhich an [dòchais,	filtering through the sand of hope,
tha mo ghaol ort-sa, nighneag.	is my love for you, lass.

Even in this early and, at first glance, slight piece, Thomson's characteristic strength of sustaining the argument of a poem to its conclusion is apparent, as is his craftsmanship, here shown in his choice of a controlled free verse to mirror the discursive nature of the poem. The first section of three verses supplies background, the second, also of three verses, advances the argument by outlining his plight, while the third section of three verses describes the physical place for the first time (in two verses) and the three lines quoted revert to the lover and describe his state of mind exactly.

One of the more remarkable poems is 'Dà Sheòmar' (Two Chambers), in which the poet begins to feel that he is recovering/has recovered from his love.

Dh'fhaodadh nach caill mi mo shuain	Perhaps I shall not lose my sleep
aon uair eile gad chionn,	ever again for your sake;
dh'fhaodadh gun chuir mi san tuam	it may be that I have put in the tomb
gach bruaillean biorach a bh'ann...	every piercing grief I had...

dh'fhaodadh gun thuit am mullach,	it may be that the roof fell in, and
['s nuair dh'fhalbh a' cheò,	[when the dust cleared,
sheas mi am meadhon an làraich –	I stood in the midst of the ruin –
[is bha mi beò.	[and I was alive.

One notices the skilled patterning of the lines and the tension as the poem proceeds to its conclusion. The beautiful third and fourth lines hint at rhythmical variety to follow, but instead are succeeded by a rapid succession of couplets rhyming with each other, with the lines becoming longer each time, until the dramatic conclusion is reached.

The poems that follow 'Two Chambers' in the first book seem more resigned than anguished, and the reader may conjecture that the process of recovery is under way, although slow. The last poem in the book is 'Clachan-meallain' (Hailstones), addressed to a woman and concluding as follows:

A' mhadainn ud thàinig thu steach [ás ùr	that morning you came in anew

air doras mo chridhe…	on the door of my heart…
a' tionndadh gu mil an t-searbhachd.	turning the bitterness to honey.

It may be that this poem is addressed to the poet's wife, like a small number of love poems published much later – such as the graceful 'I Saw a Vision of You Young', which begins 'As my grief was ebbing/I saw a vision of you young'. The link between a writer's work and his personal history is a delicate matter, but here it may not be unreasonable to conclude that the ebbing of grief in the life is connected with the fact that love poems are not so prominent from now on. Yet on occasion there are love poems, such as the striking 'Between Summer and Autumn', first published about two years after the first book came out and sufficiently important to give its title to the second book, in which it was collected in 1967 (the title fits in other ways also – in terms of the poet's age, for example). It describes a physical encounter between a couple with great vividness and has lyricism, beautiful rhythms and self-reproach, as well as a classic Thomson phrase: 'slàinte 'na chiùrradh' (healing in its hurting).

But while *An Dealbh Briste* made its impact as a collection of love poems, almost half of it was on other matters, and perhaps the best known poem from it is 'An Tobar' (The Well):

Tha tobar beag am meadhon a' bhaile	Right in the village there's a little well
's am feur ga fhalach,	and the grass hides it,
am feur gorm sùghor ga	green grass in sap closely
[dhlùth-thughadh,	[thatching it.
fhuair mi brath air bho sheann	I heard of it from an old woman…
[chaillich…	
Nuair sheall mi 'na h-aodann preasach	When I looked in her lined face
chunnaic mi 'n raineach a' fàs mu	I saw the bracken growing round
[thobar a sùilean	[the well of her eyes
's ga fhalach bho shireadh 's bho	and hiding it from seeking and
[rùintean	[from desires
's ga dhùnadh 's ga dhùnadh.	and closing it, closing it.
…Dh'fhaodadh nach eil anns an	…It may be that the well
[tobar	
ach nì a chunnaic mi 'm bruadar,	is something I saw in a dream,
oir nuair chaidh mi an diugh ga	for today when I went to seek it
[shireadh	

cha d'fhuair mi ach raineach is [luachair,	I found only bracken and rushes,
's tha sùilean na caillich dùinte	and the old woman's eyes are closed
's tha lì air tighinn air an luathghair.	and a film has come over their [merriment.

This fine poem has been taken to be about Gaelic tradition/culture/way of life/language, and it embodies the paradox of being life-affirming in its being a work of art at the same time as it is an account of loss. The sense of loss is strong in *An Dealbh Briste*, not only in the love poetry but in poems such as 'Ruins' ('On a summer's day, fifty years ago,/the village stepped back a pace, and now/the stolid grass-covered walls have taken root again,/and the thatch has sagged') or 'Harvest Field', which begins by presenting an idyll but ends shockingly ('…you fell on a scythe that another had left,/and your skin was cut, and refused healing'). These are all successful poems – indeed, 'The Well' is a modern classic – and if Thomson has published excellent work into old age, it should also be said that he matured early (his first published poem dates from about 1938) and that, while his first book is a young man's book, it remains a highly satisfying collection.

The poet's relationship with his native country begins in Lewis, but it has been said with justice of him (by Donald MacAulay in the *Festschrift*) that his is a 'political nationalism Scottish rather than Gaelic'.[4] Yet he is naturally unhappy at the state of Gaeldom, and for him this is a national matter. The poem in *An Dealbh Briste* entitled 'Faoisgneadh', first published in 1943 and not translated in the collected volume (the title means 'Unhusking' or 'Bursting from the Pod'), had addressed this directly in its first lines (my translation):

A bheanntan Chill-Fhinn, is sibh dorch le dùr-aogas a' bhròin
a laigh air mo thìr…
[O mountains of Killin, dark with the intractable face of the sorrow
that has covered my land…]

The 'sorrow' is multiform, but needs only to be outlined here. It involves the displacement of Gaelic and its associated culture from the seat of power in Scotland in the early Middle Ages, a displacement that was followed by active persecution by central government and the stigmatising of those associated with the language and culture – a process that continued, if in more refined form, until recent times, and arguably continues still. The reprisals that followed the failure of the 1745-1746 Jacobite Rising changed the Highlands forever, and these were succeeded by much depopulation well into the twentieth century, through Clearances, emigration and the toll exacted by two World Wars. This depopulation, combined with a failure by governments to foster Gaelic and to make it an educational medium (especially as part of the Education Act of 1872), meant that the language was in a parlous state when Derick Thomson began to write and publish poetry. True, it was still vigorous in rural Lewis and in all of the Western Isles, and in some of the other islands and in parts of the western mainland, but the population of these was a very small proportion of the population of Scotland.

To these difficulties some commentators (although by no means all) would add a stifling of the arts – of music and song, in particular – and of traditional communal celebration by the Protestant Churches, especially in Thomson's native Lewis.

All these matters fell under his even more detailed consideration in his second book, *Eadar Samhradh is Foghar* (Between Summer and Autumn), a highly organised volume in which nearly 50 poems are grouped in five sections, two of which are 'Heather Isle (Lewis)' and 'The Scottish Highlands'. It is a rich, well-distilled collection by a poet in his maturity, and includes some of his most highly regarded work.

Among these is 'Mu Chrìochan Hòil' (In the Vicinity of Hol), Hol being a small hill near where Thomson was brought up. A rich tapestry of scenes from the life of the poet when a boy, and from the life of his community, it extends to over 120 lines in an assured, steady rhythm that conveys the flow of the seasons, the year's round. It concludes in this way:

Chaidh Earrach 's Samhradh 'nan [aon latha buan,	Spring and Summer became [an everlasting day,
Foghar is Geamhradh suainte san [aon oidhch;	Autumn and Winter wrapped in [the same night;
na bliadhnachan air tàthadh: 's [gann gu lorgadh sgeilb	the years coalesced: a chisel [could hardly find
na clachan eadar-dhealaichte fon aol,	the separate stones under the lime,

no obair mheanbh a' chlachair air   nor the mason's intricate work on
 [a' chrìdh,   [the heart,
's e togail bhallachan – tha 'm balach   as he built walls – the boy within
 [staigh 'nam broinn   [them
's a' ghrian neo-thruasail, gheal a'   and the white unpitying sun soaking
 [drùdhadh orr'.   [them.

But the boy grew up and had to leave, and in many poems from
now on the man expresses his regret at that fact, although 'regret'
is rather a simple term for the complex of feelings for the place
that is explored in this book, as in 'Clouds': 'Waxed bandage on my
eye, so that I do not see how you have changed, dark island, long
missed./Though I left light-heartedly, in youth's brashness and gaiety, my eye on a distant horizon, my steps hurrying towards it...'
This is from 'Aig an Uinneig' (At the Window):

Ged nach faod mi cianalas
a chur ann an ionad beatha,
is stiallagan de sheann bhruadairean
a chàradh ri uinneig mo thaighe
mar nach biodh saoghal ùr ann,
's a' ghrian a' deàlradh air aodann leanaibh –
gidheadh, tha meadhon na Màigh seo
a' toirt 'nam chuimhne làithean eile.

Mun do thuit a' bhrat, mun do shrac
mi 'n cùmhnant, mun do mhùch
mi 'n t-iarrtas, mun do dh'fhàg
mi beàrn a dh'fhàg beàrn...

Though I may not put longing in place of living, nor arrange shreds of
old dreams against the windows of my house, as though there were no
new world to reckon with, nor the sun shining on a child's face – still,
this time of mid-May brings other days to my mind...

Before the curtain fell, before I tore up the agreement, smothered the
desire, left an empty place that has made an empty place within me...

The poet is mourning the loss of a secure world – which has in
any case changed, the pace of change being very swift, and the
change including a dilution of an immemorial culture. His own
occupation, which involves upholding at least one crucial part of

the culture, the language – and an occupation which, ironically, he could not have pursued except in the outside world – appears not to be a great consolation, at least to the heart. In the poem 'In Other Fields', as he is on a city street, 'I see the fields of barley, heavy-eared,/and on my nostrils strikes the rain-washed scent/of autumn acres in my own country./...Rough the stroking of the bearded ears on my hand –/here my hand falls on nothing in the street/but a smooth rail; and... I see, with a lustreless eye, the whole round world/becoming a nut, and falling to the ground'. In 'Troimh Uinneig a' Chithe' (When This Fine Snow Is Falling), he reflects on his ancestors:

Iadsan a' fàgail staid a' bhalaich,	When their boyhood came to an end
's a' strì ri fearann, 's a' treabhadh [na mara	they strove with the land, and [ploughed the sea
le neart an guaillibh,	with the strength of their shoulders,
's ag adhradh, air uairibh;	and worshipped, sometimes;
is mise caitheamh an spionnaidh, [ach ainneamh,	I spend their strength, for the [most part,
a' treabhadh ann an gainneamh.	ploughing in the sand.

But there are other important aspects to this book, and to his future work: that of commemoration and celebration and that of the exposure of injustice visited on his country, with anger being vented, however ironically. Thomson once confided that one of his reasons for writing poetry was that he wished to preserve a recollection of the life that he had seen in the very different world of his youth, and from this book onwards he produces memorable portraits of his people, whether as individuals or groups. His best known single poem is probably 'Clann-nighean an Sgadain' (The Herring Girls), the subject being the young women who travelled around Britain gutting the fish landed in the herring fishing boom of the first half of the twentieth century. In the Gaelic the image in the first two lines is unforgettable – appealing both to the eye and to the ear – and it will be seen even in partial quotation how the images are maintained:

An gàire mar chraiteachan salainn ga fhroiseadh bho 'm beul...	Their laughter like a sprinkling of salt showered from their lips...
is mara b' e an gàire,	and were it not for their laughter

shaoileadh tu gu robh an teud
    [briste.

you might think the harp-string was
    [broken.

Ach bha craiteachan uaille air an
    [cridhe,
ga chumail fallain,
is bheireadh cutag an teanga
slisinn á fanaid nan Gall…

But there was a sprinkling of pride
    [on their hearts,
keeping them sound,
and their tongues' gutting-knife
would tear a strip from the
    [Lowlanders' mockery…

The awareness of history is also displayed in poems more hard-hitting than any so far that deal with the state of the Highlands. He often deploys irony, as in 'Srath Nabhair' ('Strathnaver'), Strathnaver being a part of northern Scotland in which the Highland Clearances were especially severe in the 19th century, with many people being evicted, their houses being set on fire and the roofs being stripped off so that they could not return to them. Some of the clergymen of the time portrayed these savage events as a judgement caused by the people's wickedness.

Anns an adhar dhubh-ghorm ud,
àirde na sìorraidheachd os ar cionn,
bha rionnag a' priobadh ruinn,
's i freagairt mireadh an teine
ann an cabair taigh m' athar
a' bhliadhna thugh sinn an taigh
    [le bleideagan sneachda.

In that blue-black sky
as high above us as eternity,
a star was winking at us,
answering the leaping flames of fire
in the rafters of my father's house,
that year we thatched the house
    [with snowflakes.

Agus siud a' bhliadhna cuideachd
a shlaod iad a' chailleach don
    [t-sitig
a shealltainn cho eòlach 's a bha
    [iad air an Fhìrinn…

And that too was the year
they hauled the old woman out on
    [to the dung-heap
to demonstrate how knowledgeable
    [they were in Scripture…

In 'Cruaidh?' (Steel?), similarly:

Cuil-lodair, is Briseadh na h-Eaglaise,
is briseadh nan tacannan –
lamhachas-làidir dà thrian de ar
    [comas;
'se seòltachd tha dhìth oirnn…

Culloden, the Disruption,
and the breaking up of the tack-farms –
two thirds of our power is violence;

it is cunning we need…

Is caith bhuat briathran mìne…

And throw away soft words…

tha Tìr nan Og anns an Fhraing,	the Land of the Ever-young is in [France,
's nuair a ruigeas tu Tìr a' [Gheallaidh,	and when you reach the Promised [Land,
mura bi thu air t' aire,	unless you are on your toes,
coinnichidh Sasannach riut is [plìon air,	a bland Englishman will meet you,
a dh'innse dhut gun tug Dia, [brathair athar,	and say to you that God, his uncle, [has given him
còir dha anns an fhearann.	a title to the land.

Thomson's third book, *An Rathad Cian* (The Far Road), appeared in 1970, only three years after the second. The 56 poems in this book were composed quickly over a short period, and while some of them have echoes of earlier work, both in content and in technique, a plausible argument can be made that this book marks a new development.

From that perspective, *Eadar Samhradh is Foghar* can be seen as the high water mark of his measured, reflective style, and his status as a leading poet in the Scottish Gaelic tradition would be assured if he were the author of that book alone. It is an indication of his poetic energy and creativity that he re-invented himself to some extent at this juncture. In *An Rathad Cian* he is more demotic; the poems are still allusive, but more direct; and if they do not represent a total departure from his earlier style, they are a very striking development of it – and one that has largely set the pattern for his work since then. This remarkable sequence is made up of a succession of vivid pieces, mostly fairly short, on the theme of Lewis, Lewis and the poet, Lewis people, Lewis religion. They can be magisterial or mischievous, and are mostly in a superbly crafted free verse. A striking perspective is offered in 'Am Bodach-ròcais' (Scarecrow):

An oidhch' ud	That night
thàinig am bodach-ròcais dhan [taigh-chèilidh:	the scarecrow came into the [ceilidh-house:
fear caol àrd dubh	a tall, thin black-haired man
is aodach dubh air.	wearing black clothes.
Shuidh e air an t-sèis	He sat on the bench
is thuit na cairtean ás ar làmhan…	and the cards fell from our hands…
Bha boireannach 'na suidh' air stòl	A woman was sitting on a stool,

ag òran, 's thug e 'n toradh ás a'
    [cheòl.
Ach cha do dh'fhàg e falamh sinn:
thug e òran nuadh dhuinn,
is sgeulachdan na h-àird an Ear,
is sprùilleach de dh'fheallsanachd
    [Geneva,
is sguab e 'n teine á meadhon an
    [làir
's chuir e 'n tùrlach loisgeach nar
    [broillichean.

singing songs, and he took the
    [goodness out of the music.
But he did not leave us empty-handed:
he gave us a new song,
and tales from the Middle East,
and fragments of the philosophy of
    [Geneva,
and he swept the fire from the centre
    [of the floor
and set a searing bonfire in our
    [breasts.

In 'The Norsemen Coming Ashore at Ness', the barbaric warriors of legend become acclimatised in 28 lines and two sentences, and, by implication, take their place as yet another element that went to form Lewis. The island itself is addressed in the most intimate terms, as in 'Sweetheart of My Youth' ('How far have I fallen from you, sweetheart of my youth?/with your brown hair and your dark eyes'), 'I Got the Feel of You with My Feet' ('I got the feel of you with my feet/in early summer;/my mind here in the city/strives to know, but the shoes come between us') and 'I Lost My Heart to You' ('I lost my heart to you at the start of May,/your thighs were warm,/firm and smooth'). Nor are the people forgotten, from 'Donald Matheson' ('A gleam of gold in your teeth/and a slow smile in your eye./You knew Hoover and Roosevelt well,/or so you said,/and you were a tramp/on the roads of America./...reared in another country, you might have been a Castro at least') to 'Murdo Morrison, 1872-', a retired Inspector of Schools who lived to be over a hundred, to 'Cotriona Mhòr' – a key poem this:

Tha do dhealbh ann an cùl
    [m' inntinn
gun sgleò air,
daingeann, suidhichte
am measg nan ìomhaighean briste...
...Siud iuchair mo mhuseum,
an clàr air an cluich mi mo
    [bheul-aithris...
an ìomhaigh tha cumail smachd
    [air na h-ìomhaighean-brèige.

Your picture is at the back of my
    [mind
undimmed,
steady, set
among the broken images...
...That is the key to my museum,
the record on which I play my
    [folklore...
the image that keeps control over
    [false images.

Towards the end of the sequence comes 'An Galar' (The Disease):

Chaidh mi mach á tarraing do [phlanaid,	I escaped the pull of your planet,
chan eil mo cheum trom, ged is [trom am meadhon-latha,	my step is weightless, heavy though [middle age may be,
air na ròidean eòlach sin,	on these well-known roads,
tha mi seòladh ann a fànas leam [fhìn.	I float alone in space.

Thomson has said of *An Rathad Cian* that it is 'both a celebration of Lewis and a farewell to it', and while the next book, *Saorsa agus an Iolaire* (Freedom and the Eagle), has poems on Lewis and on relatives and friends there, we feel that the poet will not be revisiting it as often. In fact, four of the first nine poems in this book have the word 'Scots', 'Scotland' (twice) and 'Scottish' in their title, and one recalls that the early 1970s were a time of considerable political excitement in Scotland, with a resurgence in the fortunes of the Scottish National Party (in 1974 eleven MPs were returned to Westminster – there had never been so many, nor have there since then) and with much debate upon themes such as 'It's Scotland's oil', a popular slogan of the time.

Derick Thomson was and is a member of the Party, and was involved in campaigning in both the General Elections in 1974 and in local elections, and in his poetry we find him looking anew at Scotland and its condition. Often the treatment is satirical, as in 'Fòghnan na h-Alba' (Thistle of Scotland), when he finds that the national symbol or emblem smells of Old Spice (a well known aftershave). But that is not the last word:

Ach tha mi mionnaichte	But I could swear
gu bheil fòghnanan fhathast a' fàs	there are still thistles growing
am measg chreagan,	among rocks,
is fàileadh na gaoithe dhiubh.	with the scent of the wind off them.
Tha mi dol air an tòir.	I am going to look for them.

In 'A Scottish Story', which 'concentrates on the spider rather than on Bruce', 'The Poke-of-Salt [one of the spider's names in Gaelic] was weary,/all day trying to stand upright/with no backbone in him... the next day, if he were spared,/he would go on his knees/to lick the boots that were trampling him...'

In this book, too, Thomson, for the first time, embarks on longish poems made up of discrete sections, as in 'An Crann'

(*crann* has various meanings – 'plough', 'mast', 'harp-key' etc.):

Tha fonn aig a' chrann,	The plough has land/the harp-key [has a tune,
iomadh fonn aig crann mo dhùthcha,	my country's harp has many tunes,
fonn iomadh-fhillte air a clàr	it had a many-layered tune
mus deach a creachadh...	before it was smashed...
Fo na bunan seacte...	Under the withered stubble...
fon an taigh air grodadh...	under the house in decay...
Fon a' chridhe ragte	under the stubborn heart
stob a-steach an crann.	thrust the plough in.

Another longer poem, 'An Turas' (The Journey), is a superbly sustained monologue by an alcoholic: sardonic, tragic, at times farcical.

The great popularity of poetry readings that has lasted since the 1970s (and whose beginnings are often traced to the 1960s) affected Scotland as it did other places, and Derick Thomson was revealed as a fine reader of his own poetry. In 1971 he was one of the party of three Scottish Gaelic poets who inaugurated the Scottish-Irish series of exchange visits of poets and musicians that has continued ever since, and he has read at many venues at home and abroad. It also seems clear that he began consciously to write poems that would make an impact at first hearing. If one had a concern about his work, it would be that a throw-away line can sometimes be cryptic (at least to this reader) and that his facility with poems like this might tempt him to produce them too readily. But he has usually been too exacting an artist to allow that to happen.

Certainly, some of the poems in *Saorsa agus an Iolaire* and many of the group first collected in *Creachadh na Clàrsaich* – these might be thought of as forming his fifth book – are highly suitable for reading aloud. One, indeed, is entitled 'Fuaim-Dhàn' (Sound-Poem), and he reads it memorably and has elected not to translate it. But in this notional fifth book there is yet another development of Thomson's subject-matter, in the sequence entitled 'Airc a' Choimhcheangail' (The Ark of the Covenant).

Even in these relatively unregenerate days, that is a bold and resonant title, but this sequence of seventeen poems contains, to quote the critic and anthologist Ronald Black, 'an ineffable series of cameos'.[5] Thomson had, of course, written on religion and on some of its practitioners earlier, but not on this scale, and not so memorably. Not himself a believer, he is the son of parents who were – in fact, his father was a church elder as well as a poet – and he was brought up in a Lewis where the influence of a particular kind of Presbyterian religion was very pervasive. Now the poet looks back and meditates on both the loss and the beauty that entailed, on the strange carry-overs and correspondences:

'Se Glaschu an Eiphit a bh'agaibh	Glasgow was your Egypt
's chaidh cuid agaibh ann nur [n-òige	and some of you migrated there in [your youth
nuair a thàinig a' chaoile air an tìr:	when the lean years came on your [land:
chaidh sibh sìos am measg nan [diathan coimheach…	you went down among the foreign [gods…
Ach ghairm ur n-athair air ais gu [ur tìr fhèin sibh…	But your Father called you back…

('Se Glaschu an Eiphit a Bh'agaibh')   ('Glasgow Was Your Egypt')

Nuair a thogadh tu na sailm	When you began the psalms
bha sinn air ar giùlan	we were transported
air na pongan slaodach sin	on these leisurely notes
gu ionad eile:	to another place:
leitheach slighe eadar Canaan is [Garrabost…	half-way between Canaan and [Garrabost…
Rut 's Naòmi am bun na lota...	Ruth and Naomi at the foot of the [croft…

('Dòmhnall Rodaidh')   ('Donald Roddy')

…is bha thu anns a' bhàr sin a-rithist	And you were in that bar again
aig iasgach Shasainn	at the English fishing,
far an tàine tu aghaidh ri aghaidh	when you came face to face
ris a' Chruthaidhear.	with the Creator.
Cò chailleadh cuimhn' air a leithid?	Who would forget the like of that?

('Air a' Cheist')   ('When You Rose on Question-Day')

Thomson has won a rich poetic harvest from a subject on which many Scottish writers – including some very successful in other areas – have been dumbstruck or shrill. It is a highly suitable way in which to round off a volume of collected poems, and it is a measure of his sympathetic and humane (although far from uncritical) approach to his own people and culture, and of his experienced artistry, that he has brought off such a feat.

***

Liberal use has been made of quotation within this essay, so that a flavour of the poetry itself may be provided, but one repeats the caveat regarding poetry in translation – even in the poet's own translation. However, it should still be clear that, while this poetry is written in a minority language, and one still without full legal status in its own country at the beginning of the twenty-first century, it is modern poetry that deserves international recognition (which it has, to some degree, already received).

The poet has devoted his working life to making available and elucidating the Gaelic literature of Scotland, and in particular the rich canon of poetry that is still extant (although it is clear that much, especially from the earlier period, has been lost). He has also frequently been involved in making the case for the language generally. It is not a unique phenomenon that such a scholar and activist should also contribute meaningfully to a tradition as a creative artist, but it is still rare enough for it to be noteworthy. The scholar Derick Thomson and the poet Ruaraidh MacThòmais are one and the same, and although he was preceded by pioneers who did much to 'make it new' in the twentieth century, he has himself contributed vitally to the process, from whichever point of view we consider his body of creative work.

In terms of form, he was deeply aware of the tradition, but even in his early poetry he shows healthy innovation, and uses traditional features (such as rhyme and allusion) in the service of the poem rather than couching his work mechanically in a traditional format. Having shown his ease with the traditional style, he gradually moved to freer and what he would call more organic forms, and he has repeatedly demonstrated mastery of these. As to themes, he has produced fine love poetry, poetry examining the relationship between a person and the native place (in his case, a highly complex matter) and the culture of the place itself (in this instance, with a necessary focus on religious life), and he has explored his country's past, its current identity and its future. These are all matters of universal interest. He has deployed a wide vocabulary, from the resonantly poetic to the everyday, in accordance with his purpose, which may vary from the expression of deep devotion to satire.

Thomson has also been a father-figure to younger poets, the work of several of whom clearly shows his influence – but it is an influence that has been creatively assimilated.

He has also continued to publish. *Smeur an Dochais/Bramble of Hope* (1991) begins with a series of Glasgow vignettes, and while the book shows much continuity with its predecessors, there is perhaps a new mellowness of tone: the author is, after all, approaching the three score years and ten.[6] *Meall Garbh/The Rugged Mountain* (1995) takes its title from Thomson's most extended long poem yet (over 400 lines), a description of, and meditation on, the climbing of a mountain in Perthshire. The poem ranges widely over local and national history, and is one of forty poems in the book, which include the fascinating 'An t-Anam-Fàis'/'The Vegetative Soul'. Regrettably, there is no space in which to discuss these most recent books here, but it may be apt to close with part of a poem from *Meall Garbh* entitled 'Leisgeul' (Sorry). Fionn and Osgar are heroes from Gaelic mythology, and the White Cockade is a rosette associated with the Jacobites (now much romanticised), who wished to restore the Stuarts to the throne of Britain:

Gabh mo leisgeul:	Sorry:
chan eil mi de chuideachd Fhinn	I am not one of the company of Finn
no Osgair...	or Oscar...
Tha na sgeulachdan sgoinneil sin	These moving stories
ann an ciste ar n-eachdraidh	are in our history's coffin,
's tha a' chiste a' breothadh.	and the coffin is decaying.
'S e monadh is beinn	I prefer moor and hill
as fheàrr leam na cladh,	to graveyard,
's tha sòbhrag nas mìlse	and find the primrose sweeter
na suaithneas bàn.	than the White Cockade.
Ach an dèidh sin 's 'na dhèidh	But for all that
dh'iarrainn iolaire anns na speuran	I'd want to have an eagle in our
[againn	[skies

cho math ri brù-dhearg,	as well as a robin,
is bradan a bhith tighinn thugainn	to have salmon coming to us
á muir cèin,	from distant seas,
is sgeul is òran ùr	and new tales and songs
a' dol dhan chiste.	going in the chest.

Ruaraidh MacThòmais/Derick Thomson has given us many new songs, and his contribution has immeasurably enriched the chest.

NOTES

[1] It should be noted for completeness that in December 1971 an entire issue of the Scottish literary magazine *Lines Review* (no. 39) was devoted to Thomson's work. This included an introduction by his fellow-Lewisman and fellow-poet Donald MacAulay which surveyed his work to date; translations by the poet himself of all 56 poems from *An Rathad Cian*, whose English title, 'The Far Road', was also the title of the special issue; translations by the poet of ten poems from *Eadar Samhradh is Foghar*, and a new poem of 76 lines in ten sections, 'Anns an Ospadal'/'In the Hospital', printed in the original Gaelic with parallel English translation. The literary material was preceded by a strong line drawing by Linda MacEwen. The whole was also published at the same time as a book entitled *The Far Road* by New Rivers Press of New York. It is all included in *Creachadh na Clàrsaich*. The main poetry collections by Derick Thomson are: *An Dealbh Briste,* Edinburgh: Serif Books, 1951; *Eadar Samhradh is Foghar*, Glasgow: Gairm, 1967; *An Rathad Cian,* Glasgow: Gairm, 1970, with translations in *The Far Road,* Edinburgh and New York: MacDonald-New Rivers Press, 1971; *Saorsa agus an Iolaire*, Glasgow: Gairm, 1977; *Creachadh na Clàrsaich/Plundering the Harp: Collected Poems 1940-1980*, Edinburgh: MacDonald, 1982; *Smeur an Dòchais/Bramble of Hope,* Edinburgh: Canongate Press, 1992; *Meall Garbh/The Rugged Mountain,* Glasgow: Gairm, 1995; *Bàrdachd le Ruaraidh MacThòmais/Poems by Derick Thomson,* Glasgow, 2002 – CD and cassette of the poet and others reading 38 poems plus 22 translations; *Scotland o Gael and Lawlander,* Glasgow: Gairm, 1996 – includes 14 poems translated into Scots by Derrick McClure. He has also published several works, such as *Gaelic Learners' Handbook,* Glasgow: Gairm, 1973; *An Introduction to Gaelic Poetry,* London and New York: Victor Gollancz, 1974; *The*

New Verse in Scottish Gaelic: a Structural Analysis, Dublin: University College, 1974; *The New English-Gaelic Dictionary,* Glasgow: Gairm, 1981; Editor and contributor: *The Companion to Gaelic Scotland,* Oxford: Blackwell Reference, 1983; *Why Gaelic Matters,* Edinburgh: Saltire Society, 1984.

[2] David Daiches ed., *A Companion to Scottish Culture,* London: Edward Arnold, 1981, p. 376.

[3] *Scottish Gaelic Studies,* Vol. XVII, Aberdeen: University of Aberdeen, 1996.

[4] *Ibidem,* p. 3

[5] Ronald Black ed., *An Tuil: Anthology of 20th Century Scottish Gaelic Verse,* Edinburgh: Polygon, 1999, p. xliv.

[6] *Smeur an Dòchais* attracted some extra publicity in 1997 because of the plagiarism of some of the poetry by a man in Cornwall. The poet appeared unruffled by this somewhat bizarre episode, and the act of plagiarism is perhaps some kind of compliment!

CAROL GOW

Truth and Fiction in the English Poetry of Iain Crichton Smith: Unfinished Tapestry

To be claimed by a language. To feel at home within a discourse. For any writer, this is the first base. For Scottish writers, however, the sense of a discourse which inscribes self and home is problematic: Scots, English, or Gaelic? Do you choose a language, or does the language choose you? For Iain Crichton Smith, the creation of a discourse, a poetry, that offers home has involved a lifetime's journey: the creation of an 'I' is constantly tested and honed in a discourse that seeks to weave a home for the poet that is anchored in a real time and place in Scotland even though that means confronting all that seems destructive to his art. In his poetry, the journey does not end, however, and homecoming is always deferred. The closing paragraph from a late short story, 'The Boy and The Rowan Tree', is unmistakably Iain Crichton Smith's because it offers a metaphor for that lifetime's journey and looks forward, but not yet, to the completion of 'the story':

> I think the boy will find the driver of the white van. He will be taken down to Nottingham: the driver wouldn't leave him here. I'm pretty sure of that. And very soon the blackbird will return to the rowan tree. And then the story will be complete.[1]

Here is a discourse honed and claimed, fingerprinted with images of the lost boy reclaimed, the blackbird returning to the red-berried rowan tree. These images outline the large themes that underpin Crichton Smith's poetry. This essay will trace the stories the poet inhabits, show how the sense of home and completion is constantly undermined, and finally suggest that, paradoxically, home for the poet can be found only in a poetry that defers the ending of homecoming, defers completion of the story he weaves for himself.

If, as Crichton Smith has written, a language chooses you, then he was twice claimed by the Gaelic of his childhood and the English of his education. Growing up in the village of Bayble, on the island of Lewis in the Outer Hebrides, he inhabited a Gaelic world and spoke only Gaelic until he was five years old. At five, brutally and suddenly, he entered an 'English' world of education. At Bayble school he was taught in English, and the textbooks he studied were written in English. In 1933, a child could be punished for speaking Gaelic in the playground. That sudden wrench from a Gaelic to an English world Crichton Smith calls 'a blow to the psyche, an insult to the brain' and suggests to him 'the perfect recipe for schizophrenia'.[2]

Certainly it seems as if it is the entry into formal education that creates the major conflict that underpins his work. Looking at a class photograph Crichton Smith identifies 'a child whose eyes are heavy and almost dim with fright, staring into a world which he finds threatening'.[3] He recalls his sense of isolation, the sense of being an outsider, often ill with asthma and overprotected because of his mother's fear of T.B. He was kept away from school at the slightest hint of illness. His mother's fear transmitted itself to the boy and Crichton Smith recalls dreadful nightmares about haemorrhaging. Yet it is vital to note that his mother's fear of T.B. was not without cause. She had seen her husband die from the disease when her youngest son was a baby and she witnessed the old and the young on the island succumb. The disease was known on Lewis as *Galair an t-sraingear*, the stranger's disease, because it was brought back home to the island by returning fisher girls who had left Lewis to work in the herring industry or on the mainland, and who there came into contact with a disease to which they had no natural immunity. The death rate peaked in the first ten years of the twentieth century. Conditions on the island then, the typical black house, with thatched roof, smoky atmosphere, the drinking of contaminated milk, and a lack of knowledge about precautions, allowed the disease to rage on the island.

It was not just the ravages of T.B. which brought death close to the people of the island and to the growing boy. The island offered a sombre history of young men's lives lost in two world wars. Thus Crichton Smith perceived himself as growing up in a community of women and old men. Perhaps most of all, however, it was the fate of the *Iolaire* which made a deep and lasting impression on him. The yacht *Iolaire*, bringing servicemen home to the island on New Year's Eve 1918, foundered only yards from shore. Over two hundred young men from the island were drowned. 'It has had a deep influence on the way that I think about the world. It is almost a black comedy or a Greek tragedy. I can imagine these people waiting for the ex-servicemen to come home, with lamps lit, food on the table and so on. And then they are drowned'.[4] In the mind of the poet, then, homecoming and death are joined in a macabre twist of fate.

It is not hard to see, then, why the world of the Gaelic village seemed threatening to the child, not hard to see why the school-room seemed to beckon like Paradise:

> How long ago that seemed! Running barefoot to school while the head-master waited with the whistle in his mouth and you ran like the wind and the iron bell clanged and the strawberries were growing in the gar-den and the teachers – all women – were waiting to welcome you into their huge arms and bosoms and the walls were bright with all the maps of the world.[5]

Set this Paradise of strawberries, welcoming arms, bosoms and bright maps against the 'Old Woman' of Crichton Smith's poetry whose 'set mouth forgives no one', and you set a warm earth-mother against the disapproving black-gowned matriarch.[6] For the poet, a nurturing, life-giving schoolroom is set against a fear-rid-den, life-draining home. This schism, this perception of existing 'between two worlds' and being drawn inexorably away from his Gaelic home, was perhaps not so clear to the growing boy at the time.[7] The choice was innocent, and would prove irrevocable. Yet for the poet it seems a choice for life against death.

Crichton Smith flourished in the world of his English education, and not just academically. Physically, too, he became stronger. The asthma which plagued him throughout his Lewis years cleared completely when he left the island to begin his university educa-tion in Aberdeen. His memories of that period include a sense of freedom, of anonymity, in which he revelled. Implicit in the divi-sion between the discourse of the prose and the poem quoted above is division between the stuff of life and the stuff of death.

Crichton Smith's perception of his Gaelic community is challenged but understood by close friend Professor Derick Thomson:

> He didn't have a very secure family background in a way – father dead, probably very short of cash, not very fully integrated into the village, to which they had come from Glasgow. By contrast, my father was the local schoolmaster, and a prominent Gaelic activist and writer, and my mother was also very interested in Gaelic poetry and song. It was perhaps easier for Iain to see a specific identity in what came his way of current fashionable English literature (and there was, after all, nothing remotely comparable in Gaelic at the time, – no literary periodicals, scarcely any new books).[8]

For Crichton Smith, the Gaelic, Calvinist background could not offer the poet a home in which he could flourish:

> Here they have no place for the fine graces
> of poetry, unless it freely grows
> in deep compulsion, like water in the well,
> woven into the texture of the soil
> in a strong pattern[9]

Home, the discourse in which he can begin to create and develop the 'I' of his text, is first discovered not 'here' on the island and its culture, but in the language of the literature he studied, the English writers and English poets of his education on the island and subsequently at Aberdeen University. Like many Scots of his generation, Crichton Smith's education removed him from his island home not just physically, but emotionally and spiritually too. That loss was not immediately apparent to him:

> I recall with a sense of injustice my own fragmented life, the choices I had to make when I didn't realise that I was making them, the losses I endured before I well knew that I was enduring them, the contradictions I was involved in before I knew they existed. And I know that my own life has been a snake pit of contradictions, because of an accident of geography and a hostile history. I envy, for instance, those poets who have developed in a stable society, who can start from there and are not constantly analysing the very bases of their art.[10]

The loss is understood by the man, but is discovered by the poet in his text in a backward glance, too late. To study Crichton Smith's poetry is to discover a deep and unifying theme: the seeking of a

narrative of homecoming. Return, however, seems linked with all
that is dangerous and hostile, and ultimately, with the death of the
discourse of the poet.

In the early volumes, the titles themselves reveal that the discourse Crichton Smith inhabits engages him in conflict with his
background: *Thistles and Roses, The Law and the Grace*. Identity is
created in opposition, and yet constantly tested against, and judged
by, his Gaelic background. As the 'I' of the poetry is developed,
however, it begins to be undermined and challenged as a fiction. It
is undermined by fact – primarily by images of death. Crichton
Smith's poetry weaves a tapestry, an identity and a life for the poet,
but the poet becomes aware that something is overlooked: the
death's head.

Discussion of Hans Holbein's painting, 'The Ambassadors', will
illuminate this point. In the painting, the artist uses perspective to
present the watcher, on the moment of looking away, with a
death's head. The picture itself depicts two finely-robed ambassadors, who stand on either side of objects which represent learning. Holbein makes use of perspective to distort an image in the
foreground which becomes clear in the minute the eye retreats
from the work: it is a skull. The painting represents not a celebration of the sum of human knowledge but the coat of arms of
death. The crucifix behind the curtain, however, promises to
replace worldly knowledge with divine knowledge. Death is not
an ending but a transformation. Holbein reveals perspective not as
absolute, but as a certain stance.

I want to illustrate how the image of the death's head intrudes
and threatens the tapestry of identity the poet has woven for himself, because it is something he has missed out of the frame. The
idea of a creation which involves lack is something that has
intrigued Crichton Smith. In an interview in 1987, Crichton Smith
relived his mental breakdown and reflected on some of the strange
misapprehensions he had experienced which seemed, at the time,
to make perfect sense:

> I wondered, you know, if someone creates a major theory, whether as I
> was doing he leaves out the things that don't fit in and just puts in the
> things that fit in. And it could be applied on a much bigger scale. I was
> just picking out the bits out of all the flux to fit in with my own ideas.[11]

Crichton Smith's poetry too is discovered to involve lack. What has been left out of the frame in his tapestry is the death's head which will appear and make the poet falter, will insist on a review of the theory, the discourse, which breathes life in the 'I' of the poems.

In fact, the death's head was there, right from the moment Crichton Smith stepped off the train in Aberdeen at seventeen to begin his university studies. He has said he felt free, anonymous, for the first time in his life, but that sense of freedom was challenged by a moment of recognition. On the platform he was confronted by a blind beggar. The incident stayed with him throughout his life, not just because of the culture shock he experienced – such a man would be cared for, claimed, by the community on his island – but because that blind gaze was like the gaze of Teresius, questioning identity, and because, more importantly, meeting that blind gaze was like meeting a mirror in which was reflected the lost boy, the vagrant who must be claimed by his community.

If the death's head intrudes in real life, it insists on a place in the poetry, too. In 'Sunday Morning Walk' for example, the poet is a 'pack of wandering flesh' like the sheep he is to encounter.[12] There is a peripeteia however, as his literary musings are disrupted by the reality of the dead sheep before him and reveals a poet stopped in his tracks by this scene of death. The idea of grace, a poetry which is pure and untainted, removed from the world, begins to be questioned: 'Too simple this pure art's hypothesis/transforming bones and flesh into light'.[13]

Poems are continually fractured and undercut by something that has been omitted. But it is the death of Crichton Smith's mother in 1969 which finally rips apart the tapestry. In 1971 he was able to say:

> Everything I have ever done is really eventually coming to this question. What is death? What is a dead person, and in the end what is the value of writing when one is confronted by a dead person.[14]

The death's head is acknowledged. However, it poses a question to which the poet can find no response. Whereas in Holbein's painting, the death's head is absorbed and indeed transcended by faith, here it threatens to dominate the tapestry, to silence the poet. His mother has frequently represented the life-threatening Gaelic back-

ground he has denied a place as he created an Other, life-giving
discourse. Now he weighs up the choice:

> The herring in my hand,
> bloody and gutted, would be far more solid
> than this more slippery verse[15]

And in 'On looking at the dead', he writes:

> This is a coming to reality.
> This is the stubborn place. No metaphors swarm
>
> Around that fact, around that strangest thing,
> that being that was and now no longer is.[16]

The tapestry has been violated by an event in the historical world.
What is faced here, finally, is the death's head that has haunted his
poetry. Shadowy, misapprehended, misinterpreted, it can no longer
be misrecognised. In order to survive, the poet has to work
through to a position where he, like Holbein, can include the
death's head within the frame and perceive it not as the end but
within the perspective of a larger meaning:

> so I know
> that death is just a place that we have looked
> too deeply at, not into, as at a book
> held that short space too close. For we must hold
> back from a painting so as to see it whole.[17]

And the cost to his poetry of admitting the death's head? In
'Orpheus' he writes:

> And so his lyre had a graver heavier tone
> As if containing all the possible grains
> That can be found in marble or in stone.
> What he had lost was the sweet and random strains
> Which leaped obliquely from the vast unknown
> Concordances and mirrors but the gains,
> Though seeming sparser, were more dearly won.[18]

The tapestry is been reworked. The 'mirrors', the identities reflected in the poetry, were created apart from his Gaelic background.
The grains of marble and stone, in the context of 'graver', suggest

the inclusion now into the tapestry the historical world, the Gaelic background, and the reality of death.

Such a tapestry 'though seeming sparser' has yet gains. Crichton Smith has said of Sorley MacLean's work:

> One has the feeling of integrity, that his life and his work are not separate and that what he really thinks about himself is in the poetry.[19]

Here is a poet meeting the gaze of the blind beggar, the death's head, the gaze which questions the identity he has wrought for himself, and undertaking to answer truthfully. His poetry becomes increasingly stripped down:

> I have been always suspicious of the glitteringly aesthetic. Metaphor can sometimes be used to conceal insoluble contradictions in life, and Yeats's poem, 'Easter 1916' did not solve the Irish crisis, it only clarified it. In the end, society lives and works outside the metaphor, and to think the metaphor solves anything except the problems set by the poet would be silly and unrealistic. Beyond the poems of Seamus Heaney, beautiful thought they are, the masked men will stand above the draped coffins saluting an empty heaven with their guns.[20]

Heaney has argued that art is not a solution to reality and has cautioned 'to deny your life the suasion of art-peace' is an 'unnecessary Puritanism'.[21] For Crichton Smith, the movement is inexorably towards that kind of Puritanism and towards the values of his island. He has written:

> The island is the anvil where was made
> The puritanical heart. The daisies foam
> Out of the summer grass. The rigid dead
> Sleep by the Braighe, tomb on separate tomb.[22]

Perhaps the 'puritanical heart' here is seen as other, separate from the I of the poetry, but inexorably the island and its mores are discovered to be not other, but within. Crichton Smith has said of his early poetry:

> There was something self-consciously literary about it, you know, it was a kind of a pose in a way. But now I think probably images are part of what I do, the way I think.[23]

The poetry moves towards accepting the strictures and limitations of his background, towards an identity which is seen in terms of fracture and loss: 'Venus with the one arm/Apollo with the one leg'.[24]

How to continue to write, to marry the fiction and the truth? Crichton Smith begins to find an answer. Here we have a tragic hero, a Hamlet who denies tragedy as 'nothing' but who still finds a brief space in which to exist, here between one line and the next, despite the enjambement, a fractured existence which is yet triumphant:

> Tragedy is
> Nothing but churned foam,
> I wave to you
> From this secure and leafy entrance
> This wooden
> Door on which I bump my head
> This moment and then,
> That.[25]

Tragedy 'is', like a defiant slogan, and the wave is a confident gesture, which undercuts the entrance and wooden door which brand him an actor, created by text. Here is the response to Shakespeare's extended metaphor of the world as stage and the individual as actor with exits and entrances – 'this moment and then,/that' allows just enough space, hemmed in, circumscribed, to act, and to act aware of the death's head.

A lifetime's journey, seeking a truthful discourse which offers a return to home. That has been Crichton Smith's task. He has said 'sometimes the real poem is the dark companion travelling alongside the actually created one'.[26] In Crichton Smith's poetry the dark companion is death, the death's head which has represented the Calvinist background, the truth, intruding into the fiction, insisting on a presence, on recognition. Otherwise, his stance is branded as just a pose, the poet as Hamlet, the actor on stage:

> 'that flourishing... false to the realities of life for most people... didn't correlate with the experiences of people, ordinary people in a way. It was a kind of pose in a way.[27]

In his poems of exile, Crichton Smith rewrites a homecoming for Odysseus in 'Next Time':

> Next time, do this,
> Salt-bronzed veteran
> Let the tapestry be unfinished
> As truthful fiction is[28]

The first word of the poem, 'Listen', insists on story, insists on an identity created at each time of telling, and to 'let the tapestry be unfinished' is to defer the ending of homecoming. 'Truthful fiction' offers a discourse in which the poet Iain Crichton Smith can survive, wholly inscribed neither in background nor in text.

Homecoming is rehearsed in *A Life*, where the self is perceived in a text of traditional denouement involving the return of the lost boy. Crichton Smith has said of Oliver Twist: 'I seemed to identify with that waif of the streets setting out to find his identity':[29]

> So your death will be like a marriage,
> As a return of the lost boy
> To the house where he originally belonged,
>
> After he had been punished in an orphanage,
> Forced to climb sooty chimneys,
> To put varnish on coffins.[30]

The return (*nostos*) offers a home, but the poet's instinct is that it will silence him. In the novel *My Last Duchess*, the hero Mark Simmons sees himself as 'homo textual' and the text here too plays with claiming, the return of the lover to his loved one. It is not difficult to see the lover here as the Gaelic matriarch, the island and the people that formed the man:

> He would find her after many years and he would say, 'I was wrong. I will do anything you wish. I will be whatever you wish me to be. I will no longer be the mental aristocrat, the aloof ridiculous backward man'...
>
> But as he looked in to the varying patterns of the snow he knew that he had come to the end of a certain road, that he had forced himself by some inner compulsion to the limits, that after all this was where he must have wanted to be, in the coldness of truth. Everyone got what they deserved in a way the Victorian novelists did not dream of.[31]

The *nostos* of homecoming can never be written. Such a homecoming would be death for the poet. Yet the death's head can no

longer be part of the unauthorised script. It must be admitted into
the frame of his tapestry. 'Varnish on coffins' is a phrase which
acknowledges awareness of the disjunction between metaphor and
society, the self-inscription and the script. Crichton Smith's poetry
is remarkable in the way that it has explored this disjunction and in
the way that he has demanded a poetry which admits into his text
that which threatens silence. In conversation, he remarked on the
relentless nature of that exploration. He searched at that point for a
poem from the early Thistles and Roses which he felt summarised
what he meant:

> It's this one – 'Of a rare Courage'. Actually the last poem in it. Where I
> say 'For he unlike those others sees quite clearly/The fractured failure of
> the best we are./And therefore I will praise him like those other/success-
> ful darlings who discover late/a tang of burning in the acid ether/and in
> spontaneous gestures a fixed fate'. You know, I think that's roughly what
> I feel even now after all these years – that what at the time to me seemed
> to be a spontaneous gesture or a spontaneous book or poem turns out to
> have been part of an overall fixed developing theme – there's an enor-
> mous amount of conditioning in everything that we do.[32]

'In spontaneous gestures a fixed fate'. Like Hamlet's wave, the gesture turns out to be not unique, not spontaneous, but set down in
the script. His journey away, his flight towards an English discourse, and then towards the creation of an identity in poetry that
was yet still protected from his Calvinist background, has brought
him close to home again. The self-inscription turns out to be what
is already written.

In 'The Boy and The Rowan Tree', the writer is faced with the
archetypal images from his work; the figure of the vagrant who
must be reclaimed, the blackbird, the tree with its red berries. In
the text, he deconstructs the resolution:

> Let me be quite honest and plain about this. The boy caused me concern
> yet I was trying to justify the workings of the universe. That was why I
> summoned up the image of the rowan tree with its red berries. The boy
> was dripping as was the rowan tree. In the end however, poetic imagery
> may fail.[33]

Art-peace is denied the poet. The ending of the short story, the
quotation with which I began, sets out a possible *nostos*:[34]

I think the boy will find the driver of the white van. He will be taken down to Nottingham: the driver wouldn't leave him here. I'm pretty sure of that. And very soon the blackbird will return to the rowan tree. And then the story will be complete.

'I think', 'I'm pretty sure', 'very soon', 'And then the story will be complete'. The tapestry remains incomplete, a truthful fiction, the *nostos* of homecoming perpetually deferred.

NOTES

[1] Iain Crichton Smith, 'The Boy and the Rowan Tree', Internet Magazine: HYPERLINK "http://www.orknet.co.uk/oar/crichton.htm", 1996.

[2] Iain Crichton Smith, 'Real People in a Real Place', in *Towards the Human*, Edinburgh: Macdonald Publishers, 1986, (pp. 13-70) p. 42; and Iain Crichton Smith, 'Writing in Gaelic', *Lines Review*, vol. 33, no. 2, 1970, (pp. 3-9) p. 3.

[3] Iain Crichton Smith, 'Between Sea and Moor', in Maurice Lindsay ed., *As I Remember*, London: Robert Hale, 1979, (pp. 107-121) p. 111.

[4] Iain Crichton Smith, 'The Highland Element in my English Work', *Scottish Literary Journal*, vol. 4, 1977, (pp. 47-60) p. 51.

[5] Iain Crichton Smith, *The Last Summer*, London: Gollancz, 1969, p. 9.

[6] Iain Crichton Smith, *The Law and the Grace*, London: Eyne & Spottiswoode, 1965, p. 16.

[7] Iain Crichton Smith, 'Writers and Education', *Scottish Education Journal*, 31 October 1975, (pp. 1010-1011) p. 1010.

[8] Private correspondence, 25 August, 1987.

[9] Iain Crichton Smith, 'Poem of Lewis', in *Collected Poems*, Manchester: Carcanet, 1992, p. 2.

[10] Iain Crichton Smith, *Towards the Human*, cit., p. 51.

[11] Interview with the author, Taynuilt, 1987.

[12] Iain Crichton Smith, *Thistles and Roses*, London: Eyne & Spottiswoode, 1961, p. 22.

[13] Iain Crichton Smith, *The Law and the Grace*, cit., p. 58.

[14] Lorn Macintyre, 'Poet in Bourgeois Land', *Scottish International*, September 1971, (pp. 22-27) p. 27.

[15] Iain Crichton Smith, *Love Poems and Elegies*, London: Gollancz,

1972, p. 51.

[16] *Ibidem*, p. 21.

[17] *Ibidem*, p. 36.

[18] Iain Crichton Smith, *Orpheus and Other Poems*, Preston: Akros, 1974, p. 14.

[19] Interview with the author, Taynuilt, 1987.

[20] Iain Crichton Smith, *Towards the Human*, cit., p. 48.

[21] Randy Barnes, 'Seamus Heaney: An Interview', *Salmagundi*, vol. 80, 1988, (pp. 4-21) p. 21.

[22] Iain Crichton Smith, *A Life*, Manchester: Carcanet, 1986, p. 9.

[23] Interview with the author, Taynuilt, 1987.

[24] Iain Crichton Smith, *The Exiles*, Manchester: Carcanet, 1984, p. 56.

[25] *Ibidem*, p. 57.

[26] Iain Crichton Smith, 'Charts of Poetic Journeys', *Glasgow Herald*, 6 December 1979, p. 12.

[27] Interview with the author, Taynuilt, 1987.

[28] Iain Crichton Smith, *The Exiles*, cit., p.11.

[29] Iain Crichton Smith, 'My Relationship with Poetry', *Chapman* 16, vol. 4, no. 4, 1976, (pp. 12-18) p. 12.

[30] Iain Crichton Smith, *A Life*, cit., p. 56.

[31] Iain Crichton Smith, *My Last Duchess*, London: Gollancz, 1971, p. 158.

[32] Interview with the author, Taynuilt 1987.

[33] Iain Crichton Smith, 'The Boy and The Rowan Tree', www.orknet.co.uk (see note 1).

[34] *Ibidem*.

MASSIMILIANO MORINI-VALENTINA POGGI

The Poetry and the Fiction of George Mackay Brown: An Orkney Tapestry

THE POETRY

In the century which saw two World Wars and the creation of a global market, some of the most important poets in the English language have felt the need to root their verse in the history and traditions of a local community. Seamus Heaney's Northern Ireland, Basil Bunting's Northumberland, and Roy Fisher's Birmingham are very different places, but what they have in common is the way they have functioned as a focus for poems which were, under other respects, far from local and traditional. However, no poet has participated so exclusively and completely in the life of a very small place as George Mackay Brown.

George Mackay Brown was born in 1921 in Stromness, in the Orkneys, and died there in 1996, after living almost all of his life on the islands. He only spent some years in mainland Scotland after the war, when he studied at Newbattle Abbey College under Edwin Muir, and then did postgraduate research on G.M. Hopkins in Edinburgh in 1962. Muir exercised a great influence and offered encouragement, helping the young poet to get his works published in various magazines. Eventually, Mackay Brown published his first collection of poems, *The Storm*, in 1954.[1] It contained some lines of considerable promise, such as these from the title-poem:

And down the sand shot out our skiff
Into the long green jaws, while deep
In summer's sultry throat
Dry thunder stammered.[2]

However, though Muir's influence on the younger poet was great (Mackay Brown had been particularly impressed by Muir's autobiography, *The Story and the Fable*[3]), there were considerable differ-

ences between the two Orcadian writers. Muir's poetry, though
rooted in an Orkney childhood filtered through myth, was one
where the splendour of the 'Fable' was set against the squalor and
derangement of life in the modern, industrial city. Mackay Brown,
on the contrary, though he recognises the threat posed by bureau-
cracy and machinery (as seen in the novel *Greenvoe*[4]), sets most of
his poems in his native Orkneys, a landscape of which he can
name every stone and tree. Therefore, whereas Muir's poetry is
often disquieting, Mackay Brown's is supremely consoling: it is the
consolation offered by the picture of an enclosed world, where
everything and everyone have their place and even tragic events
are 'Godsent', as the storm in the poem quoted above. Mackay
Brown's Orkneys come to life in characters which can be divided
in type-groups and yet are never the same:[5] fisher, crofter, priest,
innkeeper, tinker, old woman, warrior. The islands are made of
bread, corn, and fish, they shine in gold and silver, and they are
ridden through by plough and ship. Mackay Brown's word for this
ordered web is 'tapestry', which is also a good definition for his
poems, stories, plays, and novels.

Despite the seemingly narrow confines of his universe, Mackay
Brown always manages to avoid the most dangerous trap awaiting
the local writer: the sentimental depiction of community life. His
islanders can be, and often are, greedy and violent, their purposes
exposed as inspired by malice and self-interest. In this, he resembles his great Welsh contemporary, R.S. Thomas; but unlike
Thomas, George Mackay Brown does not see the shortcomings of
his fellow-beings as evidence of the absence of God. On the contrary, he relishes depicting characters whose morality he, as a
Christian man, cannot endorse: 'The new skipper' of 'Vikings: Two
Harp-songs', for instance, boasts that 'The churches have had
enough of our swords', and threatens 'It is time the merchants
knew about us'.[6] Here is neither R.S. Thomas's despair nor
Geoffrey Hill's grim satisfaction in the unadorned facts of history:
on the contrary, it is the sheer pleasure of telling stories which
marks both Mackay Brown's fiction and his predominantly narrative poetry.

Also, George Mackay Brown is a regional poet, but certainly not
a provincial one. Though his field of vision might be seen as a lim-

ited one, he widens it indefinitely by conferring to it both historical and religious depth. His poems, like his stories, plays and novels, are set not only in contemporary Orkney, but also in the Orkney of previous centuries, of Norse times, or even of an imagined prehistoric past. Particularly important, to him, is the time when Orkney was a powerful Norse earldom. From this Germanic past, apart from a number of stories, Mackay Brown derives some of the defining characteristics of his poetic style; the use of kenningar, alliteration, and a saga-like compression:

HIERARCHY

A claret laird,
Seven fishermen with ploughs,
Women, beasts, corn, fish, stones.[7]

Another quality which saves Mackay Brown's poetry and prose from the strictures of provincialism is his ability to confer a mythical or religious dimension to his descriptions. Mackay Brown was a religious man who had always mistrusted the excesses of Northern Presbyterianism, and in 1961 he decided to embrace the Catholic Faith. Of Catholicism, he said in an interview that it was 'full of material for poets [...] a huge quarry of very rich and beautiful imagery':[8] and in his verse, he exploited these possibilities to the full. Not only did he write some memorable poems and sequences on religious subjects and Biblical stories, but he also explored, in his secular verse, the parallels between religious archetypes and everyday life: in many of his poems, the figure of Christ looms behind that of the Orcadian crofter, the furrows of the field are as many lines in the Great Book. More noticeably, and perhaps more importantly, Mackay Brown sees the history of humanity and of his native archipelago as having at its centre a small number of mystical events: as far as the Orkneys are concerned, there is the tale of Saint Magnus's martyrdom, told in the Orkneyinga Saga, which the poet defined as 'the great drama at the heart of the Orkney story'.[9] He rewrote it in different forms: poems, sequences, plays, stories, and the novel *Magnus*.[10] Earl Magnus, at the heart of Mackay Brown's vision as well as of the Orkney story, is the scapegoat who, more or less freely, renounces power and embraces death: his sacrifice is the seed of peace sown in a troubled age.

Mackay Brown's inspiration is religious in another fundamental, wider sense, in that it affirms the sacredness of both the things it describes and the words it is made of. George Mackay Brown thought that words, in the world of 'white papers and business letters, [...] lose their "ghosts" [...] their "kernel", the sheer sensuous relish of utterance':[11] in the novel *Greenvoe*, a small island community is destroyed by men whose bureaucratic jargon reflects their barrenly materialistic view of life (once again, one could see a parallel with R.S. Thomas's fixation with the 'machine'). Accordingly, Mackay Brown's poems show his desire to define neatly and accurately, but also economically, the realities they deal with: very often, as seen in 'Hierarchy', single things/words are evoked on the page as if they were runic spells 'to make the corn grow, to lure fish into the net'.[12] The wish to preserve things and the desire not to waste words are one.[13]

Therefore, though almost all of his poems are concerned with life on the Orkney islands, George Mackay Brown offers no mere realistic description. If one of his aspirations was no doubt that of being a chronicler of Orkney, he also wanted to bring out the inner qualities of objects and characters: their 'inscape', to use a word borrowed from the terminology of his beloved G.M. Hopkins. Ultimately, his verse is not about surfaces, not even about the act of witnessing (though both aspects have their importance): it is about the romantic search for depth, infinity, and causes. The poet's true task, when he has sung for the pleasure of his folk, is the 'interrogation of silence' which begins when the lights have all gone out:

THE POET

Therefore he no more troubled the pool of silence.
But put on mask and cloak,
Strung a guitar
And moved among the folk.
Dancing they cried,
'Ah, how our sober islands
Are gay again, since this blind lyrical tramp
Invaded the Fair!'

Under the last dead lamp

When all the dancers and masks had gone inside
His cold stare
Returned to its true task, interrogation of silence.[14]

Massimiliano Morini

THE FICTION

It seems apt to define the work of George Mackay Brown – in his later years a friend and collaborator of composer Peter Maxwell-Davies, who set many of his lyrics to music – in musical terms, as a brilliant series of variations on a theme. The theme is Orkney, the archipelago North-East of Scotland where Brown lived practically all his life; the variations are based on two main melodic lines: spirit of place and sense of time, human geography and history; a third strain, however, makes itself heard occasionally, increasingly as years go by: in it fantasy blends with the supernatural, and the Orcadian scene is sometimes transcended, transfigured into exotic regions or fairy-tale atmospheres, becoming a space of the soul rather than on the map, a locus of timeless and universal meaning.

In Orkney George Mackay Brown (the sixth son of humble parents, who began writing poems in his twenties while in a sanatorium, under treatment for t.b.c.), found the inexhaustible source of material he could weave into his tapestry of words, whether in the shape of poem, story, essay, novel or play. To the stark beauty of its land- and sea-scapes – radiant, bleak, or stormy according to weather and time of year – and to the wry humour of its natives, with their old traditions and idioms (that a lesser writer might have turned to the simple effect of local color), Orkney added in his eyes the deeper fascination of history and archeology: ruins and monuments pointing as far back as the Neolithic and as late as the Renaissance, connections and conflicts between peoples and nations, from Norway to ancient Rus, from Ireland to Constantinople, witnessed both by stone relics and ancient writings.

Foremost among the latter, the Icelandic Orkneyinga Saga and Njall's Saga inspired and influenced Brown's own writing in two ways: first, they impressed on his imagination the figures of the Norse Vikings, who had ruled and tilled the Orkney islands throughout the Middle Ages: strong and adventurous men, sensual and warlike, cruel and treacherous, but also capable of humour, idealism and poetry; secondly, the sagamen's terse and lucid prose came to represent a model of style to which he was to adhere all his life.

Brown's language has the evocative, musical and image-making quality of poetry in whatever genre he writes; however, elements of story and character are to be found *in nuce* in nearly all his lyrics, especially in poetic sequences such as *Fishermen with Ploughs*.[15] Therefore it is no wonder that Hogarth Press, where he had been introduced by Edwin Muir and had started publishing poems, soon suggested he should also try fiction. The outcome was the collection of short-stories *A Calendar of Love*,[16] which gave a sample of the range of narrative structures, settings and figures he was going to revisit, develop and refine on, over nearly three decades, in half-a-dozen superb collections: *A Time to Keep*, *Hawkfall*, *The Sun's Net*, *Andrina and Other Stories*, *The Masked Fisherman*, and *Winter Tales*.[17]

The title story of *A Calendar of Love* adapts to narrative a pattern already used in some of Brown's poems: twelve phases in a course of events, corresponding to as many months from January to December. The pattern became more and more of a favourite with the author, whose last published work, *Winter Tales*, shows no less than four calendar-stories. Three of them center respectively on a medieval architect and on two boys, a peasant and a tinker. A fourth, 'The Woodcarver', is to my judgement the best. Its protagonist is a type familiar to Mackay Brown's readers, the good-for-nothing, beer-loving, wife-nagged villager; who here, as the instinctive, unselfconscious, naif artist, comes to embody its creator's ideal of art as the unpretentious, disinterested making, out of the material of daily life, 'a thing of beauty' and a tribute to God. The calendar pattern allowed the author to blend character-sketch with varying seasons and situations of work and play: fishing, whaling, ploughing, harvesting, wooing and wedding, death and burial, all became stages in a progress leading inevitably toward the Winter Solstice, the time of night-and-sunrise, death-and-rebirth.

For, unlike his Presbyterian countrymen, George Mackay Brown, a convert to Catholicism, did not consider it sinful to associate Orkney's ancient Yule customs with the celebration of Christ's birth: were not the pagan rituals of the Winter Solstice an unconscious foreshadowing of the redemption of man, and of the universe with him, by the Man-God? Hence the Christmas motif recurs in many of his best poems and stories, bringing, as it were, up to date and into an Orcadian framework the Gospel narratives of Nativity and Epiphany; in 'A Winter Tale' (*The Sun's Net*) a mysterious birth looms as a good omen against a background of sterility, death and depopulation, while in the triadic stories of the Magi in *Andrina* the kingly gifts and the gifted child become symbols of poetic creativity and of the renewal of life beyond the upheavals of history.

Earlier on, in a less stylised frame, the title story of *A Time to Keep* recorded a young crofter-fisherman's one year of married life, ending with his wife's death in childbirth; though it stressed, the more starkly for the dour young husband's rejection of social sympathies and religious consolation, the uncertainty of human happiness implicit in the title's quotation from Qoelet, still the coming of Christmas marked its end with a sense of the continuity of life. In the same collection 'Celia', perhaps the most poignant of Brown's many compassionate depictions of drink-addiction as affliction rather than vice, closes on a note of hope, on a feeling that each new day may bring new life, and that charity can be found deeper and stronger among those the world looks upon as reprobates.

Besides the twelve months of the solar year, culminating in the memory of the historical event of the Nativity, the Biblical seven days of Creation function as a structuring principle in many poems and stories of Brown's. If we find only six chapters in his first novel *Greenvoe* it is because the seventh, corresponding to the day of God's rest, must remain a matter of hope, until men learn once again to love and respect one another and God's creation. The first five chapters correspond to as many days in the life of a tiny island village, which in the sixth is systematically evacuated and finally effaced in order to make room for a top-secret, political-technological Mega Project, actually never to be completed. This novel encapsulates Brown's dislike and distrust of the myth of Progress as co-terminous with Hi-Tech, standardization, and cultural imperialism – what today we call globalization – and therefore as a threat to vegetable, animal, and human life, to that variety of types and life-styles which make up the 'pied beauty' of Creation. A sense of the dignity of every person, including the mentally handicapped, the social failures, the malicious and narrow-minded, underlies these now humourous, now pathetic portraits of men, women and children, who, even when not round in Forsterian terms, are never mere stock-types, never boorish or coy *à la* kailyard.

Mackay Brown's plea for nature and for the simple life of small communities has nothing to do with ideological fads and fashions, hippy catchwords and Greenpeace policy; likewise, his love for traditional Orkney folklore figures – like the Selkie or man-seal – and his flair for atypical, 'purgatorial' ghost stories, imply no New Age sympathies. In children's books like *Pictures in the Cave* and *Six Lives of Fankle the Cat*[18] the lesson of love and respect to animals is conveyed in the language of the fairy-tale, without any concession to animalist fanaticism. And the vision of universal harmony between man and nature, ascribed to Christ by the Easter story in *Winter Tales*, which brings up to date the Gospel episode of the two disciples meeting with Jesus on 'The Road to Emmaus', is a personal, poetical interpretation of Biblical passages such as Isaiah's prophecies of universal peace, and the Pauline picture of Creation in the throes of childbirth, yearning for deliverance.

If, while dealing with the latest centuries, Mackay Brown often focuses on the evil side-effects of unbridled technology, equally often, in whatever historical age he sets a story, his attention is fixed on the timeless realities of war and cruelty, the outcome of greed and lust for power. Single historical characters, such as those in the title story of *Hawkfall*, may be mean exploiters like Scottish Earl Patrick during the Renaissance, or men of epic stature like Norse Earl Thorfinn in the Middle Ages: the latter may arouse a degree of fascination, but never sympathy or approval. From the mid-eighties on, indeed, Brown seems to have grown more alert to the ugly aberration of war, more anxious at mankind's power of self-destruction. This anxiety was distilled into an intriguing and intensely poetical book, half fantasy half novel: in *Time in a Red Coat*[19] a mysterious girl, in a white gown slowly getting soiled as she walks by bloody battle after bloody battle, travels across Asia and Europe and across centuries, from Genghis Khan to Napoleon and on, until she is granted, in a weird museum, a glimpse of the horrors of atomic war. The flute she plays along the way might be a symbol of the poetic art, helpless to avert the doom of carnage, only able to sing 'the pity of war'.

Another example of war as a compound of blood, folly, heroism and treachery is the battle of Clontarf, fought in eleventh-century Ireland, recorded in Njall's Saga and retold by Mackay Brown in *Vinland*.[20] In this novel, written five hundred years after Columbus' enterprise, and celebrating the earlier discovery of America by the Vikings, Earl Thorfinn appears again in all his lust for power, courage and resourcefulness, with other historical figures like Leif Ericson, the Irish king Brian Boru, the kings of Norway Olaf and Magnus. But at the centre stands the fictional Orkneyman Ranald Sigmundson. Unlike *Greenvoe*, where a group of villagers share the central role, or *Beside the Ocean of Time*[21] whose protagonist is rather a means to link together a series of tales than a fully developed character, but like the earlier *Magnus*, *Vinland* is a 'novel with a hero'. As a boy Ranald follows Ericson to Vinland, and for the rest of his life he is haunted by a longing to go back and make peace with the young native outraged by the violence of the Viking intruders. As a young man, after fighting in the battle of Clontarf, he decides to have nothing more to do with war. He raises a family and farms his land in Orkney successfully, but steadily refuses to mix with his countrymen in the feuds and fights pro or contra any of the rival Earls. Still in the prime of life, he withdraws from business and family ties, to concentrate on a quest after truth, wavering between the fatalism of the Odin worshippers and the promise of eternal life held out by the Irish monks.

Through this character George Mackay Brown, then a seventy-year-old ailing man, faced the realities of age, retirement and death, with serenity if not without pathos. Death finally comes to a Ranald ready and eager to sail on a long anticipated voyage, which is to take him back to Vinland's virgin land and reconcile him to the people. In fact, his is the voyage to life through death; for as he hastens toward the little monastery, he has a stroke, is given the last rites by a monk, and dies. While his body lies in the chapel 'shaped like a little stone ship', the monks sing a song that express-es, besides the Christian idea of life as a voyage to the heavenly haven, the author's conception of human work – first and foremost that which provides the essentials of nourishment and shelter, like farming and fishing and building, but surely also the poet's humble craft – as both service and worship, labour and grace:

> Christ of the workbench, be thy strength and timberwit in the long,
> [powerful keel.
> Be thou in the well-made strakes.
> Be thou in the tall mast.
>
> …………..
>
> Be thou in the bread and wine of the seamen, hidden in the sea-chest.
> Be thou, Lord, at the helm, when at last the voyager turns his face to the
> [west...[22]

Valentina Poggi

NOTES

[1] George Mackay Brown, *The Storm*, Kirkwall: Orkney Press, 1954.

[2] George Mackay Brown, *Selected Poems 1954-1992*, London: John Murray, 1996, p. 1.

[3] Edwin Muir, *The Story and the Fable*, London: G.G. Harran & Co., 1940.

[4] George Mackay Brown, *Greenvoe: A Novel*, London: Hogarth Press, 1972.

[5] Anthony Thwaite has written that Mackay Brown's material is hand led 'with such suppleness that he is seldom monotonous'. Anthony Thwaite, *Poetry Today*, London: Longman, 1985, p. 108.

[6] George Mackay Brown, *Selected Poems 1954-1992*, cit., p. 92.

[7] *Ibidem*, p. 44.

[8] Colin Nicholson, *Poem, Purpose and Place: Shaping Identity in Contemporary Scottish Verse*, Edinburgh: Polygon, 1992, p. 102.

[9] George Mackay Brown, *Selected Poems 1954-1992*, cit., p. 143.

[10] George Mackay Brown, *Magnus: A Novel*, London: Hogarth Press, 1973.

[11] Colin Nicholson, *op. cit.*, p. 106.

[12] *Ibidem*, p. 100.

[13] David Annwn has written: 'If I were asked to characterize the most fundamental tendencies of Brown's poetry, I should write on one hand of "foldings": the desire to gather up and preserve, and, on the other, of clear outline and definition'. David Annwn, 'The Poetry of George Mackay Brown', in Hans-Werner Ludwig and Lothar Fietz eds., *Poetry in the British Isles: Non-Metropolitan Perspectives*, Cardiff: University of Wales Press, 1995, (pp. 283-310) p. 285.

[14] George Mackay Brown, *Selected Poems 1954-1992*, cit., p. 24.

[15] George Mackay Brown, *Fishermen with Ploughs*, London: Hogarth Press, 1971.

[16] George Mackay Brown, *A Calendar of Love*, London: Hogarth Press, 1972.

[17] George Mackay Brown, *A Time to Keep*, London: Hogarth Press, 1969; *Hawkfall*, London: Hogarth Press, 1974; *The Sun's Net*, London: Hogarth Press, 1976; *Andrina*, London: Hogarth Press, 1989; *The Masked Fisherman*, London: John Murray, 1989; *Winter Tales*, London: John Murray, 1995.

[18] George Mackay Brown, *Pictures in the Cave*, London: Chatto & Windus, 1977; *Six Lives of Fankle the Cat*, London: Chatto & Windus, 1980.

[19] George Mackay Brown, *Time in a Red Coat*, London: Hogarth Press, 1984.

[20] George Mackay Brown, *Vinland*, London: John Murray, 1992.

[21] George Mackay Brown, *Beside the Ocean of Time*, London: John Murray, 1994.

[22] George Mackay Brown, *Vinland*, cit., p. 232.

MASSIMILIANO MORINI

Liz Lochhead's Poetry and Drama: In Her Own Voice?

Liz Lochhead (born 1947) is today widely regarded as one of the leading figures in both Scottish poetry and drama. From the publication of *Dreaming Frankenstein & Collected Poems* (1984, with an introduction by Edwin Morgan) onwards, she has firmly established herself, to borrow the title of one of her 'Recitations', as an 'Almost Miss Scotland' of literature, no doubt the most popular female poet and dramatist of the latter half of the twentieth century. This, however, is in itself problematic in a country where, as Joy Hendry wrote, 'those [women writers] who succeed are those who thrive in an adverse climate',[1] and in a culture which is still very much male-dominated. In her own career, Lochhead has had to grapple with some of the problems arising from such a situation, and the fact that she has increasingly employed Scots as her language (while at the same time largely abandoning poetry as a private form of expression) has raised some questions which are still begging answers about the relationship between gender and nationalism, and more general ones about the possibility of finding or fashioning a medium in which to express a personal and national Scottish identity.

Lochhead is fundamentally a poet of language. She is fascinated by the way cliché, stock phrases, but also different registers shape people's perceptions of the world, their opinions and affections. She declared in an interview that 'Any ideas [she has] come already clothed in language', and that she is motivated to write when 'a little bit of language goes funny. An ordinary phrase'll suddenly strike you in a new way. It'll turn itself inside out in some way'.[2] Already in her first collection, *Memo for Spring* (1972), she was exploring the way people use commonplace language so as to understand and defend themselves from the flow of experience going on around them. In a poem called 'Homilies from Hospital', the bed-ridden speaker strives to make sense of a frightening situation:

> I had my dressing changed today.
> To be honest I had not thought to be flawed
> so very visibly.
> But when all is said and done, no matter.
> Getting better is the main thing.[3]

This character, as many others in Lochhead's poetry, tries to use the platitudes of day-to-day language so as to assess her position and assuage her fears, but it is language itself which, as in that illuminating interview ('It'll turn itself inside out in some way') disturbingly becomes the subject of her speech, and reveals what she would like to keep hidden. The stock phrases ('Getting better is the main thing') and linguistic routines ('when all is said and done', 'To be honest') underscore the tangible terror the speaker is feeling, and her shocked surprise at the condition of her body is poignantly expressed by 'flawed', which is both an understatement for 'wounded' and an involuntary giveaway of the self-disgust sick people feel when confronted with their own bodies.

Much of Lochhead's poetry is concerned with the way people try to fit language to their ends, and are in their turn betrayed by words which, unlike Humpty Dumpty's, refuse to do the job they are paid for, even if they are paid double: like James Fenton in 'A German Requiem', what she tries to wrestle from her characters 'is not what they say. It is what they do not say', 'not what [they want] to know', but 'what [they want] not to know'.[4] This is particularly true as regards love relationships. Her female protagonists repeatedly attempt to deceive their (ex-) partners as well as themselves in the process of expressing their emotions and affection, but their intentions are made clear by the very intensity of their disclaimers. 'Poem for Other Poor Fools', for instance, begins with a declaration of independence ('Since you went I've only cried twice/Oh never over you')[5] which is then subtly revealed to be untrue, as the two characters the speaker has cried over are shown to be, in the context of the poem, emblems of her own loneliness and spiritual nakedness. Nor does this double nature of language spare the language-wielders themselves, the poets: in 'A Giveaway',[6] the poet-speaker proudly (if tentatively) affirms that 'Poets don't bare their souls, they bare their skill', but of course, at that stage, she has already given away a lot more than skill. In a sense, Lochhead's poetry is the exact opposite of the confessional mode: it is crowded with characters who try to conceal as much as they can, to fashion a certain image of themselves, only to discover that their real desires, fears, and expectations have already been revealed by the very words they have used.

From *The Grimm Sisters* (1981) onwards, Lochhead has extended this interest in the way language literally writes experience to a study of how the female subject is constructed by the various (male) narratives that have served for centuries as supposedly neutral models of human behaviour. Already in *Memo for Spring*, women were defined or defined themselves according to age-old received notions of femininity, often as filtered through that humblest of literary media, the women's magazine. Some of the characters in this collection, though already disillusioned about love, behave compulsively in what is commonly considered as the 'female' manner, as if under the dictation of some magazine advice column:

Our eyes are blank
of illusions
but we automatically
lengthen lashes, lacquer hair
lipstick our lips for later[7]

In *Cuba*[8], a play about the twin life of two schoolgirls at the time of the Cuba missile crisis (when Lochhead herself was more or less fourteen, as her two protagonists), Barbara and Bernadette pass the time hurling quotations from such magazines at each other. Woman's life is thus made up of odd scraps from magazines, and it is no wonder, Lochhead seems to imply, if it is often so untidy, and if a woman grows up 'expecting not too much from love –/just that it should completely solve [her]', as does the speaker in 'After a Warrant Sale'.[9]

With *The Grimm Sisters*, Liz Lochhead has tried to reach back to the roots of all such expectations and self-expectations, in order to discover the male-centred impositions on which such notions are based. In doing so, she has repeated an operation which many women writers, from Stevie Smith to Angela Carter, have felt it their duty or their need to perform: she has gone back to the stories children are told at bedtime (those of the brothers Grimm in particular), that is, to the first versions of reality men and women receive from the realm of fiction, and she has attempted to rewrite them in order to show how much of what is commonly taken for granted as a 'neutral' story is actually the product of a patriarchal culture which relegates women to ancillary roles. The traditional image of the fairy-tale heroine, patiently waiting to be saved by the knight in shining armour on white steed, is cunningly subverted, and we are not spared the boredom and the setbacks which fleeing with a snoring, garlic-breathed gipsy-king involves:

> On the fourth night
> the lady thought as she drifted off to sleep
> how monotonous it was going to be
> to live on rabbit stew forever
> & she turned a little away
> from snoring, the smell of wild garlic.[10]

'Forever', the magic formula of so many fairy tales ('and they lived happily ever after'), as well as of the pampered world of sentimental romance, is here employed in a very unsentimental context. The female protagonist is neither hopelessly (and silently) in love nor particularly virtuous, and we may foresee what happens next: 'on the fifth day,/she began to make eyes at the merchant'. Very often, it is the heroines in these poems who are impatient of their male counterparts' idealistic stances, because they know that such idealism conceals not only their male-centred assumptions, but also, quite often, a moral and intellectual void. The female protagonist of 'Rapunzstiltskin', a poem which mixes, already in the title, two different Grimm stories, is exasperated at the Prince's inability to voice anything but 'strung-together cliché', picked up, it seems, from a mixture of bad Hollywood films and half-remembered fairy tales; and her desperation is heightened by the impossibility of finding a language in which to express her own growing frustration:

> 'I'll do anything in my power' he intoned, 'but

the impossible (she groaned) might
take a little longer.' He grinned.
She pulled her glasses off.
'All the better
to see you with my dear?' he hazarded.
She screamed, cut off her hair.
'Why, you're beautiful?' he guessed tentatively.
'No, No, No!' she
shrieked and stamped her foot so
hard it sank six cubits through the floorboards.
'I love you?' he came up with
as finally she tore herself in two.[11]

The poems in *The Grimm Sisters* explore, by putting new twists to
the old stories of the fairy realm, the roles accessible to women in
a society organised according to patriarchal rules. The world of the
brothers Grimm becomes a microcosm through which conclusions
can be drawn about the condition of women in the Western civilisation of today. Here as there, 'Mother', 'Spinster', and 'Bawd'[12]
seem to be the only models available, and it is made clear that
adopting aggressive stances can be no less constricting than
accepting the submissive ones.

   Characteristically, in these poems the comic bathos is often
obtained by giving a contemporary turn to the traditional tale, and
that often means, for a poet as language-oriented as Lochhead,
employing colloquial, even slang registers which ridicule the pretensions of the original, and reveal the interests it serves. In 'Tam
Lin's Lady', this is applied to traditional Scottish ballads. As she
confronts the lady herself, the narrator assumes a no-nonsense,
contemporary stance which makes her sceptical about the idealised
plot of the ballad:

So you met him in a fairy place?
O.K.
But that's a bit airy fairy for me.
I go for the specific – you could, for instance,
say that when he took you for a coffee
before he stuck you on the last bus
there was one of those horrible congealed-on
plastic tomatoes on the table... [13]

And the happy ending itself is questioned as the speaker asks the

Lady 'how do you think Tam Lin will take/all the changes you go through?', where those changes are no doubt those of the frustrated Scottish housewife.

This poem is particularly relevant because it is spoken by a narrative voice which is recognisably female and Scottish. The quotation from Burns's version of the same ballad which opens the poem highlights Lochhead's revisionist stance; her demythologising approach challenges the male assumptions which lie at the heart of the story of Tam Lin from a feminist standpoint.[14] This is one of the first poems in which Liz Lochhead has consciously tried to face Scotland's history and literature, and to come to terms with a culture that is as ineradicably hers as she feels alienated from its patriarchal tradition.

On the one hand, Liz Lochhead tends to identify Scotland with the female subject: as she said in several interviews, she places her country in an imaginary proportion where Scotland is to England as Woman is to Man, Scotland and Woman having been for centuries the weak, subjugated half. On the other hand, she is well aware that Scotland is much more aggressively male than highly-civilised, decadent England, as is shown by the fact that women poets in Scotland are still a very small minority, if a combative one. This contradiction is one that Liz Lochhead has confronted in several poems, but above all in those theatrical productions (*Mary Queen of Scots Got Her Head Chopped Off* and her translation of Moliere's *Tartuffe* are the two most noteworthy examples) which employ Scots as a medium of expression.

Her ambivalent feelings about Scotland show for instance in 'Inter-City', one of the finest, most balanced poems in her collection of 1984, *Dreaming Frankenstein*. The train of the title is cutting diagonally through Scotland (the first sexual metaphor of the poem) which is, at the beginning, equated with female delicacy ('(my/small dark country)'). This harmony between she-poet and she-country is, however, immediately disrupted by the irruption of rough-tongued he-men ('(fuck/this fuck that fuck/everything)') at whose appearance the first reaction of the poet, and of the reader with her, is disgust. Yet Scotland, one cannot help feeling, is theirs as well as the poet's; moreover, the speaker is insidiously fascinated by the rough, muscular vulgarity of that 'swaying caveful of half-/seas over oil men', and the poem closes on a stunned numbness which does not exclude the possibility of attraction, as the puns on the female sex make clear:

> The artsyfartsy magazine I'm
> not even pretending to read
> wide open
> at a photograph called portrait of absence.[15]

Yet the speaker, however fascinated against her better judgement, is evidently ill at ease before the vulgarity of these rude males: she feels embarrassed as a woman, because as such they are reducing her to a mere tool for sexual enjoyment; but also as an intellectual, since she is isolated from them by her superior culture as much as her gender. There is, to be sure, a lot of self-irony, even self-deprecation, in the affirmation of that difference, as the sarcastic 'artsyfartsy magazine' reveals: the aggressive masculinity of the oil-men reminds her uncomfortably of her unacceptable position as a woman who thinks and writes within a misogynous culture, and therefore she defensively plays down her own pretences. The female persona of 'Inter-City' feels the threat which is implicit in the men's 'fuck/this fuck that fuck/everything', and at the same time the patriarchal order those men represent at its most (verbally) violent is threatened by this woman who refuses to be either mother or bawd, that is, to fit into the only pattern the oil-men can understand, and who dares appropriate the very role which men have traditionally kept for themselves: that of the secondary creator, of the creative artist.

Naturally, that appropriation is far from unproblematic for the woman poet herself. Getting accepted by the literary establishment, or even by society at large, is not the biggest problem women writers have to grapple with, though difficulties of publication and lack of visibility can often be overwhelming. The worst enemy of the creative woman is not outside, but within herself, the 'familiar compound ghost' which is made of all the notions of femininity which the female subject receives since childhood. Unfortunately, those notions, beside being constricting in a number of ways, do not include creative activity: if a thinking woman, as Adrienne Rich wrote, sleeps with monsters,[16] a woman who writes sleeps with those which are conceived by her own brain; and a Scottish woman writer is a sort of monster herself.

Now, monsters have haunted Liz Lochhead's poetry from a very early stage: already in 'Revelation', one of the most striking poems of *Memo for Spring*, the girl-protagonist (ostensibly the poet herself) confronts the dark, archetypal potency of a 'black bull' called Bob ('as though perhaps/you could reduce a monster/with the charm of a friendly name.'), a metaphoric beast which stands for male (sexual) aggressiveness, and which, like the oil-men in 'Inter-City', is enticing and menacing at the same time:

> Then he was immense,
> his edges merging with the darkness, just
> a big bulk and a roar to be really scared of,
> a trampling, and a clanking tense with the chain's jerk.
> [...] I ran, my pigtails thumping on my back in fear...[17]

But at this early stage, the monster is still exclusively and unequiv-ocally male, 'his anarchy/threatening the eggs', the latter ('well-rounded, self-contained') standing for a fragile, threatened female identity. In later poetry and drama, Lochhead comes to terms with the monsters which lurk in the depths of the female psyche: in *Blood and Ice*, a play that she revised several times before and after publication, Mary Shelley, the protagonist, learns to see through the high idealism of her husband ('God save all women from men who worship "Woman"')[18] which relegates the 'Woman' it worships to a passive, ancillary role; and she also comes to accept the fact that there are aspects of her personality, and parti-cularly those which are connected with the creativity of her brain, which are bound to appear monstrous in her own eyes. 'Dreaming Frankenstein', the title poem of Lochhead's 1984 collection, sums up nicely one of the main strands of the play:

> Anyway
> he was inside her
> and getting him out again
> would be agony fit to quarter her,
> unstitching everything.[19]

Mary has just been visited by the monster – representing her own creativity – which interestingly is conceived of as something exter-nal, something that compels her to write (with a violence that has sexual connotations: 'This was the penetration...'). The creative act is an unsettling one, since it disrupts, undoes the creator: 'unstitching' links the agony involved in the act of creation with the plight of the created thing itself, because we know that Frankenstein (as well as the abortive female monster) is 'stitched together' from odd scraps of dead bodies; thus, a woman writing is, again, a created thing that dares to create, or, more simply, a monster producing monsters.

In *Mary Queen of Scots Got Her Head Chopped Off,* Liz Lochhead went back to the historical moment when the political and religious (and, consequently, also linguistic) destiny of Scotland was in the making, in that troubled period when Mary's reign was beset by political dangers from outside and religious troubles within, as Calvinism, led by John Knox, grew more and more powerful. But Lochhead does not attempt any faithful historical reconstruction, though there is documentation behind her work: through metatheatrical, non-fourth-wall devices, she aims at showing the ways in which such events are relevant to present-day Scotland, because it was at that moment in time that Scotland's self-divisions (the Scottish as against the English soul, tolerance/intolerance, man/woman) were created or reinforced. In John Knox's 'first blast o' the trumpet against the *monstrous* regiment o' women'[20] we can perhaps find the origin of the reduction of the Scottish woman to a monster: but in this play, the subjugation of women is linked with Scotland's subjection to England and, as a consequence, with the historical crisis of the Scots language.

Again, in *Mary Queen of Scots,* characters are not merely described, but literally constructed by the language they wield, as Lochhead makes use of Scots with tightrope eclecticism. Here as in *Tartuffe* (which is so free an adaptation that it can be almost considered Lochhead's original work), geographical position, social condition, but also subtler distinctions between, say, sincerity and pretence, depend on exactly how much Scots and how much English the characters are speaking, and on the way they are making use of and blending them. In *Mary Queen of Scots,* virtually everyone has a language of his/her own, which may also vary in different circumstances: Mary's, though a little 'Frenchified', is always pure Scots, whereas Elizabeth's is, literally, Queen's English;

the other characters move between these two opposing poles. In *Tartuffe*, the most honest voice is the Scottish one of Dorine, sarcastically commenting on the big characters' actions, whose mixed moral nature is mirrored in the way they opportunistically mingle Scots and English.

But what is extraordinary about these two plays is the beautifully varied use Lochhead makes of Scots. In the mid-1980s, and particularly between 1986 (the year when *Tartuffe* was first staged) and 1987 (when *Mary Queen of Scots* was first performed at the Lyceum Studio Theatre in Edinburgh), she was developing her competence in this language, and at the same time re-inventing it for her purposes, because the actual Scots of today was too impoverished to allow for the dramatic subtleties she was trying to express; as she wrote in her own introduction to *Tartuffe*, what she employed in these two plays was 'a totally invented... theatrical Scots, full of anachronisms, demotic speech from various eras and areas'.[21] It was a language no more existent than MacDiarmid's synthetic Scots, and which in places baffled many of the Scottish spectators that went to see these plays; and the dramatic and lyrical peaks which it managed to reach, as well as its remarkable vitality and energy, are best illustrated by direct quotation:

> LA CORBIE: Country: Scotland. Whit like is it?
> It's a peatbog, it's a daurk forest.
> It's a cauldron o' lye, a saltpan or a coal mine.
> If you're gey lucky it's a bricht bere meadow or a park o' kye.
> Or mibbe... it's a field o' stanes.[22]

In order to find her way into that 'daurk forest', Lochhead has invented an intricate, labyrinthine language; and since Scotland is a sort of cultural and political monster, made up of Gaelic origins, Scots traditions, frenchified elements and English domination, she has acted as a philological Frankenstein, stitching together the corpses of 'various eras and areas'. But apart from the cleverness involved in this somewhat artificial construction, and its great poetical and theatrical effectiveness, the operation has also disturbing implications, because it points to the fact that in order to stage Scotland and its history, one has to employ a language which does not exist. A Scottish identity cannot be simply found, since it has suffered so many attacks in the last four centuries that it has almost been obliterated: therefore, it has to be invented.

This is not only true of Scottish culture in general but it is also relevant to Lochhead's personal experience. In the years since 1984, when *Dreaming Frankenstein & Collected Poems* was published, Lochhead has been confronting more and more directly problems related to Scotland's culture, language, history, and national identity. At the same time, the more she grappled with these problems, the more she abandoned the medium of poetry in favour of theatre in its various forms. *Bagpipe Muzak* (1991), the only major collection after *Dreaming Frankenstein* to date, is actually made up by two thirds of 'Recitations' and 'Characters', while only one third is dedicated to 'Poems', and even of these two out of ten ('Lucy's Diary: Six Entries' and 'Renfield's Nurse') stem from a play (*Dracula*) she was writing at the time. And that poetry has become an appendix of Lochhead's successful career as a dramatist has become even more evident after 1991, because since then she has written very few poems and published no collections.

This could be explained away as a mere change of preferences, where it not that Liz Lochhead continues to declare that poems are her 'favourite thing to do';[23] and doubtless her frantic dramatic activity in recent years has stolen time from the more private exercise of poetry. But there are reasons to suppose that her dedication to Scotland and her abandonment of poetry are connected. Her first collection, *Memo for Spring*, was by far the most introspective of her publications. Many poems, though they could not be called confessional, were about personal experiences which had then been transformed and refined in the process of turning them into poetry. The already-quoted 'Revelation' opens on an unmistakably personal note:

> I remember once being shown the black bull
> when a child at the farm for eggs and milk.

Now, what is significant about *Memo for Spring* is that besides being overtly personal, it is also written completely in English. And even in the later collections, from *Islands* (1978) to *Bagpipe Muzak*, whenever she is writing 'poems', as distinct from recitations, and particularly poems where a near-autobiographical 'I' is speaking, Lochhead's *personae* employ a variety of English which might, with few exceptions, be termed standard. Thus, it would seem that lyrical inspiration in poetry is not compatible with the use of Scots; after all, English is the language in which Liz Lochhead has been educated, and probably also the language that she feels is right for poetry, at least poetry of the more intimate sort.[24]

Therefore, it seems that though she has invented a language for her country, she cannot then appropriate that voice for herself: her attempts at finding a voice for Scotland have estranged Lochhead from her own voice, somehow making it impossible to write poetry, at least poetry in the same vein that she is at present exploring in drama. Thus far, Lochhead has hovered uneasily between MacDiarmid's urge to go back to Scotland's linguistic origins and Muir's resignation to use English as the only possible medium for moulding Scottish experience in verse. It is perhaps to be hoped that in the future she can find a way of coaxing her own voice into Scots, but at the moment that seems unlikely to happen. When Lochhead, after *Bagpipe Muzak*, has resumed writing verse, she has gone back to English. These lines from 'The baker', the finest poem she has written recently, have the composure and the elaborate diction of Douglas Dunn's finest poems, and moreover they are nearer to a perfect iambic rhythm than Lochhead had ever gone before:

Sober girls in black and white replenish plates
And freshen up the cooling cups with warm
As if tomorrow like live yeast could rise and prove.[25]

This is the contradiction, or rather the self-division, that Liz Lochhead's poetry has been facing in recent years, that will not leave her in the future, and that will probably remain unsolved. But far from being a limitation, it is a division which makes her drama and her poetry (and all the steps leading from one to the other) even more important and emblematic, because in her writing the rifts running through a whole country are mirrored. In this, she is akin to Heaney, and to all the poets of Northern Ireland that have felt it their painful duty to sing their country in a foreign language, with the addition that, as a woman, she is estranged both from her language and, at least partly, from her country. A Scottish identity, and particularly a female Scottish identity, remains at present a chimaera, in the double sense that it is all but impossible to find and that it is made up of various, incompatible elements. Whether or not Liz Lochhead and the other poets now writing in Scotland will forge the uncreated (or forgotten) conscience of their race, it remains to be seen: but Lochhead's willingness to risk her own poetic voice to forge one for her country is a moving example of courageous, undivided loyalty.

NOTES

[1] Joy Hendry, 'Twentieth-century Women's Writing: The Nest of Singing Birds', in Cairns Craig ed., *The History of Scottish Literature. Vol. 4: The Twentieth Century*, Aberdeen: Aberdeen University Press, 1989, p. 291.

[2] Gillean Somerville-Arjat and R.E. Wilson eds., *Sleeping with Monsters: Conversations with Scottish and Irish Women Poets*, Edinburgh: Polygon, 1990, pp. 9-10. Square brackets, here as elsewhere, are mine.

[3] Liz Lochhead, *Dreaming Frankenstein & Collected Poems*, Edimburgh: Polygon, 1984, p. 154.

[4] James Fenton, *The Memory of War* and *Children in Exile: Poems 1968-1983*, Harmondsworth: Penguin, 1983, p. 19.

[5] Liz Lochhead and *Dreaming Frankenstein & Collected Poems*, cit., p. 125.

[6] *Ibidem*, p. 42.

[7] *Ibidem*, p. 151.

[8] Liz Lochhead and Gina Moxley, *Cuba/Dog House*, London: Faber & Faber, 1997.

[9] Liz Lochhead, *Dreaming Frankenstein & Collected Poems*, cit., p. 131.

[10] *Ibidem*, p. 81.

[11] *Ibidem*, p. 79.

[12] *Ibidem*, pp. 71, 75, 76.

[13] *Ibidem*, pp. 81-82.

[14] Though Lochhead has declared that, though a feminist herself, she does not set out to write poems from a feminist point of view.

[15] Liz Lochhead, *Dreaming Frankenstein & Collected Poems*, cit., p. 34.

[16] Quoted by Lochhead herself in the interview collected in *Sleeping with Monsters*, cit., p. 14: 'I'm very interested in repressions of various

sorts, linguistic, sexual, whatever. I keep thinking of a line from a poem by Adrienne Rich: '*A thinking woman sleeps with monsters...*' Yes, that's right.'

[17] Liz Lochhead, *Dreaming Frankenstein & Collected Poems*, cit., p. 124.

[18] Michelene Wandor ed., *Plays by Women Volume Four*, London: Methuen, 1985, p. 113.

[19] Liz Lochhead, *Dreaming Frankenstein & Collected Poems*, cit., p. 12.

[20] Liz Lochhead, *Mary Queen of Scots Got Her Head Chopped Off & Dracula*, Harmondsworth: Penguin, 1989, p. 19; italics mine.

[21] Quoted in Randall Stevenson, 'Re-enter Houghmagandie: Language as Performance in Liz Lochhead's *Tartuffe*', in Robert Crawford and Anne Varty eds., *Liz Lochhead's Voices*, Edinburgh: Edinburgh University Press, 1993, p. 119.

[22] Liz Lochhead, *Mary Queen of Scots Got Her Head Chopped Off & Dracula*, cit., p. 11.

[23] Robert Crawford, Henry Hart, David Kinloch, and Richard Price eds., *Talking Verse*, St Andrews and Williamsburg: Verse, 1995, p. 118.

[24] As she admitted herself. When asked by the interviewer for *Verse* if there were 'any poems in Scots coming up', Liz Lochhead answered: 'Sort of... but they tend to be in a voice. I don't really write in Scots in my own voice'. See *Talking Verse*, cit., p. 126.

[25] Unpublished material.

TONY MCMANUS

Kenneth White:
A Transcendental Scot

Kenneth White occupies a paradoxical situation in Scottish letters. André Breton remarked upon the 'high note of originality' which he brought to literature and Lawrence Durrell praised his 'poetry with marrow and purity'.[1] However, the work of Scotland's writer of greatest European and global standing since Hugh MacDiarmid only became available in Scotland in 1989. Translated into many world-languages, he barely features as yet on the syllabuses of the Scottish universities. Founder of the International Institute of Geopoetics with centres in various parts of the globe, his essays have only recently become available in Scotland. While Scottish to the bone, White, then, cannot easily be described in national terms, nor fitted into the established categories: 'I'm what you might call a transcendental Scot', he writes in 'The Ballad of Kali Road'.[2]

White works in three forms of literary expression. His prose narrative 'way-books' follow a narrative figure out of the contemporary western context through the cultures of the earth and into its empty spaces where he is imbued with a 'sense of world' – a clarification of perception in relation to the earth itself. The essays chart a similar movement in a more analytical form. The poetry is of two kinds. The long poems White refers to as 'peregrinations' in the spaces of the earth and the mind. The short, 'diamond' poems evoke intense moments of perception. The three forms overlap considerably – analytical passages are found in the 'way-books' which are also peppered with poems; the poems can be long analyses of ideas or significant cultural figures; the essays reach moments of poem-like imagery and focus.

One of the key contributions Kenneth White has made to

Scottish cultural discourse is to indicate that Anglo-centricity means rather more than constant reference to England as that in opposition to which a distinct Scottish identity is created – Scotland and Scots always trying to define themselves as not-England, non-English. He even comes across it in francophone Canada:

> The motto of Quebec is *Je me souviens*.
> I asked somebody what the remembering was all about.
> 'The time the English came.'
> God almighty! Who cares about the English, whether coming or going?
> If I bothered about what the English did, I'd be up there in old Caledonia with a historical chip on my shoulder, scrawling long political poems in Lallans and waving a wee flag.
> Shit, you can't be a Scotsman *all* your life. At least, you can't always be harping on it. You've got to get out there and mix it more. *Make* something of it.[3]

This is a little image of Kenneth White's itinerary and of the nature of his considerable *oeuvre*. In its rejection of dominant culture, its imperative to 'get out there and mix it more' and its appeal to '*make* something of it' we can see reflected the three-part movement which grounds and permeates White's work. Firstly, there is a nihilism in the face of a western civilisation at its 'endgame';[4] secondly, 'intellectual nomadism'[5] – a movement out of this in physical and mental exploration of the world; thirdly, the apprehension of a new or re-newed 'sense of world', which requires to be expressed in a new, or re-newed, poetics. This is the movement towards 'geopoetics'.[6]

THE SUPERNIHILIST'S ITINERARY

White starts from the modern condition, the sense that things are lacking coherence. Alienation – from work, from others, from oneself, from the world – is the identifying feature of the modern context. This is not simply an intellectual severance, it is also an existential one – we feel the problem as well as think about it. Here is Barcelona in this perspective:

> ...away at the dead end of the Calle San Pablo, where there are no longer any women visible, only men humped in sordid drink-shops with pale blue TV screens flickering in the darkness, yes, this is the end, with a pale-green-painted little hospital-looking shop there advertising *lavajes-*

siphilis, the syphilitic end of the overhuman bloody world.[7]

The scene is full of signs of a civilisation at its end – the 'dead-end' street is that of St. Paul, establisher of Christian orthodoxy, the 'darkness' in which the TV screens flicker is a cultural and intellectual darkness. The human hopelessness of it recalls the extreme negativist E.M. Cioran's dark definition of contemporary man: 'a convalescent aspiring to disease'.[8]

White's 'way books', always start in this sense of the 'overhuman bloody world'. *Travels in the Drifting Dawn* searches the ports and landscapes of Europe for signs of 'something else' in the air. *Incandescent Limbo*[9] recounts White's experiences in seven rooms in Paris in the early sixties and reflects an initial interest in surrealism that later moved out, as does the book, towards a radical culture-analysis. Later books such as *The Blue Road* and *Pilgrim of the Void*[10] accentuate the more comic tone also present in the earlier books. A movement is then charted towards a 'clarified space'. In *Letters from Gourgounel*[11] a thunderstorm, 'a field of energy' in the world, gathers and breaks during the course of the book and parallels the enlightenment which gathers and breaks in the book's narrative figure through intellectual penetration into the philosophies of the east, especially through the translation of Chinese poetry, and through penetration into the landscape.

In his essays,[12] which range with great erudition and acute intelligence over the cultural map, White casts a critical eye upon the two main attempts which have been made to deal with the existential problem outlined here – the political method of Marxism and the psychoanalytical method originating with Freud. Close to European critics such as, among others, Gilles Deleuze[13] and Jean-François Lyotard,[14] he indicates how psychoanalysis' function is to repatriate the sick spirit back into the alien land which made it sick in the first place, and how political movements have offered no genuine path out of the malaise. What White proposes is a larger field of thought and action.

Along with a negativist awareness of the modern context, is an awareness of another reality which White discovers, at least in its initial signs, in his childhood territory and which becomes the potential focus for that renewal of culture which he seeks. This is the territory around the west coast village of Fairlie[15] – what he calls 'the white world of arctic gulls, breaking waves and silver birches'.[16] This sense of an 'energy-filled' and spacious reality is also an experience felt in both mind (knowledge of and mental penetration into nature) and body (sensual enjoyment of wind, tree, bird flight, salt of sea, smell of earth). Here he is instinctively aware of the presence of what is missing in contemporary culture – 'a sense of world' – and as a child the desire to penetrate, to realise that 'sense of world', is awoken. 'Morning Walk'[17] is an early poem of White's which describes that sensation:

MORNING WALK

It was a cold slow-moving mist
clotted round the sun, clinging
to the small white sun, and the earth
was alone and lonely, and a great bird
harshly squawked from the heronry
as the boy walked under the beeches
seeing the broken pale-blue shells
and the moist piles of mouldering leaves

The key word is 'seeing': this is a poem about perception. One might have expected 'looking' – what 'seeing' does is to heighten and deepen the perceptual experience the boy is having. The word's force is strengthened by its use in participial form just after two active verbs, 'squawked' and 'walked', whose rhyme helps transmit their active nature into the participial form of 'seeing': this 'seeing' is not something that is happening *to* the boy, he is *doing* it. This form also allows the word to act as a noun and a verb at the same time, that is, to make the abstract and the concrete co-exist: *this* boy seeing *those* pale-blue shells, but also the *idea* of 'seeing pale-blue shells'. This, plus the apt expression of colour, 'pale-blue shells' (the repetition of the *l* sound unites the three words into a strongly visual expression) also leads the reader, to 'see' them too. The final line is an image of the necessary focus of perception, the earth in a sensual, erotic[18] expression: 'moist, mouldering leaves'.

   The reality being perceived seems to lie outwith the parameters of western culture. This leads White to consider that perhaps it is this obsession with the socio-personal context itself which is wrong. Perhaps we need to look at the whole cultural context, its roots, ideas and expression. This is what White calls the 'superni-hilist'[19] movement, the desire to go beyond nihilism's infinite pessimism and, without indulging in facile optimism, to seek possibilities. This is to initiate a move away from the western mainstream, not just its anglo-centric manifestation, towards the study of the 'fundamental question' – culture. This requires a radical analysis of the roots of western culture. Using the image of the 'motorway of western civilisation', White traces its humanist and sacred development from Platonic idealism and Aristotelian categorisation, through the Christian paradigm of 'creator' and 'created' and the modern Cartesian dualisms of mind and body, man and nature, to the Romantics' attempt to refocus on the earth.

The real inspirational break, as far as White is concerned, arrives in the shape of two figures who, beginning a movement off this 'motorway', prefigure the geopoetic field: Rimbaud who says: 'if I have any taste it is only for earth and for stones';[20] and Nietzsche who says: 'remain true to the earth'.[21] These figures, the French philosophical poet and the German poetic philosopher, break out of the Hegelian line which led to the twentieth century's dream of the superstate and illusion of the 'supermarket of happiness',[22] and, from their movements, White develops a method, leaving the main road of culture and delving in to the wild terrain. It is a movement he calls 'intellectual nomadism'.[23]

THE INTELLECTUAL NOMAD

If White's sense of alienation is both intellectual and existential, then the intellectual nomadism which explores ways beyond this consists of intellectual enquiry – reading and writing, the cultivation of the mind – but also existential experience – errance and residence, the cultivation of the body and the senses. We separate them for the purpose of explaining and interpreting them. However, our idealising and categorising culture has seen that separation become almost permanent. In fact, as Kenneth White proceeds in to his territory he is aware that these apparent dualisms – mind and body, man and nature – are fundamentally one and this awareness can lead to a genuine perception of the world.

Dissatisfied with the 'mediocratic'[24] cultural context of 1960s

Britain, White settled in France in 1967. However, in leaving Scotland-Britain, he found himself penetrating into a more authentic Scotland which, chiming with the intuitions he felt as a child on the west coast and evoked in the poem quoted above, seemed connected to that bigger 'sense of world' which he was seeking.

Always beginning with the ground, White's vision of Scotland goes back to its origins in the glacier and its shaping movement out of which:

> the land emerges
> bruised and dazed
> in the arctic light[25]

The humans he sees inhabiting this land develop a highly poetic culture with totemic references to the natural world and cosmological considerations in their engravings.[26] In the Christian era they evolve ways of seeing and expressing which put them at the margins of establishment culture. This pelagian[27] line which, in direct conflict with the establishment,[28] holds that there is no original sin, permeates the teaching and poetry of the early Christian monks who travelled Europe teaching a Christianity which was expressed in terms of the natural world not as metaphor for 'the human condition', but as the *locus* of reality. In his essays White refers us to Ernest Renan's comment on:

> the quite particular vivacity with which the Celts informed their feeling for nature... a sort of realistic naturalism, love of nature for its own sake.[29]

White's departure from Anglo-centric mainstream culture and his adoption of alternative routes to the perception of reality is summed up in his statement: 'there is a pelagian line running through the whole of Western culture.'[30] That is, there is an alternative way to perception of reality. This movement is summed up in the poem 'Brandan's Last Voyage'[31] about the saint whose journeys inspired the remarkable medieval poem on his life which gave Europe the original model for the vision of the 'other world' and which furnished Dante with some of the models and images which inform *The Divine Comedy*. At the end of White's poem, Brandan and his followers go off in their little boat:

> farther and farther they sailed away
> into the white unknown.

White traces a Scottish line of the descendants of these 'studious philologians and rugged philosophers'[32] from Erigena's ninth century philosophy of nature[33] to Duns Scotus[34] who, in opposition to Thomas Aquinas affirms the 'thisness' (*haecceitas*) of the phenomena of the world. George Buchanan,[35] teacher of Montaigne, wrote a long Latin poem on the subject of the cosmos. Patrick Geddes[36] sought a unification of the branches of knowledge through what he began to see as an *aesthetic*. Hugh MacDiarmid's intellectual aim extended to cover world literature and philosophies, science, anthropology and grammars. The tradition of 'extra-vagant'[37] Scots reaching out from Scotland to the world and promulgating an alternative tradition of perception of reality is a long and distinguished one which Kenneth White synthesises and develops.

However, this tradition stands in opposition to Cartesian modernity with its explicit separation of human from nature, mind from body, and the ever more minute separation of the branches of knowledge and the specialising of the sciences to which it led. Ironically, as White points out in many essays on the scientific theme, that very specialising finally led to discoveries which have re-opened the cosmological perspective, notably Einstein's *Cosmological Considerations* through which 'the notion of "cosmos" returns'.[38] Subsequent developments in science have put in question the basic foundations of mainstream western culture. Quantum physicists refer to the impossibility of the subject-object dualism in a manner which reminds us of the perceptual force in the poem 'Morning walk' quoted above.

In linguistics and literary theory, the American Ernest Fenollosa comes to a parallel conclusion which is also mirrored in that poem:

> A true noun, an isolated thing, does not exist in nature. Things are only the terminal points, or rather, the meeting points of actions... The eye sees noun and verb as one.[39]

In philosophy White indicates Edmund Husserl's dismissal of objectivism as 'naivety'[40] which leads him to propose the aim of a subject who, in unencumbered contemplation of the world, can realise its essence. Here not only is modernity's subject/object dualism being questioned but so is the materialist/idealist dualism. Husserl's pupil Martin Heidegger takes this further still, attempting to re-establish the meaning of the basic concepts of western thinking as they were originally conceived, and positing an idea of 'being' where phenomena 'emerge', 'stand' and 'endure in the light' and are 'apprehended' by humans.[41] These notions, which Heidegger grounds in pre-Socratic thinking, connote movement, event, experience and presence. In post-Socratic times – White's 'motorway of western civilisation' – they become static, formulaic, to do with opinion and interpretation. This, then, is the 'loss of world' which underpins the modern feeling of alienation. It is a cultural problem to do with a weakening in thought or 'apprehension' of the world.

For White, this pelagian movement in western thought dismantles the orthodox western categories and turns the mind, at least in the first instance, towards the East, demands a re-orientation of thought. This is not, as one critic[42] put it, to embrace 'thin-witted ...international zennery' (White is as scathing of pseudo-movements as anyone), but to explore a thought and expression unconditioned by western traditions – the experience of the void, the emptiness in which the socio-personal identity is lost and one experiences an 'enlargening of identity'.[43] A major source of inspiration is the Japanese haiku and prose master, Matsuo Basho,[44] whose advice to the poet sums up the points being made in this brief survey of White's intellectual nomadism:

> You must leave your preoccupations with yourself. Your poetry issues of its own accord when you and the thing have become one... if your feeling is not natural – if the thing and yourself are separate – then your poetry is not true poetry but merely a counterfeit.[45]

GEOPOETICS

This nomadising in the byways of civilisation leads White, like the figures and cultures through which he has 'nomadised', to the conclusion that instead of attempting to understand the human in relation to itself, we must perceive the human in relation to the earth, that is develop that 'sense of world' whose felt loss had been the spur of all his work. This is the 'geo' in 'geopoetics'. The 'poetics' covers the realisation, also derived from that nomadising, that when the human being hits upon genuine perception of reality, the desire to express that perception is part of it:

> Geopoetics is concerned with 'worlding' (and 'wording' is contained in 'worlding'). In my semantics, 'world' emerges from a contact between the human mind and the things, the lines, the rhythms of the earth. When this contact is sensitive, subtle, intelligent, you have 'a world' (a culture) in the strong, confirming and enlightening sense of the word. When that contact is insensitive, simplistic and stupid, you don't have a world at all, you have a non-world, a pseudo-culture, a dictatorial enclosure or a mass-mess. Geopoetics is concerned with developing sensitive and intelligent contact, and with working out original ways to express that contact.[46]

For White, then, 'poetics is a fundamental word, underlying science, literature, philosophy, and coordinating elements arising from all these disciplines.'[47] Because the 'normal' condition of man is artificial, so is his language. Therefore, the geopoetical poem seeks a new form of expression. This leads to a radically different approach to the form of poetry than the norm in the English and western canon. For White, the language of poetry must reveal the world. Poetry as we are accustomed to it in the English canon rarely reveals world. We are offered an artefact constructed of metaphors, metrics, word and sound-play, beautifully made often, but only revealing the poet. Poetry which reveals a world will not point back in on itself like this, rather it will be, to use Gaston Bachelard's memorable description, 'the flare-up of being in the imagination'.[48] White's writing is full of such incandescent moments as this from 'In the sea and pine country':[49]

> an occasional cry
> enlarges the silence

This image pares the poet's experience down to the essential sign and simplest language but it has the opposite effect on the reader whose mind is filled, from this starting point, with the 'sense of world' which has inspired the lines. And the lines themselves reflect the poetic practice being pointed to – it's the small 'cry' of the poet which indicates the vast 'sense of world'.

This is not to say that 'form' is irrelevant. It may be correct to a certain extent, as one critic has said,[50] that White reveals a 'distrust of style and technique' (although there is a lot more craftsmanship in White's poetry than is initially apparent), but he is utterly wrong in accusing him of 'lack of form'. On the contrary the 'poetics' in 'geopoetics' refers precisely to the idea of 'composition'. The focus of the poet's attention, though, is, primarily, not on (artificial) form, but on that point at which essential perception of the world, so truly felt as to necessitate its being expressed, meets its form in its emergence into being (its voicing).

'No metaphor-mongering/no myth-malarkey', as 'Ovid' puts it in one of White's longer poems, 'Ovid's Report',[51] which offers a useful example of White's content and method. These long poems trace the development of certain key historical cultural figures from their personal-social contexts to vaster and clearer fields of perception. 'At first I found it hard to swallow,' says Ovid of his exile 'on the Scythian coast'. Then,

    the citizenship of Rome
    dropped off me
    like some old skin

and he begins to delight in this 'land of wind and shadow' which is 'at the world's edge'. Normal perception will see that phrase as meaning 'the world's end'; in the intellectual nomad's perspective, it means 'the world's beginning'. Now, Ovid contemplates the known world and speculates on unknown worlds:

    between the Scythians and the Hyperboreans
    a hundred peoples, a thousand tribes
    Rome has never heard of

and begins to discover the 'strange poetry hidden/in these barbarian lands'. The poem finishes with Ovid, echoing Brandan, seeking to 'get further into this unspoken space' and:

    find, who knows, the source
    of another light

The poem starts in apparent prosaic form, its tone bitter and proud – 'just imagine me... all alone among uncouth clods...' – with Ovid still writing his 'finely wrought discourses'. But as the rough, cold, Black Sea landscape begins to penetrate, images of it begin to accumulate in the conversational tone, signs of an enlargening and illuminating perspective growing in the Latin poet. In a river-like movement common to many of these poems, the poem's rhythm, mirroring its content, becomes slower and more open, becoming calmer as it becomes more aware of the expansive void to which the content has directed itself – the geopoetical sea of potentiality opening up at the end which is, in fact, a beginning.

Similarly, in the short poem form, a sense of apparent, prosaic-ness is the initial response to a poem such as this image of Venice:

HOTEL WINDOW, EVENING

Night falling
voices fading from the quays
gondoliers covering their barques

and suddenly, all along the lagoon
the lighting up of the hidden channels[52]

The ordinary scene from the window reveals illuminating signs of a hidden reality, the light which the darkness reveals to those who can see it. And the poet must say, as well as see it, in a language apparently as ordinary as the scene but also full of signs brought to the reader's attention by slight rhymes, alliteration and word echoes which, in unifying the poem as a complete image, offer the reader the opportunity to see exactly what the poet has seen, uni-fies the reader's mind with the poet's. The effect is, contrary to the poetry described above, to open up the reader's mind to an image of the world and its significance. As White says in 'Broken ode to white Brittany':

May it never, don't forget
smell the poet[53]

G.M. Hopkins, drawing on Duns Scotus' 'haecceitas', sought to express phenomenal reality and to forge the language which it necessitated. T.S. Eliot exposed the 'waste-land' of western culture to the critical analysis of the poetic imagination. Ezra Pound, influ-enced by Fenollosa, reoriented western poetry towards the 'image', which would, when perfected, become the building block for long, all-embracing poems. Hugh MacDiarmid pointed to the knowledge of all the disciplines of human endeavour and knowledge as the true subject-matter of poetry. Kenneth White has taken up these most significant attempts to return poetry to its central role as clear and perceptive expression of human experience in the world and renewer of culture. But more than that, he has developed them, and evolved a poetic language which is as remarkable for its simplicity, its musicality and its oral tone as it is for its intensity, profundity and formal astuteness. The 'possibilism' which he espouses does not see 'endgame' in the degeneration of western culture, but new beginnings:

> Today, for the first time in the history of humanity, winds blow from all regions of the globe at once, and each and everyone of us has access to all the cultures of the world. That can give rise to cacophony, to disarray, lassitude in front of so much accumulated richness, but it can also give rise, with analytical work and synthesis... to a new way of thinking, a great world poem, liveable by everyone.[54]

NOTES

[1] André Breton in a letter to Kenneth White in 1965 after reading a draft chapter of *Incandescent Limbo* in *Les Lettres Nouvelles* of January 1965 edited by Maurice Nadeau. Durrell quoted in 'Presenting Kenneth White', a publisher's brochure published by Mainstream in 1989.

[2] Kenneth White, *The Bird Path*, Edinburgh: Mainstream, 1989, p. 20.

[3] Kenneth White, *The Blue Road*, Edinburgh: Mainstream, 1990, p. 16.

[4] Samuel Beckett's expression. Kenneth White writes of Samuel Beckett pushing the boundaries of nihilism further and further out while White seeks to take the step across those boundaries.

[5] The expression partly originates with Emerson, but Kenneth White made it his own with a doctoral thesis on 'intellectual nomadism' presented to a jury in Paris in 1979.

[6] The word first occurred to White in the Labrador in 1979 and soon developed into the concept which unifies his life and work and gives them forward impetus especially through the International Institute of Geopoetics.

[7] Kenneth White, 'Night in Barcelona', in *Travels in the Drifting Dawn*, Edinburgh: Mainstream, 1989, p. 125.

[8] *A Short History of Decomposition*, London: Quartet Encounters, 1990, pp. 24-25.

[9] Unpublished in English as yet. French version: *Les Limbes Incandescent*, Paris: Denoël, 1976.

[10] *The Blue Road* (Edinburgh: Mainstream, 1990) recounts a journey up the St. Lawrence River from Quebec City to Ungava Bay in the Labrador; *Pilgrim of the Void* (Edinburgh: Mainstream, 1992) recounts travels in Asia and incorporates two books published separately in France: *Le Visage du Vent de l'Est* (Paris: Les Presses d'aujourd'hui, 1980) and *Les Cygnes Sauvages* (Paris: Grasset, 1990) which recounts a journey from Tokyo to Hokkaido in the footsteps of Matsuo Basho (1644-1694). French translation of White's work are by his wife, Marie-Claude.

[11] *Letters from Gourgounel* was published by Jonathan Cape in London in 1962 but is now out of print. The revised edition in translation, *Lettres de Gourgounel*, was published in Grasset's Cahiers Rouges editions, Paris 1986. It recounts Kenneth White's experiences in an old farmhouse in the Ardèche in Southern France, 1961.

[12] Four volumes of essays have been published in France: *La Figure du Dehors* (1982), *Une Apocalypse Tranquille* (1985), *L'Esprit Nomade* (1987) and *Le Plateau de L'Albatros* (1994), all Grasset of Paris. Individual essays on the likes of Victor Segalen, Antonin Artaud and Hokusaï have also been published as well as collections of interviews.

[13] Notably Gilles Deleuze and Félix Guattari, *L'Anti-Oedipe*, Paris: Les Editions de Minuit, 1972.

[14] Notably J.F. Lyotard, *Dérive à Partir de Marx et Freud*, Paris: Union Générale d'Editions, 1973.

[15] Village south of Glasgow on the west coast of Scotland where Kenneth White was brought up from the age of three having been born in Glasgow.

[16] In 'Following out world lines' an interview with Alistair Paterson in Kenneth White, *Coast to Coast*, edited by Norman Bissell, Glasgow: Mythic Horse Press, 1996, p. 78.

[17] Kenneth White, *Handbook for the Diamond Country*, Edinburgh: Mainstream, 1990, p. 17.

[18] Kenneth White's insistence on bringing together sensual and intellectual experience is expressed in phrases such as 'eros, logos, cosmos' and 'erotic logic'.

[19] Kenneth White refers to the three early books *Travels in the Drifting Dawn*, *Incandescent Limbo* and *Letters from Gourgounel* as 'a supernihilist's itinerary'.

[20] 'Une Saison en Enfer', in *Oeuvres Poètiques*, Paris: Garnier Flammarion, 1964, p. 133.

[21] In *Thus Spoke Zarathustra*, Harmondsworth: Penguin, 1961, p. 41.

[22] Kenneth White's expression for the 20th century terminus of the 'motorway of western civilisation', degeneration of the 19th century's utilitarian goal of 'the greatest happiness of the greatest number' and of Hegelian ideas of inevitable historical 'progress'.

[23] See note 6.

[24] An epithet for contemporary culture and social organisation frequently used by Kenneth White.

[25] Kenneth White, 'Scotia Deserta', *The Bird Path*, cit., p. 123.

[26] The archaeological, lithographical and mythographical records of Scotland's pre-Christian peoples constitute a tantalising field of study to which Kenneth White refers throughout his work.

[27] Pelagius, a 4th century philosopher of British origin, denied original sin and shifted the theological balance away from divine grace towards individual responsibility for salvation; excommunicated three times by the Vatican.

[28] St. Augustine sent St. Jerome, unsuccessfully, to sort out the pelagian Britons. The Synod of Whitby in 663 AD referred to the Scots as 'the only people stupid enough to put themselves out of step with the entire world'.

[29] Ernest Renan, 'La Poèsie des Races Celtique', in 'Essais de Morale et de Critique' in *Ouevres Complètes*, edited by Henriette Psichari, Paris: Calmann-Levy, 1948, II, p. 269.

[30] 'Ces moines venus de la mer', offprint (St. Malo, 1992), p. 6.

[31] Kenneth White, *The Bird Path*, cit., pp. 188-193.

[32] Ernest Renan, *op. cit.*, p. 292.

[33] John Scoto Erigena was invited to the court of Charles le Chauve, King of France, in the ninth century where, protected from the wrath of Rome regarding his pelagian ideas, he translated the Greek philosophers and wrote his great work – *Periphyseon* (*De Divisione Naturae*).

[34] John Duns Scotus, 13th century Franciscan philosopher.

[35] George Buchanan (1506-1582), renowned teacher in Paris and Bordeaux, termed 'prince of poets' by his contemporaries.

[36] Patrick Geddes (1854-1932), biologist, town-planner, teacher, ecolo-

gist... He demonstrated 'the paradoxical generalisation that (human) production – though fundamentally for maintenance – is mainly for "art"'.

[37] 'extra vagans' was an epithet used in the Middle Ages for the wandering Scots.

[38] Kenneth White, 'Elements of Geopoetics', *The Edinburgh Review*, vol. 88, 1992, p. 164.

[39] Ernest Fenollosa, *The Chinese Written Character* (1906).

[40] Edmund Husserl, *Phenomenology and the Crisis of Philosophy*, translated by Quentin Lauer, New York: Harper, 1965, p. 185.

[41] Martin Heidegger, *An Introduction to Metaphysics*, Yale: Yale University Press, 1987. See especially ch. 4: 'The Limitation of Being'.

[42] Douglas Dunn, 'Bird Path of an Exile' (review), *Glasgow Herald*, May 13th, 1989.

[43] An expression used throughout Kenneth White's work in various contexts.

[44] Kenneth White's *The Wild Swans* (in *Pilgrim of the Void*) follows Basho's footsteps *The Narrow Road to the Deep North*.

[45] Quoted widely. See the introduction to *The Narrow Road to the Deep North and Other Travel Sketches*, London: Penguin Classics, 1966, p. 33.

[46] In '"From the Centred Complex": An Interview with Tony McManus', *The Edinburgh Review,* vol. 92, 1994, p. 126.

[47] *Ibidem*, p. 128.

[48] Gaston Bachelard, *The Poetics of Space*, Boston: Beacon Press, 1969, p. xiv.

[49] Kenneth White, *The Bird Path*, cit., p. 104.

[50] Edwin Morgan, *Books in Scotland*, vol. 31, 1989.

[51] Kenneth White, *The Bird Path*, cit., pp. 34-40.

[52] Kenneth White, *Les Rives du Silence*, Paris: Mercure de France, 1997, p. 196.

[53] Kenneth White, *The Bird Path*, cit., p. 206.

[54] *Sources,* vol. 32, 1991, p. 44.

MARCO FAZZINI

Douglas Dunn's Poetry:
A Barbarian In-between Cultures

To read Douglas Dunn's poetry is to experience the sense of division that prefigures the emergence of a new radical voice in
Scottish contemporary poetry. After the strongly nationalistic and
revolutionary ideas of MacDiarmid and the attempts of the Second
Generation of the Scottish Renaissance to restore the use of vernacular Scots, Dunn is the purveyor of a transitional style which revisits the Larkinian tradition of English poetry and smashes it against
the coarsest creativity of the Scottish revival. In most of his poems
he may yearn for a social change – 'I have written about class and
the system of humiliations on which this country and the rest of the
world tick over' – yet he restores more convincingly the powers of
imagination and intuition as the best English-language contemporary poets have managed to do: 'But I don't think I *chose* these
subjects. The way I look at it is that my imagination decided that I
should show my colours. In retrospect, I think the gesture was
necessary, and I stand by it'.[1]

The uncertain interstices of historical and literary change in contemporary Scotland is where Dunn likes to move and write: from
the area of ambivalence between Tradition and Renovation; out of
an unresolved contradiction between national culture and class
struggle; from deep within the encounter of the conduct of government and the conduct of private persons. As to his own methods,
there is all the difference which separates the person from the
group, and, obviously, that alignment that colonial subjects are
familiar with: Civilised/Uncivilised, Poor/Rich, Self/Other,
Barbaric/Cultured. It is this revealing and latent list of divisions that
pushes Dunn's poetry to the lively ground of dialectics which he
exploits and climbs over. Strong is his sense of the uncertainty of
the border, that uncomfortable state of exile which, for a period of

his life, made him feel part neither of his Scotland nor of his adopted England. The poet seems to live the endless alienation of the writer whose poetry, as Larkin once said, can happen anywhere, even though it is more probable that it may exploit the local and familiar. Talking about his period spent in Hull from 1966 to 1984 the poet observes: 'Never further away than a long morning's train journey from Hull, Scotland has always been accessible and I have travelled back more often than I care to remember. Several years ago it dawned on me for the first time that these visits home were spent largely in checking facts, feelings and settings for writing, testing the sounds of voices and the cadences of a locality. It was the sort of realization that can make you feel like an exile when you know that you are not'.[2]

If, on the one hand, Dunn's Hegelianism tries to restore power to Scottish history, his use of the 'I' declares the entrance of multifaceted *personae* into a revisited sense of historiography built upon precise masks penetrating the poetical reconstruction of his external reality. In this way Dunn's agonistic method illuminates the cruelty of subjection, slavery, imperial and parochial academism by treating the privileged themes of high literature through the low and 'barbaric' intrusion of his indigenous culture. Talking about the Humber estuary in Hull, Dunn metaphorises his attraction for the meeting of contrasting elements of reality: 'It is so spectacularly grim it is beautiful. Sunlight turns the mud to a silvery grey, the colour of chrome taps'.[3] That mixture of colours and feelings is characteristic of Dunn's poetry, as well as it was characteristic of Larkin's style. The Humber estuary is beautiful and grim, silvery and muddy at the same time or, as Derek Mahon observed during a walk taken with Dunn, has the 'post-Imperial grandeur of a British port in decline'.[4] It is in this post-Imperial climate that Larkin wrote his first poems, and it is under Larkin's influence and encouragement that Dunn shaped his own style and poetics. In those years the Welfare State failed its intents, the Vietnam War broke out with a violence that shocked the young generations of, at least, three continents, and the decline of the British Empire was dissolving the illusions of many nostalgic conservatives.[5] It is in this panorama that Dunn's poetry was first published in 1969.

In articulating the idea of class struggle and cultural alienation,

Dunn's transgressive vision of truth puts into question the ambition of sharp dialectics: the trite stereotype of the civilised/uncivilised dichotomy; the fear for technological progress guaranteed by advanced neo-colonialist countries; a traditional conception of the historicist idea of time as a progressive advancement towards an idealised structure of society. So, Dunn's argumentation moves in the interstitial space between those opposing elements to show the ambiguity of any total theory and to revalue the hidden and suppressed voices of both a personal and common past.

The equilibrium Douglas Dunn has maintained since the publication of his first volume *Terry Street*, in 1969, is something that Ian Gregson describes in these terms: 'Dunn's surrealism deliberately offends against the realist mode whose dominance Larkin helped to establish – where Larkin's was a conservative dialogue with modernism, Dunn's is a subversive dialogue with realism'.[6]

Re-introduced in post-war England by the Movement poets, especially Larkin and Davie, the realism Gregson talks about mainly looked at urban landscapes with urban taste. In order to declare that 'nature poetry' and a Modernist attitude to the world was at that time impracticable, the group of poets Robert Conquest gathered in *New Lines* was considered to share his question about external reality: 'What can a poem do with a landscape?'[7] A new general tendency was introduced in contemporary poetry. Against 'The debilitating theory that poetry *must* be metaphorical'[8] and the 'irresponsible exploitations of technique in contradiction of human life as we know it',[9] the Movement poets refused the experimentations of Modernism and the richly metaphorical poetry of the new Romanticism *à la* Dylan Thomas in order to inaugurate a poetry of statement, like the one written by William Empson but without the notoriously witty ambiguities of his most cerebral word-plays.[10] The programme was based on a general downplaying of any concern for feeling and on a technique which admitted a slight narrative thread based upon a sheer descriptive listing of all the paraphernalia of post-war urban landscape.

Yet, even though the Movement poets, and Larkin in particular, refused to concede Modernism an eminent place in the development of the English poetic tradition, it seems clear, as the above-mentioned quote by Gregson has evidenced, that a dialogue with

Modernism existed and was very productive. Larkin was not indifferent to Eliot's, Auden's and Yeats's works, as can be observed in his
first book *The North Ship* or, even better, in his juvenilia.[11]

Recent criticism on Larkin's work has also evidenced that
Symbolism and, by implication, Modernism were all-important for
a book like *High Windows*.[12] This partly justifies the idea that
Larkin's poetry was much more interested in transcendence and
human endeavour than previously acknowledged, so that the conviction that an unhistorical trend in his work should be put into
focus has become relevant at least in the last twenty years. Without
going as far as to share Barbara Everett's suggestion that a 'timeless
idealism' can be applied to some of Larkin's poems,[13] a serious and
well-documented work on Larkin's engagement with the social attitudes of the post-war years seems far from being produced by the
recent critics. So, if on the one hand it is certain that the social and
historical situation of the late 1940s and 1950s may have influenced
Larkin's general tone, his sense of disillusionment and the nostalgia
Heaney talks about when referring to Hughes, Hill and Larkin,[14] on
the other his commitment to the present situation of British society was always dictated by a general aloofness from contingent
matters.

On the contrary, Dunn's revisitation of Larkin's attitudes has
always been, contextually and historically, much more open to a
direct socio-historical analysis. Dunn's observing eye is flooded by
a series of *realia* which become strong markers of a deeper historical excavation since his poetic debut. If Larkin's observation was
led by a mastering eye which tended to appropriate external reality
and extract from it the meaning of an epiphanic moment, Dunn
questions his own realistic techniques in order to open a dialogic
relationship with the world and his literary influences.[15] Since the
publication of *Terry Street*, Dunn's work has been crowded by people and their respective and respectable identities. Instead of
engaging in a 'colonizing' process of appropriation and subjection,
Dunn looks for an enriching relationship with the Other, letting
him or her enter his consciousness in a creative way:

> I want to be touched by them, know their lives,
> Dance in my own style, learn something new.
> At night, I even dream of ideal communities.

Why do they live where they live, the rich and the poor?[16]

Here Dunn shifts the axis of his poetical and philosophical attention to a de-centered account of reality in order to open his discourse to the Others' voices and attitudes. Differently from Larkin,
he does not try to generalize about Man, or Life, or Death.[17] He
places his work in a particular time and in a particular place. *Terry
Street*, for example, insists on a slum street of Hull as it could be
seen by the poet in the late 1960s, a few years before it was
destroyed. Or, again, the first section of *Barbarians*, and a few
poems from *St Kilda's Parliament*, revisits aspects of Scottish history and compares them to other historical events of the Western
colonisation of the world in a way which had always been alien to
Larkin.[18] So, even though he is often interested in some 'underdog'
or victim, as the Movement had already done by recuperating the
lessons of the Georgian poets,[19] or of Owen, or Hardy in particular,[20] Dunn's aim is not that of showing 'pity' for him or her but
that of entering the Other's feelings and expectations to discover a
new and unexpected side of Truth.[21] If the married couples
described by Larkin in 'The Whitsun Weddings' remain sheer exte-
riority to be observed and even ironised ('Struck, I leant/More
promptly out next time, more curiously,/And saw it all again in different terms:/The fathers with broad belts under their suits/And
seamy foreheads; mothers loud and fat;/An uncle shouting
smut...'), Dunn often allows the observed to become observing
subjects in their turn, and accepts to submit himself to their contemplation and judgments:

> This time they see me at my window, among books,
> A specimen under glass, being protected,
> And laugh at me watching them.
> They minuet to Mozart playing loudly
>
> On the afternoon Third. They mock me thus,
> They mime my culture. A landlord stares.
> All he has worked for is being destroyed.
> The slum rent-masters are at one with Pop.[22]

Here the poet does not only look for a way of deepening his
knowledge through a relationship with the Other; he also tries to

feel part of a place, questioning himself and his choice to live in Hull, wondering about the real existence of an 'ideal community', a 'home' to be created or recuperated, and thinking about a possible solution for his condition of exile. In a response to a request to give a brief account of his work, the poet observed: 'It just happened that I wrote a fictionalized version of what was around me. I have never self-consciously chosen to write about a particular subject in my life. An explanation of why I wrote about Terry Street, and a way of understanding the moods of these poems, is that I felt myself a stranger in the street and town in which I lived. In the community of accents and attitudes Hull represents, I still feel as if I'm not at home'.[23]

If on the one hand, in that community of proletarian workers, Dunn shared those people's background and ideological convictions, on the other their everyday dramas, idiosyncrasies, and imagined 'ideal life' were for the poet only a natural subject his imagination improvised on in a detached way. Yet, in many of his poems his desire to identify himself with those people is clearly discernible, even though hidden or understated. From a stylistic point of view, his friendship with Larkin made it easier for him to start his career in the typical Movement way:

> On a squeaking cart, they push the usual stuff,
> A mattress, bed ends, cups, carpets, chairs,
> Four paperback westerns. Two whistling youths
> In surplus U.S. Army battle-jackets
> Remove their sister's goods. Her husband
> Follows, carrying on his shoulders the son
> Whose mischief we are glad to see removed,
> And pushing, of all things, a lawnmower.
> There is no grass in Terry Street. The worms
> Come up cracks in concrete yards in moonlight.
> That man, I wish him well. I wish him grass.[24]

Yet, even in his early beginnings, there is more than a mere realistic technique. First of all, Larkin's unconsolable sense of disillusionment has been replaced by an ironic last line which stands for a kind of positive, or at least open possibility about the changing times and the conditions for that class.[25] Secondly, since the poem rests on the internal division played by the two pronouns 'they' and 'we' – the poet being a member of the second group and the proferrer of the final wish – it also ironically enacts a sort of confrontation between the poet's 'home' and his sense of alienation in Terry Street. Thirdly, being Dunn an external observer of some other people's removal, he ironically plays on the re-elaboration of the seventeenth century tradition of Marvell's 'Garden Poems' in order to underline his distance from that 'lost tribe'. The social and economic improvement he wishes to the man moving out of Terry Street ('I wish him grass') metaphorically implies not only his own longing for the rural landscape he left in Inchinnan, but also a conflictual desire that 'that man', and himself, could appropriate the exterior commodities of the upper class. So, even though, as David Montrose observes, the poet has to accept that an 'existential choice is necessary between the two cultures, between the working class and the bourgeoisie',[26] his irony maintains the choice suspended in the gap created by his own ambiguous indecision.

His 'home' desire is expressed in another poem called 'A Window Affair'. Here a kind of 'flirtation, through the glass' forces the poet to abandon his idealized relationship with the woman living opposite to him in order to become aware of her and his own delusions and frustrations ('But some ideals have passed far out of my reach'). As Linden Peach notes, in Dunn's early work there is 'a tension between a realistic, often disillusioned, documentary voice and a poetic imagination which promises, at least for a while, to transform this reality'[27] so that realism and lyricism merge to state a final declaration of belonging to some idea of 'home':

> It's come to this, that in this time, this place,
> There is a house I feel I have to leave,
> Because my life is cracked, and in a room
>
> Stares out of windows at a window face,
> Thin shifts of dust on the sunning glass,
> And does not want to love, and does not care.[28]

We are far from Larkin's crude affirmation that 'We all hate home/And having to be there:/I detest my room,/Its specially-chosen junk,/The good books, the good bed,/And my life, in perfect order...'.[29] A sense of refusal of his state of 'exile' is evident in Dunn's first sequence, but his desire to see himself definitely detached from Terry Street merges with his fear of being left alone in a solitary world made of art and contemplation. In 'Sunday Morning Among the Houses of Terry Street' he writes that what he sees is 'A city of disuse, a sink, a place' but he also says that 'Without people it would be like the sea-bottom'.[30] Along with those people's 'culture of clothes and little philosophies' Dunn also stresses the importance of that cultural environment for his own literary training, even though it can cost him being identified as one member of that 'barbarian' world. On this point Alan Robinson has something to point out:

> Dunn's strength as a political poet lies in his capacity to dramatise this unceasing process of class tensions, ranging from antagonism to embarrassment, which inform one's perception of the Other and one's awareness of the Other's returning gaze. This visual negotiation of deferentiality and mastery epitomises the wider nexus of power relationships in society and is, I shall argue, distinctively relevant to Dunn's situation as a Scottish working-class writer.[31]

The window (and the recurrent image of a frame) through which the poet observes the external occurrences and the people in them is a continuous presence to be crossed and re-crossed in various moments and situations, a space of exchange and confrontation. That window is not only the place where separation is made possible, but also the space that the poet's look has to cross in order to guarantee the existence of an interstice of negotiation.[32] As Seamus Heaney observes in his essay 'Frontiers of Writing', these dividing borders, which are borders between classes, cultures, and nationalities, exist because 'within our individual selves we can reconcile two orders of knowledge which we might call the practical and the poetic; to affirm also that each form of knowledge redresses the other and that the frontier between them is there for the crossing'.[33] The Other is always different yet familiar to the poet. So even though Dunn knows that 'they all come back,/Mysterious people without names or faces,/Whose lives I guess about, whose dangers tease./And not one of them has anything at all to do with me', he is condemned to share their presence and to accept that the Other's life enters the poet's eye and imagination. This negotiation can happen through the surreptitious framed photograph of a book, the glass of his Terry Street window, or the lenses of his spectacles:

> They will not leave me, the lives of other people.
> I wear them near my eyes like spectacles.
> Sullen magnates, hunched into chins and overcoats
> In the back seats of their large cars...[34]

Here Dunn's imaginative lyricism meets a realistic way of representing the external world.[35] If the objective mode of his work must acknowledge Larkin's influence (he says that 'There are lots of ways in which I'd defer to Larkin – obviously he's a much better poet than I am'), he also thinks that his mentor 'might see himself as a traditional lyric poet who's got fucked up on the *realia* of his particular moment of the twentieth century, which has ruined the nature of his lyricism'.[36] Dunn's desire to make lyric imagination coexist with an objective way of representing external *realia* is nothing else than a merging of Modernist (Imagist and Surrealist) elements with 'That gentlemanly verse, towards which poets like Philip Larkin and Kingsley Amis have tended', and give 'imagination the spaciousness which it has'[37] when the authorial voice of poetical and political perspectives are open to the intrusion of an enriching Alterity.

NOTES

[1] 'An interview with Douglas Dunn by Bernard O'Donoghue', *Oxford Poetry*, vol. 2, no. 2, Spring 1985, p. 44. For a short definition of the relationship between imagination and reality read the following observation by Dunn: 'Imagination is usually the faculty through which language and imagery are discovered and then transmuted into the poetic substance with which reality can be recorded in the way which poetry does that. Some poems will always be about recognizable realities more than others'. Douglas Dunn's letter to the author (dated 15.5.1992).

[2] Douglas Dunn, 'Exile and Unexile', *Cencrastus*, no. 16, Spring 1984, p. 5.

[3] Douglas Dunn, 'Living Out of London', *London Magazine*, vol. 19, nos. 5/6, August/September 1979, p. 77.

[4] *Ibidem.*

[5] Cf. John Strachey, *The End of Empire*, London: Gollancz, 1959; E.T. Salmon, *The Nemesis of Empire*, London: Oxford University Press, 1974; Franz Ansprenger, *The Dissolution of the Colonial Empires*, London: Routledge, 1989.

[6] Ian Gregson, '"There are many worlds": The "Dialogic" in Terry Street and After', in Robert Crawford and David Kinloch eds., *Reading Douglas Dunn*, Edinburgh: Edinburgh University Press, 1992, p. 27.

[7] Robert Conquest, 'Antheor', in *New Lines: An Anthology*, London: Macmillan, 1965, p. 75. See also Kingsley Amis's 'Against Romanticism' and John Wain's 'Reason for not Writing Orthodox Nature Poetry', respectively at p. 45 and p. 83 of the above-mentioned anthology.

[8] Robert Conquest, 'Introduction' to *New Lines*, cit., p. xii.

[9] Philip Larkin, *All What Jazz: A Record Diary*, London: Faber & Faber, 1985, p. 27.

[10] As for the Movement poets' appraisal of William Empson's poetry see John Wain's article 'Ambiguous Gifts' published in 1950 in *Penguin New Writing* and reprinted in John Wain's *Preliminary Essays*, London: Macmillan, 1957.

[11] See what Larkin affirms in *Required Writing: Miscellaneous Pieces 1955-82*, London: Faber & Faber, 1983, p. 29. For a critical treatment of Yeats's influence on Larkin see James Booth, *Philip Larkin: Writer*, Hemel Hempstead: Harvester Wheatsheaf, 1992, pp. 64-68; Edna Longley, 'Larkin, Edward Thomas and the Tradition', *Phoenix*, nos. 11/12, 1973/74, p. 64; and A.T. Tolley, *My Proper Ground: A Study of the Work of Philip Larkin and Its Development*, Edinburgh: Edinburgh University Press, 1991, pp. 32-45.

[12] See the following articles published in the 1980s: Grevel Lindop, 'Being different from yourself: Philip Larkin in the 1970s', in Peter Jones and Michael Schmidt eds., *British Poetry Since 1970: A Critical Survey*, Manchester: Carcanet, 1980, pp. 46-54; Seamus Heaney, 'The Main of Light', in Anthony Thwaite ed., *Larkin at Sixty*, London: Faber & Faber, 1982, pp. 131-138; Barbara Everett, 'Philip Larkin: After Symbolism', *Essays in Criticism*, vol. 30, no. 3, 1980, pp. 227-242; Andrew Motion, *Philip Larkin*, London and New York: Routledge, 1982.

[13] Barbara Everett, 'Larkin's Edens', in *Poets in Their Time: Essays on English Poetry from Donne to Larkin*, London: Faber & Faber, 1986, pp. 230-244.

[14] See in particular the following observation by Seamus Heaney: 'I

think that sense of an ending has driven all three of these writers into a kind of piety towards their local origins, has made them look in, rather than up, to England. The loss of imperial power, the failure of economic nerve, the diminished influence of Britain inside Europe, all this has led to a new sense of the shires, a new valuing of the native English experience'. Seamus Heaney, 'Englands of the Mind', in *Preoccupations: Selected Prose 1968-1978*, London: Faber & Faber, 1980, p. 169.

[15] Alastair Fowler, reviewing Dunn's *Selected Poems*, says: 'Certainly Dunn owes an enormous personal debt to Larkin, as his master in the vocation and craft of verse. But he no longer aims at the Larkinian epigram of predefined feelings: rather, at a warmer and more exploratory elegiac form. And he has dared to re-open communicative lines that lead off the modernist map altogether'. Alastair Fowler, 'Off the Raised Beach', *Cencrastus*, no. 26, Summer 1987, p. 45. Kenneth White is much more polemical when he states: 'But he does move out from the distinguished nonentity of the "contemporary English scene" in the company of writers with more existential space and more intellectual energy to their life and work (he mentions Jaccottet, Camus and Rimbaud) than anything he could find in the slough of more or less sophisticated despond'. Kenneth White, review of *St Kilda's Parliament*, *Cencrastus*, no. 8, Spring 1982, p. 44.

[16] Douglas Dunn, 'Young Women in Rollers', in *Selected Poems 1964-1983*, London: Faber & Faber, 1986, p. 16.

[17] On this general problem see what Robert Dixbury notes when he states that 'Dunn has not the ability to sustain an idea in the abstract. His gift is in his lists of details (his imagery) and in his narrative technique'. Robert Dixbury, 'The Poetry of Douglas Dunn', *Akros*, vol. 14, no. 41, 1979, p. 59.

[18] Read, for example, the following statement by Dunn: 'By the time my book *Barbarians* appeared, which was not, shall we say, right-wing, or even tending in that direction, Larkin's influence on my work must have become an embarrassment to him. It was never an embarrassment to me, although it seemed to annoy others who failed to understand how a poet who identified himself through a "left-wing of the spirit" took hints and examples from Larkin, whose wing was on the other side'. Douglas Dunn, *Under the Influence: Douglas Dunn on Philip Larkin*, Edinburgh: Edinburgh University Library, 1987, p. 11.

[19] Blake Morrison, *The Movement: English Poetry and Fiction of the 1950s*, London and New York: Methuen, 1986, p. 215.

[20] Cf. Donald Davie, *Thomas Hardy and British Poetry*, London: Routledge, 1973.

[21] With regard to the 'underdog' and his or her intrusion into his poetry, Dunn observes: 'My imagination is drawn to it, it's not a political choice or anything like that. I still have the belief that these people know truths that I don't know, and I'd like to know what they know'. John Haffenden ed., *Viewpoints: Poets in Conversation with John Haffenden*, London: Faber & Faber, 1981, p. 22.

[22] Douglas Dunn, 'Young Women in Rollers', in *Selected Poems*, cit., p. 15.

[23] P.R. King, *Nine Contemporary Poets: A Critical Introduction*, London: Methuen, 1979, p. 221.

[24] Douglas Dunn, 'A Removal from Terry Street', in *Selected Poems*, cit., p. 8.

[25] On this last line Douglas Dunn comments in the following way: 'The last line of the poem is intended as ironic. That man, and his lawnmower, setting off for a new place, perhaps a better place, and perhaps some grass for him to look after, moved me; and yet I also saw the vignette as an image of vanity, of that man's touching faith in progress, and of my own unjustifiable cynicism in an environment which perfectly embodied the shame amd wormwood of British society'. P.R. King, *op. cit.*, p. 224.

[26] David Montrose, 'Class is the Curse of the Thinking Workers', *The Honest Ulsterman*, no. 66, 1980, p. 72.

[27] Linden Peach, *Ancestral Lines: Culture & Identity in the Work of Six Contemporary Poets*, Bridgend: Seren, 1992, p. 141.

[28] Douglas Dunn, *Selected Poems*, cit., p. 19.

[29] Philip Larkin, 'Poetry of Departures', in *Collected Poems*, London: Faber & Faber, 1988, p. 85.

[30] Douglas Dunn, *Selected Poems*, cit., p. 12.

[31] Alan Robinson, *Instabilities in Contemporary British Poetry*, London: Macmillan, 1988, p. 82.

[32] See also Nadine Gordimer's use of the window as a dividing frame between a white narrator and the black *locations* of Johannesburg in her first two novels *The Lying Days* (1953) and *A World of Strangers* (1958).

[33] Seamus Heaney, *The Redress of Poetry: Oxford Lectures*, London: Faber & Faber, 1995, p. 203.

[34] Douglas Dunn, 'The Hunched', in *Selected Poems*, cit., p. 47.

[35] On this topic see Dunn's analysis of Larkin, Heaney, Harrison and

MacCaig's poetry in his lecture delivered on 28 October 1987 at Dundee University: '"Importantly Live". Lyricism in Contemporary Poetry', Dundee: Dundee University Occasional Papers 1, 1988.

[36] John Haffenden ed., *op. cit.,* p. 33.

[37] *Ibidem*, p. 34.

J.C. BITTENBENDER

The Novels of Alasdair Gray:
Subversions of Narrative Authority

The publication of the novel *Lanark* in 1981 established Alasdair Gray as the leading fictional voice in what has become known as the Scottish Literary Renaissance of the late twentieth century. His novels, short stories, and radio plays have gained a critical following and he has become increasingly well represented in academic studies both within Scotland and internationally. At the heart of Gray's work is an obsession with authority and carnivalesque responses to it. This obsession can be examined in terms of the way in which Gray manipulates language and literary convention in his fiction, particularly in the novels *Lanark*, *1982 Janine* (1984), and *Poor Things* (1992).

The authorities Gray reacts to are many and varied. While it has become fairly standard to point to the political and cultural forces of Britain (read England) as the ultimate motivators of literary defiance in modern and contemporary Scottish literature, and although many contemporary Scottish writers including Gray can be seen to respond to national and cultural repression, a close inspection of Gray's texts reveals that repression itself is represented by forces much larger than English cultural domination. For Gray, the ultimate authorities are not simply political in nature but also historical and textual since these forces work hand in hand with political power to ensure control. While control of a culture or a nation may lie in the very governmental bodies Gray dismantles in his work, he goes much farther in his investigations of what signifies individual freedom by highlighting the role of textual authority and the position of the reader with regard to the teller of the tale. An analysis of the relationships between the characters/heroes in Gray's fictions and the authors/narrators who tell their stories may reveal important ways in which authority is constructed within society and how that authority might be subverted for any number of purposes.

Lanark is a book that is anti-chronological in format. Gray begins his story in Book III, a position in the middle of the narrative, with the character of Lanark already established in Unthank and attempting to come to some sort of understanding of who he is and how he came to this surrealistic world. This section follows Lanark as he moves from Unthank to the Institute, a purgatory of sorts, where he recovers from his experiences in Unthank and finds potential answers to his identity crisis through the Oracle whose recounting of Lanark's previous life forms Books One and Two. Book One forms the second section of the novel and introduces the character of Duncan Thaw, a small boy who comes of age in post-World War II Glasgow. The penultimate section, Book Two, follows on Book One and traces the course of Thaw's life from art school through his mural painting period to his sad demise that prepares the reader for the 'birth' of the hero Lanark in Book Three. The final section of the novel, Book Four, charts the course of Lanark's escape from the Institute and his journey to Provan, the governmental center of the fantastical world that contains Unthank.

Lanark and Duncan Thaw are hero-figures who the reader is tempted to merge into one, but who, through Gray's managerial skill, are kept distinct. Both characters are deeply troubled by a sense of insufficient identity and both share a drive towards art and imagination that they sense may lead them to find an answer to the question of who they are. In the second chapter of Book Three (which is the second chapter of the novel), Lanark, who knows nothing of his past as the artist Duncan Thaw, considers the act of writing and the nature of authorship that has been presented to him by Sludden, the leader of one of the popular cliques in Unthank:

> Lanark did not wish to be an artist but he felt increasingly the need to do some kind of work, and a writer needed only pen and paper to begin. Also he knew something about writing, for when wandering the city he had visited public libraries and read enough stories to know there were two kinds. One kind was a sort of written cinema, with plenty of action and hardly any thought. The other kind was about clever unhappy people, often authors themselves, who thought a lot but didn't do very

much. Lanark supposed a good author was more likely to write the second kind of book. He thought, 'Sludden said I should write to express myself. I suppose I could do it in a story about who I am and why I have decided to write a story. But there's a difficulty.'[1]

Here, Lanark is presenting the idea that an author needs to create a self through writing. The reader has not gone very far in the book and already Gray has implicated authorship and questioned the traditional notions of what constitutes good writing. Lanark is to be an author and so must consider what that means given the limited sort of knowledge he brings to the creative act. The Russian philosopher and literary theorist Mikhail Bakhtin defines the author and hero as 'correlative moments in the artistic whole of a work'.[2] As such the author and hero are inseparable, although never the same. Lanark's problem with authoring a hero follows simply from the realization that there is a problem: '"What does it matter who I am?" he asked aloud'.[3] He seems to sense a division implicit in the act of authoring, one that requires that he define a self 'outside' himself.

Though the two principal 'heroes' of Lanark are the characters of Thaw and Lanark, their positions in the text are closely paralleled by the descriptions of the two regions they inhabit, Glasgow and Unthank. One way in which these two characters attempt to define themselves is through their imaginative uses of the cities they inhabit. While Lanark is in Unthank he seems drawn to the imaginative possibilities of a world not unlike that of the Scotland of Thaw, in which, at least there is always the certainty of the sun rising and setting. However, the imaginative world of the artist Thaw is consistently focused on making use of the raw materials of history and religion to create fantastical otherworlds that bear some resemblance to Unthank. Throughout Book Two, the reader senses that Thaw is attempting to create not only a new persona for himself, but also one for Glasgow, one that has been denied by a lack of imagination. Thaw diagnoses the problem with Glasgow as one that stems from the lack of imaginative uses that have made of the city and he shares his philosophy with his fellow art student Kenneth McAlpin:

'Glasgow is a magnificent city,' said McAlpin. 'Why do we hardly ever notice that?' 'Because nobody imagines living here,' said Thaw. McAlpin

lit a cigarette and said, 'If you want to explain that I'll certainly listen.'
'Then think of Florence, Paris, London, New York. Nobody visiting them
for the first time is a stranger because he's already visited them in paintings, novels, history books and films. But if a city hasn't been used by an
artist not even the inhabitants live there imaginatively. What is Glasgow
to most of us? A house, the place we work, a football park or golf course,
some pubs and connecting streets. That's all. No, I'm wrong, there's also
the cinema and the library. And when our imagination needs exercise we
use these to visit London, Paris, Rome under the Caesars, the American
West at the turn of the century, anywhere but here and now.
Imaginatively Glasgow exists as a music-hall song and a few bad novels.
That's all we've given to the world outside. It's all we've given to ourselves.'[4]

What is interesting about this passage is not so much the fact that
Thaw is emphasizing the importance of artistic and imaginative
uses of a place in order to secure the healthy identity of a culture
and a nation, but that in the final sentence of his analysis he suggests the responsibility each Glaswegian has to create or assume
some authority over the creation of Glasgow. If this can be
achieved imaginatively, then perhaps it can be achieved politically
and in other areas as well. Although Thaw has drawn attention to
the importance of using Glasgow imaginatively, he fails to do so
himself in his own artwork, drawing instead on the stories from the
Old Testament in constructing the mural he paints in Cowlairs
Church. This is significant though, since what Thaw chooses to
portray is his interpretation of another form of textual authority,
God and the Bible.[5] However, while Thaw is seemingly intent on
rendering his unique vision of the Old Testment, imaginatively he
is gathering materials from Glasgow that will be used to fashion a
vision of Unthank. The reader, who has already been exposed to
the world of Unthank in Book Three (which starts the novel), is
treated in Book Two to the raw materials that will go into the creation of Unthank. As Thaw travels in and around Glasgow he interprets both natural and man-made objects in ways that are reminiscent of the landscape and characters of Unthank:

The stone walls, stapled over with iron pipes, seemed to hold something
grander and stranger than the builders knew. He looked through a door-
way and saw a huge unhealthy tree. It grew in a patch of bare earth
among pale-green rhubarb-shaped weeds; it divided at the roots into two

scaly limbs, one twisting along the ground, the other shooting up to the height of the third-storey windows; each limb, almost naked of branches, supported at the end a bush of withered leaves. Thaw stared and munched for several minutes then moved away feeling triumphant. It was not a feeling he understood. It might have come from identifying with the tree, with the confining walls or with both.[6]

This passage indicates the imaginative uses that Thaw can make of the world that surrounds him and that the reader finds realized in the Unthank sections where there are 'scaly limbs' (dragonhide) and the condition of the Glasgow tree becomes that of the ordinary Unthank citizen. Thaw not only uses nature and landscape in preparing the way for Lanark's Unthank sections, he also uses characteristics of his friends and acquaintances in Glasgow to form composite characters who show up in Unthank. Lanark's friend Sludden seems to be a composite of Thaw's friends Coulter and McAlpin, while Rima seems to represent a number of female interests from Thaw's past. This might suggest to the reader that the narrative authority of the Lanark/Unthank sections of the novel is in the hands of Thaw. If the reader is tempted to interpret the text in this way, the temptation is quickly thwarted by the Epilogue, which, true to the way in which Gray subverts the textual order of the novel, appears before the end of the narrative. In the Epilogue, Lanark misidentifies the author of his own story:

'Are you the king of this place?'
'The king of Provan, yes. And Unthank too. And that suite of rooms you call the institute and the council.'[7]

When the voice of the author finally identifies itself on the following page, Lanark asks it another searching question: 'Are you pretending to be God?' God and authorship are brought together here in a way that suggests that authorship of any narrative, be it political or imaginative is an act of arrogance if it assumes an equality between narrative and interpretive control. Playing at God implies the ability to control the lives of people, whereas authorship implies the setting up of plot and character but allows the reader some freedom of interpretation that is not to be impinged upon by the author. This is a perfect world of narrative possibility for Gray as well as one with potential ideal political ramifications if govern-

ments were less dominating and citizens given more control over
their own lives. As the Epilogue progresses, Lanark begins to sense
the power that the author (known as Nastler in Provan) holds over
him and he realizes that the things he wants will be denied to him
by the one who controls the flow of narrative:

> 'I never wanted anything but some sunlight, some love, some very ordi-
> nary happiness. And every moment I have been thwarted by organiza-
> tions and things pushing in a different direction, and now I'm nearly an
> old man and my reasons for living have shrunk to standing up in public
> and saying a good word for the only people I know. And you tell me
> that word will be useless! That you have planned it to be useless.'[8]

What Lanark has desired within the plot of his story seem very like
the desires of the common person in life and the connections
between the plotting and structuring of authorship and the political
forces that direct and control individuals could not be made clearer. It is at this point that Lanark levels his most damning pronouncement concerning what he believes to be the true identity of
his interlocutor: '"A conjuror!" said Lanark with loathing. "A
damned conjuror!"'.[9] This is also the point in the text of *Lanark*
where Nastler attempts to reveal the secret power of the printed
word and Gray, through his extensive 'Index of Plagiarisms,' listed
in the margins for the remainder of the Epilogue, confesses to the
materials he has plundered in cobbling together his own narrative.
In presenting the two disclosures together on the same page Gray
unites himself momentarily with Nastler. As Nastler explains his
manner of working to Lanark the reader senses that he or she is
simultaneously being addressed by Gray:

> 'Your survival as a character and mine as an author depend on us seduc-
> ing a living soul into our printed world and trapping it here long enough
> for us to steal the imaginative energy which gives us life. To cast a spell
> over this stranger I am doing abominable things. I am prostituting my
> most sacred memories into the commonest possible words and sentences.
> When I need more striking sentences or ideas I steal them from other
> writers, usually twisting them to blend with my own. Worst of all I am
> using the great world given at birth "the world of atoms" as a ragbag of
> shapes and colours to make this second-hand entertainment look more
> amusing.'[10]

This theme of authorial entrapment of a reader corresponds to a number of more political imprisoning environments that Gray explores in his other fictions.[11] The Institute and the Council of Lanark set the tone for the sham governmental bodies of Gray's other work such as the 'Ministry of Social Stability' in *McGrotty and Ludmilla*[12] and the empire of the 'Axletree stories' from *Unlikely Stories, Mostly*.[13] These remind us as well of other satiric and prophetic fictional organizations such as the Circumlocution Office of Dickens' *Little Dorrit* and Orwell's and Kafka's worlds of censorship and imprisonment. Gray's perception of 'organized' government as being both dangerous and ineffectual at the same time indicates a concern with the unexamined nature of authority. Gray's carnivalesque portrayals bring the official into relief, focusing on the ability of the unexamined to perniciously and surreptitiously take over. It is Gray's biggest fear that the complacency of people, of Scots, and of readers, will dull their wits and intellect to the point at which the 'powers-that-be' are able to remove a sense of effective community and individual possibility from their consciousnesses. This fear and its consequent carnivalesque treatment is even more noticeable in Gray's scientific and academic satires.[14]

More frightening for *Lanark* and for *1982 Janine* is the suggestion that characters, or even character-authors in the form of Jock McLeish, might be written into their prisons by the commanding pens of an outside authority. This incarceration of the imagination is touched upon by Cairns Craig in 'Going Down to Hell is Easy: *Lanark*, Realism and the Limits of the Imagination,' where he identifies fiction itself, frequently seen as an escape from confinements of reality, as connected to the act of control and captivity: 'The very imagination through which Gray constructs his novel is implicated in that destructive process of mastery: the novel must challenge the source of its own creativity if it is not to become just another play in the power structures and the escape routes by which the world entraps us'.[15] For Nastler, however, authorial control is more than entrapment for it is a form of control that sucks the energy out of the imprisoned reader through a series of magic tricks that are misleading. Yet the authority of Nastler, the self-confessed conjuror, is greatly diminished since the magic he practices is primarily illusion. This is a somewhat comforting notion that is

borne out by the subsequent realization on the part of the
author/conjuror that he has been unable to 'create' the birth of
Alexander, Lanark's son. As Craig points out, this is the point in the
text in which Lanark succeeds in wresting the authority of fatherhood from the author/conjuror.[16]

In *1982 Janine*, Gray presents the reader with another character
in the act of writing himself. The 'hero' of this text is Jock McLeish,
'an ageing, divorced, alcoholic, insomniac supervisor of security
installations,'[17] who sits in his hotel room in Peebles or Selkirk and
attempts to author an identity out of a collection of memories and
fantasies that are so dislocated that they continually fail to help him
achieve a form of consummation. He rejects the autobiographical
in favour of the imaginative, then slinks back again when this
comes too close to affecting him in the physical world. As opposed
to Lanark's narrow self-accounting, Jock's appears to be set in a
box from which events (real or imagined) pour forth to enlarge his
world. Where authorial control lies outside Lanark (with the exception of his brief introductory bit), Jock seems to suffer from surplus
of material out of which to construct a self. Lanark's access to surplus vision is severely restricted by the control enforced by his narrators (the Oracle, the author in the Epilogue) whereas Jock as narrator maintains an overabundance, which turns out to be perhaps
as debilitating. Jock is cast as an author and as such he creates his
own fictional 'inside' characters to help him towards some understanding of the outside world. The characters Janine, Big Momma,
and others of their kind who Jock creates in his 'story within a
story' are attempts of Jock's to fill in the areas surrounding Denny,
Helen, and others who Jock has been unable to see in reality. They
are artificial constructs built by Jock to assist him in the creation of
a complete identity. Another aspect of Jock's self-authoring
attempts are the interior dialogues he engages in when constructing his fictions. He frequently narrates the process of description,
as in this early scenario in which he exerts control over his heroine
Janine:

Half an hour later she stops the car in a lay-by. Some trucks whip past on
the road and when their lights fade she crouches down, unbuttons
blouse, slips it off, removes bra then slips blouse on again, fastening just
the two lowest buttons. Can I now have her sit back and light a cigarette,

smoking with one elbow out of the window (it's a warm night) and feeling the cool silk supporting her breasts? Yes. The row with Max has upset her, she wants to calm down, she thinks, 'Let Charlie wait another five minutes, it'll make him that much keener.'[18]

This typical passage is interesting in that not only do we catch a glimpse of Jock narrating the act of writing, we see him participating in the thought process that is Janine. Here he is thinking not only as Jock the author, but as Jock/Janine the heroine. He is justifying Janine's actions by imagining how she would feel on a warm night after having a row. Jock can only condone the authorial control he wishes to exert on Janine by answering his directorial questions with feelings of empathy. However to maintain control he must distance himself from his own creation, something he finds extremely difficult to do.[19]

In *1982 Janine* we see identity formation as a debilitating activity through Jock's refusal to embrace authentic others. In essence, the others he creates in the shape of Janine, Big Momma and company are false others, and 'real' others cannot be 'authored' by a consciousness resting in isolation. So too the limiting notions of Scottish literary stereotypes fostered by antisyzygical sentiments from earlier in the century contribute falsely to a sense of Scottish literary identity.[20] It is this type of literary authority that Gray so successfully resists through carnivalizing the roles of authors and heroes and making them less answerable to sterile forms of literary convention.

In *Poor Things*, the act of authoring operates on a number of levels. Besides the authoring of Gray, which is actually passed off as 'editing,' we have the authoring of 'Episodes from the Early Life of a Scottish Public Health Officer,' by Archie McCandless and a letter by Victoria McCandless (Bella Baxter) denouncing Archie's book as pure fantasy. These are the surface, written texts to be contended with. Beneath these writings lie the creation of Bella Baxter by Godwin, the self-creation of Bella in her letters to Godwin and Archie, the letter of Wedderburn concerning Bella, and the history of Victoria Blessington as presented by her natural father and husband. Authoring is interwoven throughout the text of *Poor Things* in such a way as to bring the whole process into question. Where *Lanark* posits the initial question of authoring by presenting a hero in search of a self which is manipulated by a number of narrators, *1982 Janine* complicates the question by giving fuller authorial power to the protagonist/hero. In *Poor Things*, much as in James Hogg's *The Private Memoirs and Confessions of a Justified Sinner*, the lines between author and hero become so blurred and interchangeable that the reader is forced to choose which story to believe and which narrator to single out for authorial credibility. In posing these questions, Gray deconstructs them within the text by constant manipulation, presenting the reader with continual exposure to a subjective reality that is forever fluctuating.

The act of 'making' is very much a part of *Poor Things* as can be seen by the chapter titles in which Archie McCandless inserts his text. The first chapter, 'Making Me', reveals the very clinical personality of McCandless, especially when contrasted with the more genuine, while less assured, confession of Lanark in his attempt to gain knowledge of himself. McCandless is best when revealing how other characters attempt to author: the description of Bella's letter (complete with tear-smudged pages), and the documentation that accompanies the arguments with General Blessington. McCandless is less successful as an author of self and we reserve judgement on him and his ability to construct an identity until after reading Victoria's letter, which was written for posterity.

The nature of authorship changes in the course of *Poor Things*. Where we are first given the introduction (which might just as well have been titled 'The Making of the Makings') as an outer shell for the remaining creations, we are next given the formation of the principal characters. Once this task of authoring is complete, McCandless gives us the making of less verifiable products: 'Wedderburn's Letter: Making a Maniac,' and 'Bella Baxter's Letter: the Making of a Conscience.' If we remember that these more abstract 'makings' are the product of McCandless, regardless of whether they are simple transcriptions, we begin to detect an interchange between him and his heroes (who are actually now authors as well).[21] What we begin to sense is something not unlike the experience of Lockwood when confronting the texts of different Catherines in *Wuthering Heights*. The author/hero relationship is dependent upon the give and take of consciousnesses of the two entities, but which hero does the author embrace when confronted with different interpretations? If we consider ourselves (as individuals) as the authors of the texts we read, since we read the texts as no other reader can read them and we never read them again in the same way, then we might be tempted to relate to the heroes we create in a way that does not pigeonhole them into static and inflexible categories. Gray highlights the subjective nature of the act of reading in his novel *A History Maker* when the young Watt Dryhope questions his adopted mother Kittock's notions of literary engagement:

> 'When a lot of folk watch something on a screen they all see the same thing. What a damnable waste of mind! Readers bring books to life by filling the stories with voices, faces, scenery, ideas the author never dreamed of, things from their own minds. Every reader does it differently.'
> 'So when you and me read *The Cat That Walked by Itself* we read a different story?' said Wat disliking the idea.
> 'Exactly!' said Kittock with great satisfaction.[22]

The reader of *Poor Things* reads McCandless reading Baxter reading Bella reading McCandless. This is an endless process in which the reader/author is endlessly involved in the process of creating meaning.[23] There is a constant striving after self-identification and a reading of an 'other' in *Poor Things* that has much to do with empathy. The very title of the book suggests an act of empathy as one self tries to understand and enter imaginatively into the suffering of another.

Bella's concern for the welfare of others, whom she relates to through the loss of her own child, signifies her attempt to reach some sort of understanding about her past and her own identity. Even when confronted with the facts of her past, Bella must construct them for herself the only way she can, she must identify with a self that is both her own and not hers. Bella strives to find a consciousness that will link the two together and she comes close to it when she hears the horrible story of how, as Victoria Blessington, she was locked in a coal cellar by her cruel husband: '"I feel how the poor thing felt," she said.'[24] Here, in a sense, Bella (as a product of the author McCandless) inscribes herself in her rejection of the text presented to her by Blessington and his cronies. However, she cannot do so until she empathizes and returns to the Bella which has been authored by Baxter. Linguistically, Bella has undergone the entire range of development; she has experimented with vowels, consonants, rhymes and lyrical forms and then breaks into prose since 'it slows me down'.[25] It is with Bella's full growth into language that she realizes the power to write herself and author her own heroine, one who will partake of her former selves as she reads them as well as the 'poor things' of the world.

It is when we feel safely assured that Bella has secured her identity that Gray throws us another, and not yet final, tidbit of his 'unfinalizable' hunt for self, the letter of the late Victoria McCandless. The reader searches her confession for corroboration of the earlier boxes of authoring that have been presented to him. Failing a substantial verification, the reader must choose between authors only to find the question 'who is the real author?' always standing in the way of certainty. Gray's loophole, reminiscent of the authorial games played by Hogg in *Confessions*, is to place the 'final' author within the framework of a historical note.[26] Leaving the last word to history is very tricky of Gray. He has consistently provided the reader with instances in which history rubs shoulders with fantasy so that now the differences become nearly negotiable. The ultimate word has not been left to the heroine here as it was for the hero Jock McLeish in *1982 Janine*. Control must pass once more to the reader who monologically closes the life of Bella Victoria Hattersley Blessington Baxter McCandless (a name that suggests multiple identities) by reference to 'a' history that is chronological. In Gray's juxtaposition of the 'fictional' with the 'historical,' he seems to be making a conscious admission of how chronology misleads the reader, an idea he artistically played with in the structure of *Lanark*. The history of the final section of *Poor Things* does not partake of the author/hero relationship that has been established to an ever increasing intensity in the course of the rest of the novel. It is for this reason that Gray gives the reader an 'out,' a choice between two versions of identity formation that are based on 'empirical' and 'historical' 'facts':

Dr. Victoria McCandless was found dead of a cerebral stroke on 3rd December 1946. Reckoning from the birth of her brain in the Humane Society mortuary on Glasgow Green, 18th February 1880, she was exactly sixty-six years, forty weeks and four days old. Reckoning from the birth of her body in a Manchester slum in 1854, she was ninety-two.27

There are a number of different 'truths' being presented in *Poor Things* and they carry on a dialogue with each other. There is no need or desire to simply resolve the differences between truths and this becomes a central theme of the novel. Resolving truth is to falsify by completion. In this sense the narrative strands of *Poor Things* represent in novelistic form the 'open-ended dialogue' that Bakhtin embraces in his image of the 'world symposium':

> The dialogic nature of consciousness, the dialogic nature of human life itself. The single adequate form for verbally expressing authentic human life is the open-ended dialogue. Life by its very nature is dialogic. To live means to participate in dialogue: to ask questions, to heed, to respond, to agree, and so forth. In this dialogue a person participates wholly and throughout his whole life: with his eyes, lips, hands, soul, spirit, with his whole body and deeds. He invests his entire self in discourse, and this discourse enters into the dialogic fabric of human life, into the world symposium.28

Discussion of Gray's concern for complicating the nature of authorship is by no means exhausted by these considerations of his more 'major' works. We see a hero attempting to author a self in the form of McGrotty or Kelvin Walker, as well as in short stories such as 'Logopandocy' and 'The Story of a Recluse.'29 In *McGrotty and Ludmilla* and *The Fall of Kelvin Walker* the heroes struggle to author selves in a foreign environment, the capitalistic, upwardly (and downwardly) mobile life of London business. McGrotty is able to successfully, though fantastically, embrace another consciousness in his environment and he fulfills a sense of self almost by accident. Kelvin Walker, on the other hand, strives to fulfill a preconceived notion of self (he even authors another's identity in his own image) but is unable to escape from his Scottish roots. He is an isolated individual, like Robert Colwan in *Confessions* and Duncan Thaw in *Lanark*, unable to connect with another consciousness and return to fortify his own identity. Finally, in the novella *Mavis Belfrage* (1996), Gray revisits many of his social and political concerns as he mixes social realism with the surreal. In this work, the fantasy world of Glonda is created by Colin as a refuge from a Scotland endangered by the British government. In the end Colin destroys Glonda with books traditionally seen as masterpieces in philosophy and education and in doing so Gray may be commenting on the self-destructive nature of nations who accept too readily the inflexible systems imposed upon them by history.

Gray's responses to textual authority are perhaps his most powerful and this aspect of his work can perhaps be most fruitfully examined by exploring the relationship Gray's narrators share with the 'heroes' he creates in his fictions. In a very postmodern way, Gray's fictions make the text itself a character in the literary event. The text becomes an additional voice and carries on important dialogues with the reader, the hero, other characters within the work, as well as the author. The links between authoring and identity become clearer as the reader moves through Gray's most significant novels: *Lanark*, *1982 Janine*, and *Poor Things*. In *Lanark*, the character Lanark, like Hogg's sinner and like Orwell's Winston Smith, begins his journal in unfamiliar world. The voice of the journalistic text is born from the dialogue between a self that is striving for explanation or to make familiar an alien world and a self who will read and empathize with it. Gray's next novel, *1982 Janine*, discards the written journal for a more 'voyeuristic' self-accounting in which not only is the reader allowed a peepshow look into the head of Jock McLeish, but the hero/author Jock stands as it were outside the keyhole, seeing his life pass before his intoxicated eyes. Finally, Gray returns to the 'voice' of confessional writing with *Poor Things* in which two renditions of a life pass before the reader's eyes and ask for 'the truth' of resolution. Each of these examinations and challenges to authority engages with questions not only of how individual identities are formed, but the ways in which cultural and national identities strive for development and are frequently denied a voice. Gray's subversive fictions attack the very foundations of hegemony that have been appropriated by political as well as literary forces for the furtherance of power and the limitation of identity. Gray carnivalizes literature, not by way of dialect as can be seen in the work of a number of other contemporary Scottish writers such as James Kelman, Tom Leonard, and Edwin Morgan, but rather through an attack on static literary forms that pervade literature and history and that have become ingrained within cultural consciousness as the only acceptable forms of discourse.

NOTES

[1] Alasdair Gray, *Lanark: A Life in Four Books*, New York: Braziller, 1985, pp. 14-15.
[2] Mikhail Bakhtin's most extensive treatment of author/hero relationships can be found in the lengthy essay 'Author and Hero in Aesthetic Activity', in Michael Holquist and Vadim Liapunov eds., *Art and Answerability: Early Philosophical Essays by M.M. Bakhtin*, translated by Vadim Liapunov, Austin: University of Texas Press, 1990, p. 12.
[3] Alasdair Gray, *Lanark*, cit., p. 15.
[4] *Ibidem*, p. 243.
[5] Gray's treatment of God and the Bible as forms of authority is significant not only in *Lanark* but in his other works as well. A notable example is the discussion of God found in 'Job's Skin Game', a story from the collection *The Ends of Our Tethers: 13 Sorry Stories*, Edinburgh: Canongate, 2003, pp. 66-90.
[6] Alasdair Gray, *Lanark*, cit., p. 227.
[7] *Ibidem*, p. 480.
[8] *Ibidem*, p. 484.
[9] *Ibidem*.
[10] *Ibidem*, p. 485.
[11] For more on forms of entrapment in Gray's fictions see Robert Crawford's introduction to Robert Crawford and Tom Nairn eds., *The Arts of Alasdair Gray*, Edinburgh: Edinburgh University Press, 1991, p. 3, and Alison Lumsden's illuminating article 'Innovation and Reaction in Alasdair Gray', in Gavin Wallace and Randall Stevenson eds., *The Scottish Novel Since the Seventies*, Edinburgh: Edinburgh University Press, 1993, pp. 115-126, in which she suggests that Gray's texts participate in rather than react against the 'art' of entrapment. See especially pages 124-125. In addition to the articles and books on Gray mentioned in this essay, a good critical overview of his work is Stephen Bernstein, *Alasdair Gray*, Lewisburg: Bucknell University Press, 1999, which provides insightful readings of a number of Gray's fictions.

746 J.C. BITTENBENDER

12 Alasdair Gray, *McGrotty and Ludmilla*, Glasgow: Dog and Bone Press, 1990.

13 Alasdair Gray, *Unlikely Stories, Mostly*, London: Penguin, 1984.

14 This can be seen in a variety of Gray's short stories. 'The Crank that Made the Revolution', from *Unlikely Stories, Mostly*, serves as a comedy of early technological advances and is a preliminary to the dystopian failures of *Lanark* and the medical and scientific parodies in *Poor Things* (London: Penguin, 1993). The failure of McMenamy's 'duck tandem', and the reference illustrations make us laugh, but who is not reminded at the same time of the serious technological and scientific disasters which we have viewed either by way of old photographs or contemporary television screens such as the Tay Bridge collapse or the Space Shuttle explosion.

15 Cairns Craig, 'Going Down to Hell is Easy: Lanark, Realism and the Limits of the Imagination', in Robert Crawford and Tom Nairn eds., *op. cit.*, p. 102.

16 *Ibidem*, p. 105.

17 This description of Jock is taken from the back cover of the Penguin paperback edition of the novel.

18 Alasdair Gray, *1982 Janine*, Harmondsworth: Penguin, 1985, p. 35. All subsequent references to this book will appear in brackets in the main text.

19 This form of authorial control can be detected as well in *Something Leather* (London: Jonathan Cape, 1990), a work that has been accused of being Gray's most 'pornographic' novel, in which characters take part in a number of voyeuristic orgies that involved imaginative scenarios of domination and submissiveness.

20 In 1919 the critic G.Gregory Smith proposed the 'Caledonian Antisyzygy' as a way of looking at Scottish writing that focused on the 'two moods' that seemed to appear in Scottish literature: a concern for a detailed reality of description, along with a pleasure in revealing the 'confusion of the senses in the fun of things thrown topsyturvy, in the horns of elfland and the voices of the mountains'. See G. Gregory Smith, *Scottish Literature: Character and Influence*, London: Macmillan and Co., 1919, p. 19.

21 For more on Gray's 'makings' in *Poor Things* in relation to Bakhtin's ideas about carnival and the grotesque see Ian McCormick, 'Alasdair Gray: The Making of a Scottish Grotesque', in Federico Eguíluz, et. al. eds., *La Europa (Cultural) De Los Pueblos: Voz y Forma*, Vitoria, Spain: Evagraf, 1994, pp. 87-94.

[22] Alasdair Gray, *A History Maker*, Edinburgh: Canongate Press, 1994, p. 140.

[23] The manner in which authors attempt to control the meaning of their texts is explored as well in Gray's most recent and voluminous work, *The Book of Prefaces* (London: Bloomsbury, 2000) in which he reproduces and comments upon a vast range of prefatory material by authors writing in English from the Anglo-Saxon period to the twentieth century.

[24] Alasdair Gray, *Poor Things*, cit., p. 231.

[25] *Ibidem*, p. 115.

[26] *Ibidem*, pp. 320ff.

[27] *Ibidem*, p. 317.

[28] Mikhail Bakhtin, 'Toward a Reworking of the Dostoevsky Book', in Caryl Emerson ed., *Problems of Dostoevsky's Poetics*, Minneapolis: Minnesota University Press, 1984, p. 293.

[29] 'Logopandocy', can be found in *Unlikely Stories, Mostly*, cit., pp. 135-195; 'The Story of a Recluse' is in *Lean Tales* (London: Jonathan Cape, 1985), a collection of stories by Gray, James Kelman, and Agnes Owens (pp. 222-246).

LILIAS FRASER

New Scottish Poetry:
John Burnside, Robert Crawford, C.A. Duffy, W.N. Herbert, Kathleen Jamie, Jackie Kay and Don Paterson

John Burnside, Robert Crawford, Carol Ann Duffy, W.N. Herbert, Kathleen Jamie, Jackie Kay and Don Paterson have all published three or more collections of poetry and have received a number of UK literary prizes. They were all born in Scotland between 1955 and 1963. Yet they don't call themselves a movement, although attempts have been made to describe some of them as 'Informationists'. What they have in common as poets is that they are Scottish poets who write in English; they write poetry which is not, or not always, in Scots, but is still described as Scottish, a term more clearly related to the nationality of the poets than the nature of their poetry. In 1994, a poetry promotion called New Generation named all of these poets, with the exception of Jackie Kay, in a list of twenty young poets who were publicised through a programme of readings, bookshop promotions and national media coverage; some, like Carol Ann Duffy and John Burnside, were already familiar names in contemporary poetry, but all were under forty, or had published their first collection in the last five years, and were resident in the UK. The publicity within Scotland concentrated on the Scottish nationality of seven poets in the promotion, beginning to treat them as a group on this basis rather than a classification of their poems. In the same year as the poetry promotion, they were all included in an anthology called *Dream State: The New Scottish Poets*.[1] The title may refer to the dreamlike condition of a poetic imagination, but it may also be suggesting that the potential of both the poetry and the political state of modern Scotland was as yet unrealised. The ambivalent treatment in these poets' work of an immature or childhood language in Scottish poetry is bound up with a sense of maturity in recognising and writing a Scottish poem.

Dream State, like other recent anthologies of Scottish verse, contains Gaelic, English and varieties of Scots. Yet in his foreword, the editor Daniel O'Rourke obviously wearied of the endless hairsplitting over how a poem could be *Scottish* if it was not written in Scots or Scots Gaelic. The poets in the anthology, he insisted, were approaching their medium in the same way as Robert Crawford who 'wastes no time debating which [language] to use', but simply 'uses the language that's to hand and most appropriate for what he wants to do'.[2] In the Dream State's constitution, the construction of Scottish poetry is a matter of tangible energy rather than theoretical self-justification. But more importantly, *Dream State*'s parameters did define the recognition of Scottishness in contemporary poetry as a matter of intuition for readers, as well as for poets:

> Good writers from elsewhere who have chosen to live in Scotland were omitted not because they aren't Scottish, but because their poems didn't seem to be.[3]

The responsibility for deciding Scottishness, the editor implies, is devolved not only onto his own editorial choices but, potentially, onto whoever might read a poem. In these poems, recognising the Scottishness of poetry which is written in English is far more complex than recognising it in Scots or Scots Gaelic poems, and its recognition is dependent on something utterly intuitive within the reader. It is 'a matter of taste', O'Rourke comments on the process of selection, 'but not caprice'. Caprice may be inconstant, but taste is, at least for O'Rourke, a first language which is learned so early that it seems innate.

These poets have at some point all used some sense of Scottishness in their poems as a counterpoint to the English literary establishment, thriving like other poetry in English on a modern tradition of marginalisation. Yet it would be misleading to see a reaction against Anglocentricity as the force that drives these writers. The interaction of Scottish and English cultures is of secondary importance in their poetry to the tensions which they often describe as part of a childhood memory, or the distance or solidarity between a child and parent, and latterly about their own children's inheritance. These tensions are caused not by national boundaries but by having or not having money, or a university education, or the right to read or write poetry, or the authority to interpret the exhibits in an art gallery or a museum. The processes of cultural preservation are often examined by these poets; particularly in earlier collections, as they came to terms with their own position as writers, they write in what I would call a 'museum poem' mode. Museums, libraries, the storing of knowledge and the preservation of culture can be shown in their poems as a process of accretion and rescue. This preservation can be haphazard yet inclusive, an irrational process which is still generously critical towards the community it serves. In poems like Kathleen Jamie's 'Aunt Janet's Museum' and 'Arraheids', Robert Crawford's 'The Scottish National Cushion Survey', or Don Paterson's 'The Alexandrian Library', this museum process has the potential to satirise society. At the same time, the process of preservation can be described as exclusive or arbitrary: the museum process deserves to be satirised itself. W.N. Herbert's poem about the conversion of Newcastle's Baltic Flour Mills into galleries warns that the museum poem's satire on canon-making is ultimately a formal preoccupation with a sub-genre. It should not become an end in itself:

> galleries are not the issue; something else
> is showing here that none of us will stomach.[4]

Herbert describes how he feels trapped in the building site, 'stranded,/swinging between the two remaining walls', torn between the site's industrial past and the galleries which threaten to eclipse its former working community. The galleries should symbolise an awareness of their former function, but they could easily become wrapped up in questions of artistic form. Jackie Kay says that, when writing about Scottish voices, her present distance from Scotland has helped her to develop an 'outside way of looking back in' at where she grew up.[5] These poets all eventually look back in on how their language is sited in childhood, but writing about childhood, like writing about the collapsed industry of a community, brings with it the awareness of an adult's nostalgia. I think it becomes obvious that mature vision for these poets depends on trusting what they have seen, and heard, as children.

C.A. Duffy is the senior poet in terms of length of public profile;

in 1998 she was seen as a possible successor to Ted Hughes as Poet Laureate, perhaps a measure of how much her poems have been disseminated by anthologies and studied in schools, as well as enthusiastically reviewed. She is often claimed as a Scottish poet because she was born in Glasgow, though she grew up in Stafford and studied Philosophy at Liverpool. Early work included two stage plays, and her poetry tends to the re-examination of mono- logues and the sound of contemporary voices. Particularly in her first collection, *Standing Female Nude*[6] and again in her most recent, *The World's Wife*,[7] her poems listen acutely for the voices that never normally get their say, or the voices which are instantly recognisable because they always say too much. The voices in *The World's Wife* are waiting for the moment to deploy mature knowl- edge; all the wives in the collection have waited for their moment for too long simply to revert to an indulgence in instinct. In the significantly-titled *The Other Country*,[8] which examines home, dis- tance and alienation, a rare Scottish childhood voice appears. In a train, travelling away from the temptation of a nostalgic idea of home, repeating the phrase, '*The day/and ever. The day and ever*', the analytic voice briefly admits that this speech is an indulgence: 'I am homesick, free, in love/with the way my mother speaks'.[9]

In some ways, Kathleen Jamie's first collection, *Black Spiders*,[10] published when she was only 20, underlined her existing desire to travel outside Scotland. On winning an Eric Gregory Award at the age of eighteen, she had used her prize money to buy 'a bike, a typewriter, a ticket to Istanbul'.[11] She is a poet who writes with authority on the situation of male and female roles in Scotland, often drawing parallels with what she has seen in other countries. In 1986 she published *A Flame in Your Heart*[12] with Andrew Greig, poems which follow a relationship between a World War II pilot and his girlfriend, yet unlike Carol Ann Duffy her explorations of monologue are mostly audible only in her earlier poetry. In 1992, she published a travel book, *The Golden Peak: Travels in Northern Pakistan*.[13] It was followed by the increased stylistic freedom of a sequence of poems, *The Autonomous Region*,[14] about a journey through Tibet, combining her perspective as a modern traveller with the voices of a Chinese princess and a Tibetan monk.

Kathleen Jamie pioneered for this generation a way of writing about Scottish culture as infinitely various and, unusually, forward-looking, impulsive and youthful in much-anthologised poems such as 'The Way We Live' from her 1987 collection of the same title.[15] The lists of this poem cram together with ironic verve the different markers of identity within a modern nationality, its 'misery and elation; mixed', and form an apparently haphazard celebration of 'the way it fits, the way it is, the way it seems to be'.[16] The title poem of *The Queen of Sheba*,[17] which won the Geoffrey Faber prize, similarly rescues the dormant energy in the sceptical putdown of youthful ambition – *who do you think you are, the Queen of Sheba?*. *Jizzen*[18] asks how to deal with living in a politically transitional country, and the sometimes politicised transitions involved in growing up; more than previous collections, it is about making uncharted journeys between established certainties. It returns to explore an early theme of her work in an increasingly closely-written poetry of Scottish landscape. The collection continues to mix both recognisably Scots words like 'jizzen' (childbirth), 'bairns' (children) or 'oxter' (armpit) with words which are not necessarily Scots but are used with a sense that they are appropriate to this setting. 'Green Woman' uses an undercurrent of ecology as it inverts the Scots law verdict of 'not proven', vindicating a language formed by childbirth as well as childhood. '[T]here's a word for women like us', says the green woman who has just given birth:

> suggestive of the lush
> ditch, or even an ordeal,
> – as though we'd risen,
> tied to a ducking-stool,
> gasping, weed-smeared, proven.[19]

Like Jamie, John Burnside also incorporates a seemingly Scottish landscape in his poems, but comments on proving the individual's place within that landscape. Since his first collection, *The Hoop*,[20] he has frequently written about mysteries; mystery is discussed in its religious sense but also through his almost forensic analyses of human behaviour and memory. Later collections, from *Common Knowledge*, *Feast Days*, *The Myth of the Twin* and *Swimming in the Flood*, to *A Normal Skin* and *The Asylum Dance*[21] have developed these concerns. His prose stories and novels deal with the human capacity for darkness and threat, but his poems are more often read misleadingly as gentle evocations of the spiritual or about secure domesticity. His poems are certainly concerned with the geography of home, with moments of revelation experienced in domestic settings, but they are also about communal illumination and vindication. 'Dundee', a poem included in *Dream State*, characteristically opens with the definition of communally-felt apprehension ('The streets are waiting for a snow/that never falls') but it vindicates individual and city as one. As 'the houses on Roseangle/opt for miraculous frosts', *seeming* becomes, as it does throughout Burnside's poetry, a stubbornly inexplicable proof of identity. Like Jamie's use of the word in 'Green Woman', 'proven' does not simply let the poem remain a meditation on privacy. It reveals a subtle evocation of the individual's place in a legal and social community:

    and it seems as if a closeness in the mind
    had opened and flowered:
    the corners sudden and tender, the light immense,
    the one who stands here proven after all.[22]

Becoming proven, whether by other people's description ('there's a word for women like us') or by recognising one's place in a community, is a process where both poet and reader can describe and recognise their adult responsibility to acknowledge where, when or how they began to grow up. Something which seems as ubiquitous as motherhood, or looking out at a street, can have all the unremarkable familiarity of a 'closeness in the mind', yet it is as much a test, or proof of identity, in these poems for the poet or reader to recognise and reassess how forceful these familiar settings or words can be. For these poems, to *seem Scottish* is not about being tested to prove their difference from any other poem in English; that cannot be proved, as O'Rourke tacitly admits. What seem satisfactorily Scottish are the poems which recognise that what could be made to sound alien ('jizzen', 'oxter', 'bairn', 'proven') is instead proven as being as familiar as childhood or home.

    Kathleen Jamie's earlier poems forced both contemporary and archaic speech and image into a language which was confident that it should seem familiar to this generation of Scottish poetry. In their first collections, Robert Crawford and W.N. Herbert were acutely aware of wanting to rewrite synthetic Scots after MacDiarmid and still keep his sense of the strangeness and surprise of Scots. But they also contributed to a Scottish poetry that presumes, with an air of authority, that its Scottishness is deeply familiar. They met as postgraduate students at Oxford, Crawford working on T.S. Eliot and Herbert on MacDiarmid. *Sharawaggi*[23] contains polemics by both poets in favour of reinventing synthetic Scots, and these are coming-of-age poems in which Scots is proven as a language by its confident force. Fast-paced and multi-lingual, using jargons and neologisms as well as simply pointing outwards to other languages, the collection develops invention as a persuasive stylistic force; it bristles with challenge to readers of English-language poetry as well as to the supporters of a more conventional Scots. It was W.N. Herbert who pointed out in a 1994 anthology of like-minded poets, *Contraflow on the Super Highway*, that an explicit label like 'Informationism' would be half – but only half – a practical joke played by the arriving generation to announce their presence. Its effects could only be fully activated by solemn critical endeavour. Informationism, he explained, was the art of 'negotiating between jargons'. The Informationists themselves were:

> Scottish, male and generally suffering from Post-Academic Trauma [...] so that means we have a particular heritage, and a particular agenda. Davidson, MacDiarmid, Morgan; writers who all establish that it is as important to know as it is to feel, and that it is vital to examine what we mean by, as well as what we feel about, knowledge.[24]

Richard Price first defined the group as Robert Crawford, W.N. Herbert, David Kinloch, Peter McCarey, and Alan Riach; Robert Crawford later included Don Paterson, Kathleen Jamie and John Burnside in the grouping.[25] But Informationists, by definition of the term as well as by individual evasion, are reluctant to be corralled by alienating *-isms*, and these poets rarely advertise the term.

Latterly Robert Crawford has been more likely than W.N. Herbert to comment directly on Scottish politics. *A Scottish Assembly*[26] and *Talkies*[27] are concerned, as their titles explain, with the political as well as emotional implications of voice as enfranchisement. Yet subsequently Crawford's voice has clearly been more Scottish than Scots. This is partly a matter of accessibility;

Herbert notes dryly of his own similarly 'bilingual' poetry that writing in Scots risks only being understood by a small readership. In part it is also a conscious attempt to write not only in Scots English but in a style which 'you could give to people who weren't "poetry readers" [...] without completely compromising a sense of tonality and emotional complexity in the poems',[28] as Crawford described his poems about father-son relationships in *Masculinity*. Like *Spirit Machines*,[29] *Masculinity*[30] showed an exploration of fatherhood combined with learning which was initiated in earlier collections. In *Talkies,* he describes how as a schoolboy he watched his dozing father wake up. He talks to his younger self, watching from the distance of adulthood how he had begun to learn different languages ('carrying/Homer from school in your bag'). They are both watching Crawford's father as he wakes up, a reminder of how forming speech is a constant process of returning to a childhood state:

> he woke up sharply, almost choking
> When he started, as miraculously
> As the baby you'd been, lying there, watching,
> Swallowing, beginning to talk.[31]

Crawford's poems are often an explicit combination of intimate with public, like his love poems addressed to Scotland. They are often explicit on political issues, but their adult voices have to risk 'beginning to talk' to achieve a confident, post-MacDiarmid Scottish voice.

It is this childhood voice which constantly shapes the seemingly Scottish poem. Herbert relished its persistence in the face of later learning, which meant that 'Herbert speak with forked tongue':

> One strand wriggles back to Blackness Primary and recites 'Yir heid's daft,/Yir belly's saft,/An yir bum is medd o leathir.' The other coils around Brasenose College and dreams of Marius the Epicurean. But I don't want to choose between them; I want both prongs of the fork.[32]

A prolific and fluent poet, his ease with longer pieces enabled him to tackle the lengthy *The Laurelude*,[33] a Wordsworthian *Prelude* revisioned through the silent film figure of Stan Laurel. It is set against his new territory of the North of England, rather than the earlier mental cartography of the east-coast Scottish city of Dundee. Dundee was a city which he powerfully reimagined in his first published collection, *Dundee Doldrums*,[34] in which reconstructed, ghostly layers of the city's past were brought to life in poems written in its present. Herbert explained how in 1982 he had written the poems by going to different parts of the city and exploring an almost subconscious voice. Its language seemed to derive from 'the fact I spoke urban Scots as a child', rather than a desire to create an adult's literary Scots:

> I had just completed my first degree at Oxford. My playground voice seemed very far away. But the poetry I was writing was a curious mixture of English, American(ish), Scots English, and something not quite formed.[35]

'Whaur ur yi Dundee? Whaur's yir Golem buriit?' is the first roar of his new language of place and personal identity.[36] Rather than exorcising this embryonic voice, with its strong evocation of childhood speech, Herbert used its compelling energy as the basis of the Scots he went on to write in *Sharawaggi* and in his later collections, the Dundee-born *The Testament of the Reverend Thomas Dick* and *Cabaret McGonagall*.[37] He began 'Dingle Dell' with the assertion that 'There is no passport to this country/it exists as a quality of the language'.[38] Yet the fear involved in writing in a voice and language associated so strongly with childhood is that this voice can either aid or betray the adult voice which strives for a tough yet accessible contemporary poetry, threatening sentimentality and return to a country which exists only in the mind.

Jackie Kay was born in Edinburgh and brought up in Scotland, studying English at the University of Stirling, and her first collection *The Adoption Papers*[39] won her awards from the Eric Gregory Foundation and the Scottish Arts Council, the Saltire First Book award and the Forward Poetry Prize. She has written poetry for adults and children, plays, a book about the jazz singer Bessie Smith, a novel, *Trumpet*,[40] about a jazz musician who lives as a man although born female, and her poems have been set as a song cycle in Mark-Anthony Turnage's *Twice Through The Heart*,[41] a study of domestic violence first performed in 1997. Her work is never far from singing, and ranges through love and family relationships, blues and jazz and racial prejudice; it is necessarily informed by her experience as a black Scottish woman. *Other Lovers*[42] includes a group of poems about Bessie Smith which feature in her radio play *Every Bit of It*, an examination of the struggles which formed the singer's life and the racism she fought against. *Off Colour*[43] is a collection about sickness; physical sicknesses, like cancer, as well as social sicknesses like racism. Conversely, its poems titled 'Virus' strengthen the collection's cohesion. The sickness of nostalgia, though, does not seem to have caught in her poems, perhaps because they begin from assertions that the past was never safer or better than the present.

Don Paterson's poems, particularly in his first two collections, are not dissuaded from tackling the way things were, though they almost never mine a childhood Scots as Herbert has done, and they are acutely aware of the threat of nostalgia. He was brought up in Dundee, but moved to England and worked as a jazz musician before returning to Scotland to combine music and writing. He currently edits the poetry list of the London publisher Picador. *Nil Nil*[44] and *God's Gift to Women*[45] used Dundee's city- and seascape as one of his poems' sources of almost magical realist shifts of visual perspective, which are all played off against a sense of rampaging narratives. Yet *The Eyes*,[46] a series of translations and variations of poems by Antonio Machado, treats lyric beauty with a less feverish vision than in the two previous collections. This collection allows a distancing from earlier Calvinist guilt, and from the demonstration of esoteric knowledge as fuel for social and moral examinations. Particularly in his earlier poems, knowledge appears as a cross-section of revered human foibles subjected to iconoclastic storage systems, like the piled-up fantasy books of 'The Alexandrian Library'. He explores as well as exploits the bookish freedoms of postmodernism, putting it through the paces of rigorous formalism. Although *The Eyes* is equally questioning, it shows a more relaxed exploration of demonstrable knowledge and technical expertise.

'Ye arenae here tae wonder,/whae dae ye think ye ur?' mutter the museum-bound 'hard tongues o grannies' in Kathleen Jamie's 'Arraheids'.[47] What this generation of poets is doing is wondering at, even breaking into, any received perceptions on display in the

Scottish poetry museum. When they write in a voice that, as Daniel O'Rourke described it, 'seems Scottish', they re-examine the intuitive use of language which W.N. Herbert calls 'my playground voice'.[48] This return rejects the literally childish argument that Scottish poetry should just define itself in opposition to whatever sounds 'posh, male, English and dead', as Liz Lochhead had already suggested in the child-cum-adult's voice of 'Kidspoem/Bairnsang'.[49] These younger writers have also spoken out fiercely against returning to a perpetual childhood of modern Scottish culture, and against the deadening effects of sentimentality and nostalgia which are an obvious threat in recovering a voice associated with childhood. Yet they are returning, prompted in some parts by their own parenthood, to acknowledge the force of the underlying familiarity in their 'playground voice'.

NOTES

1 Daniel O'Rourke ed., *Dream State: The New Scottish Poets*, Polygon: Edinburgh, 1994.

2 *Ibidem*, p. xxv.

3 *Ibidem*, p. v.

4 W.N. Herbert, 'Hard Hat Heaven', in *Cabaret McGonagall*, Newcastle: Bloodaxe, 1996, (pp. 121-123) p. 123.

5, 'Don't Tell Me Who I Am: Jackie Kay interviewed by Libby Brooks', *The Guardian Weekend*, no. 12, 2002, p. 37.

6 C.A. Duffy, *Standing Female Nude*, London: Anvil Press Poetry, 1985.

7 C.A. Duffy, *The World's Wife*, London: Picador, 1999.

8 C.A. Duffy, *The Other Country*, London: Anvil, 1990.

9 *Ibidem*, p. 54.

10 Kathleen Jamie, *Black Spiders*, Edinburgh: Salamander Press, 1982.

11 'Kathleen Jamie interviewed by Richard Price', *Verse,* nos. 8/9, Winter/Spring 1992, (pp. 103-106) p. 103.

12 Kathleen Jamie and Andrew Greig, *A Flame in Your Heart*, Newcastle: Bloodaxe, 1986.

13 Kathleen Jamie, *The Golden Peak: Travels in Northern Pakistan*, (reissued as *Among Muslim*, 2002), London: Virago, 1992.

14 Kathleen Jamie, *Autonomous Region*, Newcastle: Bloodaxe, 1993.

[15] Kathleen Jamie, *The Way We Live*, Newcastle: Bloodaxe, 1987.

[16] *Ibidem*, p. 54.

[17] Kathleen Jamie, *The Queen of Sheba*, Newcastle: Bloodaxe, 1994, pp. 9-11.

[18] Kathleen Jamie, *Jizzen*, London: Picador, 1999.

[19] *Ibidem*, p. 46.

[20] John Burnside, *The Hoop*, Manchester: Carcanet, 1988.

[21] *Common Knowledge*, London: Secker & Warburg, 1991; *Feast Days*, London: Secker & Warburg, 1992; *The Myth of the Twin*, London: Cape, 1994; *Swimming in the Flood*, London: Cape, 1995; *A Normal Skin*, London: Cape, 1997; *The Asylum Dance*, London: Cape, 2000.

[22] John Burnside, 'Dundee', in *The Myth of the Twin,* cit., p. 36.

[23] Robert Crawford and W.N. Herbert, *Sharawaggi: Poems in Scots*, Edinburgh: Polygon, 1991.

[24] W.N. Herbert, 'A Defence of Noetry', in W.N. Herbert and Richard Price eds., *Contraflow on the Super Highway*, London: Southfields Press/Gairfish, 1994, p. xv.

[25] See Robert Crawford, 'The Computer and the Painted Pict', *TLS*, 15 August 1997, pp. 4-5.

[26] Robert Crawford, *A Scottish Assembly*, London: Chatto & Windus, 1990.

[27] Robert Crawford, *Talkies*, London: Chatto & Windus, 1992.

[28] Andrew Zawacki, 'Robert Crawford: An Interview', *Verse,* no. 15, 1998, (pp. 38-54) p. 46.

[29] Robert Crawford, *Spirit Machines*, London: Cape, 1999.

[30] Robert Crawford, *Masculinity*, London: Cape, 1996.

[31] Robert Crawford, 'Oral', in *Talkies*, cit., p. 79.

[32] W.N. Herbert, *Forked Tongue*, Newcastle: Bloodaxe, 1994, p. 10.

[33] W.N. Herbert, *The Laurelude*, Newcastle: Bloodaxe, 1998.

[34] W.N. Herbert, *Dundee Doldrums*, Edinburgh: Galliard, 1991.

[35] W.N. Herbert, 'Author's Note', in *Dundee Doldrums*, cit., p. 3.

[36] W.N. Herbert, '2nd Doldrum (Elephants' Graveyard)', in *Dundee Doldrums*, cit., p. 5.

[37] W.N. Herbert, *Cabaret McGonagall*, Newcastle: Bloodaxe, 1996.

[38] W.N. Herbert, *Forked Tongue*, cit., p. 40.

[39] Jackie Kay, *The Adoption Papers*, Newcastle: Bloodaxe, 1991.

[40] Jackie Kay, *Trumpet*, London: Picador, 1998.

[41] Jackie Kay and Mark-Anthony Turnage, *Twice Through the Heart*, English National Opera, 1997.

[42] Jackie Kay, *Other Lovers*, Newcastle: Bloodaxe, 1993.

[43] Jackie Kay, *Off Colour*, Newcastle: Bloodaxe, 1998.

[44] Don Paterson, *Nil Nil*, London: Faber & Faber, 1993.

[45] Don Paterson, *God's Gift to Women*, London: Faber & Faber, 1997.

[46] Don Paterson, *The Eyes*, London: Faber & Faber, 1999.

[47] Kathleen Jamie, 'Arraheids', in *The Queen of Sheba*, cit., p. 40.

[48] W.N. Herbert, *Dundee Doldrums*, cit. p. 3.

[49] Liz Lochhead, 'Kidspoem/Bairnsang', *Penguin Modern Poets 4*, London: Penguin, 1995, pp. 61-62.

ADRIENNE SCULLION

New Scottish Drama:
The Repertoire of the Traverse Theatre, Edinburgh

The Traverse aims to nurture, develop and produce the work of contemporary Scottish and international playwrights to the highest possible standards.[1]

The Traverse Theatre opened in Edinburgh on 2 January 1963. Its founders – Richard Demarco, Jim Haynes, Terry Lane and Tom Mitchell – saw that, apart from at Festival time, there was almost no opportunity to see international, experimental or avant-garde work in Edinburgh. Through the year audiences had to be satisfied with Scottish plays and mainstream production values at the Gateway, the modern classics and conventional repertory values of the Wilson Barrett company during their very successful residencies at the Lyceum, and productions of West End try outs and tours of productions that had already been successful in London. Mainstream tastes were well catered or but there was nothing radical, oppositional or political. The Traverse Theatre sought to fill this gap.[2]

When the Traverse opened – with a production of Arrabal's *Orison* and Sartre's *Huis Clos* – it was, remarkably, Britain's only professional studio theatre: within the British theatre of the time there was, quite simply, nothing else like it. Initially located in a small upper room in James Court just off the High Street, the company's policy to produce challenging works in challenging ways meant that it was Scotland's first fringe theatre. Notoriously the Traverse was based in a building that, it was claimed, had formerly been a brothel and early publicity courted associations of scandal, immorality and risk. The space – its tiny auditorium, seating just 60 people, arranged around a two-sided transverse stage, its intimacy, its informality and the audience's enthusiasm – encouraged both experimentation and imitation. Its influence quickly extended beyond the cultural life of Scotland as it was, in some measure, a point of genesis for the London fringe. It came to operate a sister venue in London at the Jeanetta Cochrane Theatre, where some of its successful productions transferred. Later it proved a model for the Arts Lab in Drury Lane, which Haynes was also instrumental in founding. Indeed one might argue that the experience of the Traverse led a shift in British theatre towards the small-scale, flexible, studio-type of theatre making that was to impact so completely on all aspects of theatre from writing and production techniques to architecture and funding.[3]

In 1969 the company moved from James Court to a venue in the Grassmarket and there the operation expanded significantly – with a main stage seating around 100 and, from 1984, a new smaller studio space seating around 60. The theatre remained in the Grassmarket through the 1970s and 1980s moving to its present site in Cambridge Street in 1992 – and, again, this is a flexible venue with two very different performance spaces and significantly popular public spaces.

This essay sees the Traverse Theatre Company as central to the development of the Scottish repertoire in the late twentieth century. It is certainly the case that all of Scotland's leading playwrights have had work produced by the Traverse and, as Scotland's leading new writing theatre, the representations and narratives that emerge from that company are of particular significance. As well as giving an overview of the company's history, and considering some of its most influential personnel, the essay will analyse in fuller detail some of the plays – in particular Stephen Greenhorn's *Passing Places* (1997), David Greig's *The Speculator* (1999), and David Harrower's *Knives in Hens* (1995) and *Kill the Old Torture their Young* (1998) – that have been commissioned and premiered by the Traverse in the last few years. Focusing on the repertoire of the Traverse, I would argue, demonstrates the diversity and the quality of contemporary Scottish drama as a whole.

POLICY AND PERSONNEL

Through the 1960s and 1970s, first in James Court and then in the

Grassmarket, the Traverse built an enviable reputation for producing new work by a roster of international playwrights including Mishima, Sartre, Jarry, Albee, Genet and Ionesco. But successive artistic directors were determined to present work by Scottish writers alongside these international writers and the first two decades of the Traverse saw premieres of work by Scottish playwrights such as Stanley Eveling, Tom Wright, C.P. Taylor, Tom McGrath and John Byrne.

The Traverse's reputation as Scotland's new writing theatre was secured by Chris Parr who was artistic director of the theatre from 1975 to 1980. During his tenure the theatre produced popular and successful work by a then new generation of Scottish playwrights, including premieres of Hector MacMillan's *The Gay Gorbals* (1976), Tom McGrath's *Laurel and Hardy* (1976) and *The Hardman* (1977), C.P. Taylor's *Walter* (1977), and John Byrne's *The Slab Boys* (1978) and *Cuttin' a Rug* (1979).

Peter Lichtenfelds, who took over the theatre from Parr in April 1980, continued the emphasis on new writing but in some sense widened the locus to think beyond particular Scottish dramaturgies and beyond the predominantly urban representations promoted by the plays of the Parr directorship. Lichtenfelds also declared a commitment to working with women writers and directors – and he determined to return to the international roots of the theatre, encouraging visiting companies and developing a new international repertoire. Early successes in Lichtenfeld's regime included Michael Wilcox's *Accounts* (1981), Liz Lochhead's *Blood and Ice* (1982) and the completion of Byrne's *Slab Boys Trilogy* with *Still Life* (1982).

Lichtenfelds's energy, however, seemed to focus more on programming, and finding and presenting international companies and plays discovered in other theatres across Britain. He increasingly left the support of new writing, and the creation of a new writing policy, to Jenny Killick who came to the theatre as Scottish Arts Council trainee director in 1983. Killick attracted a younger generation of writers to the theatre – including Peter Arnott, John Clifford, Simon Donald, Chris Hannan and Stuart Paterson. By building on Lichtenfelds's example to look out beyond Scotland and discover other dramaturgical conventions and traditions, they reinvented

Scottish playwriting.

These writers were boldly distinctive, very different from the successful writers of the 1970s. They were encouraged to be internationalist and they broke out of the gender representations and the urban milieu of the Parr-produced plays. They used ideas of myth, fable and storytelling with a determined aesthetic, if not necessarily political, intent. They recreated new writing at the Traverse as embodying cosmopolitan ambition and fantastical experimentation. This dramaturgy impacted on Scottish audiences with a triple bill of new short plays called *1984: Points of Departure*, a programme which included Stuart Paterson's *The Clean Sweeps*, Chris Hannan's *Purity* and Simon Donald's *In Descent*. The success of this season, combined with the opening of the Traverse's tiny, 60-seat second studio space in May 1984, and the appointment of Killick herself as artistic director in September 1985, announced a bold new standard in Scottish drama.

Killick's directorship was marked by a new dynamism and new, almost experimental writing, and was embodied in the influential 1985 season that included three of the most important plays of the decade: Peter Arnott's *White Rose*, a Brechtian three-hander set against World War II and story of the female fighter pilot Lily Litvak; Chris Hannan's *Elizabeth Gordon Quinn*, a radical deconstruction of the urban mythology of twentieth-century Scottish drama; and, John Clifford's *Losing Venice*, an elaborate fantasy on colonialism and end of empire angst, which proved the most immediately popular.

Despite the fact that these are outstanding, innovative and powerful plays, despite the fact that they were well received by critics and audiences, they are all to a significant degree neglected by modern theatre practice and criticism: only *Elizabeth Gordon Quinn* has been professionally revived in Scotland; and Arnott, Clifford, Donald and Hannan remain at the very least out of fashion.[4] They and their works have also fallen outwith the critical literature of Scottish theatre – marginalised because they do not quite fit the popular tradition, nostalgia, urban, gender tropes that make up the dominant critical vocabulary of Scottish theatre: this is a point to which this essay will return.

Ian Brown's tenure as artistic director of the Traverse – the period from 1988 to 1996 – signalled the consolidation of work by new writers, the breakthrough of a number of women writers and the high-profile impact of contemporary Canadian writing – in particular work by Michel Tremblay and Brad Fraser – on Scottish theatre, along with increased touring between the two countries. Although the most significant aspect of Brown's artistic directorship was, perhaps, the transfer of the theatre from the Grassmarket to Cambridge Street, important Scottish plays were produced during this time including A.M. Di Mambro's *Tally's Blood* and James Kelman's *Hardie and Baird: The Last Days* (both 1990), Donna Franceschild's *And the Cow Jumped Over the Moon* and Sue Glover's *Bondagers* (both 1991), Simon Donald's *The Life of Stuff* and *Your Turn to Clean the Stair* by Rona Munro (both 1992). These successful Scottish dramas were, again, programmed alongside an international repertoire that included Raymond Cousse's *Pig Play: A Strategy for Two Hams* (1990), Bernard-Marie Koltes's *Struggle of the Dogs and the Black* (1991), Michele Celeste's *Columbus: Blooding the Ocean* (1992), and, of course, Michel Tremblay's *The House Among the Stars* and Brad Fraser's *Unidentified Human Remains and the True Nature of Love* (both 1992).

Directing for the company from 1993, Philip Howard became the artistic director of the Traverse in 1996. Since then the theatre has renewed its commitment to new writing, developing a very active literary department that is headed by the company's literary director. During Howard's tenure this post has been filled by John Tiffany and latterly by Roxana Silbert. This department works with both commissioned playwrights and those who send unsolicited scripts. The department has a formal reading panel, offers feedback to writers, runs workshops and rehearsed readings, as well as providing dramaturgical input at each stage of a commission. The team facilitates a writers' group, organises an international festival of new writing under the banner 'Colours of the Chameleon', and develops programmes of short plays such as *Sharp Shorts* (1996) and *Family* (1999).

Howard's Traverse has made a significant impact in the development of the contemporary Scottish repertoire. He has commissioned and produced new work by Mike Cullen, David Greig,

Chris Hannan, David Harrower and Stuart Paterson, and by Catherine Czerkawska, Sue Glover, Nicola McCartney and Aileen Ritchie. His company has premiered a number of hugely popular, and perhaps also rather populist hits – including Stephen Greenhorn's *Passing Places* (1997), Liz Lochhead's *Perfect Days* (1998), Kate Atkinson's *Abandonment* (2000) and Gregory Burke's *Gagarin Way* (2001). In addition the company has also recommitted to touring to theatres beyond its Edinburgh base, including small-scale venues in the Highlands with successes including Iain Crichton Smith's *Lazybed* (1997), Nicola McCartney's *Heritage* (1999) and Henry Adam's *Among Unbroken Hearts* (2000).

WRITERS AND REPERTOIRE

Despite the company's distinguished record of premieres, where the Traverse has, perhaps, faltered is in sustaining the careers of its writers and, especially, its Scottish writers. It is, of course, not the responsibility of the company to keep producing work by particular writers; nor is it in any sense the right of playwrights to have work produced; but the seeming impossibility of sustaining a career as a writer within Scottish theatre is a distinctive and worrying issue within our culture – an issue that might be of particular concern to Scotland's new writing theatre. Peter Arnott, John Clifford and Chris Hannan – the very writers who defined what Scottish writing might be in the 1980s – have, in the late 1990s, all but abandoned theatre in favour of careers in film, television and education. On the one hand this might have the positive outcome of opening the field to a new generation of writers, to Stephen Greenhorn, David Greig, David Harrower and Nicola McCartney; but on the other it excludes a whole generation, dismissing experience in favour of youth, and colludes in a general British media frenzy to find and valorise the prodigious rather than the mature talent. Despite the success and skill of the new generation of Scottish playwrights, the loss of Arnott and Hannan to practising theatre offers a stark lesson upon which we would do well to act: it must be down to more than good fortune and happy circumstance that Scottish playwrights can work and develop and see their writing produced on stage over more than a few seasons.

Still, the ambition and the adaptability of writers like Greig,

Harrower and McCartney, along with their declared commitment to working for and in Scotland, the healthy diversity of current theatre production with its determined national commitment and international vision, and – perhaps most significantly of all – the broader social and cultural shifts in Scotland that devolution guarantees might result in more long-term changes to the infrastructure of theatre making in Scotland.

Indeed, one might also argue that the legislative revolution within Scottish society changes everything that we have hitherto understood about representation and identity. Arnott's *White Rose* and Clifford's *Losing Venice* emerged into a culture with distinctive and clear national and cultural identities, but also into a society and an industry struggling with a role as peripheral, marginal and other. The remarkable originality of these plays, so closely tied to their bold political and dramaturgical internationalism, rendered them isolated and uncontainable within contemporary criticism. Other plays of the late 1980s and early 1990s that had an easier and more obvious link to ideas and issues of Scottishness – Liz Lochhead's *Mary Queen of Scots Got Her Head Chopped Off* (Communicado, 1987), Tony Roper's *The Steamie* (Wildcat, 1987), Sue Glover's *Bondagers* – have been more seamlessly accommodated into a critical orthodoxy and into the producing repertoire.[5]

Nevertheless, it is, perhaps, only because of the new and radical work undertaken by Arnott, Clifford and Hannan in the 1980s and early 1990s that it is possible for a play like Harrower's *Knives in Hens* to be understood as deeply and significantly Scottish, and as necessarily and essentially international. Certainly when the play premiered at the Traverse in the context of the 1995 Edinburgh Fringe Festival critics and audiences acknowledged Harrower's place in the forefront of a new wave of Scottish play writing and celebrated *Knives in Hens* as a text of significant originality, maturity and sensuality: the latter not a description generally associated with Scottish drama.

Knives in Hens – the remarkable professional debut of an astonishingly poised and controlled writer – is quintessential of the new Scottish drama in its implicit challenging of dramaturgical orthodoxies. It is a play of deliberate poeticism and emotional power set against an elusive landscape of competing value systems, near-pagan philosophies co-existing with ideologies of modernisation, urbanisation and industrialisation, with a seductive, equivocal and ultimately violent narrative centring on the unnamed 'Young Woman' and her desires for sexual and intellectual freedom.

Harrower describes a rural society – or at least a society ordered around the cycles of the agricultural year – existing within a complex of belief systems: on the one hand using a Christian rhetoric; on the other referencing a pantheistic and even demonic iconography. Contemporary Scottish drama has found a useful paradigm in the recreation of the history play but Harrower rewrites this dramaturgy in a distinctive and, indeed, radical manner. Although part of Harrower's research was into the rural Clearances in Lowland Scotland around 1720,[6] one might argue that the imagined location of the text remains open and that his characters inhabit an ahistorical diegesis; existing before and after Reformation (and, indeed, before and after Christianity); before and after industrialisation and urbanisation; before and after disorder and chaos. Thus the community's distrust and fear of technology as it is personified in the character of the miller – 'All you need's hate for him... 'S a village custom.'[7] – and symbolised in the object of the pen – 'an evil stick'[8] – might be understood as pre-industrial *or* as post-apocalyptic *or* as separatist and marginalised. The point being that Harrower creates an extraordinary and completely theatrical linguistic and imagined space.

The underpinning metaphor of naming, and owning through naming, is played out within the framework of relationships between the Young Woman, her husband the ploughman Pony Williams, and the miller, the solitary and mistrusted Gilbert Horn. Harrower resists easy categorisation in his male characters: *both* are virile and seductive, *both* are in possession of knowledge. However, while Pony is sexually rapacious and overtly physical, Gilbert's sexuality is more sensual and seductive; while Pony's knowledge is based on traditional values and orthodoxies – knowledge of the land and its seasons, knowledge of the ways of his horses – Gilbert's is literate and technological, forward-looking and improving, self-aware and reflective. The Young Woman negotiates a path of growing independence learning from both men: at the end of the play she has no lover but she has economic independence – control of property and ownership of the horses – and she has attained both linguistic authority and sexual maturity. Within the context of Scottish drama this singular and positive independence sets her apart as an extraordinary heroine.

Harrower's contemporary – and one of Scottish theatre's most prolific present-day playwrights – is David Greig. In his career the distinctive diversity of the modern Scottish theatre culture and industry is usefully distilled. Greig has, of course, written for the Traverse – including *Europe* (1994), *The Architect* (1996) and *The Speculator* (1999). *Caledonia Dreaming* (1997; revised 1999) was written for Scotland's major touring company, 7:84. He also writes for and with Suspect Culture, the company he founded with director and actor Graham Eatough, with projects including *Airport* (1996), *Timeless* (1997), *Mainstream* (1999) and *Candide 2000* (2000). Greig has also had significant production success in England: Paines Plough premiered his evocative fantasy on communication, geographic and temporal dislocation, *The Cosmonaut's Last Message to the Woman he Once Loved in the Former Soviet Union* in May 1999 (the play received its Scottish premiere in a new production by the Tron Theatre in Glasgow in October 1999); and the Royal Shakespeare Company premiered *Victoria* in 2000. In addition to these commissions Greig has successfully written plays for children: *Petra* (1996; revised 1998) and *Dr Korczak's Example* (2001) were both for Glasgow-based TAG Theatre and *Danny 306 + Me (4 ever)* (1999) for the Traverse.[9]

Greig's plays are intellectually precise investigations into place and belonging. In common with so much of contemporary Scottish theatre, he writes plays that confront issues of contemporary and identity politics. *Stalinland* (Suspect Culture, 1992), *Europe, One Way Street* (Suspect Culture, 1995), *Airport* and *Cosmonaut* all describe and explore life in a post-war, post-industrial Europe, exposing a society wherein the weight of history is in constant tension with feelings of cultural displacement and disorientation. All are cool, intellectually rigorous investigations into the philosophies, politics and prejudices that shape Scottish society, but none is in any easy or predictable way *about* Scotland. *Europe*, for example, is set in the railway station of some 'small decaying provincial town', some unnamed border town, a place caught in the huge movements of history as well as the exposed setting of the small dramas of individuals and itinerant travellers.[10] In contrast *The Speculator* has the very specific setting of Paris in 1720. It interweaves a knowing and reflexive story of Marivaux writing a new play for the Comedie Italienne, with the romantic adventures of Lord Islay of Islay, a young Scottish nobleman on the grand tour, and the cautionary tale of John Law, the Scot whose scheme to move away from a gold standard of currency saw him, for a time at least, the richest and the most powerful man in Europe.

As the title suggests, the play is an elaborate fantasy. It appears huge and sprawling, being filled with dozens of characters and telling many stories. These stories are intricately and subtly linked through narrative and through metaphor. The play tells the evocative and, indeed, erotic love story of Islay and Adelaide. Their story is paralleled with the frustrated relationships of Marivaux and his wife and mistress. In addition the play is shaped through images, metaphors and debates on money, wealth and credit, ideas of the future, the forces and meaning of modernisation, and on ideas of national identity, re-imagining a socio-historical anxiety of conflicting cultural identities at the heart of eighteenth-century Europe:

Islay Why do you want to go back [to Scotland], Mr Law?
You're in Paris, man.
Paris is the centre of the fucking world –
You'ld need to be fucked up to want to go back to Edinburgh.
Law I don't need Paris, Islay.
I'm a rich man.
It's not physically possible to be richer than me. I control the assets of a quarter of the world. I can satisfy any desire it's possible to imagine.
Islay I suppose that could fuck you up.
Law There's no end to me, Islay.
No night, no day, no possible, no impossible.
I'm limitless.
[...]
French princes begging at the door.
And we're here.
Scots – the pair of us.
Islay And proud of it.
Law – weightless.
Islay But fucked up about it as well.[11]

In an essay written in the aftermath of the devolution referendum, Greig and Harrower argued that:

> Scotland has voted to redefine itself as a nation. To redefine ourselves we need to understand ourselves, exchange ideas and aspirations, confront enduring myths, expose injustices and explore our past. The quality, accessibility and immediacy of Scottish theatre make it one of the best arenas in which this these dialogues can take place.[12]

Just this investigation of myth, representation and identity is to be seen in *The Speculator*. In contrast to an earlier generation of plays this cultural exploration deliberately looks beyond Scotland and tests itself against other ideas, forms and dramaturgies. This has resulted in a new and innovative range of representations within Scottish theatre and has encouraged a reassessment of the environment, the milieu of Scottish drama. In this regard the new writing of Greig and Harrower marks a new, highly sophisticated engagement with the nature of writing in a small country distinguished by an outward-looking, internationalist dynamic.[13]

REPRESENTATION AND IDENTITY

Despite the excitement generated by the distinctive dramaturgies of plays by Harrower and Greig, the bleakly nihilistic specificity of the modern metropolitan zeitgeist that so dominates new writing for the London theatre is similarly familiar within contemporary Scottish drama. A vision of contemporary urban Scotland as a society collapsing in on itself because of drugs, unemployment and poverty has been the locus of much of recent Scottish literature, film and drama. The mainstream success of novelists like James Kelman, Alan Warner, Des Dillon and Irvine Welsh, of television programmes and films like *Looking After JoJo* (1998), *Psychos* (1999) and *Tinsel Town* (2000), *Trainspotting, Small Faces* (both 1996) and *My Name is Joe* (1998), and their tendency towards depicting a self-destructive, urban drug culture has had some significant impact on Scottish theatre. Even before the film, stage versions of *Trainspotting* (1994) brought a young and non-traditional audience into theatres across the whole of Scotland. Whilst this was unquestionably an exciting and challenging feature of the play's success, the theatrical and cultural phenomenon that was *Trainspotting* tends to overshadow the impact of other Scottish playwrights dealing with similar issues of the contemporary urban experience: Iain Heggie's *A Wholly Healthy Glasgow* (Royal Exchange, 1987) and *Clyde Nouveau* (Tron Theatre, 1989), Simon Donald's *The Life of Stuff*, Mike Cullen's *The Cut* (Wiseguise, 1993) and *The Collection* (Traverse, 1995) are all narratively and linguistically distinctive original plays and are all, like *Trainspotting*, set in a heightened, but recognisable, contemporary cityscape. This urban milieu has been of repeated concern for Scotland's playwrights, a potent feature of, for example, Chris Hannan's revisionary city comedies *The Evil Doers* (Royal Exchange, Manchester, 1990) and *Shining Souls* (Traverse, 1996), Anthony Neilson's violent ur-realistic *Penetrator* (Traverse, 1993) and *The Censor* (The Red Room at the Finborough Theatre, London, 1997), David Greig's *The Architect* and Harrower's eclectic and idiosyncratic *Kill the Old Torture their Young* (Traverse, 1998), each of which offers varyingly bleak views of the contemporary urban experience.

Hannan's most recent play, *Shining Souls*, is a sharp black comedy set in a world of loan sharking and addiction (in this case a gambling addiction). As with his earlier play *The Evil Doers*, Hannan references the Jonsonian city comedy and the core of the play is the pursuit of money. The vestiges of family are represented by a loose collection of idiosyncratic individuals, the mother and daughter Ann and Mandy, the friends are Max and Charlie, Charlie's estranged wife, Margaret Mary, and Ann's two suitors, Billy 1 and Billy 2. The play confronts the regrets and sorrows of family and of faith, with a central concern being the role of fate and self determination within a chaotic, urban now, with the play's (a)moral being distilled in Ann's question to Mandy: 'Do you not believe in happy endings...?'.[14] In response both *The Evil Doers* and *Shining Souls* Hannan creates a bleak and disordered urban environment, but one where friendship can survive and, indeed, must endure.

David Harrower's *Kill the Old* continues Hannan's contemporary and urban investigations. Like Hannan, Harrower finds contemporary urban Scotland to be a topography of psychological unease and moral uncertainty. In *Kill the Old* Harrower deconstructs the quintessential Scottish dramaturgical trope of nostalgia by removing sentimentalism and replacing it with a coolly analytical attitude towards place and, more particularly, towards ideas, myths and memories of place. The contrast is established in the nexus of the four characters of Robert Malloch, Steven, Paul and Darren, and is framed by the choric figure of the Rock Star.

Malloch is a successful London-based documentary maker, returning to the city of his birth to make a documentary about the place for television executive, Steven. This 'prodigal son' figure is a recognisable one within all marginalised and peripheral cultures, the economic emigrant whose return is celebrated and valorised, mythologised and demonised: 'You've not come back, Robert. This is a return. You've returned'.[15] Harrower gives voice to this figure's desire to leave and distance himself from the homeland: Malloch claims:

> I know what I'm doing. You don't. This's the reason I left. These people who say look, look at what's ours. This is what we're known for. Let's keep it that way. The only thing they care about – the only reason they look at anything is to make sure it hasn't changed since the last time they looked. Because if it changes they're lost.[16]

In Harrower's version the character is matched by the figure of the 'good brother', the character who stayed at home and was loyal to his father(-land). In pointed contrast to Malloch, then, Steven stayed in the city. He repeatedly declares his love of the city and demonstrates his increasing bemusement with Malloch's vision of it: indeed as Malloch's camera exposes the fragile veneer of listing magazines, cafe society and art exhibits, revealing a city of barely concealed violence and isolation, Steven's own sense of self seems to collapse: 'I don't recognise my own city. Where I was born. All dark, sinister. All shadows. Browns and greys. I don't know where I am'.[17]

Paul is the old man who has lived his whole life in the city. His relationship to it is predicated on memory and disillusionment. He remembers a time when eagles flew over the city, he remembers Malloch as a child: metaphor and narrative in close alignment. His disillusionment is symbolised in the dead bird caught in the guttering outside the window of his flat and is signalled in the fear with which he initially meets his young neighbour, Angela.

Darren, in contrast, has clear, if unlikely, expectations about the place he inhabits. He expects that, through the sheer force of him willing it to happen, the city and his life in it will be transformed.

His vision of this urban space is one where he will meet people
that he conceives of as 'interesting' – artists, designers, actors – and
that they, in turn, will alter his frustrated existence: 'I'm always
telling myself I need to get to know more interesting people'.[18]
Darren's tragedy is that he cannot see that the 'ordinary' people he
meets can validate and affirm his life and his identity more readily
than his fantasies.

The character of the Rock Singer stands outwith these conflicting and essentially emotional reactions to place. The cultural itinerant, constantly travelling from one city to the next, he attracts none
of the detritus of psychological engagement or personal involvement (this highlighted by the fact that he only refers to himself in
the third person): 'The rock singer', he says at the opening of the
play, 'is flying out of one country and time zone, across land and
sea, to get to... some others somewhere'.[19]

Kill the Old deconstructs the allure of belonging and interrogates
the theme of dislocation and alienation through extended
metaphors of flight and flying, birds, aeroplanes, panoramas,
bird's-eye views and other elevated perspectives. Indeed this play
about the nature and the idea of the city ends from another high
perspective – an aeroplane leaving the city – and focuses on the
alienated voice of the Rock Singer reflecting upon the urban experience. He identifies the potential of the audience to be understood
as individuals, but resists this in favour of their capitalist potential
as the anonymous urban crowd:

> The rock singer is leaving again, the way he always leaves, climbing
> upwards, through the air, towards other countries, other cities. He sits
> and stares out of the window and realises he is in a contemplative mood.
> His mind drifts back to the night before [...]. He remembers [...] looking
> out over the crowd and how on the fringes of it, there were people con-
> stantly moving – walking past, walking away – people who would not
> stand still like the others. This is something he will remember. The rock
> singer reclines his seat and presses the call button above him. He knows
> now these are the people he must reach. He wonders what it will take to
> get through to them; how he will make them stop and listen and
> applaud. How to make them part of the crowd.[20]

Despite the competing claims of the authority of the rhetoric of
documentary, the rights of residence, of economic or career com-

mitment, and the familiarity of longevity, none of the characters can claim an authentic vision of the city, each is partial, incomplete and resistant. And, although the city can contain and indeed trap the individual, it is also the case that it remains unknown. No matter what the perspective, comprehension slips from reach and, Harrower's point is, the city remains elusive and intangible. This is in contrast to an earlier generation of Scottish dramas wherein the city was certain and fixed and utterly knowable. In passing it is useful to remember that Harrower's play does not name the city it describes and although it is easily read as Glasgow (indeed most critics and audiences made this assumption) the fact that it remains unnamed, open to interpretation, seems intriguing; marking the play as different from this earlier generation of Scottish urban plays; hinting again at contemporary Scottish drama's fascination with exploring Scotland and its parallel disavowal of provincialism; and marking the play as being so much less about Glasgow than it is finally about the nature and the very idea of the contemporary post-industrial city.

In contrast to these city comedies and urban dramas there is, infusing all of Scottish culture, a parallel and potent tendency to acknowledge the history of Scotland as an immediate and meaningful presence, and to describe and encompass the rural experience as impacting on the imaginary and, indeed, moral well-being of all of Scotland. Underlying both these trends is a tendency to depict Scotland as magically transformative and psychologically healing – quintessentially described in films like *Brigadoon, The Maggie* (both 1954) and *Local Hero* (1983) – wherein the physical experience of being in Scotland, of being associated with a woman who functions as the personification of Scotland, returns urban man to his contented, complete and natural self. This familiar trope is not much advanced in Stephen Greenhorn's none-the-less delightful 'road movie for the stage' *Passing Places* (Traverse, 1997). The play recounts a mythic journey from Motherwell to Thurso undertaken by two young men. Along the way Greenhorn wittily interrogates the received ideas of Scottishness, nationhood and identity, and deconstructs conventional images of Scotland's history and rural life.

Alex and Brian are unlikely explorers, venturing furth of the decaying central belt – the archetypal topography of late twentieth-century Scottish dramaturgy – into a diverse and vibrant rural and Highland Scotland – the Scotland preferred in nineteenth-century cultural representation. It is a journey of unexpected incongruities:

> **Brian** (*in guidebook mode*). Inverary. A picturesque township on the shores of Loch Fyne. Notable for its carefully planned layout, its church tower and its historic court-house, now an award-winning museum.
> **Alex** White-washed tourist hell-hole.
> **Brian** Excellent sea-fishing opportunities. In season.
> **Alex** We're not stopping... We're not tourists, Brian.
> **Brian** I've not been here before.
> **Alex** We live here.
> **Brian** Not here.
> **Alex** We're only a hundred miles from Glasgow.
> **Brian** Yeah? Look though. See anything familiar?
> **Alex** Only you talking shite.[21]

Travelling *up* the west coast (as opposed to the classic road-movie motif of travelling *to* the west coast) Alex and Brian are challenged to reconsider what it is to be Scottish and what it means to belong. As they navigate their way north the quixotic pair meet with an eclectic group of new Scots all of whom seem much more knowledgeable about and comfortable in this fluid version of Scotland than are the urban and native Scots. Guided by slacker drop-out Mirren, they encounter an ex-army new-ager in Loch Creran, a Canadian geologist on Skye, in Ullapool they meet a French sculptor-cum-handyman and Ukrainian workers from a factory ship, while in Thurso they meet a Cornish surfer-chick working as a hotel receptionist. Throughout they are trailed by Binks, the quintessential late-twentieth-century Scottish theatrical stereotype, the psychopathic Glasgow hardman. These meetings and encounters lead Greenhorn's characters to reinterpret and re-negotiation the contrasts and dissonances of contemporary Scotland in the extended metaphor of 'Zen and the art of single-track roads', wherein one travels 'Optimising the way you meet other traffic. Minimising the disturbance to either side', aspiring towards 'Oneness'.[22]

Greenhorn's play is fun and witty and was a significant popular success when it was premiered in 1997: it was then revived and toured across the whole of Scotland in 1998. Increasingly, and of course with varying degrees of success, Philip Howard's Traverse makes strategic use of plays that are perceived of as rather more mainstream and popular: one might argue that the Festival-time, main stage productions of Liz Lochhead's *Perfect Days*, Aileen Ritchie's *The Juju Girl* (1999), Kate Atkinson's *Abandonment*, and Gregory Burke's *Gagarin Way* were marketed with just this intention. The company uses this mixed economy of potential popular successes (often cast with well-known actors) alongside rather more challenging examples of new writing to widen its audience-base, to raise its media profile and perhaps also to anchor its season with income-generating successes. Because whilst the production of new writing is unquestionably culturally and socially significant, it is also critically and financially risky.

CONCLUSION

Given the particular problems and challenges facing contemporary Scottish theatre makers – the pressures of economic and social diversity within the country, the geographical spread that theatre must at least aim to cover, the increasing cost of making theatre and the parallel need to make inadequate public subsidy stretch ever further, the limited appeal of some aspects of Scottish theatre making to private funders, and very limited potential for some very necessary types of theatre making to make earned income – it is perhaps inevitable that when we begin to consider Scottish theatre we almost always end up talking about crises in infrastructure, organisation and funding, and about economic malaise. However, this has to be balanced by the emergence of a whole repertoire of challenging new plays that has been encouraged by investment by the new writing companies and an expansion of the locus of production, the growth of the small touring companies and their creative and organisational diversity, a determined post-1990 international dynamic,[23] and a positive engagement with issues of social inclusion all of which has finally led to a healthy and distinctive diversity and bold eclecticism in contemporary Scottish theatre making. Much of contemporary Scottish theatre has the ambition to be a site of national political and social debate, as well as of aesthetic and dramaturgical innovation and experiment. For forty years the Traverse has been at the forefront of new writing and new theatre making in Scotland. In a context of radical political change, contemporary Scottish theatre makers are increasingly willing to experiment with historical and geographical settings, with character and narrative convention, and to challenge the orthodoxies of what it might mean to write a Scottish play. With a funding remit to support new writing, an infrastructure of dramaturgical expertise and a knowledgeable, informed and committed audience, the Traverse has particular responsibilities to support these experimentations and interventions. And it is certainly the case that the plays that make up its contemporary repertoire are as varied and challenging as our current cultural and social climate demands.

NOTES

[1] The aim of the Traverse Theatre Company given on its excellent webpages – http://www.traverse.co.uk/– and in its season brochures.

[2] The following are useful introductions to Scottish theatre and drama in the twentieth century: David Hutchison, 'Scottish Drama, 1900-1950', in Cairns Craig ed., *The History of Scottish Literature. Volume 4: The Twentieth Century*, Aberdeen: Aberdeen University Press, 1987, pp. 163-177; David Hutchison, '1900 to 1950, in Bill Findlay ed., *A History of Scottish Theatre*, Edinburgh: Edinburgh University Press, 1998, pp. 207-252; Randall Stevenson, 'Scottish Theatre, 1950-1980', in Cairns Craig ed., *op. cit.*, pp. 349-367; and Donald Smith, '1950-1995', in Bill Findlay ed., *op. cit.*, pp. 253-308. See also Randall Stevenson and Gavin Wallace eds., *Scottish Theatre since the Seventies*, Edinburgh: Edinburgh University Press, 1996.

[3] For more on this idea see Mark Fisher, 'From Traverse to Tramway', in Randall Stevenson and Gavin Wallace eds., *op. cit.*, pp. 49-56. In addition a fuller history of the Traverse is given by Joyce McMillan in *The Traverse Theatre Story*, London: Methuen, 1988.

[4] Having noted this, in September 2000 7:84 produced *A Little Rain*, a new play by Peter Arnott. This was the first premiere of Arnott's work since Hyde, his adaptation of Robert Louis Stevenson's *Dr Jekyll and Mr Hyde* at Dundee Rep in 1996. Since then his theatre work has consisted of *Mr Puntilla and his Man Matti*, his translation of Brecht's *Herr Puntila und sein Knecht Matti* in 1999, again at Dundee Rep, and the rehearsed reading of *The Wire Garden* at the Tron Theatre in

Glasgow in 1998.

[5] See, for example, Robert Crawford and Anne Varty eds., *Liz Lochhead's Voices*, Edinburgh: Edinburgh University Press, 1994; Ilona Koren-Deutsch, 'Feminist Nationalism in Scotland: *Mary Queen of Scots Got Her Head Chopped Off*', *Modern Drama*, vol. 35, no. 3, 1992, pp. 424-432; Jan McDonald, 'Scottish Women Dramatists since 1945', in Douglas Gifford and Dorothy McMillan eds., *A History of Scottish Women's Writing*, Edinburgh: Edinburgh University Press, 1997, pp. 494-513; Anne Varty, 'The mirror and the Vamp: Liz Lochhead', in Douglas Gifford and Dorothy McMillan eds., *op. cit.*, pp. 641-658; Tom Maguire, 'When the cutting edge cuts both ways: contemporary Scottish drama', *Modern Drama*, vol. 38, no. 1, Spring, 1995, pp. 87-96; Audrey Bain, 'Lose Canons: Identifying a Women's Tradition in Playwriting', in Randall Stevenson and Gavin Wallace eds., *op. cit.*, pp. 138-145; Adrienne Scullion, 'Contemporary Scottish Women Playwrights', in Janelle Reinelt and Elaine Aston eds., *The Cambridge Companion to Modern British Women Playwrights*, Cambridge: Cambridge University Press, 2000, pp. 94-118; and Adrienne Scullion, 'Feminine Pleasures and Masculine Indignities: Gender and Community in Scottish Drama', in Christopher Whyte ed., *Gendering the Nation: Studies in Modern Scottish Literature*, Edinburgh: Edinburgh University Press, 1995, pp. 169-204.

[6] See Jerome Hankins, 'Entretien avec David Harrower', in David Lescot ed., with Sebastien Derrey and Bertrand Krill, *Dossier 'Des couteaux dans les poules'*, Paris: Theatre Nanterre Amandiers, 2000, pp. 45-55.

[7] See David Harrower, *Knives in Hens*, scene 5, London: Methuen, 1995, pp. 8-9.

[8] *Ibidem*, scene 9, p. 18.

[9] *Petra* was adapted for TAG by Greig from his original play for adults *Petra's Explanation* (Suspect Culture, 1993). Established in 1967, TAG is a touring theatre company with a specific remit, and enviable reputation, for making high quality work for children and young people across the whole of Scotland: successes have included productions of *Great Expectations* (1988), *Sunset Song* (1991) and *Where the Wild Things Are* (1998). Between 1984 and 1988, and before his appointment as the artistic director of the Traverse, Ian Brown was the artistic director of TAG. See his 'Directing for the Scottish stage', in Randall Stevenson and Gavin Wallace, *op. cit.*, pp. 198-205.

[10] See David Greig, *Europe in Europe and The Architect*, London: Methuen, 1996, (pp. vii-85) p. x. For commentary on Greig's plays see:

Peter Nesteruk, 'Ritual, Sacrifice and Identity in Recent Political Drama, with reference to the plays of David Greig', *Journal of Dramatic Theory and Criticism*, vol. 15, no. 1, Fall 2000, pp. 21-42; and Janelle Reinelt, 'Performing Europe: Identity Formation for a "new" Europe', *Theatre Journal*, vol. 53, no. 3, 2001, pp. 365-387.

[11] Quotations come from David Greig, *The Speculator* in *The Speculator and The Meeting*, London: Methuen, 1999, pp. 1-119. See act 1, scene 8, pp. 29-30.

[12] David Harrower and David Greig, 'Why a New Scotland Must Have a Properly-funded Theatre', *The Scotsman*, 25 November 1997, p. 15.

[13] The irony is that this is the self-same internationalism that criticism has found problematic in the work of Arnott and Clifford and it raises the question 'what's so different about now?' In addition to the radical nature of political devolution, I suspect that one of the differences is that through increased international touring, collaboration and exchange, Scottish theatre itself has become much more outward-looking, and has caught up with the dramaturgical internationalism of some of Scotland's dramatists.

[14] See Chris Hannan, *Shining Souls*, act 2, London: Nick Hern, 1996, p. 77.

[15] See David Harrower, *Kill the Old Torture their Young*, Part 3, scene 14, London: Methuen, 1998, p. 68.

[16] *Ibidem*, part 3, scene 14, p. 68.

[17] *Ibidem*, part 3, scene 12, p. 60.

[18] *Ibidem*, part 3, scene 13, p. 63.

[19] *Ibidem*, part 1, scene 1, p. 3.

[20] *Ibidem*, part 4, scene 18, pp. 71-72.

[21] See Stephen Greenhorn, *Passing Places*, scene 17, in Philip Howard ed., *Scotland Plays*, London: Nick Hern, 1998, (pp. 137-226) pp. 155-156.

[22] *Ibidem*, scene 26, p. 170.

[23] In 1990 Glasgow was European City of Culture. The city used the year-long celebrations as an opportunity to relaunch itself as an attractive destination for international tourism and to invest inwardly in local companies and new venues – principally the Tramway, the Glasgow Royal International Concert Hall, and the Arches. The long-term benefits have been both economically and socially significant: see John Myerscough et al., *The Economic Importance of the Arts in Glasgow*, London: Policy Studies Institute, 1988, and *Monitoring Glasgow 1990*, Glasgow: Glasgow City Council, et al., 1991.

PAOLA SPLENDORE

New Scottish Prose:
Speaking, Breathing, Bullfighting in the Novels of Janice Galloway and A.L. Kennedy

> *The miracle of the I is this: wherever it speaks, it lives; it can't die – no matter how battered, or doubtful, amputated and no longer credible, this unreliable I! And even if nobody trusts it, even if it doesn't believe in itself, we must believe it.*
>
> Ingeborg Bachmann

PUTTING THE I ON STAGE

The voice in the text of many contemporary Scottish novels is that of a displaced 'I' speaking out of loneliness and despair; a fractured I, amputated, split, no longer sure of its own identity, expressing itself in broken sentences, in a wounded typography, and in the collision of registers. Critics have often commented upon the quality of such a voice and explained it as a symptom of a 'Scottish malaise', the expression of the 'damaged Scottish identity',[1] and as 'the dramatization of a society no longer capable of articulating itself'.[2] However, the anatomy of what seems to be the most typical expression of a generation of authors and their monological insistence on despair[3] has overlooked the theatrical disposition of the speaking I, its talent for performance, its narcissistic pose. The exhibition of despair and the scenery of grief are indeed very carefully orchestrated in their novels where, drawing upon an already flourishing national tradition,[4] such form is aggrandised, satirised even, in complicity with the reader called in as spectator/voyeur of very private functions.

My reading of two contemporary Scottish novelists, Janice Galloway and A.L. Kennedy, will focus on the narrator's dramatic vocation to show how the emphasis on voice and performance –

elements which can also be traced back to the tradition of oral storytelling, still so relevant in Scottish literature – combine creatively
in their work with postmodernist devices, such as the exploitation
of first-person registers, the dislocation of typographic styles, and
the re-interpretation of older Scottish motifs like dualism and the
supernatural. Among their novels, I would like to concentrate on
Janice Galloway's *The Trick is to Keep Breathing*[5] and A.L.
Kennedy's *So I Am Glad*[6] and *On Bullfighting*,[7] works apparently
very dissimilar but linked by a series of strategic and thematic elements: the exploration of female subjectivity, the splitting of the
subject, the foregrounding of the theme of death and suicide, the
rebirth paradigm, and its metafictional implication.

The three novels' narrating voices belong to subjects devoid of
authority, caught at a time of crisis; women who have lost their
grip on reality but are desperately trying to control their lives,
something they will achieve in the end by means of a curious suicidal pact with themselves. It is my intention to show how the
manipulative and rhetorical ability of the narrating voice is such as
to 'subvert' – from within – a tale of introversion and disintegration, so that what appears to be a story of self-destruction will end
up being a tale of rebirth and regeneration. The role of the voice is
very important in these novels, not only for its stubborn refusal to
be extinguished, but because in the course of the novels it actually
gathers self-assurance and a sort of healing power by which the
protagonists will regain control over their lives.[8] So, while the text
may appear monologically shut in on itself, it is made to proliferate, to expand from within in the shifting of registers, in the dou-
bling fantasies, and in a variety of typographic styles. The apparent
disarray of the text, like the 'spilling' over of the writing into the
margins, are evidence of a firm control both at a typographical
level and in the structuring of the narrative sequence.[9]

The re-interpretation of dualism is mainly effected through
masks: the interplay between I-narrator and I-subject, not always
clearly discernible in the texts, releases a series of splits and doubles that, in Galloway's novel, take the form of a dislocation
through which the 'I' manages to look at herself from a certain critical distance and with a degree of self-irony, as if dissociating the
character from an implied surrogate author (see for example the

use of playscript form as if she were a sardonic spectator of her own life); whereas in A.L. Kennedy's works, the splits tend to happen in the form of doubles, or fictional projections, in which the speaking I assumes another *persona*, as if identifying with a literary antecedent, Cyrano de Bergerac in *So I Am Glad*, and Federico García Lorca in *On Bullfighting*. Such dislocations, while allowing the characters to retrieve their own voice through a mask, or an interposed persona, convey at the same time their fictiveness, their word substance. And, in an almost Beckettian effort to translate failure into language, they make the reader aware of the healing force of literature and of words.

SPLITS AND DOUBLES

The narrators' malaise in these novels shows in their grim fascination with guilt, an almost morbid intimacy with pain and failure, and a sense of impotence and helplessness. They are women alone who shun other people's company and talk mostly to themselves or to absent interlocutors; who toy with the idea of suicide, and enjoy entertaining mortuary and sexual fantasies. They are also, in a special way, 'performers' in search of a meaningful text. Joy Stone, the protagonist of Galloway's *The Trick is to Keep Breathing*, is a young drama teacher in deep emotional crisis due to the death, by drowning, of her lover while on holiday in Spain, a fact that makes her feel obscurely guilty. Ostensibly to keep a record of what happens, a frail way of controlling what appears to be beyond control, she starts keeping a sort of diary of her mental break-down, a sequence of short sections, separated by a curious symbol, a triple 'o' or three zeros, symbols of death and absence, a 'typographic marker of temporal and textual division' which Cairns Craig reads as 'the encoded representation of the trauma from which the narrative begins'.[10] The language of the text breaks up in a variety of typographic signs and fonts, blank spaces, frames, notes in the margin, unfinished words and sentences which while showing the impossibility of making sense out of reality and feelings, also links back to a method already practised by authors like Flann O'Brien, B.S. Johnson and Alasdair Gray.

Often Joy experiences a feeling of disembodiment and virtual invisibility and can talk about herself as if she were somebody else,

like in the opening line of the novel: 'I watch myself from the corner of the room',[11] or when she describes her job at school: 'The
nice thing is that I need not be present when I am working. I can
be outside myself, watching from the corner of the room'.[12]
Talking to the doctor at the psychiatric clinic, she feels almost
reduced to a mouth and a voice, almost another being whom she
does not control, but nevertheless obscurely trusts:

> My mouth knew more than the rest of me put together. I had to trust my
> mouth. I closed my eyes and the mouth said
> > My mother walked into the sea.
> I remember the voice: chiselled as crystal. Cold as a razor. I hadn't
> known it would start like this but then I was redundant. The voice didn't
> need me...[13]

One fragment after the other, a sad personal story surfaces of an
unloving mother and an antagonistic sister, of a failed marriage and
of strained work relationships. Her clandestine affair with a married colleague at school had not encouraged her sense of being
herself, and her feeling of non-existence is most noticeable at the
memorial service at the school when the priest refers to Michael's
wife ignoring her existence: 'the Rev Dogsbody had chosen this
service to perform a miracle... The miracle had wiped me out'.[14]
The same feeling is re-inscribed as self-mockery when at one point
she takes a picture of herself to send to a friend, and the picture is
faceless because the flash has whitened out her face making her
look like 'a spider devouring a light bulb'.[15] The light bulb image
recurs again, as a transposed self-portrait, in a joke a friend tells
her about psychiatry which she later tells herself : 'Q. How many
psychiatrists does it take to change a lightbulb? A. One. But the
lightbulb must really want to change'.[16]

While Joy loses all desire to talk to people, her voice gathers
control in the course of the novel and it is her own voice, becomes
almost another self, that eventually stops her from killing herself:
'The human voice... I hear it quite distinctly, my own voice in the
empty house. I forgive you'.[17] After her failed attempt at suicide
she concludes, not without a grim sense of self-irony, that she
could learn to swim instead: 'I read somewhere the trick is to keep
breathing, make out it's not unnatural at all. They say it comes with

practice'.[18] In other words, she has to make herself pretend that 'something unnatural is natural' and it will work, it is the same with living. Besides, being a drama teacher, she's an expert in breath control.

Jennifer, the protagonist of A.L. Kennedy's *So I Am Glad*, is another 'expert' in control and breathing being a radio announcer and a voice-over, a woman who lives in a world of muffled rooms and barred doors, a world made essentially of words where she hides from the reality of feeling. A world she shuts herself in: 'Like manholes and poisonbottles I was made to be self-locking and I could no longer be bothered pretending I might have a key'.[19] She has never recovered from a lonely and difficult childhood during which she suffered sexual abuse from her parents and now she seems inclined to have only sadomasochist relationships with men. Recurring images all through the novel emphasize her sense of isolation and her suppressed guilt, and although 'Guilt is good', as the protagonist of Kennedy's previous novel *Looking for the Possible Dance* believes,[20] she punishes herself by not admitting to any feeling: 'I was pretending that I had anything to hide... I can't recall a single moment of damage that could have turned me out to be who I am today... I am empty'.[21] So, she has fabricated a cool, unromantic image of herself, always calm and in control and she enjoys describing herself as a 'voice', bodyless, invisible: 'My job involves being completely invisible'.[22]

She starts losing control when a stranger turns up at the apartment which she shares with three other young people while they are expecting a new lodger. He is awkward and fragile, a vulnerable young man with a self-produced glow and a striking voice: 'a round, open, dark tone which I like – an almost edible sound'.[23] He turns out not to be who they think he is but a ghost from the past, somebody with no memories of his identity. Later on he will reveal only to Jennifer his name is Savinien, alias Cyrano de Bergerac,[24] the supreme symbol in literature of a voice, almost dissociated from a body. They soon become soul mates: like Jennifer, Savinien-Cyrano has a violent past proved by the scars on his body, scars hidden under borrowed clothes[25] just as Jennifer's psychological scars are disguised under her controlled appearance. Through him Jennifer will literally 'come out' of herself, learn new aspects of human relationships, and the possibility of an unselfish and pure love. When by the end of the novel he 'disappears' just as he had appeared, Jennifer will be a healed woman and although pining for the loss of her friend, she will be glad, as the novel's title declares: 'What do I have instead of the calm. A voice. I remember everything of one man's voice, not a part of it fades'.[26] Through the character of Savinien, the professional voice-over has created not only her own fantasy, a double self, but also a spokeswoman for the author, flaunting the deceptive nature of her story as a fabrication, a pack of lies: 'A little advice here. If you find what I tell you now rather difficult to believe, please treat it as fiction'.[27]

In *On Bullfighting*, the pretence is gone and the person who says 'I' is clearly the author, thinly disguised as herself, represented at the outset sitting by a window considering suicide: 'I'm a writer who doesn't write and that makes me no one at all... I have nothing of value inside'.[28] An unforeseen incident – a man's voice loudly singing a folk song, a 'piece of pseudo-Celtic pap' that would diminish her suicide to a ridiculous farce, stops her. A voice, again, a saving voice. Instead, she goes to Spain to write a book about bullfighting, about 'people who risk death for a living'.[29] Accordingly, the authorial voice shifts from the confessional tone of the first chapter to a more neutral travel-essay tone. Whether the opening scene should be considered a gambit to introduce bullfighting or a way for the author to introduce a metaphor of writing[30] we cannot say, but the author takes pains all along to draw parallels between *toreros* and her own predicament: 'in attempting to control death, the toreros and I may have a little in common',[31] and 'I wanted to discover if the elements which seemed so much a part of the corrida – death, transcendence, immortality, joy, pain, isolation and fear – would come back to me. Because they were part of the process of writing and, good and bad, I miss them'.[32]

A dutiful and absorbing visit to Granada, the Spanish poet Federico García Lorca's home town, is almost a propitiatory rite to the theme of bullfighting and although she refers only cursorily to his poem celebrating the death of a famous torero, *Llanto por Ignacio Sánchez Mejías*, Lorca appears a haunting presence in the text, a 'corpo presente' very much like Ignacio's body in the poem: 'The sensation that I must have been here before is unmistakable, as is the certain knowledge that someone is missing, somehow still expected to come home'.[33] Kennedy finds Lorca's exploration of 'duende', a mysterious force, 'angel and muse',[34] relevant both to bullfighting and to artists; she seeks comfort in his life and words, and looks for possible parallels with his experience, responding above all to his obsession with death. The way Lorca was silenced through violent death becomes a sort of touchstone by which the author, being alive, confronts her own responsibility towards writing: 'Lorca was an unhappy writer who spent much of his life contemplating the horrors, the fascinations and the strengths of death... He adored the theatre, acted a little, believed in the strength of words let loose, out loud. This last point I find a particular comfort – I've suspended my belief in words, but I'm happy to be close to his. Even after all this time, I still look for company in words, I still want to believe in the possibilities of inspiration'.[35]

Thus, both literary figures evoked by Kennedy – Cyrano and Lorca – come to help, to give meaning to a disillusioned life and prove the repairing role of literature. Literature becomes a vehicle for self-reappropriation and as Joy, at the end of Galloway's novel, re-claims her life through her own voice, so the 'former' writer in *On Bullfighting* reappropriates her role through other writers' words.

DEATH IN PERFORMANCE

A crucial moment in each of the texts considered is the protagonists' attempt to commit suicide, an event which the readers are asked to witness although not to believe completely in. In fact, although the suicide scene is rather realistic in detail, there is something in it that calls for disbelief; it is the story of a failed act told in the aspiring suicide's detached voice. The *mise-en-scène* of suicide in the text nevertheless achieves an end: it allows her to enter a fiction of her own making, and become an actor in a self-directed 'therapeutic' performance. On the basis of its presentation in the novels it is therefore possible to interpret suicide as a recurring topos in contemporary Scottish fiction[36] – almost as a rite of passage which makes the aspiring suicide into a new person; a ritual performance, a sublimation, a controlling means both for living and writing, a rebirth.

Joy Stone's 'suicide act' in Galloway's novel is constructed all along as if intended for the stage, almost like a rehearsal or a simulation game, not the real thing. Taking her time, still debating suicide as a possibility, she invokes all her relatives who committed suicide before her to inspire her, her mother and grandmother among them, together with a smaller host of cousins and aunts, almost a matrilinear legacy of self-determination. 'The men are less interesting... With my father it was booze. That has possibilities'.[37] Is she serious? She almost blames her family for not infusing her with more determination:

> I toy with suicide. I toy with pills, the fresh collection in my locker saved for emergencies. I toy with broken glass and razor blades, juggernauts and the tops of tall stairwells. I toy. But there's no real enthusiasm. My family have no real talent in that direction...[38]

Decision time is getting near and then, perhaps guilty of giving in, she puts herself, or rather her 'bad' self, on trial in the role of 'defendant': 'The defendant is anxious, depressed, mildly paranoic and suffering from low self-image. Also guilty about all of these things and why not? The defendant refuses to see the Point [...] The defendant is afraid of health... Ergo....'.[39] When she convinces herself the time has come, she starts laying out the grim scenography of suicide, drawing the curtains, turning off the lights, deciding whether to have music, then, clutching her tablets, a large glass of gin, and a paper bag, she scrawls a last message: THANK YOU, chalking it on the floorboards with one of the tablets. Now she is ready for a lonely toast... The scene cannot escape a sense of deja-vu, even to the intending suicide, who behaves as if following a well memorised script. A blank page follows... filled with the anguish of void and impending death. A tap on the window, another blank space. 'If I answer I have to accept what it says about me. That I don't want to die'.[40] She answers. It was just pretending, a trial of strength with herself, as a subsequent scene makes clear, a zany scene of make-up, of hair dyeing and thorough washing, a cleansing ritual, which announces the decision to live. Joy makes lists of things to do, and finally manages a scream to break the silence in which she has been hiding, reappropriating, as if it were, her own voice.

In Kennedy's *So I Am Glad* it is Savinien, Jennifer's double self, who 'toys' with death all the time, cutting his wrists, almost killing himself with drugs and streetfights, walking backwards on the edge of water... and always with a theatrical flair to it. But being a figment of Jennifer's damaged identity, he's probably devoid of substance, and when he vanishes at the end of the novel it is as if through his death Jennifer has sublimated her own death-wish. He is Jennifer's instrument of healing; that achieved, he can disappear, leaving her with just 'a voice', herself restored. Another 'ritual' suicide is to be found in *On Bullfighting*'s opening scene, aptly titled 'An introduction to death', which shows the author considering suicide while sitting on the window sill. The theatricality of the scene is in this case even more striking: about to jump, her last thought is that she could actually enjoy her flight under different circumstances, but the wrong soundtrack erupts loudly and stops her... The analogy between her pantomime in the face of death and the corrida, as well as the almost immediate switch to bullfighting – a form of ritualized theatre – and to the plaza de toros – an open air stage –, emphasize the theatricality of the first scene. Bullfighting, which Hemingway also saw as drama rather than sport, a 'tragedy' performing the bull's death,[41] is in Kennedy's words 'a ritualised escape from destruction and a bloody search for meaning in the end of a life'.[42] The elaborate metaphor of bullfighting is the means through which the author is trying to understand the impulse behind her suicide and the value of writing against self-destruction, an act giving meaning to a life.

NOTES

[1] See Gavin Wallace, 'Voices in Empty Houses: The Novel of Damaged Identity', in Gavin Wallace and Randall Stevenson eds., *The Scottish Novel Since the Seventies*, Edinburgh: Edinburgh University Press, 1993.
[2] Cairns Craig, *The Modern Scottish Novel: Narrative and the National Imagination*, Edinburgh: Edinburgh University Press, 1999, p. 199.
[3] In a very interesting article by Donald Wesling, the author defends

the use of first person narratives as an 'oppositional form'. See 'Scottish Narrative since 1979: Monologism and the Contradictions of a Stateless Nation', *Scotlands*, vol. 4, no. 2, 1997, p. 87.

[4] According to Gavin Wallace 'The Scottish novel continues to build upon an already spectacular tradition of despair'. See Gavin Wallace and Randall Stevenson, *op. cit.*, p. 217.

[5] Janice Galloway, *The Trick is to Keep Breathing*, London: Vintage, 1999.

[6] A.L. Kennedy, *So I Am Glad*, London: Cape, 1995.

[7] A.L. Kennedy, *On Bullfighting*, London: Yellow Jersey Press, 2000.

[8] Gavin Wallace observes: 'Indeed, the directions which such novels appear to be taking would suggest that, rather than the *failure* to find a voice, the process being envisaged is – with varying degrees of confidence – the successful *retrieval* of one' [author's italics]. Gavin Wallace and Randall Stevenson, *op. cit.*, p. 222.

[9] In the already quoted volume, Cairns Craig has a very interesting chapter called 'The Typographic Muse' where he analyses in detail the use of typography both in Gray and in Galloway.

[10] *Ibidem*, p. 195.

[11] Janice Galloway, *The Trick is to Keep Breathing*, cit., p. 7.

[12] *Ibidem*, p. 12.

[13] *Ibidem*, pp. 103-104.

[14] *Ibidem*, p. 79.

[15] *Ibidem*, p. 156.

[16] *Ibidem*, p. 173 and p. 200.

[17] *Ibidem*, p. 235.

[18] *Ibidem*.

[19] A.L. Kennedy, *So I Am Glad*, cit., p. 4.

[20] A.L. Kennedy, *Looking for the Possible Dance*, London: Minerva, 1995, p. 15.

[21] A.L. Kennedy, *So I Am Glad*, cit., pp. 6-7.

[22] *Ibidem*, p. 10.

[23] *Ibidem*, p. 11.

[24] French writer (1619-1655), the hero of Edmond Rostand's play, *Cyrano de Bergerac*, 1897. A new and acclaimed translation of the play, in Scots, was made by Edwin Morgan in 1992.

[25] A.L. Kennedy, *So I Am Glad*, cit., p. 47.

[26] *Ibidem*, p. 280.

[27] *Ibidem*, p. 12.

[28] A.L. Kennedy, *On Bullfighting*, cit., p. 28.

[29] *Ibidem*, p. 5.

[30] A somewhat similar analogy is to be found in Michel Leiris' idea of 'literature as bullfighting' in *Miroir de la tauromachie* (1938).

[31] A.L. Kennedy, *On Bullfighting*, cit., p. 8.

[32] *Ibidem*.

[33] *Ibidem*, p. 65.

[34] Kennedy is referring here to Federico García Lorca's famous essay, 'Teoria y juego del duende' (1930).

[35] A.L. Kennedy, *On Bullfighting*, cit., p. 36.

[36] Suicide scenes are to be found, for example, in Alasdair Gray's *Lanark* (1981), in *1982, Janine* (1984), and in *Poor Things* (1992), while in James Kelman's *A Disaffection* (1989) suicide is a constant temptation for the narrator; a suicide is at the beginning of Alan Warner's *Morvern Callar* (1998), and, again, Kennedy's most recent novel, *Everything You Need* (2000) opens with an attempt at suicide narrated by the male protagonist, a writer.

[37] Janice Galloway, *The Trick is to Keep Breathing*, cit., p. 199.

[38] *Ibidem*.

[39] *Ibidem*, p. 200.

[40] *Ibidem*, p. 203.

[41] See Ernest Hemingway, *Death in the Afternoon*, London: Cape, (1932) 1956, p. 22.

[42] A.L. Kennedy, *On Bullfighting*, cit., p. 12.

Contributors

RICHARD AMBROSINI, Professor of English Literature, teaches at the Faculty of Political Science of the University of Roma Tre. He has written two books on Joseph Conrad – *Conrad's Fiction as Critical Discourse* (1991), and *Introduzione a Conrad* (1991) – and one on R.L. Stevenson, *R. L. Stevenson: la poetica del romanzo* (2001). Together with Richard Dury he co-edited a collection of essays, *R. L. Stevenson, Writer of Boundaries* (2005). He has written a book on the teaching of English poetry, *Il piacere della poesia inglese* (2000), co-edited with Piero Boitani, *Ulisse: archeologia dell'uomo moderno* (1998), and published essays on a variety of subjects, including Chaucer, Shakespeare, William Cowper, Coleridge, and Canadian literature. He has translated and edited, among other novels, *An Outcast of the Islands* (1994), *Treasure Island* (1996), and *The Secret Agent* (1996).

GIOIA ANGELETTI gained her PhD in Scottish Literature at the University of Glasgow and is presently a Research Fellow at the University of Bologna, where she has taught courses on Romantic and Victorian British Poetry and on English Language. Her research interests have recently turned to Romantic British theatre and drama (in particular by women) and to translation studies. She has published articles, reviews and translations in various books, periodicals and anthologies. Her most recent publication is *Eccentric Scotland: Three Victorian Poets. James Thomson ('B.V.'), John Davidson and James Young Geddes* (2004).

CHRISTOPHER BITTENBENDER is Associate Professor of English at Eastern University in St. Davids, Pennsylvania where he teaches Twentieth-century British literature. He specializes in modern Scottish and Irish literature and has published articles on Robert Burns, James Kelman, and Robert Crawford. His other areas of academic interest include Bakhtinian theory and censorship studies.

VALENTINA BOLD is head of Scottish Studies at the University of Glasgow's Crichton Campus, and Director of the Crichton Tourism Research Centre. Her publications include a CD-rom, co-edited with Tom McKean, *Northern Folk* (1999) and an anthology of the shorter works of Lewis Grassic Gibbon, *Smeddum* (2001). She has published widely on Scottish literature and culture, and forthcoming work includes a study of nineteenth-century autodidactic poetry in Scotland, *Nature's Making: James Hogg and the Autodidacts.*

FRANCO BUFFONI lives in Rome. He is Professor of Literary Criticism and Comparative Literature at the University of Cassino. Some of his poetry books are: *Suora Carmelitana e altri racconti in versi* (1997); *Songs of Spring* (1999); *Il Profilo del Rosa* (2000); *The Shadow of Mount Rosa* (2002). As a translator he edited *I Poeti Romantici Inglesi* (2005), *La trilogia delle Ballate dell'Ottocento inglese* (2005). As a journalist he collaborates with several newspapers and radio programmes and he is the editor of the journal *Testo a fronte*, dedicated to the theory and the practise of literary translation.

STEFANIA D'AGATA D'OTTAVI is Professor of English Literature at the University of Macerata. She has worked on Blake, on the Victorian Novel (Charlotte Bronte, Thomas Hardy), on Shakespeare and on Renaissance Utopias (Thomas More, Francis Bacon). Her main interest, however, is Medieval English Literature. To Geoffrey Chaucer's dream poems she has devoted a monograph (*Il sogno e il libro. La 'mise en abyme' nei poemi onirici di Chaucer*, 1992). She has completed the first Italian verse translation of Langland's poem *Piers Plowman* and has extensively studied the Medieval theatre (*The York Plays*). She is currently working on Chaucer's *Troilus and Criseyde* and on the poems of the Gawain-Poet. She is a member of The New Chaucer Society, of The Medieval Academy of America, and of the Society for Germanic Linguistics.

SARAH M. DUNNIGAN graduated from the Universities of Glasgow and Edinburgh and she is Lecturer in English Literature at the University of Edinburgh. She is the author of *Eros and Poetry at the Courts of Mary Queen of Scots and James VI* (2002), and of articles on Medieval and Renaissance Scottish literature, Renaissance women's writing, and twentieth-century Scottish women's writing. She is also co-editor of *Scottish Literature* (2002), and of *A Flame in the Mearns. Lewis Grassic Gibbon: A Centenary Celebration* (2003).

MARCO FAZZINI is a poet, critic and academic. He took a PhD at the University of Ca' Foscari, Venice, followed by further study at the universities of Edinburgh and Natal, Durban. After teaching at the University of Macerata, he is now at the University of Ca' Foscari where he teaches English and Post-colonial Literature. He has translated selections from the poetry of Douglas Livingstone, Philip Larkin, Norman MacCaig, Hugh MacDiarmid, Douglas Dunn and Charles Tomlinson, and co-edited and translated *Poeti della Scozia contemporanea* (1992) with Carla Sassi, and *Poeti sudafricani del Novecento* (1994) with Armando Pajalich. His most recent publications include: *Crossings: Essays on Contemporary Scottish Poetry and Hybridity* (2000), *L'acrobata della memoria: quattro saggi sul primo Geoffrey Hill* (2002), and *Tradurre, paradiso dei poeti* (2005).

LILIAS FRASER took a PhD at the University of St Andrews in 2003, writing a work on contemporary Scottish poetry. Now she works at the Scottish Poetry Library in Edinburgh.

WILLIAM GILLIES is Professor of Celtic at the University of Edinburgh. His Gaelic interests include both early and contemporary literature. For the Medieval period his research has centred mainly on the Book of the Dean of Lismore, from which he has published a number of poetical texts, and on the Red and Black Books of Clanranald.

CAROL GOW is a Lecturer in Media and Creative Writing at Dundee College. She wrote her PhD on Iain Crichton Smith's poetry in English and published extracts in *The Scottish Literary Journal* of an extensive interview conducted with him at that time in his home in Taynuilt. Her publications include the book *Mirror and Marble: The Poetry of Iain Crichton Smith* (1992). She has also published critical essays on a range of contemporary Scottish poets including Norman McCaig, Liz Lochhead, George Mackay Brown and Edwin Morgan. She regularly reviews contemporary poetry and writes a monthly personal column on education for *The Times Educational Supplement* (Scotland).

SEAMUS HEANEY was born in County Derry in Northern Ireland. *Death of a Naturalist*, his first book, appeared in 1966, and since then he has published poetry, criticism and translations which have established him as one of the leading poets of his generation. In

1995 he was awarded the Nobel Prize for Literature. He received the Whitbread Book of the Year for *The Spirit Level* (1996) and *Beowulf* (1999). *Electric Light*, his most recent collection of poems, appeared in 2001.

TOM HUBBARD is an Honorary Research Fellow in the Department of Scottish Literature, University of Glasgow (2004-2007). From 2004 to 2005 he initiated compilation of the new Bibliography of the Scottish Book Trade (BSBT). From 2000 to 2004 he was editor of BOSLIT (Bibliography of Scottish Literature in Translation). A widely published and translated poet and literary scholar, he is the author or editor of several books including *Seeking Mr Hyde* (1995), and *The Integrative Vision: Poetry and the Visual Arts in Baudelaire, Rilke, and MacDiarmid* (1997). He is editor of *The New Makars* (1991), *Poetry from Switzerland* (2002), and co-editor, with Duncan Glen, of *Stevenson's Scotland* (2003). His most recent poetry collections are two pamphlets, *Scottish Faust* (2004) and *From Soda Fountain to Moonshine Mountain* (2004). He is currently completing working on the Scottish poet T. S. Law (1916-1997), on the medieval polymath (and legendary 'wizard') Michael Scot, and on the reception of Walter Scott's poetry in Europe.

R.D.S. JACK is Professor Emeritus at the University of Edinburgh. He held the chair of Scottish and Medieval Literature from 1987-2004. He has published widely on Scottish Literature in all periods with special emphasis on the Renaissance, the eighteenth century vernacular revival and Victorian drama. His interest in the links between Scottish and European Literature is mirrored in the two monographs *The Scottish Influence on Italian Literature* (1972) and *Scottish Literature's Debt to Italy* (1986), as well as in his continued involvement with the online database The Bibliography of Scottish Literature in Translation. He is currently working on studies of Burns and Barrie as well as editing (with Tom Hubbard) a collection of essays entitled *Scotland in Europe*.

MARGARET LENTA was born and grew up in the north of England. After leaving Britain, she taught in Nigeria and Kenya, and since 1973 has worked at the University of Natal (now the University of KwaZulu-Natal), Durban, where she is now an Honorary Research Associate and Professor Emeritus. Her research interests in the last few years have been in the autobiographical writings of Lady Anne

Barnard, J.M. Coetzee's fiction and criticism and, in the recent past, the novels of the Botswana author Unity Dow. Her recent publications include: *The Cape Diaries of Lady Anne Barnard, 1799-1800* (1999), edited with Basil Le Cordeur, 'Choosing Difference: South African Jewish Writers' (2001), 'Autrebiography: J.M. Coetzee's Autobiographical Writing' (2003), 'White South African and Latter-day Bohemian: Two Editions of Herman Charles Bosman' (2003), 'Postcolonialism in an Anti-colonial State: Unity Dow and Modern Botswana' (2004).

DERRICK MCCLURE is Senior Lecturer of English at the University of Aberdeen. He is the author of *Why Scots Matters* (1997), *Scots and Its Literature* (1995), *Scotland o Gael an Lawlander* (1996), *Language, Poetry and Nationhood* (2000), *Doric: The Dialect of North-East Scotland* (2002), and numerous articles and papers. Chairman of the Forum for Research in the Languages of Scotland and Ulster, he is also editor of *Scottish Language*. In 2002 he was awarded an MBE for services to Scottish Culture.

IAN MACDONALD is from North Uist in the Western Isles of Scotland and is Director of Comhairle nan Leabhraichean (the Gaelic Books Council), based in Glasgow. He has edited many books and translated several others, among them *Am Mabinogi* (1984), the first Gaelic version of the famous Welsh tales. With Boyd Robertson, he compiled the *Teach Yourself Gaelic English Dictionary* in 2004.

KEVIN MCGINLEY is a graduate of Glasgow and Edinburgh universities. His thesis was on the Scholastic background to the poetry of Robert Henryson. He has published a number of articles on Scottish literature and was jt. editor (with R.D.S. Jack) of the volume *Of The Lion and Of Unicorn*, an essay collection in honour of John MacQueen.

TONY MACMANUS was an inspirational teacher, writer and musician who studied the work of Kenneth White in French and English, and gave lectures and published many articles on that work and on other subjects. He was curator of the *White World* exhibition for the National Library of Scotland in 1996, which has since toured extensively in Scotland and France. He founded the Scottish Centre for Geopoetics in January 1995, becoming its first director and securing its future before his untimely death in 2002.

COLIN MILTON is Associate Director of the Elphinstone Institute at the University of Aberdeen. The Institute, which he helped to set up, is a research centre for work on all aspects of the vernacular culture of North-East and North Scotland. A native speaker of North-East Scots, one of Dr Milton's main research interests is the expressive uses of lowland Scots in both the oral and print traditions – and in the cultural significance of non-standard language varieties generally. He teaches Ethnology and Folklore at the Elphinstone Institute, with an emphasis on Scottish lowland traditions. He has published on the history and present situation of vernacular writing in Scots, and on various aspects of the Scottish literary tradition in the period from the eighteenth to the twenty-first century.

MASSIMILIANO MORINI has a PhD in English and American Studies. He has taught university courses on translation theory and practice. His researching interests include fantasy literature (*Le parole di Tolkien*, 1999), contemporary British poetry (*Poeti inglesi del secondo Novecento*, 2001), and the theory, history, and practice of translation (*Manuale di traduzioni dall'inglese*, 2002, edited with Romana Zacchi). Among his forthcoming publications, *Tudor Translation in Theory and Practice*, to be published by Ashgate, and *La traduzione: teorie/strumenti/pratiche*. He is also a literary translator.

COLIN NICHOLSON is Professor of Eighteenth-century and Modern Literature at Edinburgh University, where his teaching includes an Honours course in Modern and Contemporary Scottish Poetry. During the 1990s he was the editor of the *British Journal of Canadian Studies*, during which time he edited collections of essays on Margaret Laurence (1992) and on Margaret Atwood (1994). In 1992 he edited a collection of essays on the Highland writer Iain Crichton Smith, followed in 1994 by *Writing and the Rise of Finance*, a study of early Eighteenth-century English Satire. In 2002 his monograph on Edwin Morgan's poetry was published, and he is currently working on a handbook for contemporary Scottish poetry.

CRISTINA OSSATO obtained her PhD in English Studies at the University of Pisa in 1998. After publishing several essays on English Victorianism and American Transcendentalism in the nineteenth century in various journals such as *Annali di Ca' Foscari, Rivista di Studi Vittoriani, Merope, Strumenti Critici* and *Rivista di Studi Americani*, she published the poems 'Truth', 'Life', 'Black/White', 'Warp and Woof' in *Revista Atenea* of the University of Puerto Rico in 2000. Her first book of literary criticism, *Sartor Resartus, ovvero la creazione di un Nuovo Mito* came out in 2001. In 2004 she was awarded a literary prize for the poem 'Obbedienza' by the *Premio Letterario Nazionale S. Egidio.* Her first collection of poems, *Foglie d'argento*, has just been published.

PAM PERKINS teaches Eighteenth-century and Romantic Literature at the University of Manitoba in Winnipeg, Canada. Her main area of research is late Eighteenth-century Fiction and Women's Writing, and she has edited, for Broadview Press, Elizabeth Hamilton's *Translations of the Letters of a Hindoo Rajah* and Robert Bage's *Hermsprong.* She has also published articles on a number of writers of this period, including Jane Austen, Mary Wollstonecraft, Frances Burney, and Anne Grant. Her current research project is a book-length study of the professional careers of several Edinburgh women writers who were working in decades around the beginning of the nineteenth century.

VALENTINA POGGI, born in Modena, graduated in 1960 at the University of Bologna and took an MA at Cornell University in 1962. Apart from a few years at Pescara, Ferrara and Padua, she has taught English Literature (and from 1991 through 1998 also Scottish Literature) at the University of Bologna since the early seventies. Her books and essays range from Shakespeare, Elizabethan drama and Metaphysical poetry to Richardson, Dickens, and other Victorians. She has dealt with most significant Twentieth-century Scottish novelists in *Voci da un paese lontano* (1992), as well as written essays on James Hogg, Margaret Oliphant, Elspeth Davie, and her favourite George Mackay Brown. She has also published her translation of stories by the two latter and by Gibbon, MacColla, Mitchson, Friel, Gray, Kesson and Owens, in the collection *Scozia controluce* (1995).

DAVID W. PURDIE is a Physician and Consultant to the Edinburgh Osteoporosis Centre. Past President of the Boswell Society, he has a particular interest in the literature of the late eighteenth century. He is a fellow of the Society of Antiquaries of Scotland.

ALAN RIACH is a poet, critic and academic. Formerly of the University of Waikato, New Zealand, he is now Head of the Department of Scottish Literature at the University of Glasgow. He is General Editor of the Carcanet Press *Collected Works of Hugh MacDiarmid*, and co-editor of MacDiarmid's *New Selected Letters*. As a poet he has published *First & Last Songs* (1995) and *Clearances* (2001).

G. ROSS ROY started teaching at the University of South Carolina in 1966. He founded *Studies in Scottish Literature*, a scholarly journal, in July 1968. He was awarded an honorary degree from the University of Edinburgh in 2002 for his work regarding Robert Burns. He is also an honorary president of the Burns World Federation and is a member of the Atlanta Burns Club. The *G. Ross Roy Collection of Robert Burns, Burnsiana & Scottish Poetry*, which consists of approximately 15,000 volumes of which nearly 5,000 are on Burns, was acquired by the University of South Carolina in 1989.

CARLA SASSI is Associate Professor of English Literature at the University of Verona. Her main fields of research are Post-colonial Studies and Scottish Literature. Her publications include: *Un'arancia panlinguistica. Espressione, comunicazione e gioco in* A Clockwork Orange *di Anthony Burgess* (1987), *Poeti della Scozia contemporanea* (edited with Marco Fazzini), *L'inglese* (1995), *Imagined Scotlands. Saggi sulla letteratura scozzese* (2002), and *Why Scottish Literature Matters* (forthcoming).

ADRIENNE SCULLION teaches in the Department of Theatre, Film and Television Studies at the University of Glasgow where her research and teaching interests focus on Scottish theatre and drama (from the eighteenth century to the post-devolution context) and cultural policy.

PAOLA SPLENDORE is Professor of English Literature at the University of Roma Tre. She has written extensively on contemporary English, Indian and South African authors (B.S. Johnson, Virginia Woolf, Doris Lessing, Anita Desai, J.M. Coetzee, etc.). Her publications include the volume *Il ritorno del narratore. Voci e strategie del romanzo inglese contemporaneo* (1991), contributions to *Storia della letteratura inglese* edited by Paolo Bertinetti (2000) and to *Writing Mothers and Daughters*, edited by A. Giorgio (2002), and translations (Raymond Williams, J.M. Coetzee, Jackie Kay, Ingrid de Kok, etc). Recently, she has translated a choice of Sujata Bhatt's poetry (2005).

Derick Thomson (Ruaraidh MacThomais) is a Gaelic poet and writer. Born in Stornoway in 1921, he was educated at the Nicolson Institute, Stornoway; Aberdeen University; Cambridge University and University College of North Wales, Bangor. He taught at Edinburgh, Glasgow and Aberdeen universities before returning to Glasgow as Professor of Celtic in 1963. He founded and was editor of the Gaelic magazine *Gairm* from 1952 onwards. He was Chairman of the Gaelic Books Council 1968-1991; President Scottish Gaelic Texts Society; former member of Scottish Arts Council and was the first recipient of the Ossian Prize in 1974. Thomson was Chairman of the Scottish National Party's Gaelic Committee in the Seventies. Author of numerous books including *An Introduction to Gaelic Poetry*, *The Companion to Gaelic Poetry*, *European Poetry in Gaelic*, and collections of Gaelic poetry, including his collected poems *Creachadh na Clarsaidh* (The Plundering of the Harp).

Anna Torti is Professor of English Literature at the University of Perugia, where she also serves as Vice-Rector. She has contributed articles on various aspects of English and Scottish medieval narrative, on Tudor drama, as well as on topics of English linguistics. Her publications include *The Glass of Form: Mirroring Structures from Chaucer to Skelton* and the Introduction to the Italian translation of Robert Henryson's *Testament of Cresseid* (1998). She has co-edited with Piero Boitani nine volumes of the 'J.A.W.Bennett Memorial Lectures' held in Perugia. She is a former Trustee and a member of the New Chaucer Society, a member of IAUPE (International Association of University Professors of English) and a Life Member of Clare Hall College, Cambridge.

Tony Voss taught at the University of Natal, Durban, until December 1995, when he retired to Sydney. He has extensively written on South African and English literature, including seminal essays on Thomas Pringle, San poetry, Shakespeare, and Joyce.

Christopher Whyte is a poet, novelist, critic and academic. He has degrees from Cambridge and Perugia, and a PhD from the University of Glasgow. He was Reader in Scottish Literature at the University of Glasgow. He has published widely in the field of Scottish poetry and fiction, with particular emphasis on the eighteenth and nineteenth centuries. He has *edited An Aghaidh na*

Siorraidheachd/In the Face of Eternity: Eight Gaelic Poets (1991) and *Dàin do Eimhir* by Sorley Maclean (2002). As a novelist, he has published five novels with Gollancz, the most recent being *The Cloud Machinery* (2000). His poetry has been collected in the volume: *Myth: Poems in Gaelic with English Translation* (1991).

Index

notes

notes

notes

Alba Literaria,
volume no. 8 in the 'Calibano' series,
has been printed in 500 copies.

The publisher has used 'Modigliani Neve' papers (95 gr./mq.),
produced by Cartiere del Nord (Cordenons, Pn),
and Garamond font.

This volume has been printed in Capodarco di Fermo (Ap)
in 2005.

Calibano

AMOS EDIZIONI

S.A.S. DI MICHELE TONIOLO E C.
VIA SAN DAMIANO, 11
30174 VENEZIA MESTRE (ITALIA)
TEL. E FAX: +39 041 98 99 80
CELL. 333 64 57 682
www.amosedizioni.it
e-mail: info@amosedizioni.it